ADDRESSES AND PUBLIC PAPERS

OF

JAMES GRUBBS MARTIN

ADDRESSES AND PUBLIC PAPERS

OF

JAMES GRUBBS MARTIN
GOVERNOR OF NORTH CAROLINA

Volume II

1989–1993

Jan-Michael Poff, Editor

Raleigh
Division of Archives and History
Department of Cultural Resources
1996

DEPARTMENT OF CULTURAL RESOURCES

Betty Ray McCain
Secretary

Elizabeth F. Buford
Deputy Secretary

DIVISION OF ARCHIVES AND HISTORY

Jeffrey J. Crow
Acting Director

Larry G. Misenheimer
Deputy Director

NORTH CAROLINA HISTORICAL COMMISSION

William S. Powell (2001)
Chairman

Alan D. Watson (1999)
Vice-Chairman

ISBN 0-86526-265-9

STATUTORY AUTHORIZATION

Section 121-6(b) of the *General Statutes of North Carolina* requires that a copy of "all official messages delivered to the General Assembly, addresses, speeches, statements, news releases, proclamations, executive orders, weekly calendars, articles, transcripts of news conferences, lists of appointments, and other official releases and papers of the Governor" be provided to the Department of Cultural Resources. From these records a selection is made by "a skilled and competent editor" who "shall edit according to scholarly standards the selected materials which shall be published in a documentary volume as soon as practicable after the conclusion of the term of office of each Governor."

2,500 copies of this volume were printed at a cost of $27,565, or $11.026 each.

FOREWORD

In accordance with G.S. 121-6(b) of the *General Statutes of North Carolina*, the Division of Archives and History, Department of Cultural Resources, has published Volume II of the *Addresses and Public Papers of James Grubbs Martin, Governor of North Carolina, 1989-1993*. Together with Volume I, the *Addresses and Public Papers of James Grubbs Martin, Governor of North Carolina, 1985-1989* (published in 1992), these volumes provide an extensive and important record of eight eventful years in the history of twentieth-century North Carolina. Included are Governor Martin's major speeches, addresses, and press releases. Volume II also contains a list of appointments made by Governor Martin during both of his terms in office.

Editor of Governor Martin's papers is Jan-Michael Poff, who has edited the governors' papers since 1983. Besides two volumes of Martin papers, he also prepared Volume II of the *Addresses and Public Papers of James Baxter Hunt, Jr., Governor of North Carolina, 1981-1985*. A seasoned editor, Mr. Poff brings a wealth of knowledge and experience to these projects. His skill in gathering, selecting, and annotating such a large collection of significant documents is evident throughout all three volumes. The quality and depth of his research and knowledge of political events are amply reflected in his many thorough notations to the papers of both governors.

Since 1923 North Carolina has published the official papers of its chief executives. The timely publication of those materials has earned the state the praise of historians, political scientists, and the general public. The *Addresses and Public Papers of James Grubbs Martin, Governor of North Carolina, 1989-1993* (Volume II) continues that proud tradition.

Jeffrey J. Crow
Acting Director
Division of Archives and History

August 1995

ACKNOWLEDGMENTS

Any attempt to compile a complete list of persons whose assistance and interest contributed to the completion of the *Addresses and Public Papers of James Grubbs Martin, Governor of North Carolina, 1989–1993* doubtless would collapse under the weight of unwarranted and embarrassing omission. Yet it would be singularly remiss not to recognize certain individuals who have earned my profound gratitude for their unfailing cooperation. Chief among them served in the Office of the Governor during the second Martin administration: Timothy R. Pittman and Nancy Jo Pekarek, successive directors, and Mary Ann Dusenbury and Joanne V. Latham of the Governor's Office of Communications; and L. Dean Myers, Jr., director, Boards and Commissions, his predecessor, Wilma Sherrill, and their staffs.

My colleagues in the Historical Publications Section, Division of Archives and History, made significant contributions. Then-Administrator Jeffrey J. Crow suggested typically perceptive revisions as he read the manuscript. Joe A. Mobley and Robert M. Topkins, two of my fellow editors, offered advice as well. Lisa D. Bailey closely proofread the text as she juggled a number of other assignments. Sandra T. Hall and Trudy M. Rayfield aided greatly in assembling the Appointments section that appears near the end of this volume; their persistence and facility with microcomputers helped speed a massive undertaking to completion.

Public servants in other branches of North Carolina government proved particularly helpful in clarifying specific issues and providing additional information. They include Raymond L. Beck, State Capitol Visitor Services Section, Department of Cultural Resources; Manfred Emmrich, Employment Service director and assistant commissioner, Employment Security Commission of North Carolina, Department of Commerce; the staff of the Division of State Library, Department of Cultural Resources, notably Cheryl W. McLean; and Chief Justice Burley B. Mitchell, Jr., and Librarian Louise Stafford, North Carolina Supreme Court. Charlie Jones, Department of Transportation-Public Affairs, shot most of the photographs used in this volume.

Beyond the halls of state government, Frank Daniels, Jr., publisher of the Raleigh *News and Observer*, deserves special thanks for granting permission to reprint Governor Martin's letter of February 24, 1990, to Editor Claude Sitton. Marilyn Avila, John Locke Foundation, Raleigh; Mary Ellen Foster, Avery County Chamber of Commerce, Newland; Sara Klemmer, head librarian, *Charlotte Observer*; Michael I. Shoop, former reference librarian, Robeson County Public Library, Lumberton; and

Frank Thomas, chief of staff to United States Senator David H. Pryor, Washington, D.C., also merit recognition for their willingness to share knowledge and experience.

Jan-Michael Poff

August 1995

EDITORIAL METHOD

Texts or notes exist for more than 730 of the addresses Governor James Grubbs Martin delivered during his second administration. Add to them the scores of press releases issued by his Office of Communications, and one has amassed a body of material too large to be reprinted in the single-volume documentary permitted each of the state's chief executives, per four-year term, by North Carolina law. The 137 items ultimately selected for inclusion in the *Addresses of Martin* most comprehensively reflect the scope of the governor's official activities during the 1989-1993 period: They discuss the aspirations and accomplishments of his administration, explain policies, focus on developments in the state and the issues he confronted, effectively illuminate some aspect of his occupational or political philosophy, or contain significant autobiographical elements.

Although Governor Martin wrote the messages he delivered to the General Assembly and other significant texts, he also depended upon speechwriters in his Communications Office, and occasionally elsewhere in state government, to generate accurate copy in terms of content. The editor elected to publish transcripts of speeches whenever possible. If transcripts were unavailable or multiple versions of an address were prepared for a single event, the text bearing the governor's handwritten emendations was favored over unadorned copy.

Because many of the texts the editor received featured Martin's personal revisions, a diplomatic transcription of those speeches initially was considered; that is, a system of textual symbols would have enabled users of this volume to distinguish the governor's additions to, and deletions from, the material prepared for him. Unfortunately, sigla-strewn prose characteristic of the diplomatic format impedes speedy comprehension of the documents themselves. Consequently, the clear text method of transcription generally was followed. Researchers eager to examine speeches fine tuned by Martin are directed to the originals kept at the Division of Archives and History, North Carolina Department of Cultural Resources.

While most of the governor's textual emendations were incorporated silently into the documents selected for the *Addresses of Martin*, there have been exceptions to the rule. Marginalia and interlinear notes that Martin added to his speeches, but which could not be incorporated elegantly into the body of a published document, were reprinted as annotations, their corresponding footnote numbers placed at the point in the text where the governor made his original insertion. Some of his jottings were so fragmentary that they defied accurate interpretation; these were not reproduced. Extrapolation was kept to an absolute minimum, and all of the editor's supplemental words have been placed in square brackets.

Overall, the documents were edited to ensure consistent spelling, capitalization, punctuation, and use of numbers. Headings were standardized. Salutations of addresses were deleted unless they contained information or a particular nuance that greatly enhanced a reader's understanding of the audience, occasion, or main text of the speech. Ampersands and esoteric abbreviations have been expanded, and typographical errors in the originals have been corrected.

Every effort was made to identify persons, legislation, reports, and quotations the first time they appear in the documentary. Presidents of the United States, the founding fathers, and others whose names are immediately recognizable did not receive biographical annotations. The editor mailed letters requesting biographical information to individuals the governor mentioned but for whom such data could not be found in standard directories. Those who failed to reply were not footnoted. Although extensive measures were employed to locate and cite all bills, laws, and studies to which the governor referred, and to check the accuracy of quotations he used, not every one could be identified.

Naturally it is inevitable that some of the same conceptual currents flow through more than one address, thus demonstrating the continuing importance Governor Martin assigned to specific issues. Annotations accompanying the documents reprinted herein mention textually identical and thematically similar items that were omitted. Deleted speeches and statements, press releases consisting primarily of Martin's direct quotations, and speaking engagements for which there was no prepared text, are listed by date, title, and place of delivery, on pages 502-533.

Finally, all governors are statutorily required to deposit their official papers with the Department of Cultural Resources—and it is upon official papers, like Governor Martin's, that documentaries such as this are based. The manner of disposal of personal records, however, is left to the discretion of the chief executive. Martin had not announced the repository chosen for his private papers by the time this volume went to press.

TABLE OF CONTENTS

1991

1993

LIST OF ILLUSTRATIONS

JAMES GRUBBS MARTIN
By Nancy Jo Pekarek*

When James Grubbs Martin was inaugurated to a second term as governor of North Carolina on January 7, 1989, he became the only Republican since Reconstruction to succeed himself in that high office. The second candidate of his party to be elected governor during the twentieth century, he dedicated his first four years to the purpose of building the "One United State" outlined in his 1985 inaugural address. With energy and determination, Jim Martin succeeded in providing better schools, better roads, better jobs, and a better environment, for a better quality of life in North Carolina. But more remained to be done, and those issues propelled his campaign for reelection.

Martin accepted the demands of a second administration with the same dedication and resolve that distinguished his first, vowing to exceed his already considerable record of achievement. Thus he adopted for his January 1989 inauguration the theme *Plus Ultra*, the Latin motto meaning "More Beyond."

In his second inaugural address, the governor told how Christopher Columbus's discovery of the New World inspired the Spanish to engrave Plus Ultra on their coins as a reminder that there was indeed more beyond the previously accepted limits of their world. In that same pioneering tradition, Martin also recognized that "there was a wider and more challenging future" for the people of North Carolina. His spirit of Plus Ultra was the spirit of globalization, evident in the governor's continuing efforts to reform North Carolina's education system, transportation network, and economy so that the state's citizens would be prepared to compete, and succeed, in the highly competitive world marketplace of the twenty-first century.

Countless challenges faced this popular governor. His efforts in building a framework for the future were hampered by such forces as a par-

*Nancy Jo Pekarek, director of communications for Governor Martin during his second term, kindly provided this essay. The opportunity for an administration spokesperson to furnish an introduction assessing the accomplishments of the chief executive traditionally has been extended as a courtesy by the editors of previous volumes of modern governors' papers. The essay represents the views of the writer and is a supplement to, rather than an official part of, the documentary.

Nancy Jo Pekarek (1960–), born in St. Louis, Mo.; resident of Raleigh; B.A., Belmont Abbey College, 1982; M.A., Marquette University, 1984. Administrative assistant to Senate Minority Leader William W. Redman, Jr., 1985; press assistant, 1985–1987, speechwriter, 1989–1990, deputy director of communications, 1990–1991, director of communications, 1991–1993, Office of the Governor; deputy director of public affairs, N.C. Dept. of Human Resources, 1987–1989. Nancy Jo Pekarek, letter to Jan-Michael Poff, December 21, 1992.

tisan General Assembly, public opposition to hazardous waste disposal, falling Scholastic Aptitude Test scores, a rising infant mortality rate, natural disasters like Hurricane Hugo, and a national recession, inescapable even in prosperous North Carolina. When slowing economic growth caused state revenues to drop significantly below anticipated levels of expenditure, Martin willingly made the hard decisions necessary to restrict government spending. His first concern in tightening the fiscal belt was to protect the jobs of thousands of state employees who depended upon their paychecks to feed, clothe, and house their families.

Jim Martin confronted those and other obstacles in his characteristic manner: rationally analyzing the problem, identifying options, and implementing the most reasonable solution. He approached the weighty responsibilities of office with innate ability and a roll-up-your-sleeves-and-get-it-done kind of attitude. A rare breed of intellectual governor, he easily understood complex issues and developed thoughtful, creative answers to seemingly insurmountable problems. Often during the most demanding of times, he would arrive early in the Capitol, armed with reams of data generated and managed on his personal computer in the Executive Mansion office. Indeed, many of his major policy addresses and fiscal proposals were crafted in the solitude of that office, where he worked in the silence after midnight, kept company only by his overriding concern for the best interests of North Carolina.

Making difficult and sometimes unpopular decisions for the greater good of the state occasionally made the governor a target for the threats and insults of angry citizens. Yet the determination to do what he knew was right, regardless of the consequences, earned him a well-deserved reputation for honesty, integrity, and fairness not often attributed to those in public life. His philosophy of government was summed up in a quotation from Abraham Lincoln: "The struggle for today is not only for today, but for a vast future also." As governor, Jim Martin worked not for himself or his political future, but for the vast future he envisioned for the people of North Carolina.

Better Schools

A self-described "mild-mannered chemistry professor in real life," Governor Martin knew that education was the key for preparing a citizenry to compete in the twenty-first century. He therefore made improving the state's system of public instruction his first priority.

During Martin's tenure in office, money spent on public schools nearly doubled from $1.8 billion, in 1984–1985, to over $3.3 billion in

1991–1992. He also thawed the teacher salary schedule and established a more competitive wage structure to compensate instructors fairly for their classroom experience. Under that new schedule, average teacher salaries rose from thirty-third to a high of twenty-ninth in the nation.

Despite the new money pouring into education, student achievement remained low. In 1989, North Carolina dropped to fiftieth in the nation in SAT scores, indicating that the education system itself, rather than the availability of funding, was the problem. Martin understood, from personal experience, that the people who best knew how to allocate resources for the greatest return on investment were local school administrators and classroom teachers, not bureaucrats in Raleigh. He therefore fought to substitute the existing three Rs—rules, regulations, and restrictions—with one R: results. Leading the charge for flexibility and accountability at the local level, the governor built the framework for education reform by establishing North Carolina 2000, an outgrowth of President George Bush's America 2000 plan.

Governor Martin was also concerned about those he called "the forgotten half," students headed to work rather than college. A survey of North Carolina employers showed that those high school graduates often lacked even the most basic skills necessary to succeed in the workplace. The governor responded by establishing the Commission on Workforce Preparedness. Its comprehensive recommendations included increased support for the community college system and statewide expansion of Tech Prep, an extremely successful technical training program at the high school level.

The governor also continued his support for Motheread, a revolutionary effort to break the cycle of illiteracy. The nationally recognized program, initiated during his first term, taught female state prison inmates to read—so they, in turn, could read to their children. During Martin's second administration, Motheread expanded beyond the prison system into communities across North Carolina.

Better Roads

Preparing a trained and trainable workforce is only one critical ingredient of economic success. To do business, companies must be able to transport their goods to the marketplace. If Governor Martin was going to attain his goal of attracting better jobs with better pay, to rural as well as urban areas, he had to build a strong infrastructure of roadways, railroads, and airports.

Politicians perennially have made highway construction promises to get elected, but few have actually delivered on all their claims.

Believing that "unpromised paving is better than unpaved promises," Governor Martin offered only one highway commitment in his first campaign for governor: to complete Interstate 40 to the coast. He dedicated the final stretch of I-40 between Raleigh and Wilmington on June 29, 1990.

But Martin far exceeded that lone highway promise. He attempted to strengthen the state's transportation system, during his first term, by proposing the Roads to the Future program and developing the Strategic Corridor Network. In his second administration, the governor expanded upon the latter concept through what became known as the Highway Trust Fund law, which provided for a 3,600-mile network of limited-access, four-lane, divided highways extending to within 96 percent of the state's population. The largest highway package in North Carolina history, it also included plans to pave all remaining 17,000 miles of secondary roads. Supporters viewed the new trust fund as a stimulus to economic development, making possible new, easily accessible commercial and industrial sites in each of the state's 100 counties.

Additionally, Martin worked to increase the proportion of federal transportation funds distributed to the state, from 79 percent to 87.5 percent of the total amount North Carolina contributed to the United States government. He also devised a more reliable construction plan that ensured the timely and fiscally responsible completion of highway projects.

But roads alone do not make an integrated transportation system. Railroads fascinated Martin, and he even taught a high school class or two on the topic during his tenure as governor. No wonder then that he was involved in saving rail lines from abandonment, restarting Amtrak's Carolinian service from Charlotte to Raleigh, and purchasing locomotives and passenger coaches for a return train, the Piedmont, from Charlotte. Governor Martin was also directly involved in establishing the Great Smoky Mountains Railway, which offered freight transport and popular scenic rail tours along sixty-seven miles of track from Murphy to Dillsboro.

Perhaps the most exciting aspect of Jim Martin's vision of a twenty-first century North Carolina was the Global TransPark, in Kinston. A project of the scale and economic potential of Research Triangle Park, GTP was a futuristic industrial complex linking air cargo transport with the latest in high-tech communications and manufacturing for the just-in-time delivery of products and materials to any point on earth. The Martin administration projected that the proposed complex would produce approximately 55,000 jobs and an annual economic impact of $2.8 billion.

Better Jobs

While a candidate for governor in 1984, Jim Martin was often accused by his opponent of "being for business." In traditional sporting humor, Martin fired back, "Sure I'm for business, 'cause that's where jobs come from." Providing new and better-paying jobs was a priority for the governor. The Martin administration helped create 471,000 net new jobs between 1985 and 1991, and per-capita personal income grew from thirty-seventh place to thirty-fourth nationally. During that same period, North Carolina's average hourly manufacturing wage rose from $7.01 to $9.19; the 31 percent increase was the highest among Southeastern states and the eighth largest in the country.

The governor also made a special effort to attract a majority of new manufacturing jobs to rural communities with a population of 10,000 or less, and the state repeatedly earned the top ranking in the nation as the location for new manufacturing facilities. However, Martin's outstanding business recruitment record was earned without penalty to existing industry. An opponent of tax breaks or other incentives for new companies, he believed such mechanisms unfairly penalized existing industries and limited their ability to expand. The strength of those new and existing industries also contributed to an average unemployment rate that remained the lowest among the eleven most populous states, even throughout the recession of the early 1990s.

The quest to attract new economic development opportunities also extended to nontraditional enterprises like film production. Thanks in part to the governor's personal recruitment efforts in Hollywood, North Carolina moved to number two or three among the nation's film-making states. Breathtaking Tar Heel vistas in motion pictures such as *The Last of the Mohicans* helped boost tourism, already a big business for the state. Travel-generated revenue swelled from $4.6 billion in 1985 to $7.3 billion in 1991.

Outstanding success in economic development was a hallmark of the Martin administration. The governor's personal salesmanship and his eagerness to meet and talk with corporate leaders, wherever and whenever they chose, was often the deciding factor in bringing new companies to the state. On his biennial trips to recruit overseas investment in North Carolina, Martin delighted foreign CEOs by addressing them in their own language. He was also strongly committed to expanding international opportunities for home-grown businesses, in part through an aggressive outreach program called Export Now. Such initiatives made North Carolina one of the few states with a trade surplus, for five years in a row, even though the country as a whole suffered from a trade deficit.

A Better Environment

In addition to better schools, better roads, and better jobs, Governor Martin knew that future economic success also depended on balancing development with the preservation of North Carolina's considerable natural resources. An avid sailor, he had a deep appreciation and respect for the environment.

As a result, Martin established the strongest environmental legacy of any previous governor. His administration levied more fines against polluters—1,719 notices for $15.79 million, through June 1992—than any other. At his urging, the state adopted storm-water runoff standards tougher than those of other states. Before Martin took office, North Carolina had no such regulations. He continued his Coastal Initiative from his first term, to balance economic development with environmental protection; the Martin administration designated nine Outstanding Resource Waters areas along the coast, to save them for fish nurseries and spawning grounds, and protected 1,100 miles of freshwater streams and rivers under the High Quality Waters classification.

The governor personally was involved in bringing together county, state, and federal agencies to establish the 47,000-acre Roanoke River National Wildlife Refuge in 1989. After years of stagnation, the state park system also benefited from Martin's leadership. Funding increased approximately 600 percent during his two terms in office, and more than 9,000 acres were added to the state parks system.

An executive order on clean air standards in 1989 led to unprecedented restrictions on 80 percent of unregulated air pollutants. A year later, regulations were approved that effectively established limits on 105 air contaminants, many of which ultimately were recognized as carcinogens. Also for the first time in state history, Martin established the Blue Ribbon Panel on Environmental Indicators, to publish an index of key ecological conditions and trends in North Carolina.

One of the governor's most popular environmental efforts was initiated by First Lady Dorothy Martin in 1985: the Wildflower Program. Throughout the spring, summer, and fall, tourists and residents alike enjoyed the beauty of bright red cannas, golden daisies, and purple bachelor's buttons that the North Carolina Department of Transportation planted along highways across the state. The floral splendor inspired hundreds of out-of-state visitors to write and express their appreciation. Combined with the efforts of Adopt-A-Highway volunteers who kept the state's roadsides free of litter, the Wildflower Progam made traveling the state's roadways an enjoyable experience.

Ironically, the governor's concern for the environment placed him at the center of what became one of the greatest challenges of his administration: the effort to locate a hazardous waste incinerator in the state. Even as opponents of the project burned and bulldozed him in effigy, Jim Martin stood firm in the midst of controversy.

North Carolina had become so successful at helping industry reduce, recycle, and reuse wastes that the Congressional Office of Technology Assessment recognized the award-winning Pollution Prevention Pays project as the "most comprehensive and focused" waste reduction effort in the nation. To further strengthen that program and increase its efficiency, in 1990 the governor combined it with the state's recycling efforts and the Waste Minimization initiative into a single, coordinated Office of Waste Reduction.

Yet as a trained scientist with a Ph.D. in chemistry, Martin knew that not all wastes could be reduced, recycled, or reused. Some were the natural and unavoidable by-products of providing the conveniences-turned-necessities of modern society. The governor believed that his duty was to provide a safe, effective method of responsibly managing the state's hazardous wastes.

At Martin's request, the legislature created the Hazardous Waste Management Commission in 1989, charged with siting a disposal operation in North Carolina. Angry citizens blocked the commission's first efforts to locate the incinerator on private property. It then chose a site on public land in Granville County.

Approval of the public site required a vote of the Council of State, composed of two Republicans—Martin and Lieutenant Governor James C. Gardner—and eight Democratic officials elected statewide. Tension over the decision reached a peak when the council met. Despite the governor's call for a reasoned discussion of the issue and a determination based on the benefits to North Carolina rather than politics, the vote split along partisan lines. The council rejected the site. Subsequent efforts by a private company to locate an incinerator in a volunteer county ultimately failed, and the state continued to refuse to accept its long-term responsibility to manage its hazardous wastes.

A Better Quality of Life

Governor Martin was keenly aware of his responsibility to ensure a better quality of life for the state's citizens, especially the very young and very old. From their first days in office, both he and Mrs. Martin demonstrated their firm devotion to improving the lives of North Carolina's children. That commitment extended into the second term, during which a number of landmark programs were introduced to increase the health and safety of the state's youngest inhabitants.

When the infant death rate rose two years in a row, Martin moved quickly to establish the Governor's Commission on Reduction of Infant Mortality to study the devastating problem and recommend solutions. He also proposed and won a $16 million expansion in Medicaid coverage to provide prenatal care for pregnant teens. Through these efforts, coordinated with state and local human service providers, the infant mortality rate dropped to what in 1992 was the lowest rate in state history: 9.8 deaths per 1,000 live births.

Ensuring that babies were born to live was only the first step. To help give those newborns a healthy start in life, the Martin administration continued the nationally acclaimed Baby Love program, begun in 1987. Baby Love offered outreach services and health care to pregnant women, infants, and children up to five years of age, with the cooperation of agencies and professionals such as local health departments, rural health centers, and physicians.

Getting a healthy start in life also meant getting a head start in school for thousands of children who benefited from the Uplift Day Care program, which Martin started in 1991. The initiative coordinated all new and existing state and federal funds for Head Start and day care into a unified structure that offered at-risk children in rural, under-served areas access to day care and the social and developmental counseling necessary to enhance their readiness to attend school. It also aided participating families that needed child care—to help them find and keep a job and thereby maintain their independence and stability as a unit. "Uplift" expanded all day-care funding by more than $36 million, through 1992, and served 29,000 needy children each month by the end of the Martin administration. This highly successful program served as a model for other states.

Children remained at risk in other ways, however. A rising tide of abuse and neglect resulted in thirty reported child deaths in 1990–1991. Governor Martin confronted the problem head-on, developing a multifaceted approach to bolster the state's child protective services system. Elements of those programs included increased funding for additional staff, strengthening staff training and supervision, better availability of child abuse information for human service professionals and the public, and the creation of county review teams to correct weaknesses in local protection systems.

The First Lady continued her active involvement in children's issues from the first term, chairing an effort to train parents across the state to guide their offspring to adulthood without falling into the trap of drug or alcohol abuse. Known as Parent-to-Parent, this grass-roots initiative had been installed in nearly fifty counties, with more than 500 parents trained as program facilitators, at the close of the second Martin administration.

The elderly, too, were in great need of expanded services, due in part to an explosion of the number of residents aged sixty-five and older. Martin proposed a comprehensive State Aging Services Plan in 1991 that recommended more than 250 key strategies to serve their needs. Indeed, as a result of the governor's appeals to the General Assembly, funding for programs for the aged grew from $1.6 million, in 1985, to $9.8 million in 1991, an increase of 612 percent even in the face of a national recession.

One area in which the Martin administration improved services for the aged was long-term care. The governor inherited a state nursing home system with a critical shortage of space, stemming from a three-year construction moratorium. Martin approved over 13,000 beds, a 55 percent increase over the 23,779 built or authorized when he took office. New construction in both rural and urban areas provided nursing home space at twice the rate of growth as the over-sixty-five population, helping to reduce the waiting period for those in need of such care.

The North Carolina Department of Human Resources program for inspecting nursing homes, hospitals, and home health care facilities was designated the nation's best by the United States Department of Health and Human Services in 1991–1992, having moved up from thirty-eighth place. Penalties for regulatory violations increased, and fines for the most serious more than tripled.

Concern over the quality of life for all citizens also meant improving the system of government. In Martin's view, good government meant open government, and he took state issues and operations directly to the people through town meetings and the Capital for a Day program begun during his first term. He also continued to open state meetings to the public and the press, believing that public business should be conducted in full view of public scrutiny. His insistence on openness even extended into the legislature, where he pushed the General Assembly to abolish closed meetings. The action helped curb pork barrel spending and brought about the demise of the "Gang of Eight" or "Supersub," a small group of very powerful legislators who for years made weighty budget decisions in secret. Beginning in late 1988, Governor Martin helped build a bipartisan coalition of state representatives that engineered the overthrow of House Speaker Liston Ramsey, a leader of the Supersub. That political coup ushered in a new era of two-party legislative cooperation.

State employees continued to benefit from the governor's policy of openness, as well. Governor Martin was vehemently opposed to the established practice of firing career state employees for political reasons with each change of administration. While he understood that every chief executive needed a core group of loyal advisers to implement administration policy faithfully, he also recognized that career employees were a valuable stabilizing influence in government and should not fear losing their jobs through partisan reprisals. Martin therefore broke with tradition and, by the end of his second term, reduced the number of state workers subject to political firings to 512—nearly 1,000 fewer than were so exposed when he entered office in 1985. He also ended political arm-twisting within state government by encouraging employees to support the candidate or party of their choice, but on their own time, using their own resources.

Believing that government must more closely reflect the composition of the general population, Martin named more women and minorities to high-level positions than any earlier administration. He became the only North Carolina governor to appoint a woman—Rhoda B. Billings, in 1986—as chief justice of the state supreme court. The governor continued breaking new ground during his second term by appointing the first female to lead the Department of Economic and Community Development, Estell C. Lee; the first African American woman to the Court of Appeals and the state Utilities Commission, Allyson K. Duncan; the second woman ever to head the Department of Revenue, Betsy Y. Justus—he named the first, Helen A. Powers, in 1985; and the first female chief of staff to a North Carolina governor, Nancy H. Temple. Martin also perpetuated his effort to expand minority involvement in state government contracts. Total annual purchases of goods and services from minority, women, and disabled vendors increased from less than $1 million, in 1985, to $47 million in 1990–1991.

Finally, providing a better quality of life also meant protecting the public from the ravages of crime. Upon entering office in 1985, Governor Martin was immediately confronted with a possible federal takeover of state prisons. He successfully avoided that crisis by proposing a plan to build a constitutionally defensible prison system that provided fifty square feet of living space per inmate.

As his second term opened, however, the state faced a prison overcrowding crisis. Correction officials were forced to parole inmates almost as fast as they entered the system. Convicted felons spent more time on the streets than they did behind bars. The crime rate rose.

Governor Martin adopted a two-pronged approach to meeting this crisis. First, he expanded alternatives to incarceration, including electronic house arrest, boot camp for juvenile offenders, treatment programs for repeat driving-while-impaired offenders, and intensive supervision, probation, and parole. North Carolina became a national leader in such programs.

Second, he developed an ambitious prison construction plan, the largest in state history, to enlarge the inmate capacity of the correction system. After a series of hearings, the Governor's Advisory Board on Prisons and Punishment recommended a bond issue to finance the program. The plan stalled in the General Assembly until Martin reached a compromise with legislative leaders to authorize $75 million in bonds immediately and another $200 million pending voter approval in a referendum. The referendum passed; when completed, authorized construction was to provide space for over 5,500 new inmates, expanding the prison system to almost 22,000 beds.

Plus Ultra: More Beyond

It is a fact of political life that the time allotted for each administration to complete its work comes to an end before all policies have been implemented and all programs established. Yet Jim Martin set the stage for important issues to be addressed by North Carolina's subsequent chief executives and legislatures. In particular, his support of gubernatorial veto and the appointment of judges and Council of State members focused attention on the most important component of the political infrastructure—sound and effective governance—and challenged the system to change as the people and needs of North Carolina were changing. It was a challenge to elected representatives to look beyond immediate issues and realize that the struggle for today's system of governance was indeed a struggle for a vast future, for more beyond: Plus Ultra.

Martin forged the way in the effort to win passage of gubernatorial veto in the General Assembly. The chief executives of the other forty-nine states and all the United States protectorates exercise such power. Each of North Carolina's living former governors supports it. In one of his strongest legislative lobbying efforts, Martin was able to win passage of a veto bill in the state Senate. But despite overwhelming public support, the House still refused to allow the people of North Carolina to decide by referendum whether their governor should have veto power.

Belief in a fair and responsive system of government compelled Governor Martin to advocate change in areas apart from the veto issue. He pushed for eliminating the partisan election of judges in favor of gubernatorial appointment, for six- to eight-year terms, subject to legislative confirmation. Convinced that the lack of defined responsibility for education was one reason the state's elementary and secondary schools had fallen below standard, Martin proposed that the governor be given responsibility for the state's education system—and the power to appoint the superintendent of public instruction. Indeed, he favored gubernatorial appointment of all Council of State members, except the state auditor and state treasurer, as well as constitutional limits on the length of service for legislators and elected Council of State officials.

Often the governor was forced to generate public demand for change, thereby persuading legislators to address an issue. That method proved effective in winning approval of his prison and road construction packages. Though less successful in such matters as veto power and merit selection of judges, the tactic still enabled Martin to raise the level of public debate on those topics.

Efforts to build a better government for the citizens of North Carolina reflected Jim Martin's hope for the future of his state—a hope he built on the conviction that government could and should operate, not for partisan advantage, but in the best interests of its constituents. At the root of his philosophy of politics and government, he believed in North Carolina and its people. Whether striving to build better schools, better jobs, better roads, a better environment, or a better quality of life, the governor responded to the needs of his state with concern and commitment. He reached for more beyond the status quo and toward his vision of North Carolina in the twenty-first century. In so doing, he created for the state a vast future of opportunity for generations to come.

Left: James G. Martin was inaugurated to a second term as North Carolina governor on January 7, 1989, the first Republican since Reconstruction to succeed himself as the state's chief executive. With First Lady Dorothy M. Martin as a witness, state Supreme Court Chief Justice James G. Exum, Jr., administered the oath of office to her husband. *Below:* James A. Graham, state agriculture secretary, views Inauguration Day festivities with Martin. (All photographs courtesy of the Office of Governor, James G. Martin, unless otherwise noted.)

The governor opened his 1991 "State of the State" message by paying tribute to North Carolina-based military personnel serving in Operation Desert Storm. He held aloft the vial of Arabian sand he kept with him "as a constant reminder of their sacrifice" in the war against Iraq. Lieutenant Governor James C. Gardner sat behind Martin.

INAUGURAL ADDRESS
PLUS ULTRA: MORE BEYOND

Today, as we begin these next four years, let us especially salute the men and women who make state government happen: our tens of thousands of fine employees who daily do their jobs with pride. They teach our children, build our roads, care for our sick, enforce our laws, and generally make our lives better through good government. One of their number is retiring today, after sixty years as a state employee, fifty-two of those years as our secretary of state, the very honorable Thad Eure. Please join with me in tribute to our friend, and the only secretary of state most of us have ever known.[1]

Let us also celebrate this bountiful land which Charles Kuralt has called, "Home far beyond all praise."[2] North Carolina is truly our "State of Grace," our "State of the Arts," and our "State of the Hearts." Four years ago, I received a poem written for me by William H. Weatherly, Jr., of Browns Summit.[3] I want to share it with you.

The State of North Carolina[4]

She lies unspoiled, snuggled amid breathless blue ridged
mountains and a distinctly romantic shore.

She is the consummate gem of America's southland.
Each season only alters her magnificence.
There is no travesty in her character.

Refresh yourself with her sparkling atmosphere,
her placid countryside and lenient people.[5]

State your pleasure, she will answer in fashion.
Have will for commerce and she'll comply, taking her place
among the giants, for within her peacefulness there is prosperity.

She will see that the student studies in excellence,
that the athlete performs at peak in any arena,[6]
and that the writer and artist are awe inspired.

She beckons you come to her and she'll make you
her lover for the time you have to share.

She asks only that you pass on the affection,
the energy and the spirit that you gather from her,
so that she, in turn, might share her gift again and again.[7]

And she will remain as always:[8]
The State of North Carolina.

North Carolina is our home! Its spirit lifts and inspires us. So, I propose to you a special year-long celebration of this spirit of North Carolina, a promotion of its heritage, and its grandeur, and its people that
will involve every community in appropriate ceremonies and events.
Let there be competitions, performances, parties, tributes, and displays.
Three years ago, there was the Tennessee Homecoming. This year, there
is the Alabama Reunion. In 1990, we will showcase the spirit of North
Carolina. Their celebrations have been excellent; ours must be better.
After all, we have North Carolina.

Four years ago, we shared here a vision of North Carolina as one
united state. Today, we can share the satisfaction of having attained so
many of our goals: building better schools, better roads, better jobs, and
a better quality of life for our people. Yet, we know there is much more
to be done to fulfill our state's potential.

We must have even better schools, with more emphasis on results
and the achievement of our students. We have focused on the inputs of
funding levels, required offerings, staff ratios, and regulations. While
those continue to deserve attention, we now see that outcomes are
really more important. The ultimate evaluation of our schools depends
not on input formulas, but on students' achievement scores, and subject
mastery, and attendance and dropout rates.

These last five years have seen unprecedented improvement in funding for North Carolina's public schools. Every budget I have submitted,
and every budget enacted by the General Assembly, has increased spending for schools even as a percentage of the General Fund. That had never
happened before.

North Carolina's greatest contribution to educational reform is our
pioneering demonstration that incentive pay for teachers can be applied
fairly—and that it works. Despite early misgivings, the vast majority of
teachers taking part in the pilot program have graded it a success. More
time is being spent on subject matter—more time on task; there is better
discipline and attention, students and teachers are better prepared for
class, and student test scores are remarkably better. It is time to offer this
program statewide, so that all teachers can have the opportunity for
classroom promotions—what I call better pay for better teachers. This
career ladder incentive-pay program will do more to improve the quality of public education than any other reform, because it will strengthen
the teaching profession.[9]

In his inaugural address in 1909, Governor William Kitchin put it this
way: "The blessings of education no good man denies, its necessity no
wise man doubts, and its opportunities no just citizen would withhold
from the public."[10] John Motley Morehead set this aim in 1841: "It is in
our Common Schools, in which every child can receive the rudiments of

an education—that our efforts should be mainly directed."[11] Jim Holshouser declared, in 1973, that "quality education will be a polar star which will guide us toward a future of promise."[12] Kerr Scott put it most succinctly, if earthily: "The most valuable crop we raise is our children."[13] I say to you that there is no responsibility more important than strengthening our financial support for public education, except to ensure that we get better results and that our children get more out of what we put in.

The next most important investment in the future of our state is transportation. Railroads, airports, and seaports are getting more attention, deservedly, as important parts of our infrastructure. When it comes to capital expenses, roads are our biggest responsibility.

In 1986, we worked together to patch a "flat tire" in our road building fund.[14] I concluded in 1987 that it is vital to the economic well-being of every part of North Carolina that we build a Strategic Corridor system of high quality, four-lane roads that would reach into every part of the state. This would bring a continuous, uninterrupted, four-lane network within ten miles of over 90 percent of our people. The Highway Study Commission is reaching bipartisan consensus on the magnitude of our need, the extent to which we can meet it over the next ten to twelve years, and the fairest and surest way for users to pay for it. I call upon you to join me in encouraging and supporting their recommendations when they are presented.[15]

How often we've heard that tired old joke that ends with, "You can't get there from here." Is that our problem? When Kerr Scott advocated paved roads in 1949 as the "repeal of the mud tax,"[16] he was echoing Governor Robert B. Glenn's observation that "next to illiteracy, mud levies the highest tax on the state."[17] Just as "farm-to-market" roads were vital ties, linking us together when we were stuck in the mud in those days, surely the Strategic Corridor system is needed today when we are stuck in traffic jams and economic stagnation. I say to you that nothing will do more to tie us together as one united state than to build this intrastate network of four-lane highways that go somewhere! It will help workers get to their jobs in our congested cities while helping to get jobs to the workers in rural areas. Then we will be able to say, anywhere in North Carolina, "You certainly can get there from here!"[18]

If better schools and better roads are our most important public investments, then the most valuable public return on those investments will be better jobs. Every governor since Luther Hodges[19] has worked at industrial recruitment and kept us ahead of the competition. What my administration has done is to add programs to help existing businesses and to identify new targets of opportunity, such as automotive components and nonmanufacturing firms. We have formed successful partnerships with local business and government leaders, so that small towns and rural communities could share in more of the prosperity, and it has worked. With investment in new and expanded manufacturing and nonmanufacturing facilities averaging $5 billion a year, creating a net gain of 100,000 jobs each year, North Carolina has clearly outstripped the nation.

While [we all][20] have shared in the concern over plant closings, this administration has been careful not to overreact or follow the call of some to take retribution, for that would have injured North Carolina's overall business climate. A recent study by the UNC Center for Competitiveness and Economic [sic] Growth found that, during the last four years, for every one job lost in the state due to plant closings, layoffs, or company moves to other states, two new jobs were created by startups, expansions, and relocations to North Carolina![21] And what about the quality of these jobs? Another study soon to be released by the same researchers has found a four-year decline in our rate of formation of low-paying jobs (under $11,200 a year), while jobs paying more than $45,000 have grown by 18 percent in North Carolina, reversing a decline of the previous four years. That is far better than the national average, or than the rest of the Southeast, which improved by only 2 percent growth in high-paying jobs. There is much more to be done if we are to reach our goal of raising our per-capita income to the national average, and our efforts must be compatible with the programs and philosophy which have produced our positive business climate.

Along with better schools, better roads, and better jobs, we must also get serious about better environmental protection. That means that we must do what it takes to identify the more serious environmental problems and to apply our resources to deal with the real wolves rather than chasing after rabbits. How can we tell the difference? The North Carolina Center for Public Policy Research has recommended taking an environmental index, both to assess the state of the environment of the state and to provide a quantitative basis for tracking our progress in dealing with it.[22] Mecklenburg County has already launched a countywide program.

I am impressed with this concept, and propose to establish a statewide effort to evaluate the quality of our air, water, and land resources. I will appoint a blue-ribbon panel of citizens from a cross section of backgrounds from all across the state. They will hold a series of hearings, and submit recommendations for standards and for action, and help us set measurable targets for improvement, so that we can know whether we are doing something useful.[23]

I am pleased that the legislature's Environmental Study Commission has just agreed to recommend enactment of my plan to consolidate environmental regulatory agencies under one department, with very few changes. This step will mean that we can now move forward with a major reorganization long sought by environmental and business leaders alike, as well as efficiency advocates.[24]

In the brief time available today to address some of our significant achievements and the remaining goals ahead of the new administration, many important topics could not be covered. There is, however, one critical problem which is so pervasive, and which poses so great a threat to society, that I must take it up before closing. Drug abuse is a costly disease in its toll on wasted education, degraded health, and jumbled productivity, as well as in the criminal activity undertaken to pay for it.

We are still just beginning to come to grips with a problem so serious that it has the potential to undermine all our major goals. To raise this concern to a far higher commitment, I will establish a special team of cabinet-rank officials to develop the best strategy for North Carolina's war on drugs. This "drug cabinet" will be chaired by the lieutenant governor and will include the attorney general, the superintendent of public instruction, and the secretaries of the departments of Commerce, Corrections, Crime Control and Public Safety, Human Resources, and Transportation.[25] I will ask them to recommend more aggressive and effective strategies for drug countermeasures by next July, with interim reports for steps that can be implemented more quickly.

Yes, there have been many satisfying accomplishments over the past four years, and there is much more to be done. With great confidence that there is a brighter future ahead for North Carolina and our people, I have chosen an antique Latin motto for the theme of this address.

Back during the fifteenth-century reign of Ferdinand and Isabella, Spanish coins were minted with the inscription: *Ne Plus Ultra*. This meant "No More Beyond," and signified the belief that there was nothing more beyond the ocean west of Gibraltar. Ne Plus Ultra also carried another meaning, signifying that no other was beyond that of Spain. It was their equivalent way of saying, "We're Number One," for so it seemed.

All this was changed by the voyages and discoveries of Christopher Columbus. Beginning with sixteenth-century Holy Roman Emperor Charles V, Spanish coins were changed to reflect the new order. As shown on this eighteenth-century silver coin, an 8 *real* piece, the negative was dropped so that they would read *Plus Ultra*, which translates to mean "More Beyond."

There was more beyond: more lands to explore and exploit, and more people to civilize. There had come a wider and more challenging future.

Plus Ultra: Let this be the watchword for this inauguration ceremony, for there are new challenges for us to face along with unfinished business from the past. There is indeed a brighter future for North Carolina. Today let us rededicate ourselves to fulfill that destiny for our state. Let us accept the responsibility to work together for better schools, better roads, better jobs, better environment, and for better quality of life for our people.

Plus Ultra. For there is truly more beyond.

---

[1]Thad Eure (1899–1993), native of Gates County; North Carolina secretary of state, 1937–1989. Previously identified in Jan-Michael Poff (ed.), *Addresses and Public Papers of James Grubbs Martin, Governor of North Carolina, Volume I, 1985–1989* (Raleigh: Division of Archives and History, Department of Cultural Resources, 1992), 283n, hereinafter cited as Poff, *Addresses of Martin;* see also *News and Observer* (Raleigh), January 1, 6, 7, 1989, July 22, 1993, hereinafter cited as *News and Observer.*

[2]The phrases "Home far beyond all praise" and "Here in my state of grace," are from the song "North Carolina is My Home," words by Charles Kuralt, music by Loonis McGlohon, as printed in Kuralt and McGlohon, *North Carolina is My Home* (Charlotte, N.C.: East Woods Press/Fast and McMillan Publishers, Inc., 1986), 7-8.

Charles Bishop Kuralt (1934-   ), born in Wilmington; CBS News correspondent, 1959-1994. Previously identified in Poff, *Addresses of Martin,* I, 43n; see also *News and Observer,* March 16, April 3, 1994.

[3]William Howard Weatherly, Jr. (1939-   ), born in Washington, D.C.; resident of Browns Summit; was graduated from Wingate College, 1960, and Wake Forest University, 1962; U.S. Army, 1957–1958. Assistant business manager, Greensboro College, 1962–1985; national marketing director, Compumed Pharmaceuticals, Inc., 1985–1988; corporate vice-president, board member, Enhanceco, Inc., 1988–1993; financial services practice, Equitable Life Assurance Society of the U.S., since 1993. William Howard Weatherly, Jr., letter to Jan-Michael Poff, February 11, 1993.

[4]The spacing and indentation of the poem remain as they appeared in the governor's text. Although those characteristics differ from the author's original version, the meaning of the work was unaffected. William H. Weatherly, Jr., "The State of North Carolina," hereinafter cited as Weatherly, "State of North Carolina," enclosed in letter to Jan-Michael Poff, February 11, 1993.

[5]The poem correctly reads, "Refresh yourself with her sparkling atmosphere, placid countryside and lenient amiable people." Weatherly, "State of North Carolina."

[6]A comma does not follow *arena* in the original poem. Weatherly, "State of North Carolina."

[7]The poet does not flank the words *in turn* with commas. Weatherly, "State of North Carolina."

[8]This line does not end with a colon in the original poem. Weatherly, "State of North Carolina."

[9]The General Assembly refrained from mandating the statewide adoption of the Career Development Pilot Program, also known as the career ladder, during Martin's second term. However, it did offer the plan to local school systems as one of five incentive-pay options for teachers under the Performance-Based Accountability Program. See "An Act to Appropriate Funds for the Implementation of the School Improvement and Accountability Act of 1989," *Session Laws of North Carolina, 1989,* II, c. 778, s. 3, hereinafter cited as *N.C. Session Laws,* with appropriate year. Although its short title was "School Improvement and Accountability Act of 1989," the measure was known most commonly as S.B. 2.

[10]The quotation is from *Inaugural Address of William W. Kitchin, Governor of North Carolina, to the General Assembly, January 12, 1909* (Raleigh: E. M. Uzzell and Co., 1909), 6.

William Walton Kitchin (1866–1924), born in Halifax County; died in Scotland Neck; B.A., Wake Forest College (later University), 1884; studied law at University of North Carolina. Newspaper editor; lawyer; represented North Carolina's Fifth Congressional

District in U.S. House, 1897–1909; North Carolina governor, 1909–1913; Democrat. *Biographical Directory of the United States Congress, 1774–1989* (Washington: United States Government Printing Office, 1989), 1319, hereinafter cited as *Biographical Directory of Congress*.

[11]"Our state possesses in her University, an institution that will compare favorably with any other in the Union, at which a portion of our youth can be well educated—we have a number of Academies and other high Schools at which another portion can receive excellent educations; but it is to our Common Schools, in which every child can receive the rudiments of an education—that our education should be mainly directed." Inaugural address of January 1, 1841, quoted in Burton Alva Konkle, *John Motley Morehead and the Development of North Carolina, 1796–1866* (Philadelphia: William J. Campbell, 1922; Spartanburg, S.C.: The Reprint Company, 1971), 215.

John Motley Morehead (1796–1866), born in Pittsylvania County, Va.; was buried in Greensboro; graduated from University of North Carolina, 1817; admitted to state bar, 1819. Lawyer; represented Rockingham County, 1821, and Guilford County, 1826-1827, 1827-1828, and 1858–1859, in state House of Commons; delegate to state constitutional convention, 1835; elected North Carolina governor, 1840, reelected 1842, champion of internal improvements, especially railroads; member of state Senate from Guilford County, 1860-1861; delegate to Confederate Provisional Congress, 1861–1862; Whig. William S. Powell (ed.), *Dictionary of North Carolina Biography* (Chapel Hill: University of North Carolina Press, projected multivolume series, 1979—), IV, 321–322, hereinafter cited as Powell, *DNCB*.

[12]"So, let us declare that quality education will be the polar star which will guide us toward a future of promise. Let us not be timid in seeking to improve our school system." "Inaugural Address," January 5, 1973, quoted in Memory F. Mitchell (ed.), *Addresses and Public Papers of James Eubert Holshouser, Jr., Governor of North Carolina 1973–1977* (Raleigh: Division of Archives and History, Department of Cultural Resources, 1978), 5.

James Eubert Holshouser, Jr. (1934–), born in Boone; North Carolina governor, 1973-1977; Republican. Previously identified in Poff, *Addresses of Martin*, I, 60n.

[13]"The most valuable crop we raise in North Carolina is our children." "Inaugural Address," January 6, 1949, quoted in David Leroy Corbitt (ed.), *Public Addresses, Letters, and Papers of William Kerr Scott, Governor of North Carolina, 1949–1953* (Raleigh: Council of State, State of North Carolina, 1957), 5, hereinafter cited as Corbitt, *Addresses of Scott*.

William Kerr Scott (1896–1958), native of Alamance County; North Carolina governor, 1949–1953; Democrat. Previously identified in Poff, *Addresses of Martin*, I, 255n–256n.

[14]Martin and Lieutenant Governor Robert Byrd Jordan III, president of the state Senate and a Democrat, announced their highway funding compromise in June 1986. The General Assembly acted the following month, passing legislation "to Provide Roads to the Future." Poff, *Addresses of Martin*, I, 365–366; see also *N.C. Session Laws, 1985, Extra and Regular Sessions, 1986*, chapters 982 and 1018.

[15]*Report of the Highway Study Commission: Report to the 1989 General Assembly of North Carolina* ([Raleigh: The Commission, February 20, 1989]); see pages 27–29 for recommendations. *N.C. Session Laws, 1987*, II, c. 873, s. 29 established the commission.

[16]"In my opinion the most inexcusable waste in our economy is the 'mud tax.' I propose repealing the 'mud tax' just as rapidly as it is possible to build and improve roads that will enable every school bus to operate every day in the year, and provide all-weather access to markets, places of employment, churches, and medical care." "Inaugural Address," January 6, 1949, quoted in Corbitt, *Addresses of Scott*, 4.

[17]Glenn's inaugural message included the line, "It is said that next to illiteracy, mud levies the highest tax on a State." *Address of Governor R. B. Glenn, January 11, 1905* (Raleigh: E. M. Uzzell and Co., 1905), 11.

Robert Brodnax Glenn (1854–1920), native of Rockingham County; was buried in Winston-Salem; educated at Davidson College and University of Virginia. Attorney; elected to N.C. House, 1880, from Stokes County; state solicitor, 1886; U.S. attorney, Western District of North Carolina, 1893-1897; elected state senator from Forsyth County, 1898; governor, 1905–1909; appointed to International Boundary Commission, 1915, by President Woodrow Wilson; Democrat. Powell, *DNCB*, II, 307.

[18]The General Assembly approved a colossal $8.8 billion, thirteen-year construction

program for intrastate highways on July 27, 1989. The measure increased the state gasoline tax and other motor vehicle-related fees to finance the project. It also routed $335 million generated by those increases into pay raises for teachers and state employees over the ensuing two years, a "raid on the Highway Fund" to which Martin strenuously objected. He argued that once money detoured into pay raises reverted to the fund, other revenues would have to be found to sustain state government's obligation to its workers. For that reason, the governor told reporters, he would have vetoed the bill had he been able—despite his having proposed and promoted a Strategic Corridor, or intrastate, system since 1987. Martin initially proposed delaying pay raises for teachers and state employees in order to finance them with recurring funds; ultimately he recommended a 1 percent hike in the sales tax to cover increases in education spending and workers' salaries. See "An Act to Establish the North Carolina Highway Trust Fund, to Provide Revenue for the Fund, to Designate How Revenue in the Fund is to Be Used, and to Raise Revenue for the General Fund," *N.C. Session Laws, 1989*, II, c. 692; "Better Pay for Better Teachers," March 9, 1989, pages 92–93; below; *News and Observer*, March 9, July 27, 28, 1989; "State of the State," January 17, 1989, pages 12–13, below.

[19]Luther Hartwell Hodges (1898–1974), born in Cascade, Va.; buried in Eden; North Carolina governor, 1957–1961; Democrat. Previously identified in Poff, *Addresses of Martin*, I, 552n–553n.

[20]The original text reads "While all we have shared in the concern over plant closings. . . ."

[21]John D. Kasarda and David L. Birch, *Job Creation in North Carolina: Where Are the New Jobs Coming From* (Chapel Hill: Center for Competitiveness and Employment Growth, Frank Hawkins Kenan Institute of Private Enterprise, University of North Carolina, November 1988), 2.

[22]The North Carolina Center for Public Policy Research devoted the October 1988 edition of its magazine, *North Carolina Insight*, to the question "State of the Environment: Time to Keep Tabs?" Among the articles featured therein were "Do We Need a North Carolina Environmental Index," 2–9, and "Recommendations: What Should Go in a North Carolina Environmental Index," 26–28.

[23]Martin appointed the Governor's Blue Ribbon Panel on Environmental Indicators in May 1989. The group established guidelines for a biennial environmental index that they envisioned would be published by the Department of Environment, Health and Natural Resources. *Final Report and Recommendations on North Carolina Environmental Indicators* ([Raleigh: Governor's Blue Ribbon Panel on Environmental Indicators], December 1990), 1, A-1, A-2; for related press release, see "Environmental Panel to Hold Public Meeting," Raleigh, August 16, 1989, Governors Papers, James G. Martin.

[24]The governor presented his plan for reorganizing state environmental regulation functions to a legislative study commission on February 17, 1988; see Poff, *Addresses of Martin*, I, 749–753. The act creating the North Carolina Department of Environment, Health, and Natural Resources was ratified August 3, 1989. *N.C. Session Laws, 1989*, II, c. 727, previously identified in Poff, *Addresses of Martin*, I, 54n.

[25]Executive Order Number 80, signed January 10, 1989, established the North Carolina Drug Cabinet. The governor later amended the order, thus including the secretary of administration among the board's membership; see *N.C. Session Laws, 1989*, II, 3094-3097, 3098. The Drug Cabinet was an outgrowth of the Challenge '87 and Challenge '88 initiatives of his first term, Martin told reporters at a January 10, 1989, news conference.

Persons initially named by Governor Martin to the Drug Cabinet included:

James Carson Gardner (1933–), born in Rocky Mount; attended North Carolina State University; U.S. Army, 1953–1955. Cofounder, executive vice-president, 1962–1967, Hardee's Food Systems, Inc.; president, Gardner Foods, Inc., Rocky Mount; chairman, state Republican party, 1965–1966; elected to U.S. House of Representatives from North Carolina's Fourth Congressional District, 1966; Republican gubernatorial candidate, 1968, 1992; lieutenant governor, 1989–1993. *Biographical Directory of Congress*, 1042-1043; *News and Observer*, November 4, 1992.

Lacy Herman Thornburg (1929–), born in Charlotte; attorney general of North Carolina, 1985–1992; candidate for Democratic gubernatorial nomination, 1992. Previously identified in Poff, *Addresses of Martin*, I, 21n; see also *News and Observer*, December 30, 1992.

Bob R. Etheridge (1941–), born in Sampson County; member, N.C. House, 1979–1988; elected superintendent of public instruction, 1988, reelected 1992; Democrat. Previously identified in Poff, *Addresses of Martin*, I, 63n; see also *News and Observer*, November 4, 1992.

Claude E. Pope (1934–1989), born in Harnett County; state commerce secretary, 1987–1989; Republican. Previously identified in Poff, *Addresses of Martin*, I, 458n.

Aaron Johnson (1933–), born in Willard; secretary, N.C. Dept. of Correction, 1985-1992; Republican. Previously identified in Poff, *Addresses of Martin*, I, 164n; see also press release, "Correction Secretary Aaron Johnson Steps Down," Raleigh, February 28, 1992, pages 430–431, below.

Joseph Wayne Dean (1944–), born in Nashville, Tenn.; secretary, N.C. Dept. of Crime Control and Public Safety, 1985–1992; Republican candidate for attorney general, 1992. Previously identified in Poff, *Addresses of Martin*, I, 121n; see also *News and Observer*, November 4, 1992.

David Thomas Flaherty (1928–), born in Boston, Mass.; secretary, N.C. Dept. of Human Resources, 1987-1993; Republican. Previously identified in Poff, *Addresses of Martin*, I, 598n.

James E. Harrington (1927–), born in Bethlehem, N.H.; secretary, N.C. Dept. of Transportation, 1985–1989; Republican. Previously identified in Poff, *Addresses of Martin*, I, 55n; see also *North Carolina Manual, 1991–1992* (Raleigh: State of North Carolina [issued biennially, 1903 to present]), 202, hereinafter cited as *North Carolina Manual*, with appropriate year.

STATE OF THE STATE

JANUARY 17, 1989

Mr. President,[1] Mr. Speaker,[2] Honorable Members of the North Carolina General Assembly, My Fellow North Carolinians:

I have come here at your invitation to present the biennial budget message, a balance of revenue and spending proposals to guide and stimulate your own deliberations for the next few months. There will be some surprises, although not many, since the Advisory Budget Commission has already publicly aired most of the requests.

So much has been written and said about the reorganization of the Senate and House last week, and I will not add to that.[3] I do wish to congratulate the new leadership of both parties, in both chambers, and express my readiness to work with you to achieve great things for North Carolina. Judging from optimistic statements many of you have voiced, the essential time of reconciliation and accommodation already has begun. I commend you for that. There is so much to be done, and so many able minds among all factions in the House and Senate, that North Carolina can reach its full potential only if all of you are involved to your full potential. Let me also personally offer to every member my pledge to work with you to serve the people of your district, for they are my constituents, too.

We meet this afternoon in a time of great change, of great challenges, and of great expectations. It is a time of revenue growth more limited than we have enjoyed in recent years, and yet, while it may not be "the best of times," neither is it "the worst of times."[4] North Carolina has continued to experience robust economic growth, with all sections of the state, rural and urban, sharing in that prosperity as never before. Economic growth cooled a fraction, from a 6 percent high, in 1987, to 5.2 percent last year, but that still exceeded the national mark, as well as our own previous three-year average.

Unemployment continued to improve for the sixth year in a row, a full 2 percent below the national average for the last four years. Factory wages climbed faster than nationally, as the number of manufacturing jobs continued a healthy climb. Jobs paying $45,000 or more rose by half again faster than the national average. While the number of counties above 10 percent unemployment steadily improved, from twenty in 1984 to only two in 1988, the number of counties with less than 5 percent jobless improved also, from just eight in 1984 to a grand total of seventy-six counties better than 5 percent unemployment last year! It is noteworthy that almost half, 43 percent, of the net gain in new jobs came from small firms with less than twenty employees.

Thanks to this robust economy and superior regulatory standards, in contrast with Texas and certain other states, North Carolina financial institutions, and businesses generally, experienced a healthier year than in many other states. By continuing to sustain a strong job market, we have a great opportunity to boost wage levels higher for the people. For that reason, my primary message to you is the strategic importance of continuing our bold investment in education and transportation. More than any other factors, those two will generate the biggest dividends of better paying jobs for North Carolinians. Through better schools, we can ensure that our workers are prepared and trainable for the more technologically demanding jobs of the future. It's one thing to bring more skilled jobs to the people; we must also bring their skills up to meet the jobs. Through better roads, we can meet a fundamental necessity upon which manufacturing investment depends. Very few of our new factories have located in a community that did not have the convenience of a four-lane highway connecting to the Interstate system.

For these reasons, my budget for the 1989–1991 biennium places its priorities on better schools and better roads.[5] In a session facing a relatively tight budget, it is even more important to keep schools at the top of our priorities, as you and I have done every year for the last four years. Every budget I have submitted, and every budget you have adopted, has increased the proportion of the General Fund operating budget allocated to our public schools. We can share pride in that constancy, because that had never happened before.

There are some important choices to be made within that top priority of public education, because there is not enough revenue growth to cover all the needs that have been submitted for schools alone. To put that in perspective, let me review the revenue picture.

Revenue

Through the first six months of this fiscal year, despite a slow start through October, General Fund revenues have grown by 6.86 percent over the previous year. That supports the confidence of both the Fiscal Research Office and the Budget Office that the current fiscal year will reach the forecast growth of 6.4 percent. Based on that, we can project the availability for the next fiscal year of only $233 million in increased recurring revenue, after allocating $80 million for mandated Medicaid costs, $65 million for construction of schools, and $75 million to continue recurring items that were funded last year with nonrecurring dollars. Then, we would expect a more normal growth level of $435 million more in the second year, 1990–1991.

This creates an unusual situation of being able to budget more generously for new programs in the second year of the biennium, while having to hold to a stricter diet in the first year. If no more than $233 million is available in 1989-1990 for recurring expenses, such as salary improvements and new programs, only our top priorities can be addressed without increasing taxes. For example, a 5 percent pay raise for all state and school employees, including teachers, would take all of the available recurring revenue, leaving nothing for added prison employees ($10 million), the Basic Education plan ($113 million), state employees' health insurance ($40 million), or services to older adults ($6 million), or anything else.

Choices must be made. Some may suggest that taxes be increased. That might have to be considered in the future if we find a chronic slowdown in revenue growth, but nobody forecasts that grim a picture. So instead I see one year in which we will have to tighten our belts to make room for some urgent improvements, while deferring others.

A Deferred Pay Increase, and How to Improve It

Let me turn, then, to the toughest part of the budget. In order to accommodate the most pressing program responsibilities for education, prisons, health, aging, environmental protection, and law enforcement, there remains only $62.4 million for pay increases in the first year, and four times as much, $250 million, in the second year. That's enough for a 4.5 percent pay increase—5.7 percent for teachers—for the entire second year, but for only one quarter of the first year, unless additional revenues can be found.

Because my recommendations need to be submitted now, several months before revenue estimates can be reliably improved, my budget reflects that tentative choice of initiating the pay increase in April 1990, but with the recommendation further that any additional savings or revenue growth be applied primarily to moving up the starting date for the pay hike. It's easy to say that's not fair to teachers and other employees, but you will have the next four months to look at possible alternatives: whether to cut programs or re-estimate revenues.[6]

The Revenue Department reports that we are already beginning to experience some surge of estimated tax payments that might reflect an anticipated windfall of capital gains tax for RJR Nabisco stockholders.[7] However, it will be April before a clear prediction of the magnitude of that effect can be made, so it is too early to rely on how much that might yield. If, for illustration only, we could be sure in June that it would generate an extra $62 million, then I would recommend that amount be used to advance the starting date for the pay increase by three months, to January. That's what it would take.

As requested by the State Employees Association (SEANC) and recommended by your study commission, part (one-third) of the increase for state employees is reserved for restoring performance pay.[8]

Your Tax Fairness Study Commission has produced a monumental package of recommendations to simplify the tax code, improve the fairness of its burden, strengthen its enforcement, and replace obsolete taxes—such as that on intangible property. This work was guided by the intention of being revenue neutral. It appears from examination that it may well raise the yield of revenues by its enforcement features, although again it is too early to predict how much with any certainty.

Meanwhile, any savings you can achieve in the Continuation Budget, over and above what I have submitted, could similarly be applied to an earlier pay increase. I have asked all departments to eliminate approximately 1 percent of their positions, and to identify user fees that might be increased, including tuition, to generate funds for an earlier pay raise, or for program improvements that could not otherwise be afforded in 1989.[9] Alternatively, you might consider deferring some part of the program expansions that I have recommended, in order to apply that to an earlier pay raise. I tried that with the Advisory Budget Commission, and got advised not to touch any sacred cows.[10]

Not even the teachers' association rose to put pay increases ahead of hiring more nonteachers, perhaps not realizing that was the only trade-off, and only one editorial response endorsed deferring the hiring of additional noninstructional personnel so that the same money could be used to improve teachers' salaries. Perhaps that was because no one understood my earlier attempt to explain what the options were. If that's so, there will be plenty of time over the next few months for you to heed any revised advice and amend the budget accordingly. I have done the best I can with this subject and certainly hope that, by springtime, revenues will be blooming in brighter abundance, and that you will have the benefit of a rosier, but less thorny, pathway than is evident now. Let me quickly highlight some of the more noteworthy program improvements being recommended.

Education

Most of the new spending goes for public education, with $113 million in the first year and $212 million in the second year for the Basic Education Program, keeping it on schedule. In comparison with the 4.5 percent pay increase for all other employees, it is proposed that a salary reserve for public schoolteachers be established, equivalent to a 5.7 percent average raise, and that the State Board of Education recommend to the General Assembly how much of this should be applied to career ladder increments and how much of it to across-the-board increases. This would likewise begin in April 1990, unless additional revenues could be identified to cover an earlier pay raise.

Other school improvements would:

(a) Double the Teaching Fellows Program, adding 400 each year;[11]

(b) Strengthen teacher education, including expansion of the summer foreign language institutes;[12] and

(c) Fund various approaches to dropout prevention, including Cities in Schools.[13]

In all, this will continue to increase, to 47.3 percent, the share of the General Fund operating budget going to public schools.

In addition to budget priorities, some exciting and challenging educational issues face you and our new state superintendent and Board of Education. A rising consensus of these and other educators and community leaders has called for a greater degree of accountability at all levels of school leadership, with the emphasis on results. After years of debating inputs of funding formulas and staffing allotments, we are now going to awaken to the real objective of public education: improving student achievement. It is my contention that the fundamental standard by which our schools should be measured is student performance. Coupled with that is the need to increase the level of local flexibility in the management of state programs, even the BEP.

At the direction of the legislature, the State Board of Education is undertaking a "mid-course review" of the Basic Education Program in order to set accreditation standards for individual schools. They will be able to recommend to you any modifications that would allow more local flexibility in allocating the positions within a school. Clearly, the typical school is not average, but has a unique combination of needs that is not likely to be met by some average prescription. One school might need more counselors and social workers for dropout prevention; others might need more math teachers.

Another reform that is having considerable success around the nation is public school choice: allowing students and their parents to have more to say about the school they attend. In North Carolina, local boards have established magnet schools to which one may choose to attend. In Maryland, Massachusetts, New York, New Jersey, Missouri, and Wisconsin it is permitted to choose any school in some systems; in Minnesota, any school in the state. This approach imposes the ultimate test of accountability on a school system: to meet the needs of the students. It is self-enforcing, through choice of enrollment, and generally strengthens teachers as academic leaders; and it should lead local boards to create more kinds of innovative schools, like "career education" high schools and combinations with community colleges.

While twenty-three states have looked at this, North Carolina has watched from the sidelines. My own reluctance arose out of a concern that such choices might lead to resegregation of schools. Other states have found ways to safeguard against this and have found a very high level of acceptance among parents of all racial, and geographic, and economic circumstances. With President-elect Bush encouraging this movement to schools of choice, the time has come for us to begin debate on this issue. I call upon the State Board of Education and this General Assembly to examine with me how schools of choice might improve education in North Carolina. It does not have to be rushed, what with so many issues on our agenda, but neither should it be ignored. Defining the concept would help public discussion of it.[14]

Many of these programs seek to build improved literacy, as do our community colleges, prisons, and many employers and volunteer tutors. To help coordinate these efforts, I propose a literacy office to be created in the Department of Administration.

In addition to programs to reduce dropout rates, we must find better ways to prepare four-year-olds to be ready to drop in when they get to kindergarten and first grade. I am convinced that we can offer appropriate readiness programs at lowest cost by utilizing our day-care providers. Accordingly, I propose $2 million for prekindergarten, developmental day care for at-risk four-year-olds.[15] This would be administered by the Department of Human Resources, with valuable input and assistance from the Department of Public Instruction, allowing the DPI to continue its concentration on improving grades K through 12.

Transportation

Turning now to better roads, I predict that this session will be historic for adopting the strategic corridor highway concept and for moving boldly to fund it to completion. The Highway Study Commission is nearing agreement on its recommendations. It is their hope to present you with a map and construction schedule of four-lane highways to be built by the turn of the century, along with improved connectors, and a tax and bond package to pay for it in the most economical way. Out of deference to the explicit request of the Highway Study Commission, I have withheld placing my own separate funding proposal before you.

When their recommendation is made public, I urge you all to be prepared to work with us on it, and to support it here and among your constituents. At long last, we will have a reliable commitment that will bring the economic benefits of four-lane roads within ten miles of over 90 percent of our people. In response to your suggestions, the package is likely to include improved funding for secondary roads and municipalities.

Railroads also have a vital place in our future, just as they had in our past. Last year, you gave me authority to acquire rail right-of-way that was about to be abandoned, albeit without funding. Fortunately, a creative financing package enabled us to strike a bargain for sixty-seven miles of railroad from Murphy to Dillsboro, which is quickly becoming a major tourist attraction. With a one-time appropriation of $1 million, we will be better positioned to respond to future contingencies in other rural areas.[16]

The Governor's Rail Passenger Task Force has been studying ways to restore passenger service along the route of the North Carolina Railroad, in which our state has held 70 percent of the shares for 140 years and along which our urban piedmont corridor has grown. This will require a significant investment in rolling stock and improvements in our track, and it is my view that this should be financed out of the state's future earnings from the railroad stock, which will be enhanced when we complete the renegotiation of our lease with Norfolk Southern.[17]

Economic Development

The public dividend from all this investment in better schools and better roads will be better jobs for our people. Yet that will also require continuation of a vigorous economic development program. To strengthen our efforts through the Department of Commerce, I propose a $2 million expansion of the business-industry development program, the International Division for export promotion and missions, and travel and tourism promotion.[18]

With migrant labor rapidly becoming the major source of farm workers, many headaches are caused by having four agencies making migrant housing inspections, using different rules and standards. My Task Force on the Farm Economy has prepared a simple bill to consolidate these inspections under one agency.[19]

I am also proposing a stronger emphasis on aquaculture to be funded within the Department of Agriculture.

Environment

In addition to moving forward with the Coastal Initiative, to protect Outstanding Resource Waters while promoting environmentally appropriate waterfront development, I will also develop and establish an environmental index to provide a frame of reference with which to gauge our progress.

North Carolina will continue to receive its distribution from petroleum overcharge settlements. Again, $24 million over the biennium will be allocated for energy conservation programs, with one-fourth of that going for the Low Income Home Energy Assistance Program.[20]

I recommend funding $9 million to the departments of Agriculture, Administration, Human Resources, and Natural Resources and Community Development to establish and strengthen programs relating to:

(a) Pesticides in groundwater;[21]

(b) Compliance of air quality standards;[22]

(c) The siting and establishment of a low-level radioactive waste management facility;[23]

(d) Our response to Mobil Oil's proposed exploratory well;[24]

(e) Water quality regulation and permitting;

(f) Clean up and replacement of leaking underground storage tanks;

(g) Hazardous waste regulation and site clean up;[25] and

(h) Assistance and permitting for solid waste management.[26]

In the second year, I propose also $10 million for a solid waste revolving fund, and $8.5 million [for] the North American pavilion at the North Carolina Zoo, and a $10 million reserve for improvements within the state parks system.[27] A study of our state parks has identified $135 million in needed park improvements and recommends funding half of that over the next five years. This will only meet the most urgent needs.

It is especially critical that we get back on track with our obligation to select a site for a facility to treat, recycle, and detoxify so-called hazardous wastes. If we fail to certify by October our ability to pick a site, we would face penalties from the federal government.[28] I must report to you that we have even less time than that to show our commitment to this responsibility.

Our neighboring state of South Carolina is considering excluding any hazardous waste delivered to its site from any state that has not taken steps to solve its own problem by March 1. The posture we have taken for the last six months is interpreted by Governor Campbell as prohibiting any solution. This will require prompt attention. I will work with you to meet both these imminent deadlines, but I challenge you either to create a framework for making a site decision, or I invite you to turn it over to me. Something has to be done soon.[29]

I am very much encouraged by progress that has been made in recent months by your Environmental Study Commission to recommend consolidation of environmental regulation within one new Department of Health and Environment, mainly along the lines that I recommended a year ago. This has now been thoroughly studied and has widespread endorsements, and it is my hope that this can also be among the first major accomplishments of this session.

Prison Overcrowding

Another issue that must be resolved early in this session is the overcrowding of our prisons. In previous sessions, we have provided for the requirements imposed under the settlement involving fifteen prisons in the South Piedmont district and moved to get ahead of the curve overall. Last month, a settlement was reached in litigation over another forty-nine prison units.[30] On tomorrow I will submit to you a package of emergency legislation to do four things:

1. Approve the terms of the settlement;

2. Commit to funding additional prison construction, using the expedited approach that has proved so successful;

3. Expand intensively supervised parole and probation, electronic monitors for house arrest, and other alternatives to prison; and

4. Extend the Prison Cap Law, amending it so as to enlarge the pool of nonviolent inmates eligible for early release under the cap, while removing from eligibility drug traffickers, rapists, and others deemed unworthy by the Parole Commission.[31]

I will also ask the Department of Correction and the Budget Office to determine whether, and under what arrangements, prison construction contractors could use inmates who are trained for construction work. As part of the rehabilitation program through Prison Enterprises, we have previously used inmates for prison maintenance; now let's see if it can be cost effective to let prisoners build prisons.

Law Enforcement

In order to maintain safe highways and address the continuing drug trafficking problem in North Carolina, I am recommending additional Highway Patrol troopers (fifty each year), State Bureau of Investigation agents (forty in the second year), and Alcohol Law Enforcement agents (thirty-six).[32] Another $20 million is proposed for a new SBI complex in Raleigh.[33] Initially, the costs of staff support for the Drug Cabinet, chaired by Lieutenant Governor Gardner, are expected from federal grants from the Drug Enforcement Agency, plus direct participation from state agency personnel.

The tragic toll of highway accidents involving alcohol- or drug-impaired drivers has been thoroughly addressed by both your Safe Roads Study Commission and my Highway Safety Commission, with nearly identical conclusions, which ought to be a good sign. I am pleased to endorse their joint recommendations:

1. To make a single Breathalyzer test admissible when appropriate;

2. To reduce the blood alcohol standard for DWI [driving while impaired] from 0.10 to 0.08;[34]

3. To reenact the lower 0.04 BAC level for truck and bus drivers;[35]

4. To increase fines for DWI convictions;

5. To clarify the revocation period for provisional licensees;

6. To increase the penalty for felony death by vehicle;

7. To prohibit open containers of alcohol in passenger vehicles;

8. To make juveniles subject to implied consent laws.

Last year, the House passed legislation I had proposed to increase the license revocation for DWI from ten days to thirty. I urge you to enact this tougher provision and to provide for revocation of the "limited driving privilege" when its terms are violated.[36] In addition, I ask you to add DWI victims as beneficiaries of the Victims Compensation Fund.[37]

Because we average daily 600 DWI inmates adding to the crowding of our prisons, I will propose that you establish one or more alcoholic treatment centers under the Department of Correction. Judges should be authorized to sentence multiple offenders to such facilities for treatment, in lieu of active prison terms. Hopefully, you will find no objection to authorizing contracts with private facilities for intensive treatment of multiple DWI offenders.

There are many facets to this DWI program. There is treatment, loss of privilege, punishment, and publicity. There is also injury, pain, and death. We must use every reasonable weapon to put a stop to it.

Health

Federal Medicaid changes will obligate an increase in the Continuation Budget of $80 million in the first year and another $64 million in the second year, as already noted. In order to assist local communities to build area mental health facilities, we are looking at developing a package of mental health facility revenue bonds, which can be paid off using anticipated federal assistance payments.

Faced with declining enrollment in nursing schools and greater need for nursing services, I will ask the Department of Public Instruction to encourage counselors and teachers to promote nursing as a career opportunity. When the revenue picture becomes clearer, I will have other measures to recommend next year to help with this.

Rising costs and utilization of health insurance for state employees continues [sic] to far outstrip available funding. For now, I am proposing yet another infusion of $40 million and $53 million, respectively, for these next two years, with a similar $4 million and $6 million for the Highway Fund. But the time has come for a re-examination of the principles of deductibles and copayments as cost restraint factors.

I also propose again to reduce the state abortion fund to cover only those abortions where the pregnancy resulted from rape or incest, promptly reported, or where the mother's life is imperiled.[38]

Older Adults

Finally, funds are recommended in the Department of Human Resources for programs related to the aging, such as Alzheimer's patients,[39] senior centers, in-home and caregiver support services,[40] and monitoring complaints against health care facilities,[41] and transportation services for the elderly and handicapped.[42]

This budget does not provide for all of the needs that have been documented and requested, and it is likely that you will adopt other amendments, reflecting any differences in priorities that you wish. I hope that you will agree that in one irregular year for which modest revenue growth is expected, if we cannot have the luxury of a lot more money to spend on new and expanded programs, then our challenge will be to do better with what we have. Rather than applying our energies toward starting up so many new operations, we can direct our attentions toward polishing up the existing ones and making them work better.

Debate and progress on many of these fiscal issues present a major challenge to this General Assembly. Continued momentum for the BEP, expanding the career ladder statewide, funding the strategic corridor highway trust fund, relieving overcrowded prisons, consolidation of environmental agencies, stronger DWI laws and drug abuse countermeasures are a full agenda for you.

Constitutional Balance of Powers

I believe chances are good that another issue also will see consummation this year, leaving its mark on history. It is certainly my hope that this will be the year in which the North Carolina Constitution will be amended to provide for the executive veto, just like every other state.[43] Already a number of bills have been introduced, ranging from an effective line-item veto, subject to a two-thirds vote of both houses to override, to a limited veto for striking an entire bill or nothing, subject to being overridden by a simple majority. The latter version is essentially the equivalent of a way to hold a bill for a fourth reading, and thus is largely symbolic.

I see this as a major issue for good government and an issue of historic dimensions. After 212 years of avoidance and denial, the time has finally come to submit the veto question to the people of North Carolina. We are the only state where the people have never been allowed to vote on whether the governor should have the power and responsibility of the veto. Let there be no doubt that they are ready.

It will not do to submit a watered-down version to the people; neither should there be any sandbagging of the issue by tying it to unpopular measures in a package so unappealing that the whole would be doomed. The people should be allowed to vote on a real veto, separate and apart from any other questions. The people are our ultimate authority for constitutional and political decisions, and they should not be put in the position of having to accept something they don't want in order to win something else that they do want. If it is desired to submit other constitutional questions to the people at the same time, they must be separate items on the ballot.

Many ideas have been put forward of companion issues that should be taken up along with the veto. Some want to eliminate the consecutive terms for future governors. Others want to adjust the balance of other powers between the governor and the legislative branch. I am among those who feel we need to change the way judges are selected; the constitution provides for partisan election of judges, but few like the judicial elections to be very partisan. Others would bargain for extraneous matters, such as electing the governor and lieutenant governor together as one unit on the ballot. I will say to you that I am prepared to discuss any proposal and will consider support of other constitutional amendments, but will not concede on any issue prematurely in advance of knowing what will be granted in return. What I would hope for is a mechanism for discussion of any proposals that might lead to a decision to place the veto amendment on the ballot, as long as it's freestanding and alone.

As you can see, there are [*sic*] a host of major challenges facing us. I offer to work with you to solve them. If we work together, with all the energy and creativity we have, and personal forbearance and respect, I am confident that we can achieve many great things for North Carolina. There are so many goals before us that could make historic achievements for us. One is so special that, if we can overcome our differences and meet its historic challenge, you can be sure that future histories of North Carolina will name this the "Year of the Veto."

---

[1]James C. Gardner.

[2]Josephus Lyman Mavretic (1934–), born in Powells Point; resident of Edgecombe County; A.B., University of North Carolina at Chapel Hill, 1956; M.S., George Washington University, 1972; was also graduated from U.S. Naval War College, 1972; U.S. Marine Corps pilot, 1956-1977. Member, 1980–1994, Speaker, 1989–1990, N.C. House of Representatives; Democrat. *North Carolina Manual, 1991–1992*, 303, 417.

[3]Both houses of the General Assembly reorganized in response to the rising Republican tide evident in the outcome of the 1988 elections. Jim Gardner became the state's first Republican lieutenant governor in the twentieth century. His victory also made him Senate president, which inspired the Democratic majority in the upper house to distribute among its members the authority it formerly granted to lieutenant governors; see "A Southern Strategy," March 30, 1990, 256n–257n, below. But while Senate Democrats consolidated control among themselves, some of their colleagues in the House of Representatives were maneuvering to share power with Republican members. A dislike of Liston

Ramsey, the formidable four-term Speaker, fueled their unprecedented desire to collaborate.

Speaker Ramsey and a close circle of lieutenants monopolized decision-making in the House, to the exclusion of most other Democrats and all Republicans, for eight years. His "arbitrary and dictatorial" control, observed Thad Beyle, "effectively provided him with the veto power the state's governors had coveted for so long." Discipline was enforced through the appropriations process.

Republican candidates, from Martin and Gardner to House hopefuls, found Ramsey and the rest of the House leadership to be an irresistible target during their 1988 election campaigns. Their rhetorical strategy proved effective. When the votes were counted, the GOP had gained ten seats in the state House of Representatives; although Democrats remained in the majority, it was the worst erosion of power the party suffered in any state legislature in the nation. There was no comparable bloodletting in the North Carolina Senate elections.

Worried their party would suffer greater losses in 1990 if Ramsey remained as Speaker, a pair of House Democrats, Daniel DeVane and Donald Dawkins, began a secret campaign on November 9, 1988, to unseat him. They soon enlisted other like-minded party members and ultimately made an overture to Republicans seeking a role in House affairs more in proportion to their numbers. Conspirators from both parties agreed on a plan, devised by Representative Josephus Mavretic, to recast the state House along the congressional model; Republicans would be given committee assignments and other power unlike any they had enjoyed that century. Both sides also agreed to back Mavretic for Speaker.

Governor Martin abetted the rebels and provided a haven for their negotiations on at least two occasions during the nine-week coup. He recalled that DeVane contacted him "'in early December and let me know what they were up to. I approved strongly of what they were trying to do, feeling that it would bring better, fairer, more representative government to the people of North Carolina. I offered to do what I could to help, but I felt the agreement should be reached by House members alone. I offered Dan the use of the Executive Mansion as a meeting place.'" Martin and the historic house exerted a steadying influence. Beyle wrote, "Both factions of the coalition seemed to regard the Executive Mansion as neutral ground. The governor played the role of guarantor. Both sides felt they could depend on the other to uphold its end of the agreement as long as Martin was involved."

The conspirators publicly declared, on January 8, their determination to overthrow Ramsey. Two days later, agents whom Martin believed to represent the Speaker called on him and urged that he persuade House Republicans to back the incumbent; in exchange, they offered "favored status" for the governor's legislative proposals and the passage of gubernatorial veto. He declined. Forty-five Republicans joined twenty Democrats on January 11, the opening day of the 1989 legislative session, to elect Mavretic as Speaker.

Speaker Mavretic reorganized the North Carolina House as promised. Yet, the unique union of Democrats and Republicans that toppled Ramsey seemed to lose its raison d'être once he was gone; its inability to enact Martin's most cherished proposal, gubernatorial veto, illustrated its ineffectiveness. "Mavretic's coalition was not cohesive enough to promote major initiatives," according to Joel A. Thompson. "The 20 Democrats ran the political spectrum and rarely voted as a bloc. The Republicans were usually split between those who sought compromise with the Democrats to influence policy and those who maintained an opposition mentality." Thad L. Beyle, "Political Change in North Carolina: A Legislative Coup d'Etat," *Comparative State Politics* 10 (April 1989): 3–15; Joel A. Thompson, "The 1989 North Carolina General Assembly: Beirut on a Bad Day," *Comparative State Politics* 10 (December 1989): 14, hereinafter cited as Thompson, "The 1989 North Carolina General Assembly."

[4]"It was the best of times, it was the worst of times." Charles Dickens, *A Tale of Two Cities* [1859], bk. I, ch. 1, quoted in John Bartlett, *Familiar Quotations: A Collection of Passages, Phrases, and Proverbs Traced to Their Sources in Ancient and Modern Literature*, ed. by Emily Morison Beck (Boston: Little, Brown and Company, fourteenth edition, 1968), 672, hereinafter cited as Bartlett, *Familiar Quotations.*

[5]Martin submitted his fiscal proposals as *The North Carolina State Budget, 1989–1991 Biennium* (Raleigh: Office of State Budget and Management, 7 volumes, January 1989) and

The North Carolina State Budget: Summary of Recommendations, Expansion Detail, Capital Improvements, 1989–1991 Biennium (Raleigh: Office of State Budget and Management, January 1989), hereinafter cited as *North Carolina State Budget, 1989–1991: Summary of Recommendations*. The *North Carolina State Budget: Post–Legislative Budget Summary, 1989–1991 Biennium* (Raleigh: Office of State Budget and Management, November 1989), hereinafter cited as *Post–Legislative Budget Summary, 1989–1991*, outlines spending authorized by the General Assembly. Joseph S. Ferrell (ed.), *North Carolina Legislation, 1989* (Chapel Hill: Institute of Government, University of North Carolina at Chapel Hill, 1990), and Thompson, "The 1989 North Carolina General Assembly," 13–17, describe the significant measures adopted.

[6]The proposal to postpone pay raises for teachers and state employees, from July 1, 1989, until April 1990, proved unpopular. It particularly rankled public schoolteachers, who recalled the governor's campaign pledge to boost salaries to the national average by 1992. The depth of opposition to the deferral became known to Martin personally in early February, when teachers booed him at an education forum in Hickory. In Raleigh, a thousand irate educators picketed the Executive Mansion the night of February 13 and shouted down the governor as he attempted to discuss the pay issue with them. The next day, more than 5,000 schoolteachers from across North Carolina converged on the General Assembly and the Executive Mansion to express displeasure with a number of issues, including the proposed raise, their frozen salary scale, statewide implementation of the career ladder, and problems with the Basic Education Program.

Martin unveiled a new pay proposal on March 8, 1989, that called for a 6 percent raise for public schoolteachers, beginning the following July, to be funded by a 1-cent increase in the state sales tax. Teacher salaries would reach the national average via the career ladder merit-pay plan; see pages 89–92, below. However, the governor's proposition was no more popular with the North Carolina Association of Educators than his initial offering, primarily because it remained tied to the career ladder. Although school system superintendents and others in the education community supported the merit-pay mechanism, NCAE opposed it. The organization adamantly maintained that enactment of a 10 percent raise, to elevate base teacher salaries closer to the national average, was a prerequisite to any earnest discussion of the career ladder.

The General Assembly approved an average pay hike of 6 percent for teachers and state employees on August 10, 1989; the raises were made retroactive to July 1. Educators received a new thirty-step salary schedule, and the career ladder was made an option. "An Act to Make Expansion Budget Appropriations for Current Operations of State Departments, Institutions, and Agencies, and for Other Purposes," *N.C. Session Laws, 1989*, c. 752, secs. 36, 38; *News and Observer*, January 10, 31, February 1, 2, 4, 9, 10, 13–16, March 14, 15, April 6, 8, 11, 12, 13, 14, 17, 23, 28, May 2, 1989; see also "Inaugural Address," page 6n, above.

[7]The governor was referring to the financial aftermath of the buyout of RJR Nabisco, in November 1988, by Kohlberg Kravis Roberts and Co. for $14.53 billion. Poff, *Addresses of Martin*, I, 459n.

[8]Jobholders protected by the State Personnel Act became eligible for 2 percent merit raises, effective January 1, 1990. "An Act to Revise the Performance Pay System in Effect for State Employees Subject to the Provisions of Chapter 126 of the General Statutes," *N.C. Session Laws, 1989*, c. 796, was ratified August 12, 1989; see also *Post-Legislative Budget Summary, 1989–1991*, 102.

[9]The General Assembly approved a 20 percent rise in tuition, beginning with the 1989–1990 academic year, for resident students attending public universities. Tuition for nonresident students was scheduled to increase 17.4 percent during the biennium. *Post–Legislative Budget Summary, 1989–1991*, 30.

[10]The *News and Observer*, December 15, 1988, reported the Advisory Budget Commission's recommendation to Martin not to cut new spending for the Basic Education Program. Later that month, the governor disclosed his intention to keep BEP funding on track; see *News and Observer*, December 31, 1988.

[11]Legislators answered Martin's call for 400 new scholarship loans, of $5,000 each, for each year of the Teaching Fellows program. *North Carolina State Budget, 1989–1991: Summary of Recommendations*, 35; *Post-Legislative Budget Summary, 1989–1991*, 20.

[12]Appropriations to enhance teacher education were provided under *N.C. Session Laws, 1989*, II, c. 752, s. 96. Lawmakers augmented summer foreign language institutes along the lines Martin proposed; compare his *North Carolina State Budget, 1989–1991: Summary of Recommendations*, 36, and *N.C. Session Laws, 1989*, II, c. 752, s. 62.

[13]*N.C. Session Laws, 1989*, II, c. 752, s. 58, financed dropout prevention and in-school suspension programs.

[14]H.B. 1256, "A Bill to Be Entitled an Act to Establish Public Schools of Choice by Election of Local Boards of Education," was introduced in the House on April 12, 1989. The measure did not become law. *N.C. House Journal, 1989*, 387–388, 1021.

[15]Martin proposed spending $2 million for his program for at-risk four-year-olds beginning with the second year of the biennium. *North Carolina State Budget, 1989–1991: Summary of Recommendations*, 50.

[16]The General Assembly ratified "An Act to Preserve North Carolina Railroad Corridors" on July 7, 1988. The following year, legislators provided over $800,000 in aid to railroads for the 1989–1991 biennium. *N.C. Session Laws, 1987, Regular Session, 1988*, c. 1071.; *N.C. Session Laws, 1989*, I, c. 500, s. 5., II, c. 752, s. 5. The Great Smoky Mountains Railway was the tourist attraction to which Martin referred.

[17]Executive Order Number 71, signed March 11, 1988, established the Governor's Task Force on Rail Passenger Service. *N.C. Session Laws, 1987, Regular Session, 1988*, III, 973–976; see also "Joint Special Meeting of Shareholders, North Carolina Railroad Company and Atlantic and North Carolina Railroad Company," August 14, 1989, pages 145–149, below.

[18]The governor's hopes for more economic development funds did not fully materialize. For the biennium, he advocated an increase of nearly $1.9 million to expand business–industry development; the General Assembly provided just $1.2 million. Lawmakers offered slightly more than the $1.2 million improvement requested for the International Division but approved nearly $60,000 less than the $546,000 boost Martin wanted for travel and tourism promotion. The $2 million figure he cited for all three categories covered only the 1989–1990 fiscal year; as adopted, the budget lifted spending in those areas by approximately $1.3 million during that time. *North Carolina State Budget, 1989–1991: Summary of Recommendations*, 60–61; *Post-Legislative Budget Summary, 1989–1991*, 74–75.

[19]"An Act to Consolidate the Regulation of Migrant Housing within the Department of Labor and to Establish Standards and Enforcement Provisions for the Regulation of Migrant Housing" was ratified May 8, 1989. Martin signed Executive Order Number 36, creating the Governor's Task Force on the Farm Economy in North Carolina, on March 6, 1987. *N.C. Session Laws, 1987*, II, 2337–2340; *N.C. Session Laws, 1989*, I, c. 91.

[20]*N.C. Session Laws, 1989*, II, c. 752, s. 150, authorized allocations from the Special Reserve for Oil Overcharge Funds. Financing for the reserve resulted from the *United States v. Exxon* case.

[21]A study of the effects of pesticides upon the state's groundwater resources was approved. *Post-Legislative Budget Summary, 1989–1991*, 71.

[22]Lawmakers appropriated nearly $1.4 million, for the biennium, in the quest to comply with state and federal ambient air quality standards. *Post-Legislative Budget Summary, 1989–1991*, 81.

[23]*North Carolina State Budget, 1989–1991: Summary of Recommendations*, 39, 161; *Post-Legislative Budget Summary, 1989–1991*, 33, 80; see also *N.C. Session Laws, 1989*, II, c. 752, s. 3.

[24]The Mobil Response Project received $337,282 for the biennium, the amount Martin requested. *North Carolina State Budget, 1989–1991: Summary of Recommendations*, 39; *Post-Legislative Budget Summary, 1989–1991*, 33.

[25]*N.C. Session Laws, 1989*, II, c. 752, secs. 3 and 144; see also "An Act to Establish an Asbestos Hazard Management Program and to Increase the Percentage of the Budget for the Hazardous Waste Management Regulatory Program Which May Come From Hazardous Waste Fees Imposed Under G.S. 130A–294.1," *N.C. Session Laws, 1989*, II, c. 724, s. 4, ratified August 3, 1989.

[26]*N.C. Session Laws, 1989*, II, c. 752, secs. 3 and 143.

[27]The legislature approved $5 million for the Solid Waste Revolving Fund during the 1989–1990 fiscal year, and $900,000 for the 1990–1991 period. *N.C. Session Laws, 1989*, II, c. 754, s. 5; *N.C. Session Laws, Extra Session, 1989, Extra and Regular Sessions, 1990*, c. 1074,

s. 2. The state zoo was to receive $4.25 million for the completion of its North American phase, provided the N.C. Zoological Park Society could raise a dollar for every four that lawmakers had set aside; see *N.C. Session Laws, 1989*, II, c. 754, secs. 4, 44. *N.C. Session Laws, 1989*, c. 754, secs. 4 and 39, earmarked $8 million for the State Parks System Reserve for F.Y. 1989–1990.

[28]Federal law required all states to prove, by October 17, 1989, that they had either the capacity to dispose of their own hazardous waste or they had joined compacts with other states that agreed to dispose of it for them. Those unable to make such certification risked losing Superfund monies. P.L. 94–580, "Resource Conservation and Recovery Act of 1976," *United States Statutes at Large*, Act of October 21, 1976, 90 Stat. 2795–2841; see also "American Chemical Manufacturers Association," below; *News and Observer*, January 19, 1989; United States Code (1988 edition), Title 42, Section 6901 et seq.

[29]Thirty–two states and Puerto Rico disposed of hazardous wastes in the GSX Chemical Services Company landfill at Pinewood, South Carolina. Of those, the largest depositor was North Carolina: The 45 million tons of waste the state's industries transported to the site in 1988 consumed approximately one–third of the facility's yearly capacity.

As concern escalated over the environmental effects of the landfill, and as the estimates rose for cleaning up the contamination it caused, Governor Carroll A. Campbell, Jr., decided it was time other states confronted their own hazardous waste problems. On January 18, 1989, he signed an executive order prohibiting states that banned disposal of such materials within their own borders from shipping them to South Carolina. The measure included North Carolina and became effective March 1.

Campbell's action in Columbia inspired activity in Raleigh. Governor Martin promulgated an executive order requiring industries to reduce the amount of hazardous waste they generated. North Carolina legislators introduced S.B. 324, which lifted the state's hazardous waste disposal ban and reopened the search for a suitable location for a waste treatment plant. Shortly after the bill passed the Senate, Campbell lifted the ban against waste shipments from the Tar Heel State for ten days, beginning March 27.

Ratification of S.B. 324 on May 30 prompted Campbell's decision to lift the ban again on July 7, 1989. But Palmetto State officials warned that it would be reinstated if North Carolina were unable to show sufficient progress in completing treatment facilities of its own. "Announcement on Executive Order Number 86," March 2, 1989, pages 85–87, below; *N.C. Senate Journal, 1989*, 119, 156, 162, 171, 198, 589, 599, 617, 618; *News and Observer*, October 14, 1988, January 19, 23, March 2, 3, 23, April 4, 9, July 8, 1989; press release, "Governor Martin's Reaction to Announcement that South Carolina Waste Facility Will Be Re–Opened to North Carolina Hazardous Waste Producers," Raleigh, July 7, 1989, Governors Papers, James G. Martin; S.B. 324, "An Act to Provide for the Management of Hazardous Waste in North Carolina, to Reorganize the North Carolina Hazardous Waste Treatment Commission as the North Carolina Hazardous Waste Management Commission, to Amend Various Statutes Relating to the Management of Hazardous Waste, and to Make Conforming Changes to Other Statutes," *N.C. Session Laws, 1989*, I, c. 168.

Carroll Ashmore Campbell, Jr. (1940–), elected South Carolina governor, 1986, re-elected 1990; Republican. Previously identified in Poff, *Addresses of Martin*, I, 908n; see also *Who's Who in America, 1994* (New Providence, N.J.: Marquis Who's Who, forty-eighth edition, 2 volumes, 1993), I, 526, hereinafter cited as *Who's Who in America*, with appropriate year.

[30]Court settlements for two major lawsuits forced the state to address its prison overcrowding problem. The consent judgment of September 1985, stemming from *Hubert v. Ward*, focused on relieving inmate living conditions in the South Piedmont prison district. *Small v. Martin*, the latter suit to which Martin referred, was settled December 20, 1988. Among that agreement's provisions were requirements for improved medical care, recreation, security, and fifty square feet of living space for each inmate in the state's forty-nine minimum- and medium-security prisons. *News and Observer*, November 11, December 12, 22, 23, 1988; Poff, *Addresses of Martin*, I, 42n.

[31]Legislators approved the terms of the *Small v. Martin* agreement with the passage of "An Act to Make an Emergency Appropriation for Correctional Programs and Projects," *N.C. Session Laws, 1989*, I, c. 8, ratified March 7, 1989. "An Act to Amend and Extend the Prison Population Stabilization Act, to Amend and Extend Community Service Parole, to

Limit the Transfer of County Prisoners to the State Prison System, and to Authorize Parole and Termination of Supervision of Misdemeanants," was ratified February 1; see *N.C. Session Laws, 1989*, I, c. 1. The original Prison Population Stabilization Act, *N.C. Session Laws, 1987*, I, c. 7, passed the General Assembly on March 11, 1987; also known as the Prison Cap Law, it set the release threshold at 97 percent of the state's correctional capacity of 18,000 inmates. The 1989 amendment pushed that number to 98 percent.

[32]*N.C. Session Laws, 1989*, II, c. 752, s. 115, authorized hiring only thirty extra state highway patrolmen during the entire 1989–1991 biennium.

[33]Legislators set aside $18.5 million, for the 1989–1991 biennium, for new SBI facilities. *N.C. Session Laws, 1989*, II, c. 754, s. 4

[34]The General Assembly lowered the blood alcohol limit for drunken driving to 0.08 in 1993. The law became effective October 1. *News and Observer*, July 8, September 30, 1993.

[35]If their blood alcohol content was 0.04 or more, drivers of commercial vehicles risked suspension of their licenses under legislation adopted on August 12, 1989; see "An Act to Provide for a Commercial Driver License System, Endorsements to a Commercial Driver License, and Disqualifying Offenses for a Commercial Driver License," *N.C. Session Laws, 1989*, II, c. 771. The General Assembly had reduced the limit from 0.10 to 0.04 in 1988, but the stricter threshold was enacted for only one month. *N.C. Session Laws, 1987, Regular Session, 1988*, III, c. 1112; Poff, *Addresses of Martin*, I, 904.

[36]The House adopted H.B. 2490, "A Bill to Be Entitled an Act to Increase the Immediate Civil License Revocation for Certain Persons Charged with Implied Consent Offenses from Ten to Thirty Days and to Provide a Fee for the Service of Pick-Up Orders," on July 5, 1988. It was not ratified by the Senate. *N.C. House Journal, 1987, Second Session, 1988*, 118, 272, 287, 293; *N.C. Senate Journal, 1987, Second Session, 1988*, 190, 207.

Republicans were the sole sponsors of the 1988 bill, and they hoped to turn the momentum that H.B. 2490 gained in the House into stricter impaired-driving laws during the next year's legislative session. However, their attempts to strengthen DWI punishments along the lines recommended by the governor, above, in 1989 proved less successful than in 1988. The following bills never escaped committee: S.B. 241, "A Bill to Increase the Immediate Civil License Revocation for Certain Persons Charged with Implied-Consent Offenses from Ten Days to Thirty Days and for Certain Other Persons from Thirty Days to Sixty Days," introduced February 22, and its companion bill in the House, H.B. 662, introduced March 16; and H.B. 356, "A Bill to Be Entitled an Act to Mandate Revocation of a Limited Driving Privilege in Certain Circumstances," introduced February 23. *N.C. House Journal, 1989*, 124, 215; *N.C. Senate Journal, 1989*, 98.

[37]See "An Act to Amend the Crime Victims Compensation Act to Include Victims Injured by Driving While Impaired Offenders, to Limit Recovery to Economic Loss, and to Provide Compensation to Residents Who Are Injured in a State That Does Not Have a Crime Victims Compensation Program," *N.C. Session Laws, 1989*, I, c. 322, ratified June 15.

[38]The legislature placed financial limitations on the state abortion fund, but the eligibility restrictions Martin suggested were not enacted. *N.C. Session Laws, 1989*, I, c. 500, s. 72.

[39]Alzheimer's Association chapters in North Carolina won four grants totaling $50,000 from the General Assembly. *N.C. Session Laws, 1989*, II, c. 799, s. 1. *N.C. Session Laws, 1989*, I, c. 500, secs. 95 and 97, addressed in-home services for Alzheimer's sufferers.

[40]In-home and caregiver support services for older adults were funded by *N.C. Session Laws, 1989*, I, c. 500, secs. 94, 95, and 97; see also *Post-Legislative Budget Summary, 1989–1991*, 53.

[41]The General Assembly authorized funds to increase investigative staff and capabilities for responding to complaints about health–care facilities; see *Post–Legislative Budget Summary, 1989–1991*, 53, 59. Lawmakers also ratified "An Act to Establish a Long–Term Care Ombudsman Program" on June 22, 1989. *N.C. Session Laws, 1989*, I, c. 403.

[42]*N.C. Session Laws, 1989*, II, c. 752, s. 105, provided $4 million for the North Carolina Elderly and Handicapped Transportation Assistance Program during the 1989–1991 biennium. G.S. 136–44.27 established the program.

[43]Martin came closer in 1989, than at any other time during his second term, to winning the executive veto; see "Press Release: Governor's Statement on Veto Efforts This Week," August 9, 1989, pages 137–139, below.

BUDGET MESSAGE TO THE JOINT SESSION
NORTH CAROLINA GENERAL ASSEMBLY

JUNE 21, 1990

Lieutenant Governor Gardner, Speaker Mavretic, Members of the North Carolina General Assembly:

I am here at your kind invitation to present a message regarding the condition of the state budget, along with my recommendations. It is highly unusual for a governor to make such an address, but you have recognized the highly unusual circumstances of the historic challenge we face. Even with a $400 million increase in state revenue this year, it is not enough to fund almost a billion dollars in new appropriations; so we must face the difficult task of amending this year's budget and the one for the second year of the biennium, which begins on July 1. Furthermore, we must face the consequences of the impact of our decisions, past and present, on future years.

I believe it will help to focus attention on what I am going to say if I first tell you what my conclusions are, and then you can keep that in mind as I review the basis for my recommendations. That way, you will not be wondering where each argument is headed. You can relate it to the conclusion that you will know is coming. Since everyone has a personal opinion on how to solve the problems, and since there is considerable disagreement on what to do, it is likely that what I propose will contain some disappointment for everyone. I only ask you not to judge the specific proposals until you hear my reasons for them.

Because I am convinced that both measures are necessary and unavoidable, I am proposing both a tax increase and major cuts in spending. A one-cent sales tax increase, effective in July 1991, is unavoidable, as I will show you; and without real cuts in spending, of 3 percent as the Senate has adopted, even greater tax increases would be needed. Therefore, I propose to you a sales tax increase for the next biennium and, for the coming fiscal year 1990-1991, enactment of something equivalent to the Senate bill, which requires no new taxes for now.[1]

Ever since the adoption of the budget last August, on the advice of my Budget Office, I have taken executive actions to restrain spending, at first by a modified freeze on vacant, noncritical positions, beginning with all departments except public schools and community colleges. Then, as revenue collections progressively weakened, I took steps to progressively tighten down on spending, with the cooperation of everyone, except some few public school leaders, who reacted instead by trying to generate firm resistance against any economy measures for school administrators.[2]

Article III, Section 5, Subsection 3 of the North Carolina Constitution obligates me to maintain a balanced budget, with language that defines balance in terms of cash accounting. Regardless of how the problem occurred, and regardless of who was at fault, here was my obligation. It directs me as follows: "To insure that the State does not incur a deficit for any fiscal period, the Governor shall continually survey the collection of the revenue and shall effect the necessary economies in State expenditures . . . whenever he determines that receipts during the fiscal period, when added to any surplus remaining in the State Treasury at the beginning of the period, will not be sufficient to meet budgeted expenditures."[3] And that's what I have done.

The constitution does not obligate me to clean up only my own mess, but to take action regardless of the cause whenever expenditures are likely to exceed combined receipts and the balance carried over from the prior budget period. There were not attractive options, only unattractive ones from which to choose. There were no permanent solutions which I was authorized to take, only temporary halts to spending authority. There were not many suggestions, frankly, but to those of you who commiserated, and encouraged me to do what I had to do to cut spending $550 million, I offer my thanks.

On May 10, I had presented to the Advisory Budget Commission a plan for spending reductions for this fiscal year, which ends this month, as well as for fiscal 1990–1991. That plan was based on consensus revenue estimates, showing that this year's revenues would be $550 million below the amount budgeted, while next year's would be $336 million lower than adopted last August for fiscal 1990–1991. I am pleased to note that in your work you have retained the concept of consensus revenue estimates.[4]

Since that time, I and all our department heads have been working with you to achieve three objectives:

1) to ensure that actual current expenditures not exceed the combined receipts and carry-over from last year, which cash balance is required by the state constitution;

2) to pass H.B. 2377 to balance the financial statement for this fiscal year, including accrued liabilities—this being one of the key factors on which preservation of our Triple-A credit rating might depend;[5]

3) to amend line-item appropriations levels for next year, not to exceed the consensus revenue estimates now expected for fiscal 1990–1991, and to accommodate new spending for education, health, and corrections.

A great deal of legislative work has gone into meeting this challenge, but there is not agreement yet as to the final form and content of the budget changes. Some insist firmly that the budget be balanced entirely by means of spending cuts, with no tax increase of any kind, while others insist that a major tax increase be a large part of the preferred solution. While both positions are courageous, because there's a political risk both in cutting popular programs and in raising taxes, there is not yet a majority to go either way, and we're running out of time. It is very important that an amended budget be enacted by June 30, or soon thereafter. In order to help move this process along to conclusion, I have decided to throw my support behind the bill which has just passed the Senate.[6] Let me tell you why.

When officials from Standard and Poor's and Moody's credit rating offices visited Raleigh earlier this month to review our budget situation, that highlighted the critical nature of our challenge. Both indicated that they were less concerned about the size of the revenue shortfall in North Carolina, or how it got there. That is a very important point: Those considerations have not cost us our lofty credit rating. What concerns them is whether we have the will and the cooperative spirit to fix it.

While Moody's has since advised us that they expect our budget problems to be resolved, and that they would continue our Triple-A rating until their review of our legislative action is completed, Standard and Poor's has placed our state on its CreditWatch list. This gives formal, ninety-day notice to the bond markets of their concerns. It cannot be overemphasized how serious this is. On average, of all the organizations which have been placed on CreditWatch, 90 percent of them have been downgraded. Meanwhile, a deep re-examination of major financial institutions is under way. Of the twenty-five largest banks in America, fourteen have been recently downgraded, some by two or more notches.[7]

In subsequent telephone conversations with officials from Standard and Poor's, I have been assured that once they are satisfied that we have adopted "permanent" solutions to the budget, we can be taken off of the CreditWatch list just as swiftly as we were put on. The factor that I must emphasize, because their emphasis of it was so firm and clear, is that our budget solutions must be permanent. Whatever the choices we make to achieve a re-balanced budget for fiscal 1990–1991, whether spending cuts, or tax increases, or some combination of both, they must not rely on one-time measures.

They have declined to write a prescription for how we solve the problem; rightly so, I think, for they should not substitute their views for yours in setting goals and policies, other than to evaluate whether the budget and its process are fiscally sound. They will not give us a prior written approval of selected features which might be incorporated into an approved budget, since those features in an otherwise defective budget would not save our credit rating. They expect the General Assembly to decide on policies needed to strengthen North Carolina's economic vitality, to decide how much we can afford to spend, and then to match up the two in a permanent way. Neither will they get specific in advance with what will be acceptable on our present timetables for the Basic Education plan, the network of four-lane highways in the Highway Trust Fund, or Senate Bill 2, the educational reform placing greater control and accountability with local schools. Their position is that legislative judgment must prevail as to what our goals are to be, including schedules for completion. They will not decide those goals for us, but will judge us on whether our funding is realistic.

If we have set too many expensive goals for the available revenue flow, then they expect us either to raise taxes to pay for them or realign our timetables more in keeping with reality. I and my financial advisers interpret that to mean that once a long-term commitment was made to boost state funding of local schools by $800 million over and above adjustments for inflation, it is our responsibility to review that from time to time, to adjust the timetable if necessary, and to revise the detailed formulas as desired; but that it would be a sign of weak character and commitment if we abandon such a goal entirely under stress. School improvements are vital to the economic future of any state, and our determination to reach our goals on a realistic schedule will reflect our worthiness for the highest, most pristine credit rating.

Consider with me what features are needed to achieve the status of being "permanent" solutions. First, the budget must be balanced not only on a cash basis, as required by our constitution, but must be balanced while including any accrued liabilities. One timely example to illustrate this distinction is the decision I have announced to delay this month's paychecks from the last working day of June to the first working day of July, which is in the next fiscal year. That does have the effect of reducing cash outlays in this current fiscal year by $170 million, which helps to meet the cash accounting standard of the constitution. It does not, however, balance our financial statement, because the $170 million in reduced spending in this fiscal year is matched by a $170 million increase in the accrued liability, namely the liability to meet that payroll on July 1, in the next fiscal year.[8]

Delaying the June payday until July does not affect the financial statement at all, on balance. It does not hurt it or help it. By itself, the delayed payday does not affect our credit rating, just as long as we also make changes that will balance the financial statement. Only the General Assembly can make those changes. The change which I have made will not help correct the financial statement but was intended solely to meet the constitutional requirement that "total expenditures . . . not exceed the total of receipts . . . and the surplus remaining in the State Treasury at the beginning of the period."[9] Remember that we have that obligation regardless of whether we can also balance the financial statement including accrued liabilities. Fortunately, the action taken earlier this week to enact the accounting amendments in H.B. 2377 takes the remaining necessary steps to balance the financial statement for 1989–1990.

The second standard we must meet in order for our budget to be "permanently" balanced is that recurring expenditures must be covered by recurring revenues. It is essential that this be clearly understood and honored. Another way of saying that is: There must be sufficient revenues from permanent sources to cover all expenditures that continue into subsequent years. One-time windfall, that is, nonrecurring revenues, must be used only for nonrecurring expenses, like capital projects. Part of the problem we face is that we have strayed from that standard under pressure to increase salaries and program spending without raising taxes to pay for it, and now we must restore the discipline of using nonrecurring revenues only for nonrecurring expenses.

These, then, are the two standards by which we will be judged as to the permanence of our balanced budget solutions: 1) the financial statement, with its accrued liabilities, must also be balanced as well as cash flow, and 2) recurring expenses must not be funded with nonrecurring revenues. If we restore those two standards, I am confident that our Triple-A credit rating will deserve to be reaffirmed. If our solutions are of lesser quality, we might receive a good credit rating, as good as most states, but we will lose our distinction of having earned the highest, most pristine credit rating.

Even if we did not intend to sell bonds for any capital projects, the loss of our Triple-A credit rating would be a severe loss to North Carolina. It would injure the reputation for sound fiscal policies that has attracted many large employers to consider locating new facilities here. It would have the side effect of undercutting the reputations of the cities and counties whose own credit ratings reflect their status as subdivisions of North Carolina, and it would erode the value and marketability of our outstanding bonds, presently held by individuals and foundations who acquired them in reliance on our fiscal reputation.

The measures available to me as governor are not permanent. I have the authority to reduce spending levels by freezing vacancies, halting construction projects before the contracts are awarded, delaying purchases, and the like, but such administrative measures do not change the levels of authorized spending in any permanent way. If you were to adjourn without action on the budget amendments, in theory I could then proceed to reorganize government in ways that might produce some permanent savings, but that would not reassure bond rating agencies that North Carolina was serious about the kind of fiscal policies worthy of a Triple-A rating. I can order reductions in the amounts disbursed to any departments and have indicated to you that I will do so to make temporary savings, if a permanently balanced budget is not enacted by June 30, but permanent solutions must be made by the General Assembly if they are to be accepted as credibly permanent.

Now that I have explained the necessity for long-term, permanent budget solutions, let me turn to specifics. It is possible for these standards to be met either by a) cutting program spending to the level of available revenues, or b) by raising sufficient taxes to cover the level of spending adopted last August, or a combination of both. The Senate bill comes very close to achieving the goal, while relying entirely on spending cuts. It gives me authority, if needed, to make another $42.5 million in real cuts, by providing a "negative reserve" whereby I can reduce the Base Budget by that amount. It would be a great help, and I think would be well received by state employees, for you to pass a spending bill providing a window of opportunity for early retirement for those with twenty-eight years of service.[10] But only when we know how much it would save would I then decide on other cuts.

What I now propose to you, from the context of where we stand, is to begin with the Senate approach or something like it, making cuts on the order of 3 percent in all departments. I had earlier advocated that level of cuts to be administered by department heads who would be given management flexibility to get the job done. That was dropped in deference to your wish to retain responsibility for specific cuts, but it would be a serious mistake, in my view, for you not to order at least the Senate level of spending cuts. For one thing, the credibility of our case for tax increases depends on our ability to show that we have cut spending as much as possible. Based on the work done in the Senate bill, it would be difficult to argue that maximum spending cuts had been achieved if we accept less than the Senate's reductions. At this point, the Senate bill has been properly repaired to eliminate $30.2 million that was earlier being shifted over onto local governments.

So, I recommend that we start with the cuts in the Senate bill. That means that we get close to that level of spending reductions. Some will argue that no cuts be made in public school appropriations, but I believe that before we raise taxes in this election year, we should show that the non-instructional bureaucracies in education are not insulated from the economies we order. After all, that's where most of the growth in school spending has occurred, most of it in the administrative hierarchy, with lesser amounts in teaching positions.

The Basic Education plan was scheduled to grow by an additional $116 million next year, but that was based on the erroneous assumption that this would be affordable from growth in revenues, which has not turned out to be the case.[11] Fortunately, there is a way for you to allow a major improvement in public schools without a major tax increase until the next session. If you increase the local control and flexibility in the management of our schools, local superintendents will be able to achieve better results than if you just insist on adding specific positions in the Basic Education plan's six-year-old-formula.

I would recommend, then, that as you slow down the growth of funding mainly for nonteaching positions in the BEP, that you again consider the advantages of giving local school systems greater flexibility in allocating the positions that they do receive. When S.B. 2 was enacted, local boards were given encouragement to seek waivers of laws and regulations if they could show the State Board of Education how those waivers would help them achieve the goals they set for student improvement. For some reason, the BEP was specifically exempted from that flexibility of S.B. 2, thus requiring local schools to employ precisely the mix of positions prescribed in the BEP, with no adjustment for local needs that might differ from the BEP formula.

If you will now amend that law to extend local control over the positions allocated from the Basic Education plan, I believe local boards can do more to improve student performance with flexibility over the positions already allocated than if required to stay locked into a prescribed pattern of staffing which bears little relation to their local needs. If one school system needs more guidance counselors, social workers, and psychologists to deal with an unusually severe dropout problem, they should have the flexibility to exchange some of their allocated positions accordingly. If another school system has a very low dropout rate, they ought not to be required to hire the statewide average of such positions, but should be given flexibility to exchange some of those positions they don't need for other positions they decide they do need. A school system with a higher than average number of college-bound students would probably need a higher than average number of math, science, history, language, and advanced placement courses.

It should not be required that every school system be locked in to the same rigid formula based on some average statewide need. The typical school is not average. All you have to do is remove the exemption excluding BEP allocations from the School Flexibility and Accountability Act, S.B. 2, and depend on local boards and superintendents to get the most out of their total number of positions.

For the past five years, we have steadily budgeted increasing percentages of the General Fund for public schools. You have, and I have. That has gone unnoticed by educators and editorialists, but it never happened before. We can and should continue that pattern, even if we order some reduction in the rate of growth for schools. With everybody else being cut 3 percent in the Senate bill, schools will have to take only 2.4 percent.

Schools have in fact become, and must remain, our number-one priority, but they're not our only priority. We have other needs, too, in corrections, environmental protection, higher education, health, law enforcement, et cetera, and these other departments cannot be expected to be the only ones to economize. If they must tighten up their administrative overhead, the schools can certainly follow the same example to a lesser extent—and why not? The argument that schools can only be improved by laying on ever greater infusions of money and bureaucracy is clearly a fallacy. It should be obvious by now that adding another $116 million will only expand the variety, but will not improve the performance, of our schools. Had that argument been true, our schools would have shown more improvement by now.

Let's not lose sight of the fact that we have seen some improvement in dropout rates and in CAT [California Achievement Test], if not SAT [Scholastic Aptitude Test], scores.[12] But after having increased funding for schools by $1.2 billion over the last five years, it would be ridiculous to contend that no real progress will be possible unless and until another $355 million is added on a strict timetable of three more years. No, my advice to my fellow educators is, if you want to help sustain momentum to keep the BEP on schedule, maybe you ought to show more appreciation for what has been provided so far, exceeding any other state in relative terms, and maybe show more results.

Some have argued that we should not cut public schools at all, but should only cut departments which have been inefficient. Public schools are the only departmental function of state government which have not had to tighten spending practices or administrative costs in recent years. In fact, that's where most of the growth in management positions has gone. It's time, then, to ask school administrators to do what others in government have been willing to do: to reorganize with leaner, more responsive management. And if you will grant them the flexibility to realign BEP positions to fit their local needs, they, and we, and the taxpayers will all come out ahead, and so will our students.

You have under consideration a bill to grant a much higher degree of management flexibility to the University of North Carolina.[13] I would strongly encourage passage of this measure. Again, we would expect to get much more mileage from the talented chancellors who head up these institutions, and the same would be expected from our local school superintendents if we will give them more flexibility over the BEP.

Now let me turn to the issue of tax increases. When the budget for the next biennium is considered, when you return in January, we will face another major challenge in the General Fund. For one thing, we will have to confront the end of the two-year diversion of Highway Trust Fund moneys to the General Fund. That will no longer be available. What then? Fortunately, the Senate bill has already faced up to half of the problem that was created last August, by reducing the General Fund spending levels to correct for the money that isn't there in fiscal 1990–1991. That $94 million has to be cut out before the next biennium, leaving another $92 million to be found when you meet in January.

Add to that the remaining expansion of BEP and S.B. 2, and that's another $152 million in 1991–1992, rising to $520 million in four years. Then we have to anticipate covering the rising cost of health insurance, on top of at least cost-of-living pay raises. If we do what we have to do for prison expansion, that will kick in at only $47 million in 1991–1992, and rise to $142 million. Unless you really think the General Assembly is going to dodge most of these responsibilities, or somehow find another 6 percent across-the-board cuts on top of what we've already done, then we're looking at $500 million a year more than we would have available to spend without a tax increase.

Just as it is essential to put school needs, and Medicaid, and prison needs on the table as we approach the next long legislative session, I recommend strongly that we also put alongside them the needs for improving services of our vital community college system. This will be our key asset for meeting the educational needs of that half of our young people who go to work after high school. My Commission on Workforce Preparedness will be recommending to us in November how best to strengthen this resource, by expanding the training programs for expanding existing businesses and by going statewide with the Tech Prep collaborations between high schools and community colleges.[14] Let's be ready in 1991 to make the most of that.

I hope I have made clear that the problem just described for the next biennium is not the result of postponement from this year. It's primarily a recognition of new requirements coming just over the horizon having little to do with this biennium. That's one reason we must resist raising major taxes well before they are actually needed. That would only put that revenue in play too soon, with an irresistible temptation to spend it right away. Then it's gone. Then we will still have to face the same future budget problem, after having already spent one big tax increase and with little room or will left for another. Then we would be in a bigger fiscal mess than we have now.

It is important for us to face up to these consequences now, rather than ignore the long-term effects. It is essential that as you go into the election campaigns this fall, you know and understand that after the General Assembly has cut spending as far as is practical, there will still be a need for another $500 million a year to start the next biennium. Your opponents may not know it, but you and I know it. You might disagree as to whether you favor more cuts, but if you can enact the level of cuts in the Senate bill, and no more, there will remain no room for disagreement as to whether substantially more cuts will be made.

We have cut administrative costs almost every year I've been here. With the guidance of the Efficiency Study Commission, we saved $120 million. Each biennium, we've cut out many vacant positions. Again this year, we will have cut $262 million out of the Base Budget continuation for next year.

Yet, after all this we will still have to provide for anticipated cost increases of another $500 million a year. The only way to raise that kind of money without injuring the economic health of the state is to raise the sales tax one cent for items already covered by the full five cents, producing $529 million in 1991–1992.

Some like to argue instead for an increase in personal income taxes. The problem with that is that those who pay the income tax already got a big increase last year, because 700,000 other taxpayers got excluded from having to pay income taxes.[15] Even so, North Carolina raises more income tax per capita, on a basis of the total population, than all but seven other states. We're also in the top ten states in the total corporate income taxes raised per capita, and that, too, just got raised two years ago.[16] So neither of those income taxes should take another hit for $500 million, unless you want to savage the competitiveness of manufacturers here, in the number-one state with the highest percentage of the workforce in manufacturing of all fifty states.

The current 5 percent sales tax, however, is not among the top ten states. While it is regressive, with lower-income taxpayers paying a relatively higher fraction of income for retail purchases, it should be remembered that 700,000 lower-income workers were relieved of any income tax just last year, and those with [the] lowest income no longer have to pay sales tax on food stamps. So I conclude that the sales tax is the fairest way of all for us to raise $500 million. At least, let's be sure we get something for our money.

Now comes the hard part. What do we do about it? Many of you made solemn promises not to vote for a tax increase this year. It is an election year. But most of you have also taken an honest position of acknowledging that a tax increase will have to be passed next year. The safest thing to do, facing review by Standard and Poor's and Moody's, is to vote now for the tax increase to take effect next year. But the worst thing to do would be to have it voted down now. If we wait until next session, we will still be vulnerable to a downgraded credit rating, unless we can take credible action to prove the character of our intentions. Is that possible?

There is a bill being introduced today, by the chairman of the Senate Appropriations Committee,[17] which will state your resolution of intent to increase the sales tax by one cent early in the next session. It would show future anticipated expenditure growth that is not included in the amended budget for 1990–1991, along with the consensus estimate of revenue growth, so that there will be no disagreement again on that subject. It will show that the sales tax is needed, because of requirements that go beyond what is required in fiscal 1990–1991.

If it is not possible to enact a future tax increase until the time comes that it is needed, then I hope you will give this resolution of intent the strongest possible endorsement, including bipartisan support, to undergird its credibility. Then I will do the best I can, with my financial advisers, to persuade the bond rating houses that you are with me in a commitment to the future. We can get no guarantee in advance. That is not their way. The only way to ensure that we keep that Triple-A rating would be [to] adopt the tax increase now, this session. However, ironically, the only way to ensure that we lose that vaunted rating would be to defeat the needed tax increase, which is likely to happen if we force it to a vote before it is actually needed.

We have raised taxes as needed in the past five years—sales taxes, individual income taxes, corporate income taxes, gasoline taxes, you name it—but we have never had to raise a tax over a year before it was needed. Not in thirty years of the highest rating has such a politically indefensible move been demanded of us. I will try my best to show the bond rating houses that our fiscal policy is still as strong as it ever was, if you will at least give me the strongest possible endorsement in passing this resolution of intent, and clear up any misperception about the future fiscal picture.

For those who continue to bemoan the responsibility we have to tighten our belts before we raise taxes, those who have never yet shown the slightest appreciation for what we've done, let me ask them to look at how far we've come in five years. Look at what we've done already to strengthen school funding as a percentage of the budget, and in real dollars over inflation! Look at what we've done to add $450 million so far in the BEP, even in the tightest budget years! Look at what we have insisted on doing with Senate Bill 2, to require better results for all these unappreciated appropriations that have gone to schools, to start getting something for our money.

Look at what we've done to raise taxes for a magnificent boost in highway construction, rivaling the combined total of every previous legislature and governor combined! Look at what that will do to open every community to share the blessings of economic development!

Look at what we have done together to save our prison system from federal courts throwing open the doors because of overcrowding! Look at what we will do to increase our prison capacity to contain the rising tide of dangerous criminals and make them spend more time in prison and less time in our homes and neighborhoods!

Look at what we've done to tighten our administrative belts, so that other than education, health, and corrections, there has been very little growth in administrative costs of general government! And, look at what we've done in 1989 to unfreeze the salary schedule for our teachers that was frozen in 1982, while providing justifiable pay increases for school and state employees, which we're retaining even in the pressure of this greatest revenue shortfall we've ever seen![18] And look at what we're going to do to establish a $140 million permanent reserve for major emergencies, later rising to $200 million, a "rainy day fund" to safeguard future shortfalls.[19]

Look at what we've done, and look at what we're doing! Is it too much to ask some recognition for the fact that right here in North Carolina over the last seven years, we have increased total expenditures, state and local, on a per-capita basis by 60 percent, most of that coming in the last five years, and most of it for public schools? Friends, only four other states have done more. Isn't it time for somebody to say "thank you," and isn't it time for us to begin to expect better results?

Today I have recommended to you that there is a need for a major tax increase, but in 1991–1992, not in 1990–1992 [1991?], our most immediate fiscal year. I have recommended that you move rather promptly to balance fiscal 1990–1991 as the Senate has done, realizing that there will be some justifiable differences in details of the House version, but with the realization that it can be achieved with permanent cuts in levels of spending that never should have been so high if the real revenue growth had been forecast accurately. If instead of spending cuts for fiscal 1990–1991 you were to use tax increases to balance that second year of this biennium, you would still have to face another big tax increase next January. But by relying primarily on spending cuts for the fiscal year beginning next week, we can show that a tax increase is clearly a last resort, not the first.

I do understand that the House is reluctant to accept some cuts and may be able to find alternative areas for savings to take to conference. Should you be unable to agree on such savings and find that you have to rely on a modest tax increase in the coming year, then I have no objection to that, but urge you to do so promptly so we can go to conference.

Maybe now it can be seen that this tax increase should have been enacted last year; but my purpose is not to say, "I told you so," but rather to help build bipartisan support for what will need to be done.[20] And to give me ammunition with which to reassure Moody's and Standard and Poor's of the clarity of our intentions, I am asking you to enact a resolution of intent to adopt that sales tax increase next year, in timely fashion, to fund the needs that are not a part of this biennium but will need attention in the next. This is not easy medicine, but with your favorable response, I believe that we can not only meet the needs of North Carolina but also deserve the confidence of those whose judgment is valued so highly in evaluating credit worthiness.

The problem is real, and it is serious. Let's work together, without rancor, and without panic, and do what we must do to fix it. Thank you for your attention and for what you do for North Carolina.

---

[1]S.B. 1426 passed the Senate on June 18, 1990, and became the basis for "An Act to Modify the Current Operations Appropriations for North Carolina for the 1990–91 Fiscal Year and to Make Other Changes in the Budget Operation of the State," *N.C. Session Laws, Extra Session, 1989, Extra and Regular Sessions, 1990,* c. 1066. The legislation was ratified July 28, the day the General Assembly adjourned its short session. Although state lawmakers departed without increasing taxes, they approved other measures to generate additional funds during F.Y. 1990–1991, including an $18 million boost in annual fees due the state and changes in accounting and tax collection strategies that amounted to a further $252 million. Legislators raised the base rate of the state sales and use tax by a penny in 1991, despite Martin's call earlier that year for only a half-cent, local-option increase. *News and Observer,* July 29, August 17, 1990; "State of the State," January 31, 1991, 47.

[2]See *News and Observer,* May 12, 1990, and related press release, "Governor Martin Challenges Superintendent Etheridge to Find Cuts in Administrative—Not Teaching—Positions," Raleigh, May 14, 1990, Governors Papers, James G. Martin.

[3]North Carolina Constitution, Article III, Section 5(3), quoted in *North Carolina Manual, 1991–1992,* 627.

[4]Among his fiscal recommendations of May 10, 1990, Martin proposed "a permanent 3.0 percent reduction in departmental and institutional operating budgets and a 2.23 percent reversionary reduction to be accomplished by allowing departments and institutions the necessary management flexibility to make the reductions." Legislators ultimately adopted the 3 percent permanent reduction as well as a new provision for making further cuts, the negative reserve, that allowed state agencies to devise their own strategies to manage funds stemming from lapsed salaries and excess receipts for one year. The 3 percent cut totaled $244.5 million, while the negative reserve amounted to a further $97.9 million in General Fund savings for F.Y. 1990–1991. *The North Carolina State Budget: Post-Legislative Budget Summary, 1990–91* (Raleigh: Office of State Budget and Management, September 1990), 1–2, hereinafter cited as *Post-Legislative Budget Summary, 1990–91*; press release, "Governor Signs Executive Order as Budget Analysts Revise Shortfall Estimate to $504 million for F.Y. 1990," Raleigh, May 8, 1990, Governors Papers, James G. Martin.

[5]The General Assembly adopted H.B. 2377 on June 21, 1990. See "An Act to Require Utilities to Pay Certain Taxes in Fiscal Year 1989–90 that Would Otherwise Be Payable in Fiscal Year 1990–91 and to Change the Accounting Method that Applies to Revenue Distributed to Local Governments from Certain Taxes Levied by the State," *N.C. Session Laws, Extra Session, 1989, Extra and Regular Sessions, 1990,* c. 813.

[6]S.B. 1426.

[7]North Carolina enjoyed a Triple-A bond rating, the credit industry's top classification, since 1970. As Martin reminded the General Assembly, the ability to retain that exemplary designation depended upon the state's willingness to address the disparity between budget needs and income. Were either of the country's two major credit assessment firms, Moody's Investors Service, Inc., and Standard and Poor's Corp., to discern a lack of sufficient determination to confront those fiscal difficulties, they could downgrade the value of the state's bonds and thereby further exacerbate the budget situation. Lower bond ratings would have meant increased costs for the state and a heavier burden for North

Carolina taxpayers. A reduction from Triple-A to Double-A, for example, translated into a one-half percentage point increase in interest the state had to pay on money it borrowed.

Moody's Investors Service, on June 12, 1990, expressed its confidence in the state's ability to manage its financial affairs. Standard and Poor's was more cautious, however. Four days earlier, the company announced it had assigned North Carolina to its CreditWatch list. But the budget cuts the General Assembly adopted for the second year of the 1989–1991 biennium, approval of a fiscal note acknowledging the need to take sterner measures to address revenue requirements during the legislature's 1991 session, and other factors prompted Standard and Poor's to maintain the state's Triple-A bond rating. *News and Observer*, May 22, August 25, 1990; press releases, "Governor's Reaction to Decision by Standard and Poor's," Raleigh, June 8, 1990, "Moody's Investor Service Reaffirms State's Triple-A Bond Rating," Raleigh, June 12, 1990, "Governor Martin, Treasurer Boyles Optimistic North Carolina Will Maintain Triple-A Bond Rating from Standard and Poor's," Raleigh, August 10, 1990, and "North Carolina's Triple-A Bond Rating Reaffirmed by Standard and Poor's, CreditWatch Lifted," Raleigh, August 24, 1990, Governors Papers, James G. Martin.

[8]Press release, "Governor Chooses Option to Relieve Revenue Shortfall," Raleigh, May 17, 1990, Governors Papers, James G. Martin, announced the postponement of the June pay period for state employees.

[9]"The total expenditures of the State for the fiscal period covered by the budget shall not exceed the total of receipts during that fiscal period and the surplus remaining in the State Treasury at the beginning of the period." North Carolina Constitution, Article III, Section 5(3), quoted in *North Carolina Manual, 1991–1992*, 627.

[10]H.B. 2383 and H.B. 519 would have allowed state employees with twenty-five and twenty-eight years of service, respectively, to retire with full benefits. Neither measure was enacted. *N.C. House Journal, Extra Session, 1989, Extra and Regular Sessions, 1990*, 82, 502.

[11]The state budget adopted by the General Assembly reduced appropriations for the Basic Education Program from $116 million to just under $44.5 million for 1990–1991. Hiring of new teachers and instructional support personnel slowed, and funds for increasing the number of administrative and clerical positions were eliminated. *Post-Legislative Budget Summary, 1990–91*, 16–17.

[12]The California Achievement Tests were a battery of standardized examinations in language arts, reading, and math given to North Carolina schoolchildren. *News and Observer*, March 16, 1993.

[13]"An Act to Implement the Joint Report to Provide Management Incentives and Flexibility for the Constituent Institutions of the University of North Carolina and to Require the Creation and Enhancement of a Program of Public Service and Technical Assistance to the Public Schools" was ratified July 16, 1990. *N.C. Session Laws, Extra Session, 1989, Extra and Regular Sessions, 1990*, c. 936.

[14]Martin signed Executive Order Number 107, establishing the North Carolina Governor's Commission on Workforce Preparedness, on March 14, 1990. *N.C. Session Laws, Extra Session, 1989, Extra and Regular Sessions, 1990*, 1028–1033.

[15]"An Act to Enhance the Simplicity and Fairness of the State Income Tax System," also known as the "Tax Fairness Act of 1989," was ratified August 7, 1989. It brought North Carolina's individual income tax code into closer conformity with its federal counterpart and removed many low-income taxpayers from the tax rolls. *N.C. Session Laws, 1989*, II, c. 728.

[16]"The School Facilities Finance Act of 1987" raised state corporate income taxes from 6 percent to 7 percent, effective January 1, 1987. *N.C. Session Laws, 1987*, I, c. 622, s. 8, ratified July 16, 1987.

[17]Kenneth Claiborne Royall, Jr. (1918–   ), member, 1973–1992, majority leader, 1973–1974, 1977–1986, deputy president pro tempore, 1989–1992, state Senate; chairman, Advisory Budget Commission, 1981–1991, and of Senate Appropriations Committee; Democrat. Previously identified in Poff, *Addresses of Martin*, I, 602n; see also *News and Observer*, March 22, June 18, August 2, 1992; *North Carolina Manual, 1989–1990*, 242–243, 299, *1991–1992*, 230–231.

[18]A severe economic recession plagued the nation during the early 1980s, and North Carolina's unemployment rate stood at 10 percent. Rather than raise taxes to continue funding step increases for teacher pay—or, alternatively, fire some educators so those remaining could be paid more—the General Assembly opted to freeze salaries in 1982. See "An Act to Modify Current Operations and Capital Improvements Appropriations for North Carolina State Government for the Fiscal Year 1982–83, and to Make Other Changes in the Budget Operation of the State," N.C. Session Laws, 1981, Regular and Extra Sessions, 1982, c. 1282, s. 7; Poff and Crow, Addresses of Hunt, II, 477.

[19]A budget stabilization reserve of $141 million was established for the 1990–1991 fiscal year. N.C. Session Laws, Extra Session, 1989, Extra and Regular Sessions, 1990, c. 1066, s. 10.

[20]See "Better Pay for Better Teachers," March 9, 1989, pages 92–93, below.

STATE OF THE STATE

JANUARY 31, 1991

[Martin saw precious few victories when reflecting upon the legislative session that met from January 30 to July 16, 1991. The most significant accomplishment, the governor noted to reporters on July 18, was the progress made in establishing the Global TransPark air-cargo facility. Otherwise, the General Assembly, dominated by Democrats, largely dismissed the proposals he made in his 1991 State of the State address for tougher drunken-driving and drug laws, revisions to the budget process, and proposals for school reform, workforce preparedness, and the Mountain Area Planning System.

Regarding fiscal matters, Martin observed that the legislature "'didn't pay much attention to the budget I put forward.'" Although the adopted spending plan countered a $1.2 billion revenue shortfall and ensured the state's Triple-A bond rating, funded prison construction, and authorized programs to fight infant mortality and child abuse—facets the governor favorably acknowledged— he also said it contained "'tax increases that are far too high, with spending reductions that are substantial but are not nearly as deep as they could have been.'" Legislators raised the state sales tax by a penny, boosted the corporate income tax rate, and increased the personal income tax rate on the state's wealthiest citizens from 7 percent to 7.75 percent. The tax on a pack of cigarettes went from two cents to five cents. The governor found much he would have vetoed, had he been granted the power.

See "An Act to Make Base Budget and Expansion Budget Appropriations for Current Operations of State Departments, Institutions, and Agencies; to Make Appropriations for Capital Improvements for State Departments, Institutions, and Agencies; to Make Appropriations for Other Purposes; to Provide for Budget Reform; and to Provide for Revenue Reconciliation," N.C. Session Laws, 1991, II, c. 689, ratified July 13, 1991; "Editorial Opposing Anti-Jobs Taxes Proposed by the General Assembly," July 1, 1991, pages 353–354, below; News and Observer, July 14, 18, 21, 1991; North Carolina State Budget, 1991–93 Biennium: Post-Legislative Budget Summary (Raleigh: Office of State Budget and Management, September 1991), 165–169, hereinafter cited as Post-Legislative Budget Summary, 1991–93.

Side headings employed in this address were inserted by the editor.]

Lieutenant Governor Gardner, Speaker Blue,[1] Honorable Members of the North Carolina General Assembly, Ladies and Gentlemen:

Once again, in response to your kind invitation, and in response to the challenges facing our state, I have come to present my biennial budget message, and to review with you the state of the state of North Carolina.[2]

We meet at a time of great national distress and profound responsibility, a time when once again North Carolina has been called upon for a greater portion of duty and sacrifice. We begin this occasion with our prayer for an honorable conclusion to war and for the safe return of those men and women whose courage, and training, and patriotism represent us and our nation in the Middle East. I want you to pause with me for a moment of personal, silent prayer, remembering those who have fallen and our beautiful friend, Senator Jim Ezzell.[3]

As a constant reminder of their sacrifice, I carry with me or keep visible on my desk this small bottle of Arabian desert sand sent to me by National Guard Sergeant First Class S[usie]. C. Davis, tactical communications chief with the 139th Rear Area Operations Center. Over there. It was delivered by her proud husband, Chester.

In addition to the highly acclaimed Operation Family Shield to help all our National Guard and reservists with emergency expenses, we have already provided our 211 state employees over there that their job is waiting when they return, and we're going to extend their paid personal leave benefits ten working days to help them resettle.[4] And all North Carolina military over there will be allowed to delay filing income taxes until June 15. They are all our neighbors, and we are very proud of them.

We meet today amid growing concern over the competitiveness of our state and national workforce, both now and in the coming century. We know that too many of our workforce are undereducated, and our community colleges underfunded. Too many reports point to the inadequacy of our investment in our most important resource, our people—not so much in terms of the financial magnitude of that investment as in the effectiveness of the programs in which we have invested. We know we must do more, and we know we must do better. That is our greatest challenge for the nineties, and that is why, if this year is to have a focal theme, it must become the "Year of the Worker" in North Carolina: the year of the educated, trainable, globally competitive worker.

Clearly, we must change how our schools prepare for work those students who do not intend to go to college. Unless they are trainable for higher skill levels, they will not qualify for higher paying jobs in an increasingly technical workplace, where the unskilled jobs have almost disappeared: down to 30 percent of the total now and 15 percent by the next decade.

That doesn't mean easier frill courses so everybody can graduate, nor does it mean teaching specific job routines in school. No, it means more math, science, and language, just like in every other industrial country, so they understand the underpinnings of zero-base defects, just-in-time deliveries, and flexible automated manufacturing. We don't teach that, but we will.

We meet, too, amid the second consecutive year of severe fiscal constraint, in which our capacity and determination to meet our challenges with fiscal integrity will be profoundly tested. We face a time of grim national economic recession, with at least twenty-eight sister states experiencing the bleakest fiscal conditions since 1982. This follows a period of eight years of uninterrupted economic growth which have seen increasing Growth, and Opportunity, and Prosperity for North Carolina.[5] Per-capita personal income has risen relative to other states. At the same time, so have tax levies and the per-capita tax burden risen, relative to other states. In return, we have seen a corresponding rise in spending on vital services such as education, transportation, health, environmental protection, and public safety.

Many strategic public investments have been made in these areas: (1) public schools, (2) highway infrastructure, (3) public safety, (4) environment and health, and (5) economic development. Yet, in each of these areas of major state responsibility, we know there is much more to be done. Let's examine these policy areas in turn.

Public Schools

For seven years in a row, spending on public schools has been the number-one priority. Nothing else has come close. Rarely before has our schools' share of the General Fund been increased in even one isolated year; indeed, in only two of the twenty-four years preceding this administration, namely in 1966 and 1984. Yet for five of the last six years, the percentage of the General Fund going to public schools has been raised both in budgets submitted by me and in those adopted by you. For that, I congratulate you, and share with you an otherwise unrequited satisfaction for putting our priorities right where they should be, whether or not anyone noticed.

Stated another way, over the last six fiscal years, public school appropriations have grown from $1,887,000,000, in 1984–1985, to $3,329,000,000 in this fiscal year, 1990–1991. I do not intend to burden you with many statistics today, but I do want you to know that one: a 76 percent increase of almost one-and-a-half billion dollars in six years. Even with today's reductions.[6] That's about a billion-dollar increase over and above the combined 30 percent inflation rate.

Do we see a billion dollars' worth of improvement? In inputs, yes. We provide more teachers, more support personnel, more administrators, and with better pay. Are we catching up yet?

Still, there are many shrill voices today calling for massive increases in spending for schools, as if throwing more money is the path to excellence in education. It isn't. We already tried that. It didn't work.

My proposals for education spending increases are limited because of the extremely tight budget picture. Nevertheless, with the help of a recent summit meeting of leading educators and education study commissions, I can bring you their consensus list of strategic, vital needs for educational investments which must not be deferred, which we cannot afford to delay until a stronger economy comes along.[7] Indeed, the budget improvements I am recommending for education are of a kind and quality that without them, we might injure North Carolina's ability to grow again after this recession.

There are many other very good ideas for schools which I do not believe we can afford just now, but I urge you to provide $22 million for continuing the reforms of last session's Senate Bill 2, the Public School Improvement and Accountability Act. Community college literacy and job training programs, including statewide extension of the resoundingly successful Tech Prep, will require an additional $40 million to better serve the needs of adults and those young people who plan to go to work after high school.

That summit consensus also endorsed even greater local control and flexibility, especially for block grants for the existing funding of the Basic Education plan, which should not be abandoned, but held accountable for better student performance. Therefore, I will ask you to honor the local leadership of our schools by granting to those meeting the requirements of Senate Bill 2 almost total flexibility, for them to decide the specific allocation of BEP positions; subject only to a limitation on the number of nonteaching positions. With more flexibility in the form of block grants, I believe they will get better results with the same money.

It was strongly felt by summit participants that more academic rigor should be built into all course work. We want to see higher standards not only for graduation, but for certifying mastery of a core of basic skills at the eighth-grade level. That would be followed by offering a career-oriented curriculum to better prepare those students who plan to go to work after high school.

One of the top recommendations was for the elimination of tenure for school administrators to increase accountability at every schoolhouse.[8] And at the state level, there was strong support for having the state superintendent appointed by the State Board of Education, so they have to work together, and decentralizing the state Department [of Public Instruction].[9]

The need to develop much greater parental involvement, both in school policy formation and in the supervision of their children's work, was a strong consensus. A third of the participants supported schools of choice as the ultimate in accountability. Many other states have experienced a high degree of success with this, with safeguards to prevent resegregation. Everywhere, the results are too good to ignore. Now it's our turn.[10]

It was shown that schools in small counties are inadequately funded by the uniform allocation based solely on enrollment. The best idea for remedying this was the proposal from the Public School Forum for $12 million for a minimum allocation to schools in counties with less than 3,000 students. My budget phases in $6 million beginning in the second year of the biennium.[11]

I am at the same time proposing that the state fund only one central office staff per county. That is in no way intended to dictate school merger or consolidation to unwilling districts, for that should remain a local decision. It just means that any county preferring multiple school systems must raise the money locally for any extra administrative staff—or take it out of their BEP.

Certainly, no educational improvement is more desperately needed today than a more widely available developmental day care for four-year-olds, especially those who are at greatest risk of failing to master the basic skills in their primary grades. Generally, these are youngsters who have no one to lap-read to them at home. If their parents cannot read, or are too tired after two jobs, or if there is the violence of child abuse or spouse abuse, or drug abuse (often the root cause of the violence), then these children will not experience the excitement and satisfaction of the English language, or the family bonds which encourage them to believe in themselves.

Here's how we fix that. We have resources available for a substantial improvement, thanks to congressional passage of the Day Care Act of 1990.[12] My budget will include $26.6 million of this to enhance state and federally funded day care for 15,610 more children, including 5,225 additional at-risk four-year-olds. Secretary Dave Flaherty and staff, who have developed our plan for Uplift Day Care, will give you a full report tomorrow morning. It will improve the staffing ratio for babies, as recently recommended by Day Care Commission Chairman Donna Ballenger, will reach all the current waiting list for Head Start and state day care, and raise the eligibility line from 60 percent to 75 percent of median income—and with the help of private foundations will reach all

15,000 currently identified at-risk four-year-olds, statewide! All this through an emphasis on parental choice. What a great advance for a worthy cause: to ensure their future.

On a related front, I am again proposing an increase of $12.8 million for similar preschool advantages for those four-year-olds handicapped with developmental disabilities.

My budget also proposes an additional $28 million for the University of North Carolina, without specifying for what purposes it is to be allocated, only that it should come from optional tuition increases. Part of that increase in tuition should be set aside, on the order of 25 percent, for grants-in-aid based on need, as recommended by the UNC Student Body Presidents Association, so that the increase not price our university out of the reach of lower income families. No institution would be required to raise tuition if its respective board of trustees did not believe that to be desirable, but each would retain its own tuition proceeds for university enrichment.[13]

I endorse the suggestion from Chancellor Paul Hardin that each institution's trustees select and develop a list of ten to thirty peer institutions across the nation as representative of those against whom they would want to be compared academically, and submit their peer list to the Board of Governors for review.[14] The median of combined tuition and fees among its comparison group would be regarded as a maximum to which each particular UNC campus could raise its tuition and fees over a period of three to five years.

As an additional option, I will ask you to allow at least two of the sixteen institutions to be funded by means of a block grant, with the complete flexibility to allocate that resource and to operate beyond that as an enterprise. This has been successfully demonstrated at Memorial Hospital in Chapel Hill since 1989. The Board of Governors could be directed to establish criteria and standards and to review the documented "Showing of Readiness" for the first two institutions to complete their plan.

The North Carolina Constitution, Article IX, Section 9, requires that "The General Assembly shall provide that the benefits of the University of North Carolina and other public institutions of higher education, as far as practicable, be extended to the people of the State free of expense."[15] "As far as practicable" has never been taken to mean free tuition. Indeed the level of tuition as a percentage of the cost of the undergraduate instructional program is far lower than in earlier years. The low tuition for graduate and professional schools is even more startling and indefensible. Setting aside part of the proceeds from higher tuition for need-based grants will protect the access of students from lower income families, but there is no good reason not to charge more for those who can afford to pay for one of the best educational bargains in America; and at a time like this, it is no longer "practicable" for middle income taxpayers to subsidize low tuition for wealthy parents.

Budget

It is at this point that I believe I should talk to you about the overall budget and how we can pay for these improvements. After conferring with many legislators, department heads, front-line employees, and business leaders, culminating with the Advisory Budget Commission, I have developed, first, a proposal to balance the 1991–1992 Continuation Budget within the limited revenues available. In this way, no forced lay-off of dedicated workers, and no tax increase, will be necessary to balance the Continuation Budget.

But we can't stop there. I then propose to cover these strategic improvements, along with restoration of the rainy day reserve, by authorizing a local-option, half-cent sales tax, coupled with elimination of the $242 million reimbursement to local governments for the earlier repeal of the inventory tax and the intangibles tax on bank deposits.[16]

This approach was proposed and endorsed by both the North Carolina Association of County Commissioners and the League of Municipalities. It will give them a more reliable source of the same revenue, and it will free up $242 million for other state expenses. I do not believe a larger tax increase can be justified at this time. There is a timing problem: This must be passed in February, so the local governments can decide whether to start collecting in April if they are going to receive it to replace the lost inventory reimbursement in June.

This will not be enough for a general, across-the-board increase in salary levels. It will give teachers protection from another pay step freeze as hit them in 1982, which caused such unfair hardship and aggravation, and they will get the next installment of S.B. 2 performance pay. And it will provide in January for a comparable increase, $32 million, to cover performance increments and market adjustments for state employees and other school (nonteaching) staff. While they all certainly deserve better, it would be difficult to justify raising a larger tax on an economy with rising unemployment in order to finance higher pay raises for those fortunate enough to have a job.[17]

Another urgent problem for which there is still no money is the increased cost of premiums for state employees' health insurance, a very costly program, with high benefit levels coupled with low deductibles and copayments. It has been estimated that rising costs of benefits would require another $125 million of appropriations. Not only is that unaffordable in the limited budget we face, but it has also become unaffordable for our employees to elect coverage for their dependents. You have placed that program within the Insurance Department, to insulate it from my direction and control, so it is difficult for me to recommend any solution to you. However, I am willing to try. If your leadership will work with the State Employees Association and me to study options, I believe that within ninety days we can develop a plan for holding down costs by raising levels of deductibles and copayments and other measures.[18]

Let me assure you that the first objective, balancing the Continuation Budget without layoffs or tax increases, is not a simple matter. No, we've already cut spending levels this current year by $700 million (repeat: $700 million) below the appropriation levels which were deemed necessary, for this year, in 1989; and what my Continuation Budget does basically is force all departments to continue next year at that same reduced level, 9 percent lower than had been budgeted originally for this year. So for those who properly contend that we should cut spending at least 6 percent before we consider any tax increase, I agree and reply that we have now already and responsibly cut back half again more than 6 percent! That's $700 million of a $7.6 billion budget.

Many of you share with me the conviction that no tax increase should be considered ever, except as a last resort. Well, I'm afraid you're right: We have now come down to that last resort. This is also clearly the time to consider carefully the suggestion of Senator Goldston and Representative Pope for a zero-growth revenue estimate.[19] It would not make much difference in 1991–1992, because there isn't much growth. In 1992–1993, however, there will be growth due to any post-recession recovery. Even then, I urge you to be careful not to disregard all that new revenue, for that could force you into another tax increase for the transition. My budget for that second year reflects the new policy of consensus revenue estimates, but I will be anxious to see if Dr. Malcolm Gillis's Economic Future Study Commission can figure out how to do with less.[20]

Our foremost and most difficult assignment in this legislative session will be to adopt a balanced budget in a time of unusually slow economic growth. We must forgo any desired improvements which we cannot now afford, deferring them until a brighter period of renewed, robust economic growth, while taking care to identify those investments in education, infrastructure, and public health and safety which we cannot afford to delay any longer. We must take care to provide for those strategically vital needs, without which we would surely jeopardize our hopes for recovery and the future economic competitiveness of our workforce.

Transportation

Let me turn now to transportation issues, and there are some exciting ones. Spending on highway improvements has also been dramatically improved, but not as much as for schools. Passage of a major construction funding program in 1989, coupled with a more modest levy in 1986, has set the stage for the greatest expansion of road building projects in history. Thanks to a determination we share to unite rural and urban North Carolina as one truly united state, we have committed the resources to complete over 3,000 miles of a strategic, unbroken network of limited access, four-lane, divided highways—a veritable intrastate highway system which will bring within ten miles of 96 percent of our people an industrial development corridor, a four-lane highway that goes somewhere. That, and completion of paving all secondary roads. The only amendment I would request is to reduce, to the cost of handling, the highway user tax on any title transfer within a family.[21]

Just as the Research Triangle Park generated enormous economic potential for this one part of the state, our intrastate system, combined with more effective schools, can do the same for all of North Carolina. Rural counties must have better schools; they also must have access to strategic four-lane highways that go somewhere, or else all you get will be, hopefully, better educated graduates who have to move away from home to find work.

This magnificent economic boon will be paid for, as it should be, with higher taxes on highway users, which I ask you again to hold in trust for that purpose. Some are critical of the fact that we will spend $9.3 billion on highways. That's a matter of opinion, of course, but they are false to suggest that is more than we have committed to schools. That $9.3 billion is not the figure for just one year, but is spread over the next sixteen to seventeen years, initially at a rate of $450 million a year—if it ever is allowed to start. For comparison, over these same six years we've increased annual school spending by over three times as much, by $1.44 billion. At least with the highway construction program, the largest such improvement in our history, there is no doubt that we will get something for our money.

My proposal for the coming biennium includes no further enhancement for highways, but will insist that this money from highway user taxes not be diverted again for any other purpose than that for which the tax was levied. I will not tolerate another raid on the Highway Trust Fund; and yet, I must tell you there will be another effort to raid this Highway Trust Fund, which was set up with increased taxes on highway users, and divert it again to other worthwhile purposes which already get far more of our tax money.[22] The education of our children is certainly our number-one priority—certainly these last six years more so than ever before—but there are some who argue that it is our only priority.

If you agree with me that the competitive viability of our rural and urban communities require [sic] both better schools and better roads in order to build for better jobs, then we must draw a line in the paving and fight hard to preserve and defend this Highway Trust Fund. Let's do what is necessary to fund those educational improvements which are strategically vital to North Carolina. Let's also insist that other needs, long overdue, are also strategically vital. Let's insist that part of our strategic investment will go for this intrastate highway system, so that we will have something measurable to show for our money.

Now, you've heard about a proposal I am exploring for a major airport development for international air cargo shipments. I invite you, and need you, to join with me to make it happen. Like the Research Triangle Park, this 5,000-acre facility offers us a rare opportunity to dominate a rapidly growing market. The potential is enormous, because any easternmost state to provide such an airport will be in a commanding position for exports to Europe and will lose little or nothing to western states for exports to Asia, because modern flying speeds nearly match the rotation of the earth. So, for export-oriented manufacturing, as well as automotive component and other just-in-time suppliers, North Carolina would be able to offer the most advantageous plant locations: immediately adjacent to, or integral to the taxiways of, this global-industrial complex in which aviation performs the primary distribution role. We must be attentive to the need to accommodate to the noise impacts at night, but the prospect of generating more than 30,000 jobs, roughly comparable to the Research Triangle Park, and its $50 billion yearly impact, according to Dr. Jack Kasarda of the UNC Kenan Institute, make it worth our best effort.[23]

We are also working on exciting initiatives for our seaports and railroad improvements, which I will bring to you in a separate message.

Public Safety

The cause of public safety has been well served by recent General Assemblies with long overdue improvements in corrections, both prison facilities and in alternatives to imprisonment. Passage of our $200 million bond issue now gives us the ability to move forward with our commitment to increase capacity by 6,000 inmates, to ensure that the most dangerous ones will spend more time in prison and less time in our homes and neighborhoods. It was a close vote, but it passed.[24]

My proposal will be for us to move as planned with this badly needed construction, but delay selling the bonds until after a September issuance of $40 million in two-thirds bonds. That way the fiscal impact in the tight budget of the first year will be a modest $1.5 million, for initial debt service. Allocation and planning, however, should not be delayed.

If this promise is kept, I will also support amending the constitution to provide for alternative punishments. At present, our constitution allows only five kinds of punishment to be ordered by a trial court: (1) the death penalty; (2) imprisonment; (3) fines; (4) removal from office; and (5) disqualification from office.[25] Parole and probation, electronically monitored house arrest, victim's restitution, and community service are possible only upon the option of the convicted person. Yet, even if the constitution is amended to provide for these alternative sentences, they could not be enforced unless there is a realistic threat of imprisonment as an alternative to the alternatives. Without adequate prison space as reinforcement, the terms of probation, community service, et cetera, could be ignored without substantial risk of imprisonment.

I am pleased to commend legislative leaders for working with us to approve in concept our first-ever privatized facilities for treatment and confinement of those sentenced for drug abuse, repeated drunk driving, and the like.[26] Unanimous support from your Joint Committee on Governmental Operations is a welcome, encouraging sign. Hopefully, this session also will move forward to a stronger limitation on blood alcohol level for drivers and stricter enforcement of all DWI laws.

My budget can only accommodate modest improvement in programs to combat and treat drug abuse, as recommended by the Drug Cabinet: $1.4 million this year and $3.3 million next, in addition to other money for prenatal exposure and more alcohol enforcement officers. I urge you to support those proposals, too, for this is an aggravated problem and we are so dangerously far behind.[27]

Thanks to increased use of seat belts and strict enforcement of drunk-driving laws, recent years have seen dramatic improvement in traffic fatalities. Now the Board of Transportation has committed $5 million to install nighttime reflectors on all our major highways in hopes of greater savings of lives. Older drivers will love it. So will I.

Environment and Health

North Carolina has made great progress for better environment and health, but again much remains to be done. Let me give you some examples. Our infant mortality rate is still higher than acceptable, even though last year it improved to the lowest level ever in history. Thanks to the recent expansion of the Baby Love program initiated in 1988, with your $10 million of added funding last year, and the new privately funded Healthy Start Foundation initiated by my Infant Mortality Commission, we can expect to see even better results this year and next. We have learned from painful experience, though, not to relent, so I am asking for a $2 million increase followed by another $2 million in 1992–1993.

Many families face the anguish of Alzheimers, epilepsy, diabetes, and other degenerative or memory loss afflictions. It won't cost much to help. Based on the lead of Guilford County, I am asking the Center for Missing Persons to establish a statewide program with guidebooks, registration, and identification bracelets to help these neighbors be returned home safely. We can ask charitable agencies to help cover the cost of such bracelets for the indigent.

Another problem: The recession, combined with stricter regulatory requirements, threaten [sic] closure for many of our rest home operators. Accordingly, I am asking for [a] $3.4 million increase in state support for this vital service for the elderly poor in rest homes. That's comparable to what Medicaid has built in for nursing homes.

No health or environmental problem ever has been as difficult to solve as hazardous waste, which means ordinary, daily, industrial, commercial, and household chemical wastes which are a normal and unavoidable part of a modern, industrial society. The only reason it's called hazardous is because that's what it is when not properly treated or disposed of. As a chemist, I had hoped to get this problem responsibly solved by now, but the resistance has been enormous. After two years of searching, with a bewildering array of restrictions—not all of which have any relevance to environment or health—our Hazardous Waste Management Commission has found only one site meeting all requirements. That site at Butner was on state property, once allocated for agricultural research but recently not used for anything. It was not a particularly good site; there's no such thing. It was simply the only site to meet all requirements. However, the Council of State refused to approve transfer of that property for the incinerator-and-recycling complex. That means our search is at an end unless you can help.[28]

I will ask you first to do one of three things. Either (a) enact legislation approving that as the preferred site, or (b) take that authority away from the Council of State so that the commission can do the job without obstruction or help from the timid, or (c) modify or clarify some of those requirements which exceed any environmental consideration—like the four-lane highway access and the overreaching wetlands prohibition—so that the commission can start looking for other sites across the state, if that's really what you want. Meanwhile, we need your support for concessions to any county which will come forward as a possible volunteer, although it would not be wise to blithely depend on that succeeding. I would ask you please not to enter independent negotiations, but to designate a committee to work with my administration on this.

This year we must try to join with our neighboring states as they seek to establish a multistate compact with shared facilities for hazardous waste disposal. This is the only route for them or us to be able to meet our needs in a way that can prohibit outside states from dumping on us. It must be done. But first, North Carolina needs to move forward to show our neighbors that we can finally deliver on our responsibility to deal properly with at least a part of such wastes. Our record these past fifteen years has left us with an untrustworthy reputation with hazardous wastes, because we have insisted on dumping on our neighbors. If there's going to be a hazardous waste compact, with constitutional safeguards to block outside generators from our facilities, then let's move to show that we deserve to be in it.

Meanwhile, my budget contains additional funding—$264,000 on an annualized basis, beginning in January—for the Pollution Prevention Pays program, for technical assistance to businesses in reducing the amount of their hazardous waste. That has been a successful effort, but cannot eliminate the need for commercial treatment facilities. Already this week, two major industrial prospects, both clean, with the capacity to handle most of their own chemical waste, have raised a concern whether we will have the courage to meet this challenge. Apparently, rival states are beginning to tell the truth on us.

North Carolinians have responded to most other environmental challenges with vigor and enthusiasm. However, too often the issues are not clear or the facts are subject to disinformation campaigns, either to obscure the extent of damage or to make it appear worse than it truly is. For that reason, I had asked Secretary Cobey and a special task force headed by Dr. David Moreau to develop and recommend an environmental index for North Carolina.[29] Their report is about to be released. I believe you will be very pleased with the prospect of having a realistic frame of reference for environmental problems, so that we can intelligently direct our resources to those which are significant. There are some real wolves out there, after all, and we can defend better against them if we are not distracted by overreaction to those less significant.

I have another special concern for the lack of coordinated protection for the natural attractions of our mountain region. Far too often, lovely vistas are spoiled by clutter; unattractive commercial properties jam up against picturesque churches or quaint villages, and no one seems willing to take the lead to save this natural treasure. The time has come to do for our twenty-four mountain counties what the Coastal Area Management Act (CAMA) has done for twenty-two eastern counties. Let's give them the same authority and sense of obligation to develop land-use plans, and zoning controls, and watershed protection through a Mountain Area Planning System (MAPS). Fifteen years later, let's do it before it's too late.[30]

I do not propose zoning decisions made in Raleigh, or by state agencies, but locally enacted ordinances and locally adopted maps. But unless we begin now to protect the beauty of this priceless asset, it won't be long until all of highways 19, 64, 74, 221, 321, 421, and 441, along with dozens of others, will have become so cluttered with wall-to-wall strip development that they will add nothing but eyesore to the natural grandeur of our mountains and will detract from their accessibility for tourists. As difficult as land-use planning and zoning can be—and I know first-hand, having led the first county-wide zoning in the state in 1973—it is the only way left to protect the value of homes, and tourist attractions, and church sites from having junk next door; to keep billboards more discreet, so they don't look so trashy; and to save the ancient New River from being "developed" into a drainage culvert. What an exciting challenge!

Economic Development

For the last three consecutive years reported—1987, '88, and '89—North Carolina led the nation in new factories and ran about third place in nonmanufacturing. Not bad! Certainly, this has helped to build a cushion against recession and unemployment, which otherwise would surely be worse. There are serious concerns about how to keep the pipeline filled with potential projects, but Secretary Broyhill and his people are working very hard at it.[31] It is likely that this month will reach the all-time high for new project commitments. Stay tuned; and, speaking of pipelines, our efforts to get an alternate source of supply for natural gas, especially for down east, are being answered affirmatively in the industry.

Travel and tourism continues [sic] to thrive in North Carolina, having just passed $7 billion a year. Related to that, we now offer valuable assistance to sports promotions, both professional and amateur. This can have the same impact as the highly successful motion picture office. It deserves note that one traditional production industry has shown good growth: Agribusiness continues to prosper, with food processing becoming more and more modern.

The most critical need in this area is to reorganize economic development for better coordination and better results. The auditor's report showed that we spend $136 million a year on forty-three—far too many—independent, uncoordinated, even duplicative operations scattered across the state "dealing with" economic development. Too often there is no accountability for their separate efforts, nor any practical way to keep score of whether each of them is doing anything really useful or not. Therefore, I propose that we direct all of this expenditure through the Department of Economic and Community Development, so that someone will have authority and accountability for it; so that we can expect to get better results for less money. And while we're at it, wouldn't it be nicer and simpler to name it just the Department of Commerce?[32]

State Government Reform

Each session in recent years has dealt with important reforms in the workings of government. This is to be no exception. One troubling issue which needs to be addressed is the question of ethical standards for public officials. This deserves your careful attention. We should clarify policies relating to the acceptable nature, and magnitude, and purpose of gifts. That does not mean that an absolute prohibition is needed, for reasonable standards with adequate reporting requirements will reassure the public. Especially for elected officials and those appointed to positions having any regulatory, purchasing, or other decision-making authority, I would hope that we could work together to clarify what is expected.[33]

The most important reform expected by the people is the veto. Every year I have urged you to authorize a vote of the people for the veto for the governor of North Carolina, just like every other state. This will not be an exception. We remain the only state where the people have never once been trusted to make that historic, fundamental, balancing decision between executive and legislative branches. It should be an embarrassment to you.

Recognizing that you are not likely to apply that historic amendment during my remaining term, it will nevertheless be a major objective for me to achieve that legacy for my successors. Having tried unsuccessfully last session to win enough votes in the House either for a balance-of-powers package or for the veto alone, I will propose this time that we work for a bill limited to the veto and nothing else. It should be done right, and that means a line-item veto, subject to two-thirds override, just like most other states. The people of North Carolina will support that.[34]

There also should be a renewed effort to change the process for merit selection of judges. I will support that but will send you a message later calling for appointment of appellate courts, while changing trial court judges to nonpartisan election by districts. It would be nice to have one branch of state government not involved in partisan politics. Until a change is made, however; as long as partisan elections are required, then you must expect them to become increasingly partisan. Trust me on this.[35]

I will also send you my thoughts on legislative and congressional redistricting. That is probably not a subject on which a lot of advice will be beneficial, but I will want you to know that I am interested and watching.

Bond Issue

Even with these increases in revenues, there is another difficult problem which we must face: There would be no money available for capital improvements. It would not be wise fiscal management to defer again so many overdue construction projects which have had to be postponed these last two years. To enable us to meet these needs responsibly, I am proposing a $355 million bond issue for capital projects, as follows:

(a) University buildings $ 100 million
(b) Community college buildings $ 25 million
(c) Local water-sewer financing $ 75 million
(d) Public schools in small counties $ 130 million
(e) Mental health facilities $ 25 million

The university and community college project lists should be developed by their respective state boards. The water-sewer bonds would only provide lowest-cost loans for local government needs. The mental health package is being developed by the Department of Human Resources in concert with state associations in this area; and, as recommended by the Public School Forum, the public school bonds would be solely for construction in those small counties with less than 3,000 pupils ADM [average daily membership], and would be paid for on a 3:1, state:local, matching basis, with the state's share of debt service being in lieu of the $10 million-a-year appropriation we currently allocate to the critical needs formula.

Conclusion

It is clear, then, that there are many opportunities, and responsibilities, for us to serve the needs of North Carolina, even in a time of fiscal crisis. There are many needs, some of which must be dealt with now if we are to reach the next century with all the vitality and preparation expected of us. That does not, however, mean that we must do everything on every menu. We must be careful and selective. Until this recession is over, we could severely damage our economic viability if we raise taxes any more than is absolutely necessary. I am just as convinced that it would risk our economic future even more if we neglect those educational improvements which are strategically most vital to our capacity to come out charging after the recession.

But to reassure the people that we will raise no tax that is not absolutely necessary, let us continue to look for more ways to control the size of government, especially within administration costs. That course might not please everyone: not those who want no tax increase, and not those who want a larger tax increase, or who want me to propose a larger tax increase so they can shoot it down like they did in 1989. But in this case, the test of leadership is to find the right course, to help identify and meet the most urgent needs, and to restrain our appetite for other nice but unaffordable improvements which could wait for the normal revenue growth of a burgeoning economy. That's the course I choose. Meanwhile, there are many nonbudgetary issues which deserve attention, and which usually get neglected when an abundance of revenues absorb [sic] all our energies. I have placed before you at least twenty proposals of that kind, which will give us plenty to do in this session.

It is to be expected that some will be critical that this budget goes too far in a recession. Others will just as surely complain that it doesn't go far enough, and that we should levy crippling tax burdens on our businesses. I take comfort in the light retort from Governor Luther Hodges about a certain local paper which, he said, "always values its opinions above the judgment of governors and state officials." As with Hodges's leadership and that of others, these times call not for radical excess on either side, but "for careful steering between the extremes," as he put it. What better model?[36]

You would understand my approach if you've ever tried to bring a small sailboat through a convulsive inlet in a storm. With dangers on all sides, you must be prepared and disciplined if you're to avoid the rocks and shoals. You must not panic, or try extreme maneuvers, or try to run too fast, lest you broach. Rather, you must keep a firm hand on the helm, and know the warning signs, and steer very carefully—always mindful that your objective is not to fly, or drive it aground, but to come through safely to the other side.

This recession is not forever. It will end, and then there will be revenue growth; and if North Carolina will tend to its strategic needs and not get drawn into a spending binge when income is down, we will be ready when recovery comes—ready with those vital programs and resources in place, and ready to move forward with other important improvements which we'll then be able to afford. That's the test of leadership: to come through safely on the other side.

TABLE I. **Educational Priorities for 1995**
Consensus of 40 Participants
Education/Workforce Preparedness Summit
January 11, 1991

A. Reforms with Little or No Budget Cost:

Overall Rank	Item Description	Weighted Score (g)	Number of Participants	Top 3
1	Appointed State Superintendent	176	27	10
2	Flexibility and Local Control	169	25	13
3	Academic Rigor, Basic Mastery and other Curricular Reforms	168	26	11
7	End Tenure, for Administrators	112	18	9
10	Parental Involvement	96	18	4
11	Accountability	91	15	8
12	Training for Administrators	90	17	4
15	Career Curriculum	75	9	6
16	Parental "Choice" of School	71	12	4
17	Fewer Interruptions in School	66	11	4
18	Stronger Attendance Laws	56	13	1
21	End Tenure for Teachers	37	5	3

B. Programs with Substantial Budget Costs:

Overall Rank	Item Description	Weighted Score (g)	Number of Participants	Top 3
4	S.B.2 Flexibility/Accountability	145	21	11
5	Professional Salary Increases	133	18	10
6	Tech Prep/Workforce Training	119	19	7
8	Basic Education Program (BEP)	101	16	6
9	Community College Improvements	97	15	7
13	Pre-School/"At-Risk" 4-year-olds	81	17	2
14	Professional Staff Development	76	16	2
19	Rural Tax Equalization Funding	49	10	2
20	Adult Literacy	39	10	2

Note: (g) Relative scores are weighted based on ten points for first priority, nine points for second, eight for third, and so on until 1 point is awarded for tenth priority or less. (Maximum possible = 400 points)

TABLE II. **Educational Priorities for 1991–1992 Budget**
Consensus of 40 Participants
Education/Workforce Preparedness Summit
January 11, 1991

			No. of Participants			
Overall Rank	Description of Program	Weighted Score (a)	Top 3	Top 5	Total No.	Median (b) $ Amount
1	S.B. 2	161	28	34	35	$ 22 million
2a	Comm. College	103	12	22	28	$ 20 million
2b	Adult Literacy	30	3	6	12	$ 8 million
2c	Job Training	30	4	6	10	$ 20 million
3	Preschool (c)	103	13	22	29	$ 22 million
	(d)	17	2	3	7	$ 16 million
4	Pay Step (e)	100	14	21	24	$ 19 million
5	Tech Prep	87	14	18	20	$ 4 million
6	BEP	85	12	18	27	$ 30 million
7	Pay Increase	70	6	12	24	$ 72 million
8	University	61	3	11	24	$ 20 million
9	Curriculum (f)	49	3	8	20	$ 4 million
10	Staff Developmt	45	2	9	20	$ 3 million
11	Equity/Minimum	31	2	6	14	$ 20 million
12	Drug-Free	19	2	2	8	$ 3 million
Total:		240	38	38	38	$283 million

Footnotes
(a) Weighted score, based on:

	Priority Order	Score Awarded
	1st	6 points
	2nd	5 points
(Maximum possible = 240 points)	3rd	4 points
	4th–5th	3 points
	6th–7th	2 points
	Other	1 point

(b) Median recommendation when participant assumes $150 million to be available for all education expansion.
(c) Developmental preschool for at-risk 4-year-olds.
(d) Preschool for 4-year-olds handicapped with developmental disabilities.
(e) This item represents the cost of not freezing the existing pay step schedule, funding only the seniority step increase.
(f) An assortment of curricular reforms, including: career curriculum and career guidance, more rigorous graduation requirements; basic skills mastery; advanced placement; enhanced testing of students.

[1]Daniel Terry Blue, Jr. (1949-), born in Lumberton; resident of Raleigh; B.S., North Carolina Central University, 1970; J.D., Duke University, 1973. Attorney; member, since

1981, Speaker, 1991–1994, N.C. House of Representatives; Democrat. *News and Observer*, November 10, 1994; *North Carolina Manual, 1991–1992*, 305–306.

²The governor offered his spending plan in long and short formats: *The North Carolina State Budget, 1991–93 Biennium* (Raleigh: Office of State Budget and Management, 6 volumes, [January] 1991), and *The North Carolina State Budget, 1991–93 Biennium: Summary of Recommendations* (Raleigh: Office of State Budget and Management, January 1991). The *Post-Legislative Budget Summary, 1991–93*, is a single-volume guide to approved funding. Joseph S. Ferrell (ed.), *North Carolina Legislation, 1991* (Chapel Hill: Institute of Government, University of North Carolina, 1992), hereinafter cited as Ferrell, *North Carolina Legislation, 1991*, reviews the major laws enacted by the General Assembly.

³James Earl Ezzell, Jr. (1936–1991), native of Rocky Mount; B.A., 1960, LL.D., 1963, Wake Forest University. Attorney; recorder's court solicitor, 1964–1968; district court judge, 1980–1983; member, N.C. House, 1977–1980, and Senate, 1985–1991; chairman, Senate Constitution Committee; Democrat. He was killed in a motor accident on January 30, the opening day of the 1991 legislative session. *News and Observer*, January 31, 1991; *North Carolina Manual, 1989–1990*, 263.

⁴For more on Operation Family Shield, see pages 308–309, below. Martin authorized the ten-day extension on March 7, 1991, upon signing Executive Order No. 134, "Granting Special Readjustment Leave to Employees of the State Who Have Served with the Nation's Armed Forces During the Persian Gulf Conflict," *N.C. Session Laws, 1991*, II, 2661–2663.

⁵Martin frequently capitalized the words *Growth, Opportunity*, and *Prosperity* when he used them together in his texts, for obvious reasons.

⁶The reductions to which the governor referred were enacted in July 1990 to help balance the state budget for F.Y. 1990–1991.

⁷For related press releases, see "Governor Announces Final Plans for Education Summit on January 11," Raleigh, January 4, 1991, and "Governor Sets Education Summit Agenda," Raleigh, January 10, 1991, Governors Papers, James G. Martin. The summit members' spending recommendations are listed in Table 2, "Educational Priorities for 1991–1992 Budget," page 59.

⁸Representatives Joe H. Hege, Jr. (R-Davidson), and Julia C. Howard (R-Davie) offered H.B. 1015, "A Bill to be Entitled an Act to Phase Out Career Status for all School Employees Except for Classroom Teachers," for consideration by the House on April 19, 1991. Their proposal for tenure changes was assigned to the Committee on Education. *N.C. House Journal, 1991*, 358.

⁹Three bills creating an appointed state superintendent of education were introduced in the North Carolina Senate during the 1991 legislative session. S.B. 318 and S.B. 806 were assigned to the Constitution Committee for study, and neither reemerged. However, the committee looked somewhat more favorably upon S.B. 250, introduced by Kenneth Royall (D-Durham) on March 21. His "Bill to Amend the Constitution to Change the Composition of the State Board of Education, to Make the Governor the Chairman of the State Board of Education, to Make the Superintendent of Public Instruction an Appointee of the State Board of Education, and to Make Corresponding Statutory Changes," was revised to eliminate the provision naming the governor as head of the education board. This substitute measure passed the Senate and was sent to the House, which closeted S.B. 250 in its Rules Committee. *N.C House Journal, 1991*, 1077–1078; *N.C. Senate Journal, 1991*, 149, 176, 290, 417, 652, 678, 679, 742, 744–745.

¹⁰H.B. 937, "A Bill to be Entitled an Act to Authorize a Schools of Choice Program in Counties with a Population of More than 300,000 People and in which There is More than One Local School Administrative Unit," was introduced April 19, 1991, by Representatives Stephen W. Wood (R-Guilford) and George W. Miller, Jr. (D-Durham). It was assigned to the House Rules, Appointments, and Calendar Committee, where it remained through the end of the session. *N.C. House Journal, 1991*, 348.

¹¹Supplemental funds for small school systems were included in "An Act to Make Base Budget and Expansion Budget Appropriations for Current Operations of State Departments, Institutions, and Agencies; to Make Appropriations for Capital Improvements for State Departments, Institutions, and Agencies; to Make Appropriations for Other Purposes; to Provide for Budget Reform; and to Provide for Revenue Reconciliation," *N.C.*

Session Laws, 1991, II, c. 689, s. 201.1, ratified July 13, 1991. Section 201.2 made available $6 million in additional financial assistance for education in low-wealth counties for the 1991–1992 and 1992–1993 fiscal years. Both sections of the legislation were later amended under "An Act to Make Technical Corrections and Other Changes to the Law," *N.C. Session Laws, 1991*, II, c. 761, secs. 47.1–47.3, ratified July 16, 1991.

[12]Martin likely was referring to the "Child Care and Development Block Grant Act of 1990," P.L. 101–508, *United States Statutes at Large*, Act of November 5, 1990, 104 Stat. 1388–236 to 1388–250.

[13]The General Assembly approved tuition increases for member institutions of the University of North Carolina system. Education costs for in-state students rose between 15 percent and 20 percent, while nonresident students were required to absorb rate hikes ranging from 12.5 percent to 25 percent. Lawmakers also earmarked $8.9 million for need-based student aid to help offset the effect of tuition increases on low-income students. *Post-Legislative Budget Summary, 1991–93*, 48.

[14]Paul Hardin (1931–), born in Charlotte; resident of Chapel Hill; A.B., 1952, J.D., 1954, Duke University; honorary degrees; U.S. Army, 1954–1956. Attorney, 1954, 1956–1958; faculty member, Duke University School of Law, 1958–1968; president of Wofford College, 1968–1972, of Southern Methodist University, 1972–1974, and of Drew University, 1975–1988; member, N.J. Board of Higher Education, 1983–1988; became chancellor, University of North Carolina at Chapel Hill, 1988. *North Carolina Manual, 1991–1992*, 739.

[15]Constitution of North Carolina, *North Carolina Manual, 1991–1992*, 645.

[16]The plan endorsed by local governments to replace "state reimbursements for legislative deletions from the property tax base," with a half-cent, local-option sales tax increase, found favor in the House. But the Senate steadfastly opposed the idea and instead won a one-cent hike in the state sales tax. Ferrell, *North Carolina Legislation, 1991*, 110–111.

[17]The massive budget shortfall that faced state government in 1991 prevented school-teachers and public employees from receiving any pay raise that year. However, the General Assembly indicated it would fund the last phase of a revised teacher salary schedule in F.Y. 1992–1993. Lawmakers promised nonteaching state employees cost-of-living increases as soon as finances allowed; they also restored an extra vacation day at Christmas that earlier had been converted to the Martin Luther King, Jr., birthday commemoration. The new law awarded state workers twelve paid holidays per year, instead of eleven, when Christmas fell on Tuesday, Wednesday, or Thursday. "An Act to Restore the Traditional Christmas Holiday Schedule to State Employees," *N.C. Session Laws, 1991*, II, c. 750, ratified July 16, 1991; Poff, *Addresses of Martin*, I, 44–46; *Post-Legislative Budget Summary, 1991–93*, 163.

[18]State workers saw major increases in their health costs under "An Act to Make Benefit, Eligibility, Clarifying, and Other Technical Changes in the Teachers' and State Employees' Comprehensive Major Medical Plan," *N.C. Session Laws, 1991*, I, c. 427, ratified June 27. The legislation raised employee and dependent deductibles, from $150 to $250 per year, and the aggregate maximum deductible went from $450 to $750 per family per year. Copayments were also higher, and reimbursement for prescription drug costs changed from a flat fee to a percentage basis.

[19]The General Assembly traditionally based the state budget for each biennium upon revenue projections. But with the state confronting a third consecutive revenue shortfall in 1991, along with another round of deepening budget cuts, Senator William D. Goldston, Jr., and Representative J. Arthur Pope advocated change: Base each new budget upon actual revenue collections from the previous year. Goldston offered S.B. 5, "A Bill to Restructure the Budget Process so as to Assure More Stable Budgeting, by Providing for Use of the Prior Calendar Year's Collections as the Revenue Estimates, Limiting Use of Reversions to One-Time Expenditures, Providing for Annual Budgets, and Streamlining the Legislative Process as a Result," on January 31, 1991. Representative Arthur Pope introduced a similar bill in the House on March 4. Although their proposals enjoyed bipartisan support, they were not enacted. *N.C. House Journal, 1991*, 108; *N.C. Senate Journal, 1991*, 24, 147, 242, 340; *News and Observer*, February 13, 1991.

William D. Goldston, Jr. (1925–), born in Charlotte; resident of Eden; B.S., High Point College, 1947; was also educated at University of North Carolina at Chapel Hill; U.S. Army

Air Corps, 1944–1945; N.C. National Guard, 1947–1950. President, Goldston, Inc., 1952–1983; member, 1961–1969, chairman, 1967, Leaksville School Board; president, N.C. Motor Carriers Association, 1972–1973; member, state Senate, 1985–1992; Senate majority whip; Democrat. *North Carolina Manual, 1991–1992,* 234. Speaking at ceremonies dedicating a portion of highway N.C. 14 in Rockingham County in honor of Goldston, January 5, 1993, Martin praised the senator's effectiveness in transportation and budgetary matters.

James Arthur Pope (1956–), born in Fayetteville; resident of Raleigh; B.A., University of North Carolina at Chapel Hill, 1978; J.D., Duke University, 1981. Attorney; retailer; senior vice-president, Variety Wholesalers, Inc.; state director of organization, Jim Martin for Governor, 1984; special counsel to Governor Martin for state boards, commissions, and agencies, 1985; elected to state House, 1988, reelected, 1990; Republican candidate for lieutenant governor, 1992. *North Carolina Manual, 1991–1992,* 313, *1993–1994,* 1049–1050.

[20]The Economic Future Study Commission was established under *N.C. Session Laws, 1989, Extra and Regular Sessions, 1990,* c. 1066, s. 22, ratified July 28, 1990. The body was directed to submit its final report to the General Assembly by February 1, 1991.

Malcolm Gillis (1940–), born in Dothan, Ala.; resident of Houston, Tex.; B.S., 1962, M.A., 1963, University of Florida; Ph.D., University of Illinois, 1968. Dean, Graduate School, 1986–1991, vice-provost, 1986–1991, dean, faculty of arts and sciences, 1991-1993, Duke University; president, Rice University, since July 1993. Malcolm Gillis, letter to Jan-Michael Poff, October 10, 1993.

[21]The General Assembly exempted motor vehicle title transfers, within a family, from the highway use tax; for specific examples, see *N.C. Session Laws, 1991,* c. 689, s. 323(a).

[22]The state legislature approved the transfer of $340 million from the Highway Trust Fund to the General Fund for the 1991–1993 biennium. *Post Legislative Budget Summary, 1991–93,* 148.

[23]John Dale (Jack) Kasarda (1945–), born in Wilkes-Barre, Pa.; resident of Chapel Hill; B.S., 1967, M.B.A., 1968, Cornell University; Ph.D., University of North Carolina at Chapel Hill, 1971. Assistant professor, University of Chicago, 1971–1974; associate professor, Florida Atlantic University, 1974–1976; professor of sociology, since 1976, Kenan Distinguished Professor, Sociology Department chairman, 1980–1990, and director, since 1990, Kenan Institute for Private Enterprise, University of North Carolina at Chapel Hill; author. *Who's Who in America, 1994,* I, 1812.

[24]"An Act to Authorize a Bond Referendum on the Issuance of Two Hundred Million Dollars General Obligation Bonds of the State, to Be Voted on by the Qualified Voters of the State, to Provide Funds, with Any Other Available Funds, for State Prison and Youth Services Facilities," *N.C. Session Laws, Extra Session, 1989, Extra and Regular Sessions, 1990,* c. 935, was ratified July 16, 1990. Held during the November 6 general elections, the referendum passed with support from just over 50 percent of the voters. *News and Observer,* November 8, 1990.

[25]Constitution of North Carolina, Article XI, Section 1, *North Carolina Manual, 1991–1992,* 647.

[26]For legislation regarding privately run correction facilities, see *N.C. Session Laws, 1989, Extra and Regular Sessions, 1990,* c. 1066, s. 121, and *N.C. Session Laws, 1991,* II, c. 689, s. 67.

[27]Legislators appropriated $620,000, for F.Y. 1991–1992, and $1,020,000, for F.Y. 1992–1993, to support programs aimed at helping pregnant alcohol and drug abusers. Ferrell, *North Carolina Legislation, 1991,* 134.

[28]North Carolina joined with South Carolina, Alabama, Kentucky, and Tennessee in a hazardous-waste disposal compact in 1989. To meet its part of the agreement, the state had to file an application, by December 31, 1990, to build a hazardous-waste incinerator, a landfill to retain the ash, and a solvent recovery plant. The facilities were to be constructed by 1992.

Charged with the task of locating those facilities, the state Hazardous Waste Management Commission initially favored privately owned tracts of land in Granville County and on the Iredell-Rowan County border. But months of persistent opposition from local residents persuaded the commission to examine state-held acreage instead. The John Umstead Farm, near Butner, emerged as the top choice on which to site the incinerator and solvent recovery plants. Questions remained whether the depth of the soil on the 1,000-acre plot conformed to state landfill regulations.

Before construction could begin, the Council of State had to approve the transfer of the land to the Hazardous Waste Management Commission. The council, consisting of the state's ten highest elected officials, eight of them Democrats, met December 13, 1990, to vote on the matter. Governor Martin spoke in support of the transfer; see "Notes for Remarks to Council of State," pages 306–308, below.

Despite the encroaching deadline and the urgency of the governor's request, approval by the Council of State was far from assured. Umstead Farm belonged to the state Department of Agriculture, and its commissioner and council member, James A. Graham, led the opposition to the land transfer. According to state law, it was the commissioner's duty to maintain the property exclusively "'for research, teaching, and demonstration in agriculture, forestry, and aquaculture.'" The state auditor believed it "'virtually impossible'" to evacuate the patients at nearby Umstead state psychiatric hospital, and the Murdoch Center for the mentally retarded, were "'a serious accident'" to occur at the proposed hazardous waste installation. Other opponents on the council contended that the location selection guidelines and process were flawed and also cited the threat to local wetlands and drinking water.

Graham correctly predicted that the measure would fail: Governor Martin and Lieutenant Governor Gardner were the only members to vote in favor of the transfer. Afterward, the governor excoriated the council's decision that left him searching for answers to the state's mounting hazardous-waste problem. In a rare expression of support for Martin, the lead editorial in the December 16 edition of the Raleigh *News and Observer* criticized the council's majority for "shooting down more than a year of Governor Martin's dogged effort to find a hazardous-waste processing site and fulfill North Carolina's obligations to its people and its neighbor states."

Failure to meet the December 31 deadline eliminated North Carolina from the five-state compact. Although Alabama and South Carolina attempted to punish the state further by halting hazardous-waste shipments to their landfills effective January 1, 1991, federal courts declared the bans unconstitutional as restraints to trade. Transport of toxic materials to out-of-state locations continued for the remainder of the Martin administration, as did the search for a disposal site within North Carolina. *News and Observer*, June 3, December 5, 6, 12, 13, 14, 15, 16, 17, 18, 19, 20, 22, 1990, January 3, 12, 14, June 11, 1991; press release, "Governor Martin's Reaction to Inclusion of North Carolina in Regional Hazardous Waste Treatment Agreement," Raleigh, November 22, 1989, Governors Papers, James G. Martin.

[29]William Wilfred Cobey, Jr. (1939–), deputy state transportation secretary, 1987–1989; secretary, Department of Natural Resources and Community Development, 1989, and of Department of Environment, Health, and Natural Resources, 1989–1993. Previously identified in Poff, *Addresses of Martin*, I, 105n; see also *North Carolina Manual, 1991–1992*, 167.

David Humphreys Moreau (1938–), born in Jackson, Miss.; resident of Chapel Hill; B.S., Mississippi State University, 1960; M.S., North Carolina State University, 1963; M.S., 1964, Ph.D., 1967, Harvard University. Faculty member, University of North Carolina at Chapel Hill: assistant professor, 1968–1971, professor, since 1976, City and Regional Planning and Environmental Sciences and Engineering depts.; associate professor, 1971–1976, Dept. of City and Regional Planning; associate dean for planning and programs, 1978–1983, acting dean, 1983, College of Arts and Sciences; director, since 1983, Water Resources Research Institute. Chairman, Governor's Blue Ribbon Panel on Environmental Indicators, 1989–1990, N.C. Sedimentation Control Commission, 1991–1993, and of N.C. Environmental Management Commission, since 1993; consultant; author. David Humphreys Moreau, letter to Jan-Michael Poff, November 16, 1993.

[30]Although inspired by the successful Coastal Area Management Act, the proposed Mountain Area Planning System was never adopted. However, the Mountain Area Study Commission was created to examine the effects of then-current land-use practices in western North Carolina and determine whether stricter guidelines should be adopted. "The Studies Act of 1991" [short title], *N.C. Session Laws, 1991*, II, c. 754, s. 16.1, ratified July 16, 1991; see also *News and Observer*, March 29, April 7, 9, May 11, 1991. The Coastal Area Management Act was ratified April 11, 1974. *N.C. Session Laws, 1973, Second Session, 1974*, c. 1284.

[31]James Thomas Broyhill (1927–), native of Lenoir; member, U.S. House, 1963–1986, and Senate, 1986; state economic and community development secretary, 1989–1991; Republican. Previously identified in Poff, *Addresses of Martin*, I, 105n; see also press release, "Jim Broyhill Resigns from His Post as Secretary of the N.C. Department of Economic and Community Development," Raleigh, March 28, 1991, Governors Papers, James G. Martin.

[32]The Department of Economic and Community Development reverted to its former title, the Department of Commerce, effective January 1, 1993. "An Act to Change the Name of the Department of Economic and Community Development, and to Make Technical and Conforming Amendments to Various Laws," *N.C. Session Laws, Extra Session, 1991, Regular Session, 1992*, c. 959, ratified July 15, 1992.

[33]*N.C. Session Laws, 1991*, II, c. 754, s. 2.6, established the Governmental Ethics Study and permitted the Legislative Research Commission to examine the "advisability of, by law, adopting or authorizing the adoption of ethical codes for State and local government officials and employees in North Carolina."

[34]Perpetuating what had become an apparent biennial ritual since 1985, the General Assembly again refused, in 1991, to authorize a referendum on the granting of veto power to the state's chief executive. H.B. 3, sponsored primarily by House Republicans, would have established a veto requiring a two-thirds vote to override and included a line-item provision for trimming appropriations bills. Neither that measure nor a companion proposal favored by GOP senators, S.B. 156, emerged from committee.

Apart from Republican efforts, Democrats made three attempts at submitting the veto question to a popular vote. Two bills never escaped their respective houses: H.B. 67, which called for referendums on both the veto and the repeal of gubernatorial succession, specified a three-fifths majority to override. It died in committee, as did S.B. 233 in the Senate.

A third proposal was longer lived. S.B. 244, "A Bill to Provide for a Referendum in November 1992 to Amend the Constitution to Provide for a Gubernatorial Veto Requiring a Three-fifths Vote to Override," passed the Senate on May 8, 1991. However, the House referred it to the Committee on Courts, Justice, Constitutional Amendments, and Referenda, which reported unfavorably on the bill in early July and offered no legislative substitute. *N.C. House Journal, 1991*, 42, 66, 617, 1078–1079; *N.C. Senate Journal, 1991*, 70, 129, 145, 323, 358, 368; see also press release, "Governor Responds to Committee Vote on Veto," Raleigh, July 2, 1991, Governors Papers, James G. Martin.

[35]Legislation establishing merit selection of appellate court judges became stalled in the House Committee on Courts, Justice, Constitutional Amendments, and Referenda in 1991. See H.B. 102, H.B. 103, S.B. 71, and S.B. 72 (Committee Substitute), *N.C. House Journal, 1991*, 76, 159, 167; *N.C. Senate Journal, 1991*, 52, 130, 142–143.

[36]Neither of the two quotations Martin attributed to Governor Hodges has been verified. However, the second seems to paraphrase a portion of Hodges's address, "The Segregation Issue—Message to the Special Session of the General Assembly," delivered June 23, 1956: "I know there are extremes on this issue; those who would go far to the left, and those who would get equally as far to the right. It is neither fear nor lack of conviction that makes me stay nearer the middle; it is a sincere desire to be the governor of all the people of whatever belief, of whatever extremes, and to lead as best I can the state in a moderate fashion to help solve this problem pressing down upon us." Quoted in James W. Patton (ed.), *Messages, Addresses, and Public Papers of Luther Hartwell Hodges, Governor of North Carolina, 1954–1961* (Raleigh: Council of State, State of North Carolina, 3 volumes, 1960), I, 42, hereinafter cited as Patton, *Addresses of Hodges*.

DRAFT TESTIMONY FOR U.S. DEPARTMENT OF DEFENSE-U.S. DEPARTMENT OF TRANSPORTATION HEARING ON MILITARY AIRSPACE

FAYETTEVILLE, JANUARY 10, 1989

Military airspace is a problem for my state, and you have an important decision to make for us: Is more airspace needed for special use, and how do you know? Intensive military training at low altitudes is an airspace use that is incompatible with residential growth and resort development, and must be separated from civilian aircraft. We accept that principle, but how much is needed?

At the same time, military training needs have grown, especially the need for low-level penetration and evasive maneuvers. We understand that. We respect that. We are proud of the military presence in North Carolina. We want the best training for them. They are on our side. But how much military airspace is really needed, and how can anyone know?

At the same time, our population is growing—rapidly. Much of that growth is concentrated in the coastal region where fighter pilots practice their skills. That is a conflict, and it's a serious one. It has become more serious in the past few years as the navy, marine corps, and air force each proposed even more low-level training and an even greater infringement upon civilian airspace.

Senator Helms requested that the General Accounting Office carefully analyze airspace decisions across the nation. On August 5, 1988, GAO condensed months of study to a single finding: "FAA is not effectively managing special use airspace to ensure its efficient and appropriate use." That is a very significant finding.[1]

It is not my purpose here to argue the merits of the several standing proposals for new MOAs [military operating areas] and the elimination of others, or the expansion of restricted areas in North Carolina; we continue to pursue those issues in another forum. Instead, I wish to emphasize a single message more properly the concern of this panel. The message is this: The system currently employed to render special-use airspace decisions is not credible or rational.

First, the system operates piecemeal. Airspace over North Carolina is a resource in finite supply. Yet there exists no plan that rationally weighs the competing demands for the resource and sets forth principles under which it will be managed in the public interest. Such a plan does not exist in the Department of Transportation, where the granting authority lies, nor does it exist in the Department of Defense, where the requesting services reside. No, it is not that rational.

Each request is taken up in isolation as it emerges from an independent service branch. No attempt is made within the Department of

Defense to coordinate these requests. No attempt is made at the Federal Aviation Administration to evaluate them collectively. Thus the system is not credible because it provides no assurance that airspace will be used efficiently, or that requests for additional airspace will be denied until airspace presently assigned has been fully utilized.

Secondly, the system has been in chronic violation of the National Environmental Protection Act.[2] On one side, the Federal Aviation Administration historically has refused to accept responsibility for application of NEPA requirements to special-use airspace decisions, arguing that the requesting military service must bear whatever obligation NEPA creates. Then, for their part, military compliance has been halfhearted and erratic, although a more insistent position by the Council on Environmental Quality and pressure from Congress seems [sic] to have nudged both the military services and the FAA toward compliance in recent months. To the extent it is heeded, NEPA is the FAA's only compulsion to consider the environmental costs of military training alternatives—including the inconvenience and danger to ordinary citizens in the vicinity of low-level overflights—simultaneously with the benefits that accrue to the national defense. And let me again assure you we know that's our national defense that's at stake. We know that. What we don't know is how much airspace in eastern North Carolina is being fully utilized and how much more is really needed. There is no way for anybody to know, and we believe that the FAA must fully embrace the letter and the spirit of NEPA.

Finally, the process lacks credibility because of the results it has produced during the last decade. Between 1978 and 1987, according to a recent GAO report, special-use airspace was expanded by 22 percent—more than 100,000 square miles. During this period, 129 new military operating areas were added, along with seventy-two restricted areas.[3] I am told that the Federal Aviation Administration virtually never denies a request from the military services for a special-use designation. Is that true? We have not had a balanced and thorough analysis of current airspace utilization, future military needs, or the cumulative problems caused by special-use airspace expansion. The policy has been to approve whatever is requested.

We wish you well in decisions you will make on how to balance our conflicting needs. Let me offer five recommendations that, if implemented in good faith, will satisfy the state's present concerns:

1. The Federal Aviation Administration, collaborating with the military branches and with state and local governments, should prepare a national airspace management plan, at least for North Carolina, incorporating both special-use airspace and military training routes. This management plan should be developed as a composite of regional segments. It should carefully balance military training needs, now and through the foreseeable future, with the competing needs of civil aviation and the concerns of affected residents. It should be updated periodically, probably every three years, in light of utilization rates, changing patterns of surface development, and evolving military requirements. I will be pleased to have my people help you with that—both our Department of Transportation and our Department of Natural Resources and Community Development, and especially our Military Affairs Commission.

2. Special-use airspace decisions by the Federal Aviation Administration and military training route designations should be subjected to thorough environmental review consistent with the requirements of NEPA. Although the FAA may choose to rely in part on information prepared and submitted by the requesting military agency, the evaluation of impacts must be an independent exercise conducted by the FAA, and the FAA must accept responsibility for execution of the environmental review processes. Pending and future airspace decisions should be made only after preparation of an analysis of cumulative impacts.

One unfortunate consequence of the present piecemeal system is that neither the respective military agencies nor the FAA has been obliged to pay attention to the combined effects of past and pending airspace designations. While individually some designations may seem inconsequential, they take on a new importance when viewed in the context of prior actions. A cubic mile here, and a cubic mile there, and soon it runs into real airspace. That importance would be exposed by the cumulative impact analysis required in NEPA.

The state supports recommendations by the Council on Environmental Quality that no further special-use airspace designations be made until cumulative impact analyses are completed for each proposal currently before the FAA. Any new designations should reflect the NEPA review through incorporation of conditions on time of use, extent of use, and type of use that limit impacts to the level assumed in the environmental analysis. Military training routes are currently established by the FAA without environmental analysis and with little or no public notice or review. That practice should be discontinued in favor of compliance with the requirements of NEPA.

3. No special-use airspace should be established in areas where gaps in radar and communication coverage preclude traffic separation by radar advisory. We are courting disaster in the airspace west of Manteo, North Carolina, where restricted areas to the north and south funnel east-west traffic along the south shore of Albemarle Sound. There spillover military traffic, most of it operating at high speeds, mixes with low-speed commercial and recreational traffic. The situation might be acceptable if aircraft using this corridor had access to air traffic control radar advisory services, but they don't. Present radar facilities will not, however, support advisory services at altitudes below 5,000 feet. At these altitudes, pilots must rely exclusively on the see-and-be-seen principle to avoid other aircraft. This situation is especially dangerous during summer haze. We hope you can help us on this.

4. *The FAA should approve no additional special-use airspace in North Carolina until it has demonstrated that existing special-use airspace is fully utilized.* The recent General Accounting Office study done at the request of Senator Helms concludes that inefficient airspace use continues to occur, but that the data required to correctly evaluate and manage military airspace allocations does not exist. Nor are there any guidelines indicating when underutilized military airspace should be restored to civilian use. North Carolina supports recommendations made by GAO requiring full reporting of usage data, periodic review of usage levels, and criteria that could lead to release of unneeded airspace.[4] We think further special-use airspace designations in North Carolina should be deferred until those procedures have been established.

5. *Special-use conditions should be consistent with minimum flight altitudes contained in FAA regulations, unless the appropriate military agency owns or controls the underlying land or water surface, or unless property owners have been compensated for loss of property value.* FAA regulations currently impose a speed limit and minimum altitude restrictions on flight in U.S. airspace. The speed limit at altitudes below 10,000 feet is 250 knots; altitude restrictions make it illegal to fly lower than 1,000 feet over heavily populated areas or closer than 500 feet to any person, vehicle, or structure over sparsely populated areas.

The speed restriction is lifted in specially designated airspace to allow military training, and that practice is acceptable so long as radar services are made available to minimize the danger of collision. The altitude restrictions are not suspended, however. We think they should be strictly enforced as a minimum safety buffer and as protection against excessive noise. Regulations require that minimum flight altitudes in restricted areas be 1,200 feet unless the underlying surface is owned or controlled by the military user. This regulation should be applied without exception, and the grandfather clause that gives military control to ground level in some areas where underlying property is privately owned should be canceled.

We want to thank you for coming here to give us this hearing, and we hope you will be able to make good use of our recommendations. We are proud to host the fine men and women of our armed forces and want them trained as well as possible. We just don't want to concede any more space than is absolutely needed—and want to be sure that there's a rational, credible basis for it.

[1] At this point in his prepared text, Martin wrote "[Repeat it]." The governor accurately quoted General Accounting Office, *Airspace Use: FAA Needs to Improve Its Management of Special Use Airspace; Report to the Honorable Jesse A. Helms, U.S. Senate* (Washington, D.C.: Resources, Community, and Economic Division, General Accounting Office, August 5, 1988), 1, hereinafter cited as General Accounting Office, *Airspace Use*.

Jesse A. Helms (1921–), elected U.S. Senator from North Carolina, 1972, reelected in 1978, 1984, and 1990; Republican. Previously identified in Poff, *Addresses of Martin*, I, 106n.

[2] The governor actually meant to refer to the National Environmental Policy Act of 1969. See General Accounting Office, *Airspace Use*, 14.

[3] General Accounting Office, *Airspace Use*, 16.

[4] General Accounting Office, *Airspace Use*, 8.

MARTIN LUTHER KING TRIBUTE

Raleigh, January 13, 1989

Thank you for the honor of being part of this program. Today we celebrate the birthday, not only of a great American and humanitarian, but a reaffirmation of the brotherhood of all humankind, for the very best of our human qualities. We come together to celebrate a great man's dream and to pledge ourselves to its reality. It is noteworthy that few people so well embodied the motto of our great state as did Dr. Martin Luther King, Jr.: *Esse quam videri*, "To be, rather than to seem."

If Dr. King were here today, I am sure he would say that we don't need to just talk about concepts like brotherhood, and racial equality, and equal job and equal educational opportunities; that we must put our words into action, however noble our words may be. Indeed, we must be willing to translate our rhetoric into programs to benefit all our citizens. We must all work together as one united state to redress inequities spawned by circumstances of birth and by social and economic conditions. We must continue to be committed to the conviction that the role of government is a continuing stewardship of service, designed to foster ever greater human possibilities—helping our citizens to be all they can be.

We know well that Martin Luther King was more than a man with a luminous vision and the power of moral persuasion. He was a force with a vision, a man calling us to action. The bottom line is results.

Human talent is a terrible thing to waste, no matter that the talent may reside within the skin of a person of a given pigment, or gender, or nationality. Human beings, or what economists are now referring to as human capital, are beyond question our state's most precious resource; and as we race toward the next decade and the twenty-first century, we must dedicate ourselves to its fullest possible development and use. No lesser goal than this will suffice.

In my brief remarks, I want to tell you some of the things our administration has done to help make Dr. King's dream a reality—and some of the things we must do if we are to bring to fruition his dream of brotherhood.

The best way to lead continues to be by example. Over the first four years of my administration, action, not empty rhetoric, has been the order of the day; and let's all pray that what we have done will set a precedent for administrations to come. Consider just a few of the people around me in top-ranking positions: Mary Deyampert,[1] director of social services; Aaron Johnson, secretary of correction; Dr. Lee Monroe,[2] senior education adviser for all education; David Solomon,[3] director of the Minority Business Agency in the Department of Commerce; William A. Webb,[4] assistant secretary of crime control and public safety; Felicia Pine,[5] the first black to serve in the International Division of the Department of Commerce; Lattie Baker,[6] assistant secretary for correction; in the number-two position of deputy secretary in the Department of Administration, Henry McKoy;[7] Morgan Edwards,[8] assistant secretary of transportation; as the very first black on the Industrial Commission, Harold Davis; as special assistant for minority affairs, Jim Polk;[9] and the person who is closest to me at the office every day, and is privy to more confidential information than almost anyone else in our administration, my personal secretary, the other Dottie in our life, Dottie Fuller.[10] Would all of those named, who are attending this function, please stand? Let's give you a big hand.

The list of talented women and men holding positions of great importance in my administration goes on. Everyone on the list has one thing in common: They are all competent. They are in positions of high responsibility because they are highly qualified to do their jobs. In fact, they each held a reputation for considerable competence before they joined our administration. We are extremely fortunate to have their services, and each of these accomplished people, in his or her own way, provides a daily demonstration that equal opportunity works when qualified minorities work. It's that simple. Of equal importance, all of the persons named serve as extraordinary role models for all races.

To be rather than to seem: We need daily to live out our state's motto. Can we do better? Yes, we can, and we shall. To put it in the words of Winston Churchill, "This is not the beginning of the end, but it is the end of the beginning" in providing equal opportunities for all our citizens.[11] What better occasion than this to declare that our creed must continue to be, "We can do better."

I truly believe that if future administrations build on our record of equal employment opportunities, there will be "more beyond" for all our citizens. It is entirely fitting that state government should become a model of equal employment opportunity. It is noteworthy that our appointments of blacks has [sic] been made not just in traditional minority affairs positions, but in positions that serve all people, not just minorities.

Our administration has been pioneering in true integration in the workplace. I have moved aggressively because I believe it is the right thing to do, and because I know that the fullest possible utilization of all people's talents and abilities will benefit not only those who serve but the citizens of our state as well. I do confess, however, that fuller use of minorities is not entirely unselfish: We need to get as many qualified people in state government as possible, so why overlook a rich source of manpower?

Our efforts on behalf of blacks, however, extend beyond these efforts.

—Item: First governor to issue policy directive concerning equal employment opportunity. This action ensures that positive steps are taken in state government to employ minorities, women, handicapped persons, and older persons.[12]

—Item: First governor to initiate a program specifically for historically black colleges and universities. This program provides support from state agencies, increased private-sector involvement through the United Negro College Fund, and recruits black teachers.[13]

—Item: First governor to serve as chairman of the statewide fund-raising drive for the United Negro College Fund. For the very first time, more than $1 million was raised for UNCF.

I could go on. I could tell you about the awarding of more than $14 million in discretionary funds to historically black colleges and universities in 1987, of which $700,000 went to improve our state's teaching profession—which is seriously short of black role models. If we had more time, I could tell you how we have increased the dollar amounts of state contracts awarded to minority businesses from almost $8.5 million in FY 1986 to better than $17.9 million, or more than double, in FY 1987, and to almost $26 million for the period covering July 1987 to November 1988. In fact, in an executive order issued in February 1985 we doubled the state's target percentage for minority contracting, and we have consistently exceeded our target.[14]

All of these are testimony that we remain committed to the concept of inclusion and expansion, to borrow the words of Jesse Jackson.[15] An open agenda, openly shared, is what you are entitled to—and what representative government must provide. I have said repeatedly that good politics is good government. By the same token, good government is good politics. They are inseparable entities. Good government comes about when we embrace the words of Frederick Douglass, who said, "I would unite with anybody to do right and with nobody to do wrong."

With the theme of our inaugural, *"Plus Ultra:* More Beyond," held firmly in mind, and with our hearts and hands together, we shall continue to span the distance between our straining reach for a greater good and our talents and abilities. With God's and your help, there will indeed be "more beyond" for all North Carolinians.

---

[1]Mary K. Deyampert (1940–), born in Dallas County, Ala.; resident of Raleigh; B.S., Tuskeegee University; M.S.W., University of North Carolina at Chapel Hill. Before serving as director, Division of Social Services, N.C. Dept. of Human Services, 1987–1995, Deyampert was the department's chief of social services for the state's south central region. Mary K. Deyampert, letter to Jan-Michael Poff, June 29, 1992; *News and Observer,* December 22, 1994.

[2]Lee Everett Monroe, Jr. (1943–), born in Wilmington; senior education adviser to Governor Martin, 1985–1990; appointed president, Florida Memorial College, 1990. Previously identified in Poff, *Addresses of Martin,* I, 164n.

[3]David Solomon (1944–), born in Wilmington; resident of Durham; B.S., North Carolina A&T State University, 1966; M.B.A., St. Louis University, 1976; U.S. Air Force, 1966–1976. Director, Minority Business Development Agency, N.C. Dept. of Commerce, 1988–1991; director, Office of Civil Rights, N.C. Dept. of Transportation, since 1991. David Solomon, letter to Jan-Michael Poff, July 7, 1992.

[4]William Arthur Webb (1943–), born in New Haven, Conn.; resident of Raleigh; B.S., University of New Haven, 1971; J.D., University of Connecticut, 1974; served in U.S. Air Force. Attorney; commissioner, U.S. Equal Employment Opportunity Commission, 1982–1986; assistant U.S. attorney and chief, Organized Crime and Drug Task Force, 1986–1989; assistant secretary, 1989–1992, appointed assistant secretary and general counsel, 1992, N.C. Dept. of Crime Control and Public Safety. William Arthur Webb, letter to Jan-Michael Poff, June 30, 1992.

[5]Felicia Renee Pine (1957?–), was graduated from Ball State University with degree in production management and industrial technology; daughter of Sylvania Wilkerson, Sr., assistant secretary for planning and programs, state Dept. of Transportation, 1985–1987. Former cleaning business owner, Charlotte; hired as entry-level trade specialist, International Development Division, N.C. Commerce Dept., November 1985. *News and Observer,* November 30, 1985; Poff, *Addresses of Martin,* I, 165n.

[6]Lattie Baker, Jr. (1944–), born in Willow Springs; resident of Raleigh; B.A., St. Augustine's College, 1960; U.S. Army, 1970–1972. High school teacher, 1965–1969, guidance counselor, 1967–1969; director, St. Augustine's College-N.C. State University Educational Talent Search Program, 1969–1970; held various supervisory positions with N.C. Dept. of Correction from 1972, including assistant secretary, programs and development, 1984–1987, and assistant secretary for substance abuse programs, since 1987. Lattie Baker, Jr., letter to Jan-Michael Poff, July 6, 1992.

[7]Henry E. McKoy (1946–), native of Raeford; assistant secretary, 1979–1981, appointed deputy secretary for programs, 1981, Dept. of Administration. Previously identified in Poff, *Addresses of Martin,* I, 165n.

[8]C. Morgan Edwards (1938–), born in Charlotte; resident of Raleigh; B.S., Johnson C. Smith University, 1961; was also educated at University of Pennsylvania; U.S. Navy, 1961–1965, and Reserve, 1965–1982. Industrial engineer, project manager at Campbell Soup and Philco-Ford, 1965–1969; quality assurance director, Townland Corp., 1969–1971; president, owner, CME Associates, Inc., 1977–1985; assistant secretary, N.C. Dept. of Transportation, since 1987. C. Morgan Edwards, letter to Jan-Michael Poff, July 7, 1992.

[9]James K. Polk (1927–), born in Charlotte; special assistant for minority affairs, Office of the Governor, since 1987. Previously identified in Poff, *Addresses of Martin,* I, 727n.

[10]Doris (Dottie) Irving-Fuller (1943–), born in Tucson, Ariz.; personal secretary to Governor Martin, 1985–1990; assistant secretary, N.C. Dept. of Administration, 1990–1991;

assistant secretary for community development and housing, N.C. Dept. of Economic and Community Development, since 1991. Previously identified in Poff, *Addresses of Martin*, I, 185n; see also Dottie Irving–Fuller, letter to Jan-Michael Poff, June 30, 1992.

[11]"Now this is not the end. It is not even the beginning of the end. But it is, perhaps, the end of the beginning." Sir Winston Churchill, Speech at Lord Mayor's Day Luncheon, London, [November 10, 1942], as quoted in Bartlett, *Familiar Quotations*, 924.

[12]Martin promulgated his policy on equal employment opportunity in state government via Executive Order Number 18, July 1, 1985. *N.C. Session Laws, 1985*, 1467–1470.

[13]Executive Order Number 24, signed February 13, 1986, established the Governor's Program to Strengthen Historically Black Colleges. *N.C. Session Laws, 1985, Extra and Regular Sessions, 1986*, 678–682.

[14]No executive order issued in 1985 addressed the doubling of the state's minority business contract target. However, Martin recommended a goal of 4 percent under Executive Order Number 34, signed February 27, 1987, which established the Governor's Program to Encourage Business Enterprises Owned by Minority, Women, and Disabled Persons. *N.C. Session Laws, 1987*, 2330–2333.

[15]Jesse Louis Jackson (1941–), born in Greenville, S.C.; Baptist minister; founder, executive director, since 1971, Operation PUSH (People United to Save Humanity); candidate for Democratic presidential nomination, 1984, 1988; chairman, Rainbow Coalition. Previously identified in Poff, *Addresses of Martin*, I, 466n.

GOVERNOR'S PROGRAM OF EXCELLENCE IN EDUCATION DEPARTMENT OF PUBLIC INSTRUCTION WINTER LEADERSHIP CONFERENCE

CHARLOTTE, JANUARY 30, 1989

[Elements of the following address were repeated in the governor's remarks at the Emerging Issues Forum, Raleigh, February 8, 1989, and to the North Carolina Association of County Commissioners, Raleigh, February 23, 1989.]

Surely, education is the strategic issue for North Carolina's future. That's why we're here for this leadership conference. This luncheon seeks to recognize and celebrate Schools of Excellence in our state.

Schools which have achieved special distinction during the past year certainly deserve public acclaim and honor, because they have honored us. Certainly that is true for the fourteen schools and their fifteen Programs of Excellence which we announce today. They are at the forefront of innovation to improve the quality of public education in North Carolina. They are pioneering in drug prevention, dropout prevention, family nurturing, preschool readiness, recognition of excellent teaching, as well as programs for career education, science, art, business management, visually impaired students.

This is indeed an exciting time for public schools in North Carolina! This is true for many reasons. We have made a commitment to stronger financial support for public schools than ever before. For the last four years, every budget I have submitted has increased the percentage of the General Fund going to schools. That has never happened before.

Our General Assembly can take rightful pride in achieving that rare result for five consecutive years. Not once in the previous twenty-five years was the schools' share of the budget raised even for two consecutive years. In only two of those years was it raised at all, before I became governor.

For many decades, we were content to rationalize our inadequate funding of schools. There were so many other requirements. We were making a strategic investment in our universities. We protested that we could not support our public schools as well as other states because, after all, our per-capita income was not up to the national average.

No longer are we making such excuses. We are putting schools first among our priorities, as never before—not to the exclusion of all other needs, but sustained over enough time to bring our schools to a position among the best in America. Does that mean that we have gone about as far as we need to go? Of course not. It just means that we must continue to strengthen our commitment to what we now agree is the most essential investment we can make in the future prosperity of our state.

Then what about my most recent budget proposal? Is that same commitment there? You bet it is. Let me show you: If my budget proposal for the next biennium is adopted, it will mean seven consecutive years of back-to-back increases in the schools' share.

There is a great deal of criticism, however, focused on an inadequate schedule for pay increases, both for teachers and other school and state employees; rightly so. It is axiomatic that no matter how far we can reach, or how much we can afford, there must always be choices among our goals. My budget is not the final word. It is a starting point, a way to focus those choices.

My budget shows that, after meeting all emergencies and critical needs, there is only enough revenue growth for a modest, deferred pay increase, starting in April 1990. But it is designed so that any additional revenues which can be identified, such as even a one-time windfall from the capital gains tax on the buy-out of RJR Nabisco stock, can be used to improve the pay increase by starting it earlier. That is, in fact, what I will propose when we know the revenue picture better in a couple of months. The same should be done with any money saved by eliminating less essential positions, as I have directed my department heads to do, or by sharp scrutiny by the Base Budget committees.

Why, then, is revenue growth limited? Is it because we expect a recession? No. In fact, the growth in recurring revenue for next year is nearly normal, $457 million. But $75 million of that will be needed to continue last year's pay raise, and another $70 million was dedicated last year to fund the school construction plan that was adopted instead of my bond financing proposal.[1] Take out, also, $80 million mandated by Congress for state matching for Medicaid, and all we have left in availability for next year is $232 million. How far will that go? It would take every cent of that to increase pay for school and state employees just five percent, leaving nothing for the Basic Education Program [BEP], or teaching fellows, or to relieve prison overcrowding, or for stronger law enforcement, or waste management, or anything else.

On the other hand, if these expansions are given priority, less would be available for improved compensation. While there is enough available growth in revenue in the second fiscal year, 1990–1991, for a 5.7 percent increase for teachers and for 4.5 percent for everybody else, only one fourth of that amount is available in the first year. It is for that reason that the budget I submitted can only carry a pay increase for the last quarter of the first year. Then, in April or May, when we know more than is certain now regarding RJR Nabisco stockholders, or when Base Budget scrutiny is completed, the budget can be amended to advance the date of the pay increase.

There are other options for improving the pay picture. The General Assembly might decide that it is more important to raise pay for existing positions rather than increase the number of nonteaching positions. When I suggested the Advisory Budget Commission consider deferring one year the nonteaching part of the BEP in favor of an earlier pay hike, not even the teachers' associations supported the idea. Of course, it may be that I did not explain the trade off very well. If so, there's plenty of time for the General Assembly to take into account any revised advice they receive. Either way, the BEP would be up to the same level in the second year of the biennium, $212 million more than this year. That's important, because it ensures that no momentum would be lost.

Meanwhile, I think it would be very helpful for you to support the teachers in their appeal for better pay. Just help us think through how to do it. Some don't want to make such choices and find it easier to call for a tax increase. The key to that is whether we are ready to insist on greater accountability as a guiding principle in the pay schedule. Higher taxes just to spend more money, without changing the system, has [sic] little appeal. If you want to talk about raising taxes, show me how we can get more for our money—not just more spending, but better results.

I have advocated a goal of raising our teachers to the national average in four years, using a combination of across-the-board, cost-of-living adjustments, plus statewide implementation of the career ladder. The best thing we can do for our schools is to offer all of our teachers the same opportunity for classroom promotions, with better pay for better teachers. I believe very strongly that incentive pay, based on performance and effectiveness, will do more to strengthen the quality of public education and to improve student achievement than any other reform anyone is trying. It is time to build that kind of accountability into our pay schedule; that is critical at a time when more emphasis is being directed toward outcomes and results, rather than inputs and rigid prescriptions for staff ratios and the like.

There is too much controversy over the career ladder pilot program. The State Board of Education has found widespread support for it among teachers who have participated in it. Few would want to relinquish the extra pay for which they have qualified. More importantly, they have generally agreed that better preparation led to better quality of work in the classroom—their own and those around them. Most importantly, the state board found that students' achievement on standardized tests was definitely improved, and that should be the ultimate measure of what works. Never mind that the NCAE [North Carolina Association of Educators] continues to undermine confidence in it, as with the recent NCAE survey which reported opposition to the career ladder by 93 percent of their member teachers.[2]

Did you wonder how they took that survey? They don't tell you, but I will: I've been told they voted by proxy, that's how. It was not a survey of all the teachers, but only of the NCAE delegates. In other words, a delegate representing 400 teachers could cast the whole 400 votes against it, regardless of how the rest felt. No wonder it was so lopsided!

It is time to stop arguing about it and start working together to make it even more successful statewide. If you want to talk seriously and responsibly about raising taxes, then show how we can build broad support among educators for extending the career ladder statewide to all school systems. The public is more likely to go for it if we can show a way to get better results for our money. We have already proved that we know how to spend more money on schools. From now on, if we are going to justify even more spending, we will have to show that better results will be required in return, and that our students will get more out of what we put in. That will be the true test of our commitment.

Before I conclude my remarks, let me tell you directly what I had in mind by mentioning the issue of schools of choice in my "State of the State" address two weeks ago. To correctly understand my purpose in raising that subject for discussion, you need to know, first of all, that I have not yet advocated any major change in policy for North Carolina. What I have recommended is that we begin to examine the success of other states and school systems which allow students and their parents to have more say about the schools they attend, and see if we can agree on a suitable variation of it which would work in North Carolina.

The advantage claimed for this policy is that it imposes the ultimate test of accountability on a school system: namely, to meet the needs of the students. It is said to be self-correcting through the consequences of marketplace choices. It is demand oriented. It leads to much greater parental involvement in the school, and it generally strengthens the prominence of teachers as academic leaders.

As I said then, my own reluctance to consider this before arose out of my concern that such choices might lead to resegregation of schools. That must not be the objective or the result. Many other states, however, have found ways to safeguard against that and have found a very high level of acceptance among parents of all racial, geographic, and economic circumstances.

In North Carolina, many of our local boards have established magnet schools which one may choose to attend. In Maryland, Massachusetts, Missouri, New Jersey, New York, and Wisconsin, it is permitted to choose any school in some systems. In Minnesota, any school in the state may be chosen, but it remains to be seen whether there is any advantage to that. The general experience of the twenty-three states which have tried schools of choice is that local boards create more kinds of innovative schools, like career education high schools, and versatile combinations with community colleges.

All I suggest is that we begin a public discussion of this issue, which is certain to come anyway as a result of the strong degree of encouragement from President Bush. For that reason, it would be better if educational leaders defined the concept and helped set parameters for discussion. I have called on the State Board of Education and the General Assembly, and I call upon you to examine with me how schools of choice might improve education in North Carolina. That would be the only criteria. It is not something that would have to be rushed, what with so many other issues on the agenda, but neither should it be ignored.

Once again, let me thank you for being here and for the vital leadership that you give to public education all across our state. Schools are our most strategic investment in North Carolina, and that is why we are here.

Budget Facts

A 1 percent across-the-board raise for teachers and state employees	$ 47 million
A 5 percent raise for teachers and all others	235 million
A 5 percent raise for teachers only	85 million
Fiscal 1989–1990 growth in recurring revenue	457 million
1988 Expansions without recurring funds	- 75 million
Pre-allocated to school construction	- 70 million
Medicaid, federally mandated	- 80 million
Net availability of new, recurring revenue (1989–1990)	$232 million

Fiscal 1990–1991 additional recurring revenue growth	$400 million
BEP scheduled increase for 1989–1990	113 million
Additional scheduled increase for 1990–1991	+99 million
Total combined BEP increase for 1990–1991	$212 million

---

[1]Martin recommended, in October 1986, a statewide referendum on a $1.5 billion school construction bond package that was projected to build 10,000 classrooms in five years. The proposal was introduced in the state Senate in April 1987 as S.B. 434. Supported by the state treasurer, the superintendent of public instruction, education groups, and county commissioners, the bill was virtually ignored by lawmakers, according to the governor, and remained marooned in committee. However, S.B. 434 did prompt the General Assembly "to enact a tax increase on business to build half as many classrooms in ten years." Poff, *Addresses of Martin*, I, 41n, 42n, 414–418, 598–603, 772–773, 944.

[2]District leaders of the North Carolina Association of Educators signified their displeasure with the career ladder, voting 34,111 to 2,607 against the plan during a winter meeting in the capital city. *News and Observer*, January 22, 1989.

VETO: LET THE PEOPLE DECIDE
STATEMENT TO THE CONSTITUTION COMMITTEE
NORTH CAROLINA SENATE

RALEIGH, FEBRUARY 2, 1989

Chairman Ezzell and Members of the Constitution Committee:
You have begun a deeply historic process that has eluded North Carolina for 213 years: the process of placing before our electorate the fundamental question of amending the state constitution to provide executive veto authority for the governor of North Carolina. Out of profound respect for the serious and responsible approach you have taken in commencing this step, I will neither lecture you nor provoke anyone to the detriment of this historic purpose. Indeed, I will first commend and congratulate you for the leadership you have shown to ensure that this issue receives the full, and careful, and positive consideration it deserves.
The issue, of course, is not new. Let me offer you a quote from our state's history that sounds as current as 1989: "The veto power should be given to North Carolina's governors. At present, our governor is the only one in the fifty states who does not have the veto power and the privilege and responsibility of signing a bill into law." Those words were not spoken by me or by any of my predecessors testifying today. They came from Governor Luther Hodges more than three decades ago.[1] I offer this historical footnote as a way to reiterate the fact that you stand now, in 1989, at the threshold of a significant moment in North Carolina history. Again, I applaud your work thus far, and I hope for the sake of the people of North Carolina that this good work goes forward.

In 1985 when debate began anew on this issue, I argued that the responsibility of veto is a just and proper role for a governor. On the tough issues of the day, courageous positions must be taken by legislators who stand alone under the pressure of opposition. With veto power, a governor must bear that pressure with you. A governor must take a position and explain that position. In modern day North Carolina, legislators alone bear the pressure and heat of tough issues. Those responsibilities should be shared with the state's chief executive. The challenge of leadership belongs also, in both the simple and the difficult decisions, with the state's top elected official.

I come before you today to make three [sic] important points:

First, this is an issue that belongs to the people in a statewide referendum. We serve them and for them, an issue of this importance belongs in their hands. It is wrong to deny them, again, an opportunity to vote on an issue in which they have demonstrated a great interest.

Second, the issue of veto for the governor of North Carolina deserves to stand alone on the ballot. I do not want to see this historic issue linked to other unrelated "trade off" questions such that all rise or fall together. There certainly are other important constitutional issues that may deserve to be put before the people, but they should not be combined with the veto in a way that could bring it down to defeat in its first referendum ever. I cannot support a referendum that links veto power vitally to such issues as succession. Let each stand on its own merits. Constitutional questions of this gravity should stand alone on the ballot.

Third, I will ask that the veto become effective upon ratification. Our citizens have indicated already that the time has come for this issue to be resolved. If the veto is ratified by the people, it should be operational immediately. There should be no reason to postpone it, except as an affront to one particular incumbent.

There has been much comment about the balance of power among the three branches of our state government. Thoughtful and legitimate questions have been raised about the veto; the appointment and confirmation power; the question of limitation and length of terms for both the executive and legislative branches. To be sure, this constitutes a healthy and productive discussion.

Fourth, one of the major responsibilities of the executive is the sound and proper management of the state budget. In Article III, Section 5(3) of the state constitution, the people direct that the governor shall prepare, recommend, and administer the budget of the government of the state. In that same section the people direct that state government operate within a balanced annual budget. This vital and central responsibility placed on the executive branch by the people would be carried out more efficiently and rationally if North Carolina joined with the majority of the states in allowing the executive the flexibility and responsibility of the line-item budget veto, subject at all times to the overrid[ing] check of the legislative branch. The sound accounting principle of the line-item veto has been demonstrated in state after state.

We must never forget, however, that these issues are basic constitutional questions that Section 2 of the North Carolina Constitution inalienably vests in the people. These words from our constitution provide the clearest mandate possible for letting the people decide the question of a veto for the governor, a right denied to the citizens of our state for well over two centuries. We are engaged today in constitutional debate; I offer these words from that document as guidelines for what we are about: "All political power is vested in and derived from the people; all government of right originates from the people, is founded upon their will only. . . ."[2]

The resolution of so fundamental a question as the balance of power is for the people to decide. The people expect the opportunity to exercise that right. To ensure that right is the most serious obligation of this session of the General Assembly.

It is incumbent upon this body to make certain that this historic question of executive veto is presented to the people in a simple, straightforward form, unencumbered by collateral or auxiliary matters which, though important, would jeopardize a clear understanding and decision of executive veto. Some of our people will favor veto but not succession; some will favor succession but not veto. Some will oppose both veto and succession. Some will favor extending the terms of legislators; some will favor limiting the number of terms a legislator may serve. Others favor initiative and referendum. Some of our people favor all these changes; others oppose all. Everyone agrees, however, that the people have the unquestioned right to vote on these issues, and it follows that these issues should be presented directly to the people, clearly and directly.

Just as our people are not obligated to vote a straight ticket, but can pick and choose individuals of their choice, so too they should not be presented with a take-it-or-leave-it package. Trust the people to strike the proper balance between separation of powers and balance of powers. If you give the people the chance to exercise fairly their right to balance, then the people will make the right choice, and it will be respected and honored for all time, because the people will have spoken.

---

[1]The quotation Martin attributed to Governor Hodges could not be verified. However, Hodges was indeed a proponent of the veto and urged lawmakers to grant that prerogative, in tandem with gubernatorial succession, during his "Special Message to the General Assembly," March 12, 1959: "Based on my own experience of working on a long-range state program, I think a governor should be allowed a second consecutive term if the

people vote to return him to office. Under no conditions should such a change, if made, apply to me, but I hope you will look seriously at the second term and at the lack of veto power. It is somewhat difficult to understand why our state is the only one in the United States in which the governor lacks the veto power." Patton, *Addresses of Hodges*, III, 49–50.

Former governors Robert W. Scott, James E. Holshouser, Jr., and James B. Hunt, Jr., testified with Martin before the Senate Constitution Committee in support of the executive veto. United States Senator Terry Sanford submitted a statement favoring veto power. *News and Observer*, February 3, 1989.

[2]Constitution of North Carolina, Article I, Section 2, quoted in *North Carolina Manual, 1991–1992*, 619.

FARM BUREAU PRESIDENT'S LUNCHEON

Raleigh, February 22, 1989

It is always a distinct pleasure to join in fellowship with a group that is such a vital force in the economy and life of our state. This occasion also affords me the opportunity to thank all the Farm Bureau presidents for their advice on, and support for, agricultural issues over the past four years. It goes without saying that without you, without your passionate devotion and hard work on behalf of agriculture in North Carolina, we could not have come as far as we have over the past four years. You have truly shown yourselves to be a force with a vision; and as great as the progress has been in those years, I say to you with absolute confidence that, with your continued counsel and support, you ain't seen nothing yet. Not only does agriculture continue to be the centerpiece of North Carolina's economy, agriculture's future promises to be even more productive in the coming years.

Why do I say this with such assurance? Why is our administration so confident that agribusiness will be one of the major waves of North Carolina's economic future, eclipsing past performances? As you all well know, agriculture is changing and becoming more diversified, with aquaculture showing great potential: a multi-million dollar source of income, with the potential to dwarf in economic impact even such grandiose projects as the multibillion-dollar super collider. Catfish production and mountain trout, as a recent report of the Governor's Task Force on Aquaculture confirms, hold potential for great expansion in the coming years. Already we are number two in the nation in mountain trout production. There is no reason to believe that we will not become the top producer of mountain trout.[1]

With the completion of ag parks, which I will say more about later, we will increase the potential production and sales of fruits and vegetables exponentially; *exponentially* is just a fancy word for dramatic doubling and redoubling. That's what I see happening. In short, agriculture has the potential to become our largest growth industry.

We're also seeing a dramatic upsurge in floriculture and turfgrass production.

The truth is, those who are telling us that agriculture in North Carolina is on its deathbed just haven't been paying attention. No, we're not using crystal balls, nor are we consulting psychics for our rosy forecasts concerning the future of agriculture in our state. Basically, our confidence is born out of a growing trend in agriculture: the steady and recently accelerating progression from a production-driven to a consumer-driven, market-oriented agriculture.

This fundamental shift, from a production-driven to a consumer-driven point of view, carries with it implications as profound and as far-reaching for rural economic development as any shift in our economic thinking. A consumer-driven, market-oriented approach to agriculture carries with it the necessity for diversification and the ability to convert raw products in our state into consumer products, thus ensuring that the value added remains in North Carolina. You know, some economists define a colony as any place that must send its goods to other jurisdictions to be processed and marketed. With our ag parks, we are moving toward the complete decolonization of North Carolina.

Development of our agricultural parks is the linchpin of an improved and diversified agricultural economy. We are continuing to make progress in the development of these parks, with Nash/Edgecombe/Rocky Mount being the most advanced in development. Also, what will be called a shipping point market, in Roseboro, is a North Carolina Department of Agriculture project that is moving along. Two other ag parks are in the initial stages of development, as well as the Hendersonville ag park.[2]

We are convinced that ag parks will be successful, as indicated in the last two years. Consider Wanchese Seafood Industrial Park, which has seen the development of two large seafood processors, a restaurant, and other marine-related enterprises.

A consumer-driven agricultural model, like any other viable economic system, must have all essential components in place: production of raw materials, processing, and distribution. The driving force behind a consumer-driven economy is demand. It should be noted that few states are in as good a position to profit from a consumer-driven economy as we are. We are blessed because we have highly productive soils and favorable climatic conditions, excellent port facilities, and roads to respond to a growing demand for all manner of agricultural products. But of most importance is our human capital: an industrious people, one of the outstanding agricultural research universities in the world, and a committed and knowledgeable people like those you represent. In a word, we've got a winning combination.

Being consumer-driven means that we will continue to seek and to exploit consumer demand, both domestic and foreign, to the fullest extent. In this sense, farmers are becoming more and more entrepreneurial, and the beauty is that, with proper diversification and responsiveness to consumer demand, you don't have to be big farming operations to profit.

Marketing will continue to play probably the most important part of our emphasis on rural development and agricultural diversification. Working closely with the Marketing Division of the North Carolina Department of Agriculture, we are developing marketing programs for our agricultural products, both in domestic and foreign markets. Two recent examples serve to illustrate our marketing success: the promotion of North Carolina Irish potatoes and the current promotion of North Carolina soybeans and soybean products. An addition[al] effort is our recently organized marketing program for Outer Banks seafood.

Tobacco is still king in North Carolina, and its importance to our state's economy will continue for the foreseeable future.[3] Indeed, our tobacco program has stabilized and is improving, but producers must be cautious in planning for 1989, especially about making large capital expenditures. The reason for urging caution is that the tobacco program is facing rather serious obstacles from the standpoint of smoking and health; proposed excise tax increases, which could reduce consumption; also, we are having to rely increasingly on foreign markets for the sale of cigarettes. These factors, singly or collectively, could further decrease future usage of tobacco. For these reasons, I strongly suggest, in making your plans for 1989, that you lease equipment, or purchase used equipment, or rent from your neighbors, or have joint use of equipment in order to hold down production expenses and prevent large capital outlays for equipment.

Tobacco is a good thing; farmers are wise to stick with a good thing. But at the same time, they should always be on the lookout for exploitable opportunities in farming. This means greater diversification. The farmer cannot afford to believe as the great American financier, Andrew Carnegie did: He advised people to put all their eggs in one basket— and watch the basket. For today's farmer, the first part of the advice is a road map to financial disaster; the conventional wisdom is, "Put your eggs in a number of baskets and watch all the baskets."[4]

Over the last four years we have added a number of baskets to our rural economic collection, with the result that we have strengthened not only agriculture but the overall rural economy, as well. Just look at our 1987–1988 performance as an example. Over two-thirds of all manufacturing plants were announced or built in communities with populations of 10,000 or less. Some of these new plants were Rocco Poultry, Saint

Pauls; Sara Lee Kitchens, Tarboro; Carolina Pride Seafood Processing, Plymouth; Carolina Classics Catfish Farm, Incorporated, Ayden; Van Brown Mountain Trout Processing Plant at Andrews. These processing plants will be able to process aquaculture and other agricultural products which hold such great potential for North Carolina farmers as a source of additional income.

One of the world's greatest speeches is "Acres of Diamonds," written by Russell Conwell, founder of Temple University. The speech is a parable for our times: A man left his home in search of diamonds in other lands. After years of searching, he died impoverished and alone. A little girl, playing in the yard of the man's long since abandoned home, chanced upon an interesting rock. It was to sit on the fireplace mantle for years before the discovery of its real value. It turned out that the farm the man had left to seek his fortune was to become the site of the largest diamond mine in the world. The story also happens to be true.[5]

You, who represent Farm Bureaus across our great state, are possibility thinkers. You know we are blessed with bountiful riches, but the riches will not yield up their value without our combined imagination and perspiration. There's a saying that most people wake up in the morning and go to work, but that the farmer wakes up surrounded by work. I'd like to suggest a slight change to that saying: The farmer in North Carolina wakes up each morning surrounded by opportunity.

The exploiting of our "acres of diamonds" will be a major priority over the next four years. You can rest assured that we shall continue vigorously to promote North Carolina agriculture, and that we shall continue to look to the Farm Bureau for advice and counsel as we have in the past. Thank you, one and all, for all you have done to help our state in its straining reach for its God-given potential in agriculture.

---

[1]North Carolina produced 7 million pounds of mountain trout in 1987, second to Idaho—whose aquaculturists raised 32.5 million pounds that year. *Aquaculture Development Plan for North Carolina: Report of the Governor's Task Force on Aquaculture* ([Raleigh]: State of North Carolina, 1988), 35.

[2]Agribusiness parks had been discussed for Hendersonville, Rocky Mount, and Concord. Although land had been purchased for the Agriculture Department's Southeast Shipping Point Market in Roseboro, construction had not started by the end of the Martin administration. Ross F. Williams, assistant director, Marketing Division, N.C. Dept. of Agriculture, letter to Jan-Michael Poff, February 16, 1993.

[3]Martin told the Tobacco Growers Association, February 8, 1991, that farm income from their commodity exceeded $1 billion in North Carolina the previous year.

[4]It was Mark Twain, not steel baron Andrew Carnegie, who admonished readers to "Put all your eggs in one basket and—watch that basket." The American humorist revised the opinion offered centuries earlier by Miguel de Cervantes: "'Tis the part of a wise man to keep himself today for tomorrow, and not venture all his eggs in one basket." See Cervantes, *Don Quixote de la Mancha* [1605], and Twain, *Pudd'nhead Wilson: Pudd'nhead Wilson's Calendar* [1894], quoted in Bartlett, *Familiar Quotations*, 195, 762.

[5]Russell Herman Conwell (1843-1925), born in Worthington, Mass.; died in Philadel-

phia; LL.B., Albany Law School, 1866; U.S. Army, 1862-1865. Attorney; immigration agent, 1867-1868; foreign correspondent, *New York Tribune, Boston Traveler*, 1869-1871; was ordained Baptist clergyman, Lexington, Mass., 1879; pastor, Grace Church, Philadelphia, 1881-1891, and of the Baptist Temple, from 1891; founder, 1888, and president, Temple University; hospital founder; author. *Who Was Who in America, 1897-1942* (Chicago: Marquis Who's Who, Incorporated, fifth printing, 1962), 253, hereinafter cited as *Who Was Who in America*, with appropriate years.

Conwell built his motivational speech, "Acres of Diamonds," upon a story that an Arab guide told him while traveling to Nineveh. As the guide related it, the man who bought the farm from the ill-fated gem hunter was watering his camel from the garden brook when he saw "a black stone having an eye of light reflecting all the hues of the rainbow." He plucked it from the streambed, put it on his fireplace mantle, "and forgot all about it." Days later, a visiting Buddhist priest told the farmer that the rock on his mantelpiece was a diamond. The farm, according to Conwell, became the Golconda, India, diamond mine. Robert Shackleton, *Acres of Diamonds, by Russell Conwell: His Life and Achievements* (New York: Harper and Brothers Publishers, 1915), 5-8, 164.

ANNOUNCEMENT ON EXECUTIVE ORDER NUMBER 86

RALEIGH, MARCH 2, 1989

[Across the top of this press conference text, Martin wrote: "Announcement—important on its own merits, but also in the context that it will help us to resolve issues that caused South Carolina to close Pinewood to waste generated in North Carolina."]

We have an enormous problem in North Carolina, a problem that is the inevitable result of our economic success. That problem is waste disposal. Each day North Carolina industries produce 6 million pounds of air emissions, 15 billion pounds—2 billion gallons—of wastewater, 7.7 million pounds of hazardous waste, and 33 million pounds of solid waste. The activities that bring about this waste make life better for all of us: high-paying jobs, low unemployment, products that enrich our lives, and a quality of life unparalleled in human history.

But what about all that waste? As our population numbers grow and our economic prosperity increases, we are beginning to see in North Carolina an erosion of our quality of life. Fish and crabs are dying of mysterious diseases in our sounds and estuaries. Trees are dying of unexplained causes in our mountains. Groundwater is being polluted daily by leaking underground storage tanks of petroleum and other products.

Our environment is obviously ailing, and it is time for all of us here in North Carolina to take our medicine. Responsible leadership demands that we take our heads out of the sand, acknowledge our problems, and set about to deal with them as quickly and effectively as we can. The day of the "not-in-my-backyard" syndrome is past. This problem exists in all of our backyards, and we can no longer hope to shove our waste management problems off to another state, another county, or another town. In fact, this announcement today, this executive order that reflects my commitment to improving our environment, also has a direct bearing on a timely issue with our sister state to the south.[1]

New legislation introduced Tuesday by Senator Tally and Senator Daughtry—and strongly supported by me and this administration, Lieutenant Governor Gardner, Senator Barnes, Speaker Mavretic—would remove prohibitions so that we can move forward to meet North Carolina's responsibility for our own waste treatment and disposal. It is my hope that the provisions contained in Senate Bill 324, and in this executive order, will resolve the most serious concerns of many legislators and other environmental leaders about the minimization and proper handling of hazardous wastes.[2]

Now let me go a step further, to tell you what's in the executive order. It will require this state to expand its commitment to preventing, minimizing, and recycling wastes by incorporating waste reduction as a goal in all decisions by pollution control agencies in the following manner: First, each applicant for a wastewater discharge or incinerator permit— new, modified, or renewed—related to treatment and disposal of solid and hazardous wastes should be able to document that (a) source reduction and recycling techniques have been considered and undertaken to reduce the volume, pollutant level, and toxicity; and (b) the discharge or emission levels are the lowest technologically and economically feasible after waste reduction.

Second, regarding hazardous waste, the state shall exercise its authority to obtain, review, and certify information from each facility that generates, treats, stores, recycles, or disposes of hazardous waste to ensure that it has a waste minimization program in place as required under federal statutes.

Third—separate goal, extremely important—I am ordering the state Environmental Management Commission to expedite the development and promulgation of rules to control the emissions of toxic air pollutants from waste incinerators. I am also directing the commission to use its existing authority to require any such incinerator permits issued after the date of this order to provide adequate control of toxic air emissions.

Fourth, I have asked the commission to use its authorities and powers to develop ambient air standards for toxic pollutants as soon as possible.

These steps, taken together, represent a dramatic step forward for North Carolina. I certainly understand that industries in this state may see a threat to their security and their competitive position in the marketplace when they are faced with complying with these significant actions. However, this state's nationally recognized Pollution Prevention Pays program has demonstrated time and time again, to our own industries, that waste reduction increases their competitive position through significant reductions in production costs. To help our industries meet this challenge, our Pollution Prevention Pays program and our solid and hazardous waste section will continue to provide technical assistance on waste reduction strategies. With the help of these agencies, North Carolina industries can continue to be good environmental citizens and gain a head start on their competitors in other states.

These measures, this executive order and Senate Bill 324, will start us moving in the right direction. Hard work lies ahead, and so do tough decisions. But when industry, state government, and the citizens of the state work together to improve our system and our environment, we will begin to see immediate progress.

---

[1]Martin signed Executive Order Number 86, concerning the "minimization of solid, hazardous, and infectious waste and the control of toxic air pollutants," on March 1, 1989. *N.C. Session Laws, 1989*, II, 3107–3111.

[2]Senators Tally and Daughtry were two of the eleven members of the upper house who introduced S.B. 324 on March 1, 1989. The bill, as amended, was ratified May 30 as *N.C. Session Laws, 1989*, I, c. 168; see also *N.C. Senate Journal, 1989*, 119, 156, 162, 171, 198, 589, 599, 617, 618.

Lura Self Tally (1921–), born in Statesville; resident of Cumberland County; A.B., Duke University, 1942; M.A., N.C. State University, 1970. Teacher, guidance counselor, Fayetteville City Schools; adult education instructor, Fayetteville Technical Institute; member, state House, 1973–1982, and Senate, from 1983; Democrat. *North Carolina Manual, 1991–1992*, 283.

Namon Leo Daughtry (1940–), born in Newton Grove; resident of Johnston County; B.A., 1962, LL.B., 1965, Wake Forest University; U.S. Air Force, 1966–1970. Attorney; partner, Johnston County Hams; owner, operator, Farmers Tobacco Warehouse, Smithfield; member, state Senate, since 1989; Republican. *North Carolina Manual, 1991–1992*, 254.

Henson Perrymoore Barnes (1934–), born in Bladen County; resident of Goldsboro; A.B., 1959, J.D., 1961, University of North Carolina at Chapel Hill; U.S. Army, 1953–1956. Attorney; blueberry farmer; member, state House of Representatives, 1975–1976; member, 1977–1992, president pro tempore, 1989–1992, state Senate; Democrat. *News and Observer*, January 22, 1989, February 28, August 2, 1992; *North Carolina Manual, 1991–1992*, 227, 229.

BETTER PAY FOR BETTER TEACHERS: A PROPOSAL FOR
SALARY REFORM AND HOW TO PAY FOR IT

CHAPEL HILL, MARCH 9, 1989

[Speaking before the State Board of Education on March 8, 1989, Martin advocated a one-cent increase in the state sales tax to implement fully the career ladder pay plan for public schoolteachers. That address was nearly identical to the one he delivered a day later, in Chapel Hill, to a joint meeting of the State Board of Education, the University of North Carolina Board of Governors, and the State Board of Community Colleges. The governor also discussed the advantages and funding of the career ladder concept in his remarks to the Asheboro-Randolph Chamber of Commerce, March 14, 1989.]

This is truly an historic occasion, a first in the history of our great state, the first annual meeting of the North Carolina education boards. This is indeed an historic milestone. This extraordinary meeting is a message in itself. What this meeting says, loud and clear, is that we must have a coordinated system of education in North Carolina, from kindergarten through graduate school, if we are to solve the growing problem of declining academic fitness among our students. By coming together, we are saying we cannot afford to pay for one part of education at the expense of other parts.

Marshall McLuhan proclaimed that "the medium is the message."[1] By coming together this evening, this meeting is the medium that says education is a continuum, and for us to serve our students most effectively, all our state education institutions—public schools, community colleges, and [universities] must work together collaboratively and cooperatively.

There is a story about a college in the Midwest that had a sign [on] the campus lawn that read, "It is the tradition at this college not to walk on the grass." Added were the words: "This tradition starts at noon." Well, I know that with this meeting, we have the start of a new and exciting tradition in our state. What a way to start a tradition: to have the first meeting hosted by the State Board of Education and conducted on the campus of one of North Carolina's great prides, the University of North Carolina at Chapel Hill.

When any individual, or any society, reaches a crossroads in life, a strategic choice must be made: which way to turn, whether to go forward or to turn back. North Carolina and its public schools are at such a crossroads. The choices before us are whether to move forward to establish a professional salary schedule for our teachers, with better pay for better teachers, or to turn back, or simply to halt. The choice must now be made.

At the same time, we have the excellent report just issued by the Commission on the Future of the North Carolina Community College System, *Gaining the Competitive Edge*. Their excellent findings and thoughtful recommendations must become part of our educational agenda, and the steps we will be taking through our tax increase [will] address some of these. On next Monday afternoon, at the second monthly education summit, I have asked Bob Scott to put that report before us and to lead a discussion of where we need to be going with this brilliant resource of our fifty-eight community colleges.[2] I will need to arrange with President Spangler a timely opportunity for consideration next, or soon afterward, of our prize university system.[3]

We must start somewhere, and while acknowledging the urgent needs of our community colleges and universities, I felt that we had to move aggressively, now, to alleviate some serious conditions at the public school level, K through 12, a level that strongly impacts on resource requirements and programs in our community colleges and universities. It is important, therefore, that this forum be used to emphasize, as strongly as possible, our commitment to improving matters across the entire educational continuum—not just at one level.

This week, I have reached a new and clearer commitment. After nearly four years' experience in developing our career ladder pilot program, it is time now for us to choose to move forward on a road that has been explored and found to improve productivity in the classroom and improve our students' learning and test performance. It is my strong recommendation, both as an educator and as governor of North Carolina, that we make the commitment this year to extend the career ladder and its opportunities for promotion and advancement to every school in North Carolina, and on the fastest schedule already recommended by the State Board of Education, consistent with the best things we have learned from the sixteen pilot systems.

For lack of funds, and for lack of any strong coalition of support, I chose earlier to defer this recommendation until I could give it more study and enlist broader support. Yet I feared that, if we did not move forward soon, we would lose momentum, and we would find our way blocked. Thanks to the steadfast commitment of Superintendent Etheridge and the State Board of Education, many local boards, superintendents, and principals, and many teachers whose views have been shared with me, as well as the emerging coalition of support in the North Carolina Public School Forum, the time has come to make our choice. Many legislators have concluded after careful study that this is one innovation which, with all the opposition and controversy, has emerged as not only a reform deserving the firm backing of the people, but one which can produce the results we seek.

Last month, legislation was introduced by Senator Ward and Representative Blue incorporating some excellent ideas for fixing the frozen pay schedule.[4] In developing my proposal, I have borrowed heavily from the work and ideas of all those who believe that better schools will result from greater accountability at all levels. Through opportunities for classroom promotions based on careful evaluation of a teacher's effectiveness in the classroom, we can have the most accountable system for raising our teachers[' salaries] to the national average, in a way that can raise our students' achievement to the national average, too.

Unfreezing Pay Steps

It also became clear, as I listened to and learned from some of the quieter discussions, and as I dug into the details of the current pay schedule, that there was another problem that had to be corrected first. Even though average pay for teachers had been increased faster than inflation, gaining on the national average three out of the last four years, automatic raises along a series of pay steps had been frozen in 1982. Two unintended consequences of prolonging that freeze have been (a) the compression of all experienced teachers onto lower steps than their seniority would otherwise entitle them, and even worse, (b) the discrimination in favor of those who came from another state, or who took several years off, and who were paid at higher steps than teachers whose continuous experience was in our schools. Thus, to use a familiar metaphor for this time of year, I found some awesome potholes in the entire network of roads, which threatened to damage our machinery no matter which way we chose to turn, and decided that these potholes had to be fixed.

To eliminate the frozen steps as swiftly as possible, I recommend for next fiscal year an increase in teachers' salaries, to begin this July, averaging 6 percent overall, to be applied so as to increase starting pay by 4.3 percent and to create a schedule of twenty-nine annual increments above that—for a total of thirty pay steps. The pay steps will average being about 2 percent higher than each preceding step, with the lower steps being increased slightly less than 2 percent and the higher steps being increased slightly more than 2 percent. Longevity increments would be absorbed at each step, with room to spare, and would no longer be computed separately.

Starting teachers with no prior experience would then be paid $19,120, and the most senior teachers, with twenty-nine years or more experience, would be paid $31,380, except that any teacher with a master's degree or higher would receive an additional 5 percent. It is intended that no teachers will receive less than their present salary during this change, but will receive either the 1988–1989 salary or the new step for 1989–1990, whichever is larger. For all other school personnel and for all other state employees, including those of the university and community colleges, I propose the same overall increase of 6 percent, effective July 1. For state employees, to meet the request of their association, the increase for each pay grade across the board would be 4 percent, with an additional 2 percent in money to be used for performance-based increments. To do all this will require revenue availability in 1989–1990 of $307.9 million.

For 1990–1991, the second year of the biennial budget, I now recommend an additional 5 percent overall increase for all categories of workers. For teachers, this would be applied in such a way that the pay steps would remain unfrozen and the average salary increase would be $1,300. This second-year proposal is the final budget adjustment before teachers will begin receiving the annual, average 2 percent increases in 1992–1993. For state employees, I will work with the state employees association to determine the best split between cost-of-living increases and performance pay.

Taking the Career Ladder Statewide

The state board already has approved a fast-track schedule for extending the career ladder statewide. This would provide for hiring and training the evaluators in the remaining school systems next year, 1989–1990. The intent of this action is that we begin evaluating teachers' progress for promotion to Career Level I, during 1990–1991, so that they would be promoted and begin receiving the additional 5 percent for that level in the 1991–1992 school year.

In previous discussions, the board has advised me that it would not want to rush this schedule for statewide implementation, because experience with some of the sixteen pilots showed that far less confusion and anxiety is created when the evaluators are well trained and prepared. That is a convincing argument. It is worth some consideration, perhaps, that evaluators hired in 1989–1990 might do actual evaluations on volunteering senior teachers, almost all of whom might be expected to score well enough for promotion to Career Level I. If this approach is approved, it should be an inducement for volunteers, in that those who are successfully promoted would be paid the extra 5 percent immediately in 1990–1991. For illustration, if the most senior teachers, those with twenty or more years' experience, were allowed to volunteer in the first transition year, 1989–1990, that would add an additional $25 million to the revenue requirements for 1990–1991.

One added advantage of this approach is that the number of teachers to be evaluated for Career Level I, in 1990–1991, would be reduced by roughly one-fourth, so that the number of evaluators needed in that principal transition year could also be reduced by one-fourth. A more important benefit is that the senior teachers, so promoted, would be rewarded with the extra pay a year earlier, as partial amends for their having to endure the worst impact of the frozen schedules. It goes without saying: These are special people deserving our undying gratitude. They have stayed with us out of devotion. This would be one good way of saying thanks.

Paying for Excellence

As I began my homework with my advisors, it soon became evident that such a dramatic departure from the recommended budget would require a major tax increase. Intellectually, politically, and spiritually, I was ready to accept that responsibility. My personal political philosophy had never led me to promise "no new taxes" in any election campaign, nor would it now.

In previous years I have proposed tax increases when needed, especially when I felt that such a move would improve the economy or quality of life in North Carolina. In 1986, for example, I proposed a tax increase on motor fuels, to pay for a stronger highway construction program, and on the local sales tax to replace lost federal revenue sharing. At other times, I have proposed tax cuts when I believed that would strengthen the economy. The elimination of the intangibles tax and inventory tax come [sic] to mind, as does the 1987 reduction on the unemployment tax on employers.

With that background, I approached the funding requirement of this objective with the same readiness to do what had to be done, accepting the necessity of a tax increase only as a last resort. I was determined to look into every nook and cranny to find as much alternative revenue as possible, in order to minimize the size of any tax increase.

The Last Resort—But the Right One

My proposed changes, if adopted by the General Assembly, will require $307.9 million in 1989–1990, and $609.5 million in 1990–1991. The numbers, understandably, increase from there. The cost is high, but so are the benefits.

Obviously, these costly but beneficial changes will require a tax increase. I chose to give careful study to the various taxes before making my decision. Since the corporate income tax has just last year been increased to a level higher than in neighboring states, and since there is legislation pending that would raise the personal income tax on all individuals who are not exempted, the only generally applicable tax that would yield the magnitude of revenue needed would be the sales tax.

Increasing the state sales tax from 3 cents to 4 cents on the dollar will generate a revenue increase of $510 million a year, substantially more than is needed. If that path were to be taken, not only would it cover the proposed pay increase, but it also allows us to restore a merchants discount of approximately $18 million a year. In addition, it gives us the budgetary freedom to look at other strategic needs, both in additional funding for programs and in the possibility of further tax cuts. The reserve, for tax cuts, for instance, might reach nearly $180 million in 1989–1990, and will grow each year. North Carolina has other obvious needs that can be met through a separate reserve, such as the university and community colleges, our programs for the elderly, and our mental health programs.

It is generally understood that most North Carolinians will support a tax increase on themselves if that were necessary as the only way to raise teachers' pay, especially if that were done in a way that would be expected to show better results: improved student performance. I, for one, am not going to propose a tax increase just to spend more money doing the same things we've been doing for so long with such little success. I believe our taxpayers and our educational consumers hold the same view.

Summary

In closing, it needs to be clearly understood that I am proposing a full, twelve-month pay increase—6 percent overall next year, and 5 percent in 1990–1991—for all state employees, including teachers. Using a modification of the schedule developed by the North Carolina Public School Forum, my plan would unfreeze the pay steps in the first year and establish an average 2 percent increase between each of the thirty steps. Following the strong recommendation of the State Board of Education, my plan would begin statewide implementation of the career ladder in all remaining school systems right away, on a timetable that will lead to an additional 5 percent performance-based pay increment for teachers in 1991–1992, with a possibly earlier boost for our senior teachers who volunteer to participate.

I would propose, in summary, that we explore the creation of a "Fund for Public Schools" through which we can channel these tax dollars directly into the future of our schools. It is critical that these tax dollars be used to improve the performance of our teachers and, in turn, the performance of our students. This fund would guarantee accountability for our tax dollars, a guarantee that these tax dollars are being used for teachers and children.

I am convinced that the future of our public schools, and indeed our community colleges and universities, will be much brighter if we can straighten out the mess caused by the long-frozen salary-step schedule for teachers and put into place a North Carolina innovation that will offer performance-based promotions to teachers in every school, with better pay for better teachers. Such a move will give us a mechanism for real salary growth in excess of the inflation rate, but [also] salaries based on accountability, which carries with it the confident expectation that students will find a better learning environment and achieve better learning results. It will cost us, to be sure, but we will get something for the money.

We do not need to accept having North Carolina's teachers paid below the national average, even if the cost of living is lower than in most other states, but neither should we accept having North Carolina's students performing well below the national average. The time has come for us to adopt a reform program which will enable us to solve both problems in an interrelated way: better pay, for better teachers, for better students.

---

[1]Herbert Marshall McLuhan (1911-1980), born in Edmondton, Alberta, Canada; died in Toronto; B.A., 1933, M.A., 1934, University of Manitoba; B.A., 1936, M.A., 1940, Ph.D., 1942, Cambridge University. English professor; communications specialist; faculty member at St. Louis University, 1937-1944, and at Assumption University, 1944-1946; appointed professor, University of Toronto, 1952; appointed director, Centre for Culture and Technology, University of Toronto, 1963; author of *The Medium is the Message: An Inventory of Effects* (1967), and other works. Charles Moritz (ed.), *Current Biography Yearbook, 1967* (New York: The H. W. Wilson Company, 1967), 270-273, hereinafter cited as *Current Biography Yearbook*, with appropriate year; see also *Current Biography Yearbook, 1981*, 468.

[2]Commission on the Future of the North Carolina Community College System, *Gaining the Competitive Edge: The Challenge to North Carolina's Community Colleges* ([Raleigh: North Carolina Department of Community Colleges], 1989).

Robert Walter Scott (1929–), North Carolina lieutenant governor, 1965-1969, and governor, 1969-1973; president, state Department of Community Colleges, since 1983; Democrat. Previously identified in Poff, *Addresses of Martin*, I, 177n-178n.

[3]Clemmie Dixon Spangler, Jr. (1932–), president, University of North Carolina system, since 1986. Previously identified in Poff, *Addresses of Martin*, I, 474n.

[4]Both Senator Marvin M. Ward and Representative Daniel T. Blue, Jr., introduced bills in their respective houses on February 15, 1989, intended to thaw the teacher pay scale. Neither Ward's proposal, "A Bill to Establish New Salary Schedules for Public School Teachers and Administrators," nor Blue's similarly titled bill was enacted directly into law; see H.B. 216, *N.C. House Journal, 1989*, 90, 853-854; S.B. 163, *N.C. Senate Journal, 1989*, 82, 633-634. The General Assembly did, however, approve a new salary schedule for teachers on August 10, 1989; see *N.C. Session Laws, 1989*, II, c. 752, sec. 38.

Marvin Martin Ward (1914–), born in Morrison, Va; resident of Forsyth County; B.A., Appalachian State University, 1934; M.A., University of North Carolina at Chapel Hill, 1940. Former superintendent, Winston-Salem/Forsyth County Schools; member, state Senate, since 1979, and chairman, Appropriations on Education Committee; Democrat. *North Carolina Manual, 1991-1992*, 285-286.

INDIAN UNITY CONFERENCE

Fayetteville, March 17, 1989

It is a distinct honor and pleasure to have this opportunity to share in your fellowship—and to talk to you about some of the problems confronting us and some of the initiatives we are taking to address those problems. In saying "we," I am referring to all of you who are striving so tirelessly to improve the quality of life for 65,000 Indians who live in our state. The "we" also includes members of the Commission of Indian Affairs and other Indian groups and committees, all of whom are working to make a difference in the life and affairs of our Indian citizens. The progress we have made is truly a group achievement. I would like to share a few of the things we have accomplished together.

As part of the celebration of "1986: The Year of the Native American," the Commission of Indian Affairs sponsored a symposium on Indian education at Pembroke State University. This proved to be an historic milestone in our state's Indian affairs. The symposium's recommendations resulted in the creation, by the General Assembly, of a State Advisory Council on Education in July 1988.[1]

In the establishment of an advisory council, we can begin to make greater progress in addressing the needs of our Indian citizens and reducing the largest educational deficit suffered by any subpopulation in North Carolina. The task before us, admittedly, is a formidable one, as attested to by just one statistic: According to the 1980 U.S. census report, 61.4 percent of Indians over the age of 25 have not completed high school.

As we all know, education and poverty are constant companions, so it should come as no surprise that Indians also suffer a greater economic deficit than other citizens in our state. Part of the reason for this is that 78 percent of Indians live in rural areas with a low level of economic development, with three-quarters of Indians working in traditionally low-paying occupations.

A significant initiative is taking place in economic development. Since 1984, the commission has received an annual legislative appropriation to provide for an economic developer staff position. The duties of the economic developer include providing assistance to the state's Indian tribes and organizations for the development of economic opportunities in their communities; assisting Indian citizens in the development, improvement, and expansion of businesses; and assisting in the development of major economic enterprises for the state's Indian population, such as the North Carolina Indian Cultural Center.

We can be proud of other accomplishments, one of which is embodied in two people in attendance here this afternoon. I refer to the

Honorable Dexter Brooks and Gary Locklear. It is a source of considerable pride that I participated in an event of great historical significance: I had the honor to appoint Judge Brooks to the bench as a Superior Court judge. Of equal historic importance was the election of Gary Locklear to the bench as a District Court judge.[2]

These events represent much more that has been taking place to achieve a more balanced and equitable criminal justice system. In February 1987, the Commission of Indian Affairs appointed a twelve-member Ad-Hoc Committee on Indians and the Criminal Justice System. This committee examined the treatment of North Carolina Indian citizens throughout the entire law enforcement process in Columbus, Cumberland, Guilford, Halifax, Hoke, Jackson, Mecklenburg, Robeson, Scotland, and Swain counties—a truly awesome undertaking. Ten major recommendations were submitted by the committee in its final report to the commission in October of 1987, including the establishment of a public defender's office in North Carolina's sixth, sixteenth, and thirtieth judicial districts.[3]

More progress was indicated by the fact that the General Assembly appropriated almost $400,000 in the short session for the creation of a public defender's office in the sixteenth district. Mr. Angus B. Thompson has been employed as the public defender.[4] Furthermore, a full staff has been selected to operate the Robeson County Public Defender's Office. Still another development is the establishment of a board of directors for the Dispute Settlement Center in Robeson County. The board is now in the process of securing an executive director for the center.

Other developments offer encouragement that things are on the move. In May of 1986, the North Carolina Indian Housing Authority was awarded a contract totaling over $7 million to build 204 units of subsidized, low-income housing in Indian communities in our state. Sites were selected and purchased in Hoke, Robeson, and Cumberland counties. Construction was completed on March 1, 1988, with assigned units per county as follows: Cumberland, 92; Hoke, 62; and Robeson, 50.

In the cultural area, two significant developments, not only for Indians but for all North Carolinians, took place. The first is the bold undertaking to establish a national Indian cultural center, involving six state-recognized tribes and three urban Indian organizations of the state. The center will be built on 500 acres in Robeson County.

January 1989 saw the completion of the center's master plan. Upon completion, the center is expected to include Indian villages, arts and crafts displays, museums, art exhibits, recreational facilities, and other related operations. In 1987, the North Carolina Department of Administration contributed approximately $75,000 to repair damage to the dam on the center site's lake and to upgrade the facilities of the site's amphitheater. In August of 1987, the commission was awarded a legislative appropriation of $125,000 to assist with the development of the center and the Robeson Historical Drama Association, which operates the popular outdoor drama, *Strike at the Wind*, located on the center site. In July 1988, the cultural center was awarded a legislative appropriation of $50,000 and was notified of a $70,000 grant award from the Administration for Native Americans; both awards are being used for the center's general support. In January 1988, the Henry Berry Lowry House was donated to the center, further commemorating Henry Berry Lowry, the subject of *Strike at the Wind* and the legendary hero of the Lumbee tribe. In addition, a challenge grant of $5,000 was made by a Robeson County businessman, facilitating the house's restoration and movement to the center site.[5]

Almost 500 miles to the west, more history was being made. With the 150th anniversary of the Trail of Tears, we have authorization to develop a "Historic Trail of Tears" as part of the National Trail System.[6] This development is important not only for cultural reasons, but for economic reasons as well. It is important that the Cherokee should be the main beneficiaries of what should become a prime tourist attraction in North Carolina, but beyond economic considerations, information provided about the injustices done to a proud and courageous people should help future generations learn the lessons from this tragic page in our country's history.

Along our trail to achieve a better life for our Indian citizens, we know we still have many more miles to go. It need not be a trail of tears; it must be a trail of hope. Winston Churchill, commenting on the turning of the tide in the Battle of Britain, remarked that the English were not seeing the beginning of the end of the war, but the beginning of the beginning. I have a similar optimism that what we are seeing—in the work that you are doing, in the splendid work of the commission, in a growing private-public partnership, and in a positive momentum toward improved conditions for Indian citizens—is the beginning of the beginning of greater things for Indian citizens throughout North Carolina.

---

[1]See *N.C. Session Laws, 1987, Regular Session, 1988*, III, c. 1084.

[2]Sandy Dexter Brooks (1943–), born in Robeson County; B.S., 1965, Master of Mathematics, 1971, N.C. State University; first Native American to graduate from University of North Carolina law school (J.D., 1976); U.S. Army, 1966–1968. Mathematics instructor, Southeastern Community College, 1971–1972, and at Robeson Technical Institute, 1972–1973; attorney, 1976–1988; adjunct professor of business law, Pembroke State University, 1977–1983; resident Superior Court judge, District 16B, since 1989, and state's first Native American judge. Dexter Brooks, letter to Jan-Michael Poff, July 5, 1992; *News and Observer*, October 22, 1989.

Gary Lynn Locklear, a Lumberton lawyer and a Democrat, was elected judge of District 16B in 1988. He was assistant district attorney for the Sixteenth District from 1979–1982. *North Carolina Manual, 1991–1992*, 494; *Robesonian* (Lumberton), November 6, 9, 1988.

[3]See Ad-Hoc Committee on Indians and the Criminal Justice System, "A Report on the Treatment of Indians by the Criminal Justice System," previously identified in Poff, *Addresses of Martin*, I, 786n.

[4]The 1988 General Assembly established public defender offices in districts 16A (Scotland, Hoke counties) and 16B (Robeson County); see *N.C. Session Laws, 1987, Regular Session, 1988*, III, c. 1056, s. 8(a).

Angus B. Thompson II (1952–), native, resident of Robeson County; B.A., Morehouse College, 1974; J.D., N.C. Central University, 1977. Attorney; member, Interim Board, 1988–1989, and of Board of Education, since 1989, Robeson County Public Schools; public defender, District 16B (Robeson County), since January 1, 1989. Angus B. Thompson II, letters to Jan-Michael Poff, August 14, September 3, 1992.

[5]The Henry Berry Lowry House was moved to the North Carolina Indian Cultural Center in 1987. Adolph Dial was the Robeson County businessman who offered the challenge grant for the movement and restoration of the dwelling. Haynes Deese, operations manager, North Carolina Indian Cultural Center, telephone conversations with Jan-Michael Poff, March 15, 1993.

Henry Berry Lowry was born circa 1846, near Pembroke. By the end of the Civil War, he had become the leader of a group known as the "Lowry band," which was engaged in a guerrilla campaign against Confederate conscription officers and the Home Guard. In December 1865, Lowry was charged with the wartime death of a Confederate scout and jailed in Whiteville. He escaped and was declared an outlaw; agreeing to surrender terms, Lowry turned himself in to authorities in 1868. Confined in Lumberton, threatened by persistent rumors of a lynching attempt, and skeptical of the protection offered by the state's Republican government, he fled captivity a second time. Lowry remained an outlaw and a "Robin Hood-like bandit," finding support among the Indians, blacks, and poor whites of Robeson County, until he disappeared in February 1872. Powell, *DNCB*, IV, 104–105.

Adolph Lorenz Dial (1922–), born in Prospect; A.B., Pembroke State College for Indians (later Pembroke State University), 1943; Ed.M., Boston University, 1953; honorary degrees; U.S. Army, 1943–1945. Businessman; historian; real estate developer; principal, Prospect High School, 1955–1958; professor, American Indian studies, Pembroke State University, 1958–1988; cofounder, board member, 1971–1986, Lumbee Bank; founder, board chairman, outdoor drama *Strike at the Wind*, 1976; member, state House, 1990–1992, from Robeson County; Democrat; author. *News and Observer*, March 13, 1988, October 3, 1993; *North Carolina Manual, 1991–1992*, 346.

[6]P.L. 100–192, "An Act to Amend the National Trails System Act to Designate the Trail of Tears as a National Historic Trail," *United States Statutes at Large*, Act of December 16, 1987, 101 Stat. 1309. "Trail of Tears" describes the forced removal of 16,000 Cherokee, in 1838 and 1839, from their southeastern homelands to Oklahoma. Theda Perdue, *Native Carolinians: The Indians of North Carolina* (Raleigh: Division of Archives and History, North Carolina Department of Cultural Resources, third printing, 1991), 40, 64.

MOBIL OIL PRESS CONFERENCE

RALEIGH, APRIL 5, 1989

[Mobil Oil Corporation announced plans, in September 1988, to explore for natural gas approximately forty miles northeast of Cape Hatteras. The proposed drilling site, on the Atlantic floor, bordered the Gulf Stream. Swift ocean currents and the frequent risk of foul weather aroused concern among coastal residents that an oil spill—it was possible that Mobil might discover oil as well as gas—would jeopardize the environment, seaside tourism, and the fishing industry. Onshore development related to petroleum exploration and processing also posed problems.

Martin demanded federal assurance that Mobil's offshore drilling could be executed safely. He wrote to the Minerals Management Service, in October 1988, requesting a new environmental impact statement. Mobil obtained its EIS, a lengthy assessment of the consequences of a project upon its surroundings, in 1981, the year it acquired the offshore leases. However, in light of later scientific research, the governor deemed the original study inadequate. He also declared that "Direct and indirect onshore impacts from a discovery the size Mobil is projecting were never sufficiently analyzed." Geologists believed that Mobil's undersea tract could contain as much as 5 trillion cubic feet of natural gas.

The state's request for a new environmental impact statement appeared to have been firmly grounded. After all, Mobil's original EIS required a second such statement "at exploration." However, Washington subsequently changed the rules: In cases of exploratory activity, such as Mobil's, the Minerals Management Service no longer required an exhaustive environmental impact statement before drilling could commence. A full EIS was needed only in instances where oil or gas had been discovered and production was to occur.

When the federal Minerals Management Service replied in November that it would not order another EIS, state officials reviewed the alternatives. In April 1989, Martin and the attorney general urged Mobil to join with the state of North Carolina in obtaining a "voluntary" environmental impact statement from the federal government. They also discussed the possibility of a lawsuit. *News and Observer*, December 2, 1988, July 15, October 6, 1989; Poff, *Addresses of Martin*, I, 916–918.]

Attorney General Thornburg and I have a brief, joint statement to make regarding Mobil Oil's proposed offshore drilling.[1] You are all aware of the firm position North Carolina has taken on Mobil's plan to explore for oil and gas off our coast, by demanding that a new environmental impact statement be prepared. As the lessons of the tragic oil spill in Alaska are revealed,[2] I am even more convinced that we must have a new EIS to lead us—the Minerals Management Service as well as the state—into what for North Carolina is a new environmental frontier off our coast.

As this Alaskan incident reemphasizes, human error is always a possibility, and therefore we must conduct our environmental studies and create our oil spill contingency plan on the assumption that a serious event, which could jeopardize our critical resources and economies, is very possible during offshore exploration. Even in situations where the oil companies tell us "it can't happen," or they say "if it does happen, we have plans in place to control the damage," the state cannot rely on such reassurances alone.

In contrast with states on the Gulf of Mexico, for whom the federal laws took into account their long experience with offshore drilling, this is a totally new challenge for us. I believe that the frontier nature of the type of drilling that will occur, the extreme conditions that exist at the Mobil exploration site, the potential for injury to the state's commercial and recreational fisheries and tourist attractions, and the need for adequate public participation compels [sic] my demand that stricter standards be met.

After a thorough analysis of the facts provided to me by my top advisers, and after consultation with the attorney general on the federal law applicable to Mobil's proposed activities, the attorney general and I are prepared today to make the following commitment, as a way to insist upon an environmental impact statement.

I have asked my staff and the Attorney General's Office to contact Mobil and its attorneys to advise Mobil of the state's position and to ask that Mobil join with North Carolina to develop a plan for voluntary preparation of an exploratory drilling EIS. We will negotiate in good faith with Mobil and Mobil's attorneys over the next few days with regard to terms, timing, and conditions. We sincerely hope that Mobil will join with the state in requesting that the MMS prepare this environmental impact statement, starting right away in the interest of time. It is not our intention to arbitrarily oppose or obstruct Mobil, but if we are to meet our responsibilities, we must insist that we be fully informed on the basis of an EIS, since this would be our first major well.

If the Minerals Management Service of the Department of Interior refuses to prepare an adequate EIS, and proceeds to approve Mobil's plan of exploration and allows drilling to commence off our coast without cooperating with our need to be fully informed, then the state will have no option but to go to court to delay any drilling, and to insist on our right to an EIS. That position is nonnegotiable.

Additionally, I have contacted our congressional delegation to explain the state's position regarding our essential need for an exploratory drilling EIS and to ask that the delegation support the state's position.

Thank you for your attention, and before I take any questions on this matter, Attorney General Thornburg will provide you with a brief statement of the state's legal position.

---

[1]For related press releases, see "Governor Calls for Mandatory Environmental Impact Statement for Mobil Oil Offshore Drilling Exploration," Raleigh, April 5, 1989, and "Governor, State Delegation to Meet in Washington with Allen Murray, CEO of Mobil, Inc.," Raleigh, May 31, 1989, Governors Papers, James G. Martin.

[2]The supertanker *Exxon Valdez* ran aground in Prince William Sound, Alaska, on March 24, 1989, spilling ten million gallons of crude oil. It was the most environmentally destructive and most expensive tanker accident in history. Art Davidson, *In the Wake of the* Exxon Valdez: *The Devastating Impact of the Alaskan Oil Spill* (San Francisco: Sierra Club Books, 1990), 3–20, 294.

LEADERSHIP CONFERENCE FOR A DRUG-FREE
NORTH CAROLINA

CHARLOTTE, APRIL 22, 1989

[Martin focused on the topic of substance abuse in the the following address
and in his remarks to the "Challenge for the 90s" Conference, October 24, 1989,
held in Raleigh.]

Let me thank each of you and the city of Charlotte for working so
hard to make this important statewide symposium on drug abuse a reality. During the past two days, you have talked with representatives
from schools, from law enforcement, from government, and the private
sector about the severity of the problem in our society, and you have
shared possible approaches to this major challenge that faces our society.

During your discussions, I hope you have pondered what I consider
the central question before us: What will it take to make North Carolina
a drug-free state? Certainly it will take stronger enforcement and stricter
penalties against drug traffickers. It will also take more effective education, treatment, and intervention to help the victims of this menace to
society. We in North Carolina have developed a strong tradition of partnership and cooperation between government and the private sector, in
economic development and in the field. Now, in that same spirit of cooperation, we all must work together to try to alleviate the human suffering that is the inevitable consequence of substance abuse.

You are, of course, familiar with the problems. Despite our efforts,
substance abuse has continued to increase. Studies show that approximately 160,000 North Carolinians have used cocaine in the last month.
A Department of Public Instruction survey shows that 6.2 percent of
North Carolina students in grades seven through twelve also have used
cocaine. That figure is slightly ahead of the national average of 5.2 percent.

The drug trade is profitable. Marijuana is estimated to be the leading
North Carolina cash crop in 1988, with a gross value of $1.5 billion. To-
bacco, in comparison, grossed only $738 million. Only three states—
Oregon, California, and Kentucky—had larger marijuana harvests than
North Carolina in 1988.

Our law enforcement officers have been working relentlessly to stem
the tide of drug trafficking: 1987 figures show a single-year increase of
23.3 percent in the number of juvenile arrests for possession of cocaine,
and 20.9 percent for possession of heroin. We arrest more people for

driving while impaired—and alcohol abuse is part of the overall sub-stance-abuse problem—each year than for any other single offense. These law enforcement efforts are important, and our officers are to be com-mended, but the problem of substance abuse remains.

Law enforcement can only use the tools at its disposal. We have tried to increase and to improve those tools through legislative initiatives. Some of those initiatives, such as our anti-DWI proposals, have been partially successful. Other efforts, such as our proposals to make sure drug kingpins serve every day they are sentenced to serve, have been rejected by the General Assembly. I will continue, however, to make sure our laws are as tough as they can be to punish those who try to make a profit from the drug-scarred lives of our young people.

Tough laws and strict enforcement are needed, but they aren't the total answer. That's why we have developed a three-part strategy of enforcement, treatment, and education. We are focusing our efforts in state government on drug treatment and education. Our State Employee Assistance Program, begun in 1982, has counseled over 13,000 individu-als; a confidential, statistical evaluation of the first 300 referrals indi-cates that 73 percent of the employees who used this service have re-turned to their jobs and are doing good work. Our state Department of Correction has also begun a comprehensive substance abuse program that treats offenders, tracks proven substance abusers through the cor-rection system, and beefs up enforcement efforts.[1]

To coordinate anti-substance abuse efforts on the state government level, I established the Governor's Inter-Agency Advisory Team on Al-cohol and Other Drug Abuse, in July 1987. This bipartisan group of lead-ing government officials has built cooperation between state agencies, eliminated duplication, and maximized the use of resources—even shar-ing funds with other agencies.[2]

Our education and treatment efforts are not limited to state govern-ment, however. To expand our fight against substance abuse statewide, I established the Governor's Council on Alcohol and Drug Abuse among Children and Youth in 1986. The council supports education, preven-tion, and treatment programs to reduce alcohol and drug abuse prob-lems among our young people and helps develop legislative programs and public policy. The governor's council also oversees the ongoing ef-forts of Challenge '89, a community-based planning process that helps communities develop local responses to alcohol and drug problems.[3]

My wife, Dottie, has also joined the effort by working to establish Parent-to-Parent programs statewide. As many of you know from her presentation on Thursday, Parent-to-Parent teaches parents how to rec-ognize signs of substance abuse in their children and how to deal with it in the home. Sixteen counties have Parent-to-Parent chapters, and more chapters are being planned across the state.

Our most recent initiative has been to establish the North Carolina Drug Cabinet, headed by Lieutenant Governor Jim Gardner and composed of top-ranking state government officials. Since January, the Drug Cabinet has been holding round-table meetings across the state to discuss the drug problem and seeking a consensus on the most effective strategy we can develop in our war on drugs. The cabinet is developing a comprehensive strategy to combat drug trafficking and illegal drug use in North Carolina. That strategy will include recommendations for appropriate punishments and for educating and treating our citizens who suffer from drug use and dependency.

To paraphrase a Biblical proverb, "Where there is no vision, the people perish."[4] This proverb is particularly apt when applied to substance abuse. We have developed some strong, effective programs in this regard, and we are continuing to try to improve and strengthen these programs. But as conferences such as this show, we have more ideas to discuss, and more programs to improve and to develop, before we can win this war on drugs.

This meeting is appropriately called a leadership conference. All of you are leaders in this quest for a drug-free North Carolina. That is our challenge: to work together to free our state from the pain and agony of substance abuse. I thank you for accepting this challenge, and hope you will continue them with renewed commitment and dedication. The lives of our children and the future of our state may depend on how quickly and how successfully we meet this challenge.

Much hard work lies ahead. Our task is truly formidable. We can't shy from it just because it is difficult; the stakes are too high. That's why what you are doing is so important and why I wanted to thank you for your efforts toward the goal we all share: the goal of a drug-free North Carolina.

---

[1]See N.C. Session Laws, 1987, II, c. 738, s. 111; c. 830, s. 13; and c. 876, s. 7.

[2]Executive Order Number 53, promulgated July 30, 1987, created the advisory team. N.C. Session Laws, 1987, II, 2393–2396.

[3]Martin signed Executive Order Number 23, establishing the Council on Alcohol and Drug Abuse among Children and Youth, on January 29, 1986. N.C. Session Laws, 1985, Extra and Regular Sessions, 1986, 675–677.

[4]Prov. 29:18.

GOVERNOR'S ADVOCACY COUNCIL FOR PERSONS WITH DISABILITIES

Raleigh, April 28, 1989

[Addressing the Governor's Advocacy Council for Persons with Disabilities, April 23, 1992, Martin recounted the efforts of his administration on behalf of the disabled. He reported that from January 1985 to October 1991, state government increased its total annual purchases of goods and services from minority, women, and disabled-owned business enterprises, from $15 million to $47 million. Accessibility to existing buildings on University of North Carolina system campuses and in the state government complex had improved, and the first comprehensive beach access on the southeastern coast, for people with disabilities, was opened at Fort Macon State Park. Finally, the governor noted that the council itself was reorganized to ensure a broader representation of disabled people.]

Ladies and gentlemen, I appreciate the opportunity to be with you today, to honor those individuals and organizations who have demonstrated, through their actions, a commitment to the disabled citizens of North Carolina. I also appreciate the chance to share the head table with the chair of the Governor's Advocacy Council for Persons with Disabilities, Deborah McKeithan. Deborah is an inspiration to everyone who believes in something, then finds a way to do it. I can tell you she was not [a] stranger to Capitol Hill when I served in Congress. She is continuing to carry the banner for change for disabled people and their families here in North Carolina and across the nation. I also want to thank Mayor Upchurch and the city of Raleigh for their hospitality in hosting this event once again this year.[1]

This is truly a day of thanks. Thanks to all of you for the contributions you are making in your communities across the state to increase awareness of the abilities, rather than the disabilities, of North Carolina's disabled citizens. Thanks to public officials and business leaders for your commitment and support. Thanks to the members of the Governor's Advocacy Council for Persons with Disabilities and local councils for the critical advocacy role you are playing to improve opportunities for disabled people; and a special thanks to those who we honor today, the men and women whose personal commitment has done so much to improve the quality of life for all disabled people.

In 1987 when I proclaimed Barrier Awareness Day, I said, "It is our responsibility . . . as individuals and as a society . . . to ensure that our disabled citizens are offered the same opportunity to succeed that everyone else has."[2] The individuals and organizations we honor today have put those words into practice. They have proven what can be done when we focus on an individual's strengths rather than weaknesses.

I'm proud that North Carolina has been a national leader in efforts to improve opportunities for people with disabilities. I'm particularly pleased about the success of the Supported Training Employment Program, or STEP. This innovative, cooperative, public-private program is one of the keys to providing competitive employment opportunities for the severely disabled. There are eighty-one programs across the state helping 510 individuals with severe disabilities to succeed in supported-employment jobs. These are individuals who would not have jobs otherwise. My thanks to the Division of Vocational Rehabilitation, the Division of Mental Health, Mental Retardation, and Substance Abuse Services, and the Developmental Disabilities Council for their efforts to make STEP a success in North Carolina.

Independence is something most of [us] take for granted. It should, in fact, be treasured. STEP is giving people independence, a sense of self-worth, and an opportunity for accomplishment. Employers praise the supported-employment program. They have found a new workforce that is competent and motivated. STEP is an important part of this administration's commitment to helping disabled people help themselves.

Independence and opportunity through employment, though, is more than new programs. Changing attitudes is the constant challenge. I know many of you are aware of a 1986 Lou Harris poll, the first national, comprehensive survey of disabled people. It showed that 40 percent of all disabled adults did not finish high school, two-and-a-half times the ratio among people without disabilities. Only one in four disabled individuals works full time; another 10 percent work part time. The poll showed that disabled people are the poorest, least educated minority in America.

We cannot ignore these findings, that unnecessary segregation and exclusion have deprived 36 million disabled Americans of what was promised to us all: freedom of choice and full participation in society. Building a society that offers genuine opportunity in our schools and universities, in public accommodations, in public transportation and employment, is our greatest challenge.

Last fall I participated in a public hearing in Raleigh to hear testimony from disabled North Carolinians about their experiences with discrimination. That testimony is providing the impetus for the reintroduction of the Americans with Disabilities Act in this session of Congress. As I said at that hearing, I feel this legislation is a long-overdue recognition of many of the inequities suffered by people with disabilities and their families. The Americans with Disabilities Act can move us toward a society that guarantees dignity, security, and opportunity for all Americans.[3]

Although it's impossible to legislate attitudes, the Americans with Disabilities Act recognizes the crucial need for attitude changes. The act extends full, enforceable civil rights protection to all citizens with disabilities. It also recognizes the disabled as self-directed and active participants in society. I mentioned polls a moment ago; another Harris poll taken during the presidential campaign in 1988 showed that disabled people who vote are twice as interested in public affairs, and attend public rallies twice as often, as voters without disabilities. It also showed that 84 percent of disabled people who vote said knowing a candidate's position on disability issues was more important to them than that candidate's party affiliation.

The impact and influence of disabled people have grown and are growing. You vote, and you take the issues seriously. So, attitudes will change. The power for change is in you.

I am very interested to learn of the conclusions from this morning's council meeting on accessibility for disabled people in the electoral process. Full participation by the disabled in elections is the key to permanent and lasting change. While I must tell you that I have reservations about providing election-day registration to vote, unless safeguards can be designed to prevent the opportunity for some to corrupt such a process, there are many good, sound suggestions; and I pledge my support for efforts to ensure each person's constitutional right to participate fully in the electoral process.

Often when I speak to groups across the state, I talk about the economic good news in North Carolina. In March I announced that North Carolina was again the leader in new manufacturing plants announced from 1986 to 1988. During that period, the state revealed plans for 275 new manufacturing plants. North Carolina also enjoys the lowest unemployment rate—3 percent—among the eleven largest states in the country. This is good news for North Carolina, but it's also good news for disabled people, and it is time for the disabled to be able to take full advantage of this economic boom.

Our problem and our challenge is to convince employers that the advantages of hiring a disabled person far outweigh any perceived liabilities. *Perceived* is the key word. It is that perception that we need to erase. Many misconceptions exist. An employer may fear that he will have to spend thousands of dollars to modify the workplace, and what about his other employees? Will they expect extra compensation if accommodations are made for a disabled employee? He's also heard the stories of soaring workers' compensation costs. He questions how productive a disabled worker will be. Will his medical costs go through the roof? Those are actual perceptions.

Yes, evidence shows all these fears are groundless. Studies reveal that modifications to a work station cost an average of a couple of a hundred dollars, often much less. Workers' compensation is based on the type of industry, not on one individual hired. In truth, it is the disabled person receiving Social Security disability insurance that places him or herself at risk when seeking employment. I know this has been a longtime crusade for Deborah.

If someone is receiving Social Security disability insurance and earns over $3,600—that's one-third of the federal poverty level—they are considered employable and lose all benefits. Obviously, $3,600 is not enough to support anyone, even without large medical expenses. It is this type of disincentive to work that must be changed. A bill is pending in Congress that would do just that. This bill has wide, bipartisan support and would make it possible for disabled people to return to work while maintaining their federal health benefits. It's high time this bill was adopted.

Looking ahead, we can see that we've got our work cut out for us if we are going to meet the challenge of improving opportunities for the disabled. None of us can do the job alone. We must work together to create an atmosphere in which each person is valued, where self-esteem is strengthened, and where each of us can live with a sense of dignity and independence.

You will continue to play an important role in this effort. Your courage and your commitment have gotten us where we are today. More disabled people are working. More children with special needs are being served in public schools. More disabled adults are being rehabilitated and are being helped to get meaningful jobs. I want to continue to be part of the effort to ensure that we don't stop now.

I am sorry that I can't stay for the award presentations this afternoon, but I know who you are, and I want to add my congratulations and personal thanks for the outstanding work you've done on behalf of the disabled. I look forward to working with you.

----

[1]Deborah Crouch McKeithan (1953–), born in Shelbyville, Ky.; resident of Charlotte; educational background in nursing. Despite her affliction by legal blindness, cerebral multiple sclerosis, and epilepsy, McKeithan is a national advocate for the needs of the disabled; founder, Handicapped Organized Women, 1979; founder, 1988, and president, Learning How, Inc., an organization that mainstreams the physically disabled; member, N.C. Council on the Status of Women; co-developer, Independent Living Center, Charlotte; community college instructor; consultant. Deborah Crouch McKeithan, letter to Jan-Michael Poff, February 26, 1993.

Avery C. Upchurch (1928–1994), mayor of Raleigh, 1983-1993. Previously identified in Poff, *Addresses of Martin*, I, 966n; see also *News and Observer*, July 1, 1994.

[2]"Barrier Awareness Day, 1987, by the Governor of the State of North Carolina: A Proclamation," March 1, 1987, Governors Papers, James G. Martin.

[3]President Bush signed P.L. 101–336, "Americans with Disabilities Act of 1990," into law on July 26, 1990; see *United States Statutes at Large*, 104 Stat. 327–378. Martin testified in support of the bill September 29, 1988, in Raleigh. Poff, *Addresses of Martin*, I, 1004.

GOVERNOR'S CONFERENCE ON TRAVEL AND TOURISM

Boone, May 4, 1989

Hello! Thank you, Secretary Broyhill, for that introduction. I'd like nothing better than to take you up on that golf challenge—at a later date.

Before I go on, let me share with you the sad news of the death, last night, of former secretary [of] commerce Claude Pope. You and I know how he faced his illness by devoting the last two years of his life to building a stronger job future for our people—in manufacturing; nonmanufacturing services; travel, tourism, entertainment, and sports; and housing. We have lost a good friend.[1]

This is truly a distinguished group gathered here today, and Boone has done a fine job welcoming us all to the High Country. So before I tell you our good news, I think you deserve a round of applause.

Thanks to your dedication and hard work, 1988 was a tremendous year for North Carolina's travel industry. Travel expenditures totaled $6.2 billion last year. Pat yourself on the back: Try it with your nose to the grindstone, your shoulder to the wheel, your ear to the ground, and keeping your chin up—just try to pat yourself on the back, and see if chiropractic helps!

Six point two billion dollars: That's the largest amount in the history of this state, an 8-percent increase over last year's record-setting revenues. $6.2 billion. Let's all say it together: $6.2 billion. Sounds great, doesn't it? That's an incredible figure for an industry that is so clean and trouble free.

Let's take a few minutes to look at how we reached the $6.2 billion mark. To begin with, attractions across the state reported record attendance:

—Our coastal waters and beaches had a banner year, enjoyed by many millions, including me.

—The Blue Ridge Parkway had more than 25 million visitors in 1988, including me.

—Biltmore Estate, in Asheville, entertained 600,000 visitors last year, including me!

—The North Carolina Zoological Park, in Asheboro, had 587,000 visitors. Kwanza, the first lowland gorilla born at the zoo, has attracted a record number of visitors since his birth, including me!

—The Mint Museum's "Rameses the Great" exhibit brought more than 634,000 visitors to Charlotte, and the Charlotte Hornets played before record crowds during their first basketball season, both including me. The expansion Hornets sold almost a million tickets! That exceeds any NBA franchise ever, or any NFL franchise, for that matter! You know, you're looking at the number-one sports fan and the number-one tourist, right here!

I could go on with individual examples, but when attractions as diverse as those do so well in one year, you can sense that your convention bureaus, visitor centers, chambers [of commerce], and accommodations are working harder and competing more aggressively.

There's more good news. I wanted personally to share the results of our most recent conversion study of the Travel Division's advertising program. These figures, which are almost as impressive as these magnificent mountains, were prepared for the Travel Division by the Office of Park and Tourism Research at North Carolina State University. We wanted you to hear these results first.

Of the more than 400,000 [travel] inquiries in 1987, approximately 261,200 can be directly connected to a specific advertisement promoting North Carolina as a destination. That's 65 percent! Of those 261,000 people who requested North Carolina travel information in 1987, 55.9 percent actually visited our mountains, beaches, or piedmont. That means that once we get our travel packet into a potential visitor's hands, there's more than a 50 percent chance his or her next vacation will be in North Carolina. To break that down even further, for every 1,000 inquiries, 808 actual visits occur. That's phenomenal.

Our conversion study also showed us that the media program proposed by McKinney and Silver, the division's advertising agency, draws visitors from top states such as Florida, New York, Pennsylvania, Ohio, and Michigan. And once they get here, 64.8 percent of our visitors' time is spent enjoying our scenic areas, 47.4 percent spend their time at our historic sites, and 30.5 percent visit our beaches. I don't [know] how, but that adds up to 142 percent! Don't worry. And they spend an average of $596 during a vacation—almost $600.

So, what is the economic result of the division's advertising program? Well, for every $1.00 spent on advertising in 1987, the state received $5.28 in taxes, and that's from folks outside North Carolina who came here to enjoy our numerous attractions and to spend their money.

Let's review those figures again: A visitor spends an average of $596 a trip; tax revenues from each inquiry averages [sic] $55; and for every dollar spent on advertising to attract that visitor, we received $5.28 in taxes. That's a good return. The bottom line is that our award-winning advertising program works. This administration is committed to continuing the success story of North Carolina's travel industry, and we're committed to boosting promotional efforts through local and regional organizations.

That analysis was based on 1987; 1988 was another outstanding year for our travel industry. Inquiries totaled 460,145, which represents a 10.1 percent increase over the previous calendar year. More than 8 million visitors passed through our eight welcome centers. The division received almost a half-million-dollars' worth of free advertising from travel articles generated by its publicity program, while its own travel features reached 5.7 million readers. The division participated in trade shows in Florida, Pennsylvania, and London, and worked with all of you in flying in tour operators, travel agents, meeting planners, and writers for the first Great American Fly-In hosted in Raleigh; and there are many other successes. We're here today, however, to talk about the future in the tourism industry.

I am especially pleased to have the opportunity to tell you that in 1989, the Travel Division is a leader in responding to travel inquiries. We now have one of the quickest response times for travel literature among the fifty states. By summer, our travel office will have its toll-free telephone lines answered by inmates at the North Carolina Correctional Institution for Women.[2] While you probably read about this change, I wanted to provide some additional details.

Approximately 75 percent of our packaging operation is now being handled at the women's facility.[3] This program is expected to save North Carolina taxpayers more than $62,000 in labor costs alone each year. We realize, however, this savings would be meaningless if our potential visitors were not provided factual information or treated in a professional and courteous manner. The Department of Commerce, as well as you in the travel industry, have always been committed to providing excellent service in our hotels, attractions, and resorts, and we realize southern hospitality begins with the potential visitors' first contact with the state. That's why specific measures have been taken to train inmates in this program. The inmates will soon begin studying North Carolina history and geography and will be talking with some of you about the attractions, and other components, that make up the travel industry in your region. In many respects, the training is very similar to that received by our welcome-center information specialists.

Requests for North Carolina travel information is [sic] at an all-time high. In March, the division responded to more than 90,000 inquiries. The figures for the months of January and February exceeded 108,000. As you can see, our packaging section and operators have their hands full, and this cooperative program with the Department of Correction will allow us to meet the demand for our travel literature promptly.

This is a win-win program for the taxpayers, the inmates, state government, and the travel industry. This program will provide the travel office with twice as many toll-free operators as they currently employ and free up badly needed help for other travel-related projects. Our private business community has donated furniture, supplies, and other material for this project. This support says to us that North Carolina is supporting this innovative solution to fulfilling the labor needs in the tourism office.

The division will also install video computers at its eight welcome centers this year. By simply touching a TV screen, travelers can get information about what to see and do, or where to eat, or spend the night. In addition, the publications department has proposed a consolidated travel guide which would combine our current publications in an easy-to-read, comprehensive volume.

Clearly, North Carolina's travel industry has a bright, tremendous future. Your daily efforts helped us exceed the $6 billion mark. Right now, today, let's set [a] $7 billion figure as our goal for 1990. Let me tell you, I need your support on another $8.6 billion goal to help pass the intrastate/strategic corridor highway construction program, the largest in our history.[4]

Before I close, let me take this opportunity to thank the members of the Governor's Advisory Board on Travel and Tourism, the leadership of the Travel Council of North Carolina, the Economic Development Board, and our good friends at American Airlines and Piedmont/USAir. And while I'm at it, may I ask you to join me in a big round of applause for our hosts here in the High Country!

---

[1] The governor inserted this entire paragraph into his prepared text and concluded, "Memorial service tomorrow 11:00 A.M. in Raleigh." Pope died of cancer; funeral services were held May 5 at White Memorial Presbyterian Church, Raleigh. *News and Observer*, May 5, 1989.

[2] Martin announced the plan to staff the tourism hotline with sixteen inmates from the women's correctional center during a February press conference. *News and Observer*, February 3, 1989.

[3] Prison inmates distributed promotional material in 1988, after it was discovered that the Division of Travel and Tourism was lagging in responding to over 93,000 requests for information from potential visitors to the state. Some inquiries received during the first five months of the year went unanswered until mid-September. The delay deprived North Carolina of approximately $10 million in tourism revenue, according to a report issued by the state auditor in January, 1989.

Three weeks after the release of the auditor's findings, Martin told reporters that tourism revenues had increased from the previous year: "'You'll find we didn't take a nose dive. It's my guess that we lost some people because of not responding timely.'" As 1989 closed, the North Carolina travel industry had generated $6.5 billion, $300 million more than 1988. Governor's Conference on Travel and Tourism, Atlantic Beach, May 9, 1991, Governors Papers, James G. Martin; *News and Observer*, September 22, December 16, 1988, January 12, February 3, 1989.

[4] Martin also jotted "Acid Rain Alliance . . . Bonner Bridge . . . Hatteras, Great Smoky Mountain RR, Kentucky Derby, [and] 1991 Reunion" at this point in his speech.

DEDICATION OF CRAGGY AND BUNCOMBE
CORRECTIONAL CENTERS

Asheville, May 4, 1989

[The original Craggy Prison, a "fortress-like dungeon" erected at an abandoned Buncombe County quarry in 1924, was the oldest penal facility in the state when it finally closed in 1989. Living conditions at overcrowded and undermaintained Craggy had become notorious. Inmates were triple bunked, roofs leaked, rats infested the kitchen, and the obsolete plumbing worked intermittently. Two hundred twenty-five convicts were incarcerated in space originally designed to hold 150, when the stabbing of an inmate instigated a riot and the burning of a cellblock in 1975. Other stabbings, an escape, and three murders followed.

North Carolina legislators and correction officials knew that Craggy had to be replaced. Two inmates emphasized that point, in 1986, when their lawyers filed suit in federal court to close the prison. The state and the plaintiffs settled the case, in October 1987, with a consent agreement to cut Craggy's population to 119 prisoners.

The legal action filed for the Craggy inmates, like the earlier suit brought on behalf of convicts jammed into overburdened facilities in the South Piedmont prison district, threatened to supplant the state's oversight of its correctional system with federal control. The General Assembly forestalled such a transfer of power when it adopted a $29 million emergency prison construction package in March 1987. Funding for a replacement for Craggy was included. On May 4, 1989, Martin dedicated the new 314-bed Craggy Correctional Center, for medium-security prisoners, and the Buncombe Correctional Center, a minimum-security compound for 104 inmates. *Asheville Citizen*, May 4, 5, 1989; *News and Observer*, May 31, 1986, November 21, 28, 1987; for related press release, see "Governor Martin's Statement Regarding Decision on Site for Western North Carolina Prison," Raleigh, April 9, 1987, Governor's Papers, James G. Martin.]

Introduction

More than a decade before I was born, Craggy Prison was carved out of the side of a mountain. For sixty-five years, the prison has served as the major correctional facility in western North Carolina. It has stood as a symbol for our state's determination to protect public safety and to preserve public order.

Unfortunately, Craggy Prison had in recent years grown to symbolize what was wrong with our state's correctional system. An overcrowded and aging prison, it had become the target of several lawsuits. Those lawsuits, filed on behalf of inmates, claimed that incarceration in Craggy violated the constitutional prohibition against cruel and unusual punishment.

Of course, this situation was unique to neither Craggy Prison nor

North Carolina. Prison systems across America have found themselves in the same fix. Each state, in due course, has been confronted with having to take bold action to correct the problems or to step aside and have a federal judge dictate his own solutions.

It was at Craggy Prison where North Carolina was faced with that choice, and it is here, at this new facility, that we see North Carolina's answer. Rather than turning our prisons over to the federal government, we sought to resolve a serious problem. Just as the old Craggy Prison was a symbol of our state prison system's past, the new Craggy and Buncombe correctional centers symbolize its future and signal this state's commitment to a correctional system that is just, humane, and constitutionally defensible.

The Price of Neglect

When I took the oath for my first term as governor, North Carolina's correctional system was in disarray. Our prisons were old and decaying. They were severely overcrowded. They were understaffed. What staff they had was overworked and underpaid. The environment in which the department was operating had been highly charged with politics. Employee morale had hit rock bottom. The federal courts were breathing down our neck. People whom I admire and respect were telling me that it wasn't a question of whether the federal government was going to seize control of our prison system, it was only a question of when.

We all knew that major changes were needed within our prisons. I couldn't help but wonder why a judge was needed to force these changes. Why hadn't the leadership of this state taken strong action to avert the prison crisis? It's not because we didn't know that trouble was coming our way. There were storm clouds visible on our horizon. Yet the record shows that the state failed to take strong action.

I'd like to quote from a 1978 Department of Correction study funded by the federal Law Enforcement Assistance Administration. It says, "At this time, North Carolina still has the initiative for coping with the vexing problems of corrections. If that initiative is to be retained, rather than relinquished to the federal courts, the state must continue to act." That was 1978.[1]

It sounds familiar, doesn't it? It is almost as if that statement was taken out of the pages of this morning's newspaper. It is clear that the concern then, as it is now, was whether North Carolina could take the actions necessary to avert a federal takeover of our prison system.

That same report also advocated a two-pronged approach to solving the problem of prison overcrowding: new construction combined with community-based punishments. In many respects, these 1978 strategies, which were to be implemented over a ten-year period, sounded very much like the Ten Year Plan my administration unveiled in March 1986.[2] Unfortunately, those that asked the pertinent questions in 1978 didn't like the answers they received, so the report was placed on a shelf to collect dust.

The Citizens Commission on Alternatives to Incarceration issued a similar report four years later. That report, commonly referred to as the "Whichard Report," outlined many of the same problems and solutions.[3] Unfortunately, state government's response was the same as it had been before.

Why is there a prison crisis? There are many reasons. It is a very complex issue. However, I believe one of the most important reasons has to do with [the] nature of corrections itself. Prisons and prisoners have no political constituency. There are no powerful special interest groups to speak out in their behalf. From a political standpoint, corrections is not a popular subject.

However, it is important to remember that when a person is elected to public office, he or she promises to uphold the constitutions of our state and nation. Nowhere in that oath of office does it say we should uphold the constitution only when it is politically popular. I am not here today for the purpose of pointing the finger of blame at others. However, I do believe it is important that we acknowledge the errors of the past. It is also important that we learn from those errors so that they may not be repeated.

Solving the Problems

I believe that this state has learned that lesson, and the fact that we have been under intense pressures from the federal courts doesn't diminish the significant improvements made to North Carolina's prison system in just four short years:

—The state has built or is in the process of building sleeping quarters for almost 4,300 offenders to eliminate triple bunking.

—We have begun to expand cost-effective, community- based supervision.

—We have made significant improvements in inmate health care, supervision, and educational programs.

—We have launched offender treatment programs that target drug and alcohol abuse.

—We have launched an Employee Assistance Program, too, to help our people cope with the stress of being a correctional professional and established the Honor Guard as a salute to the families of [incomplete].[4]

—We have strengthen[ed] management through an increased emphasis on training.

—We have standardized many of the policies so that, for the first time, all of our employees are operating under the same set of rules regardless of where they work.

—Recognizing the special needs of female offenders, North Carolina has become one of only a handful of states to place the management of our women's facilities under a separate command.

These are all very significant accomplishments. They could not have been achieved without the bipartisan cooperation of the executive and legislative branches of state government. Our differences have been well documented by the news media. What often has been ignored is the high level of cooperation and consensus that has developed in many areas, most notably corrections. When the time came to make crucial decisions about the future of the state's prison system, we put our differences aside, rolled up our sleeves, and did what had to be done. It just took leadership.

While these significant changes were taking place, it was good to know that we enjoyed the support of the thousands of North Carolinians who serve as volunteers within our prisons and at our probation and parole offices. More than 4,700 of our citizens served as teachers, ministers, clerks, and community sponsors during the past year. Others served on various boards, commissions, and as members of community resource councils. Without the generous contribution of their most valuable possession—time—many good things that have happened within our prisons would have been left undone.

Of course, I would be remiss if I were not to express my gratitude to Secretary Johnson and the employees of the Department of Correction. No other department has been as much under the gun as has Correction, and no other agency has made as much tangible progress in such a relatively short period of time. Aaron Johnson has demonstrated both the strength and compassion necessary to manage this agency. He has shown grace under pressure, and he has earned my respect and gratitude.

The Solutions

Today, as we dedicate this facility, let us rededicate ourselves to the difficult task that lays ahead. Overcrowding continues to be a serious problem. There are also more legal challenges to be met.

Despite the great progress we have seen in the past four years, we still face a considerable challenge. A solution rests in "fixing" the entire prison system, bringing the entire system up to the constitutional standards we have already agreed to in a number of legal settlements. If we bring all eighty-nine prisons up to the same standards we have established here at Craggy and Buncombe correctional centers, we would greatly diminish the threat of federal intervention.

Let there be no mistake: Fixing the system will carry with it a hefty price tag. It will take a lot more than the $150 million that has been set aside during the next biennium. Exactly how much will largely depend on the outcome of pending litigation and legislation. However, it is a price we must pay.

Once the system is fixed, it will have to be maintained on a consistent basis. As I have already said, we must learn from the errors of the past. We must not let our failure to act sow the seeds of a prison crisis for the next generation to solve. If we fail to resolve this problem now, then the millions of dollars we have spent would have only bought us time, not solutions.

We must also recognize that the problems facing the state's correctional system are symptomatic of much larger problems facing our criminal justice system. When we talk about prison overcrowding, we are not talking about a Department of Correction problem. We are talking about a criminal justice problem, and it is a problem we must address in a comprehensive manner.

Public confidence in the criminal justice system has been sorely shaken in recent years. The public is tired of a system that is seemingly slow to respond and fails to adequately punish those that break our laws. Some feel that the system serves criminals more than their victims. I have been deeply troubled about the early release of convicted offenders to ease prison overcrowding. That is why I proposed recent changes in the prison cap to make sure that drug traffickers, sexual offenders, and drunk drivers do not get an early ticket out of prison. That is also why I have supported the expansion of community-based punishments: to provide adequate supervision for lesser offenders and to free up scarce prison space for the more serious offenders.

We must also take dead aim at those who threaten to undermine our society. That is why my administration has placed a special emphasis on combatting substance abuse and drunken driving. The creation of the Drug Cabinet, headed by Lieutenant Governor Gardner, is an attempt to bring all of government's resources to bear on this most serious social problem. However, we will be doing more than putting these people behind bars. We will also be looking at ways to treat them in order to break the vicious cycle of addiction.

We also need to strengthen our state's educational system. Education is as much a deterrent to future criminal activity as are tough laws and new prisons. Ninety-five percent of those in our prisons have been skill tested at less than a twelfth-grade level. More than half have been tested at less than a sixth-grade level. When we strengthen our state's economy, we are creating a social environment that is more conducive to lawful activity. That is why this state must continue its aggressive efforts at both attracting new industries to our state and assisting those traditional industries that have called North Carolina home for many years.

However, as we look for solutions to the many challenges facing the criminal justice system, let us not lose sight of our limitations. Government can and should go only so far. If we are to stem the rising tide of criminal activity in our state, we must address these issues within the family. The family is the basic foundation upon which our society and its values rest. This is why my administration has placed such a heavy emphasis upon family issues. We, as individuals, have to take an active role in our families, communities, and churches. We, as parents, must not be spectators in our children's lives. We can, and must, tap into the inner strength of all North Carolinians.

Conclusion

Those of us here today can look at what we have accomplished and take a measure of pride in that accomplishment. But let us not forget the way it used to be. Let us not forget how far we have come, and let us not forget that many of the problems that existed in the old Craggy Prison still exist within our prison system today. We need to remember. We need to remember the high cost of neglect, inaction, and indecision. We need to remember so that we don't walk that same path again.

Let the new Craggy and Buncombe correctional centers remind us of what concern, decisive action, and political courage can accomplish. After many false steps, North Carolina and its prisons have come a long way. The challenge now is to continue that journey. It is a challenge we can't afford to ignore, and with the support of the legislature and our citizens, it will not be ignored.

---

[1]"1978–1987 Strategies" ([Raleigh: Department of Correction, 1978]), 7.

[2]The governor was referring to "Corrections at the Crossroads: Plan for the Future" (Raleigh: Department of Correction, 1986).

[3]See *Report, Citizens Commission on Alternatives to Incarceration, 1982* (Durham: [The Commission, 1982]). The popular name for the study was taken from its chairman, Willis Padgett Whichard. Whichard (1940–), born in Durham; A.B., 1962, J.D., 1965, University of North Carolina at Chapel Hill; U.S. Army National Guard, 1966–1972. Attorney; member, state House, 1970–1974, and Senate, 1974–1980; judge, N.C. Court of Appeals, 1980–1986; elected associate justice, 1986, N. C. Supreme Court; Democrat. *North Carolina Manual, 1991–1992,* 471.

[4]The twenty-two-member Division of Prisons Honor Guard was activated on April 14, 1987. It represented the division in funeral ceremonies for workers who died while

employed by the state and for its deceased retirees. If requested, the group also attended the last rites of law enforcement officers killed in the line of duty. Members were chosen from the division's four commands and had been divided into two squads: one served the area east of Raleigh, while the second covered the remainder of the state. See Governor's Remarks, Commissioning of Honor Guard, Central Prison, Raleigh, April 14, 1987, and press release, Department of Correction, Raleigh, April 14, 1987, Governors Papers, James G. Martin.

NORTH CAROLINA WORLD TRADE ASSOCIATION

CHARLOTTE, MAY 4, 1989

I am delighted to be here tonight to talk to you about North Carolina's efforts to develop a stronger export market and to present the Governor's Award for Exporting.

Improving foreign language instruction, so that the entrepreneurs of tomorrow will be able to do business in the language of their foreign clients and customers, is one method we are using to educate and prepare ourselves to compete in the global market. According to the U.S. Census Bureau, 4.6 million workers owe their livelihoods to the exportation of U.S. products. This is 12.6 percent of all manufacturing jobs. The growth in exports in 1988 was about 27 percent; however, export growth has tapered to about 18 percent during the past twelve months.

There are several reasons for this slowdown. One reason, you know, is that the value of the U.S. dollar has increased about 10 percent since last summer. Also, many of our country's largest exporters are now producing at capacity and are said to be reluctant to make the investment necessary to increase that capacity. Still, America's total export volume is now greater than Japan's, and we are catching up with the Federal Republic of Germany. In January, for the first time in five years, the United States sold more goods to Western Europe than it purchased.

In a recent edition of *Business America*, North Carolina was listed as the tenth-largest exporting state in the union and the leader in the Southeast. We are the leading state in the export of tobacco products, textile mill products, and furniture. Furthermore, we are among the top five states in exporting paper and allied products, in lumber and wood products, and in stone, clay, and glass.[1] The range of export products in our state is truly amazing: lawn mowers, balloons, eels, popcorn, air filters, chain saws, and yachts, and telephone switching equipment.

It is important that U.S. firms dedicate a portion of their plant capacity to export sales. This will increase opportunities for sales and profits when demand decreases in the domestic market. Also, a firm's involvement in the overseas market gives that firm the advantage of meeting competitors on their home turf.

I believe that American firms already are taking steps to make their products better and their plants more efficient. The new North Carolina business creed is, "We don't just inspect or measure quality; we produce it." Now is the time for our companies to produce world-class products that are appropriate to foreign markets with regard to electrical standards, labeling requirements, and metric measurements. It is also time for a sustained marketing effort offered in the language of a firm's potential customers.

The third significant impediment to continued export growth involves barriers to foreign trade, barriers often imposed by countries to protect their local industries or to encourage foreign investment. The Korean automobile market is a case in point. In 1987, Korean auto makers sold 420,028 cars in Korea and exported 564,310 cars. During the 12 months ending July 1988, only 138 foreign cars, including 38 from the United States, were sold in Korea. America imported 81 percent of Korea's export production. Credit should be given to the highly literate and hardworking Korean worker—who works 40 percent longer, on an annual basis, than the average American worker and 25 percent longer than the average Japanese worker. But the bottom line is that the United States can no longer continue to function as Korea's number-one auto dealer while American exporters are denied fair and equal access to Korean consumers.

Last Friday, a decision by the cabinet-level Economic Policy Council was announced by U.S. Trade Representative Carla Hills.[2] The announcement concerned trade sanctions against Japan for failing to keep an agreement to open its fast-growing telecommunications market to American cellular phone and mobile-radio firms. Mrs. Hills released a 214-page list of "foreign trade barriers" that will be used next month to target countries if they refuse to end practices that the United States considers unfair to American exporters. That should prove most beneficial in meeting the trade barrier challenge.

On a related front, the International Division of the N.C. Department of Commerce recently requested information from a number of North Carolina exporters asking them to identify specific problems they face in overseas markets. This information will be compiled and sent to the office of the U.S. trade representative. My administration is working hard to ensure that any trade complaints you have are directed to the proper channels, so we can get results. We stand ready to assist our exporters and trade negotiators in any way we can. We want to help find solutions to those problems and to promote foreign trade in every way possible.

I have mentioned some of the challenges we face. Those challenges are real, but they shouldn't dampen the spirits of any firm seeking to compete in the global market. In fact, in looking at the opportunities available now, it is apparent that the export climate is excellent. The new Canadian Free Trade Agreement, for example, offers new sales prospects.[3] The big winners from this agreement should be our North Carolina textile, apparel, and furniture industries—especially upholstered furniture.

On another front, Europe's unification plans for 1992 offer a single market of 320 million consumers who will be easier to reach if a firm is properly positioned. At the reception earlier this evening, I found many who were preparing to be ready for that. The North Carolina Department of Commerce just returned from a very successful mission to Italy and France promoting trade for North Carolina products. The Commerce Department was supported by North Carolina allies including export managers, attorneys, accountants, and trade and reverse investment developers. One of the highlights of the trip was the North Carolina trade booth at the Milan Trade Fair.

I will lead a mission of North Carolina delegates to the Pacific Rim in October.[4] The delegation, comprised of business leaders, economic developers, and trade promoters, will attend the SEUS conference in Tokyo, the KUSEC conference in South Korea, and official meetings in Hong Kong and Taiwan.

Services now account for more than two thirds of America's gross national product and almost 70 percent of our employment. The U.S. Department of Commerce estimates that America accounts for 20 percent of all trade in international services. That makes us the leader, number one in the world. Well, that's relatively good news.

There's more good news in the service sector. The trade agreement with Canada that I mentioned earlier marks the first time that such an agreement has created binding rules in service exports. It is being used as a model for U.S. negotiators at the General Agreement on Tariffs and Trade, in Uruguay.

We also have another weapon in our export arsenal that exporters should remember: the foreign sales corporation. If an exporting firm establishes a foreign sales corporation, it can save up to 6 percent of its pretax profits on export sales. There's no need to tell you that this can add up to substantial savings.

Stepping back and looking at the overseas trade picture, it is apparent to me that if America is to overcome its trade deficit, many more new firms, particularly small and medium-sized manufacturers, must become actively involved in exporting. Statistics show that new industry growth is coming from these small and medium-sized firms. Our people at the North Carolina Department of Commerce, working with the United States Department of Commerce, the North Carolina Department of Agriculture, the North Carolina World Trade Association, the Export Council, and the Department of Community Colleges believe that we are in good position to help firms learn the basics of exporting, establish overseas representation, and increase sales in international markets. We can do more; we must do more.

Secretary Broyhill and I seek your support for what we are trying to do legislatively. We want to have a trade specialist, assigned to our Tokyo office, and a trade office in the western Pacific and in Canada.[5] We have also requested funds to create an export finance program to ensure that small and medium-sized firms will have easier access to import financing. We are also seeking funds to create a shared foreign sales corporation.

These initiatives will provide a strong foundation for a stronger North Carolina presence overseas, but they need your support. We are depending on you to become even more committed to exporting. I want to thank you for what you have already done to make North Carolina successful in the world marketplace. I look forward to working with you to make our state a leader, not just a participant, in that marketplace.

In October, I will be leading a trade mission to Japan, South Korea, and Taiwan. Later, we will go to England and Scandinavian countries.[6] Let me invite you to consider whether that can help your business. Yes, we will be cultivating prospects for reverse investment here by foreign firms, but my main goal is to help you find export markets and wedge them open.

Increasing our share of the export market is a key part of our continuing effort to promote economic prosperity and to enhance the quality of life for all North Carolinians. This is a noble goal, a goal that demands the best from all of us, a goal that will help us build the kind of future we all want for ourselves and our children.

---

[1]"California Continues to Rank First in Manufactures and Agricultural Exports," *Business America*, 27 March 1989, 9–10.

[2]Carla Anderson Hills (1934–), born in Los Angeles; A.B., Stanford University, 1955; LL.B., Yale University, 1958; honorary degrees. Attorney; assistant attorney general, Civil Division, U.S. Justice Department, 1974–1975; U.S. Housing and Urban Development secretary, 1975–1977; appointed U.S. trade representative, 1989, Executive Office of the U.S. President. *Who's Who in America, 1992–1993*, I, 1558.

[3]Prime Minister Brian Mulroney and President Ronald Reagan signed the Canada-U.S. Free Trade Agreement on January 2, 1988. The pact went into effect January 1, 1989. Duncan Cameron (ed.), *The Free Trade Deal* (Toronto: James Lorimer and Co., 1988), i; *New York Times*, January 2, 1989.

[4]The governor's economic development mission to the Far East lasted from October 4 to October 19, 1989. Near the end of the trip, and again in 1991, he approved sister-state accords with Taiwan. See Governor's Schedule for Weeks of October 1–October 15, 1989, October 9–October 22, 1989, and press releases, "Governor Signs Sister-State Agreement with Taiwan," Taipei, Taiwan, October 16, 1989, "Governor Signs Sister-State Agreement

with Taiwan," Taipei, October 15, 1991, "Media Advisory," Raleigh, October 17, 1989, Governors Papers, James G. Martin.
[5]North Carolina's Canadian trade office opened April 23, 1990, in Toronto. *News and Observer*, April 24, 1990.
[6]Martin visited England, Germany, Sweden, and Austria during the European tour, November 8 to November 20, 1989. Governor's Schedule for Weeks of November 6–November 19, 1989, November 13–November 26, and November 20–December 3, 1989, Governors Papers, James G. Martin.

SWEARING-IN OF WILDLIFE RESOURCES COMMISSION

RALEIGH, MAY 10, 1989

[A new Wildlife Resources Commission was installed in May 1989, following the enactment of S.B. 560. Martin sought the legislation, which reorganized the board, after Commissioner Robert W. Hester interfered in a personnel decision involving the wildlife commission staff. Hester, a Martin appointee, convinced other board members to join him in derailing the promotion of wildlife officer Terry L. Waterfield in 1988. The governor initiated an investigation into the affair and also signed an executive order requiring that commissioners confine their activities to wildlife policy and avoid personnel issues. Hester declined two requests from Martin to resign.

Martin admitted that he would not have pursued a new state law if Hester had stepped down. "'That would have gotten the message across and others would have gotten the message by it,'" he said. S.B. 560 gave the state's chief executive undisputed control over the dismissal of the eleven commissioners whom he appointed to the thirteen-member wildlife board. *News and Observer*, February 17, March 12, 16, 21, 23, April 28, 1989; press release, "Governor Martin Names New Wildlife Commission Members," Raleigh, April 27, 1989, Governors Papers, James G. Martin.]

Speaker Mavretic, Secretary Cobey, "future" members of the Wildlife Commission, I am extremely pleased to call this meeting to order and to welcome each of you—especially those who will soon be sworn in as members of the North Carolina Wildlife Commission. I'm happy to see that many of you have brought family members and friends with you to mark this occasion. They will be invaluable in providing the support you need to deal with the many challenges you will face as members of this commission, so I'm glad they are with you here, today, as you begin this important task. Before we begin, let me ask the Reverend Tom Dorman to offer the invocation.

(Reverend Dorman gives invocation.)

I want to talk to you about that task and what we hope you will be able to accomplish, but first we need to administer your oaths of office. To do that, I will now call upon Judge Robert Orr of the North Carolina Court of Appeals.[1]

(Judge Orr swears in commission members.)

The oaths that each of you just swore culminates [*sic*] a bipartisan effort by my administration, the General Assembly, and the North Carolina Wildlife Federation to correct a long-standing problem. You are here today because that problem was recognized and rectified. Senator Barker, who introduced the bill, and his colleagues in the General Assembly deserve credit for their efforts. Their action has given me and future governors clear authority in commission matters. That authority was necessary to ensure that the reform we have instituted within this commission is a true and lasting reform, a reform that will work to the benefit of the commission and especially to the public it serves.[2]

As I said in announcing my appointments to this commission last month, the most important aspect of the legislation is that we have now given the staff of the Wildlife Commission the tools it needs—the authority to do a job without undue interference. With your support and commitment, we have taken politics out of the offices of the Wildlife Commission. We have freed the staff to concentrate its full attention to the job at hand. That's real reform and real progress.

Time now to turn to policy issues that confront you. The problems we have had in the past, and the attention those problems have received from the news media and the public, means [*sic*] that you as a commission will find yourself in the spotlight. That spotlight brings a formidable challenge. We can no longer tolerate baited duck blinds that earned our northeastern counties the unfavorable "Gold Coast" moniker. We must find ways to restore our dwindling population of quail, rabbit, and pheasant that once were mainstays of a thriving small-game population. North Carolina citizens are concerned about preserving our wildlife resources—they tell us so when they purchase licenses and subscribe to *Wildlife in North Carolina*—and those citizens will be watching you closely to make sure things have changed for the better.

The greatest challenge is to restore an aura of professionalism to this commission. I chose you because you have the ability to meet that challenge. I have faith in you, and I know you are going to give your best efforts to the task ahead. We look, today, to a new dawn for the Wildlife Commission—as full of promise as a winter dawn in a duck blind in northeastern North Carolina. I am counting on you to lead us down the right paths, to develop programs and policies that work to the benefit of all our citizens and to help us protect our priceless wildlife habitats for generations to come.

Now it is my pleasure to recognize the immediate past president of the Wildlife Resources Commission, Gene Price.[3] Gene, I want to commend you for the job you have done, under some very trying circumstances, and I wanted to take this opportunity to thank you for your good work. Because of your efforts in working to protect our wildlife resources, and because of your many efforts on behalf of the people of North Carolina, it is my pleasure to present to you the Order of the Long Leaf Pine.

[Martin presents certificate to Price.]

Now, Gene, I would like for you to serve as temporary chairman of the Wildlife Resources Commission in order that this agency can elect a new chairman and get on with the important tasks it faces.

---

[1]Robert Flynn Orr (1946–), born in Norfolk, Va.; A.B., 1971, J.D., 1975, University of North Carolina at Chapel Hill; U.S. Army, 1968–1971. Attorney; Buncombe County Republican Party chairman, 1983–1985; appointed judge, N.C. Court of Appeals, 1986, by Governor Martin; first Republican elected to state Court of Appeals during twentieth century, 1988, and the first to be reelected, 1992. *News and Observer*, November 25, December 12, 1992; *North Carolina Manual, 1991–1992*, 487; Robert F. Orr, telephone conversation with Jan-Michael Poff, May 6, 1993.

[2]S.B. 560, "An Act to Provide for the Appointment of a new North Carolina Wildlife Resources Commission," was ratified April 25, 1989. *N.C. Session Laws, 1989*, I, c. 68.

William H. Barker (1944–), born in Oriental; B.A., 1968, J.D., 1969, University of North Carolina at Chapel Hill; U.S. Navy, and Reserves, 1962–1968. Attorney; farmer; member, state Senate, 1987–1990, and chairman, Marine Resources and Wildlife Committee; Democrat. *North Carolina Manual, 1989–1990*, 253.

[3]Martin named H. Eugene Price, editor of the *Goldsboro News-Argus*, to the Wildlife Resources Commission in July 1985. Price was elected chairman two years later. *News and Observer*, March 7, 1989.

NORTH CAROLINA BANKERS ASSOCIATION

PINEHURST, MAY 13, 1989

[The governor's remarks to a meeting of the state's bankers in Pinehurst, below, essentially echoed his speeches at the Chamber of Commerce Luncheon during Capital For A Day festivities in Laurinburg, May 1, and at the Business-Industry Appreciation Dinner, May 3, 1989, in Elizabeth City.]

It is an honor to speak to you, today, as this Ninety-third Annual Convention of the North Carolina Bankers Association draws to its successful conclusion. You are the core of our financial community, true partners in progress toward a future of prosperity in North Carolina. The last time I spoke to a group like this, the microphone went dead just as I stepped to the podium. So I called out to a gentleman in the back row and asked him whether he could hear me. When he said no, another gentleman in the front row stood up and hollered back, "Well, I can, and I'll be glad to change places with you." Well, I hope you can all hear me, today, because I want you to remember what I have to say.

Since 1897, the North Carolina Bankers Association has witnessed a phenomenal growth of banking in our state and has helped to promote the continued progress of this industry. In 1960, North Carolina was home to approximately 200 banks. Today, through consolidations that have strengthened the banking industry statewide, seventy-one North Carolina banks hold assets of $66 billion and deposits of $48 billion. I'm proud to say that the last bank to fail in North Carolina occurred on March 18, 1943.[1]

The outstanding success of this industry in North Carolina is due in great part to progressive banking laws that fostered branch banking state-wide. Branch banking increased the availability of capital and credit in our communities and, in turn, expanded investment opportunities for business and industry. But branch banking also taught the financial industry how to manage and maintain growth so that when regional interstate banking was approved in 1985, North Carolina was catapulted into its current leadership role.[2]

Unfortunately, not all North Carolina banking laws are so progressive. This association sponsored Senate Bill 377 in the General Assembly to authorize credit card banks, amend interest and fee rates, and allow credit card facilities to write insurance contracts. That bill has been amended to authorize a legislative research committee to study these issues. The committee substitute is currently held in the Senate Appropriations Committee awaiting funding.[3]

I believe that the best way to regulate credit card interest rates is to allow competition in the marketplace, to respond to supply and demand. When government arbitrarily decides a cap for fees and interest, the entire financial community will organize around that cap. Allowing the free market to adjust fees and interest will strengthen the banking industry through competition and will most likely result in lower costs for the consumer.

We cannot forget that a strong banking industry is the cornerstone of a strong economy. It supports the growth and expansion of all other business. A dramatic example of this occurred just two years ago as our farmers suffered from a crippling drought. The banking community rushed to the farmers' aid, restructuring loans rather than foreclosing. The members of the Governor's Farm Finance Task Force, a veritable who's who in banking, put their financial wizardry into action and developed a better credit system for farmers to protect them in the future.[4]

That same effect is evident in the strong economy we have enjoyed during my administration. In 1987 alone, businesses invested a total of $5.4 billion in North Carolina: $2.5 billion in the manufacturing sector and $2.8 billion in the nonmanufacturing sector. We expect 1988 figures to be even better. North Carolina also led the nation in the number of new manufacturing facilities in both 1987 and 1988.

I said that North Carolina bankers are true partners in our progress to the future. That is why I am coming to you once again, just as I did during the farm crisis, to solicit your support for two programs that are critical to the future of our state. These are the career ladder and the highway trust fund proposals under consideration in the General Assembly.

All of you are familiar with the education crisis in North Carolina and all across America. A survey of American college students revealed that many thought Beirut was in Ireland and that Joseph McCarthy was a famous communist. Most cannot properly identify the location of the fifty states in our own country. This month, too, U.S. education secretary Lauro Cavazos rated our nation's students as "merely average" despite our determined efforts to improve our public schools.[5]

The extent of this crisis is overwhelming, particularly when you realize that the high school graduating class of the year 2001 is just finishing kindergarten. Something must be done to improve education in our schools, and I believe that a key to that improvement is better pay for better teachers. As managers and financiers, you are familiar with the greatest management principle in the world: If you reward people for a job well done, they will do the job well. I believe we have to put that management principle to work in our schools, and reward good teachers for doing a good job in the classroom. I believe we can do that by implementing the career ladder statewide.

Until now we have said to our teachers, we may not pay you much, but we will pay you the same salary whether you can teach or not. With the career ladder program, we can say the better you are as a teacher, and the better you become, the better you will be paid. Sixteen pilot programs across the state have tried the career ladder program, and for fourteen of those pilots, the program has been an outstanding success. As a result of the career ladder, these fourteen systems showed improvement in student classroom performance, standardized test scores, class attendance, college acceptance, and lowering the dropout rate. The remaining two pilots have identified some problems in the system, problems that can and will be fixed before the program is offered statewide.

So how does the career ladder work? I am proposing to raise the starting pay for teachers from the current level of $18,000 to $20,500. Additional years of experience would offer additional salary increases so that teachers with thirty or more years of experience would earn up to $36,000. But it doesn't stop there: As each teacher completes one of the four career ladder levels of achievement, he or she receives a five to ten percent salary increase on top of that. That means experienced teachers can earn up to $42,000 a school year. I think you will agree this is a professional pay scale, one that says to our teachers, we intend to pay you well as long as you are doing a good job in the classroom.

So who determines whether a teacher is good? Under the career ladder program, trained evaluators visit each classroom four times during the year to evaluate a teacher's performance. These evaluations then serve as guidelines for improvement. In addition, experienced teachers counsel new teachers to help them improve their lesson plans and classroom style. Instead of fostering competition, these procedures actually increase cooperation among teachers and improve classroom performance.

Being bankers, you probably want to know how we propose to pay for this program. The career ladder requires a sweeping overhaul of our educational system, and that takes money. To provide the necessary funds, I am proposing a one-cent increase in the sales tax for nonfood items, from four to five cents on the dollar. That would provide approximately $450 million each year to improve education in North Carolina.

Of course, no one likes a tax increase. As taxpayers, we all work hard for our money. But I believe most taxpayers in North Carolina would be willing to pay an additional one cent per dollar at the cash register if it means the difference between a good education and an average or below-average education for their children. We don't mind paying a little more in taxes if we know that money will be used to pay good teachers for doing a good job in the classroom.

But improving schools isn't the only critical issue we are facing. We have another challenge to meet in North Carolina, and that is the challenge to build a system of "intrastate" highways that unites our state—north and south, east and west—in one united state as never before. To meet this challenge, I have endorsed the major highway improvement program now before the General Assembly. That program would build a system of uninterrupted, limited-access, four-lane, divided highways that reach within ten miles of 96 percent of our entire population.

As you are well aware, good roads are vital to bringing good jobs to our state, particularly into our rural areas, and good jobs are the key to a strong economic future for North Carolina. The state Highway Study Commission has recommended a 5-and-a-quarter-cent motor fuel tax increase and a 2 percent title transfer tax to pay for this ambitious highway program, but other proposals are also being considered. Whatever the pay plan, the result will be better roads and better jobs for our citizens.

These programs are innovative, they are ambitious, and they are critical to the future growth and prosperity of our state, but we cannot ensure these programs will become reality without your help. I need your support for these proposals if they are to be adopted by the General Assembly. I urge you to contact your legislators and tell them how important the career ladder and the highway trust fund bill are for better schools and better roads are to you and the future economy of our state. Join with me in helping to build a better North Carolina for all of us, especially for our children. Help me in this quest for better schools, better roads, and better jobs, so that when the twenty-first century dawns, North Carolina, and especially North Carolina's children, will be ready.

---

[1]The state-chartered Bank of Black Mountain, in Black Mountain, and its Old Fort and Weaverville branches, "were placed in liquidation on March 18, 1943." *Reports of the Condition of the State Banks at the Close of Business on December 31, 1943* (Raleigh: State of North Carolina, Banking Department, [1944]), 4.

[2]"The North Carolina Regional Reciprocal Banking Act" was ratified July 7, 1984, and became effective January 1, 1985. *N.C. Session Laws, 1983, Extra and Regular Sessions, 1984*, c. 1113.

[3]Democratic state senators William W. Staton, Kenneth C. Royall, Jr., and Aaron W. Plyler sponsored S.B. 377, "A Bill to Authorize Credit Card Banks, to Amend the Rate of Interest and Fees Applicable to Credit Card Accounts, Open-End Credit, and Revolving Charge Accounts, and to Repeal the Prohibition Against the Use of Credit Card Facilities to Solicit Contracts of Insurance." The Senate Banks and Thrift Institutions Committee held the measure for two months before reporting unfavorably upon it on May 4. However, the committee's substitute bill was adopted by the Senate, and the study of "Deregulation of Revolving Credit and Authorization of Credit Card Banks" was included in *N.C. Session Laws, 1989*, II, c. 802, s. 2.1(5); see also *N.C. Senate Journal, 1989*, 146, 463, 1428.

[4]The Farm Finance Task Force was launched October 20, 1986. Poff, *Addresses of Martin*, I, 421–423.

[5]Secretary Cavazos called American pupils "merely average" on May 3, as he unveiled his department's sixth-annual state-by-state evaluation of student performance. *New York Times*, May 4, 1989; *Washington Post*, May 4, 1989.

Speaking to the North Carolina Alliance for Public Education on May 16, 1989, Martin further described Cavazos's findings. "Among the statistics compiled for the Department of Education's State Education Performance Chart, North Carolina ranked thirty-seventh among the fifty states with a graduation rate of 67.8 percent. The department's chart also shows national SAT scores fell from an average of 906 to 904 from 1987 to 1988. Fourteen of the twenty-two states in which the SAT is the dominant college entrance exam registered declines. Unfortunately, even with the national average on the decline, North Carolina ranked twentieth of those twenty-two states with an average score of 841."

Lauro Fred Cavazos (1927–), born in King Ranch, Tex.; B.A., 1949, M.A., 1951, Texas Tech University; Ph.D., Iowa State University, 1954; U.S. Army, 1945–1946. Faculty member, Medical College of Virginia, 1954–1964; faculty member, 1964–1980, dept. chairman, 1964–1972, dean, 1975–1980, Tufts University School of Medicine; biological sciences professor, professor of anatomy, and president, Health Sciences Center, 1980–1988, Texas Tech University; secretary, U.S. Dept. of Education, 1988–1990; author. *Who's Who in America, 1992–1993*, I, 566.

INDEPENDENT COLLEGE FUND ANNUAL MEETING

RALEIGH, MAY 31, 1989

For thirty-six years, the Independent College Fund has supported and sustained our private colleges and universities in their effort to educate our young people. As every college president knows, finding enough money to offer a quality education and maintain facilities presents a major challenge to any school administrator. All those involved with the Independent College Fund, administrators and donors alike, deserve our sincere thanks for their support and commitment to higher education in the state of North Carolina.

North Carolina boasts an outstanding system of higher education, both public and private. The University of North Carolina system, our fifty-eight community colleges, and our independent colleges and universities train and educate our citizens of every age so they can provide a better life for themselves and their families. I know you share my pride in the outstanding work done in each of these fine institutions, just as I share your pride in the strong liberal arts tradition found in our independent colleges and universities.

It is often said that a liberal arts education teaches the whole person: mental, physical, and spiritual. As both a student and teacher, I learned to appreciate a liberal arts education as much for what it taught me about life as for what it taught me about books. My professors at Davidson College drilled me in history, science, literature, and the arts, but they also taught me to think. In graduate school at Princeton University, I learned the advanced principles of chemistry, along with the principles of hard work, discipline, and study which remain with me to this day. I may not easily call to mind when Milton wrote *Paradise Lost*; I may be a bit rusty on some of the more involved chemical theories I once knew, but I do know how to think.

This, then, is the great gift you offer your students through a liberal arts education. While they think to learn, they learn to think. Technology changes, job skills change, but the thinking person masters change and turns it to his or her advantage. The world offers possibilities; a strong liberal arts education teaches students to turn possibilities into reality.

We share a common belief: that a quality education opens the door of opportunity for our citizens. We share a common goal: to kindle the spark of knowledge into a bright and healthy flame that will light the path through and beyond that door of opportunity. But the excellence of our higher education is threatened. Falling enrollment isn't the problem; overall, enrollment increased in private colleges during this past school year. Finances are a big problem, but not the central problem. The financial gap between public and private institutions remains. To partially offset that, I have again sponsored legislation in the General Assembly that will increase state funds provided for the North Carolina Legislative Tuition Grant and the Contract Grant—this time by $50 per person, per grant.[1] The General Assembly also approved my emergency request for funds to cover the shortfall caused by that increased student enrollment.

The problem we face is more serious than enrollment or finances. The problem we face is educating high school graduates who don't have the reading and writing skills to handle college. This problem is your problem, too, because these are the students some of whom eventually end up in your classrooms.

I believe that improving the quality of our public schoolteachers is the way to correct this problem. I have submitted a proposal to the General Assembly that would improve our public school system by providing better pay for better teachers. This plan would restructure teacher pay scales to consider years of experience and promote good teachers in the classroom through the career ladder program. I believe so strongly in the success of this program that I have proposed a one-cent increase in the sales tax to pay for it. The career ladder is the only way to ensure accountability in our public schools and to ensure that good teachers receive the financial compensation they deserve.

The time for educational reform in North Carolina is now. Our young people cannot continue to suffer from our indecision. We must act quickly. We must act now, or I fear we will lose an important opportunity to prepare our young people to compete in the economic marketplace of tomorrow.

Just a few hours ago, Lieutenant Governor Gardner announced his support for my education and pay scale proposals. Since I announced these proposals, he has spent much of his time talking with legislators, comparing notes, and sounding out teachers' views, and looking at other alternatives. After weeks of independent investigation, he has concluded that my education proposals offer the best way to meet our state's most critical needs. His endorsement comes at [a] critical time for these proposals, as the members of the legislature draw close to a vote on these issues.[2]

I want to publicly thank Lieutenant Governor Gardner for his support and commend him for his independent investigation of the pay and education proposals before the General Assembly. If another proposal could have provided these sweeping reforms without a tax increase, both he and I would have joined the bandwagon in support of that proposal. Now, however, Lieutenant Governor Gardner has come to the same conclusions I drew earlier this year: We must move forward now with education as well as highway improvements, we must provide better pay for better teachers with the accountability provided through the career ladder, and we must have a tax increase to pay for it.

Lieutenant Governor Gardner's support is vital support for educational reform that is being built all across North Carolina. We need your help to build a tower of educational excellence on this foundation. I urge you to unite as never before, with one another, with me and with Lieutenant Governor Gardner, and legislative leaders, in voicing your support for my educational reform package.

Some members of the legislature do not yet see the importance of these measures and may not fully realize the crisis in our public schools. We need you to tell them. I urge you to contact our legislators, tell them what you see in your freshman composition courses, and tell them they need to support my educational reforms if we are to turn the system around.

North Carolina is on the verge of great things in education, and you are a part of that effort. It is time to get our students thinking, as well as reading and writing, long before they come to you in college. Help me in this effort, and you will find that the students in your classrooms will be more ready and more willing to learn what you have to teach.

---

[1]The $50.00 per student increase was authorized by *N.C. Session Laws, 1989*, II, c. 752, s. 93.

[2]Gardner and other Republican lawmakers had been leery of the one-cent hike in the state sales tax that Martin recommended in March to fund his education and pay scale proposals. But, as the lieutenant governor concluded at his May 31 press conference, he put his philosophical objection to a tax increase aside. "'I boiled it down for what I thought was best for the children of this state. . . . We've had time to look. There is no other good plan out there.'"

Along with Gardner, approximately forty GOP legislators also declared their acceptance of Martin's proposal. Such a showing, the governor said, indicated that intraparty differences over his suggested sales tax increase had ebbed and that it was time to build a coalition with Democrats to pass it: "'As long as there were so many news stories that there was a potential rift in the Republican Party, there was no chance of getting the Democrats to come and do the work for us that I had proposed. The Democrats said to me, "Can you get a majority of the Republicans?" As of today, we can show them visually with names and with a nose count that yes, we've got support on the Republican side. Now can we get the support on the Democratic side? I believe they are ready.'" As it turned out, the Democrats were unwilling to heed Martin's call for a penny sales tax increase in 1989. *News and Observer*, June 1, 1989; press release, "Governor Martin's Response to Endorsement of Education Proposal by Lt. Gov. Gardner," Raleigh, May 31, 1989, Governors Papers, James G. Martin.

PRESS RELEASE: GOVERNOR MARTIN'S STATEMENT ON
SUPREME COURT DECISION ON THE BURNING OF
THE AMERICAN FLAG

RALEIGH, JUNE 27, 1989

[Gregory Lee Johnson burned a United States flag, as a participant in a larger demonstration against Reagan administration policies, outside the 1984 Republican National Convention in Dallas. Found guilty of breaking Texas's law against flag desecration, Johnson appealed his case to the United States Supreme Court. On June 21, 1989, the court declared that he had been wrongly convicted: Johnson's deed was an expression of political protest protected by the First Amendment of the United States Constitution.

The *Texas v. Johnson* decision overruled extant federal and state statutes against desecrating the U.S. flag. It also ignited public indignation and sparked a call by President Bush for a constitutional amendment banning flag burning. However, as Congress debated the merits of amending the Bill of Rights, the angry protests that swirled about the court's ruling cooled. In the end, federal lawmakers left the Constitution intact.

While members of Congress considered constitutional change, Martin urged the General Assembly to enact his flag desecration bill. Based on legislation originally proposed by Governor Mario Cuomo of New York, the measure would have made the destruction or mutilation of either the United States or state flag punishable by up to two years in prison and/or a fine. Persons disposing of a worn flag in compliance with the Code of Flag Etiquette were to be exempt. According to a press release, Martin "said the legislation would protect the flags in a manner consistent with First Amendment rights under the U.S. Constitution."

State senator N. Leo Daughtry (R-Johnston) introduced S.B. 1331, "A Bill to Make it Unlawful to Intentionally Destroy or Substantially Mutilate a Flag of the United States or of the State of North Carolina," on July 13, 1989. The Senate unanimously approved the proposal and sent it to the House, where the measure remained with the Judiciary Committee through the end of the 1989 session. *Congressional Quarterly Almanac, 101st Congress, 1st Session, 1989, Vol. XLV* (Washington, D.C.: Congressional Quarterly, Inc., 1990), 307, hereinafter cited as *Congressional Quarterly Almanac*, with appropriate year; *N.C. House Journal, 1989,* 1221; *N.C. Senate Journal, 1989,* 989–990; press release, "Governor Urges General Assembly to Adopt Legislation to Protect American, North Carolina Flags," Raleigh, July 13, 1989, Governor's Papers, James G. Martin.]

Governor Jim Martin has issued the following statement on the U.S. Supreme Court's decision extending First Amendment protection to political protesters who burn the American flag: "While I understand and respect the U.S. Supreme Court's role in our constitutional system of checks and balances, I am deeply concerned by its recent decision that, in effect, decriminalizes the destruction and desecration of the U.S. flag. Our flag—a symbol of our freedoms, and those who have died defending those freedoms—deserves special recognition and protection.

Surely those who advocate political change can do so without destroying the foremost symbol of their right to seek such change.

"To protect our flag, to remain true to the thousands who have died in its defense, I am announcing my readiness to work for congressional action that would make the act of destroying an American flag a criminal offense. I think this approach offers the quickest possible way of redressing what I consider to be an erroneous interpretation of the Constitution by the U.S. Supreme Court, and I urge those who agree with me to join me in this effort."

ANNOUNCEMENT OF MEMORANDUM OF UNDERSTANDING ON MOBIL OIL OFFSHORE DRILLING

RALEIGH, JULY 14, 1989

[Appearing at a news conference with Attorney General Thornburg in April 1989, Governor Martin described his demand for an environmental impact statement on Mobil's proposed drilling for natural gas off Cape Hatteras as "nonnegotiable." Three months later, the governor announced an agreement among the state, Mobil Oil Corporation, and the federal Minerals Management Service on a study that embraced the salient components of a full environmental impact statement but was placed on a much tighter schedule. A complete EIS would have required upward of two years to prepare. Under the new plan, the Minerals Management Service intended to release preliminary findings in two months and conclude the survey in approximately nine months.

Martin and a representative of Mobil Oil expressed satisfaction with the agreement. The state would learn the environmental risks associated with the project and could effect an appropriate response before natural gas exploration could begin. The petroleum company, thanks to the "fast track" adopted for the study, stood a much better chance of beginning drilling before many of its offshore leases expired in August 1991. Some environmentalists, however, were angered that a full EIS was not in the offing. See "Mobil Oil Press Conference," pages 98–100, above; *News and Observer*, July 15, 1989.]

We have an announcement today regarding an agreement that has been reached between the state of North Carolina, Mobil Oil Corporation, and the Minerals Management Service of the U.S. Department of the Interior.[1] With me for this historic occasion are the attorney general of North Carolina, Lacy H. Thornburg, who has been a valuable ally and partner in this project; and Mr. Ed Cassidy, deputy director of the Minerals Management Service, whose creative ingenuity first suggested the innovative concept that was the basis for our unique memorandum of understanding. What we announce today is also a special tribute to the leadership and dedicated hard work of Donna Moffitt, outer continental shelf director for the North Carolina Department of Administration, and Dan McLawhorn and his associates in the Justice Department.[2]

This memorandum of understanding sets forth a schedule of requirements for public records and information to be shared, and public meetings and hearings to be conducted over the next year, leading to a thorough environmental report covering the consequences and risks associated with offshore drilling and the plans for minimizing those risks. We believe it will best meet the needs of North Carolina to fulfill our responsibilities under the federal laws governing Mobil's proposal to drill an offshore exploratory well off our coast.

We believe that this agreement is even superior to the provisions of an environmental impact statement, such as we had previously sought, and gives us certain valuable advantages not otherwise available to us. For example, it would extend the area of review to more than the single nine-square-mile lease block, designated by Mobil, to include twenty-one such contiguous blocks for a total of 189 square miles. Second, our agreement would extend the scope of study to include developmental wells and production facilities, if any ensue. The detailed environmental report will analyze how drilling could affect marine life, tourism, and commerce, and do so more extensively than any alternative approach.

Third, we have agreed on a more extensive series of three public meetings to allow public input to identify issues of concern to be addressed in the draft report, followed by three more public hearings for public discussion of the specific information contained in the draft report. More than any traditional method, this approach makes the public a full partner in this entire environmental review process. All of this goes well beyond anything we could expect from an environmental impact statement, as defined by federal law.

Fourth, because we can already anticipate the period of fishery spawning—especially menhaden spawning—in the test-well area, the memorandum of understanding limits any test drilling to a period from May 1 through October 31. This will minimize the effect of drilling sediments on this valuable commercial resource.

Fifth, because we have built a mutual basis of respect and good faith in our dealings with Mobil and the Minerals Management Service, the memorandum of understanding expressly protects our rights to litigation if that later proves necessary.

In short, this custom-made environmental report will do everything North Carolina sought under a legally preconceived environmental impact statement, and much more. It especially suits our situation as a novice state with no prior experience dealing with offshore wells and their environmental effects. Mobil Oil and the Minerals Management Service have been persuaded to respect the problems we faced: Neither our staff nor our interested public had the benefit of having dealt with extensive drilling and had less backlog of understanding in comparison with producing states, such as those along the Gulf Coast. Therefore, as a rookie, we had a greater need for more information, more public participation, and more time for thoughtful review than states which had been through the drills many times. We also believe that we have unique circumstances due to the conditions of the Gulf Stream and its eddy currents, the great depth of the water, and the weather intensity at this site.

The state of North Carolina has no predetermined intent arbitrarily to oppose this exploratory well. Some organizations and individuals may seek that agenda, regardless of what the report will show, but that is not the policy of the state. We respect the national need for energy production, including a great diversity of resources. Someone must explore for it, or we will soon find our nation at risk, with a growing dependency on foreign sources.

It is our responsibility to ensure that this first well and any subsequent wells not pose a serious or uncontrollable threat to the environment or to a vast recreational and commercial economy based upon our natural assets. We must specifically find that this plan of exploration has features, safeguards, and procedures consistent with our Coastal Area Management Act before we can agree to it. But on the other hand, if the report shows that offshore drilling will pose unacceptable risks to the environment, or our people and their livelihoods, or our visiting tourist[s], then I must do everything in my power to oppose such drilling. I believe that this memorandum of understanding, more than any other alternative, strengthens and protects our rights to ensure that this will be done in the safest way, or not at all.

This is an agreement that we can be very proud of, as well as the teamwork that made it happen. I've mentioned Judge Thornburg and Mr. McLawhorn, Mr. Cassidy, Donna Moffitt and her boss, Administration Secretary Jim Lofton.[3] I especially want to thank our congressional delegation for backing us effectively at every step, with special thanks to Congressman Walter Jones,[4] who pushed legislative alternatives in case this failed, and Senator Jesse Helms, who interceded for us to convince Mobil and MMS officials that this innovative agreement would work and would be far superior to trying to operate under traditional procedures.

Ordinarily, all parties are isolated in adversarial roles. The reason we were able to come together in a partnership for this agreement is largely because of the leadership of my friend, Manuel Lujan, secretary of the U.S. Department of Interior.[5] His personal guidance led us to work together to solve problems rather than to create problems. That means that as we go forward under this memorandum of understanding, the concerns that North Carolina raises will be more readily understood by a partner than by an adversary.

Now let me call on Attorney General Thornburg to come forward to give us his views on this, with my thanks for his partnership in obtaining a sound, practical, environmental review that will help us protect our coastal resources.

---

[1]For related press release, see "Governor, Attorney General Announce 'Custom Made' Environmental Report on Mobil Exploration," Raleigh, July 14, 1989, Governors Papers, James G. Martin.

[2]Edward M. Cassidy (1954–), born in Miami, Fla.; resident of Alexandria, Va.; was educated at Fairfield University and Georgetown University. Legislative assistant to U.S. Rep. Larry Hopkins, R-Ky., 1979–1980; press secretary to U.S. Rep. Paul Trible, R-Va., 1980–1981; legislative director, National Republican Congressional Committee, 1981–1982; executive assistant to U.S. Rep. Thomas Ridge, R-Pa., 1983–1984; director, intergovernmental and public affairs, Appalachian Regional Commission, 1984–1989; campaign manager, Bill Clements for Governor (Texas), 1985–1986; chief press spokesman, Bush-Quayle Inaugural Committee, 1988–1989; appointed deputy director, Minerals Management Service, U.S. Interior Dept., 1989. Ann L. Brownson (ed.), *1990 Federal Staff Directory* (Mount Vernon, Va.: Staff Directories, Ltd., 2 volumes, 1990), II, 912.

Donna D. Moffitt (1947–), director, Outer Continental Shelf Office, 1988–1992, N.C. Dept. of Administration. Donna D. Moffitt, telephone interview with Jan-Michael Poff, July 27, 1994; see also Poff, *Addresses of Martin*, I, 917n–918n.

Daniel F. McLawhorn (1948–), born in Morehead City; resident of Raleigh; B.A., Davidson College, 1970; J.D., University of North Carolina, 1974. Attorney; chairman, Legal Dept., N.C. Justice Academy, 1977–1979; assistant attorney general, 1979–1985, special deputy attorney general, since 1985, N.C. Justice Department. As special project attorney with the Justice Department's Environmental Protection Section, 1985–1990, he served as principal adviser on Mobil offshore drilling project, expansion of military airspace, and Oregon Inlet stabilization project. Daniel F. McLawhorn, letter to Jan-Michael Poff, February 9, 1993.

[3]James Shepherd Lofton (1943–), secretary, North Carolina Dept. of Administration, 1987–1993. Previously identified in Poff, *Addresses of Martin*, I, 153n.

[4]Walter Beaman Jones (1913–1992), born in Fayetteville; resident of Farmville; B.S., N.C. State College (later University), 1934. Office equipment dealer; Farmville mayor and Recorder's Court judge, 1949–1953; member, N.C. House, 1955–1959, and Senate, 1965–1966; member, U.S. House of Representatives, from North Carolina's First Congressional District, 1966–1992, and chairman, Committee on Merchant Marine and Fisheries; Democrat. *News and Observer*, September 16, 1992; *North Carolina Manual, 1991–1992,* 510.

[5]Manuel Lujan, Jr. (1928–), born in San Idlefonso, N.Mex.; B.A., College of Santa Fe, 1950. Insurance business; member, 1969–1989, U.S. House of Representatives, from New Mexico's First Congressional District; appointed secretary, U.S. Department of the Interior, 1989; Republican. *Who's Who in America, 1992–1993,* II, 2117.

PRESS RELEASE: GOVERNOR'S STATEMENT ON VETO EFFORTS THIS WEEK

RALEIGH, AUGUST 9, 1989

[Throughout his campaign for a second term as governor, Martin stressed the theme "Better Schools, Better Jobs, Better Roads, and a Better Environment." He also sought to make his reelection a referendum in favor of awarding veto power to the state's chief executive. Martin's victory at the polls over Lieutenant Governor Jordan in 1988, the increase in the number of GOP candidates elected to the General Assembly that year, and his role in forming the Democratic-Republican coalition that replaced Liston Ramsey with Josephus Mavretic as Speaker of the House would have seemed to give the governor the popular and political momentum to achieve the legislative goals he set forth on the stump. But turning that momentum into the three-fifths majority of the membership of each house, necessary to approve a constitutional amendment establishing gubernatorial veto, proved to be a difficult challenge. In the end, Martin and his allies were unable to persuade enough state representatives to alter the centuries-old balance of power between the legislative and executive branches.

The state Senate adopted S.B. 3, "A Bill to Provide for a Gubernatorial Veto," on March 2, 1989. Riding the crest of a better than three-fifths majority, the proposal sailed to the House of Representatives—where it remained stalled in the Judiciary Committee for over four months. When the committee's version of S.B. 3 finally came to a vote before the full House on August 3, it failed to pass: The 60–43 tally in favor of veto was 12 votes short of the 72 needed to approve a constitutional amendment.

Martin worked extremely hard to generate House support for gubernatorial veto in the final days before the vote, interrupting his attendance at a National Governors' Association conference to return to the capital and rally lawmakers to the cause. He was determined to keep the issue alive. On Friday, August 4, the governor's lobbyists queried Speaker Mavretic on the likelihood of another House vote, and negotiations between Martin and the legislative leadership lasted through the weekend. Within ninety-six hours of the bill's defeat, a compromise was reached: the Speaker agreed to revive the issue of executive veto in exchange for the governor's endorsement of a constitutional amendment extending lawmakers' terms from two to four years. Proponents hoped the plan would sway the votes of legislators apprehensive that executive veto alone, without concessions for the General Assembly, would shift the balance of power too far in favor of the governor.

Mavretic informed the House of the discussions with Martin and recommended resurrection of the veto bill. State representatives, voting 55–29 on the evening of August 7, agreed and sent it to the Rules Committee. Seventy-two votes were still required for adoption, and the governor needed the backing of the entire Republican delegation, along with the goodwill of at least twenty-six House Democrats, for success. The votes of twelve lawmakers who offered their support for executive veto, but who left Raleigh for the National Conference of State Legislatures meeting in Tulsa, Oklahoma, were too valuable to ignore.

The governor received two pieces of heartening information by Tuesday morning, August 8. First, the minority leader had won GOP support for the bill.

Second, recalled Donald R. Beason, a lobbyist for Martin, the Speaker was "'confident of the additional votes needed to amount to 72.'" With those assurances, the governor dispatched two state airplanes to Oklahoma to retrieve the veto advocates.

Once the aircraft were aloft, Martin learned that House Democrats who had backed executive veto, on August 3, were not solidly behind the agreement with Mavretic. Lacking sufficient support to pass the measure, the governor recalled the planes, empty of passengers, to Raleigh. The Speaker's executive assistant later denied that Mavretic ever assured Martin that he possessed the requisite votes. He allowed only that the compromise package "'. . . was a more palatable proposal that had the potential of reaching the magic number.'"

Martin's decision to order airplanes to Tulsa had its critics. Among them was Representative Dennis A. Wicker (D-Lee), who declared, "'To send two planes out there before he had the votes, costing $6,000, is a waste of the taxpayers' money. . . .'" From his viewpoint, however, the governor felt that the risk had to be taken: "'The costs of sending those two planes out there, I wish it could have been avoided. I wish even more that it would have been productive, that we had had the votes, brought them back, and been able to pass the veto resolution. The cost of it is about equivalent to one hour of work or one hour's recess over at the Legislative Building.'" No further attempt was made to revive the veto issue during the 1989 session of the General Assembly. *N.C. House Journal, 1989,* 170, 1287, 1315–1316, 1327–1328, 1343; *N.C. Senate Journal, 1989,* 25, 96, 118, 124, 129–130; *News and Observer,* March 3, August 1, 3, 4, 8, 9, 10, 11, 13, 19, 20, 1989; press release, "Governor Returns to Raleigh to Work for Veto Legislation," Raleigh, July 31, 1989, Governors Papers, James G. Martin.]

The combined strenuous efforts over the past two weeks to build the necessary coalition of seventy-two votes in the House for the veto amendment have produced only sixty-eight commitments to be present and vote for the latest compromise. That represents a gain above the sixty House votes that supported the veto last week as a single-issue referendum. However, it still leaves us well short of the "magic number."

Accordingly, I reached a decision late last night to request that the bill be left for safekeeping in the Rules Committee, to which the House had sent it on Monday evening. The state airplanes were recalled this morning from Tulsa, Oklahoma. It was my decision to have them there on standby, so that a dozen or more House members could be brought back in the event their votes would produce the seventy-two required to approve a referendum to amend the North Carolina Constitution. Since their votes would have brought us only to the total of sixty-eight, it was my decision not to ask for a vote and not to ask them to return.

Some have asked whether any members should have been ferried back from Tulsa who wished to vote against the veto compromise, and the answer is yes, of course. Since the outcome depends solely on the number voting for the bill, 60 percent of the total membership being required, few opponents cared to return, since their absence would have the same effect as voting *no*. Only one indicated a wish to return to speak against the compromise.

NORTH CAROLINA ASSOCIATION OF COUNTY COMMISSIONERS

RALEIGH, AUGUST 11, 1989

It's a pleasure to see you again and to address the North Carolina Association of County Commissioners at this, your eighty-second annual conference.[1] Since 1906, this association has played coach and referee for a diverse team of players, sharing ideas, coordinating policies, and encouraging regional cooperation for solving common problems while helping counties retain flexibility to best address local needs.

The slide presentation we just saw, "Crossing County Lines," meant a lot to me. I know what [the] project involves. [It] reminds us how difficult such tasks are. Yet how important it is to address these issues. Decisions made in courthouses from Currituck to Cherokee—on issues ranging from distributing welfare benefits and treating waste, to encouraging economic growth and discouraging substance abuse—directly affect the lives of the people you represent. The leadership of the North Carolina Association of County Commissioners has enabled us to step across those county lines that separate our individual interests and to move into the broader realm of regional and statewide cooperation. That cooperation is the cornerstone for success in building a healthy, effective working relationship between local, state, and federal governments.

Cementing that cooperative relationship takes on added significance as the federal government returns more power, and more responsibilities, to state and local governments. We welcome the opportunity to decide our local affairs, but we realize, too, that we have opened a Pandora's box of critical needs, which used to be funded via the growing national debt; needs that now place an ever-increasing burden of funding on counties and local communities. That burden hits hardest those counties that need services the most, but which can afford those services the least.

How do we finance all the programs we need with limited revenues? Cooperation is the key. Cooperation and creativity can help us shoulder increased responsibility while we develop effective, practical programs to meet the needs of our citizens both now and in the new millennium that lies just ahead. As the theme for this conference states, we must work together now if we are to accept the "Leadership Challenges for a New Century."

Accepting these challenges requires the kind of vision and determination of Senator David H. Pryor. While a teenager in Camden, Arkansas, David Pryor saw a movie filmed in part in Washington, D.C. Inspired by scenes of the capital city, he sought appointment as a congressional page. He got the job and vowed to return someday as a member of Congress.

To reinforce his goal, while he was serving as a page, he hid a dime in a crack behind a statue in the Capitol, vowing to retrieve the coin when he succeeded. Fifteen years later, as a newly elected member of the House of Representatives, he found his dime still hidden in the statue. Reflecting on this experience, Pryor now says it proved two things: that anything is possible if you have the determination to make it happen, and that they don't do a very thorough job in cleaning our nation's Capitol.[2]

Keeping the Capitol clean may be beyond the scope of our elected offices.[3] But working with determination to meet the leadership challenges of the next century is a goal all of us must seek if we are to get the job done for the good of the people we serve.

On the state level, I'm proud to say that our efforts met with some success in the 1989 session of the General Assembly. This legislature has passed the most extensive prison package yet, designating $79 million for development of community-based alternative punishments and a two-year prison construction schedule.[4] The General Assembly also passed the largest highway construction package in the history of this state, designed to build 3,000 miles of 4-lane, divided highways reaching within 10 miles of 96 percent of our population; this association supported my original proposal, and for that support I am truly grateful.[5]

Unfortunately, the highway package the legislature passed is a "divided highway" package, taking a wrong turn on an exit ramp by diverting highway revenues to pay for teachers' salaries over the next two years. That diversion of funds will cost us in the future. In two years, we will find a budget full of serious potholes and a huge stop sign looming over funding for many critical programs.

Diverting highway funds to pay for teachers' salaries also does little to improve the crisis we face in our educational system except to maintain the status quo. While the General Assembly rejected my proposal to implement the career ladder statewide, despite a record success in pilot programs, I am pleased to see that a model similar to my proposal for step increases for public teachers has indeed been adopted. Throughout debate on my education plan, I have insisted that we look at major reform in teacher pay, reform achieved through performance-based pay. This plan from the General Assembly will help bring teacher pay to professional levels through step increases similar to my proposals, but we will have to continue to look toward merit pay for teachers through career ladder. I will continue to propose ways to do that.

I am also pleased to report that merit pay will apparently be a part of the state employee raises the General Assembly has approved. Merit pay is a concept I believe in deeply. Ask the state employees' association: They will tell you how important they consider merit pay. We're on the way to a better merit plan that includes teachers. I believe that eventually teachers will insist on it as a way to build professionalism through accountability.

I promise you, I have not ended the fight to improve teacher salaries and performance. The General Assembly has agreed to allow local school systems to decide what form of career development plan they would like to implement, if any. I regard this as an important first step. Those options include the career ladder, which I believe is still the best method yet for improving both teacher and student performance.

I know I'm preaching to the choir when I tell you how important education is to your communities. I underscore this point, though, because you have the power to help decide how to improve the opportunities for your children's future education. Consider your options well. This is a decision which requires true leadership—and a decision with important implications for the quality of life of the people in your home counties into the next century.

Highways, merit pay, veto, prison construction: These are complex issues; issues that have been debated intensely; issues that, in many cases, we have addressed inadequately. Yet if we are to compete in the workforce of tomorrow, if we are to aspire to a better life for ourselves and our children, we must continue to fight for more progress in areas where we have achieved our partial successes. We must also, however, look to our future and work to prevent crisis situations that have left us scrambling for solutions to our highway, education, and prison problems. One of the problems looming large on the horizon is the problem of solid waste disposal.

I don't have to tell you that county landfills are rapidly reaching their capacity, drawing us ever closer to a crisis. A third of the counties represented here today have landfills that will be full within five years. We can't stop producing solid waste. We must develop ways to dispose of it properly, and we must do it quickly.

If that wasn't bad enough, the EPA is expected to announce new regulations governing landfills in late December. These new rules, over the next two years, will require more recordkeeping, extensive groundwater monitoring, and protective liners in all existing landfills. When you look at the bottom line—and that, after all, is one of your main jobs as a county commissioner—these new regulations could also increase the cost of operating landfills by $200,000 per acre, not including the cost of the land.

Solid waste won't go away by itself. We must act, and act quickly. With that in mind, we have taken the first of several positive steps in that direction. Two weeks ago, the General Assembly adopted my proposal to consolidate state environmental agencies under a new Department of Health and Environment. This agency will oversee all aspects of environmental regulation, including permitting, landfill inspection, and air and water quality standards. This reorganization will streamline operations, simplify procedures, and increase our ability to monitor the environment carefully and effectively.

You'll be pleased to know that as part of our environmental efforts, we have obtained the funds to hire some—but not all, unfortunately—of the technical assistants we need to address our backlog of permit and planning requests. We're pleased at our progress, but we will continue our efforts to hire more personnel so that we can get the job done. I am also pleased to point out that for the first time, the General Assembly has appropriated $5 million for an historic solid waste financing program.[6] Leveraged with private funds, the loan pool is expected to average $50 [million] to $100 million each year. Local governments can use these funds to construct new high-tech landfills, build recycling facilities, and develop liners and leachate collection systems.

Designing better landfills will help us to properly treat waste, but we must also attempt to lessen the amount of trash going into our landfills. Senate Bill 111, headed for passage in the General Assembly, requires that 25 percent of the total waste stream be recycled by January 1993. That bill also requires each county to submit a comprehensive solid waste management plan to the state for approval. The state would have to provide planning, technical, and financial assistance to local governments for the reduction, recycling, reuse, and processing of solid waste.[7]

This bill goes a long way toward improving our waste disposal methods and reducing the amount of waste in our landfills. Success in implementing the complex and far-reaching provisions of this bill will require the full cooperation and support of state and local agencies working together toward the common goal of a cleaner, safer environment.

Solid waste disposal isn't our only challenge. We must also accept increased responsibility at the state and local levels for human service programs such as Medicaid and other welfare programs, infant mortality, and substance abuse. Every county must deal with its tangled web of welfare paperwork. But despite having one of the most complicated Medicaid systems in the country, we have just been notified that North Carolina has once again earned the lowest Medicaid error rate in the nation: 0.2 percent over the last six months, for the second time in two years. Let me remind you that the federal government considers 3 percent the tolerance level. Last year, we averaged an annual rate of 0.32 percent. Only Alaska tallied a lower rate of 0.302 percent, and they have a significantly smaller program.

Your county eligibility workers are to be congratulated for attaining this stunningly low error rate. Their efficiency and response to corrective action planning are giving us a good name all across the country.

Despite our obvious ability to deal with the intricacies of the system, simplifying the Medicaid eligibility process would greatly assist counties in reducing their paperlog. Your 1989 association resolution calls for support of automatic Medicaid eligibility for SSI [Supplemental Security Income] recipients. Many citizens eligible for SSI are already being assisted in part as catastrophic-qualified Medicare beneficiaries. Federal reclassification of our state option would ease the county eligibility burden without placing an overwhelming increase on the state's finances. We will be working with our Department of Human Resources to explore this reclassification option.

We are also working on another of your association resolutions: the people-versus-paper issue of simplifying the welfare system. As you well know, separate application and eligibility processes are required for Medicaid, AFDC [Aid to Families with Dependent Children], and food stamps, and each of those programs is administered by a different and wholly separate federal agency. It's time we eliminated some of that paperwork and freed our social services personnel for more important duties.

The Department of Human Resources and our congressional delegation are discussing legislation to create a national commission on public assistance administration. If enacted, this commission would help state and county officials present their ideas how to simplify welfare programs to the proper national officials and agencies. Simplifying these programs may actually enable us to assist more people who need help and reduce other critical problems such as our high infant mortality rate.

At the end of fiscal year 1989, 21,214 pregnant women received Medicaid benefits. A number of them were enrolled in Baby Love, a case-management program that provides comprehensive prenatal care services to pregnant women. Because of extensive local government and private sector involvement, this program has been an outstanding success, increasing birth weights and ensuring a higher percentage of prenatal care visits among high-risk groups. In light of its success, the General Assembly has expanded eligibility for the Baby Love program from 100 percent to 150 percent of the federal poverty level. That will enable an additional 6,900 pregnant women and 7,200 new infants to receive proper prenatal care.

Through programs such as Baby Love, we are attacking the infant mortality issue and reducing societal costs of caring for disabilities that easily could have been prevented through adequate prenatal care.

Finally, let me mention what I think may prove to be our greatest leadership challenge of the new century: the fight against substance abuse in every community in our state. We have already accomplished a great deal, but our efforts to promote drug treatment and prevention must continue. My wife, Dottie, has taken this fight directly to the local level by supporting the establishment of Parent to Parent programs in many communities across North Carolina. Parent to Parent is a substance abuse prevention program that trains parents how to get their children through adolescence drug free. At last count, twenty-five programs have been established in communities across our state. Through Parent to Parent, we are fighting drug and alcohol abuse at the grassroots level: in the home.

To help coordinate Parent to Parent and other such substance abuse efforts statewide, I created the North Carolina Drug Cabinet this year, chaired by Lieutenant Governor Jim Gardner. During its eighteen-month tenure, the cabinet will investigate the causes and, more importantly, recommend solutions to the problem of substance abuse in our state while coordinating existing prevention and treatment programs. As part of that effort, the lieutenant governor and I will convene a one-day conference on substance abuse at the McKimmon Center, in Raleigh, on October 24. At this Challenge for the '90s conference, we will focus on the development of local business and community coalition partnerships for combating alcohol and drug abuse across our state. I invite each of you to attend. We need your advice. We need your leadership if we are to meet and overcome this most critical challenge of the '90s. That's October 24, at Raleigh's McKimmon Center.

We have accomplished a great deal, but a great deal more remains to be done. As state and local leaders, we must work together to meet the challenges of a new century. The promises and possibilities of that century will be measured, in large part, by the successes we achieve during this century. Join with me, and together we will ensure that new century will be a century of hope and promise for all our citizens. Thank you for your commitment to the future. Thank you for what you bring to that commitment and for all that you do.

---

[1]At this point in his text, the governor jotted "Many old and good friends. In fact, waited out by the booth for Governors Waste Management Board. Few came by—afraid: volunteer/LLRW [low-level radioactive waste] or Haz. Waste incinerator. Understand[.]"

By way of introduction, Martin wrote at the top of this speech, "Started in County Gov[ernmen]t[;] worked my way down[.]"

[2]The story of the dime is true, according to Frank Thomas, chief of staff of the Washington office of Senator David H. Pryor. However, he did not recall the senator mentioning a statue during the many occasions he recounted the anecdote. The film *Born Yesterday* moved young Pryor to write Representative Oren Harris (D-Arkansas) about becoming a congressional page. Following his appointment, he was so captivated by the experience of working in Congress that he hid a dime "way back in the Capitol," in an area that was later closed off, as a token of his intention to return as an elected official. Pryor succeeded Harris, whom he had served as page, when he was elected to the U.S. House in 1966. Frank Thomas, telephone conversation with Jan-Michael Poff, March 3, 1994.

David Hampton Pryor (1934–), born in Camden, Ark.; was graduated from University of Arkansas, 1957, and from its law school, 1964. Attorney; founder, publisher, *Ouachita Citizen*, 1957–1960; elected to Arkansas House of Representatives, 1960, reelected 1962, 1964; member, U.S. House of Representatives, 1966–1973; Arkansas governor, 1975–1979; elected to U.S. Senate, 1978, reelected 1984, 1990; Democrat. Michael Barone and Grant Ujifusa, *The Almanac of American Politics, 1994* (Washington, D.C.: National Journal, Inc., 1993), 64, hereinafter cited as Barone and Ujifusa, *Almanac of American Politics*, with appropriate year; *Biographical Directory of Congress*, 1678.

[3]"Often volunteers," added the governor. "Mrs. Martin saw an idea in Macon County and promoted it statewide as 'Adopt-A-Highway' program."

[4]*N.C. Session Laws, 1989*, I, c. 8

[5]Here Martin inserted a flurry of notes. "Railroads[—] Jeopardy: 2200 miles of rail[,] even country sidings[;] Loss of ROW [right of way]; loss of passenger service[.] Intrastate highway[,] People to Jobs[—]vice versa[,] 'Road to Future[.]'"

[6]"An Act Creating the North Carolina Solid Waste Management Capital Funds Projects Financing Agency, Authorizing the Issuance of Agency Revenue Bonds to Make Loans to Units of Local Government for Solid Waste Management Projects, Authorizing Units of Local Government to Issue Special Obligation Bonds for Solid Waste Management Projects, and Amending Certain General Laws," was passed August 11, 1989. *N.C. Session Laws, 1989*, II, c. 756.

[7]The General Assembly approved "An Act to Improve the Management of Solid Waste" on August 12, 1989. The measure became effective the following October 1. *N.C. Session Laws, 1989*, II, c. 784.

JOINT SPECIAL MEETING OF SHAREHOLDERS
NORTH CAROLINA RAILROAD COMPANY AND
ATLANTIC AND NORTH CAROLINA RAILROAD COMPANY

Raleigh, August 14, 1989

[The General Assembly established the North Carolina Railroad and the Atlantic and North Carolina Railroad in the nineteenth century to spur economic development in the eastern and Piedmont regions of the state. Shareholders voted on August 14, 1989, to merge the two state-controlled rail lines. The new system, known as the North Carolina Railroad Company, connected Morehead City with Charlotte, a distance of 316 miles. Proponents of consolidation reasoned that such a move would safeguard rail service in eastern counties and buttress the state's position in negotiations with the Norfolk Southern Corporation, whose undervalued lease on the tracks expired December 31, 1994. Martin addressed the shareholders following the merger decision. *News and Observer*, August 15, 1989.]

It's a pleasure to be here for this historic event, another milestone in the colorful and dramatic history of railroading in North Carolina. It is a history that can be traced to Joseph Caldwell's wise and stirring editorials in the 1820s that so eloquently championed his vision of an intrastate railroad system, immediately after the invention of the steam locomotive. One memorable and crucial historical event was Calvin Graves's courageous tie-breaking vote in the 1849 session of the General Assembly that ensured the east-west trunk line in the face of a north-south route proposed by a group of Virginia planters and speculators.[1]

Then there was John Motley Morehead's eloquent speech promoting a statewide rail system that would "strike its roots deeply in the shore of the Atlantic, and . . . stretch its noble trunk through the centre of the state . . . until it becomes the Tree of Life to North Carolina."

That history also includes the strategic but vulnerable role of railroads in the Civil War, which afterward left southern railroads ripe for the plucking by northern businessmen more interested in interstate profit than in intrastate economic development. That history includes the presence, today, of Albert Bell, Jr., whose father, Albert Bell, Sr., grandfather, George Green, Jr., and great-grandfather, George Green, Sr., all of whom served on the board of the Atlantic and North Carolina Railroad since the beginning.

The economic trials of the late nineteenth century eventually led North Carolina to lease its great state rail line so that we have become a collector of rents for the 316 miles of track that run from Charlotte to Morehead City. But the railroad is still there. It lives on. In recent years, though, interest has been renewed in the great potential that railroads offer, both as people movers and freight haulers.

The need to provide adequate transportation looms as one of the major challenges we will face in the twenty-first century, and it is becoming more and more certain that railroads must help meet that challenge. With this in mind, railroads have come to play a resurgent role in our short- and long-term transportation planning. In recent years, for example, at our request the General Assembly has enacted legislation that permits the Department of Transportation to acquire and lease rail lines that otherwise would be abandoned and has provided some funding to purchase rail lines.[2] Our first venture saved the Dillsboro-to-Murphy rail line and leased that sixty-seven miles of track to a group of shippers and investors who formed the Great Smoky Mountains Railway, which has been a roaring success. Adding to my satisfaction of having been able personally to negotiate that settlement with Chairman Arnold McKinnon of Norfolk Southern, I am pleased that shipping on that line has increased since the line was acquired, and the weekend excursion trips often must turn away customers.[3]

Despite the success of this venture, it is only the first step in a long, uphill climb we face if we are to preserve rail corridors, revive rail transportation, and make it an integral part of an overall transportation strategy for the next millennium. With this in mind, I appointed the Governor's Rail Passenger Task Force, in 1988, to study the current, near-term, and long-range needs for rail transit service to connect major cities in our state. In March, I received an interim report from the task force. A key recommendation in that report called on the North Carolina Railroad and the Atlantic and North Carolina Railroad to "make an aggressive entry into railroad operations" so that you can play an increasingly important role in moving people and freight.[4] With your historic decision today, you have taken the next major step in that direction.

What does this merger mean for North Carolina? With negotiations scheduled to begin soon with Norfolk Southern on its lease of this rail line, we can now speak as a single voice and play a stronger hand in seeking a more flexible lease arrangement, an arrangement that can let us use this railroad in creative and innovative ways. We can look toward the day when we can implement the task force's major passenger recommendation: providing intercity service in the Charlotte-Greensboro-Raleigh corridor.

We can also look toward a number of intriguing possibilities that address both transportation and economic challenges. For example:

—We could market the merged railroad as a package with the state port at Morehead City.

—We could lease the railroad right of way for uses that take advantage of access to the port. These uses might include a fiber-optic communication cable or pipelines for shipping natural gas or crude oil.

—We could use rail access and timely, reliable rail service as inducements to industry along rail corridors in much the same way we use multilaned highways to attract new industry or to help existing industries to expand.

These are some of the possibilities that have been discussed, and we need to explore them and others that may arise. We also need to remember that railroads are an efficient, practical way to move people from one place to another. As time goes by, this will become ever more important to our transportation network. This may seem an outmoded concept in a year when the General Assembly has just adopted the most far-reaching, expensive highway construction program in this state's history, but it is not. Bear in mind that this highway program primarily will allow us to catch up on road building projects that have been neglected far too long. If we are to grow and prosper into the twenty-first century, we cannot travel by highway alone. Our airports—particularly our regional airports—our mass transit systems, and our railroads all have crucial roles to play in getting us from here, to there, to where we want to go in the future.

The potential of light rail and multimodal transportation, the possibilities that superconductivity experiments may provide—all must be taken into account as we prepare for tomorrow. What you have done here today is an important step in that preparation, in coming to grips with the challenges that lie ahead and in acting to meet those challenges. The single rail line you have forged here today is, in the words of your attorney, Allen Foster, "more than the sum of its parts."[5] It is now a unified ribbon of steel, stretching from Charlotte up and around to Morehead City, with the potential to become once again the economic "Tree of Life" foretold by Governor Morehead for the communities through which it travels.

I thank all of you who have been working on the railroad. You've done a great job. Now our challenge is to make this railroad work for us even better to fulfill its role as another major resource in making North Carolina a better place to work and live. It is a challenge we must meet if our state is to continue to grow and prosper. Working together, I know we will prevail.

---

[1]Joseph Caldwell (1773–1835), born in Lamington, N.J.; died in Chapel Hill; was graduated from College of New Jersey, 1791; honorary degrees. Mathematician; Presbyterian minister; astronomical advisor for laying of boundary separating North Carolina from South Carolina and Georgia, appointed 1807; public education advocate. First president, University of North Carolina, 1804–1812, reappointed 1817; career at UNC also included appointment as professor of mathematics, 1796, and presiding professor, 1797. Author, *A Compendious System of Elementary Geometry* (1822) and other works, including essays written under the pseudonym "Carlton" on the benefits of rail transportation for North Carolina. Powell, *DNCB*, I, 303–304; see also Joseph Caldwell, *The Numbers of Carlton, Addressed to the People of North Carolina, on a Central Rail-Road through the State* . . . (New York: G. Long, 1828).

Calvin Graves (1804–1877), born, died in Caswell County; admitted to state bar, 1827. Attorney; farmer; member, N.C. Constitutional Convention of 1835; represented Caswell County in state House, 1840–1845 (Speaker, 1842–1843), and Senate, 1846–1849 (Speaker, 1848–1849); member, N.C. Board of Internal Improvements, 1849–1854; Democrat.

Speaker Graves's deadlock-ending vote in favor of funding the North Carolina Railroad was indeed a politically courageous act. Western North Carolinians, desperate for rail service, endorsed a proposed north-south line from Danville, Va., to Charlotte, and it would have been logical for the senator from Caswell to back his co-regionists—especially because the railroad would have traversed his home county. Convinced, however, of the greater commercial benefit of an east-west route linking Goldsboro and Charlotte, he threw his support to the North Carolina Railroad. Unfortunately for Graves, his act of economic altruism estranged him from his fellow Democrats and ended his political career. John L. Cheney, Jr. (ed.), *North Carolina Government, 1585–1979: A Narrative and Statistical History* (Raleigh: Department of the Secretary of State, 1981), 310, 312, 313, 315, 316, hereinafter cited as Cheney, *North Carolina Government*; Thomas E. Jeffrey, "Internal Improvements and Political Parties in Antebellum North Carolina, 1836–1860," *North Caro-*

lina Historical Review 55 (spring 1978): 138–141; Powell, *DNCB*, II, 342–344, and *North Carolina through Four Centuries* (Chapel Hill: University of North Carolina Press, 1989), 288–289.

[2]"An Act to Authorize the Department of Transportation to Condemn Property for Railroad Corridor Preservation, to Expand the Authority of the Department to Provide Rail Revitalization Funds, and to Permit Cities and Counties to Preserve Railroad Corridors," was ratified July 11, 1989. *N.C. Session Laws, 1989*, I, c. 600.

[3]Arnold Borden McKinnon (1927–), born in Maxton; resident of Norfolk, Va.; A.B., 1950, LL.B., 1951, Duke University; was graduated from Advanced Management Program, Harvard Business School; U.S. Army, 1946–1947. Attorney; began career with Southern Railway Co. (later Norfolk Southern Corp.), 1951, as law assistant; vice-president, law and accounting, Southern Railway Co., 1971–1982; executive vice-president, marketing, 1982–1987, chairman, president, chief executive officer, 1987–1992, Norfolk Southern Corp. *News and Observer*, December 27, 1992; *Who's Who in America, 1992–1993*, II, 2280.

[4]"This corridor together with an aggressive entry into railroad operations would allow these companies to play a significant role in the state's transportation future. This could include passenger, freight, and other railroad activities." The North Carolina Railroad, extending from Charlotte to Goldsboro, and the Atlantic and North Carolina Railroad, linking Goldsboro to Morehead City, spanned two-thirds of the state and formed the corridor mentioned in the quotation. *Interim Report of the Governor's Rail Passenger Task Force* ([Raleigh]: North Carolina Department of Transportation, [1989]), 8.

[5]The comment Martin attributed to C. Allen Foster was accurate. Foster (1941–), born in Monroe, La.; resident of Gibsonville; B.A., Princeton University, 1963; B.A. in jurisprudence, 1965, M.A. in jurisprudence, 1971, Oxford University (Brasenose College), England; J.D., Harvard Law School, 1967. Attorney in private practice, 1967–1973, 1975–1981, 1983–1988; partner in law firm of Patton, Boggs and Blow, Greensboro, since 1988; secretary, director, general counsel, Spanco Industries, Inc., Greensboro, 1973–1975; commercial and labor arbitrator, since 1981; senior lecturer in law, Duke University, since 1981; U.S. rep. to International Energy Agency Dispute Resolution Centre, Paris, since 1983; advisor, Governor's Task Force on Passenger Rail Transportation, since 1988; author. C. Allen Foster, letter to Jan-Michael Poff, February 2, 1994.

AVERY COUNTY CHAMBER OF COMMERCE

LINVILLE, AUGUST 22, 1989

It's good to be back here in the "Fraser Fir Capital of the World." I want you to know, when Dottie told me she wanted a nice "fur" for Christmas, I knew where to get a nice tree to decorate the Mansion for Christmas!

It's good to be here and enjoy some good country cooking with my friends here in the Avery County Chamber of—Economic and Community Development?—Commerce. Tomorrow I'll be in Spruce Pine with Secretary Broyhill to celebrate the new Ethan Allen furniture plant, and on Thursday I'll be speaking up for [the] Champion paper mill in Canton and the thousands of jobs we're about to lose.[1]

Tonight I want to talk about progress: where we are, where we are going, and how we plan to get there from here. Contrary to what you might have been hearing from Raleigh, North Carolina did move forward during the past General Assembly. There are signs of reform and progress in many areas. Tonight, I want to share some of those with you.

As leaders of government and business in Avery County, you are no strangers to progress. You've been working together long and hard to develop new ideas, to strengthen the local economy, and to provide more and better jobs for your friends and neighbors. That kind of cooperative partnership has made the story of progress in Avery County a real success story. Because of your own success, you'll appreciate even more what we are trying to do in Raleigh with education and transportation, two key building blocks of true progress. But before I get into that, let me take a moment to salute you for your accomplishments.

Already one of the top twenty-five vacation meccas in North Carolina, Avery County earns over $50 million each year from travel and tourism, its number-one industry. Now the whole nation is finding out what we in North Carolina have known all along: The July issue of *Snow Country* magazine named Avery County one of the top twenty fastest growing ski counties in the nation, actually ranking sixteenth in America.[2] Now that's what I call a real ski lift.

Your partnership for progress has been riding that ski lift up the mountains of industrial recruitment, as well. In just a few short months, January of 1990, Fasco Controls will open its new plant at the old Norris site, bringing 250 new jobs to the area—and that will be a definite plus for economic growth and diversity in Avery County.[3]

Increased growth brings with it increased opportunity, but taking advantage of opportunity means managing that growth: coordinating industrial development with tourism, agriculture, and the environment. Here, too, you've already made great progress, obtaining funds from the General Assembly to develop a growth management plan with the state, through Jim Broyhill's new Department of Economic and Community Development, your county commissioners, and the Avery County Economic Development Commission. When it's completed in two years, this growth management plan will be a model for other North Carolina counties seeking to develop a coordinated response to economic growth and environmental protection.

The key to successful development anywhere in North Carolina—or anywhere in the nation, I believe—is mapping and managing a pathway to progress. You've done that in Avery County. Your elected leadership and other members of the local Economic Development Commission are to be congratulated for their roles in making that progress possible.

Fortunately, in keeping with that theme of mapping and managing progress, I'm glad to say that we in Raleigh are trying to help, too. You saw news reports last week about my appointments to the Western North

Carolina Environmental Council.[4] In the coverage of that announcement, you probably heard critics charging that the council was "weighted" toward timber interests.[5] I feel compelled to challenge that assertion by point[ing] out that seven of the seventeen members represent environmental interests, including the Sierra Club and the North Carolina Nature Conservancy, and Hugh Morton, Sr. Apparently, they weren't radical enough for the critics. Only three have direct ties to the timber industry—a fourth, if you count a tree farmer with a strong environmental reputation, who chairs the state parks commission. The remaining seven could best be described as holding objective positions, like the mayor of Franklin and the chief of the Cherokee Nation.[6]

Always, we will hear criticism. That goes with progress. But I believe this council will serve the interests of the twenty-three western counties with skill and judgment.[7] The council's work represents our ongoing effort to continue to balance growth and environmental concerns. Just as you have made progress to develop a local growth management plan, the council will be charged with that task on a regional level.

Progress, I believe, also is measured by the paved mile, and I'm proud to point out that the new road-building package adopted by the General Assembly offers us plenty of measuring sticks. This highway package, developed over two years by a blue-ribbon task force appointed by the legislature and me, is the most ambitions construction package ever in North Carolina history. The road package will follow through on my campaign proposal to build 3,000 miles of uninterrupted, four-lane, divided highways reaching within ten miles of 96 percent of our population. Sounds great, doesn't it? But listen to how good it sounds for Avery County: It means completing the job of four-laning N.C. 105, from Boone to Linville; U.S. 19 and 19E to N.C. 194, in Ingalls; N.C. 194, from U.S. 19E to U.S. 221; and U.S. 221 from Linville to South Carolina.

Other highway projects are likely to be moved up in our planning process, including the upgrading of N.C. 194 from U.S. 19E, near Elk Park, to the western corporate limits of Banner Elk. The entire High Country and Smoky Mountain economy will benefit from the completion of I-26 as a two-state project from Mars Hill to Erwin, Tennessee. In addition, we're going to pave a lot of dirt roads. Of the remaining 144 miles of unpaved roads in Avery County, 115 miles should be improved by the year 2001, with the twenty-nine remaining miles to be improved by 2004.

I don't have to tell you how important these road improvements are to Avery County. Better roads bring more industry, and more industry brings better jobs for our citizens. Better roads and better jobs create a broader tax base and more revenue to improve our schools: Those are the critical building blocks to a better future.

Unfortunately, the largest highway package in our state history, bringing us all those divided highways, is itself a divided highway. One lane of this package leads to much needed highway progress, like those projects I've just mentioned. The other lane leads to a big pothole, which the state budget is going to hit, and hit hard, in 1991.

I regret that the General Assembly raided the Highway Fund, for two years, to pay for other expanded items in the state budget—which they won't have the money to pay for after the two years. I predict that state leaders will be in a serious bind within two years, with no way to fix that budgetary pothole. By using one-time money for major expansions and pay raises, this threatens the fiscal integrity of state government. This scheme was the brainchild of the chairman of the Senate Finance Committee, who boasts that this was just "creative financing."[8] Well, it was the same kind of creative financing that has Governor Dukakis in such a fiscal mess in "Mess"-achusetts.[9]

While increasing teacher salaries and improving our educational system are important goals, I proposed a way to reform those old, outdated teacher pay schedules with a one-cent sales tax [increase]. I'm proud to say that the new teacher pay schedule, which ends a seven-year freeze that began in the previous administration, is indeed similar to one I proposed. But it doesn't go far enough. We needed the one-cent sales tax proposal for schools to move toward true, lasting, educational reform. Nobody wants any such tax increase if it just goes to spend more money on the same results. That's why I proposed the tax only if it was tied to merit pay, as in the career ladder.

You will continue to hear me talk about career ladder—better pay for better teachers—because I believe it is the best way to improve our teachers' performance and our students' learning. It establishes accountability. While the General Assembly rejected my proposal to implement the career ladder statewide, despite a record of success in sixteen pilot programs, I believe that it will catch on with our teachers; and ultimately, the teachers will bring the career ladder, or some form of it, into North Carolina's public schools.

I promise you I have not ended the fight to improve teacher salaries and performance. Yes, I want to get our teachers' pay to the national average, but I also want to get our students' achievement up to the national average, too. I believe we deserve results for the billion dollars a year we're adding to schools. The General Assembly has agreed to permit local school systems to choose some form of career development plan they would like to implement, if any. I regard this as an important next step.

I know that you know how important education is to your community. I underscore this point, though, because you have the power to help decide how to improve the opportunities for your children's future education. I'm asking you to join me in achieving progress in our educational system the same way you are working to achieve progress in the economic sector: by teamwork and cooperation.

Local businesses can help reduce our dropout rate and encourage academic excellence by encouraging students to stay in school. Follow the example of your chamber board members who adopted a student for a day through the Shadowing Program and showed those students how a good education relates to the workplace. We may not have the state funds to pay for every educational reform, but we can still begin to reform the system through determination and involvement. You can be a part of that educational reform, just as you are a part of the economic reform here in Avery County. Look around, adopt a student, adopt a school, and promote excellence to education in North Carolina.

Yes, here in North Carolina, and here in Avery County, we know where we are, we know where we are going, and we are working hard to develop responsible, effective ways of getting there. Together we are a partnership for progress. It is a partnership that is paying big dividends now. It is a partnership that will pay even bigger dividends in the future.

---

[1]Opposition from Tennessee to an EPA waste-water discharge permit for Champion International Corporation's Canton, North Carolina paper mill threatened the plant's viability and the livelihoods of its 2,200 employees. Objection to the license stemmed from the composition of effluent evacuated from the plant and into the Pigeon River, which ultimately flowed into the Volunteer State. Martin appealed to the EPA on behalf of Champion at a hearing on August 24, 1989, defended the company's willingness to clean up the discharge, and emphasized the economic benefits the paper maker brought to his state and its western neighbor. The governor offered similar testimony a year earlier; see Poff, *Addresses of Martin*, I, 721–725, for the text of that speech and further information on the Canton mill. The U.S. Environmental Protection Agency awarded Champion a waste-water permit in September 1989.

[2]See David Rowan, "Where the Growth Is," *Snow Country*, July 1989, 28–31. The chart on page 29 ranks Avery seventeenth among the nation's nineteen fastest-growing ski counties.

[3]The necessity of layoffs at the Fasco Controls plant in Shelby halted the company's plans to open auxiliary production facilities at the former Norris Industries site near Pineola. Mary Ellen Foster, Avery County Chamber of Commerce, letter to Jan-Michael Poff, October 4, 1993.

[4]Executive Order Number 92, signed May 31, 1989, established the Western North Carolina Environmental Council. *N.C. Session Laws, 1989*, II, 3129–3133.

[5]Critics of the composition of the membership of the Western North Carolina Environmental Council included representatives of the Clean Water Fund of North Carolina, Blue Ridge Environmental Defense League, and the Western North Carolina Alliance. Monroe Gilmour, leader of the movement that halted timber harvesting in the Asheville watershed, called the council a "'Trojan horse for pushing the [timber] industry agenda at the expense of the environment.'" Speaking of the Western North Carolina Alliance and its efforts against clear-cutting, Gilmour said "'It seems interesting that an organization that

generated a petition with over 16,000 signatures is not represented.'" *Asheville Citizen,* August 17, 1989.

⁶Apart from ex-officio members and the lieutenant governor, who served as chairman, Martin named eighteen persons to the board; see press release, "Governor Appoints Members to Western N.C. Environmental Council," Raleigh, August 16, 1989, Governors Papers, James G. Martin. The following biographies of the eighteen were compiled from information provided in the press release and by other supplemental sources, as listed:

William A. Banks, of Burnsville; president, Banco Lumber, Inc.; board member, Multiple-Use Council, and of Western Carolina Development Assn.; board chairman, Blue Ridge Savings and Loan.

Joe Eugene Beck, associate professor, environmental health sciences, and director, Environmental Health Program, Western Carolina University; chairman, Technical Committee on Hazardous Waste, Governor's Waste Management Board.

Charles Alvin Brady III, of Sugar Grove; attorney; member, since 1989, past national director, Trout Unlimited, and president, Table Rock Chapter, N.C. Council of Trout Unlimited; member, N.C. Nature Conservancy. See also Charles Alvin Brady III, letter to Jan-Michael Poff, October 6, 1993.

Shirley Crisp, self-employed at Crisp and Crisp Contracting Co., Robbinsville; member, Graham County Social Services Board; board member, Graham County Chamber of Commerce.

Bjorn Martin Dahl, formerly of Fairview; resident of Vienna, Va. Career with U.S. Forest Service included branch chief, 1984–1988, policy analysis staff reviewing forestry policy and the national forest timber sale program; and forester supervisor, 1987–1992, for all national forests in N.C. See also Bjorn Martin Dahl, letter to Jan-Michael Poff, October 15, 1993.

David E. Henson, dentist from Franklin; Franklin mayor; chairman, Cherokee Historical Assn., and of the Region A Council of Governments; director, Cherokee Indian Museum.

Linda G. Hogue, third-grade teacher, Bryson City Elementary School; president, Nonpartisan Citizens Against Wilderness in Western North Carolina, and "an outspoken advocate of wise multiple use of public lands;" was married to a logger. See also *News and Observer,* March 18, 1990.

Lee Q. McMillan, resident of Crumpler; retired U.S. Navy commander; owner, Shatley Springs Inn, Mountain Impressions Printing, Ashe Memorial Works, and a marina; tobacco and Christmas tree farmer; president, Ashe County Tomorrow.

Richard Maas, of Weaverville; assistant professor of environmental science, and director, Environmental Quality Institute, University of North Carolina at Asheville; board member, Buncombe County Metropolitan Sewage District, and of Clean Water Fund of N.C.

Hugh MacRae Morton, Sr., tourism advocate; conservationist; president, Grandfather Mountain, Inc.; former chairman, Western N.C. Tomorrow, and of N.C. Botanical Garden Foundation; board member, Keep N.C. Beautiful. Previously identified in Poff, *Addresses of Martin,* I, 584n.

Christian Lewis Rust, of Hendersonville; senior engineer, department manager, Procter and Gamble, 1953–1959; vice-president, Booz, Allen, and Hamilton, Inc., 1960–1985; part-time consultant on waste reduction since retirement. See also Christian Lewis Rust, letter to Jan-Michael Poff, September 27, 1993.

Robert S. Scott, resident of Franklin; retired U.S. Army Reserve captain; reporter, *Asheville Citizen;* board member, Western N.C. Associated Communities; past president, Franklin Area Chamber of Commerce, and of Franklin Rotary Club. He was replaced on the council by Tom Rhodarmer, environmental affairs manager, 1988–1991, and corporate director, environmental affairs, from 1991, Dayco Products, Inc., Waynesville. Press release, "Governor Appoints Rhodarmer to the Western N.C. Environmental Council," Raleigh, October 19, 1989, Governors Papers, James G. Martin; and Tom Rhodarmer, letter to Jan-Michael Poff, September 28, 1993.

Charles H. Taylor, registered forester; managing director, Transylvania Tree Farms; member, state House, 1967–1971, and Senate, 1973–1974; vice-chairman, Western N.C.

Environmental Council; chairman, N.C. Parks and Recreation Council; elected to U.S. House of Representatives from North Carolina's Eleventh Congressional District, 1990, reelected 1992, 1994; Republican. Cheney, *North Carolina Government*, 541, 544, 545, 547; *News and Observer*, November 4, 1992, November 9, 1994; *North Carolina Manual, 1973*, 602–603, *1991– 1992*, 520.

Jonathan L. Taylor, of Cherokee, was chief of the Eastern Band of the Cherokee Indians.

William R. Thomas, Jr., of Cedar Mountain; award-winning environmentalist; thirty-three-year career with E. I. Du Pont de Nemours and Co. as research associate; cofounder, Friends of the Horsepasture, 1984, which won National Wild and Scenic River status for the watercourse in 1986; cofounder, Jocassee Watershed Coalition, 1987, formed to fight Duke Power's $3 billion pumped-water storage project, which the utility abandoned in 1989. Executive Committee member, since 1987, and chairman, 1989–1991, N.C. Chapter, Sierra Club; member, Western N.C. Alliance. See also William R. Thomas, Jr., letter to Jan-Michael Poff, November 15, 1993.

Sherry S. Thompson was self-employed as an apple farmer near Hendersonville.

John B. "Jack" Veach, of Asheville; retired forest products executive; past president, N.C. Forest Assn. and of Appalachian Hardwood Manufacturers, Inc.; past president, chairman, National Forest Products Assn. and of American Forest Institute; president, Asheville Chamber of Commerce, 1978.

Charles D. Woodard, resident of Sylva; executive director, Multiple-Use Council; board member, Western North Carolina Tomorrow; Forestry Commission chairman, Western North Carolina Development Assn. See also *News and Observer*, March 18, 1990.

[7]The twenty-three counties were: Alleghany, Ashe, Avery, Buncombe, Burke, Caldwell, Cherokee, Clay, Graham, Haywood, Henderson, Jackson, Macon, Swain, Madison, McDowell, Mitchell, Polk, Rutherford, Transylvania, Watauga, Wilkes, and Yancey. Press release, "Governor Appoints Members to Western N.C. Environmental Council," Raleigh, August 16, 1989, Governors Papers, James G. Martin.

[8]Senate Finance chairman Marshall Arthur Rauch defended his plan to transfer money from the Highway Fund to the General Fund, saying, "'At worst, we've saved taxpayers two years of paying additional taxes. At best, we avoid it altogether.'" Expanding state revenues would, he believed, compensate for any budgetary shortfall once the highway funds were restored, "'[b]ut if it doesn't, we'll revisit the issue in two years.'" *News and Observer*, July 27, 1989.

Rauch (1923–), born in New York, N.Y.; resident of Gastonia; was educated at Duke University; served in U.S. Army during World War II. Chairman, president, Rauch Industries, Inc.; director, treasurer, E.P. Press, Inc.; director, president, P.D.R. Trucking, Inc.; director, president, S.L. Rauch, Inc.; member, state Senate, 1967–1990; Democrat. *News and Observer*, August 11, 21, October 22, November 8, 1990; *North Carolina Manual, 1989–1990*, 282–283.

[9]The rising economic tide that swept the Bay State in the 1970s and 1980s, a phenomenon the *Boston Globe* named the "Massachusetts miracle," had ebbed by 1989. Unemployment rose. Locally headquartered minicomputer giants, especially Digital and Wang, and software producers such as Lotus, became uncompetitive. Congressional cuts in military spending, that Massachusetts politicians had demanded perennially, caused even more joblessness as defense contractors curtailed or closed operations. New England's plummeting real estate market crushed major financial institutions.

Private-sector economic troubles adversely affected the financial stability of the government of Massachusetts, the budget of which had grown 9 percent per year in the 1980s. By the end of the decade, wrote one observer, the state "essentially went bankrupt: spending had ballooned, revenues were falling and higher tax rates only decreased them more, services were cut, [and Governor] Dukakis," who touted the Massachusetts miracle in his failed campaign for U.S. president, "was ridiculed and announced his retirement from office." Barone and Ujifusa, *Almanac of American Politics, 1994*, 595.

Michael Stanley Dukakis (1933–), born in Brookline, Mass.; B.A., Swarthmore College, 1955; LL.B., Harvard University, 1960; U.S. Army, 1955–1957. Attorney; member, Massachusetts House of Representatives, 1962–1970; moderator, "The Advocates" public television program, 1970–1973; Massachusetts governor, 1975–1979, 1983–1991; Democratic nominee for U.S. president, 1988. *Who's Who in America, 1992–1993*, I, 923. Martin also maligned Massachusetts's fiscal affairs in remarks to the North Carolina League of Municipalities, October 4, 1988; see Poff, *Addresses of Martin*, I, 940, 948n.

NORTH CAROLINA TRUCKING ASSOCIATION

PINEHURST, SEPTEMBER 11, 1989

[Martin delivered a similar address to the North Carolina Bus Association, February 5, 1990.]

What a pleasure it is to join the North Carolina Trucking Association for its sixtieth anniversary celebration. You've developed quite a record of success over the past sixty years, serving your industry's needs here in North Carolina. That experience has guided the phenomenal growth of trucking in our state and will provide leadership far into the twenty-first century.

We've seen a lot of changes in those sixty years, and your association has learned a lot, too. At least you've learned enough to put the politicians last on the program before lunch and promise them a round of golf afterward so they'll keep the speeches short. Well, President Tyler, in honor of the association's sixtieth anniversary, I promise to be brief no matter how long it takes.[1]

Dr. Catlett has already discussed the rapid changes we've experienced in our economy due to increased technology, changes that continue to modify the way we do business.[2] Just look at the effect deregulation of the transportation industry has had on trucking. Trucks are larger, heavier, and equipped with more complex controls. Improved roads, economic growth, and increased competition have brought more of these trucks onto highways already overcrowded with private automobiles.

Under these conditions, we are beginning to view our truck drivers in the same way we view airline pilots: as highly skilled professionals who can safely handle complex equipment in complex situations. That emphasis on skill and safety increasingly requires our truckers to be well trained, experienced, and safety conscious. I'm proud to say that our North Carolina truckers are among the nation's best in all three of these areas. To maintain that reputation for excellence, and to ensure that other interstate truckers maintain the same level of expertise, the state of North Carolina is instituting changes that will promote industry growth and improve safety at the same time.

Progress, I believe, is measured in part by the paved mile, and I'm proud to say that the new road building package adopted by the General Assembly provides us with plenty of measuring sticks for progress.

This highway package, developed over two years by a blue-ribbon task force appointed by the legislature and me, working with a visionary secretary of transportation, Jim Harrington, is the most ambitious construction package in North Carolina history. We already have the largest state-maintained highway system in the country, but this highway plan will triple our construction program and will follow through on my 1987 proposal to build an uninterrupted network of four-lane, divided highways reaching to within ten miles of 96 percent of our population. Until now, the history of North Carolina transportation acclaimed the pioneering vision of John Motley Morehead, Cameron Morrison, and Kerr Scott.[3] This new commitment, Senator Goldston, will triple all that went before.

I don't have to tell you what good roads mean to economic development in our state. Good roads mean faster deliveries, and faster deliveries reduce inventory storage costs for business. Lower costs lead to increased productivity and that leads to economic growth, which means even more business for the trucking industry. Yes, I think you'll agree that better roads mean better business for North Carolina. Just think how much better business will be when I-40 is opened all the way from Barstow, California, to Wilmington.

Back in 1984 when I first ran for governor, I did an unprecedented and risky thing. I made one highway promise, but it was strategically important: to have all of I-40 under construction by 1988. We met that goal easily, with six months to spare, and now I expect to be cutting the ribbon opening the final segment of I-40 next summer—just nine months away. That just goes to show, by the way, that if you don't make any more promises than you can keep, you can keep more promises than you make! We've built a lot of other roads, too, thanks to the 1986 highway bill, so instead of more unpaved promises, we delivered a lot of unpromised paving. You tell me which way is better! And what's more, we're doing more than just paving the way. In other modes, we're promoting air freight, too, and rescuing railroad rights-of-way from abandonment, and working to restore railroad passenger service by next year.[4]

To bring our state into compliance with the Commercial Motor Vehicle Safety Act of 1986, the legislature approved requirements for a new commercial drivers license. As of April 1, 1992, all drivers will be required to take both a written and skills test to receive commercial licenses. Drivers with a clean record for the past two years will not have to take the skills test. This legislation also lowers the blood alcohol level for commercial drivers from .10 to .04 percent in North Carolina. Drivers blowing more than .04 will lose their license for one year on a first offense. If they're caught a second time, they will lose their commercial license for keeps. That's a tough standard, but we cannot afford anything that would undermine public confidence in the good reputation you have built for trucks. Requiring a single commercial drivers license for interstate trucking will go a long way toward getting the bad drivers off the road and improving safety for all of us.[5]

North Carolina has also joined a growing number of states with authority to adopt a uniform fuel tax reporting system. Interstate truckers may soon be able to report and pay the fuel-use tax for their total travel directly to the state. Each state will then serve as a clearinghouse for distributing taxes owed to other states. When the new uniform fuel tax reporting system is adopted, it will significantly reduce the paper logjam currently overwhelming the trucking industry. Instead of filing quarterly reports for each state you travel, you will submit one form and one check to the state of North Carolina. We will do the rest.[6]

In addition to streamlining the tax reporting system, we will simplify your permitting and licensing procedures by improving our existing one-stop shopping center for commercial truckers effective December 1989. We've been operating a limited one-stop service center for two months in each of the last two years. We will be one of the first states in the nation to set up such a service full time, year-round. This special center will be staffed by representatives of the Department [sic] of Motor Vehicles, the North Carolina Department of Revenue, the U.S. Internal Revenue Service, International Registration, and the Utilities Commission to take care of all your fees, permitting, licensing, and fuel tax needs. The center will be located in Raleigh, near I-40.

The legislature also approved a provision making North Carolina part of a growing movement to allow 53-foot trailers to travel on designated routes throughout the state, effective next January.[7] The North Carolina Department of Transportation is responsible for adopting rules for reasonable access to those routes by December 1. This provision will require significant investment by the trucking industry, but states are finding that they must approve longer trucks in order for their businesses to remain competitive with other states.

The 1989 General Assembly also provided for elimination of the $10 decal fee by January 1, after the U.S. Supreme Court ruled such fees unconstitutional. By eliminating the fee, North Carolina will lose $5.5 million in revenue, but avoid an eventual court battle. By moving ahead quickly to eliminate the fee, North Carolina has paved the way to become a member of the Base-State Fuel-Tax Compact in the East.[8]

Many of these innovations have grown out of an effort by the National Governors' Association and the North Carolina Motor Carriers Advisory Council to improve uniformity of regulations across state lines. Because the North Carolina Motor Carriers Advisory Council proved such a success in the two years it existed as an ad-hoc committee, I granted the body permanent status by executive order four months ago.

The council will now serve as a permanent forum for coordination and cooperation between state agency and industry representatives.[9]

These rapid and major changes in the trucking industry are designed to improve efficiency and highway safety by creating uniform requirements for all interstate truck drivers. I'm proud to state that North Carolina is considered a leader in motor carrier safety, and we want to keep that reputation intact. Our emphasis on safety must continue to grow as 53-foot trailers appear on North Carolina highways and equipment becomes even more complex. Some states are already experimenting with onboard computers that can track truck locations by satellite. Enforcement sections are also moving toward biometric identification on driver's licenses through fingerprints or retinal scans. Digitizing photographs on licenses will also allow photos to be transmitted across the country by computer.

As we build new roads into the future, we will also begin to think in terms of building intelligent highways instead of simply laying pavement. Highway sensors and central control points will someday communicate with onboard computers to inform motorists about traffic jams just around the bend, or the nearest accommodations or service stations, for example. General Motors is already experimenting with such systems in California. Some states are also innovating with using simulators in place of road tests for commercial licensing.

Better roads and better interstate enforcement are moving us toward the future. The trucking industry, too, must help meet the challenges and seize the opportunities that lie ahead. The North Carolina Trucking Association has provided vital leadership during the past sixty years, and believe me, we will look to you for your continued leadership well into the twenty-first century and beyond. Thank you for all that you mean to North Carolina.

---

[1]Ben J. Tyler (1933–), born in Loudon, Tenn.; was graduated from University of Tennessee, 1955, and UNC Senior Executive Program, 1982; twelve-year veteran, U.S. Army Reserve. President, Burlington Industries' Trucking Division, 1982–1990; vice-president, National Private Truck Council, 1985–1990; president, 1989, N.C. Trucking Assn., and of Alamance County Chamber of Commerce. Ben J. Tyler, letter to Jan-Michael Poff, February 1, 1993.

[2]Lowell B. Catlett (1948–), born in Dalhart, Tex.; resident of Las Cruces, N.Mex.; B.S., West Texas State University, 1973; M.S., New Mexico State University, 1974; Ph.D., economics, Iowa State University, 1980. Assistant professor, 1978–1982, associate professor, 1982–1986, and professor, since 1986, New Mexico State University. Lowell B. Catlett, letter to Jan-Michael Poff, February 3, 1993.

[3]Governors Morehead, Morrison, and Scott were widely known for emphasizing the relationship between transportation and economic growth. During his two terms in office, Morehead was a determined supporter of state-aided railroad development, highway construction, and navigation improvements. Morrison was instrumental in winning passage of the Highway Act of 1921, historic legislation authorizing a $50 million bond package that launched the construction of a 5,500-mile system of state highways; two years

later, he garnered a further $15 million in road bonds. The highway program contributed significantly to the transformation of North Carolina into a modern commonwealth during the 1920s. Kerr Scott's "Go Forward" program paved 14,000 miles of secondary farm-to-market roads. Corbitt, *Addresses of Scott*, ix–xxvi; Powell, *DNCB*, IV, 321–322, 328–330.

Morehead and Scott are identified elsewhere in this volume. Cameron A. Morrison (1869–1953), born near Rockingham; was buried in Charlotte. Attorney; mayor of Rockingham, 1893; elected to state Senate, 1900; governor, 1921–1925; member, U.S. Senate, 1930–1932, and of the U.S. House, 1943–1945; Democrat. Morrison's support of the Highway Act of 1921 earned him the nickname, "Good Roads Governor." *Biographical Dictionary of Congress*, 1538; Powell, *DNCB*, IV, 328–330.

[4]Revenue shortfalls caused Amtrak to terminate prematurely the Carolinian, its one-year experiment in rail passenger service between Charlotte and Richmond, in 1985. However, subsequent planning by the Governor's Rail Passenger Task Force and an annual state subsidy of $2 million resurrected the train nearly five years later. The new Carolinian, which crossed the piedmont daily from Charlotte to Rocky Mount and returned, made its inaugural run on May 11, 1990. *News and Observer*, May 12, 1990; Poff, *Addresses of Martin*, I, 747, 749n.

[5]See Title XII, "Commercial Motor Vehicle Safety Act of 1986," P.L. 99–570, *United States Statutes at Large*, Act of October 27, 1986, 100 Stat. 170–189. *N.C. Session Laws, 1989*, II, c. 771, secs. 2–19, brought North Carolina standards for commercial driver licenses into compliance with federal regulations.

[6]See "An Act to Authorize the Secretary of Revenue to Enter into Cooperative Agreements with Other States to Administer the Fuel Tax and to Make a Conforming Change to the Definition of Motor Carrier," ratified July 24, 1989, and effective January 1, 1990. *N.C. Session Laws, 1989*, II, c. 667, s. 1.

[7]"An Act to Amend the Limitations on Semitrailers on Certain North Carolina Highways" was ratified August 12, 1990. *N.C. Session Laws, 1989*, II, c. 790.

[8]The United States Supreme Court declared decal fees unconstitutional in *American Trucking Associations, Inc., et al., v. Scheiner, Secretary, Department of Revenue of Pennsylvania, et al.*; see *U.S. Reports, Volume 483*, 86–357, 266–267. *N.C. Session Laws, 1989*, II, c. 667, s. 2, changed the state's listing of vehicles for road taxes in accordance with the court's decision.

[9]Executive Order Number 91, signed May 18, 1989, made the North Carolina Motor Carrier Advisory Council a permanent entity. *N.C. Session Laws, 1989*, II, 3125–3128.

STATE EMPLOYEES ASSOCIATION OF NORTH CAROLINA

CHARLOTTE, SEPTEMBER 15, 1989

Good morning![1] Before I begin, I'd like to thank our immediate past executive director, Butch Gunnells; our legislative director, Alice Garland; and President Wijnberg for their cooperation during the past year.[2] You all did a terrific job representing the association membership, and we are grateful for your leadership and direction. Thank you.

I also look forward to working with our new executive director, Dr. Bob Berlam,[3] and all our new officers who are taking the reins of leadership for the coming year. I know I'll be seeing quite a lot of you in coming months.

At the end of the Second World War, he [Winston Churchill] was visited by a delegation from the Temperance League. One of the women in the group chastised him by saying, "Mr. Prime Minister, I've heard that if all the whiskey you've drunk since the war began were poured into this room, it would come all the way up to your waist." Churchill looked down at the floor, then at his waist, then all the way up to the ceiling. After a moment, he replied sorrowfully, "Ah, yes, madam. So much accomplished and so much more left to do."

Like Churchill, we've accomplished a great deal, but we still have much more to do if we are going to meet the goals we've established for our membership. I'll be working closely with the association to meet those goals. As you know, my door has always been open to SEANC officers and staff. We've had many meetings during past years to improve conditions so our membership can say with pride, "I work for the state of North Carolina."

Continuing that tradition of cooperation, for the second year in a row I appointed a special committee, chaired by my chief of staff, Phil Kirk, to discuss in detail each issue addressed in our policy platform.[4] Then we met with a similar committee from the association to discuss the platform further. These meetings have been highly profitable and will continue to be so in the future. In talking together, we found we agreed on many issues, disagreed on some others, and following standard bureaucratic procedures, we asked for more information on almost everything.

I remember, back when I submitted my first budget to the General Assembly early this year, your officers came to my office and politely but firmly urged me to see the error of my ways, and do better. What they said made sense, so I thought about it a while longer and submitted a new proposal. I promise that Butch Gunnells' imposing physique and the baseball bat he was hiding behind his back had nothing to do with my change of perspective. No, actually your association went about it the right way.

The second proposal I submitted called for a 4 percent salary increase for state employees to be paid for by a penny hike in the sales tax, coupled with a 2 percent merit pay option. The legislature approved the salary increase, but unfortunately they also approved a raid on the Highway Fund to pay for it. By failing to approve my permanent financing plan, the General Assembly will find itself in a serious budget crisis in two years.

I regret the short-term solution carried the day in the legislature. Not only have they jeopardized the stability of our state budget, but they'll probably come back to us in two years, wanting us to come up with a patchwork proposal to repair the damage. You know, dealing with the legislature on the state budget is a bit like what you go through when your supervisor comes into your office with a big smile and says, "You've been such a good employee, we're going to give you a bonus. If you could have anything you need in the whole world, for under $5.00, what would it be?"

Money is tight—the plan isn't perfect—but by working together, we still achieved a respectable pay raise for state employees. More importantly, we were able to persuade the General Assembly to set aside the money to reinstate merit pay. Together, we agreed on the need for funding the performance pay plan, and we were successful. In the last two months of this session of the General Assembly, it wasn't a question of whether the state employees would get a salary increase, but how much of a salary increase and merit pay they would get. I believe that was our number-one goal as state employees. Of course, more money would certainly be helpful if we are going to help you get anything you need in the world—for over $5.00.

Just as with North Carolina's teachers, I believe state employees are career professionals and therefore should be provided opportunities for career growth, something besides a cost-of-living increase. The salary structure we have now is not based on career growth. We need to adjust the present system to allow for more flexibility. The Salary Adjustment Fund remains a top priority with you and with me. Unfortunately, the General Assembly has cut the funding I've asked for in recent budgets. I will continue the fight, however, and have agreed to seek $6 million in salary adjustments next year. I will need your continued support on this proposal if we are to be successful.

But salary adjustments and merit pay aren't the only issues demanding our attention. The General Assembly, for the second time, rejected our plans for a model day care center for state employees on the Dorothea Dix campus. Next to salaries, day care is probably the most important issue confronting the majority of our state employees. I promise you we will continue to search for ways to address this issue. In this and in all other issues, your opinions will always be welcome.

I am also committed to thoroughly studying health and workplace standards for video display terminals. This is a relatively new, uncharted area for the state, but I have asked State Personnel Director Dick Lee to turn his attention to this issue.

We are also working to improve our retirement and insurance plans. Sometimes it seems insurance plans are like warranties: The thing that goes wrong is sure to be the one thing that isn't covered. I promise we will continue working with you to make certain our retirement and health insurance plans remain healthy.

I believe in the state employees and in our association. Without a doubt, professional state employees are the backbone of state government, and I applaud the association's continuing efforts to increase

professionalism among our membership. The strength of this association lies in its cohesive approach to problem solving. We are not polar-
ized between management and workers. We work together, as a team,
for the benefit of the entire group. That's why I'm a member, and that's
why I encourage my cabinet and staff to join and be active in SEANC.

You know, they say there are three kinds of people: those who make
things happen, those who watch things happen, and those who say
"What happened?" Well, we are the kind of people who are going to
make things happen. Together, we will define our goals, then work for
them until we succeed. I'll be right there, working with you and supporting our association throughout the next three years of my administration. You can take that to the bank. Thank you, and have a great
convention!

---

[1]Here Martin wrote: "Proud to be a state employee and SEANC member. Some day
delegate? Missed dance last night. So many at breakfast (Winston-Salem 3 years ago)."
The governor hosted breakfast for state employees' association convention delegates on
September 11, 1987, prior to his address to them in Winston-Salem. Poff, *Addresses of Martin*, I, 655.

[2]Durward Franklin "Butch" Gunnells III (1949–), born in Mobile, Ala.; resident of
Raleigh; B.A., Duke University, 1971; J.D., University of North Carolina, 1974. Staff attorney, North Carolina General Assembly, 1974–1977; staff attorney, assistant director and
general counsel, North Carolina County Commissioners Assn., 1977–1984; executive director, State Employees Assn. of North Carolina, 1984–1989; president, North Carolina
Soft Drink Assn., since 1989. Durward Franklin Gunnells III, letter to Jan-Michael Poff,
February 24, 1993.

Alice D. Garland (1951–), born in Greenville, Tenn.; resident of Raleigh; B.A., College
of William and Mary, 1973; Master of Urban and Regional Planning, University of North
Carolina at Chapel Hill, 1975. Chief lobbyist/policy and research director, State Employees Assn. of North Carolina, 1985–1989; assistant commissioner, N.C. Dept. of Insurance,
1990; government affairs director, ElectriCities of North Carolina, since 1990. Alice D. Garland, letter to Jan-Michael Poff, February 26, 1993.

Kay Cox Wijnberg (1943–), born in Indianapolis, Ind.; resident of Carrboro; was edu-
cated at University of North Carolina at Chapel Hill. Various positions with University of
North Carolina at Chapel Hill, since 1972, including director of administration, School of
Law, since 1985; president, State Employees Assn. of North Carolina, 1988–1989, and of
Chapel Hill-Carrboro League of Women Voters, 1991–1993. Kay Cox Wijnberg, letter to
Jan-Michael Poff, March 15, 1993.

[3]Robert A. Berlam (1936–), born in Providence, R.I.; bachelor's degree, Rhode Island
College, 1958; M.A., University of Rhode Island, 1965; Ph.D., Nova University, 1974. Government relations director, National Assn. of State Boards of Education, 1976–1978; managing director, Close-Up Foundation, 1978-1984; staff and faculty development director,
N.C. Dept. of Community Colleges, 1985-1989; executive director, State Employees Assn.
of North Carolina, since 1989. *News and Observer*, November 15, 1992.

[4]Phillip James Kirk, Jr. (1944–), secretary, N.C. Dept. of Human Resources, 1985-1987;
chief of staff to Governor Martin, 1987-1989; became president, N.C. Citizens for Business
and Industry, December 1989. Previously identified in Poff, *Addresses of Martin*, I, 60n; see
also "New President Phil Kirk Will Lead the Association into the 1990s," *North Carolina*,
December 1989, 12-15; *News and Observer*, November 14, 1989.

PRESS RELEASE: GOVERNOR MARTIN ESTABLISHES
HURRICANE HUGO RELIEF FUND

RALEIGH, SEPTEMBER 26, 1989

[Hurricane Hugo hurtled ashore at Charleston, South Carolina, before midnight on September 21, 1989. It churned through the Palmetto State, struck Charlotte in the early morning of the twenty-second, and crossed North Carolina's western Piedmont on a northwesterly track. Later that day, Martin surveyed stricken areas by helicopter with Charlotte mayor Sue Myrick. He also approved a request from Charlotte city and Mecklenburg County governments for National Guard assistance in stemming the "looting, break-ins and thefts that broke loose in Hugo's aftermath."

President Bush declared Union, Mecklenburg, Gaston, and Lincoln counties disaster areas on September 25, enabling residents there to claim federal disaster assistance. Another twenty-five North Carolina counties were added to the list by October 5. One of the worst storms in the state's history, Hugo caused $964 million in damage and took seven lives; nationally, it killed forty-one people. Combined property losses in the United States and the Caribbean totaled approximately $9 billion. *Charlotte Observer*, September 23, 24, 1989; *News and Observer*, September 23, October 6, 1989, September 22, 1990; see also press releases, "President Bush Issues Disaster Declarations for Mecklenburg, Lincoln, Gaston, and Union Counties," Raleigh, September 25, 1989, and "Governor Proclaims State of Disaster in North Carolina," Raleigh, October 3, 1989, Governor's Papers, James G. Martin.]

Governor Jim Martin and Secretary of Crime Control and Public Safety Joe Dean Wednesday established a North Carolina Hugo Relief Fund to channel contributions to people who need assistance the most. "Many North Carolina counties have been hit much harder than people realize," Governor Martin said. "This relief fund will help us assist those who will not benefit from existing emergency programs."

Governor Martin said the fund will help channel financial contributions to people who need assistance. The money will be distributed on a per-capita basis in counties where it is most needed. Governor Martin praised the efforts of businesses, churches, and public service organizations to create similar relief efforts across North Carolina.

Tennessee governor Ned McWherter Tuesday notified Governor Martin that many organizations, including churches, power distributors, and others in his state have sent assistance to North Carolina.[1] In a telegram to Governor Martin, Governor McWherter said that Tennessee "will respond with any resources we have which can accommodate the people of North Carolina."

"Thank you for the generous offer of assistance from the kind and caring people of Tennessee," Governor Martin wrote to Governor McWherter in a telegram to the Tennessee governor. "Hurricane Hugo dealt us a very severe blow; your offer of help means a great deal. Thank your citizens on our behalf."

---

[1]Ned McWherter (1930–), born in Palmersville, Tenn. Farmer; businessman; member, 1969–1986, Speaker, 1973–1986, Tennessee House of Representatives; elected governor of Tennessee, 1986, reelected 1990; Democrat. Barone and Ujifusa, *Almanac of American Politics, 1992,* 1144, 1149.

MARKET ACCESSIBILITY SESSION
SOUTHEAST UNITED STATES-JAPAN ASSOCIATION

Tokyo, October 6, 1989

As I said in my opening remarks to the session this morning, I am excited to be able to participate in this breakout session o[n] "Market Accessibility." This issue is at the forefront of the trade relations dialogue between our countries. It is an issue of great importance to our economic growth and to the prosperity of our citizens. We have an opportunity today, perhaps not to resolve this issue, but to offer some constructive suggestions that can help our countries meet their individual goals while building a stronger economic partnership.

North Carolina is in a special position to contribute to this dialogue because our state exports more to your country than it imports. We have strong markets for our agricultural and chemical products, for lumber and furniture, for paper and textiles, and we have growing markets for other products like medical, biochemical, and telecommunications equipment. We are proud of our trade arrangements. They are important to our state and to our state's sustained economic growth. We realize, however, that the trade between our country and yours is drastically out of balance and that this situation must be rectified if the economic relationship between the United States and Japan, and between North Carolina and Japan, is to continue to grow and prosper.[1]

Japan's distribution systems are seen as major obstacles to U.S. exporters seeking visibility in your markets. While we respect the cultural, economic, and historical conditions that have limited the accessibility of Japan's markets for many products, we request your understanding and dynamic assistance in bringing out the fair playing field our exporters are offered in other markets and generally support in our own market. On our part, we intend to do all we can to keep an open market for your products so that mutual prosperity can evolve from a more balanced trading platform. This, rather than a succession of import restraints from each side, would ensure the best values for our citizens and the economic good health that is our mutual challenge for the years ahead.

I'm sure that we will hear many other reasons, from many different perspectives, for our current trade challenge during today's session. I hope that as we discuss this issue here today, our discussion will be framed in the spirit of friendship and cooperation we have developed over the years. I hope we can concentrate on looking for cooperative opportunities between our great nations. Others have found the symptoms of our division. We must find the remedy.

Because North Carolina has developed such a strong export program with Japan, we think we have a unique ability to contribute to meeting this challenge. We have the know-how to work with our Japanese counterparts in seeking ways to increase trade and market accessibility, ways that will prove beneficial to both countries.

I announced earlier today that I will be forming a Japan Business Council in North Carolina, a council of top North Carolina and Japanese business officials in our state who will work on common challenges and opportunities.[2] The major purpose of this council will be to ensure mutual understanding and early attention to problems affecting Japanese investment in our state. But I will advise this council that I will also welcome their thoughts on what should be done on the issues of market accessibility that we should share with our federal representatives and the government of Japan. I am confident that if we approach the issue using these resources, we can make a meaningful contribution to resolving this challenge.

To resolve any challenge, of course, we must begin, and we are doing just that here today. As we begin, I urge all of us to remember how far cooperation and friendship have brought us, and how far they can take us, as partners for economic growth for our countries and our people. I also hope we can take advantage of this conference, and the friendship we have built and nurtured from previous conferences, to develop ideas and approaches that can serve as models in the process of adjusting conditions for trade that impede its flow in either direction.

I look forward to exploring this issue with you today. I am confident that our exploration will lead us to a common ground of mutual cooperation and an even stronger alliance.

---

[1]North Carolina exported $5.4 billion in agricultural and manufactured goods in 1988, yielding a trade surplus of $69.8 million, a state record. Japan absorbed approximately 15 percent of those exports, making it the state's largest foreign trading partner, Martin told a Duke University audience on March 7, 1989. He also noted that Japanese business investment in the state exceeded $1 billion during the previous eight years. Over sixty Japanese companies maintained operations in North Carolina, with thirty-eight of them engaged in manufacturing; furthermore ASMO, Central Yoshida, Deere-Hitachi, Kawai

American, and NGK Ceramics announced new factories in 1988 that were projected to employ a total of 990 people.
[2]The North Carolina-Japan Business Council was to be comprised of three senior Tar Heel business leaders and representatives of the three Japanese business organizations in Charlotte, the Triad, and the Triangle. Martin, in his opening remarks at the Southeast United States-Japan Association meeting, October 6, 1989, dubbed the council "the first of its kind in the nation."

SMALL BUSINESS DEVELOPMENT CONFERENCE

RALEIGH, OCTOBER 23, 1989

[The remarks to the Small Business Development Conference, below, were similar to those Martin delivered at the launching of the state chapter of the Inc. Council of Growing Companies, Raleigh, December 6, 1989.]

Welcome to the State Treasurer's 1989 Informational Conference on Financing Small Business Development in North Carolina. I am pleased to see such a well-represented group of our state's business leaders here to discuss how better to do business and economic development in North Carolina. Small business and its continued development in North Carolina is an important agenda, and I am glad Treasurer Boyles asked me to be here today.[1]

For many years, North Carolina has been recognized both nationally and around the world as an outstanding state in which to do business.[2] In both 1987 and 1988, our state was number one in the nation with the most new manufacturing plant announcements. Our state has enjoyed strong economic growth across the board; 1988 was another record year. New and expanded businesses invested $6.2 billion; there was a net gain of 144,000 new jobs. That means that over the last five years, we averaged better than $5 billion per year and 100,000 jobs per year—and the year's average unemployment rate fell to 3.6 percent, the lowest in ten years!

This reputation and record did not develop overnight, nor did it occur by chance. Leaders from all walks of life, from the mountains to the coast, from big business and small businesses, all of these have worked diligently to make North Carolina's business climate what it is today: the better business climate.

Small business is the backbone of our state and national economy. According to a Dun and Bradstreet report issued earlier this year, small businesses are expected to contribute more than half of the 2.6 million new jobs to be created this year. Small businesses, those with fewer than 100 employees, historically account for nearly 56 percent of all new jobs created. In North Carolina, the percentage is significantly higher.

Companies with fewer than 100 employees account for nearly three quarters of the 400,000 jobs that have been created in our state over the past four years. Add to that statistic the fact that over 95 percent of businesses operating in our state are classified as "small," and you have a bright picture of small business in North Carolina.

More and more people each year have been bitten by the entrepreneurial bug and started their own businesses. Nearly forty years ago, some 50,000 new businesses were created each year. Now, almost 700,000 are begun each year. Here in North Carolina, this explosion in the small business sector of the market has added significantly to our economic base.

Yes, small business is alive and well in North Carolina, but just like the state's overall economic climate, it did not happen overnight. North Carolina is an attractive business address for many reasons. Our workforce is dedicated and hardworking. We are a ready-to-work state! We have one of the best statewide highway systems in the nation—and have just begun a commitment to make it much better. The state's community college system and its training programs provide excellent opportunities for employee training, and North Carolina is made up of outstanding communities that offer a quality of life that is second to none.

But there is something else that makes our state attractive to businesses of all sizes. We are a fiscally responsible state. We have taken the steps necessary to make fiscal policy conducive to business development and economic opportunity. We have been working hard to maintain an environment in North Carolina that will support and encourage the development and growth of small businesses.

Nineteen eighty-seven was a very productive year for us, and our state instigated a series of new financing initiatives designed to provide small firms greater access to capital resources. In cooperation with the state treasurer, it is now possible for up to $30 million of state General Fund reserves and highway funds to be invested in venture capital companies.[3]

We established a new pooled industrial revenue bond program to allow small firms greater availability of this low-interest financing. Pooled IRBs have been issued totaling $8.15 million. Right now the state Department of Economic and Community Development is processing twenty-seven applications totaling $37 million for two upcoming bond issues.[4]

We created a new, statewide SBA certified development company so small businesses will have improved access to federal loan and loan guarantee programs.[5] Also in 1987, the General Assembly enacted a repeal of the inventory tax, which I had proposed in 1985; since that time, we have seen the number of state and regional distribution centers locating across North Carolina increase tremendously. Other legislation addressed rural economic development activity, including the creation of the Industrial Building Renovation Program. In the first eighteen months of this program, it has helped create over 4,200 new jobs as it made commitments for $4 million in funding. In 1989, new legislation allows the use of money for the Industrial Building Renovation Fund to provide water and sewer to proposed manufacturing or industrial projects in the twenty-five most severely distressed counties, which also qualify for the jobs tax credit.[6]

Also during this past session of the General Assembly, the Small Business Division of the Department of Economic and Community Development led the lobbying efforts to repeal the intangibles tax on venture capital companies. By rolling back this law, we expect to entice more venture capital firms to establish operations in North Carolina, thus creating more financial opportunities for our fastest growing businesses.[7]

One other vital ingredient: the personal touch of our treasurer, Harlan Boyles. It seems two cows had just returned to pasture from [a] milking session [incomplete].

Sound fiscal leadership, combined with our loyal, hardworking people, and our many natural resources, and the personal touch, have made and will continue to make North Carolina the better business climate.

---

[1]Harlan Edward Boyles (1929–), elected state treasurer, 1976, and returned in subsequent elections; Democrat. Previously identified in Poff, *Addresses of Martin*, I, 41n; see also *News and Observer*, November 4, 1992.

[2]At this point in his prepared text, Martin jotted "*Business Week*—one state stood out. *Manufacturing Week*—same state . . . which one?" The answer to the governor's rhetorical question was North Carolina.

[3]*N.C. Session Laws, 1987*, II, c. 751.

[4]*N.C. Session Laws, 1987*, I, c. 517.

[5]*N.C. Session Laws, 1987*, I, c. 214, s.1(3).

[6]The Industrial Building Renovation Program described by Martin was established as the Industrial Development Fund; see *N.C. Session Laws, 1987*, II, c. 830, s. 111. *N.C. Session Laws, 1989*, II, c. 754, s. 54, ratified August 10, was the "new legislation" to which the governor referred.

The renovation fund was "designed to assist industries in our less-developed counties by providing $1,200 for each new job created, up to a total of $250,000," explained Martin at the Harriet and Henderson yarn mill grand reopening, August 30, 1989, in Clarkton. At that time, the program was financing thirty-eight projects in twenty-four counties across the state; one of the first to be completed was the water tower Bladen County needed to ensure the expansion of the Harriet and Henderson plant.

[7]"An Act to Exempt Venture Capital Companies from Intangibles Tax," *N.C. Session Laws, 1989*, II, c. 704, was ratified July 31, 1989.

BUSINESS COMMITTEE FOR EDUCATION AWARDS

Charlotte, October 26, 1989

My fellow educators and friends of education, welcome to the 1989 Governor's Business Awards in Education.[1] It's a pleasure for me to be here in Charlotte to honor some of our state's most outstanding teachers. It is also a pleasure to recognize a few of the many businesses in our state that are helping to educate our young people as part of their corporate responsibility.[2]

Back in 1963, President Lyndon Johnson proclaimed, "We have truly entered the Century of the Educated Man."[3] Well, that was 1963, during the Age of Sexspeak! Yet, just twenty-six years later, technological advancements have so far outstripped our system of education that even those who can read and write are being left behind. No longer can a college graduate assume that he or she has the necessary skills to perform adequately in the job market.

Through complacency and inattention, we have allowed our education system to fall behind. LBJ's century of the educated person has quickly turned [in]to the Century of the Functional Illiterate. Even by the 1960 standards, we have fewer dropouts and fewer unable to read, but by 1989 standards we have more who cannot read well enough and use math well enough.

You all know that North Carolina ranks last in the nation in SAT scores. That is painfully well known. Maybe if we had faced up to the pain of being next to last, we might have decided years ago to do something about it. Instead, we made excuses: A high[er] percentage of our students take the SAT than among those states with the highest averages. Yes, but many states have a higher percentage [of] participation than we. Among all states with over half the students taking SAT, we're still last. No matter how you cut it—among states with names with the initial *N*, among states with two-word names, among Appalachian states, whatever—we're last.

What are we going to do about it? We're going to bring those scores up, that's what. Let's not fool around with gimmicks, like having fewer students take the test! Let's help them do better.

How do we propose to do that? Will we prompt our children to achieve by answering multiple-choice questions? Are we going to drill them in arithmetic, grammar, and history? Will we give them old SAT tests for practice, to sharpen their skills? Yes, these activities will very likely help to improve our students' SAT scores and basic skills. Superintendent Etheridge has proposed that, and I think we ought to do it.

Improving basic skills alone is not the only goal of our educational reform movement, but for years we've acted like it was not a very important goal. Some say that we should not teach the test. That's silly. For those who want to go to college, we should at least teach what college admissions require. Then we can go on to other education goals.

To compete in today's world, we do need to structure our educational system to encourage development of thinking and reasoning beyond the memorization of facts, and this process must start in the primary grades. But you can't do much thinking and reasoning if you don't know the fundamentals. Not even a computer will help if you don't know English and math.

We must find ways for teachers, parents, and community leaders to guide our young people so that learning becomes an interesting challenge and a pathway to the creative mind. Why is this necessary? Take a look for a moment at changes in the textile and furniture industries. Years ago, these industries were production oriented. Now competition has forced them to be product oriented, changing styles frequently, searching constantly for new combinations of function and attractiveness. In such a marketplace, creativity, reasoning, and thinking are essential. The same principle holds true in virtually every business and industry seeking to compete in the global marketplace.

We have to think beyond the basics if we hope to survive against the knowledge and creativity of our competitors in Europe and the Far East, but that's no reason to neglect the basics. That's precisely the area where they do far better than we. I recently returned from a trade mission to Japan. The chairman of Toyota had been asked how many functional illiterates worked at his plants. He tried to be kind: "By American standards, none—zero percent.["] By his standards, there were 10 percent illiterate, could not use [a] computer.

Can we raise our SAT scores while creating an atmosphere for lifelong learning? The work of the North Carolina Business Committee for Education proves that we can. We must do a better job getting college-bound students ready for college. The SAT is one of many indicators showing we have room for improvement, and that's only half the story. What about those students who will not go to college, who will go directly into the workforce? We need a much stronger commitment to prepare them for today's jobs.

Businesses are telling us they need better-educated workers. We need a career curriculum, not just a buffet of vocational courses. English, and math, and citizenship ought to be at the core of career education. That's today's five *R*s: reading, 'riting, 'rithmetic, respect, and responsibility. Then we should offer an introduction to office skills and tools that are relevant to today's jobs. We owe it to these young people, so that when they graduate, their diploma will mean something. It ought to be a warranty to show their first employer, and we should be prepared to back up this warranty by reprocessing those workers who cannot perform as warrantied. Right now the failure/defect rate is too high, and world competition proves it.

We've got a lot of work ahead of us, North Carolina. We've got a lot to be proud of, but it's time to go beyond that. This year our General Assembly set the stage for a profound reform, offering every school system, every schoolhouse, greater freedom from regulations, to allow more local decision making, more school-based decision making, and more pay for better teachers—according to local plans which the teachers must help devise and must support on a secret ballot.[4]

Why? What do we get in return? The only catch is that each school must evaluate what it is doing well and doing poorly, and set reasonable goals for improved student achievement. It might be SAT goals overall, and it might be SAT goals for the top 10 percent of the student body, the next 10 percent, and so on. It ought to include writing sample improvement, CAT [California Aptitude Test] scores for third grade, sixth, ninth, and eleventh grade. It should include basic attendance and drop-out/retention rates. It must include reasonable, achievable, measurable, important goals for students to do better, to do as well as they are capable of doing. That's what we get in return. The catch is that if a school does not show substantial progress in a few years, the extra money will be forfeited and the extra freedom will be replaced with central edict regulations—until you reorganize under new management and try again.

Now is that exciting, or what?

Howard Haworth likes to point out: "America's system of public education was designed seventy to eighty years ago. It should tell us something that no other country is copying us."[5] It's time to reorganize for the next century, and North Carolina is committed to school-based decision making, with better pay for better teachers as the way to get there, all based on higher standards for student performance.

I recently read an education covenant written by the Forsyth County Public Schools. In that covenant, our Forsyth County educators state:

> We believe that in the high country of the human mind lies the most exciting frontier for exploration.
> We believe that every person is endowed with incalculable power.
> We believe that the seeds of possibility lying at the core of our being can be brought to fruition only through caring and nurturing—and that it is our divine obligation and destiny to help not only ourselves, but others along the "Yellow Brick Road" to greater opportunity and human becoming.[6]

With that kind of commitment, with winners like you working together, we cannot fail to succeed. Congratulations, and keep up the good work.

---

[1] At this point, Martin inserted into his text, "Good to see legislators . . . miss them in Raleigh—."

[2] The teachers and businesses commended at this event were listed in the press release, "Governor Awards 32 for Excellence in Education," Raleigh, October 26, 1989, Governors Papers, James G. Martin.

[3] Vice-President Johnson described the transformation of the twentieth century, from the "Century of the Common Man" to the "Century of the Educated Man," in a commencement address at Tufts University, June 9, 1963. Martin quoted the line straddling pages 130–131 in Lyndon B. Johnson, "The Century of the Educated Man," *A Time for Action* (New York: Atheneum Publishers, 1964).

[4] The governor was briefly summarizing some of the provisions of Senate Bill 2.

[5] Howard H. Haworth (1934–), state commerce secretary, 1985–1987; elected chairman, 1988, State Board of Education. Previously identified in Poff, *Addresses of Martin*, I, 127n–128n. The quotation was properly attributed and is accurate, according to Haworth, although the date and specific occasion that prompted it were unknown. He recalled that he made the observation, as commerce secretary, while discussing the important relationship between economic development and an educated workforce. Bertha Deal, secretary to Howard H. Haworth, telephone conversation with Jan-Michael Poff, March 19, 1993.

[6] Neither the source nor accuracy of this quotation could be verified. A spokesman for the Winston-Salem/Forsyth County Public Schools, in an interview with the editor, March 8, 1993, denied that his school system had produced the covenant Martin cited.

EIGHTH NATIONAL RECYCLING CONGRESS

CHARLOTTE, NOVEMBER 1, 1989

[An advocate of recycling by both the public and private sectors, Martin addressed the topic of reusable resources in his remarks at the Mayor's Award of Excellence Banquet, February 2, 1990; the Decision-Makers Forum on Cutting the Cost of Waste, September 12, 1990; and the presentation of the 1991 Governor's Award of Excellence for Outstanding Achievement in Waste Management, May 21, 1992. See also his instructions to the Governor's Task Force on Recycling, January 26, 1990, pages 221–224, below.]

Ladies and gentlemen, welcome to the friendly state of North Carolina for this Eighth National Recycling Congress in our Queen City of Charlotte. I got all excited when I heard you were in favor of recycling Congress—I used to work there.

We're glad to have you here, and I know you're glad to have a chance to see old friends and to make new ones. Renewing acquaintances is one of the best things about these meetings, and I suppose this is especially true of a recycling conference. You know what they say about recycling: What goes around, comes around—again, and again, and again—and around, and around, and around!

Today I'm going to do something I don't often do. I'm going to talk trash in public.

In modern society, the goods and services available to us create an overwhelming amount of garbage: 3.6 pounds of trash per day, per person, according to the EPA—two-thirds of a ton a year. In the course of a year, we Americans throw away enough trash, about 160 million tons, to bury 2,700 football fields under mounds of garbage 10 stories high. What's worse, we don't pile it on football fields; no, we bury it under the ground. We're talking dirty, friends! Most people don't concern themselves with these statistics. They just dump their 3.6 pounds of garbage in the bag and leave it on the street corner to be collected.

Until recently, public knowledge of solid waste disposal ended at the trash can, but things are changing since the "garbage barge" debacle created such a stir on the nightly news.[1] As landfills reach their capacity, the question of how to handle solid waste responsibly is one more and more people are raising. Increased awareness of our waste disposal challenge unfortunately hasn't been matched by public support for new landfills and waste incinerators.

Recycling, though, does have broad public support. According to the National Solid Waste Management Association, however, 84 percent of the American public support recycling as a best solution to the solid waste disposal problem. Now, how do we get 84 percent to do it? We can take advantage of this support by developing recycling policies at the state level, by assisting local communities to implement those policies, and by encouraging recycling efforts in every home, and in every community of our state. Long-term planning and community support: That's what we are going to need to make a molehill out of the solid-waste mountain.

Here in North Carolina, we've taken the first steps in this direction. Along with other states, we're combining source reduction, recycling, resource recovery, and landfills in a comprehensive approach to waste management. Many of our businesses and industries are using waste minimization and recovery practices at plant sites. Our local governments are working to upgrade existing landfills and find sites for new ones.

In 1987, I set a goal for reducing North Carolina's use of landfills by 90 percent by the year 2000. I also called for a solid waste state revolving loan fund, an idea that was adopted by the 1989 General Assembly, that will help local governments get equipment and facilities for dealing with solid waste. North Carolina also has consolidated the state agencies that deal with waste issues into one central agency: the Department of Environment, Health, and Natural Resources. Now instead of bouncing between five or six state agencies, local governments know where to go to find the people who can help with their waste-disposal needs.

We've made other progress in coordinating efforts and planning for the long term. For example, the North Carolina General Assembly passed Senate Bill 111 that established a statewide, comprehensive, waste-management plan and waste reduction targets for local governments. This bill calls for local governments to establish recycling programs by July 1, 1991, and calls for 25 percent of the total waste stream to be recycled by January 1, 1993. Detachable rings on beverage containers are now prohibited—so Dr. Rathje's tie tack is illegal—and plastic bags and polystyrene foam containers must be recyclable.[2] A statewide recycling coordinator and field operation units will provide local governments with technical assistance and program development in recycling.

But government alone can't solve the problem. We must encourage business, industry, and private citizens to recycle, as well. One way to lead this effort is by personal example. That's why we're recycling paper, glass, and aluminum products at the Executive Mansion. On a larger scale, I've asked the Department of Transportation to recycle the paper and glass products they collect from along our roadsides as part of our Adopt-A-Highway program. The tons of trash these volunteers collect should keep the recycling centers working overtime.

Yet as you well know, collecting trash doesn't do much good if we don't have recycling centers to reclaim the waste and a market for recycled materials. In this sense, recycling is an economic, rather than an environmental, issue. Perhaps we in state government can once again set an example for business and industry across the state by recycling whenever possible. That's why I am announcing, today, a new recycling initiative in state government.

I have directed the departments of Administration, Transportation, and Environment, Health, and Natural Resources to develop an interagency task force to conduct a recycling feasibility study for state government. The task force will be directed to do two things: first, develop a coordinated approach to recycling in all state government offices; and second, to design for us a policy for purchasing recycled materials. Recycling paper and aluminum cans in state government snack bars and offices may encourage our state employees to bring recycling home and help develop community support for the idea. By purchasing recycled goods, we may also help create a demand and reduce the cost of recycled goods in the marketplace.

Communities all across North Carolina have joined in the recycling effort. As one example, the curbside recycling program operating right here in Mecklenburg County has gained national recognition for its outstanding success.

I believe that the responsible disposal of society's waste—solid waste, low-level radioactive and hazardous waste—is rapidly becoming a major issue of the next decade. It's no longer simply a question of management; it's a matter of survival. Thanks to some irresponsible or ignorant practices of the past, which gave the town dump a bad name, it has become nearly impossible to find sites for proper facilities to handle the stuff. Yet, that failure is itself irresponsible. If we fail to manage our wastes properly, we will soon find our environment irretrievably polluted, our resources depleted, and the quality of our lives diminished. That's why your leadership is so important. Recycling must be part of the answer. Recycling will be a major part of the answer.

It's time to bring the garbage problem out of the can. It's time to develop a long-term plan to dispose responsibly of society's waste and to establish strong community support for the program. It's time for us to clean up after ourselves so that our children and our children's children have something left to clean up. It's time!

---

[1]The two-month voyage of the barge *Mobro 4,000*, packed with 3,186 tons of baled garbage from Islip, New York, brought widespread attention to the mounting waste-disposal problem facing municipalities across the United States. When the barge came calling in eastern North Carolina, residents were disinclined to welcome it.

The *Mobro* departed the Empire State on March 22, 1987, carrying the first load of a 100,000-ton garbage shipment envisioned by Lowell L. Harrelson. A waste-disposal contractor from Alabama, Harrelson planned to pay Jones County $600,000 for the privilege of burying New York refuse in a landfill near Trenton, North Carolina. He would then siphon methane from the decomposing trash and share the profits, from the sale of the gas, with the county and with local farmers who might later agree to bury garbage bales on their property.

Public outcry greeted the vessel and its pungent, potentially toxic cargo when it docked near Morehead City at the end of March. That opposition, combined with North Carolina's intricate permitting process, soured Jones County leaders on the disposal idea. Pasquotank, Pender, and Washington counties also refused Harrelson's overtures. When state environmental officers obtained a court order that barred the offloading of the *Mobro* and demanded that it be moved, the contractor towed the barge to the Gulf of Mexico.

Denied entry into Florida, Louisiana, Mexico, and Belize, the *Mobro* returned to New York in May. That same month, Islip supervisor Frank R. Jones begged Martin to take "'any significant fraction'" of the 1,000 tons of refuse the city produced daily. "'As you are by now probably aware, the Town of Islip is in the midst of a severe solid waste disposal crisis,'" he wrote.

The governor would have none of Islip's trash. To avoid that city's plight, Martin told Jones, his administration was devising a program "'to encourage the development of alternatives that will minimize landfill disposal of solid waste by the year 2000. Therefore, to accept or encourage out-of-state solid waste for disposal in North Carolina is an unacceptable burden for the citizens of North Carolina.'" "Don't Be a Litterbarge," *Time*, May 4, 1987, 26; *News and Observer*, April 3, 4, 5, June 9, 1987.

[2]Archaeologist William L. Rathje was director of Le Projet du Garbage at the University of Arizona and a speaker at the recycling conference. His research methodology included the study of landfill refuse to gain insight into modern American life. *Charlotte Observer*, November 3, 1989.

GOVERNOR'S CONFERENCE ON INFANT MORTALITY AND
MORBIDITY IN NORTH CAROLINA

CHAPEL HILL, NOVEMBER 2, 1989

As I play with my fifteen-month-old granddaughter, Kathren, I am
once again amazed by nature. Kathren's tiny fingers are marvels of engineering—so small and delicate, but with a grip like a vise if they get
hold of your hair or eyeglasses—and those huge eyes gazing on the
world, full of trust and innocence. Nothing in the world compares with
the joy that comes from a child's laughter. Even when she had no teeth,
Kathren's smile could light up the room and turn her grandfather to
mush.[1]

For Kathren and most of the 97,000 other healthy babies born each
year in North Carolina, awakening into the real world begins the way it
should, with a lusty cry that clearly announces another new presence in
the world. Yet for too many others, life outside the womb begins too
early, or never has a chance to begin at all. You've spent the morning
addressing infant mortality and morbidity in our state. We face a critical
challenge in North Carolina: the unnecessary death and disability of
newborn babies who won't experience the joys and sorrows of life as
healthy children. It's heartbreaking to know that most of the 1,227 infants that died before their first birthday, in North Carolina, died unnecessarily. It's also heartbreaking to learn that another 300 low-birth-weight
babies survived to live out their lives with moderate or severe handicaps, handicaps that were preventable.

What causes babies to be born too soon? The complicating factors are
legion. Children having children often don't know how to care for the
new lives inside them. Mothers continue to smoke, drink and take drugs,
and eat improperly during pregnancy. AIDS-infected mothers pass on
their deadly disease to their child. Low-income mothers can't afford to
visit the doctor to properly care for their babies. We must use every
weapon in our arsenal to fight prematurity by ending teenage pregnancy,
substance abuse, AIDS, and poverty. Though we should continue our
efforts to erase these problems, we know we can't accomplish this overnight.

While we work on these problems, we must also take another
approach: We must ensure that all pregnant women get prenatal care.
Early and regular prenatal care is the best health policy for babies.
Prenatal care not only gets the mother to the doctor, but also teaches
women good health habits and ways to reduce the risk of having a low-
birth-weight baby. Through prenatal care, health professionals teach

expectant women good nutritional habits and help them identify high risk factors in their life-styles.

If we know the solution, then, why do we still have a problem? Just tell the health care professionals to do their job and get these women into prenatal care programs. Well, it's not that simple. Infant mortality and prematurity is not just a health care issue but a social and economic issue, as well. Pregnant teenagers may be too frightened to seek help or may not know where to turn. Unemployed women or the working poor may not have the necessary insurance to cover the cost of prenatal care visits. Women in rural counties have an especially difficult time getting prenatal care even if they want it, because the high cost of malpractice insurance is driving rural obstetricians out of business. Those women for whom prenatal care is both affordable and available may not realize its importance for the health of their baby.

No, if we are to end premature births and infant mortality, we will have to join the health care professionals and fight the problem as a community. Business, religious, and civic leaders, parents, educators— we must all unite our energies and our resources to get the word out that prenatal care is a must for pregnant women. Why is something so personal as the birth of a baby a community concern? In addition to the human suffering involved, infant mortality and prematurity mean high economic and social costs for our society.

First, let's consider the economic issues. Women of childbearing age make up 30 percent of the workforce. The longer premature babies remain in the hospital, the longer businesses have to suffer from absentee employees who must skip work to care for their children.

The longer those babies stay in the hospital, the higher the medical bills continue to mount. Neonatal intensive care costs, early in the first year of life, often exceed $100,000. Premature babies that survive, but who are severely handicapped as a result, require average health care and support costs exceeding $23,000 per year. When the parents have insurance, businesses wind up paying for these health care costs. If the parents are uninsured, society ultimately pays the bill through higher taxes or an increase in health insurance premiums.

And what about the loss of future workers and consumers? Birth rates in the West have declined in general over the past ten years; fewer people will be available for the jobs of the next century. Losing babies unnecessarily through premature death and disability will reduce the number of potential employees and consumers even further.

Then there's the emotional strain suffered by parents who lose a child in infancy or who must care for a handicapped child. Family and friends, at home or in the church, must often help these parents bear their emotional and financial burdens.

What can we do, working together as a community, to meet this challenge? At the state level, we've begun a number of programs to get the word out that prenatal care is necessary for having a healthy baby. The Baby Love Medical Assistance Program, now in its third year of operation, is the most successful prenatal care effort to date. As part of Baby Love, the General Assembly has extended Medicaid eligibility to pregnant women and infants whose family incomes are at or below 150 percent of the poverty level. Through Baby Love, program participants receive a full range of prenatal care services, including case management—we call it care coordination—childbirth education, and parenting classes. Baby Love also provides information to potentially eligible clients and health care professionals about Medicaid changes and new benefits.

Building on success, the new Healthy Generations program expands on Baby Love by offering additional services to women planning pregnancy and infants who are at risk. This program is currently operating in six counties.

Not all mothers are indigent, of course. Unfortunately, too many mothers-to-be from all walks of life fail to care for themselves even before pregnancy. The state's Preconceptional Health Program encourages women to think in terms of a twelve-month pregnancy—getting healthy before getting pregnant.

The Preconceptional Health Program is based on the idea that pregnancies are not diagnosed for many women until critical weeks of fetal development are well under way and the period of greatest environmental sensitivity of the developing fetus has passed. The program assesses a woman's social and medical history and identifies potential problem areas. Health professionals then recommend changes to lessen the risks and help women make informed decisions about future childbearing.

On a broader scale, the Office of Prevention, in the Division of Maternal and Child Health, established in 1987, is coordinating a statewide network of prevention activities and increasing public and professional awareness of how to prevent disabilities. To get more and better prenatal care to pregnant women, the General Assembly passed the Rural Obstetrical Care Incentive in 1988. This program helps cover insurance costs for family physicians and attract obstetricians to counties where they are needed.[2]

We're moving ahead on the state level, offering services and providing leadership to communities across North Carolina, helping them promote preconceptional, prenatal, and postnatal care for healthy mothers and healthy babies. So where do you come in? I need you to help get the word out on these programs and to encourage all pregnant women in your communities to seek prenatal care early in their pregnancy. Preach the word from your pulpits, hang prenatal care posters in your office lunchroom, sponsor prenatal care seminars through your civic organization. If you're a medical professional, help us lean on the insurance companies to adjust obstetric insurance premiums based on the number of deliveries, so that rural physicians won't be priced out of serving their patients.

If you own a business, consider following the example of Burlington Industries, in Greensboro, which offers prenatal care classes to women employees on their lunch hour. Review leave and insurance programs to make prenatal care both more affordable and more available to your employees. Become informed and involved in public issues.

Public-private partnerships work. The Appalachian Regional Commission and the Kate B. Reynolds Foundation have combined private foundation and federal monies for grants to help communities reduce infant mortality. We will soon be launching an infant mortality and morbidity prevention media campaign to preach the virtues of preconceptional, prenatal, and infant care. This campaign will target women of childbearing age through the use of TV, radio, and other news media. I invite you, our business, religious, and community leaders, to join our health care professionals in this effort with your leadership, your expertise, and your resources.

Today I am announcing a new public-private partnership: the Governor's Council on Infant Mortality and Morbidity.[3] This council will coordinate public and private resources for greatest effectiveness at the local level; provide a forum for ideas from business, religious, and volunteer organizations; and ensure an ongoing focus for infant mortality concerns. Because infant mortality and morbidity are more than health problems, it will take more than the health care community to develop the ultimate solution. We need the help of both the public and private sector to ensure the health and well-being of all our infants and pregnant women.

We know we can do better. Over the last fifteen years, North Carolina's infant mortality rate has been cut in half, from 27 per 1,000 to 12. Now it's back up a little to 13 per 1,000, probably due to the loss of rural practice resulting from malpractice premiums going too high.

Let's fix that. Let's work together, as partners in every community across this state, to ensure that our children will live to know and enjoy the simple pleasures of childhood. Let's become a society that cares for its children before they are born so they can live their lives to the fullest.

---

[1]Kathren Downing McAulay Martin (1988–) was the daughter of James Grubbs Martin, Jr., and his wife, Patricia. She was also the governor's first grandchild. Betty F. Dean,

personal secretary and administrative assistant to First Lady Dorothy M. Martin, letter to Jan-Michael Poff, September 22, 1988.

²The Rural Obstetrical Care Incentive was established under "An Act to Create and Continue Various Committees and Commissions and to Make Changes in the Budget Operation of the State," *N.C. Session Laws, 1987, Regular Session, 1988,* c. 1100, s. 39.3, ratified July 12, 1988.

³Martin signed Executive Order Number 99, establishing the Governor's Commission on Reduction of Infant Mortality, on December 13, 1989. *N.C. Session Laws, 1989, Regular Session, 1990,* 1009–1015; for related press release, see "Governor Intensifies Infant Mortality Effort," Raleigh, December 14, 1989, Governors Papers, James G. Martin.

AMERICAN CHEMICAL MANUFACTURERS ASSOCIATION

Washington, D.C., November 6, 1989

It is good to be back with you after about five years, and what an honor to be wedged in between two profound addresses of great international importance. My assignment is to "talk trash."

How fortunate we are to live in America, where we enjoy a better life-style and longer life-span than at any time in our history, thanks to the benefits of technology. But as we praise the wonders of microwave ovens and telecommunications, synthetic foodstuffs and clothing, CAT-scanners and laser surgery, we must not forget that our technical wizardry also produces harmful by-products that must be disposed of properly. Are we living longer, and better, and worrying about it more? Well, it's not a new problem.

Many of the mistakes of the past occurred out of ignorance. Two hundred years ago, haberdashers in England spread mercury on their hands to treat the felt used in making hats. Eventually, high mercury levels in their systems drove them insane, thus the term *mad as a hatter*. How could they know? Even Marie Curie, a genius in chemistry and physics, failed to understand the destructive power of the radium she discovered. Long years of close contact with the element is believed to have eventually caused the leukemia that claimed her life, but how could she know?

Well, education and experience have finally taught us to respect chemicals and their industrial by-products. We have overcome ignorance in a rational way. Unfortunately, that shift in direction has swung the weather vane of public opinion to another, and I believe just as dangerous, form of ignorance. The horrors of past misuse have caused too many government leaders, and many among the public, to race one another to the rooftops, shouting, "Stop production! Ban hazardous waste!" In their hysteria, these alarmists use fear to build a wall of opposition against any legitimate effort to provide for the responsible treatment and disposal of waste materials.

Just two weeks ago, our state sponsored a public meeting on a proposed low-level waste facility in North Carolina. In a newspaper interview, a local participant at the hearing was quoted as saying, "I think whoever's making all this stuff, we ought to make them stop it." That's a great answer, and the news media find it, and viewers feature such statements rather than inform readers what their consequences would be.

Well, we're not about to turn off our electricity, close our hospitals, and change our life-styles just to stop making all this hazardous "stuff." But by opposing proper treatment and disposal facilities, these demagogues are helping create the very problem they condemn: the irresponsible contamination of the environment. If no legal ways are available to properly dispose of it, is it any wonder that some will resort to illegal, improper ways? It's time we recognized we are an industrialized nation, and as such, we must accept the responsibility to protect our environment and preserve our resources while continuing the technologies which improve our quality of life.

Let me tell you what kind of situation this "informed ignorance" has wrought in North Carolina. We have no hazardous waste landfill in North Carolina. Public opposition, justified by plant mismanagement, closed our only commercial hazardous waste incinerator.[1] Our off-site hazardous waste management capacity in North Carolina is limited to an aggregate kiln and small chemical treatment facilities, primarily for water containing metal wastes.

North Carolina produced 2.8 billion pounds of waste in 1987, 90 percent of which was handled on site. The remaining 176 million pounds had to be shipped mainly to other states, about half of it to South Carolina's landfill. Understandably, our welcome in neighboring states is wearing thin. Earlier this year, both South Carolina and Alabama issued bans against accepting our waste until we showed a commitment to developing a responsible disposal plan of our own.[2] They certainly felt justified.

Our refusal thus far to accept responsibility for waste production has placed us in a very awkward position. The political trend has been (1) to pass laws requiring proper disposal, then (2) place strict limitations on legislation so that (3) no facility can possibly be built to meet specifications. That happened in North Carolina. The General Assembly stripped the governor's power to appoint an independent siting commission, then passed legislation that required facilities treating contaminated water to also dilute it 1,000 to 1. Under this legislation, even if the water with 1 percent contaminant was purified to remove all 99.9 percent of it, all but 10 parts per million—or parts per billion, whatever it would take to [render it] biologically insignificant—it would still have to be diluted 1,000 to 1. That means that each thousand gallons of treated water, even if it had only 1 ounce of other chemicals safely dispersed in it, would have to have another 1 million gallons of water added for dilution, but for no other purpose except to eliminate every river but one in North Carolina![3]

Basically, each gallon of water, no matter what was in it, would require another thousand gallons of water to be added, even though it no longer contained an unsafe level of any hazardous chemical. Right now we are being sued by the Environmental Protection Agency—properly, in my opinion—to overturn this law, the sole purpose of which was to block proper treatment of such waste by making it technically impossible. Ironically, I am obligated to legally uphold that law, but I don't have to agree with it.[4]

When it appeared that the facility would be designed so that the original water would just be distilled off to reduce the amount of water that would have to be added (!), our legislature saved the day again by passing another law to prohibit any site, anywhere, unless a volunteer county could be found. Needless to say, none have come forward! Well, actually, one did—until existing businesses in that county decided they didn't want such a neighbor. Now there's a modern-day irony for you![5]

The sole purpose of such legislation as this is to make politicians appear to be doing something environmentally sound for the state while ensuring that no hazardous-waste facility would be built in their backyards. What it really does, though, is prevent proper waste cleanup facilities and thus increases the risk of illegal waste disposal: dumping it in creeks, gutters, and gullies when no one is looking—the moral equivalent of "corking" household sewers, then blaming someone else for the overflow.

I don't mean to suggest that environmental groups have been no help at all. They have helped us to identify ways to recycle waste. By supporting our nationally recognized Pollution Prevention Pays program, they have also helped to encourage chemical and other technology-based industries to minimize waste. That has worked pretty well. As a result, North Carolina has about the lowest waste generation rate per industrial job in the nation. But when it comes to going a step further and helping us build a proper waste-treatment facility, the environmentalists become obstructionists, not supporters. Contrary to their stated purpose, the environmentalists are not willing to support responsible waste management when they can get more new dues-paying members by opposing a treatment facility.

The federal government says states have to handle their RCRA—

Resource Conservation and Recovery Act—waste by establishing disposal facilities, or they will forfeit Superfund money for abandoned waste dumps.[6] Some environmentalists say we have to handle our waste by not producing any more. So, some politicians say we have to handle our waste, as long as the disposal facility is built in someone else's district. It's time for someone to say we have to handle our waste because that is the responsible thing to do: simply that.

I believe governmental leaders must set a responsible course of leadership for the reduction, treatment, and disposal of industrial waste, despite public opposition. That's the stand I'm taking, a stand for the common good. As proof of my commitment, I have set an ambitious goal for North Carolina to reduce our hazardous waste by 30 percent, by 1995, through technical assistance to generators, and to get approval for the facilities and sites that we will need for the remaining waste that has to go off site.

Yes, we are committed to reducing hazardous waste, but reducing waste cannot and will not eliminate the need for proper treatment and disposal facilities. While a chemical plant might readily reduce or recycle its waste, and would certainly have the technology base to do it, the same could not be expected at the neighborhood laundry, or service station, or house painter, or even a small textile mill or furniture factory. Incidentally, we recently had a noxious fire that required evacuation of several hundred residents when a dustbin full of lacquer dust, from finishing furniture, caught fire and smoldered. Ironically, it was being collected and stored for transshipment at the former incinerator that had been shut down.[7]

To deal with these matters, I asked our General Assembly for the authority to determine what treatment facilities will be established in North Carolina, to oversee facility development, and to negotiate interstate agreements.[8] Under the authority of this legislation, I began negotiations with other southern states earlier this year to develop a regional waste treatment agreement. Such an agreement was designed to share our existing and proposed facilities instead of each state having to build the full, comprehensive range of different types of treatment facilities to comply with federal regulations.[9]

At this point, four of the original eight states in the negotiations have settled on their own agreement.[10] Given our past record, the four states with existing facilities need to be convinced we could overcome public pressure against building our proposed facility—in this case, a chemical incinerator—in the future. As these regional negotiations continue, my task is to show them that, yes, we are committed to doing something about hazardous waste in North Carolina, and I am committed to providing the necessary leadership to see that the job gets done, and gets done right.

But if government provides the leadership, we need your help, too, in promoting waste-minimization efforts. You can set an example for all industries by reducing and recovering waste on site and by supporting public treatment facilities. Your cooperation and concern for the environment will also go a long way toward educating the "informed ignorant" that chemicals can be used and disposed of safely and effectively.

I'm proud to say that several companies in North Carolina are setting great examples in this area. Sandoz Chemical Corporation, in Charlotte, North Carolina, which produces chemicals for the textile industry, reduced its hazardous wastewater by 90 percent, to 300,000 tons per year in 1986, through manufacturing process and product changes—and it's now treated on site. DeSoto Chemical Company, in Greensboro, a paint manufacturer, used waste segregation and process modification to reduce waste chemicals by 98 percent while significantly cutting production costs.

You don't have to be a big company to practice waste minimization, either. Daly-Herring is a small business in Kinston, North Carolina, that formulates pesticides. Through waste segregation, avoiding mixing it with water, they reduced their waste volume by 450,000 pounds at a savings of $10,000 per year.

To multiply the good examples, I'm asking you to take the lead in minimizing waste like these and other North Carolina companies have done. To help small companies who don't have on-site treatment capabilities, I'm asking you to help support development of commercial disposal facilities. Finally, I'm asking you to help us make the public aware of how much we depend on chemicals in our daily lives, and how important it is that we provide a safe, effective, responsible method for dealing with industrial by-products.

With government leadership and private sector support, we can and will build a cleaner, safer, healthier environment for the next generation. We must do it without retreating to a simpler, shorter life, when everyone raises their own food and makes their own clothing; but we must do it by showing the people—our constituents, our customers—that we can manage both our products and our waste, and that we can do it right. That's much of my job now, and of yours.

---

[1]Residents of the Lick Mountain area, near Hudson, Caldwell County, had long blamed an increase in respiratory illnesses and other health problems on the hazardous waste incinerator operated since 1977 by Caldwell Systems, Inc. Local protests, county government investigations, and EPA scrutiny of the site forced CSI to halt waste burning in May

1988. Afterward the facility was used as a transshipment station for hazardous materials until it was shut down completely on December 1, 1989. A lacquer-thinner dust fire at the plant finally forced its closing; see footnote 7.

Although waste disposal operations had ceased in late 1989, the effects of CSI's business lingered in Caldwell County. In July 1990, federal authorities released studies indicating that the incinerator indeed had a harmful effect on the health of some nearby residents. However, they were most alarmed by the incidents of severe neurological and respiratory damage found among former plant workers. The Environmental Protection Agency established a task force to investigate whether the nation's other hazardous waste incinerators posed health threats similar to those at Caldwell.

County and federal government agencies took the lead in investigating complaints about, and finally closing, the Caldwell incinerator. The state drew fire for its apparent slowness to act on the situation, prompting speculation whether North Carolina could safely operate the incinerator it promised to build as a requirement for inclusion in the regional hazardous waste management agreement of November 1989. *Independent Weekly* (Durham), April 12, July 18, 1990; *News and Observer*, April 28, 1988, September 19, December 2, 1989, July 26, 27, 28, 31, August 1, 3, 5, 14, 15, September 11, 12, November 11, 1990, February 22, 1992.

[2]Alabama declared a ban on hazardous waste shipments, effective September 14, 1989, to its mammoth Emelle landfill from North Carolina and twenty-one other states. The action was authorized by legislation prohibiting the removal of such material to Alabama if the states in which it was produced did not permit its disposal within their own boundaries or lacked a cooperative agreement with Alabama. Montgomery lawmakers based their statute on South Carolina's model; federal judges later ruled that the bans enacted by both states violated the U.S. Constitution's provision granting Congress the authority to regulate interstate commerce. *News and Observer*, August 30, 1989, August 10, 1990, June 11, 1991; see "State of the State," January 17, 1989, 25n, for more information on the closing of the Pinewood, South Carolina, landfill to North Carolina's hazardous wastes.

[3]"An Act to Specify an Additional Requirement Applicable to the Permitting of Any Commercial Hazardous Waste Treatment Facility for the Purpose of Protecting Public Health" established dilution guidelines for contaminated water; see *N.C. Session Laws, 1987*, I, c. 437, ratified June 22, 1987.

[4]GSX Chemical Services and a trade group, the Hazardous Waste Treatment Council, petitioned the U.S. Environmental Protection Agency to rescind North Carolina's power to manage hazardous wastes after the General Assembly passed S.B. 114. GSX protested that the "arbitrary" legislation was adopted to block construction of its proposed regional hazardous waste treatment plant near Laurinburg, Scotland County, and ran afoul of the U.S. Resource Conservation and Recovery Act. In general terms, opponents of the state law claimed that it unjustly barred all hazardous-waste treatment operations from North Carolina.

Proponents of S.B. 114 argued that the measure was needed to safeguard public drinking water. The GSX facility would have dumped upwards of 500,000 gallons of treated waste per day into the Lumber River. The small river was the primary source of water for a significant number of Robeson County residents.

The Environmental Protection Agency conducted hearings in 1989 on the implications of S.B. 114. The administrative law judge attached to the case ruled in favor of the state in April 1990. The following June, EPA dropped the challenge to North Carolina's authority to regulate hazardous waste under the federal Resource Conservation and Recovery Act. The decision upheld S.B. 114 and the state's prerogative to enact environmental standards stricter than those adopted by the federal government.

Announcing the end of the challenge, EPA regional administrator Daniel W. McGovern declared that S.B. 114 "'cannot be said to act as a prohibition on the treatment, storage or disposal of hazardous waste in North Carolina.'" While the law indeed prevented GSX—later Laidlaw Environmental Services Co.—from erecting the plant near Laurinburg as initially designed, it still allowed two options. The firm could either build the same facility elsewhere in the state or locate a downsized operation in Scotland County. "'A smaller facility of the type routinely operated across the country could be constructed at the GSX Laurinburg site in compliance with the act,'" noted McGovern. "'Recall that under Senate Bill 114 the maximum allowable discharge would be 72,000 gallons a day. The average flow rate of commercial aqueous hazardous-waste treatment facilities is significantly less— 45,000 gallons a day.'" *News and Observer*, June 2, 1990; for related press release, see "Governor Martin's Reaction to EPA's Announcement of Hearings on Withdrawal of RCRA Authority from North Carolina," Raleigh, April 19, 1989, Governors Papers, James G. Martin.

[5]Edgecombe County officials briefly floated a proposal in 1988 to host a waste management park for the disposal of hazardous and low-level radioactive materials. They abandoned their offer after a local business organization passed a resolution calling for a referendum to determine whether the county should volunteer for the project. Of greatest concern was the fear that Kitchens of Sara Lee would cancel its plans to build a bakery employing 600 people, near Tarboro, if the waste facility were approved. *News and Observer*, May 12, 19, 20, 21, 22, June 7, 8, 1988.

[6]P.L. 94–580, "Resource Conservation and Recovery Act of 1976," *United States Statutes at Large*, Act of October 21, 1976, 90 Stat. 2795–2841; see also *United States Code* (1988 edition), Title 42, Section 6901 et seq.

[7]The lacquer-thinner dust fire occurred September 13, 1989, at the Caldwell Systems, Inc., hazardous-waste treatment facility. Two-hundred fifty of the plant's neighbors were evacuated, and fifty-four were briefly hospitalized for respiratory and other ailments. Afterward, the Caldwell County inspector and his counterparts from the U.S. Environmental Protection Agency discovered infractions of local, state, and federal waste-handling regulations by CSI. The county official determined that "the fire was preventable and the result of poor management." *News and Observer*, September 19, December 2, 1989.

[8]*N.C. Session Laws, 1989*, I, c. 168.

[9]Martin and other state officials were negotiating North Carolina's entry into the waste disposal pact formed by Alabama, Kentucky, South Carolina, and Tennessee. In case those talks failed, the governor directed the state Hazardous Waste Management Commission, on October 26, 1989, to determine an alternative "solo strategy" for the handling and treatment of toxic materials. Less than a month later, however, he announced that North Carolina had won admission into the regional agreement. The terms of participation required the state to "provide an incinerator, a solvent recovery unit, and a small residuals management unit to handle the ash and residue from the incinerator." Press releases, "Governor Asks Hazardous Waste Management Commission to Explore Options for State Treatment Plan," Raleigh, October 26, 1989, and "Governor Martin's Reaction to Inclusion of North Carolina in Regional Hazardous Waste Treatment Agreement," Raleigh, November 22, 1989; see also News Conference on Hazardous Waste, Raleigh, October 26, 1989, Governors Papers, James G. Martin.

The General Assembly ratified North Carolina's participation in the disposal plan on December 7, 1989. See "An Act to Approve Entry by the Governor into an Interstate Agreement for the Management of Hazardous Waste, as Defined in G.S. 130A–290, as Set Out in the Document Entitled 'Expansion of the SARA Capacity Assurance Regional Agreement,' and Attachments as Filed with the Department of the Secretary of State on 5 December 1989, and to Adjourn the 1989 Extra Session of the General Assembly *Sine Die*," *N.C. Session Laws, Extra Session, 1989, Extra and Regular Sessions, 1990*, c. 1.

[10]Alabama, Kentucky, South Carolina, and Tennessee were the first states in EPA's eight-member Region IV to reach a hazardous waste disposal agreement. The others eligible to become party to the plan were Florida, Georgia, Mississippi, and North Carolina. Press Conference on Hazardous Waste, Raleigh, October 26, 1989; see also "SARA Capacity Assurance Regional Interstate Agreement," 1, attached to press release, "Governor Announces Briefings for Legislators, Plans December 7 Extra Session on Hazardous Waste," Raleigh, November 27, 1989, Governors Papers, James G. Martin.

PRESS RELEASE: GOVERNOR MARTIN'S STATEMENT ON SITE
AREA ANNOUNCEMENTS BY LOW-LEVEL RADIOACTIVE
WASTE AUTHORITY

RALEIGH, NOVEMBER 8, 1989

[The landfill at Barnwell, South Carolina, in which North Carolina and other states disposed of low-level radioactive waste, was statutorily mandated to close December 31, 1992. Members of the Southeast Compact Commission for Low-Level Radioactive Waste Management elected, in September 1986, to site a replacement facility in North Carolina. Tar Heel officials pledged to begin operating the new disposal plant by January 1, 1993; it was to remain open for twenty years or until it had swallowed 32 million cubic feet of refuse, whichever occurred first.

On November 8, 1989, the state Low-Level Radioactive Waste Management Authority announced four tracts of land as potential locations for the storage project: 2,000 acres in southeastern Richmond County; 1,000 acres in southeastern Rowan County; 1,000 acres in southeastern Union County; and 750 acres straddling southwestern Wake and southeastern Chatham counties. From those choices, two finalists, Richmond and Wake-Chatham, were selected in February 1990.

Neither of the two sites was prepared to succeed Barnwell by the end of 1992. A number of factors—including geological considerations, licensing procedures, contractor delays, and vigorous, sustained protests from Chatham and Richmond residents—combined to postpone the opening of the project until 1996 at the earliest.

The revelation in July 1990 that North Carolina would not meet its original target date disturbed many in the Palmetto State, who were tiring of their role as the nation's dump. Seventy percent of the country's low-level waste was shipped annually to Barnwell; South Carolina also hosted an interstate hazardous-waste facility, at Pinewood, and the controversial Savannah River nuclear weapons complex near Aiken. Environmental and legislative opposition to prolonging the landfill's life seemed to ensure that it would close on schedule whether or not a replacement was on line.

Without a ready alternative to Barnwell, hospitals, research laboratories, and other producers of low-level radioactive waste faced the unpleasant prospect of storing refuse on site. Such a potential environmental and regulatory nightmare ultimately was dispelled, however, by the economic recession early in the decade. Like many states in 1992, South Carolina experienced difficulty attracting sufficient tax revenues; a functioning Barnwell had the ability to generate $125 million in disposal fees. In a decision that "divided politicians and angered environmentalists," the South Carolina House of Representatives backed the state Senate and voted, in May 1992, to keep the landfill open until 1996. On December 8, 1993, North Carolina officials finally designated the Wake County site, redrawn to exclude Chatham, as their choice to host the successor to the Barnwell facility. *News and Observer*, November 9, 1989, February 22, 1990, July 14, 18, 1990, October 24, 1991, March 14, 15, May 24, 30, 1992, December 9, 1993; see also Poff, *Addresses of Martin*, I, 348–351.]

The task of siting and operating a low-level radioactive waste disposal facility is a commitment the state of North Carolina has made and one which I am personally committed to keeping. From the start, I have actively supported North Carolina's decision to accept this responsibility and to move ahead as quickly as possible to meet the goals we have set. I commend the North Carolina Low-Level Radioactive Waste Management Authority for the progress we have made thus far.

The candidate sites that they have selected fulfill an extremely difficult assignment which they have undertaken on behalf of all North Carolinians. It is understandable that those living near any potential site will oppose it, but I hope all will respect the fair-minded and evenhanded approach taken by this authority in meeting its duty. Open and honest communication is vital to the success of this project. Many questions and concerns will no doubt be raised. I urge all North Carolinians to become informed, to be active and constructive participants in the process, and to bring their questions and comments before us.

I have been briefed on the progress made thus far, and I am confident that [the] Low-Level Radioactive Waste Management Authority and its contractor, Chem-Nuclear Systems, will proceed rapidly with the siting process while ensuring the utmost safety of the public and protection of the environment. North Carolina is fulfilling its obligation to our neighboring states, and we have their commitment that they will in turn accept their responsibility. Working together, I am fully confident that the people of North Carolina can meet our common challenge.

HIGH POINT CHAMBER OF COMMERCE

High Point, December 5, 1989

It is great to be back in High Point, to be among so many who have given special meaning to the wor[d] *entrepreneur*. You know, when George invited me to speak with you, today, he asked me to discuss the importance of economic development in North Carolina and to talk a little bit about foreign investment.[1] We happened to be together on an economic trade mission to the Far East at the time.

A wise man once said, "Commerce has made this country what it is, and it cannot be destroyed or neglected without involving the people in poverty and distress." These are words for our time, but they are words of the past, spoken by John Adams in 1797. They are also words of truth, words that clearly define commerce as the foundation of our national progress and the cement that supports and strengthens growth in this state.

You've seen evidence of that truth right here in High Point. Look how far you've come since M. J. Wrenn, T. F. Wrenn, John Tate, and E. A. Snow founded the High Point Furniture Company here in 1881. From its beginnings, manufacturing wooden beds and sideboards, this first furniture factory in the state led the way for High Point to become the "Furniture Capital of the World."

If you want to know about progress, just ask the folks at Wright's Clothing Store and R. K. Stewart and Son, Builders and Contractors. When they started out, they built their business without having a television, a computer, or a fax machine—neither did the competition, because that was seventy-five years ago! What about the thirty companies that have chosen to locate or expand their operations in High Point during the past year? They not only understand progress, they are progress.

Tonight we've honored High Point's 100-year-old, 75-, 50-, and 1-year-old companies. At the same time, we renew our commitment to help them continue to grow and prosper into the next century. During the past 70 years, the High Point Chamber of Commerce has lived up to its motto of "Good People Promoting Good Business." As economic recruiters, community boosters and developers, and all-around problem solvers, you've taken an active role with your membership to make High Point a city of progress in North Carolina.

Sometimes it hasn't been easy, but your cooperation and commitment to progress has [sic] brought you success. When the furniture market decided to come to town and you realized you didn't have enough hotel rooms to handle the business, you developed the Housing Bureau and made the transition by welcoming your visitors into your private homes. In the early '70s, when businesses began moving out of downtown, your revitalization efforts led to the establishment of the High Point Economic Development Corporation and the Radisson Hotel. When it looked like the Furniture Market might leave High Point for Dallas, you jumped right in and developed incentives, such as shuttle services, welcome centers, and free parking to say, "We're glad you're here, and we want you here to stay," and it worked! That's cooperation and commitment, and that's progress, right here in High Point.

We're part of that cooperation and commitment at the state level. Let me give you an example or two. When I first came into office, I called for a repeal of the inventory and intangibles taxes. I believe that repeal of the inventory tax has particularly helped attract many of the distribution companies that have come to High Point, and it has helped save our manufacturing companies by making them more competitive. I also pledged to get I-40 under contract to Wilmington, and now it looks like the whole project will be open to traffic by the end of summer. Just think how that will increase distribution opportunities for new and existing businesses in High Point. Our seaports can help your exports!

A number of companies here have also taken advantage of the technical training program offered by Guilford Technical Community College. When you expand or retool, we pledge to train your employees, your way, at our expense. Now that's what I call a good deal.

Yes, that's cooperation and commitment, and that's progress, right here in High Point. But we need to keep that cooperation and commitment going if we expect to continue that progress on into the twenty-first century. As John Adams said in 1797, commerce was and still remains the foundation of this nation, but commerce in 1797 and 1990 are different animals. The small, local markets and limited foreign trade of Adams's day have given way to competition in the global marketplace. That's where we need to be if we hope to continue the economic progress we currently enjoy.

What will it take to compete in the global marketplace of the twentieth century? It will take the same kind of cooperation and commitment that has brought us where we are today. We must begin a regional approach to marketing, similar to the approach you and other cities in this region are taking to develop a world trade expo at the Piedmont-Triad International Airport.

When we visit Europe and the Far East on trade missions, we don't just promote Charlotte or Raleigh to foreign investors, we promote all of North Carolina and, especially, our many first-class smaller communities under 50,000. We also promote the southeastern states as a region. Developing a regional approach to industrial recruitment, and foreign investment, and hazardous waste, by the way, combines the resources of an entire area to make it more attractive to investors. Investment then helps to strengthen the economy of that entire area.

I feel the same way about regional development within North Carolina. That's why I want to work with you and challenge you to develop and promote a Triad, multi-county, stronger unity and presence—with a research park, here, a major airline hub or air freight service, rail passenger service, and on and on. Challenge me. Show me how we can make this happen.

Fortunately, our international economic recruitment efforts have paid off for North Carolina. Foreign companies investing in and buying from North Carolina mean more and better jobs for our citizens, more work for our vendors and contractors, more orders for supplies from local manufacturers, and an improved tax base for the region. The recent wave of political reforms sweeping eastern Europe promises to increase our opportunities for foreign investment and trade in the future. We must be ready to compete with other states for import as well as export opportunities with those nations.

But the opportunities won't last forever. In a recent edition of *Fortune* magazine, George Baeder, director of the Pacific Rim Consulting Group, in Hong Kong, was quoted as saying "U.S. and European companies have only the coming decade to establish leadership positions in the Asian market." I believe the same is true of opportunities in the European market. No one can accurately predict what will happen when a common currency links the European Common Market in 1992. We need to firmly establish our foothold now, so that we will remain trading partners with the Common Market nations even if they restrict trade with other, less well established partners.

What can we do to open those markets for North Carolina goods? First, we can continue our face-to-face dealings with foreign entrepreneurs. I've just returned from my biannual trade missions to the Far East and Europe, both of which were successful and will lead to several announcements of new plant locations in our state in the coming weeks. Also, our state Department of Economic and Community Development will continue to work with the High Point Economic Development Commission, and the chamber of commerce, to open foreign markets for local goods and bring new companies to the Triad.

But more remains to be done. Participation in the global marketplace means global competition, competition that we must be prepared to meet and overcome. I've already said North Carolina has a reputation for excellence among foreign investors, but competition is strong, and we can easily lose that reputation if we fail to provide the kind of workforce we need.

In a recent address at the Kenan Institute at Chapel Hill, Texas entrepreneur Ross Perot said, "We can't win an international competition unless we have the best-educated workforce."[2] With SAT scores ranked the lowest in the nation, North Carolina may lose its edge in the global marketplace if we lose the edge in education here at home. The legislature did partially approve my plan to improve education by increasing accountability and providing better pay for better teachers. Now we have to find other ways to promote better teaching and greater student achievement. That's where you come in.

We must stop thinking of the education of our young people as just an institutional issue. We must begin thinking of education as an economic and community issue. Without a properly educated workforce, commerce will fail, and the foundation on which we hope to build our future economic progress will crumble.

If we fail to deal with dropouts and underachievement, it could eventually force North Carolina to drop out of the competition in the marketplace. That's why I've asked Secretary Jim Broyhill to develop a plan of action to better educat[e] our young people for jobs, to meet the needs of employers. "Workforce preparedness," he calls it. He will recommend to me ways in which we can better use our resources to keep North Carolina competitive.

One option is for businesses to become directly involved in education in their communities, either by offering hands-on training or developing incentive programs through local schools. An example of such hands-on education is available right here in High Point. By encouraging local industries' taking responsibility for the economics education of high school juniors and seniors in the area, your chamber's Economics in Action program is helping teach young people what it really means to run a business, to be [an] entrepreneurial risk-taker.

On the state level, the Business Committee for Education, located in the Governor's Office, creates partnerships between businesses and the schools to improve educational opportunities for young people in our state. I'm pleased that Thomas Built Buses of High Point is a member of that committee. I'd like to encourage more High Point businesses to join the Business Committee for Education in their efforts to improve student performance.

Incentive programs sponsored by local businesses across North Carolina can also help to improve student attendance and performance while rewarding good teachers for excellence in the classroom. In some schools, simple programs such as annual teaching awards and door prizes for perfect attendance can help lower the dropout rate and improve student achievement. On a larger scale, RJR Nabisco recently announced a $30 million incentive program, called Next Century Schools, that will distribute 3-year grants to schools that are willing to take risks in developing innovative approaches to improving education—entrepreneurial educators!

In announcing that grant, Louis Gerstner, chairman and CEO of RJR Nabisco, said that "the biggest risk in education is not taking risks."[3] He's right, and that's why I'm asking you to take a risk for education in whatever way you can. Sponsor an apprentice from the local high school to learn your business. Support the chamber's new Mentor and Match program, or lend an area school the expertise of one of your employees as a teacher. Join the successful Cities in Schools program already operating here in High Point. Donate some product that can be used directly in the learning process or as an incentive to better learning. Pool your resources as a group and help support an innovative educational program in an area high school.

I said before, the High Point Chamber of Commerce has proven itself to be a problem-solver and catalyst for progress. Now I'm asking you to help us solve our educational problems so that we can continue our economic progress in the global marketplace of the twenty-first century.

Aristotle once said, "All who have meditated on the art of governing mankind have been convinced that the fate of empires depends on the education of youth." I'm convinced that the fate of North Carolina depends on the education of our youth. What kind of education those young people receive is our responsibility.

We must accept the education of our youth as a community responsibility. By working together as a community, as a state, we can take the necessary risks to develop schools that will enable our young people to compete in the global marketplace of the next century. Join me in taking that risk for our children and the future of North Carolina. Surely it's our biggest challenge, and you can do it.

———————

¹George S. Erath (1927–), born in Chicago; resident of High Point; B.S., High Point College, 1952; M.A., University of North Carolina, 1954; U.S. Army, 1945–1947. Board chairman, chief executive officer, Erath Veneer Corp. of Virginia, since 1968, and of Euro-American Wood Products, Inc., since 1977; board chairman, N.C. Education Assistance Authority, 1987, and of High Point Chamber of Commerce, 1989; chairman, board of trustees, High Point Regional Hospital, 1990–1991, and of Presbyterian Home of High Point, Inc., 1991–1992. George S. Erath, letter to Jan-Michael Poff, January 20, 1993.

²According to the Raleigh *News and Observer*, November 16, 1989, Perot said "'We can't win an international competition unless we have the best-educated workforce, and right now, we're just talking about it.'" The observation was part of his keynote speech, November 15, 1989, to the first Kenan Conference on International Competitiveness. The Frank Hawkins Kenan Institute of Private Enterprise and the University of North Carolina MBA Student Association sponsored the two-day event; see also *News and Observer*, November 17, 1989.

H. Ross Perot (1930–), native of Texas; was educated at U.S. Naval Academy; U.S. Navy, 1953–1957. Data processing salesman, IBM Corp., 1957–1962; founder, 1962, chairman, chief executive officer, 1962–1984, director to 1986, Electronic Data Systems Corp., Dallas; founder, Perot Systems Corp., 1988; independent candidate for U.S. president, 1992; author. *Who's Who in America, 1994*, II, 2688.

³"The biggest risk in education is not taking one," said Louis Vincent Gerstner, Jr., upon the launch of the Next Century Schools initiative in Raleigh on November 1; see *Asheville Citizen*, November 2, 1989. The phrase also headed a single-page advertisement, featuring an open letter from Gerstner, that ran in state newspapers on November 5, 1989; for example, see *Charlotte Observer, Greensboro News and Record*, Raleigh *News and Observer*, and *Winston-Salem Journal*. Gerstner (1942–), born in New York City; B.A., Dartmouth College, 1963; M.B.A., Harvard University, 1965. Director, McKinsey and Co., 1965–1978; executive vice-president, 1978–1981, board vice-chairman, 1981–1983, executive committee chairman, 1983–1985, president, 1985–1989, American Express Co.; chief executive officer, RJR Nabisco, Inc., 1989–1993; chief executive officer, IBM Corp., since 1993. *Who's Who in America, 1994*, I, 1251.

NORTH CAROLINA HOUSING FINANCE AGENCY AND NORTH CAROLINA HOUSING PARTNERSHIP

RALEIGH, DECEMBER 14, 1989

[The governor delivered remarks similar to those reprinted, below, to the Housing Coordination and Policy Council, December 8, 1989, in Raleigh.]

Thank you, Mr. (Bill) Boyd, and thank you all for your hard work to provide affordable housing for our North Carolina citizens.[1] The importance of this mission is never more evident than this time of year, when winter's chill takes its greatest toll from those who most need affordable, quality, housing. Maslow was right, of course: The sociologist-philosopher included the need for shelter as one of the greatest human needs.[2] All of you, I am sure, understand this priority. Today I call on you to place that priority at the top of the list for 1990 and beyond. That's why I have come today, to offer my help in defining this challenge for the 1990s.

Before I begin my remarks, let me share with you a personal story that my staff in the Governor's Office has encountered. Some of you have heard this before, but bear with me. You're going to be hearing from me often—this issue is one of my top priorities—so you may hear me repeat myself once or twice.

My staff has "adopted" a family through the holiday season and, in the process, has learned a great deal about the trials and tribulations of those most in need. When they began the project, we discovered that the family was just about to be thrown out of their trailer, because they could not pay the November rent. A good Samaritan came through with the November rent, but the mother and her five children—her husband is in jail—certainly face moving to a temporary shelter after Christmas.

We're working with Social Services to find this family a more permanent home, day care for the youngest child, and a job for the mother. You can see the problem this family faces. I hope my staff can come up with a solution.

But this individual story is one of thousands in North Carolina. This situation may be more dramatic than most, but the problem is very real. That's where you come in. Fortunately, we have two outstanding partners in this quest for quality, affordable housing: the Housing Finance Agency and the Housing Partnership. Challenges such as the one I have described can be met with your coordinated efforts.

The Housing Finance Agency is the envy of the nation, having been recognized by the National Council of State Housing Agencies this fall for initiating the most outstanding home ownership program in the country: the Home Ownership Challenge Fund. Our meeting today comes at an appropriate time to highlight that honor, since the agency just signed its 20,000th mortgage yesterday, with Robin and Karen Tuttle of Winston-Salem. That's 20,000 success stories for your efforts to make home ownership affordable for working families, the elderly, and families with moderate and low incomes. Like the Tuttles, many of those 20,000 families assisted are households with two working parents.

Through a variety of financing programs, the Housing Finance Agency has proven to be an effective vehicle for bridging the gap between government and the private sector, as well as for enlisting the support of private business in helping provide affordable housing for North Carolina families. I knew that when I appointed Bill Boyd as agency chairman back in September, he had what it takes to provide the continued leadership we need to meet the challenges ahead.

Like the Housing Finance Agency, the North Carolina Housing Partnership has also established a clear record of success in just a few short years. Seventy-two percent of the partnership's $25 million in state funds already committed have [sic] helped families that earn less than half the area median income. Some of those success stories include projects like converting unused nurses' dormitories in Wilmington and Valdese into apartments for the elderly; creating shelters for the homeless in Durham and Greenville; and repairing twenty-two substandard homes scattered throughout Avery, Mitchell, Watauga, and Yancey counties.

These are genuine success stories. From the mountains to the coast, literally, in cities and small towns, people now enjoy adequate shelter thanks to your work. My challenge to you today, and my challenge for the next three years, is to keep these programs moving forward. Use your creativity and your individual energy to bring excitement to this good work.

But let me take a few moments to talk about the depth of our challenge. Despite your past success, we still do not have sufficient housing in this state. Here are a few grim statistics that help define your work, and my work, in the years ahead:

—Federal-funded housing starts in our state declined by 72 percent between 1981 and 1987.

—At the same time, a shortage of 48,000 rental units for low-income families is further reducing the ability of our citizens to find shelter. Between 1980 and 1985, this apartment shortage increased by 87.5 percent.

—And what about families who want to buy a home? The median income in North Carolina increased by 58.4 percent between 1980 and 1987, but median home prices increased by a whopping 87.5 percent. In fact, the number of households able to buy a median-priced home is only half of what it was in 1970. In ten North Carolina counties, 70 to 90 percent of the households cannot afford the median price of a new home. In the ten "most affordable" counties, that figure is 45 to 50 percent.

The trend line is obvious. The situation grows worse. It's unacceptable. That's where you come in.

We must be able to provide decent and affordable housing for our citizens if we expect to continue social and economic progress. We must have an adequate supply of affordable housing if we ever hope to create a secure environment for the education of our children, a stable workforce for our businesses, and active, concerned citizens in our communities. It is worth repeating here that home ownership brings a ripple economic impact to every government entity through property taxes. It is also worth repeating here that home ownership brings with it a sense of pride, and self-worth, and enhances our spirit of community.

You've already demonstrated an ability to identify underutilized structures such as schools and hospitals and convert them into housing structures. We need to do more of that.

You've also worked hard at involving the private sector and local government in the housing business through financing plans and other alternatives. We need to do more of that, too.

We also need to encourage more businesses across North Carolina to invest in their workers by providing equity funds for home ownership opportunities. When business helps employees become homeowners, business helps itself by keeping good workers, improving productivity, and building morale. A certain chemistry professor I know was able to take advantage of just such a program at Davidson College back in 1960. When my wife, Dottie, and I decided to buy our first home, we obtained a very attractive fixed-rate mortgage through Davidson College—with a rate adjustment when we launched into another line of work!

Let me close by repeating the challenge. I am committed to spending a great deal of time in the last three years of my term taking the lead on the housing issue. It ranks at the top of the list of North Carolina's challenges for the 1990s.

As the National Football League players like to say, "Thanks to you, it's working."[3] But it's not working well enough. You need to help us build a public consensus and a link to the private sector that will funnel our energies to make a difference. It will take personal creativity and energy. It will take leadership and cooperation. I expect all of those, and more, from you in the thirty-six months ahead.

---

[1]William Thomas Boyd (1941–), native, resident of Asheboro; attended Appalachian State College (later University). President: Piedmont Construction of Asheboro, Inc.; Boyd Realty and Builders, Inc.; Integrity Group, Inc.; and Joshua Corp. Chairman, Randolph County Board of Commissioners, 1982–1983; member, state House, 1985–1988; unsuccessful candidate for Republican lieutenant governor nomination, 1988; appointed chairman, N.C. Housing Finance Agency Board of Directors, September 1, 1989, reappointed April 3, 1991. *North Carolina Manual, 1987–1988*, 392, *1989–1990*, 935–936; see also press releases, "Boyd Replaces Crosland on N.C. Housing Finance Agency," Raleigh, September 14, 1989, and "Governor Reappoints Boyd to N.C. Housing Finance Authority Board of Directors," Raleigh, April 15, 1991, Governors Papers, James G. Martin.

[2]Abraham Harold Maslow (1908–1970), born in Brooklyn, N.Y.; died in Menlo Park, Ca.; B.A., 1930, M.A., 1931, Ph.D., 1934, University of Wisconsin; honorary degree. Psychologist; philosopher; educator; faculty member, Brooklyn College, 1937–1951; faculty member, 1951–1969, dept. chairman, 1951–1961, Brandeis University; named Humanist of the Year, 1967, by American Humanist Assn.; author; editor. *Encyclopaedia Britannica*, 15th ed., s.v. "Maslow, Abraham H(arold)"; *Who Was Who in America, 1969–1973*, 463.

[3]"Thanks to you, it's working," was the tag line for United Way commercials televised during NFL games. The spots, typically narrated by professional football players, described aspects of the relationship between their league and the charity.

COMMUNITY JUSTICE FORUM, NORTH CAROLINA CENTER ON CRIME AND PUNISHMENT

RALEIGH, DECEMBER 15, 1989

[Like the speech at the Community Justice Forum, Martin's addresses to the Governor's Crime Commission, February 7, 1990, the N.C. Victims Assistance Network, April 10, 1990, and the Criminal Justice Summit, April 20, 1990, focused on alternatives to incarceration and the problems of prison overcrowding and funding. During the February occasion, he announced the creation of the ad-hoc Governor's Advisory Board on Prisons and Punishment. Information gathered from the committee's statewide hearings on Martin's prison proposals was to be incorporated into a correctional system construction and reform program to be submitted to the General Assembly in May 1990. Scheduled to disband once legislative action on the reform package ended, the nonpartisan committee was composed of judges, district attorneys, sheriffs, and victim and prisoner advocates. It was chaired by state Supreme Court associate justice Burley B. Mitchell, Jr.]

You will earn the everlasting gratitude of the people of North Carolina for your willingness to take part in this conference, and to offer and defend your beliefs about the future direction of our troubled corrections system. There is a great deal of concern among the public these days about the credibility of criminal justice. Our General Assembly has set in motion an outside study of our prisons and their needs. You have already had the benefit of presentations from Justice Whichard, who has given much thought to this vital subject, and from Dr. Krisberg[1] and Mark Corrigan, analyzing the current state of corrections and alternatives for reform in the '90s. You will be pleased to know that I, too, have studied the reports provided to you by our consultants. My purpose is not to summarize them again, but to give you some policy considerations that I hope will be welcome and useful to you.

Crisis to Crisis

When I took office in January, 1985, I found a severe crisis facing North Carolina's criminal justice system: overcrowded prisons. We had 17,000 to 18,000 inmates in a prison system big enough for only 13,000. Very little had been done to implement a 1977 study that had forecast the need to accommodate growth from 13,000—then—to 20,000.[2] So in 1985, either we had to risk federal courts releasing 5,000 of them, or we had to build constitutionally defensible space for 5,000.

With the support we needed from the General Assembly, we launched the largest prison construction program in state history and avoided the unhappy fate of thirty-six other states. Currently authorized construction will eliminate triple-bunk crowding in the sixty-four institutions where litigation had originated, but we must build another $92 million worth, over the next two years, to provide the same standards of fifty square feet of sleeping space and twenty-five square feet of dayroom space, per inmate, at every facility in the state's prison system. Meanwhile, a statutory cap requires special action by the Parole Commission to release any inmates not judged to be dangerous when the prison population exceeds 17,640—98 percent of 18,000—for fifteen consecutive days.

That crisis is being resolved, but it is important to note that this program only fixes the space requirements for the 18,000 or so population we found in 1985, along with improved education, health care, recreation, et cetera. It does not raise capacity. Now we face another crisis, related but different. The rate of imprisonment is growing rapidly, too fast for our capacity. One result is that more inmates are serving shorter sentences, which is eroding public confidence in the protection they feel they are getting from our criminal justice system. So, either we must expand alternative sentencing, or we must expand our prison capacity beyond 18,000. I will propose that we must do both, but first, let me build the case for both.

Alternatives to Incarceration

This administration believes in the concept of rehabilitation through such motivational measures as parole, work release, and "gain time."[3] We believe that good behavior must be reinforced through such traditional rewards. We have been innovative and have advocated a greater utilization of new techniques.

I am pleased that editors across the state are beginning to give Secretary Johnson and me credit for advocating alternatives to incarceration, even though their tone is as if we had just discovered the concept. In fact, for four years he and I have been promoting (a) intensively supervised parole and probation, (b) electronically monitored house arrest, (c) victim restitution by the assailant, (d) halfway houses, and (e) treatment centers for DWI offenders; such principles were a vital part of our Ten-Year Plan for construction and alternative sentencing in 198[6] and still are our goals. The recently successful BRIDGE forestry and IMPACT discipline programs for youthful offenders are more examples of how this administration has been committed to alternatives to incarceration where appropriate.[4]

We must continue to expand such programs and create new ones, but it is not as though we were neglecting alternatives. Indeed, that is the only area of expansion since 1985. The state hasn't increased the number in prison; rather, we have increased the number out on parole and probation by 15,000.

There are presently almost 100,000 criminal offenders under the Department of Correction. Over 80,000 of those are outside the prison walls serving some alternative confinement or restrictions, as we speak.[5] This places a great stress on the supervisory capacity of the department. Nearly 70,000 of those are on court-ordered probation, a number rising at the rate of 7 percent a year. The annual number of paroles issued used to be relatively modest, at 8,000 or so, but is rising very rapidly since the cap was instituted in 1987. It will reach 19,000 this year, nearly two-and-a-half times the rate of 1985! A significant number of those are repeat paroles, having earlier had their paroles revoked.

The point is that we are already relying very heavily on alternatives to prison. We need to give more attention to better alternatives to the alternatives! One place to look would be expansion of the electronic house arrest program. Begun by this administration in cooperation with the courts in Forsyth County, it has now spread to fourteen counties in its third year and is expected to accommodate over 2,000 offenders this fiscal year.

The house arrest program may be worthwhile, as a last chance to stay out of prison, for first offenders convicted of lesser property crimes—of whom there are [a] thousand or so at a time. You may want to recommend it for DWI offenders after an appropriate term in treatment and rehabilitation centers separate from the traditional prisons. I favor that.

In some cases where a violation of one of the terms of the probation or parole now sends the offender directly to prison, some consideration of the magnitude or character of the violation might justify house arrest or intensively supervised probation as a suitable alternative. After all, last year 8,300 admissions, 37 percent, were for violation of probation or parole. Would stricter nonprison alternatives be suitable for a thousand of those?

These measures would surely provide some relief for the prison system, but not nearly enough. There the most serious problem we face is that very few of those convicted of very serious crimes serve enough [of] their sentence. We cannot fix that unless we build more prisons.

Supreme Court Justice Burley Mitchell was thinking of me the other day in a speech when he said, "The prison system is the problem simply because we do not have enough prison space for those criminals who absolutely must be put in prison if we are to have any hope of reducing our crime rate." He wanted his governor to fix it.[6]

Now, some will argue that we cannot solve all our problems by building prisons alone, and that the cost of building and operating prisons is prohibitively high. Well, it may be that the cost to society from increased criminal activity is far greater if we do not keep some of the worst cases locked up longer. A 1987 research study by the National Institute of Justice [NIJ] found strong evidence, based on a survey of the average number of crimes—187 a year—committed by typical prison-bound criminals, that we will pay far more by releasing repeat offenders than by expanding prison capacity.[7] Far more. To apply its findings more cautiously to North Carolina, I looked at the distribution of crimes per inmate at the median, because, as I will show you in about ten minutes, that is about the cutoff margin where we need to differentiate those inmates for whom we need to impose longer terms of actual imprisonment.

On that basis, the NIJ study supports a conclusion that the marginal number of crimes committed by the average prisoner sent back into society would be fifty. Using the study's average cost per crime nationally, $2,300, for fifty hits would run up $115,000 per criminal. That's not as dramatic as the $430,000 figure cited in the NIJ study, but $115,000 is still almost five times the cost to society of locking up more of the dangerous felons for longer terms. By the way, that study didn't include the cost of drug abuse, which would add enormously to the social cost of crime.[8]

Yes, we can agree that building more prisons will be very expensive; and if we aren't wearing blinders, we must also agree that for most felons in our prisons it will cost us a lot more if we let them out. Yet, I have an even better, more compelling argument for building more prison capacity.

Build More Prisons as One Alternative to the Alternatives

Now I want you to pay very close attention and take some notes, because what I have to say next is not what some want to hear, and [I] will load enough statistics on you to make your eyes glaze over. But it is essential for you to understand what I am about to say, because it will answer the crucial argument of those who oppose building any more prisons.

Let me begin this with the premise that we need a change in policy that will, first, keep those convicted of the more serious crimes in prison longer, while second, releasing more of the less dangerous offenders to serve less time in prison but more time in community-based alternatives. I believe that strongly. If you agree with me on that premise, hang on, because you can't get there from here without building more prison capacity.

While we were proceeding since 1985 to modernize our prison capacity for 18,000 inmates, our courts responded with dramatic increases in the number and duration of active prison sentences. They may have perceived our construction program as an opportunity to open up the pipeline and give active sentences to more offenders who previously might have gotten suspended or probationary sentences. In a way, that's the good news, and I will not criticize them for heeding public appeals to get tougher. Another factor was the rising tide of drug abuse and the vast criminal activity that surrounds and sustains the drug market. Surely all will agree that we must deal severely with drug traffickers and dealers, for most of whom rehabilitation is irrelevant.

Whatever the causes of increased admissions, the consequences for the system, with its 18,000-bed limit, was to erode the average time served as a percentage of the sentence. It has to be clearly understood that the average term served in prisons is solely and exclusively determined by only two things: (1) the total number of prison beds available and (2) the total number of persons admitted to these prisons per year. For all the value and importance we may ascribe to alternative sentences, they do not affect the average term served per prisoner one way or another. You have to understand this—call it Martin's Law if you wish: Whatever the number of prison spaces available, whether or not they meet federal standards, divide that by the number of persons admitted per year to get the average term served in years.

For example, if we have only 15,000 prison spaces, they will all be filled, and 15,000 will be the average population. Then if we send 10,000 offenders in during the year, 10,000 must come out, and the average term will be one and a half years, regardless of whether or not there are any alternatives. For every 100 inmates in, 100 must come out. If we then send 20,000 inmates into those same 15,000 spaces, 20,000 must come out, some after less than a year, and the average stay will be— 15,000 divided by 20,000, or 0.75 years—nine months. The only way for 20,000 admissions to stay in for an average of one and a half years is to double the number of spaces to 30,000. That's an illustration with numbers rounded to thousands.

By the way, I am not lamenting the one-to-one ratio: For every one sent in, we have to let one out. That's not the problem. It's not our goal to reach some other ratio either greater than, or less than, one to one. The problem is with the magnitude of the numbers. They are getting too big for our prisons.

Now what were the real numbers? Rather than launch a lot of five-digit numbers at you, let me just say that I have them in a table if you want a copy of this.

TABLE I

Year	Average Population	Total Admissions	Average Term	
			Years	Months
1985	17,330	13,978	1.24	15.0
1988	17,400	17,471	1.00	12.0
1989	17,500	18,100	0.96	11.5

What it shows is that the average time served in 1985 was fifteen months, and by 1988 it was down to twelve months and falling. If the number sent to prison continues to rise without an offsetting increase in prison space, then the average term will continue to get shorter. This year is expected to average 11.5 months, about one fourth less time than the 1985 average. Is that what we want for North Carolina? What message does that send to someone calculating the wages of crime?

Already I'm told that we are beginning to see more offenders decline alternative sentences, as they are permitted to do under our constitution, in favor of taking whatever active sentence the courts might apply. Why? Is it because they are figuring out that they won't have to stay in prison long, especially if they plea bargain for a misdemeanor, in which case their actual time away from their criminal profession won't pose a severe hardship? Perhaps we need to amend our constitution to add specific community-based alternatives and victim restitution to the five types of punishment that now may be imposed without the offender's consent. Did you know that was a problem?

Now let's look at the average fraction of the sentence served. For all categories, it was a fairly uniform 40 percent of the sentence, on average, in 1985, but had dropped to about 30 percent today. That is indeed shocking testimony to what has happened in just four years.

TABLE II. **Percentage of Sentences Served by Inmates and its Effect on the Prison Population**

Category	Population 6/88	Percentage Served		Space Needed	
		1985	1989	at 40%	at 35%
Assaultive Felons	8,426	39%	35%	10,931	9,565
Repetitive Property Felons	2,472	37	31	3,677	3,217
Drug Felons	1,531	43	31	4,458	3,901
Subtotal	12,429	40	33	19,066	16,683
Nonrepetitive Property Felons	2,485	42	28	5,184	4,536
All Other Felons and Misdemeanants	1,964	39	19	5,465	4,782
Subtotal	4,449	41	25	10,649	9,318
Grand Total	16,878	40	30	29,715	26,001

NOTE: For drug traffickers to serve 100 percent of sentence, without "good time"[9] or "gain time," would require an additional 1,647 spaces.

What if we take the most serious general categories of assaultive felons, drug felons, and repetitive property felons. For these more dangerous crimes, the sentence served has dropped from 40 percent to 33 percent on average. As shown in Table II, just to get those three major categories back up to 40 percent would require 19,000 prison spaces! That exceeds the 18,000 spaces that we have, even if all the other convicts served no active sentences at all! This, then, is today's crisis.

I have become convinced that, just as we have made a bold move to build a highway system to meet the needs of our people and are working to improve the output of our schools, we now must recognize the results of neglect of our prison system and move as boldly to fit it to meet the needs of our people. I would begin with the reasonable objective of restoring the reliability of the system so that once again the more dangerous offenders will serve an average of 40 percent of the court's sentence. That alone will require 17,000 spaces.

Then I would eliminate parole, "good time," and "gain time" for drug traffickers so that they will have to serve 100 percent of their sentence. For them, rehabilitation is irrelevant. This will take another 1,700 prison spaces, half close security and half medium [security]. Then for those other less-threatening offenders, I would want to at least keep them serving the same average percentage of sentence as now, which would need an additional 6,800 [spaces].

A $500 Million Bond Issue

It seems to me, then, that the conclusion is twofold: (1) We must continue to expand innovative alternatives to imprisonment, but (2) we must also finance a real expansion of our prison capacity to 27,500. It can be estimated that this would cost $490,500,000 to build, including the $92 million needed to finish eliminating triple bunking. All of this could be paid for with bond financing, and the debt service on that would run $49 million a year. In addition, it would cost about $141 million a year to operate the additional prison space. Combined with the debt service, the annual cost would be $190 million.

So, you see where I come out of this issue of how to balance effective punishment within our Correction Department. With all the justification that I can muster for alternative punishment, for the goals of rehabilitation and cost savings, I am just as firmly convinced that we must also expand the capacity of our prisons for the vital necessity of deterrence, incapacitation, and public protection.

I am willing—in fact, eager—to ask the public to help make this critical decision. That's one reason why I propose that the construction be financed with general obligation bonds, in the amount of $490,500,000, to be submitted to a vote of the people. I have no doubt that the public uneasiness of what has the appearance of becoming a revolving door will be further hardened by education campaign about the erosion of the fraction of the sentence being served, especially in the more dangerous crime categories. Unless you are prepared to argue that murderers, rapists, professional burglars, and drug dealers should spend less time in prison, you must agree that more prisons are needed. To sharpen the focus on this proposal, I will call a high-level conference, in April, of those interested in the subject: a criminal justice summit.

I believe that, faced with a choice between having $190 million of their tax money taken to pay for prisons, versus having a lot more of their money stolen by criminals, the people of North Carolina will vote "Yes" for prison bonds. It will cost them a certain $190 million a year in taxes, but that will insure them against the probability of losing $1.09 billion a year to crime—based on the $115,000 estimate per criminal, times the 9,500 more criminals which I propose to keep away from society per year. This is not related to the likelihood of rehabilitation. What I'm saying is that if we have to spend another $190 million a year to keep the worst 9,500 locked up for another year, they just cannot steal the usual billion dollars while locked up.

In any case, I say it's time to ask the people. To paraphrase an analogy of Justice Mitchell, the basic question would be, "Would you pay one dollar in order to save five dollars from being stolen?"[10] That's what it comes down to: one dollar or five, $19.00 or $109.00, $190 million or $1.09 billion.

I will agree that construction alone is not the way to go. It never has been. We haven't gone that way at all in decades. Neither is it the way to go for us to avoid expansion of our prison capacity, as we have done for at least twelve years.

The crime rate has risen.[11] A new scourge of widespread drug abuse has fueled a raging wildfire of crime. If we don't do something about it, it will be our fault. That will not be my legacy to North Carolina. I am ready to continue to push the General Assembly for stronger commitments to alternatives. Will you join me? But I want you also to join me in making a successful case for more prison capacity. Will you join me? I believe that the people will.

Table III. Estimate of Construction and Operating Costs

Construction Cost

Medium Security (as additions to existing sites)	$38,000/bed	$163,400,000	for	4,300	beds
Drug Traffickers (close and medium security)	$76,500/bed	$130,050,000	for	1,700	beds
Close Security (new, for other serious cases)	$96,100/bed	$ 48,050,000	for	500	beds
Minimum Security	$19,000/bed	$ 57,000,000	for	3,000	beds
Total for Real Expansion		$398,500,000	for	9,500	beds
Commitment to Eliminate[12]		$ 92,000,000			
Bond Issue		$490,500,000			
Bond Amortization: $49,050,000 per year					

Annual Operating Cost

Drug Traffickers	$15,410/bed	$ 26,200,000	for	1,700	beds
Medium Security	$15,000/bed	$ 64,500,000	for	4,300	beds
Close Security	$18,750/bed	$ 9,371,500	for	500	beds
Minimum Security	$13,580/bed	$ 40,740,000	for	3,000	beds
Total for Additional Operating Cost		$140,815,000	for	9,500	beds

Note: This would be phased in over a five-year construction period and thus is shown as 1989 constant dollars.

Recapitulation	Bond Financing Cost	$ 49,050,000	per year
	Operating Cost	$ 140,815,000	per year
	Grand Total	$ 189,865,000	per year

[1] Barry Alan Krisberg (1945–), born in Brooklyn, N.Y.; resident of Berkeley, Ca.; B.A., 1967, M.A., 1968, Ph.D., 1971, University of Pennsylvania. Assistant professor, School of Criminology, University of California-Berkeley, 1971–1977; senior research associate, 1977–1979, research director, 1979–1983, and president, since 1983, National Council on Crime and Delinquency, San Francisco; author. Barry Alan Krisberg, letter to Jan-Michael Poff, March 23, 1993.

[2] It is unclear what "1977 study" offered the forecast Martin cited. One assessment indicates that during the first six months of 1978, the state's average daily prison population stood at 14,450 inmates and was projected to reach 20,650 by 1987. Using a standard of sixty square feet per inmate, state correctional facilities had space for only 9,842 prisoners in 1978. See "1978–1987 Strategies" ([Raleigh: Department of Correction, 1978]), 23, 38, 39, 43.

[3] Gain time previously defined in Poff, *Addresses of Martin*, I, 53n.

[4] BRIDGE trained medium-security prisoners in forest fire control and forest management operations. The acronym stood for Building, Rehabilitating, Instructing, Developing, Growing, Educating. Poff, *Addresses of Martin*, I, 357–358, 603–604.

Boot-camp-style discipline for youthful criminal offenders arrived in North Carolina on October 30, 1989, when IMPACT—Intensive Motivational Program of Alternative Correctional Treatment—admitted its first class of thirty young men at Morrison Youth Institution in Richmond County. Participants in the ninety-day "shock incarceration" program, all first-time offenders, performed manual labor and took basic education courses in a military atmosphere. *News and Observer*, October 29, 1989.

[5] Martin told the audience attending the Criminal Justice Summit, April 20, 1990, that 82,000 convicted criminals were participants in alternative punishment programs. Governors Papers, James G. Martin.

[6] Burley Bayard Mitchell, Jr. (1940–), resident of Raleigh; B.A., N.C. State University, 1966; J.D., University of North Carolina, 1969; U.S. Navy, 1958–1962. Attorney; assistant attorney general, N.C. Dept. of Justice, 1969–1972; district attorney, Tenth Judicial District, 1972–1977; Court of Appeals judge, 1977–1979; secretary, N.C. Dept. of Crime Control and Public Safety, 1979–1982; associate justice, state Supreme Court, since 1982. *North Carolina Manual, 1991–1992*, 467. The quotation is from page 14 of Mitchell's address to the Law Enforcement Associations' Presidents' Planning Conference, Raleigh, June 20, 1989. Burley B. Mitchell, Jr., letter to Jan-Michael Poff, March 10, 1993; copy of LEAP speech, attached, hereinafter cited as Mitchell, LEAP.

[7] Edwin W. Zedlewski, "Making Confinement Decisions," *Research in Brief* (Washington, D.C.: National Institute of Justice, U.S. Department of Justice, July 1987), hereinafter cited as Zedlewski, "Making Confinement Decisions."

[8] Zedlewski, "Making Confinement Decisions," 3–4.

[9] For a definition of "good time" see Poff, *Addresses of Martin*, I, 53n.

[10] The governor summed up portions of Mitchell, LEAP, 11–12. The judge originally stated:

Assuming that this federal study was wildly inaccurate, and that the cost of new crimes committed by released prisoners was only $200 billion—well less than half the actual estimate—the cost to the taxpayers of those new crimes by released prisoners each year would still be twenty times as great as the entire cost of running all the prisons of the nation.

Unless I have missed something, simple math with a short pencil stub shows that every $1.00 spent on prisons has the potential of saving the taxpayers as much as $20.00. The question we need to put to the taxpayers, the legislature, and the governor is about as simple as this: Would you pay $1.00 for a $20.00 bill?

[11] Crime in North Carolina increased at triple the average national rate between 1985 and 1988, spurring a climb from fortieth to twenty-eighth place, according to State Bureau

of Investigation figures released in 1990. N.C. Victims Assistance Network, April 10, 1990, Governors Papers, James G. Martin.
    [12]This figure reflects the cost to halt the practice of triple bunking.

INFANT MORTALITY TASK FORCE

Chapel Hill, January 5, 1990

I'd like to thank each of you for agreeing to serve on the Governor's Commission on Reduction of Infant Mortality. You have an important mission on this commission: to unite the public and private sectors in an effort to give babies born in North Carolina a fighting chance at life.

When I announced your appointments in mid-December, I said this commission would focus on results, not reports. We've done enough studies to know what the problem is: Too many babies are dying in North Carolina. Now we must act.

Together, we must help babies be born to live, not die, in North Carolina. Part of the answer is education. This commission must develop effective ways to teach pregnant women how important adequate and regular prenatal care is to having a healthy baby. We must get the word out that babies will be born to die unless their moms take good care of themselves during pregnancy.

But teaching pregnant women the importance of prenatal care doesn't help much if that care isn't available. Perhaps you saw the recent news reports that one of the major problems facing our public health clinics is inadequate staffing. If you saw those reports, you know that another part of the answer to the problem of infant mortality lies in making sure every pregnant woman in this state has access to early and adequate prenatal care. That's your mission. It isn't an easy job, but each of you has been carefully chosen for the task by virtue of your knowledge and concern. I have great confidence in your abilities and in your determination to succeed.

As you consider these challenges, I would ask you to give special consideration to the plight of pregnant teenagers. It's no secret that another major factor contributing to our state's high infant mortality rate is the number of children having children in North Carolina. The statistics are sobering: A baby born to a teenager is one-and-a-half times as likely to die as a baby born to a woman in her twenties. One infant in ten born to a pregnant teenage mother is likely to have a low birth weight and need extensive medical treatment, possibly for life. So it's clear that teenage pregnancy is one risk factor to focus on, to see if some new approach is needed and will work.

The North Carolina Division of Health Services reports that for all of the past decade, the percent of live births for which there was inadequate prenatal care, technically defined, was 6 percent. We can take some comfort in the fact that this has been the best in the Southeast. As you would expect, for teenagers it is 14 percent, and the number of teenagers getting no care in the first trimester is 43 percent (U.S. average: 48 percent).

These teens present us with special challenges. Often they are too frightened and confused to seek help and don't know how or where to find it. That's certainly not among their most pressing concerns early in the pregnancy, is it?

The results of that fear and confusion can be tragic for the family, and for the teenage mother, and also for her newborn child. I know you were as shocked and saddened as I was by the recent news report of a fourteen-year-old pregnant teen whose abandoned newborn was found dead in a local landfill. We failed that child—both of them, really—and our failure may have resulted in the death of another unfortunate victim.

But even when pregnant teens seek help, they lack the money to pay for prenatal care on their own. For a pregnant teen living at home, if the parents try to help their child financially, they soon find that most health insurance policies do not cover maternity care for dependents. Ideally why should it, right?

Another problem is current Medicaid eligibility rules say that, if a pregnant teen lives at home, her parents' income is counted in determining her eligibility for Medicaid services. If her parents have an income above 150 percent of the poverty level, or if they refuse to supply information to verify eligibility, the pregnant teen will not qualify for Medicaid. All too often these eligibility restrictions force an already frightened and confused teen out of her home and into the streets, just to qualify for Medicaid. If she does stay at home, she will still need public assistance to get prenatal care.

All too often these pregnant teens don't get the money or the prenatal care. All too often their babies are born to die. So what can we do? I propose that we expand Medicaid eligibility to cover prenatal care services for pregnant teens living at home. We can do this simply by not including the parents' income in determining a pregnant teen's eligibility for prenatal care services. Now that's what I call a drastically simple idea: Just count the teenager's income for this purpose of offering prenatal care.

A new interpretation of the federal law, which we requested, now allows North Carolina to change these eligibility requirements for pregnant teens. That would require amending the Administrative Procedures Act and the state Medicaid plan. After that, Health Care Financing Administration approval is required to amend the state plan. So, we've got several steps ahead of us. I support this idea, and I'm ready to back that support with action. By adopting this plan, North Carolina would become a leader in Medicaid expansion for teen pregnancy services. Only one other state has received federal approval for a similar program.

What does this change mean in dollars and cents? A $16 million Medicaid expansion in state fiscal year 1991 would buy prenatal care services for an estimated 3,800 teens under age twenty-one. That $16 million would require a $10.7 million appropriation from the federal government, matched by $4.5 million from the state and $800,000 from the counties. The counties may also need to add staff to help with enrolling new mothers.

This eligibility change shouldn't be too complicated. It means we can deliver early pregnancy care to very young mothers—how to care for themselves, what to eat. It would also mean that teen mothers on Medicaid would be taught about Medicaid programs available for their babies, like WIC [Women, Infants, Children program], if they're eligible for that, too. That awareness could result in other medical coverage for many of these 3,800 babies who now qualify for Medicaid but are not enrolled.

Ordinarily, changing Medicaid eligibility rules, under the Administrative Procedures Act, takes six to seven months, unless emergency rule making is allowed. Federal changes can be made effective in the state fiscal year. I propose that we move now to put this plan into effect by April, if we can, or at least have it ready to go as soon as we can get legislative approval, unless we can get earlier encouragement to go ahead in April.[1] On Tuesday I'll take this up with the Advisory Budget Commission to see what they think about it.

The $400,000 in state funds necessary to implement this plan between April 1 and July 31 could be reallocated from the existing budget. To fund this through the full 1990–1991 fiscal year, I plan to propose that the General Assembly appropriate $4.5 million in the short session.[2]

That's the dollars part of the equation. The "sense" part, I hope you will agree, is simply that: good sense. It makes good sense to help pregnant teens get the prenatal care they need to have a healthy baby. It makes sense to provide some safety and security to a confused and frightened teenager at an extremely difficult time. It makes sense to help her child be born to live in North Carolina.

Earlier I had asked Secretary Dave Flaherty at the Department of Human Resources to ask his staff for some creative, innovative suggestions on how we could attack the infant mortality challenge. This idea for helping teenagers arose from those discussions. I hope you will like it as much as I do, but what we do with this idea is up to us. I hope you will consider supporting this Medicaid expansion as one way to make sure babies are born healthy and happy here in North Carolina.

Now I'm sure as I'm standing here that some critic will object to solving this problem until we first solve something else! It's happened to every initiative so far, but I say, let's just take 'em one at a time! On this one, we've got a good idea. Let's make it work.

You've accepted an immense challenge and an immense responsibility. You have also accepted an immense opportunity to help babies be born to live, and not to die, in North Carolina. Thank you for your commitment, and thank you for caring about the children of North Carolina.

---

[1]The Baby Love program was increased to provide Medicaid benefits to "almost all pregnant adolescents" in April 1990. Task Force on the Reduction of Infant Mortality, Raleigh, July 13, 1990, Governors Papers, James G. Martin.

[2]Medicaid coverage for pregnant women, infants, and children was expanded under *N.C. Session Laws, Extra Session, 1989, Extra and Regular Sessions, 1990*, c. 1066, s. 72.

ONE HUNDRED TWENTY-FIFTH ANNIVERSARY OF THE CIVIL WAR IN NORTH CAROLINA

Raleigh, January 5, 1990

No conflict is so devastating as one that divides a nation against itself. The conflict that threatened to destroy our union of states engulfed every aspect of society, pitting neighbors and families against one another in anger and in sorrow.

We must remember that war as a part of our history and as a part of ourselves. We remember the great courage and agony of soldiers facing bullets and cannon fire on the field of battle. We remember the overwhelming poverty and suffering of the women and children left behind to tend crops, and livestock, and home, while supporting the war effort by making do with little help and even fewer resources. We remember, too, the pain and suffering of African Americans caught in the tug-of-war between slavery and freedom that raged around them.

"First at Bethel, farthest to the front at Gettysburg, last at Appomattox," North Carolina soldiers paid a heavy price for what they accepted as their duty in this War Between the States. North Carolinians supplied one-sixth of the total Confederate army, and 40,000 of them—fathers, husbands, and sons—lost their lives as casualties of war. That was one-fourth of the total North Carolina enlistments, killed in action.[1]

There is no victory in civil war, only the bittersweet thankfulness for peace and the eager hope that the nation and her people would some-day recover from their self-inflicted wounds.

It is fitting that we begin this commemoration here, at the State Capitol. For me, this very building stands as an historic symbol of the division that tore our Union and the healing that restored it. Governor Zebulon Vance[2] directed the state's war effort from the same office I occupy today—the same office General William Tecumseh Sherman also occupied after the surrender of Confederate troops in April 1865.

During the war, regimental banners captured from defeated Union troops were hung from the balconies of the House and Senate chambers as a symbol of Confederate hope for victory. Here, as well, Confederate wives and daughters would gather under those same banners to share stories of suffering and loss, while making military uniforms, bandages, and equipment for their sons, and husbands, and fathers in the army.

It was here, in these House chambers, that elected officials ratified the secession legislation that catapulted North Carolina into the Civil War on May 20, 1861, and established her place in history as the last state to make the decision to secede. In these chambers also, in December 1866, the legislature repealed that secession legislation to once again join us to the Union of these United States. The original document annulling that legislation hangs today in the Executive Mansion.

It was here, too that Lieutenant George C. Round set off the signal rockets that delivered the final message of the war: "Peace on Earth, Good Will to Men."[3] A stronghold of Confederate and Union leadership, a center of Confederate hope and Confederate pain, a site for the beginning of war and the herald of peace, these massive granite walls still stand as a monument to what we were, but just as surely, the foundation of what we have become. The "stillness at Bennett Place" resonates today in these halls and in each one of us, for we are products of that Civil War and the generations who gave their lives in defense of their beliefs.[4]

Ancient Egyptian mythology tells the story of a beautiful winged bird, called the phoenix, that lived in the Arabian desert for more than 500 years before consuming itself in fire. From its ashes, the phoenix was reborn to begin another long and beautiful life. Like the phoenix, a new South was reborn from the ashes of the Confederacy. Glittering cities have sprung from wasted fields of battle. The division of war has given way to the union of peace.

A new and vigorous rebirth has made us stronger than ever before, one united state in this union of states we call America. In his Memorial Day address in 1915, Woodrow Wilson said, "[The Civil War] created in this country what had never existed before—a national consciousness.

It was not the salvation of the Union; it was the rebirth of the Union."[5]

Today, as we remember the war in these chambers, we also celebrate the peace that healed our division and built for us a new society rededicated to the principles of freedom and the United States Constitution. Like rival siblings in any large family, we will always have our differences with other states. The issues we face are no less passionate, no less important than those faced by our ancestors in antebellum America. Yet, today we resolve our differences through the ballots and the courts, not on the battlefield.

The national consciousness that is the legacy of this war has brought us strength and unity in our diversity. Should we ever doubt that legacy, we need only to look to Eastern Europe. The American experience of democracy, that survived its greatest threat 125 years ago, today shines as a beacon of peace, hope, and freedom to the world. Today, forty scholars assembled at Gettysburg College are busy translating the words of Abraham Lincoln into Polish, to help guide that nation toward democracy even as they once guided this nation in its fight to preserve the Union.

Supported in hope, guided by wisdom, and determined to succeed, our European neighbors now share with us the love of freedom and democracy so eloquently declared by Abraham Lincoln to the United States Congress in 1862. Let me close by repeating his eloquence: "In giving freedom to the slave, we assure freedom to the free—honorable alike in what we give and what we preserve. . . . The way is plain, peaceful, generous, just—a way which if followed the world will forever applaud and God must forever bless."[6]

---

[1]North Carolinians often summarized their troops' role in the Civil War with the words "First at Bethel, farthest at Gettysburg and Chickamauga, and last at Appomattox," according to Hugh T. Lefler and Albert R. Newsome. The first Confederate soldier to die in battle, Tarboro resident Henry L. Wyatt, was killed June 10, 1861 at Bethel, Virginia. During the Battle of Gettysburg, Tar Heel soldiers advanced the greatest distance in a fruitless attack, July 3, 1863, popularly known as Pickett's Charge. Some credited the Fifty-eighth North Carolina Infantry with the deepest penetration of Union lines on Snodgrass Hill at Chickamauga, September 20, 1863, but at least one historian wrote that battle conditions made the claim difficult to prove. Finally, the men of Company D, Thirtieth North Carolina Regiment, fired the last shots on Federal forces at Appomattox, April 9, 1865, the day General Robert E. Lee surrendered.

The Tar Heel boast, as Martin explained, implied a harsh reality. Although only one-ninth of the population of the Confederacy inhabited North Carolina, the state nevertheless furnished approximately one-sixth of the southern fighting force. Of the 125,000 soldiers North Carolina offered to the Confederacy—111,000 "offensive troops," including 19,000 draftees; 10,000 reserves; and 4,000 home guards—19,673 were killed in action. Disease claimed another 20,602 men. By war's end, one-fourth of all Confederate battle dead were Tar Heels. Walter Clark (ed.), *Histories of the Several Regiments and Battalions from North Carolina in the Great War, 1861–'65* (Goldsboro, N.C.: State of North Carolina, 5 volumes, 1901), V, 169–173; Hugh T. Lefler and Albert R. Newsome, *North Carolina: History of* a *Southern State* (Chapel Hill: University of North Carolina Press, third edition, 1973), 455, 456, 457; Glenn Tucker, *Front Rank* (Raleigh: North Carolina Confederate Centennial Commission, 1962), 11, 12, 14, 54, 78–79.

[2]Zebulon Baird Vance (1830–1894), born in Buncombe County; died in Washington, D.C.; was buried in Asheville; was educated at University of North Carolina; served in Confederate army. Attorney; member, state House of Commons, 1854; member, U.S. House, 1858–1861, and U.S. Senate, 1879–1894; North Carolina governor, 1862–1865, 1877–1879; Democrat. *Biographical Directory of Congress*, 1973; *North Carolina Manual*, *1991–1992*, 19.

[3]Lieutenant Round sent the message, during the evening of April 26, 1865, from a signal station posted atop the Capitol dome. George Carr Round (1839–1918), native of Wyoming Valley, Pa.; post-Civil War resident of Manassas, Va.; alumnus of Wesleyan University (Conn.), law degree from Columbia University; enlisted in First Conn. Artillery, 1861, and later transferred to U.S. Army Signal Corps. Manassas civic leader, town attorney, public schools superintendent; wrote Manassas town charter, donated land for courthouse; member, Virginia General Assembly; organized "Peace Jubilee" of 1911, the first reunion of Union and Confederate soldiers on a battlefield since 1865, to mark the fiftieth anniversary of the Battle of First Manassas; successfully lobbied U.S. Congress to establish Manassas Battlefield National Military Park. Information courtesy of Raymond L. Beck, History Museum Specialist, State Capitol Visitor Services Section, N.C. Department of Cultural Resources, May 18, 1993.

[4]Bruce Catton's book on the final year of the Civil War, *A Stillness at Appomattox* (Garden City, New York: Doubleday and Co., 1953), no doubt prompted Martin's turn of phrase. Bennett Place, the Durham County farmhome of James Bennett, was the site of General Joseph E. Johnston's surrender of the Army of Tennessee to Union general William T. Sherman, April 26, 1865. The event, which followed by more than two weeks Lee's capitulation to Grant in Virginia, concluded the Civil War in the Carolinas, Georgia, and Florida. Michael Hill (ed.), *Guide to North Carolina Highway Historical Markers* (Raleigh: Division of Archives and History, Department of Cultural Resources, eighth edition, 1990), 56.

[5]See Bartlett, *Familiar Quotations*, 841.

[6]Abraham Lincoln, Second Annual Message to Congress [December 1, 1862], quoted in Bartlett, *Familiar Quotations*, 638.

GOVERNOR'S ADVISORY COUNCIL ON LITERACY

Raleigh, January 25, 1990

Good morning to all of you, and thank you for coming to this first meeting of the Governor's Advisory Council on Literacy. You are the successor to the Commission on Literacy which I named two years ago, headed by Bill Friday. You are, in fact, one of their recommendations. I [spoke] with Bill this morning and told him I would welcome Sharon Darling, president of the National Center for Family Literacy, and introduce her to this meeting.[1]

America's First Lady, Barbara Bush, recently chaired her National Foundation on Literacy, featuring presentations by Harold McGraw and its president, Joan Abramson. But the clear highlight of the conference was a presentation by Sharon Darling about the family-based literacy program in North Carolina and Kentucky, her home state, and its success. She introduced a young Madison County mother, who advanced from illiteracy to an A average in college, as illustrative of the many heart-warming success stories that will continue to drive your commitment.

Bill told me about a film produced for that occasion by WQED/Pittsburgh which featured three outstanding programs from across America—one of which was Fayetteville's part in this Kentucky-North Carolina effort. A national leader—Sharon, we are so pleased to have you on our team, sponsored by the Kenan Literacy Project.

By agreeing to serve on this council, you have accepted what I believe will be a great challenge and a great responsibility: to build on the work of the Governor's Commission on Literacy and develop a long-range plan for attacking illiteracy in North Carolina. Throughout this campaign against illiteracy, we have continued to build on and grow stronger from each other's work. So it was with the original commission, and so it is now with the council. Our responsibilities don't suddenly begin or end. They don't shift suddenly from one group to another. We need a continuum of commitment in the fight against illiteracy, and I believe the creation of this council, a key recommendation of the Commission on Literacy, mirrors our commitment to the fight against [il]literacy.

We do have a problem in North Carolina. As the Commission on Literacy stated in its report, *Literacy for the 21st Century*, 40 percent of adult North Carolinians aged sixteen and older do not have a high school degree.[2] Clearly, many of those people cannot read and write. According to statistics from the 1980 census, 14 percent of the North Carolina population is functionally illiterate. They lack verbal and math skills to handle their jobs.

Every day, we grow more and more dependent on a skilled and educated workforce. Every day, illiterate and functionally illiterate North Carolinians grow more at risk of dropping out of society altogether. Sadly, some of them already have.

A 1987 National Governors' Association report on literacy stated that "The concept of literacy must now encompass a continuum of skills from the most basic reading skills to significantly more complex communication, analytical, and quantitative skills." Your basic challenge is obvious: Ensure that every North Carolinian knows how to read and write. But just as the "concept of literacy" is broader and wider, so is your challenge. As a council member, you must help guide North Carolina toward a workforce where our people have the skills to earn a living wage, to provide for their families, and educate their own children. We're not just working to improve literacy in North Carolina, we're working to improve the lives of our citizens.

Let me take a moment to relate a simple story that speaks volumes about this issue. Earlier this week, the *Winston-Salem Journal* reported a personal experience told by Bob Greene, president of Forsyth Technical Community College. Greene related that he met an elderly couple in a downtown parking garage. As he got off the elevator, he noticed an elderly man and woman who were frustrated because they couldn't remember where they had parked their car. While trying to help them, President Greene soon became aware that the couple could not find their car because they could not read the directional markings in the garage.[3]

In the parking garage that day, the handicap meant frustration and delay. What did it mean when they tried to read the label of their medicine, or a letter on Social Security benefits, or a bank deposit slip? Multiply this experience by thousands of other similar cases—some merely frustrating, others clearly dangerous—and you begin to sense the toll of illiteracy.

With our resources and abilities, there's no excuse for our people not knowing how to read, write, and function in our society. I am determined to end the cycle of illiteracy in North Carolina, and you are the catalyst for that progress. As my Executive Order Number 90 outlines, I'm asking you to get involved in every aspect of the literacy question, from family and work place literacy programs to funding and long-range policy issues. Let me mention just a few of those goals that I believe deserve special emphasis.

You must begin your efforts with a serious look at family literacy programs in our state. To break the cycle of illiteracy, we must work with parents as well as their children. Children learn by example. If they see their parents reading, they will be more likely to want to read themselves. Few activities bond a child and a parent more than reading together and sharing the joy of imagination and learning.

We've used that parent-child bonding to teach female inmates in our prison system to read through the Motheread program. Motheread requires that female inmates read to their children on family visits, and so far, this program has been an outstanding success. One inmate, a mother of four, offered an insightful quote that illuminates the value of reading to her children: ". . . it will make you feel good inside that you can relate to them, read to them. . . . If you can't relate to them while you're in prison, you can't relate to them when you get out." We're not just working to improve literacy through these programs, we are improving lives.

Another highly successful family reading program is the Kenan Trust Family Literacy Project, first begun in Kentucky. Supported by Bill Friday and Tom Kenan,[4] who also serves on this council, the Kenan Family Literacy Project is a cooperative venture between public schools and community colleges. The model works to improve parents' basic skills and attitudes toward education, improve children's learning skills, improve parents' child-care skills, and unite parents and children in a positive educational experience.

A student in that program described her experience, saying, "When I heard about this program, I didn't think I would be able to go back to school, with all my problems. But the staff came to my home, and they made me so at ease that I felt that whatever happens, I can do it. I always wanted my GED, and this program provided meals, transportation, and a program for my child. Social Services let me count the program instead of going to work. That was encouraging, and I just ran out of excuses. . . ."[5]

It's time all our North Carolinians run out of excuses for not learning how to read, write, and become productive members of our society. These and other outstanding literacy programs, such as Head Start and the FRED [Families Reading Every Day] program in the Charlotte-Mecklenburg School System, are taking away the excuses. I am asking you to take a hard look at these and other similar family reading programs. See what's working and what's not. Find out how we can incorporate the successes into our existing programs, and what new programs we might want to start, and where.

Family literacy programs are a good start in breaking the cycle of illiteracy, but we must also consider work place literacy options as well. At least 200 businesses and industries in North Carolina are involved in on-site literacy education programs. Business involvement in education isn't just a matter of civic consciousness, it's a matter of survival. As the Commission on Literacy reported, deficiencies in writing, math, speaking, and listening skills lead to employee frustration, low productivity, high turnover, and the loss of income and profit.

But businesses are fighting back. Burlington Industries, for example, has developed a model program in conjunction with the Caldwell Community College and Technical Institute to provide adult basic education classes at the work site. This program represents a major breakthrough in reaching workers who need help by bypassing such barriers as transportation, time, and child-care problems.

We need to find out what other programs are out there and which ones are succeeding. We also need to make sure we are targeting the population that needs help. We can have all the best programs in the country, but they won't mean a thing if the people who need help don't know how or where to get it.

I also want you to determine how to implement the literacy trust fund recommended by the Commission on Literacy.[6] This fund would be used to support innovative literacy programs across North Carolina. I need for you to tell me where we get the money, who would be eligible to receive grants from the fund, and how the money would be distributed.

Beating the challenge of illiteracy requires one central ingredient: cooperation. Many of the programs I've mentioned involve the cooperation of a number of literacy groups. Others operate autonomously. We need to encourage cooperation and coordination, not just among the membership of this council, but in every literacy program statewide.

You've got a big job ahead of you, building on the work already accomplished by the Governor's Commission on Literacy. They surveyed the landscape. Now it's your turn to lay the foundation for future progress by proposing the options and advising me on how to develop a comprehensive literacy policy for this state.

Among all these challenges, don't forget that each of you individually is an advocate for literacy. Your interest and example can inspire others to join us in this battle for the future of our citizens. Together, we can beat illiteracy. Together, we can write our own success story here in North Carolina.

---

[1]The Governor's Advisory Council on Literacy was established by Executive Order Number 90, signed May 18, 1989; see *N.C. Session Laws, 1989*, II, 3119–3124. Executive Order Number 32, of February 1987, created the Governor's Literacy Council; less than a month later its name was changed, to the Governor's Commission on Literacy, by Executive Order Number 38. See Poff, *Addresses of Martin*, I, 43n.

William Clyde Friday (1920–), president, 1956–1986, president emeritus, since 1986, University of North Carolina system; appointed chairman, Governor's Commission on Literacy, March 20, 1987. Previously identified in Poff, *Addresses of Martin*, I, 43n; see also James G. Martin, letter of appointment to William Friday, March 20, 1987, Governors Papers, James G. Martin.

Sharon K. Darling (1944–), president, National Center for Family Literacy, Inc., since 1989. Previously identified in Poff, *Addresses of Martin*, I, 893n.

[2]*Literacy for the 21st Century: Recommendations of the Governor's Commission on Literacy* ([Raleigh]: Office of Policy and Planning, North Carolina Department of Administration, July 1988), 5, hereinafter cited as *Literacy for the 21st Century*.

[3]The *Winston-Salem Journal*, January 20, 1990, told of President Greene's encounter with the elderly couple. Bobby (Bob) Hamp Greene (1936–), born in Boone; B.S., 1957, M.A., 1961, Appalachian State University; Ed.D., Nova University, 1981. Former elementary school and high school principal; director, secondary education, Winston-Salem/Forsyth County Schools, 1972–1973; president, Forsyth Technical Community College, since 1981; Democrat. *North Carolina Manual, 1987–1988*, 1093.

[4]Thomas S. Kenan III (1939–), born in Durham; resident of Chapel Hill; A.B., University of North Carolina at Chapel Hill, 1959; U.S. Navy, 1959–1961. Director, Kenan Transport Co., since 1972; trustee, William Rand Kenan, Jr., Charitable Trust, since 1984, of the N.C. Museum of Art, 1985–1990, and of the Duke Endowment, since 1991. Thomas S. Kenan III, letter to Jan-Michael Poff, March 14, 1994, hereinafter cited as Kenan correspondence.

[5]Quotation by Regina Osteen Lynn, of Marshall, North Carolina, a young mother who entered the Kenan Family Literacy program in 1989. Kenan correspondence.

[6]*Literacy for the 21st Century*, 11.

Above: Martin's sole highway-related campaign promise in 1984 was to put the Raleigh to Wilmington portion of Interstate 40 under contract in four years, a goal his administration reached in 42 months. Ceremonies at Newton Grove, June 29, 1990, opened the final section of roadway and signaled the completion of the entire route between Wilmington and Barstow, California. The governor handed commemorative mile markers to the mayor of Wilmington, Don Betz (left), and Mayor Bill Pope, of Barstow (right). *Below:* The governor promotes the Adopt-A-Highway program during a visit to eastern North Carolina. Martin launched Adopt-A-

Highway in 1988, and the program continued throughout his second term. Volunteers contracted with the state Department of Transportation to keep a two-mile stretch of road clear of litter for a year. DOT furnished safety training and orange vests, trash bags and bag pickup, and roadside signs acknowledging the participants.

An accomplished tuba player as well as a composer of music, Martin conducted the orchestra during the March of the Maestros program, April 25, 1991, Queens College, Charlotte.

PRESS CONFERENCE AND INTRODUCTION OF
DR. DAVID ALLAN BROMLEY

DURHAM, JANUARY 25, 1990

Dr. Bromley, we're pleased and honored that you have come to North Carolina to visit our School of Science and Mathematics and to deliver a lecture on science policy here at Duke University. We're also delighted that you were able to come here today to discuss some of the important national science issues with us. I also want to welcome Dr. Thomas Ratchford, an old friend and classmate at Davidson and former staff colleague in Congress, who now serves as Dr. Bromley's associate director of the Office of Science and Technology Policy. I'm proud they are with us today.[1]

As a fellow scientist, I was, of course, extremely pleased when President Bush elevated the position of science advisor to Cabinet level. The president's choice of such an eminent scientist and scholar as Dr. Bromley clearly strengthened the importance of the position of science advisor. Before we hear from Dr. Bromley, I'd like to take just a few moments to discuss science policy from the perspective of a governor, a scientist, and a former congressman who served on the Science, Space, and Technology Committee.

Science policy has drawn more attention lately because of the technological challenges we face from countries like West Germany and Japan. These nations have challenged our preeminence in the production of automobiles, electronics, and a host of other areas. Japan's moon probe does not escape notice.[2] We must wish them well, of course, but we must do more than wish for ourselves.

While some have taken the challenge itself as a sign of technological defeat, I am of a different opinion. While we need to do a better job, particularly in manufacturing technology, I don't think we need to throw up our hands in despair and rush to make fundamental changes just for change['s] sake. America remains the most productive and creative nation in science and technology, thanks to our entrepreneurial spirit and our marketplace of ideas. We must, however, coordinate our scientific activities and learn how to cooperate better with one another. For one thing, our historic antitrust laws handicap collaborative efforts by American companies, of the kind used against us by foreign competition, against whom the antitrust laws offer no defense whatsoever.

Science policy in my administration follows a similar pattern to that of the federal government. My science advisor, Dr. Earl Mac Cormac, serves as a cabinet-level coordinator of activities in science and technology ranging from the environment to basic research.[3] He serves as executive director of the North Carolina Board of Science and Technology, of which I am chairman. Let me briefly mention three policy initiatives that have been developed from this structure:

—In 1987, the board began to explore the development of aquaculture, harvesting seafood from what might be considered state-of-the-art farm ponds. Through the formation of the Aquaculture Task Force, a plan was developed, and later approved by the General Assembly, to form an office for aquaculture within the Department of Agriculture.

—A cooperative effort by the Science and Technology Board, the departments of Public Instruction and Community Colleges, and our universities has led to a recent project to improve science and math education from kindergarten to the twelfth grade in our public schools. The heart of this program involves partnerships between local schools and industries to promote science and math education. In two pilot programs, teachers have been participating in summer internships in industries learning how science and math are actually used. This will be expanded as a major part of our efforts to prepare a better educated workforce.

I've spoken many times about how important it is for us to train our workforce to be prepared for the challenges and opportunities in the workplace of tomorrow. To accomplish that goal, we've got to give students the science and math education they need today. Secretary Broyhill will soon present me an action plan to improve workforce preparedness.

—Finally, let me remind you of the agreement we recently signed with North Rhine-Westphalia to form the International Center for Advanced Study of Microstructure. This project offers unparalleled opportunities for discoveries in microelectronics, biomedicine, chemistry, and the development of new materials. It will be located in North Carolina.[4]

These are some of the areas of science that North Carolina is helping to explore. As I said earlier, cooperation and coordination are keys to our success in this exploration, and we are certainly fortunate to have a scientist of Dr. Bromley's stature and knowledge to work with on the national level. He is truly one of the world's foremost nuclear physicists and a leading spokesman for U.S. science and for international scientific cooperation. Ladies and gentlemen, it is a distinct honor to be able to introduce you to the assistant to the president for science and technology and the director of the Office of Science and Technology Policy in the Executive Office of the President, Dr. Allan Bromley.

---

[1]David Allan Bromley, Bush's assistant for science and technology, visited Durham to promote the president's proposals for math and science education; see *News and Observer*, January 26, 1990. Bromley (1926–), native of Westmeath, Ont.; resident of North Haven, Conn.; B.S., 1948, M.S., 1950, Queen's University, Kingston, Ont.; Ph.D., University of

Rochester, 1952; honorary degrees. Award-winning physicist, educator; senior research officer, section head, Atomic Energy Canada, Ltd., 1955–1960; faculty member, since 1960, physics department chairman, 1970–1977, Henry Ford II professor, 1972–1993, Sterling professor, since 1993, Yale University; assistant to U.S. president for science and technology, 1989–1993, and director, Office of Science and Technology Policy, Executive Office of the U.S. President, 1989–1993; author; editor. *Who's Who in America, 1994*, I, 428.

J. Thomas Ratchford (1935–), born in Kingstree, S.C.; resident of Alexandria, Va.; B.S., Davidson College, 1957; M.A., 1959, Ph.D., 1961, University of Virginia. Assistant professor, Washington and Lee University, 1961–1966; physicist, Office of Science Research, Dept. of the Air Force, 1964–1970; science consultant, U.S. House Committee on Science and Technology, 1970–1977; associate executive officer, American Assn. for the Advancement of Science, 1977–1989; associate director, Policy and International Affairs, Office of Science and Technology, Executive Office of the U.S. President, appointed 1989. *1990 Federal Staff Directory*, II, 1097–1098.

[2]With little fanfare, Japan launched its pilotless Muses-A lunar orbiter in late January 1990. The project was envisioned as the first step in a space program that would send unmanned probes to the moon's surface and "explore the atmosphere of Venus." "Japan Goes to the Moon," *Time*, February 5, 1990, 58.

[3]Earl R. Mac Cormac (1935–), appointed science advisor to the governor and executive director, North Carolina Board of Science and Technology, 1986. Previously identified in Poff, *Addresses of Martin*, I, 552n.

[4]The International Center for the Advanced Study of Microstructure was to be based in Research Triangle Park. Martin and Dr. Johannes Rau, minister-president of the German state of North Rhine-Westphalia, signed the pact establishing the center on September 18, 1989. It was "the first international agreement between two states from different countries for a specific scientific endeavor," according to the Governor's Office. North Carolina and North Rhine-Westphalia embarked on a scientific and cultural exchange, in May 1984, with the announcement of their "Joint Declaration Concerning Economic and Scientific-Technological Cooperation." Press release and attachments, "North Carolina, West Germany to Sign Historic Microstructure Research Agreement," Raleigh, September 15, 1989; see also press release, "West German Cabinet Minister to Visit Microelectronics Center," Raleigh, October 5, 1989, Governors Papers, James G. Martin.

RECYCLING TASK FORCE

Raleigh, January 26, 1990

Let me welcome all of you to the first meeting of the Governor's Task Force on Recycling, and thank you for serving. Now it's time for the warning: We have much to do in this arena. You're not starting from ground zero, because we've already set some activities in motion. We've been recycling at the Executive Mansion the past year, to cite just one example, and we're now beginning to recycle glass, aluminum, and plastic collected during our Adopt-A-Highway program.

Your challenge is to coordinate the many good ideas now underway within state government.[1] Several departments have loosely formed recycling programs, and these efforts do good, but no comprehensive policy exists involving all departments. I'm proud that we have started these individual efforts within the departments, but the situation cries out for a guiding presence. That's where I come in as governor, and that's where you come in as members of the task force.

Senate Bill 111 has given us a statutory reason to make formal arrangements for what many of us have been doing informally. Recycling is now the law in North Carolina, and it's now your mission to help us comply with that law as efficiently and effectively as possible. I see four major issues for the task force:

1. First, you must study current recycling activities in state government. Find out what types of waste we produce and in what volume, how much and in what way that waste is being recycled, and what obstacles to recycling exist in the bureaucracy.

2. We also need a cost assessment: How much will it cost to recycle various materials? On the other side of the issue, what kinds of recycled materials are available for purchase, and how much will they cost?

3. Third, we need a plan of action that coordinates all this information into a comprehensive recycling policy for the state.

4. Finally, I need your advice on how to raise the consciousness of our employees—in short, let's make recycling a reflex! Sounds like a poster slogan, doesn't it? "Recycle—it's a reflex." Well, I hope you can do better.

In short, I want state government to be a good example to others.

Now let's talk about specifics. I believe that, in addition to those broad goals you face as task force members, I can point you toward a few specific milestones I expect you to reach:

—Immediately ask employees to separate paper and aluminum waste and use the recycling bins we've already put in place in some agencies, and let's get recycling bins in as many buildings as possible.

—Let's set one goal, to immediately increase tenfold the amount of paper being recycled. Let's aim to increase the current total by 75 percent more by year's end. We will keep score!

—We can join in a recycling effort with N.C. State University to recycle aluminum cans and prime paper from the Dorothea Dix campus.

—Let's review contracts to purchase envelopes with plastic windows and stop their use as soon as possible.

—By March, let's place special dumpsters around the state government buildings to recycle old phone books.

—Put away those Styrofoam cups and start using paper products instead. We're using up the ones we purchased in the Governor's Office, but soon we will be using paper products exclusively. I've asked my agencies to do the same. The legislature has jumped the lead on this.

You've got a lot to do, and you need to do it quickly, but we have already given you a head start of sorts. Let me tell you where we stand today as far as recycling in state government. State government now recycles about thirty tons of paper a month, compared to an average 1,300 tons purchased and used per month. Plenty of room to improve there. Is a 500-ton goal reasonable?

The Department of Transportation has instituted a major recycling program for asphalt used on state roads and highways. Last year, the department recycled 1.6 million tons of asphalt. Most contractors now have the surface grinders to do it, because otherwise they would be priced out of the bidding.

Another important, but less heralded, good deed is that DOT has also started buying rebuilt vehicle parts and recapped tires. That's an important part of recycling. A recycling task force within the Department of Transportation is also looking at several projects: use of recycled oil in road construction, a review of bid specifications to spur the use of recycled products, and the potential use of ground-up rubber from tires and mixed plastic to resurface highways. Obviously, you'll need to incorporate the work of the DOT task force with your own work.

I have also asked the DOT to recycle aluminum, glass, and plastics collected through the Adopt-A-Highway program. While at my Capital for a Day in Elizabeth City this past Monday, I helped kick off the first Adopt-A-Highway program in the state that is specifically designed for recycling those materials.[2]

To assist local governments who also are mandated by law to begin recycling, the Department of Environment, Health, and Natural Resources has established a Planning and Education Branch within the Solid Waste Section. A statewide recycling coordinator within the branch will work with regional waste management specialists to assist local governments in planning and implementing local recycling policies.

I've also joined in the effort by establishing a recycling program at the Executive Mansion. We've been recycling paper, aluminum, and plastics there for several months. It's fun to recycle newspapers: What you do is like physically rejecting their criticism—and tossing it right back. And they like it.

I believe we can, and should, serve as examples of leadership in a statewide recycling effort, not just for government, but for business and individuals as well. The more we raise awareness of recycling in the workplace, the more we will succeed in raising the same awareness of recycling at home. We've made some progress, but there is much, much more to do. Your job is to coordinate and increase these efforts as efficiently and effectively as possible. I want to thank you, again, for your time and willingness to support this recycling effort. Now let's get to work!

<hr />

[1]Martin publicly unveiled, on July 19, 1990, *Recycling Development Plan for North Carolina: Report of the Governor's Task Force on Recycling* ([Raleigh: The Task Force], 1990).

[2]Elizabeth City served as Capitol For A Day on Tuesday, January 23. The visit to the Adopt-A-Highway site on River Road was the final event listed on Martin's agenda. See Governor's Schedule for Weeks of January 22–February 4, 1990, Governor's Papers, James G. Martin.

PRESS CONFERENCE: SCIENCE AND MATHEMATICS EDUCATION PROJECT

RALEIGH, FEBRUARY 1, 1990

On the eve of the president's visit, I want to share with you a preview of an innovative science and math education project which we have under development—and which I intend to outline for President Bush tomorrow.[1] It has already been discussed with his science advisers.

A. The Need for Change

North Carolina suffers with all states in the poor performance of its students in science and math education, resulting in few students going on to careers in science, mathematics, and engineering, and many students inadequately prepared for technical demands of the present workforce. Those job requirements will get tougher and higher; so must we. With North Carolina rapidly becoming one of the leading high-technology states in the United States, the need for excellent preparation in science and math at all levels, from elementary school through graduate study, is even greater.

B. Initiative

Recognizing these needs, two years ago I asked the North Carolina Board of Science and Technology—a fifteen-member statutory board, representing universities, government, and industries, on which I serve as chairman—to begin a thorough exploration of how to improve science and mathematics education in North Carolina. Last July and August, our plan began to come together.

C. An Alliance For Change at the Highest Levels

We are currently forming an alliance among leaders of industry, the superintendent of public instruction, the community college system, and the university system to forge a program to improve science and math education in North Carolina, funded by state, federal, and private-sector monies. I believe that the importance of this problem requires [the] bipartisan cooperation of the governor, lieutenant governor, the major leaders of education, the major leaders of government, and especially the General Assembly of North Carolina. I also believe that North Carolina can play a major leadership role for the United States, in cooperation with various agencies of the federal government—including the White House—through its Office of Science and Technology Policy, the National Science Foundation and its Directorate for Science and Engineering Education, and in the various initiatives represented by proposed bills presently in Congress. I would like to preview for you the basic outline of our program, still in the development stage, which I expect to announce and present by the end of March.

D. Goals For Our Program

1. Excite students and teachers about science, engineering, and mathematics by conducting workshops and summer internships in industry for teachers.

2. Bring scientists and engineers from the public and private sectors as volunteers into grades K through 12 to assist teachers in promoting and guiding activities designed to help students understand how science and engineering works [sic].

3. Make the public aware of the importance of science and mathematics for the workforce of the twenty-first century. Public awareness, coupled with statewide models of how to instill excitement and improve performance in students and teachers, will translate into grass-roots pressure for statewide changes in science and mathematics education, including more adequate funding.

4. Identify skills in science and mathematics necessary for the jobs that will be available in the twenty-first century. This will involve a projection of what skills we need to teach in order to meet the rapidly changing demands of a high-technology economy in the twenty-first century. This innovative work will be done by the Labor Market Information Office of the Employment Security Commission.

E. Program

The heart of the program to improve science and mathematics education in North Carolina will be the formation of local partnerships among schools, industries, colleges and universities, and community colleges to serve as demonstration programs. At least ten geographical areas will be selected, distributed statewide, including at least one near each of our two research parks—University Research Park, in Charlotte, and Research Triangle Park—and one associated with the Forsyth Technical High School.

F. Local Partnerships

Each partnership will establish an advisory council composed of teachers, parents, school administrators, industrial, and college or university representatives. They will meet regularly and oversee the operation of the program, ensuring that it meets local needs and receives local support. They will be served by a full-time coordinator who will:

1. Establish, enhance, and expand workshops and internships for teachers in local industries, community colleges, and universities;

2. Assist teachers in the creation and use of materials that will bring practical scientific and engineering experience into the classroom;

3. Recruit and coordinate the scientists and engineers from industries and local academic institutions to participate in all aspects of the program;

4. Administer a grant program for scientific equipment with the advice of the local council to support teachers in the classroom;

5. Work with local community colleges and universities to improve teacher preparation, and to establish closer relationships between these institutions and school systems;

6. Work with local industries to facilitate their interest and participation in the local school system; and

7. Establish programs to support the interests of women and minorities in science, engineering, and mathematics.

The Educational Reach for Technological Literacy Program, funded by the National Science Foundation, has operated for two years on a pilot basis in the Wilmington and Lumberton areas under the auspices of our Board of Science and Technology, and has already demonstrated that teachers who participate in summer internships do come back to the classroom with changed attitudes about what can be accomplished and improved subject mastery. The Semiconductor Research Corporation has operated a similar internship program in the Triangle area, with excellent results. We intend to draw upon these pilot experiences and enhance and expand them.

Denis DuBay, of North Carolina State University, has operated a successful program of bringing scientists and engineers from the university and industry into classrooms in the Triangle area.[2] He has had excellent results and today has accepted the position as director of the science and mathematics education project. Our program thus draws upon prior successful experiences in improving science and mathematics education and will expand them into a larger arena, where they will bring about a statewide change through increased awareness and participation in cooperative efforts.

G. Workforce Preparedness

Since many students will enter industry directly, without going to college, their awakened interest in science and mathematics will be channeled into a Tech Prep program to be developed at each of the demonstration programs. The successful Tech Prep programs in Richmond County and Lincoln County will serve as models for the development of similar programs. The coordinator and the local advisory council of each demonstration program will have the responsibility for this development.

H. Recruiting Students to Become Scientists and Engineers

A program to interest students who may later attend college, majoring in science and mathematics, will be developed. This will be done in cooperation with local institutions of higher education. A special program to interest women and minorities in careers in science, engineering, and mathematics will be developed in each of the ten regional demonstration programs. A number of successful models already exist in North Carolina and elsewhere, such as the North Carolina Council on Minorities in Science and Engineering and the Math-Science Network of the University of North Carolina.

I. Teacher Preparedness

A program to improve teacher preparedness in science and mathematics will be developed with schools of education in the universities. This program will follow the partnership concept, where teachers work together with scientists and engineers to design courses. One possible development might be to offer internships in industry for those preparing to become science and mathematics teachers. The North Carolina School of Science and Mathematics will also play a supportive role in providing advice and experience on the needs of teachers in science and mathematics.

J. Public Awareness

A significant effort will be devoted to making the experiences of the ten demonstration projects known statewide. This will be accomplished through the preparation of brochures, videotapes, public service announcements, and visits by teachers from other schools to the demonstration schools. Special efforts will be made to keep local government officials at the city and county level informed of the development of the demonstration projects. An integral cooperative relationship with the university system, the community college system, the Department of Public Instruction, and the local school boards will be maintained.

K. Evaluation

Finally, there will be a carefully designed evaluation [that] will be conducted to measure the results of the program, including: improvements in student attitudes and performance, increased public awareness of the importance of science and mathematics, improved performance of teachers, changes in programs of teacher preparedness, and measures of numbers of students, especially of women and minorities preparing to enter careers involving science and mathematics.

---

[1]President Bush visited a North Carolina State University physics laboratory, on February 2, to emphasize his determination that the United States remain a leader in science and technology. The nationally televised tour was intended to generate support for the education proposals contained in the budget he submitted to Congress earlier in the week. During the trip from Washington to Raleigh, Bush told reporters accompanying him aboard Air Force One that he would create the President's Council of Advisers on Science and Technology to heighten the nation's competitiveness. Riding with the president from Raleigh-Durham International Airport to the N.C. State campus, Martin described plans for the state's own science and mathematics education project. *News and Observer*, February 3, 1990.

[2]Denis Thomas DuBay (1952–), born in Baltimore, Md.; resident of Cary; B.S., University of Notre Dame, 1974; M.S., 1979, Ph.D., 1981, Emory University. Founding director, Scientist-Teacher Partnership, N.C. State University, 1989–1991; project director, principal investigator, N.C. Science and Mathematics Alliance, from February 1990; adjunct assistant professor, Dept. of Botany, N.C. State University; author; consultant. Denis Thomas DuBay, letter to Jan-Michael Poff, September 24, 1993.

EMERGING ISSUES FORUM

Raleigh, February 9, 1990

[The following address is similar to the governor's speech at the Take Pride in America awards ceremony, February 2, 1990.]

It's a pleasure to join so many of my distinguished fellow scientists, public policy specialists, and concerned citizens again this year at the Emerging Issues Forum. This year's topic is the environment, with emphasis on worldwide effects. I will address a more local perspective.

One of the great challenges facing North Carolina is the need to pioneer a path between preservation and progress. We must balance the economic growth, which we need to feed, clothe, educate, house, and employ our people while protecting the natural resources that support and inspire our very existence. Yes, the decade of the '90s has brought with it enormous challenges for better schools, better roads, better jobs, and a better environment.

For the next few minutes, I'd like to tell you about what we're doing to strike the balance between economics and environment in North Carolina. Unfortunately, unless I tell you personally, there's no other source where you can read or hear about it, because good news has little news value—at least, not enough to warrant repetition.

Those of you who live on or visit our coast understand the importance of preserving its natural beauty while also providing the businesses and services that make tourism thrive. That's why in North Carolina, we refuse to allow bulkheads and beach walls that would obstruct the natural sand flow of nature, harden the beach, and restrict public access. But here, too, balance must be maintained. We cannot allow these concerns to threaten the safety of our citizens and visitors at Hatteras Island by failing to construct a rock-wall groin to protect the Bonner Bridge at Oregon Inlet. To let it wash away would be foolish and would not preserve anything at all, except a closed mind![1]

We are also working to preserve the few maritime forests that remain along our coast, even with limited funds. Last month we announced a unique agreement to save more than 450 acres of Kitty Hawk Woods. The trade-off was to allow development of nearby property at the same time. It's a balanced agreement that protects and enriches both the public and the private good.[2]

The Coastal Initiative I announced back in November of 198[7] has that same goal of balancing high-quality development of existing coastal towns while preserving the natural resources that surround and enrich them. We will fight to keep marinas and high-density development out of marshes and productive shellfish beds, but we will actually encourage them in the existing towns that otherwise have inadequate payrolls.

Following the lead of my Coastal Initiative, the Environmental Management Commission adopted realistic, tough storm-water runoff controls, and designated the first coastal Outstanding Resource Waters in September. It was a tough fight, but because of that, these waters will remain pristine and productive for the wonder and enjoyment of future generations of North Carolinians.

Now we face another major challenge to our ability to balance preservation and progress with Mobil Oil's proposal to test drill for natural gas off our coast. As the natural gas shortage during Christmas showed us, our nation must have sufficient gas resources to keep our homes heated and our businesses and industries running. Clearly, we must have necessary gas reserves. We want to do what's best for our nation, but we don't want to jeopardize the fisheries, tourism, or safety of our coastal waters and sounds. How do we balance that? Some argue that we should not even try! Their advice is to block exploration, regardless of how it's planned—badly or well. Unfortunately, some of these critics would block gas, and oil, and coal, and nuclear, and hydroelectric resources. That would not leave many alternatives for any practical kind of fuel or electricity to power our economy. I'm counting on Bill Lee to help us think through that.[3]

Others argue we must block gas production to prevent a shipping accident like the *Exxon Valdez* tanker that grounded off Alaska, or like the spill in California on Wednesday.[4] Well, I would want to know whether we could expect more oil tanker traffic if they find gas or if they don't. If they find gas, will that make us more dependent, or less dependent, on oil tankers?

We told the federal government and industry that we must have all the facts before I decide whether to oppose or endorse off-shore drilling along our coast, even for that one test well. That's the first time any state in this nation has ever succeeded in demanding a full environmental study of how drilling would affect our coast—both exploratory wells, production wells, and pipelines. We won that agreement, and we're holding both Mobil Oil and the federal government to a strict standard of performance. We recently had to reject the first study submitted by the federal agency because it failed to include all the information we needed and had asked for. Offshore drilling would be a first-time [experience] for us, so we want to be sure in advance that it's done right or not at all!

Yes, we're working to balance progress and preservation along our coast, but that isn't the only place we're working to preserve and protect our natural resources. Last year I appointed the Western North Carolina Environmental Council, headed by Lieutenant Governor Jim Gardner, to develop a comprehensive strategy for protecting our mountain resources, consistent with attracting some better-paying jobs for western North Carolina.

If you've visited Mount Mitchell lately, or seen Hugh Morton's photographs, you know the serious problem we face with acid rain. Acres of lifeless trees stand as silent testimony to the devastation caused by sulfur dioxide emissions from other states, carried over the mountains and deposited on our trees and soil. North Carolina, I'm proud to say, is doing its part to limit sulfur dioxide emissions from our power plants by paying the extra cost for low-sulfur coal. We've done our part, and we've joined with sixteen other states who are concerned about this problem in a coalition that actively supports President Bush's efforts to reduce acid rain.[5]

The Western Environmental Council endorsed our efforts. Ironically, they got bad press for it because some national environmental organizations want us to pay the cost of cleaning up acid rain emissions from Ohio, Indiana, Tennessee, and Alabama. In effect, they've formed an alliance with the polluters, who have agreed to clean up if we pay their bill. I do not want acid rain poisoning the life out of our mountains, but I do not believe we should pay other states to stop polluting us.

We're also working to preserve our mountain streams. Last year our Environmental Management Commission adopted a new water classification called High Quality Waters. Under this classification, more than 1,000 miles of streams have been proposed for special protection. The Western Environmental Council had proposed that county governments be allowed to veto protection for streams.[6] I could not support that position, so I have helped work out a compromise. Local governments should have the right to express their opposition to stream protection if an area is preferred for development—and have that view considered—but they should not be able to control the outcome. Once again, the balance of progress and preservation is working to provide a means for planned, orderly development to take advantage of our outstanding mountain resources without destroying them.

We have tough environmental regulations in North Carolina—some of the toughest in the nation—but regulations don't matter without enforcement, and we're very serious about enforcing environmental regulations in North Carolina. That's why we consolidated into one department all the agencies in state government that deal with environmental, health, and natural resource permits and regulations. For ten years, environmental and business groups had sought that change, but state and local bureaucracies had opposed it. In 1988, I personally drafted a plan which won their confidence, and it was enacted last July.

We are serious about enforcement. In five years, this administration has issued more fines, for more dollars, than any previous ten-year period! Our programs—to persuade farmers to use Best Management conservation practices, to get Texasgulf to recycle their mining water, and get municipalities to use chemical or biological technologies to remove phosphate—will do more than any other program in America to reduce phosphate loads in our surface waters.

Despite our progress, we face other environmental challenges in this decade of decision and in the years beyond. One major challenge is what to do with our waste: solid, hazardous, and low-level radioactive waste.

Solid waste—the papers, bottles, aluminum, and other garbage we throw away in our homes and offices each day—is rapidly clogging our landfills with a glut of 3.6 pounds per person, per day. We're going to need new landfills, but we can minimize that if we reduce the amount of trash you and I throw away. We can do it by recycling at home, at school, and at the office. That will be a major theme for the '90s: to make it a reflex to recycle!

I want you to know that state government is working to set an example by developing a comprehensive recycling program for all state offices. My recently created Governor's Task Force on Recycling is charged with developing this plan and putting it in place, both for collection of solid waste and purchasing of recycled products. I've also personally started a recycling program at the Executive Mansion. Maybe that's a small thing—not exactly a global response—but sincerity, like charity, begins at home; we've been recycling all our aluminum, glass, and paper products there for months. Together, we're working to make recycling a reflex in North Carolina. If we all work at it, it won't be a small thing, will it?

Waste reduction is a challenge we must meet, but the special case of hazardous waste may present an even bigger challenge. One cynical suggestion is, don't make any, and you won't have to get rid of it!

Back to reality. Physically, everything we enjoy in this society—electricity, electronics, clothing, newspapers, food, medical care—is produced along with some hazardous waste as a by-product. Our innovative Pollution Prevention Pays program works with industry to adopt ways to minimize the amount of waste they produce and have to treat. That program has been so successful that it serves as a model for other state and federal programs, and most of our chemical companies treat or recycle their own waste on site: 90 percent of it, in fact.

Yet, even with waste minimization and on-site treatment, we still have tons of waste to deal with. Nearly all of that is shipped to other states for treatment, but they don't want to take our waste anymore, not if we continue to dodge responsibility. To meet this challenge, I negotiated an agreement with four other southeastern states whereby we will build a chemical incinerator with a companion ash landfill and solvent recovery—recycling—unit. We will accept a minimal amount of waste from those states, and they, in turn, will dispose of all the remaining hazardous waste we can't get rid of in our own incinerator or on site. Because of my professional scientific concern about the elimination of toxic gases from this incinerator, our Environmental Management Commission adopted yesterday a schedule of specific standards for both prolonged and brief exposure for each of 105 major chemicals, most of which are not covered by EPA.

That's another balanced approach to progress and preservation. Some don't like it that we have agreed to a multistate partnership, but some of those same people oppose every facility ever proposed anywhere for proper handling of hazardous waste. It's time we grow up and start accepting some responsibility for that mere 10 percent of our own hazardous waste that cannot be treated on site.

The same situation exists with the regional storage facility for low-level radioactive waste, which we also have to site in North Carolina. Under that 1983 compact with seven other southeastern states, North Carolina must assume its responsibility on January 1, 1993, as the next state to build and operate a storage facility for twenty years. At the end of that time, our facility would close, and we would then ship our waste to a new facility in another state. Certainly I would have preferred some other state to have been honored first, but it's our turn, and it would be foolish to pull out and go it alone, for then we would have no legal protection against all forty-nine other states using our facility.

Through recycling and waste minimization efforts, we can have more industries that create less waste in our state. We are committed to reducing the amount of waste, not increasing it. As we head into the twenty-first century, we must encourage growth, but that growth doesn't have to come with a high environmental price tag. We've already proven that we can manage our natural resources to balance progress and preservation, and with this improved department, we're going to continue working toward that goal. It may not be global, [but] it is, after all, our own backyard—on the coast, in the mountains, and in the industrial piedmont.

Thanks for letting me present this report. It's the only way you would ever know about it. I hope it helps to reassure you that this administration has been proactive and effective in protecting our environment.

---

[1]For press releases on the Herbert C. Bonner Bridge, see "Martin Endorses Groin Project Proposed by Lt. Gov. Gardner," Raleigh, March 14, 1989, "Statement on Bonner Bridge," Raleigh, March 20, 1989, "Governor to Visit White House for Acid Rain Announcement, Senators' Scheduling Conflict Postpones Oregon Inlet Trip," Raleigh, June 9, 1989, and "Governor Praises Issuance of Permit for Project to Protect Herbert C. Bonner Bridge," Raleigh, June 15, 1989, Governors Papers, James G. Martin.

[2]Maritime forests once blanketed the Outer Banks; of those remaining at the end of the twentieth century, Buxton Woods, Nags Head Woods, and Kitty Hawk Woods were the three most valuable. Real estate developers owning a 455-acre tract of Kitty Hawk Woods offered the land to the state in exchange for the state's permission to construct a shopping center on protected wetlands. The property to be donated, bounded by U.S. 158 and S.R. 1206, was worth approximately $2 million. News and Observer, January 10, June 4, 6, 1990.

[3]William States Lee (1929–), chairman, chief executive officer, 1982–1994, president, 1989–1994, Duke Power Co. Previously identified in Poff, Addresses of Martin, I, 856n; see also News and Observer, January 11, 1994.

[4]The tanker American Trader apparently struck her own anchor on February 7, 1990, as

the crew attempted to position the vessel to pump her cargo into an offshore oil pipeline, two miles from Huntington Beach, California. A significant portion of the 400,000 gallons of light Alaskan crude that poured from her torn hull polluted the southern California coastline from Anaheim Bay to Newport Harbor, a distance of fourteen miles. As damaging as the accident was, the *American Trader* spilled only one twenty-seventh the amount of oil disgorged by the *Exxon Valdez* in March 1989. *New York Times*, February 9, 14, 15, 20, 1990.

[5]The Alliance for Acid-Rain Control was comprised of sixteen governors and former governors intent on solving the acid rain problem. Martin joined the organization in May 1989 and was appointed vice-chairman of its research group, the Center for Clean Air Policy, in January 1990. Press releases, "Governor Martin Attends President Bush's Acid Rain Announcement, Pledges to Protect Western North Carolina Mountains," Raleigh, June 14, 1989, and "Governor Named Vice-Chairman of National Environmental Group, Announces Support for Lieutenant Governor Gardner's Efforts," Raleigh, January 11, 1990, Governors Papers, James G. Martin.

[6]The council passed the veto resolution, presented by Charles H. Taylor, on January 10, 1990. *News and Observer*, January 11, 26, February 3, 9, 1990.

PRESS RELEASE: GOVERNOR REJECTS PROPOSAL TO SELL
PORTION OF UMSTEAD PARK, URGES CITIZEN SUPPORT FOR
ADEQUATE FUNDING OF STATE PARK SYSTEM

RALEIGH, FEBRUARY 13, 1990

Governor Jim Martin issued the following statement on Thursday about the proposal from the staff at the Department of Environment, Health and Natural Resources to sell a portion of Umstead State Park to raise funds to buy other parkland in the Triangle, upgrade existing parks, and underwrite park operations. "After careful review, including a personal visit to the park on Monday, I have decided not to support or consider further the proposal to sell part of Umstead Park. I remain committed to seeking additional funds from the legislature for our state park system, but I need help. Last session, I asked for $25 million for capital improvements for this current biennium and $120 million to improve the park system during the next eight years. The General Assembly approved only $6 million for capital improvements and declined to make a long-term commitment to our parks.

"The Umstead proposal was, I am sure, born of the frustration caused by the General Assembly's continued lack of adequate funding. Our parks employees, both in Raleigh and across the state, have a long history of dedicated service, and I want to thank them for seeking a creative solution to the funding dilemma in which they find themselves. The interest and concern that many citizens have expressed in this matter is sincerely appreciated. If only they would apply their energies and commitment to helping us obtain the funding we need for our parks. Twenty years ago, there was little legislative support for needed repairs

and improvements to the Governor's Mansion, which badly needed renovation. When Governor Bob Scott suggested that the Mansion be closed
and a more modern residence be provided, only then did the shock
awaken the public and inspire the legislative commitment to fix up the
grand old treasure, now ninety-nine years of age."

PRESS RELEASE: GOVERNOR ISSUES STATEMENT ON
RESEARCH OFFICE AUDIT

RALEIGH, FEBRUARY 20, 1990

[The Governor's Research Office performed many duties. It tracked and
helped develop legislation, gathered information on topics of state importance,
and collected newspaper reports on contemporary political figures so that Martin could stay abreast of their views on particular subjects. The office also followed Martin's official activities, both to ensure consistent gubernatorial policy
and to verify—if requested by a government agency or private citizen—his stance
on an issue.

The office conducted its affairs in relative obscurity until November 6, 1989,
when an article in the Raleigh *News and Observer* questioned the relationship
between the agency and the governor's reelection campaign. The story focused
on the report the research office assembled on then lieutenant-governor Robert
B. Jordan III, Martin's opponent in the 1988 gubernatorial race. The governor
contended that compiling the file "'was a legitimate function of the administration to keep the governor informed and to have a source of information about
the positions taken by the leader of the loyal opposition in the legislature.'"
However, the political commentary outlining Jordan's vulnerability on a number of issues moved the document beyond the bounds of a dispassionate collection of press excerpts and into the realm of campaign material, according to the
News and Observer.

The story prompted State Auditor Edward Renfrow to investigate whether
the office had been conducting campaign business using state funds, as the newspaper had suggested. His report, released February 20, 1990, concluded that the
agency improperly spent tax money making suspect telephone calls and undertaking political research on Jordan and others.

It appeared to Renfrow and his staff that a certain blending of official and
campaign functions had occurred within the office. But their report further stated
that, without "'any meaningful accountability system in place to account for
employee activities, we are unable to quantify the amount of questionable uses
of taxpayers' funds'" expended by the agency in conducting reelection-related
research. The auditor instructed the research office to limit its activities to the
requirements of state business and establish tighter controls over its operations.

Renfrow also urged Martin to monitor more carefully telephone use in the
offices under his control. Six hundred fifty-one long-distance calls, dialed at
state expense to the governor's political advisers, were discovered as the audit
unfolded. Of those, the Martin campaign reimbursed the state $15.35 for twenty-
three calls to consultants in Washington, D.C. Many of the remaining 628 phone
calls were placed to J. Brad Hays, Martin's longtime political counselor, in

Charlotte. Hays, declared Nancy Temple, Martin's chief of staff, often conferred with the governor and senior administration members on many issues "not related to politics." The cost of those calls was not repaid.

The audit proceeded with the governor's complete cooperation, noted Renfrow. Martin vowed to institute the report's recommendations.

Following the release of the auditor's findings, Attorney General Lacy Thornburg declared his intention to meet with Renfrow and the Wake County district attorney to "determine whether an investigation was warranted into possible misuse of state property." The threat of a probe by the State Bureau of Investigation roused Martin from his sickbed, where he had been battling a severe throat infection for days. He called a press conference for Thursday, February 22, 1990, to defend himself and his administration. See Appendix I, page 677, below; see also *News and Observer*, November 6, 7, 22, December 1, 1989, February 15, 21, 22, 23, 24, 1990.]

Governor Jim Martin issued the following statements [*sic*] on Tuesday after receiving a report from State Auditor Ed Renfrow on his review of the Governor's Research Office:

"I'd like to thank the state auditor for his insistence on being fair as well as thorough in his review. We have already repaid the state for mistakes that were made in telephone usage. The auditor also questions internal messages on certain files. I agree that some were not appropriate. However, there appears to be no reasonable way to determine how to set a dollar figure on inappropriate notes in margins.

"In studying the auditor's report, I have come to the conclusion that there is a need to review the management practices in the research office. I have instructed my chief of staff, Nancy Temple, to initiate such a review.[1] In fact, changes in office management techniques and operations already have been accomplished. The public can have full confidence that we are working diligently to learn from our mistakes and to prevent them from happening again."

---

[1]Nancy Huey Temple (1948–), born in Philadelphia, Pa.; resident of Raleigh; was educated at Salem College, University of North Carolina at Chapel Hill, University of North Carolina at Greensboro, and North Carolina State University. Congressional campaign finance director for W. Eugene Johnston, 1980, 1982; executive campaign director, Reagan-Bush North Carolina, 1984; chief assistant to the secretary, 1985, assistant secretary for administration, 1985–1987, N.C. Department of Human Resources; deputy chief of staff, 1987–1988, chief of staff, 1989–1993, Office of the Governor; assistant secretary, parks and community resources, N.C. Department of Natural Resources and Community Development, 1988–1989; assistant secretary, community development and housing, N.C. Department of Economic and Community Development, Sept.–Dec. 1989. *News and Observer*, November 9, 1989, April 7, 1991.

JOINT MEETING OF EDUCATION BOARDS

RALEIGH, MARCH 8, 1990

[Martin unveiled the Governor's Committee on Workforce Preparedness at the second annual combined meeting of the State Board of Education, Board of Community Colleges, and University of North Carolina Board of Governors; his text for the event follows. He also addressed the committee's work in his Beta Gamma Sigma Distinguished Lecture, East Carolina University, March 20; at an economic development seminar, Southwestern Community College, April 4, and a Wilkesboro luncheon, April 17; and before the N.C. World Trade Association, May 10, the Association of Community College Trustees, May 18, and the Cleveland County Chamber of Commerce, September 25, 1990.]

I want to talk to you today, both as governor and as an educator, about the future of North Carolina—about the future of our economy and of the men and women who fill the jobs that fuel that economic progress. Today I am announcing a major new initiative: the creation of the Governor's Committee on Workforce Preparedness.

You'll see some familiar names on this committee when I announce all the members in about two weeks. Jim Broyhill, secretary of the state Department of Economic and Community Development, and Bob Scott, president of the community college system, have already agreed to help us by serving as vice-chairmen on the committee—as has Superintendent Etheridge, as has university vice-president Jay Robinson[1]—and I will be talking with others of you. And I will have a surprise chairman, a well-known personality who is just right for this, but I am going to make you wait in suspense for a couple of weeks. This chairman will join me at a news conference later this month.[2]

This committee is not expected to study the problem again. That's been done! Its purpose is to get action and results by building support for the ideas generated previously by such groups as the Commission on the Future of the Community College System, chaired by Sherwood Smith;[3] the Governor's Commission on Literacy, chaired by Bill Friday; and the SAT study commission, chaired by Richardson Preyer;[4] and some of our own ideas.

The SAT study commission, in particular, considered the needs of half of our students: those planning to attend college. The Governor's Committee on Workforce Preparedness will address the needs of that other "forgotten half" who do not take the SAT, because they do not expect to go to college, but who need desperately to be better prepared to enter the workforce after graduation. As a partnership between government, business, and industry, the committee will initiate educational reform to improve student achievement in a curriculum that is designed to be career oriented, that considers the workplace and its need for train-able workers who have the basic skills.

The committee will serve to build a greater consensus between business and education. We've seen good examples of how business and education can communicate and develop public-private partnerships that work for workforce preparedness. Now we need to spread this success. To open those lines of communications, the Governor's Committee on Workforce Preparedness will hold a series of hearings across the state in the next few months, meeting with leaders of business and industry to discuss and develop programs to meet their needs. Those hearings will culminate in a business and education round table sometime in the fall.

Why do we need such a committee? For the third year in a row, *Site Selection Handbook* has rated North Carolina number one in the nation for new manufacturing investment.[5] That's great. *Inc.* magazine has just rated Raleigh-Durham, Charlotte, Hickory, and Wilmington-Jacksonville as four of the top fifteen national entrepreneurial hot spots for job growth, business starts, and the proportion of high-growth companies; three more North Carolina cities—that's nine in all—made it into the top 100 out of a field of 192.[6] That's better than any other state.

Our economy is strong, healthy, and growing. But the future competitiveness of our state economy and our workforce is threatened. Let's face it: For too long we have accepted the results of an educational system which fails to prepare students for the changing demands of the workforce and often doesn't even recognize that as a part of its mission.

John L. Clendenin, CEO of BellSouth Corporation and chairman of the U.S. Chamber of Commerce, has said, "The bottom line is, America's fight for long-term competitiveness ultimately will be won or lost not in the halls of Congress, not in the boardrooms around the world, but in America's classrooms."[7] He's right! Unless we initiate radical reforms in our education system, our state stands a very real chance of plummeting drastically from our number-one ranking in the national competition for jobs and investment.

We must reform our education system, not just to strengthen scholastic aptitude among the college bound, but among the "work bound" as well. We must develop and promote a career-oriented curriculum which will prepare our students to enter the workforce, and open—not close—the door to attending college if they change direction at a later date.

What is a career-oriented curriculum? That's what we've got to figure out. That's the innovation we must design. I see it as a curriculum that stresses the basics: with English language and arithmetic as the ultimate vocational courses! It will offer programs shaped to the needs of major job sectors and will prepare high school students for jobs after graduation—jobs, for example, in technical support and assembly, office administration, health and home care, agriculture marketing, and general business. These and a few others would be intentionally broad categories so that the students' options would not be narrowed too much, too soon. If the student should later decide to attend college, even after working a few years, the career-oriented curriculum would not be wasted for that, because the community college system would by then have a working knowledge of this individual and will have the flexibility to help with the transition. That's better than what we offer now for the academic late bloomer.

Some critics will discount this and object that some students may take the wrong track and miss their chance for college. I say the forgotten half don't go to college now, and for them all we offer is a "wrong track." Is that too harsh?

Let me share with you a few comments of business people, from around North Carolina, to show just how much we have forgotten our work-destined students. A state manufacturer employing 340 workers says, "I am dismayed at the poor educational level of some of the high school graduates. A high school graduate who cannot correctly perform simple multiplication, read a ruler, or punctuate a sentence is of no use to our company.[. . .]"[8]

Another health care employer writes, "It is my perception that the majority of new graduates now entering the labor market have marginal basic skills at best, no work ethic, and take no pride in their performance. These graduates take little or no responsibility for their performance on the job and enter the workforce with the opinion that the world owes them something for nothing. They are difficult to motivate, find no challenge, and have little initiative. If basic skills and attitudes do not both markedly increase, I see a very dismal future for both the employees and the employers."[9]

A major retailer found that employees could not even handle their time cards properly, so some were being overpaid, and some were being underpaid, and neither group had the foggiest idea whether their pay was over or under! That employer has now changed to bar-coded time cards. How's that for a lack of confidence?

Finally, a mid-sized manufacturer states, "It is my opinion that North Carolina will lose industry in the future unless it can supply a well-educated workforce."[10]

These comments are culled from those of 2,500 employers who took part in a 1989 North Carolina Business and Industry survey on workforce preparedness.[11] That survey was compiled by the Governor's Office and our state departments of Administration and Economic and Community Development. Each of you should have copies in front of you.

These results, to be honest, are chilling. This survey, released for the first time, today, reveals a deplorable lack of confidence in the trainability displayed by our students when they leave school to enter the workforce. Of the responding employers, 32 percent say that applicants' reading skills are inadequate, while only 54 percent say reading skills are adequate; but that's the highest approval rate in any of the five skills studied in the survey. Does it surprise you that 52 percent of the respondents say writing skills are inadequate; that 48 percent say math skills are inadequate? Forty percent say the ability of the applicants to think and solve work-related problems is inadequate, and 51 percent say communications skills of North Carolina's high school graduates are inadequate.[12]

Every cloud has a silver lining, and the silver lining in this storm cloud of educational inadequacy seems to be the strength of our community colleges, and colleges and universities. Eighty-four percent of the businesses and industries responding to the survey said that the average college and university graduate is well prepared for the workforce. Seventy-two percent agree that graduates of community colleges are also well prepared. That's good. We've demanded excellence in postsecondary education, and it shows![13]

Employers say they have confidence in the product of our postsecondary schools, but they lack confidence in the product of our secondary schools. If our colleges and community colleges can prepare students to enter the workforce, and they do—that's what my chemistry degree was for; if career preparation is not too anti-intellectual for them, why can't our elementary and secondary schools do the same? Why must our public schools alone neglect preparation for the workplace? Is it beneath their intellectual dignity, but not for colleges?

The leader of the largest state teachers' organization recently scoffed at such reports, saying it's not the schools' or the educators' responsibility to prepare students for jobs in the workforce.[14] Whose is it, then? I say that attitude is a big part of the problem. I say that radical education reform is not a luxury; it's necessary for survival.

In our increasingly competitive and technological economy, the forgotten half of children need a career curriculum, not to train them for any specific job, but to educate them and give them the basic skills so that they will be trainable for a job. Their diploma ought to be a product warranty, but it's not. We need our educational leaders to understand and respond to the needs of business and prepare these students to meet those needs with adequate grounding in the basics, as well as appropriate advanced training. Business, for its part, must help educational leaders understand their needs and take an active role in educating and training the workforce of the future. That's part of the mission of my Committee on Workforce Preparedness.

I would like to commend Governor Scott and the Community College Board for recognizing the needs of our work-bound students and for recommending the creation of a committee such as the one I envision. I hope you will use your considerable knowledge and insight to support and direct this new committee to achieve true educational reform and improved workforce preparedness in our state. Help me get ready for my 1991 budget that will be my last biennial budget message as governor.

Business is ready to work with us. The Kenan Family Literacy Project, which we visited with Mrs. Bush at lunch, is only one of several outstanding business-education partnerships operating in North Carolina.[15] Cities in Schools, Adopt-A-School, Tech Prep partnerships between high schools and community colleges, and related programs are successfully combining the resources of business and education for improved student motivation and achievement.

Over 500 businesses across this state are directly engaged in some form of educational program in their local schools. The Governor's Business Council on Education has stimulated and shared many ideas that work. Good examples are all around us. My Committee on Workforce Preparedness is going to help us apply what we know that works.

James D. Robinson III, CEO of American Express, has said, "The collaboration between business and schools is the wave of the future. The question is not whether to get involved, but when and how. There is simply too much at stake, for business and students alike, for us to sit back and hope that our country's education problems will solve themselves."[16]

It's time to follow our business leaders and reform our educational system to meet the changes and challenges of the twenty-first century. I intend to do that by making workforce preparedness a high priority for the remaining three years of my administration. It will be based on partnerships between business and schools, and it will be innovative in developing a career curriculum that will be worthy of promotion, not a demotion.

I want to remember the forgotten half of our educational system. I want to be a catalyst for reform in elementary and secondary schools across this state. I want well-educated high school graduates, whether they are ready for college or ready for the workforce.

I know you share my dream, and I hope all of you here, as members of the combined boards of community colleges, education, and the UNC Board of Governors will join forces with me and business leaders in supporting the Governor's Committee on Workforce Preparedness. Working together, we can redeem the forgotten half and build a brighter future of opportunity for them. We owe it to them, don't we?

Thank you for listening. Now I would like to introduce to you our next speaker, the man who serves as President Bush's assistant secretary for postsecondary education in the U.S. Department of Education. Dr. Leonard Haynes III is the man with the educational purse strings, overseeing a $10 billion annual budget—almost half of the total budget of the Department of Education. That $10 billion funds more than 1,000 employees and more than forty programs for student financial aid, institutional aid, and international education under Dr. Haynes's direction. With his extensive educational experience, both in teaching and administration, Dr. Haynes is more than adequately trained to handle the challenges of his particular job. Will you please join me in welcoming Dr. Leonard Haynes.[17]

---

[1]Jay M. Robinson (1928–), native of Mitchell County; B.S., Appalachian State University, 1950; M.A., University of North Carolina at Chapel Hill, 1957; Ed.D., Duke University, 1976; U.S. Army Air Force, 1946–1948. Educator; superintendent, 1965–1977, Cabarrus County Schools; superintendent, Charlotte-Mecklenburg Schools, 1977–1986; served as vice-president for public affairs and as vice-president for special projects, University of North Carolina General Administration, 1986–1993. News and Observer, September 24, 1993; Jan-Michael Poff and Jeffrey J. Crow (eds.), Addresses and Public Papers of James Baxter Hunt, Jr., Governor of North Carolina, 1981–1985 (Raleigh: Division of Archives and History, Department of Cultural Resources, 1987), 431n, hereinafter cited as Poff and Crow, Addresses of Hunt.

[2]Martin revealed the identity of the "surprise chairman" of his Commission on Workforce Preparedness on March 21, 1990: Tom E. Smith, chief executive officer of the Food Lion supermarket chain. Smith (1941–), born in China Grove; A.B., Catawba College, 1964; U.S. Army Reserve, 1968–1972. Joined Del Monte Co., 1964; hired by Food Lion, Inc., as buyer, 1970, and subsequently promoted to vice-president for distribution, 1974, executive vice-president and board member, 1977, president, 1981, chief executive officer, 1986, and board chairman, 1990. His appearances in Food Lion television commercials made him very popular, and his work ethic was legendary. Regina Oliver, "Tom E. Smith of Food Lion, Inc.: Doing a Thousand Things 1 Percent Better," North Carolina, February 1992, 8–11; see also Workforce Preparedness Press Conference, March 21, 1990, Governors Papers, James G. Martin.

[3]Sherwood H. Smith, Jr. (1934–), native of Jacksonville, Fla.; resident of Raleigh; A.B., 1956, J.D., 1960, University of North Carolina at Chapel Hill. Attorney practicing in Charlotte and Raleigh, 1960–1965; associate general counsel, 1971–1974, executive vice-president for administration, 1974–1976, president, 1976–1992, chief administrative officer, 1976–1980, chairman and chief executive officer, since 1980, Carolina Power and Light Co. Previously identified in Poff and Crow, Addresses of Hunt, II, 266n; see also News and Observer, August 25, 1992.

[4]The Scholastic Aptitude Test scores of North Carolina's high school students were the worst in the country in 1989, having fallen from second worst a year earlier. Formed to investigate the factors resulting in such poor performance, the SAT study commission was entrusted with the first critical statewide evaluation of secondary education in a generation. Secretary Bobby R. Etheridge, state superintendent of public instruction, announced

the formation of the twenty-four-member study commission in October 1989 and directed that it furnish recommendations for legislative action by May 1, 1990.

The commission, led by L. Richardson Preyer, released preliminary findings two months in advance of its deadline. It recommended that students learn to analyze information, rather than merely regurgitate facts, and take all coursework necessary for admission to the University of North Carolina system, as well as advanced electives. The group also advised college-bound students to take the Preliminary SAT in ninth grade and to retake the PSAT and SAT each year in high school, using the tests as indicators of areas for further study and improvement. *News and Observer*, October 14, 1989, March 29, April 29, 1990; Poff, *Addresses of Martin*, I, 941.

Lunsford Richardson Preyer (1919–), native, resident of Greensboro; A.B., Princeton University, 1941; LL.B., Harvard Law School, 1949; served in U.S. Navy during World War II. Superior court judge, 1956–1961; Democratic candidate for governor, 1964; senior vice-president, trust officer, city executive, North Carolina National Bank, Greensboro, 1964–1966; member, U.S. Congress, 1969–1981. *Biographical Directory of Congress*, 1673.

[5]North Carolina and Florida tied for first-place honors, each having announced 106 new manufacturing facilities in 1989. However, the Tar Heel State alone held the record for new plants during the 1987–1989 period, with 320; Texas was second with 278. Deborah S. Fusi, "Site Selection's '89 Scorecard Posts Record Number of New Facilities," *Site Selection and Industrial Development*, February 1990, 16–24.

[6]Las Vegas was the best city for starting a new business, according to the 1990 *Inc.* survey. Raleigh/Durham ranked ninth, Charlotte eleventh, Hickory twelfth, Wilmington/Jacksonville thirteenth, Asheville fifty-third, Greensboro/Winston-Salem fifty-sixth, and Fayetteville ninety-seventh. John Case, "The Most Entrepreneurial Cities in America," *Inc.*, March 1990, 42–43.

[7]John L. Clendenin (1935–), born in El Paso, Texas; B.A., Northwestern University, 1955. Telephone company executive; vice-president, operations, Pacific Northwestern Bell, 1978–1979; vice-president, AT&T, 1979–1981; president, 1981–1982, board chairman, 1982–1984, Southern Bell Telephone and Telegraph Co.; board chairman, president, chief executive officer, BellSouth Corp., since 1984; chairman, U.S. Chamber of Commerce, 1989. *Who's Who in America, 1994*, I, 644. The quotation attributed to him could not be verified.

[8]Michael L. Vasu and Andy Frazier, "Workforce Preparedness for Economic Development: Report on the 1989 North Carolina Business and Industry Survey" ([Raleigh]: Office of Policy and Planning, N.C. Department of Administration; Division of Employment and Training, N.C. Department of Economic and Community Development; N.C. Business Committee for Education, Office of the Governor, [1990]), 17, hereinafter cited as Vasu and Frazier, "Workforce Preparedness for Economic Development."

[9]Vasu and Frazier, "Workforce Preparedness for Economic Development," 17.

[10]Vasu and Frazier, "Workforce Preparedness for Economic Development," 18.

[11]Actually, the bar-code anecdote, above, cannot be found in "Workforce Preparedness for Economic Development."

[12]Although the governor rounded off many of the percentages to the nearest whole number, the figures are essentially accurate. Vasu and Frazier, "Workforce Preparedness for Economic Development," 8.

[13]These percentages were adjusted to the nearest whole number. Only 29 percent of the survey's participants felt that the state's high school graduates were adequately prepared for the working world. See Vasu and Frazier, "Workforce Preparedness for Economic Development," 9.

[14]Martin was referring to remarks by Julia P. Kron, president of the North Carolina Association of Educators. *News and Observer*, October 31, 1989.

[15]Carver Elementary School, in Henderson, one of seven participants in the Families in School Together literacy project, received a visit from Barbara Bush on the morning of March 8, 1990. The First Lady came to North Carolina to advocate support for the experimental program, which was administered by the National Center for Family Literacy and funded by the William R. Kenan, Jr., Family Trust. She spent an hour at Carver and later addressed literacy experts at a luncheon in Chapel Hill. *News and Observer*,

March 7, 9, 1990; see also Introduction of First Lady Barbara Bush, March 8, 1990, and Response to Barbara Bush Speech, March 8, 1990, Governors Papers, James G. Martin.

[16]James Dixon Robinson III (1935–), born in Atlanta, Ga.; B.S., Georgia Technical Institute, 1957; M.B.A., Harvard University, 1961; honorary degrees; U.S. Naval Reserve, 1957–1959. Various managerial positions with Morgan Guaranty Trust Co., 1961–1968; general partner, Corporate Finance Dept., White, Weld and Co., 1968–1970; executive vice-president, 1970–1975, president, 1975–1977, board chairman and chief executive officer, 1977–1993, American Express Co.; president, J. D. Robinson, Inc., since 1993. *Who's Who in America, 1994,* II, 2901.

[17]Leonard L. Haynes III (1947–), born in Boston, Mass.; resident of Silver Spring, Md.; B.A., Southern University, 1968; M.A., Carnegie-Mellon University, 1969; Ph.D., Ohio State University, 1975; honorary degrees. College professor, administrator; desegregation policy director, Institute for Services to Education, 1976–1979; director, Office for Advancement of Public Black Colleges, 1979–1982; assistant superintendent, Office of Academic Programs, Louisiana Dept. of Education, 1988–1989; assistant secretary, U.S. Dept. of Education, 1989–1991; consultant, HHS, Washington, D.C., since 1991; consultant, academic programs director, U.S. Information Agency, since 1991. *Who's Who in America, 1994,* I, 1515.

PRESS CONFERENCE: CELEBRATION NORTH CAROLINA

RALEIGH, MARCH 15, 1990

Thank you all for coming today. Celebration North Carolina is an important program, and I am glad to have the opportunity to officially announce its formation.

On January 7, 1989, in my second Inaugural Address, I proposed a year-long celebration of the spirit of North Carolina, a promotion of our state's heritage, and grandeur, and its people that would involve every community in ceremonies and events. After hearing from business leaders across our state, I have been persuaded that while these elements of heritage should be featured, Celebration North Carolina can be much more meaningful if we make our main emphasis on the future: how to improve the quality of life now and thereby enrich the heritage we prepare for future generations. To do this, we will ask sponsors to support programs to improve education, health, environment, housing, recreation, and cultural resources.[1]

Over the past fourteen months, we have been hard at work developing Celebration North Carolina and putting together the right team to manage this undertaking. I want to take a moment and introduce you to the Board of Directors of Celebration North Carolina: Secretary James T. Broyhill, chairman; Secretary William W. Cobey; Secretary Patric Dorsey;[2] Stephen R. Conafay; Phillip J. Kirk, Jr.; Anne S. Peden.

This board is working with several planning committees developing programs that can be adapted in every community across North Carolina. The programs center around the areas of education, health, agriculture, environment, cultural enhancement, housing, and sports and recreation. We want each North Carolina community, no matter how small or how large, to take one or more of the Celebration North Carolina programs and mold it to fit their particular needs and interests.

North Carolina was founded on the idea of *plus ultra*, more beyond. Over the past five years, our goals have reflected this idea: better schools, better roads, better jobs, and a better quality of life for our people. Celebration North Carolina carries on that spirit. Our goal is to promote volunteer programs which will help those less fortunate. North Carolina's spirit is not to stand still, to not accept the present. The public-private partnerships we have put together in the formation of Celebration North Carolina are founded on that ideal.

For these goals to be met and real programs developed, we needed a true public-private partnership. The issues we are examining are issues that transcend the boundaries of politics. They are concerns and opportunities in which every segment of every sector needs to become involved.

I recently met with a group of business leaders from across North Carolina and asked them to serve as members of the financial committee to Celebration North Carolina. At that meeting, I explained our ideas for the celebration and its goals. I was met by tremendous support and commitment.

We have representatives from two of North Carolina's finest corporate citizens with us today, and I am pleased to present them to you so that each can make his statement of support.

[Martin introduced John McAlister, community relations manager, Duke Power Company, and Stephen Conafay, senior vice-president of corporate affairs, Glaxo, Inc.]

Thank you both for the leadership of your commitments and support. Together we can make a difference.

Celebration North Carolina can move us a step closer to fulfilling our state's potential. Celebration North Carolina is, in the truest sense, plus ultra.

---

[1]Donations offered through Celebration North Carolina during 1990 included free medicine to community health centers and migrant health care centers, courtesy of Praxis Biologics; funds from Cone Mills and Centura Banks to bolster literacy and education programs; and enough bricks from Cherokee Sanford Brick to build two houses for Habitat for Humanity. Centura Donation for Celebration, November 15, 1990, and Celebration North Carolina Reception, December 18, 1990, Governors Papers, James G. Martin.

[2]Patric Griffee Dorsey (1924–), secretary, N.C. Department of Cultural Resources, 1985–1993. Previously identified in Poff, *Addresses of Martin*, I, 556n.

PRESS RELEASE: GOVERNOR MARTIN'S REACTION TO THE
PROPOSAL BY THE SPECIAL COMMITTEE ON PRISONS

RALEIGH, MARCH 22, 1990

[Representative Anne Barnes and Senator David Parnell presented their
four-part corrections reform proposal to the Special Committee on Prisons,
March 22, 1990. The plan balanced the need for expanded prison capacity with
alternatives to incarceration, local jail funding, and a reevaluation of sentencing. The prison construction component elicited a skeptical response from Governor Martin, below.

Barnes and Parnell, the committee co-chairs, recommended that the state build
accommodations for 3,274 new inmates by July 1, 1992. The additional space
would enlarge the state correctional system to "an actual legal capacity" of 20,597
persons—a 20 percent increase over 1990 levels—allowing fifty square feet per
inmate, as mandated by the *Small v. Martin* court decision. The construction
deadline offered the state the opportunity to evaluate the effects of the "expansion of community-based sanctions on the prison system," examine the "impact
of modifications to our sentencing laws," and "to consider whether it needs to
incur massive debt or obligations in building prisons." Were further construction necessary, it could be accomplished between July 1992 and July 1, 1994, the
date federal courts were to review state compliance with *Small v. Martin*.

The committee co-chairs called their construction plan a "measured and reasonable approach" that permitted the legislature "to balance the corrections need
with other budgetary needs, such as education." No state had yet "succeeded in
building their way out of overcrowded prisons," they observed. "Before over-
spending and overbuilding, a rational policy for the use of incarceration should
be fully developed. This committee is dedicated to recommending a comprehensive policy to the voters and taxpayers of the state." Attachment 3: Proposal
to the Special Committee on Prisons, March 22, 1990, pages 3–4, from Representative Anne Barnes and Senator David R. Parnell, Minutes of the Special Committee on Prisons, 1988–1990, vol. 3, Legislative Library, Research Division, N.C.
General Assembly, Raleigh.]

The Special Committee on Prisons has received the recommendations
of the co-chairs, Senator David Parnell and Representative Anne Barnes.[1]
The work and study devoted to this issue are greatly appreciated. They
address the needs for (a) further expansion of alternative sentences, (b)
prison construction, (c) matching grants for jails, and (d) a review of
sentencing policies. The obvious shortcoming of the recommendations
of the special committee's co-chairs is the near neglect of desperately
needed prison expansion. They have recommended adding 3,274 spaces
to raise the prison capacity [to] about 20,600. That would be barely
enough to meet the goals of having drug traffickers and kingpins serve
100 percent of their sentences—no parole, no good time or gain time—
and to have all other drug felons, assaultive felons, and repetitive,
nonassaultive felons serve only 40 percent of their sentences. For

adequate punishments for these most dangerous criminals, it would take 20,700 spaces.

What about the others? With no additional capacity, all the other felons and misdemeanants would have no fear of ever having to go to prison for more than a few weeks and would have no meaningful requirement to obey the rules of their alternative punishment. Currently, 40 percent of prisoners are admitted for revocation of probation or parole.

For all the other meritorious ideas in this report from these two respected legislators, they need to add more prison beds. Otherwise, their emphasis on unenforceable alternatives will not protect the public. The reason we want to build more prisons is so we can lock up the more dangerous offenders for a longer time and make alternative sentences mean something through fear of having to go back to prison. I will continue to push for real solutions.

---

[1]Anne C. Barnes (1932–), born in Gaston County; resident of Orange County; was graduated from Mount Holly High School, 1950. Former ballet instructor; chairwoman, Orange County Democratic Party, 1974–1976; elected to Orange County Board of Commissions, 1978, chairwoman, 1980–1981; member, state House of Representatives, since 1981, and chairwoman, House Education Committee. *North Carolina Manual, 1991–1992*, 320–321.

David Russell Parnell (1925–), state senator from Robeson County since 1983; Democrat. Previously identified in Poff, *Addresses of Martin*, I, 906n; see also *North Carolina Manual, 1991–1992*, 268.

DRUG SYMPOSIUM FOLLOW-UP

Charlotte, March 23, 1990

[The governor officially received the North Carolina Drug Cabinet's report, *A Plan of Action for the State of North Carolina*, on March 19, 1990. His brief remarks on that occasion provided the basis for the speech printed below.]

Thank you, Mayor Sue Myrick,[1] Chairman DuPuy,[2] and Lieutenant Governor Gardner, and thank all of you for joining us to discuss what I believe is the greatest menace our state and nation faces: the menace of drug abuse that threatens every community in North Carolina. One year ago in April, we met to share concerns and ideas about how to build a strong defense against drugs and alcohol. From that meeting, we gained an understanding about what is being done, an idea about where we ought to go, and a commitment to work together to cage the lion in our midst.

That commitment has brought us here today to proclaim, for

ourselves and for those who look to us for leadership, that we are, and will remain, committed to the fight against substance abuse. We're here to say we will fight to make our neighborhoods safe from drugs and get drug-related crime out of our neighborhoods and out of our homes. We're here to say we will teach our children to beware the false temptations of drugs and alcohol, and we're here to tell drug addicts that we'll help them kick the habit and get back on track toward a full and productive life. And we're here to tell drug kingpins and drug traffickers, these predators that threaten our society, that the only place we want them is behind bars, serving 100 percent of a stiff sentence for preying on the pain and suffering of others.

That's why we're here, but now it's time to move on. This past Monday, I received the long-awaited report of the North Carolina Drug Cabinet, which was chaired by Lieutenant Governor Gardner.[3] I said then that this is not another study: It's a plan of action for a drug-free North Carolina. For the first time in North Carolina, we have a plan that outlines a coordinated drug strategy, a strategy that involves treatment and education as well as prevention and law enforcement.

It's a bold step, but it's only the first step. Now we must prepare for the long march through the legislature. There will be critics and obstructionists. Some are already complaining about false myths that they themselves created, complaining falsely that it neglects education, treatment, intervention. It does no such thing—they just know they can't be held accountable for false witness! It does deal with these prevention issues, because Dr. Jonnie McLeod[4] insisted that it do so, and because State Superintendent Bob Etheridge worked with us on a bipartisan basis to ensure that we identified the problems and needs in our public schools.

Our critics ask how we expect the legislature to fund a $50 million drug plan on top of a $190-million-a-year prison expansion proposal, particularly when we are struggling with a $200 million revenue shortfall in this fiscal year. Tough choices must be made, but it is time to choose, and sacrificing our children and their futures to drug abuse is not one of our options. It is my intention to include the top priorities in my budget amendments for the short session in May, and include the rest in January; and I mean a cross section of priorities from each general area: education, treatment, intervention, and law enforcement.

We cannot think of drugs as a separate problem from those that plague our prisons, our schools, our businesses, and our families. Drugs are to blame for many of the crimes that victimize our citizens and fill our jails to bursting. Get drugs off the streets, and we will reduce the crime rate. But it will take more prison capacity to get drugs off the streets.

Addiction to drugs and alcohol are to blame for many of the children who drop out of our schools before ever really dropping in. Teach our young people to avoid addiction, and we can teach them what they need to know to find and hold a job in an increasingly competitive economy.

Drugs are also to blame for the pressures that tear our families apart. Close the door to drugs and violence, and we will ease the pain suffered by those families who live in the shadow of substance abuse.

Drug abuse is not a separate problem from crime, illiteracy, or the economy. It's part of the same problem. I want to implement this drug plan and cage the raging beast of drug abuse so we can reduce our crime rate and ease some of the burdens borne by our prisons and school systems across this state.

Your commitment and expertise have helped us in the fight against drug abuse, and I thank every one of you for your involvement. I must ask you now to continue that involvement and join us in our efforts to get the General Assembly to adopt this plan. We need you, your families, your neighbors, and your friends to contact your legislators and encourage them to support this plan. I think they will. There really are only a few controversies among nearly 200 proposals, all of which I endorse. We should be able to get 90 percent of it done with little argument. It's that bold. It's that good! But more than anything else, we need your continued leadership. When this plan passes the General Assembly, as I believe it will, you must help us to build on the foundations we have already laid and erect a strong, solid defense against substance abuse for a drug-free North Carolina.

Back in December 1988, when we learned that the state Senate leaders were going to strip the legislative powers of the new lieutenant governor, Jim Gardner and I discussed the constitution's provision that he would have such duties as the General Assembly or the governor might assign! So I felt positive about having a partner to whom I could assign major goals. Jim Gardner immediately identified the drug issues as the greatest area of policy inadequacy and suggested that instead of being spread thin with smaller roles in dozens of areas, he would rather take a few major responsibilities and do them well and thoroughly. Surely, this report fulfills that ambition, Jim. You have done your work well and thoroughly!

I would like to call on Lieutenant Governor Gardner to tell you more about the work of the Drug Cabinet and the specific provisions outlined in its action plan for the state of North Carolina.

---

[1]Suellen W. Myrick (1941–), born in Tiffin, Ohio; resident of Charlotte; attended Heidelberg College. President, chief executive officer, Myrick Advertising, Marketing, and Public Relations; at-large member, Charlotte City Council, 1983–1985; Charlotte mayor, 1987–1991; candidate, Republican nomination for U.S. senator, 1992; elected to U.S. Congress,

1994. *Charlotte Observer*, November 9, 1994; *City and State*, April 8, 1991; *News and Observer*, November 22, 1987, May 6, 1992.

[2]Carla E. DuPuy (1947–), born in Bellefountaine, Ohio; resident of Charlotte; B.A., University of Florida-Gainesville, 1969. Vice-president for public affairs, Charlotte-Mecklenburg Hospital Authority; chairwoman, N.C. Community Development Council, 1984–1988, and of Mecklenburg County Board of Commissioners, 1984–1990; member, Governor's Advisory Board on Prisons and Punishment, 1990; board member, 1979–1984, chairwoman, 1982–1984, Public Library of Charlotte and Mecklenburg County; vice-chairwoman, Charlotte-Mecklenburg Drug Commission; numerous honors and awards. Carla E. DuPuy, letter to Jan-Michael Poff, November 9, 1993.

[3]North Carolina Drug Cabinet, *A Plan of Action for the State of North Carolina* ([Raleigh: The Drug Cabinet], March 1990).

[4]Jonnie Horn McLeod (1923–), pediatrician; professor; leader of Charlotte community efforts in sex education and drug abuse prevention; appointed chairwoman, 1986, Governor's Advisory Council on Alcohol and Drug Abuse among Children and Youth; appointed chairwoman, 1989, Governor's Inter-Agency Advisory Team on Alcohol and Other Drug Abuse. Previously identified in Poff, *Addresses of Martin*, I, 499n–500n.

A SOUTHERN STRATEGY: AN ADDRESS TO THE SOUTHERN REPUBLICAN LEADERSHIP CONFERENCE

RALEIGH, MARCH 30, 1990

Yesterday's panel of polling experts raised an interesting discussion with you about the future role of the Republican party in the South. On the one hand, we have campaigned on the principles of limited government; but on the other, we intend for government to safeguard the rights of innocent victims, including the unborn. On the one hand, we have waged many campaigns against taxes and other unpopular causes; while on the other, we have found that winners then have to try to fix problems that plague our cities, our schools, our transportation systems, our prisons, and our environment. While the anti-tax sentiment seemed strong as ever yesterday, it was acknowledged that there are some problems which responsible elected officials must not ignore. While we believe that if it's not broke, we're not going to fix it, what will we do for something that is broken? Will we be the party to fix it?

So where do we go from here? Can we just throw bricks at Democrats' programs, or must we come up with real solutions of our own? In those cases where we are in charge, are we willing to be held accountable if our ideas are tried and don't work? And what about taxes? We like to be against taxes, right? Do we oppose all taxes equally? Can we help make choices favoring some taxes as preferred over others, and thereby lose our chastity, or do we opt to let the Democrats make those tough decisions, which means they will choose the taxes we like least? To help with your digestion, let me tell you some things that Republicans are doing to try to solve problems, but in a way that will bear our stamp, to show we can make a difference for good—and for good government.

Republicanism in North Carolina draws its roots from many sources: We are the party of Abraham Lincoln and of Ronald Reagan; we have a strong element of Libertarian philosophy on many issues. Yet when it comes to building a stronger economy in the South, we spring from the mid-nineteenth century political movement known as the Whigs.

History records the period of our four Whig governors, from 1837 to 1850, as the greatest era of progress in North Carolina.[1] They did not just spend money for its own sake; they only spent public money if it would strengthen the economy in ways that private money would not or could not do. The Whigs built the first public schools. The Democrats have recently tried to claim that their dynasty began the commitment to schools in 1901, but that is partisan revisionist history, designed to ignore their Whig and Republican enemies. The Whigs also built the first plank roads and the first railroads, as well as the coastal canal system. For our purposes, all these things helped get North Carolina on its feet and greatly increased personal economic liberty. Throughout my two terms, their example has been the inspiration I needed.

Like the Whigs, my own goals became the improvement of education, of transportation, and of personal economic growth for our people. That became the powerful theme of my 1988 campaign for reelection, and I expect every Republican here can recite it with me: "Better Schools, Better Roads, and Better Jobs"; to these I added "Better Environment and Better Government." You might recognize this prescription as basically the same thing as my version of GOP: Growth, Opportunity, and Prosperity.

Well, how has it turned out? Have we made a difference for schools, roads, jobs, environment, government? The Democrats and the local newspaper, which is the same thing, try to argue No. They try to cast our efforts in a bad light, by comparing my first year's record with my Democrat predecessor's eighth year! Is that fair? To them it is. But let's not wait until 1992. This administration will settle for our first five years compared to Jim Hunt's full eight years.[2]

Better Schools

For five years every budget I have submitted, and every budget adopted by the legislature, actually increased the percentage of the General Fund going to our public schools. Now it would be comforting to assume that has always been the case, but it has not. For the previous twenty-four years the schools' share went down twenty-two years, rising only in 1966 and 1984. If public schools are our number-one priority, who has done the most for North Carolina's schools: a Democrat who reallocated resources away from schools seven out of eight years, or a Republican who reallocated resources toward our schools? Yes, the budgets were adopted by Democrat-dominated legislatures, but only in one biennium did they enact more than I had recommended, while enacting less in the two more recent biennial budgets.

The way I see it, two-party competition has greatly benefited schools. Schools have fared far better with two strong parties vying with one another to see who could do the most for schools. When there was only one party, our schools suffered. So our five years compare favorably with their eight.

Better Roads

In eight years, the Democrats' hero was unreliable on promised paving. We have paved more with less promises. He waited until safely into his second term to propose a timid 3-cent-a-gallon gas tax increase, which barely covered maintenance and repairs.[3] In our first term, I submitted a bolder gas tax increase for badly overdue construction and got it passed in time for the people to see results for their money.[4] Then last year, the General Assembly enacted my plan to build a network of four-lane, limited-access, divided highways to tie North Carolina together as one truly united state, although they fouled it up badly by promptly raiding the highway trust fund for other unrelated programs. Even so, it is no contest, in that my administration has won legislative enactment of seven times as much highway improvements [sic] in five years as the previous Democrat hero could dare achieve in eight years. Who, then, has done more for better roads?

Better Jobs

You might not know this, but North Carolina has been a national leader in economic development. A Democrat, Luther Hodges, pioneered the concept, and both parties have worked hard at overachieving to bring jobs here. It has become very competitive, but for the last three years North Carolina has led the nation in new industrial facilities—each year. It may console you that Florida tied us in 1989, Georgia was a close second in 1988, and Texas was runner-up in 1987, but over the three years nobody was close.

My point, though, is that no previous Democrat administration has done better. Some states have lost interest in manufacturing, preferring service jobs. That's nice, but we believe that the only way to increase wealth for our people is to mine it, grow it, make it, or construct it. All the rest is the moral equivalent of taking in each other's wash, burying each other, or lending each other money. Those are important, but don't create new wealth.

Part of the proof of our strategy is that for each of the last two years, North Carolina has exported more than we imported. That's right—by encouraging manufacturing, we have proven that we can have a net favorable balance of trade two years in a row! Without manufacturing, you cannot do that.

Has this benefit gone to the average worker? Absolutely: Over the last nine years North Carolina has progressed steadily, from forty-fourth in the nation to thirty-third, in per-capita income. Another record gain is that over the last five years, we have added an average of 100,000 net new jobs a year. In comparison, Massachusetts was more myth than miracle!

Better Environment

The Democrats would have you believe they alone care about the environment. They do care, but their record is not as good as ours. My proposal to consolidate regulatory programs from six agencies into one was enacted, while they backed down from such a goal. We now have the strongest surface water protections in the country. It yet remains to be seen whether we can meet our responsibility for hazardous and radioactive waste treatment facilities, but our showdown is near, while they never met theirs; and while the Democrats will attack us at every opportunity for trying to work with businesses so they can meet our environmental standards, our enforcement record is far better than theirs. Compared with the previous Democrat administration, we have levied twice as many fines for three times as many dollars in five years as they did in eight years. Who protects the environment?

What I've tried to show you is that Republicans can fix it when it's broke; that we are not limited to opposing Democrat ideas, but can improve the quality of life for our people with a Republican approach that is bolder and more progressive than their best could do, even with all the assumed advantages of leading the majority party. They didn't do badly; we just did better. But what about the remaining goal:

Better Government

Running all through the record I've cited is the question of how to pay for it. Obviously some taxes had to be raised, but some were cut. How did we choose? My approach has been very practical: If a tax cut would be expected to strengthen the economy for our people, then I was for it. So, we won reductions in taxes on the job market. The inventory tax was eliminated; the intangibles tax on stocks, bonds, receivables, and deposits was reduced; and the unemployment insurance tax was greatly reduced.[5] But if it can be shown that another tax increase will strengthen the economy, my Whig instincts support it. So, I advocated a major tax increase on highway users, but only so that we could afford to pay for badly needed improvements; so our people would get something for their money. Nobody really likes the gas tax, but they sure do want the four-lane highways that go somewhere!

Another example is how we resolved the difficult problem of building minority participation into the system, but without [the] quotas and mandatory set-asides of so-called Affirmative Action. The previous Democrat administration set a goal of 5 percent of state purchasing contracts for minority businesses and achieved only 0.015 percent. What we did was start with a more modest goal of 2 percent, took some ridicule for it, but achieved 5 percent—600 times better success, even with more modest promise. And we did it without quotas, just by reaching out to new businesses, including minorities, to share in sales that previously had been reserved for the same old Democrat firms which had always had all the action.

Is this approach acceptable? Well, we recently launched the same approach for sharing road contracts, as well as other construction, and—listen to this—the Associated General Contractors liked the idea and worked with us to implement it, as a welcome contrast to the old set-asides which the AGC had strongly opposed as being discriminatory and too costly. Our approach works.

When it comes to hiring and promoting black employees in state government, the equal employment opportunities office will tell you my administration has not achieved any ideal; but that we have done much better than the Democrats, even though they owed a lot more in return for the near unanimous vote they've won in black precincts. We owed less and delivered more, you might say, and we have no apologies about treating people fairly. That more and more black business and professional leaders are switching to our party just shows that some want in on the Republican action—no less honorable than the other side—and that many others want to show their appreciation for fair dealing. I certainly feel good about the effort, the results, and the response.

One final illustration of better government: We have all had to struggle with drug abuse and its insidious market. Dottie has been helping parents with training on how to deal with it. Our problem was that our efforts were too uncoordinated, but we soon found a Republican solution.

Just after the last election, when we elected a better lieutenant governor, Republican Jim Gardner, the Senate Democrats promptly rejected the people's choice and stripped him of many traditional responsibilities in the Senate. Well, the constitution says he will have such duties as the legislature or the governor may assign. They think they're legally right, but [they are] morally wrong. But, they can't stop me from utilizing his talents.[6]

He and I talked, and Gardner suggested that instead of adding him to dozens of operations he would prefer to start with one or two and work hard at that. His choice was the most neglected policy area, drug abuse. So, he chaired our Drug Cabinet of top officials, bipartisan, and has just produced what Bill Bennett calls the most comprehensive package of drug countermeasures in America.[7] Now we're ready to move.

To our Republican guests, let me say that this was intended to show what can be done with the opportunity we have had to make a difference in North Carolina. Your Governors Bellmon,[8] Campbell, Clements,[9] Hunt,[10] and Martinez[11] have done the same. Some of our Republicans still prefer to stand firm against government, and that is their right, of course. I can even grant that they may turn out to be right, and I might be wrong, but my goals have been to build upon Republican political efforts to win the opportunity to lead this state—a state which, like yours, had suffered from dominance almost exclusively by one political party for far too long. Our schools, our roads, our economy, our environment, and our government had some problems of inadvertent neglect, and I wanted to prove that Republicans would not just look away but would roll up our sleeves and fix it.

You may agree with my approach, or you may have a better idea, maybe less costly, but I think you will have to agree that if future historians are at all fair about it, they will have to recognize two eras of great progress for North Carolina: that of the mid-nineteenth-century Whigs and that of their spiritual and philosophical descendants, the late-twentieth-century Republicans. If not, if the Democrats get to write the history again, at least they will have to admit that when we had our chance to govern, we faced the state's needs, we worked hard, and we definitely did make a difference—which was about the best one might have hoped for.

Thank you for listening, and we hope you will come back in a few years to see what else we can fix. And better yet, we'll be watching to see the great things that your Republican governors, and legislators, and local governments can do. That's why it's so great to be on the forward crest of the Republican wave of the future, because, as I told some of you yesterday, the southern Democrats have their wave of the future, too. Their wave is "Bye-Bye," because pretty soon, they're out of here!

[1]Whig governors during the period 1837–1850 were Edward B. Dudley (1836–1841), John M. Morehead (1841–1845), William A. Graham (1845–1849) and Charles Manly (1849–1851). Cheney, *North Carolina Government*, 160–161.

[2]James Baxter Hunt, Jr. (1937–), served two terms as North Carolina governor, 1977–1985; was reelected to third term, 1992, with a 10 percent margin of victory over Lieutenant Governor Jim Gardner, the GOP candidate. Previously identified in Poff, *Addresses of Martin*, I, 7n; see also *News and Observer*, November 4, 1992. The "local newspaper" Martin referred to was, of course, the *News and Observer*.

[3]Governor Hunt called for more than just a 3-cent boost in the state sales tax, on each gallon of gasoline, to fund highway construction and repairs; see "Address to the General Assembly on Highway Needs," April 28, 1981, in Poff and Crow, *Addresses of Hunt*, II, 24–30. The General Assembly authorized the increase, and other revenue generating measures proposed by Hunt, on June 26, 1981; see "An Act to Increase the Gasoline Tax, the Special Fuels Tax, and the Tax on Carriers Using Fuels Purchased Outside the State; to Increase Powell Bill Funds for Municipalities; to Provide for Construction of Secondary Roads; to Transfer Sales and Use Taxes on Motor Vehicle Parts, Accessories and Lubricants to the Highway Fund; to Increase Motor Vehicle Fees; to Increase the Registration Fees on Property Hauling Vehicles; and to Establish Fees for Oversize and Overweight Vehicles," *N.C. Session Laws, 1981*, c. 690.

[4]Martin was referring to the Roads to the Future package passed in 1986.

[5]Taxes on manufacturers', retailers', and wholesalers' inventories were eliminated by the "School Facilities Finance Act of 1987," *N.C. Session Laws, 1987*, I, c. 622. *N.C. Session Laws, 1985*, c. 656, addressed intangibles taxes, while *N.C. Session Laws, 1987*, I, c. 17, cut unemployment taxes.

[6]Jim Gardner's constitutional responsibilities as lieutenant governor—to preside over the Senate and to vote in case of a tie—remained intact during his four years as the state's second-highest elected official. Many of his traditional duties, however, were conferred upon him by the upper house. The 1988 elections were barely over before Gardner discovered that that which the state Senate gives, it can also rescind.

During Republican administrations, the Democratic majority in the Senate granted broad powers to the number-two officeholder when that person was also a Democrat, circumstances true for lieutenant governors Jim Hunt (1973–1977) and Bob Jordan (1985–1989). But when the GOP won both the state's top executive posts in 1988, the Senate Democratic caucus was compelled to reexamine the rules under which the upper house and its presiding officer, the lieutenant governor, operated. On November 25, 1988, the caucus took the power to appoint committee chairmen, as well as the ability to refer bills to committee, from Gardner. The new rules were formally adopted on January 11, 1989, in a vote of the entire Senate.

Senator Henson Barnes (D-Wayne), elected president pro tem on January 11, explained that the revisions were necessary because the upper house had ceded too much of its power to the lieutenant governor during previous gubernatorial administrations. The authority to name committees and assign legislation resided with the majority party in the Senate, he declared. Apart from the practice of majority rule, Barnes cited two other precedents for the change: the limited role of the U.S. vice-president, and the principle that "'In all states and in every nation in the free world, the House or the Senate has a right to organize itself.'"

Republicans greeted Barnes's justification of the rules changes with skepticism. Interestingly, what appeared to Governor Martin and others as nothing more than a partisan mugging of Jim Gardner by Senate Democrats turned out to be a reconsolidation of power in the legislative leadership of the upper house—particularly in the president pro tem—that survived the 1992 elections. When Dennis Wicker won the lieutenant governorship that year, fellow Democrats, holding a majority in the Senate, did not restore to him the powers taken from Gardner. Ran Coble, "The Lieutenant Governorship in North Carolina: An Office in Transition," *North Carolina Insight* 11 (April 1989): 157–165; *News and Observer*, December 21, 1992, September 1, 1993. Article III, Section 6 of the North Carolina

Constitution describes the duties of the lieutenant governor; see *North Carolina Manual,
1991–1992,* 628.

[7]William John Bennett (1943–), U.S. education secretary, 1985–1988; appointed director, Office of National Drug Control Policy, by President Bush, 1989. Previously identified
in Poff, *Addresses of Martin,* I, 277n; see also *Who's Who in America, 1990–1991,* I, 242. Bennett's
pronouncement on the Drug Cabinet's plan followed his review of their preliminary recommendations during a visit to Raleigh; see *News and Observer,* February 9, 1990.

[8]Henry Louis Bellmon (1921–), born in Tonkawa, resident of Red Rock, Okla.; B.S.,
Oklahoma State University, 1942; U.S. Marine Corps, 1942–1946. Farmer, rancher; mem-
ber, Oklahoma House of Representatives, 1946–1948; chairman, Oklahoma Republican
Committee, 1960–1962; first Republican governor of Oklahoma, elected 1962, reelected
1986, retired March 1989; U.S. senator from Oklahoma, elected 1968, reelected 1974. Barone
and Ujifusa, *Almanac of American Politics, 1992,* 1004; *Biographical Directory of Congress,* 605;
Robert Sobel and John Raimo (eds.), *Biographical Directory of the Governors of the United
States, 1789–1978* (Westport, CT: Meckler Books, four volumes, 1978), III, 1254–1255.

[9]William Perry Clements, Jr. (1917–), born in Dallas, Texas. Founder, board chairman,
chief executive officer, SEDCO, Inc., Dallas, 1947–1973, 1977; deputy secretary, U.S. Department of Defense, 1973–1977; Texas governor, 1979–1982, 1987–1991; SEDCO board
chairman, from 1983; Republican. *Who's Who in America, 1992–1993,* I, 628.

[10]H. Guy Hunt (1933–), was elected governor of Alabama, 1986, reelected in 1990; was
removed from office, 1993, upon conviction of feloniously channeling $200,000 to per-
sonal bank accounts from a nonprofit fund established to pay his inauguration expenses;
Republican. Previously identified in Poff, *Addresses of Martin,* I, 1039n–1040n; see also *New
York Times,* April 23, 1993.

[11]Bob Martinez (1934–), born in Tampa, Fla.; B.S., University of Tampa, 1957; M.A.,
University of Illinois, 1964. Teacher, Hillsborough County (Fla.), 1957–1966; director,
Hillsborough County Teachers Assn., 1966–1975; president, Cafe Sevilla Spanish Restau-
rant, 1975–1983; Tampa mayor, 1979–1986; Florida governor, 1987–1991; appointed direc-
tor, 1991, Office of National Drug Control Policy, by President Bush; Republican. *Who's
Who in America, 1992–1993,* II, 2201.

STATE EMPLOYEES ASSOCIATION OF NORTH CAROLINA
MEMBERSHIP KICKOFF

RALEIGH, APRIL 3, 1990

This is that time of year when we make our major effort to show state
employees the value of our state employees association to our fellow
workers. Other membership groups have put on more strident pep rallies in favor of their "demands," but none have been more effective or
successful than SEANC. That's because you understand the workings
of the legislature, and you respect the good-faith efforts of your fellow
members who are in management—and it's because you have avoided
becoming part of either political party's machine.

It has been impressive to see the way in which you have worked
with my management team to identify problems and then to help us
develop solutions that are good for North Carolina. You have done that
without rancor or confrontation. In all the issues facing us, personnel

and otherwise, it is comforting to know that you will always take the SEANC[1] overview!

So I feel good about being with you to show my support and to add my voice to urge others to join us in SEANC. This is an organization which truly involves the input and participation of its members.

We meet at a time of great stress on the state budgetary process. For that reason, we have to expect difficulty greater than normal in addressing many needs. That means that it will take a combination of determination and forbearance to ensure the consideration of our major goals within the limits of a balanced budget. Your help and professional leadership are needed as never before, both by our members and by the people whom we serve.

We face an overall budget shortfall of $311 million for the current fiscal year ending June 30. Of that total, $205 million lies in the traditional tax base of the General Fund. We now know that there is another $106 million shortfall in the new highway users tax on [vehicles].[2]

Most of the shortfall in traditional General Fund revenues has already been absorbed, mainly by leaving unfilled the less-critical vacant positions. Even so, that has stressed all departments and the university system. The most recent episode has necessitated asking our public schools and community colleges to share with the rest in a round of belt tightening. I am proud to report that the response has been positive—indeed, even patriotic in character.

That had allowed my current efforts, until last week, to be focused on how to accommodate an additional shortfall for next fiscal year, 1990–1991, of about $150 million less than the General Assembly had enacted when the biennial budget was enacted last summer. That is still a major challenge, for which I expect to have a recommendation on May 10, when the General Assembly appropriations committees meet, prior to the May 21 session. But now, because of the added complexity of the shortfall in that part of the Highway Trust Fund diverted to the General Fund by the legislature, we would expect to face another $129 million shortfall—a total $279 million shortfall—as we begin the next biennium.

How did we get into this predicament? It's not the result of any slowdown in the economy, which to the contrary is very healthy. Economic factors are fairly close to what my budget office had forecast in April 1989. But when the budget was amended and adopted by the General Assembly, major new uncertainties were built into revenue projections. The profound changes in the personal income tax code, to parallel the federal tax law, were optimistically assumed to be revenue neutral, and the expected capital gains tax to be derived from the RJR Nabisco leveraged buyout were similarly overestimated. You may remember that in my own budget projections, I asked that we not include the RJR Nabisco revenues.

That led to a gross overestimate of revenue growth, in the legislative budget, of a whopping good 13.8 percent growth rate. Instead, what we are now getting is on the order of 7.5 percent, roughly equal to the total of the inflation rate plus the real growth in the gross state product.

That combination of errors was the result of Senate resistance to my proposal to raise the state sales tax by one penny, coupled with a partially offsetting cut in the state sales tax on food. They wanted to be able to adopt the popular improvements in schools and salaries, which I had recommended as higher expenditures, while appearing to take credit for rejecting the taxes to pay for it properly. Then they raided the new Highway Trust Fund, without regard to whether these new levies could be reliably estimated. I have already frequently pointed out the folly of that two-year diversion, for it sets the stage for a major tax increase after the next election, when the 1991 session convenes.

Last week, as I have already stated, we discovered another problem, in that Highway Trust Fund revenues from the new users tax on vehicles were running short by about $106 million, to which I have previously referred. In any normal year, that could be taken in stride by just deferring highway contracts until the money was available. That would not have involved the General Fund at all, because it would have been budgeted to meet its needs from its own taxes, without raiding the Highway Fund. A number of proposals have been put forward, all of which have certain shortcomings.

The same legislators who originally created the problem, by their insistence in paying for your salary increase by raiding the highway user taxes for two years, are now suggesting we just dig a little deeper into the Highway Trust Fund, a "trust" created as assurance that it would be insulated from such diversions. While I search for alternatives, I have directed DOT Secretary Harrelson to withhold any new construction project contracts, just in case there are no adequate alternatives.[3]

But I must insist that this is a travesty of budget policy and would not have been necessitated at all had not the Senate leadership indulged what the Senate Finance chairman boasted as "creative finance." The sad experience many financial institutions have had with "creative financing" schemes should have persuaded the General Assembly to reject this experiment and its dependence on uncertain new taxes that were more appropriate anyway for capital improvements on our highway system, for which they were originally intended.

Another unworthy proposal has been the suggestion that we lay off state employees to cover the additional $106 million shortage from the highway user tax that had been purloined for the General Fund pay increases and educational improvements. This is not a very productive source of savings, because to achieve the savings necessary, all within the two months remaining to the end of this fiscal year, it would take elimination of almost one-fourth of our employees. That's not possible, and I won't support that. We have already reduced employment levels to the limit of what is prudent by imposing a freeze on certain vacancies. My sentiment is the same for suggestions that we cut back on pay increases already enacted: Employees and their families have already made obligations with that raise in mind. I will do my best to protect the scheduled raise.

Let me repeat: I believe we can and should avoid any layoffs or delayed paychecks. But to be honest and fair, I cannot guarantee that at this point. As I have explained, the budget shortfall I now face—not of my own making, I will repeat—has forced the state into a difficult spot.

If things don't get any worse than we now can predict, I am confident that the problems can be handled without such drastic measures. But we must remind ourselves that tax returns for the crucial month of April are not yet in hand. I promise to keep you updated, through your association leadership, about our budget situation.

At my request, the budget office is preparing a list of alternatives from which to put together a package of budget amendments to present to the General Assembly after we have a better idea of April revenues. It is my hope that you will review these with an eye to helping us resolve this fiscal mess. Throughout our work in the next month, I hope you will heed my request for assistance and patience.

When the time comes to solve the basic flaw in all this mischievous "creative financing," when we must consider the taxes in 1991 that should have been considered in 1989, I hope you will remember this lesson and join me in opposing a repeat of distortions of the budget process such as those enacted last year. This is a prime example of the way in which careful use of the veto could have prevented a crisis of the budget. With veto power, I might have been able to urge some sense in that legislative budget.

The potential use of veto power would have helped me get the attention of the General Assembly and work toward a responsible budget. That's another reason why I hope you, as concerned state employees, will see that it is in your interest to support the veto. Believe me, it will help you do your jobs with pride. It will make your lobby a more effective organization because it can focus attention on the governor, who will have veto power.

Just as I am part of SEANC, you are part of this administration. You have the same stake in good government that I have. For that reason, I ask you to join with me to insist that budget decisions return to the standard of fiscal responsibility that has been so reliable in the past and reject any more flights of "creative financing."

---

¹SEANC was pronounced as *scenic*.

²*N.C. Session Laws, 1989*, I, c. 692, s. 4.1 imposed a highway use tax of 3 percent "of the retail value of a motor vehicle for which a certificate of title is issued."

³Thomas J. Harrelson (1941–), born in Greensboro; resident of Raleigh; A.B., University of North Carolina at Chapel Hill; M.A., University of Pennsylvania. Financial analyst, Chevron Oil Europe, 1967–1968; junior partner, Harrelson Supermarket, 1968–1976; member, state House of Representatives, 1970–1974; president, owner, Harrelson Enterprises, Inc., Southport, 1976–1987; chairman, state Environmental Management Commission, 1985–1986; deputy secretary, 1987–1989, secretary, 1989–1993, state Department of Transportation; Republican. *North Carolina Manual, 1991–1992*, 201. Martin praised Harrelson's accomplishments as transportation secretary during ceremonies naming a thirty-five-mile segment of U.S. 17 in his honor; see Tommy Harrelson Highway Dedication, Brunswick County, January 6, 1993, Governors Papers, James G. Martin.

EARTH DAY

Research Triangle Park, April 24, 1990

[This address was delivered at the United States Environmental Protection Agency complex on the twentieth anniversary of Earth Day. Some of the same text reappeared in Martin's remarks for the Governor's Hazardous Waste Management Awards presentation ceremony, May 17, 1990.]

I've just come from celebrating another special event: the twenty-fifth anniversary of IBM's Research Triangle Park facility. When IBM first opened its doors here in 1965, the Research Triangle Park was just beginning to crawl in its infancy. But look around you today, and you'll see how the Triangle has grown into adulthood, the proud parent of progress in pharmaceuticals, microelectronics, biotechnology, and, of course, the environmental health sciences.

We've come a long way in twenty-five years, but progress has its price. Our food, our clothing, our jobs, the electricity we use, the medical care we depend on: All these daily essentials use up our natural resources and yield some form of waste that must be dealt with reliably and responsibly.

Mark Twain once said, "Thunder is good, thunder is impressive; but it is lightning that does the work."[1] What kind of lightning can we expect to cut through the thunder of rhetoric that surrounds Earth Day 1990? As one honored to have been considered for administrator of EPA in 1981, and who has followed the quality and professionalism of your work, I would suggest that since the founding of EPA, for almost two decades you have been Mark Twain's "lightning that does the work!"

In just a moment, I want to help cut through the rhetoric of the past week by announcing important new steps we in the Martin administration will take to mark real advances in environmental protection. As we enter the 1990s, it is my intention that we take up the banner for environmental progress as partners, not as adversaries.

Earth Day 1970 helped us understand that we are the caretakers, not the masters, of planet Earth. I have to admit, though, that I was turned off by what I saw of it, because I was busy personally putting together the first attempts to enforce North Carolina's laws against air pollution and water pollution, organizing our first stream monitoring volunteers, and presiding over the first countywide zoning in North Carolina. None of that seemed to fit into Earth Day organizers' agenda, so I got left out. It seemed to be characterized by too much blame—and too little progress.

I hope that the emphasis selected for Earth Day 1990 will help us understand that all of us, individuals as well as industry, are partners in pollution. Instead of pointing fingers at each other, I want us to join hands as partners in preservation. We must learn to balance the economic growth that sustains our quality of life with the preservation of our natural resources—to create an ecological and economical give and take. We must learn to use only what we need, replace what we can, and preserve the rest for future generations. Perhaps Greer Tidwell said it best himself in an article published last week in the Raleigh newspaper: "Some people would pit the economy against the environment, but the truth is that a strong economic base requires environmental control and vice versa."[2]

A recent survey of North and South Carolinians supports that ideal of a balance of progress and preservation. Eighty percent of the respondents said they were willing to pay higher taxes or higher prices to protect the environment. Similar huge majorities were unwilling to accept environmental degradation or economic stagnation. They want both, and it's our challenge to deliver.[3]

The answer is balance: economic growth and development designed to preserve our natural resources. How do we achieve that balance? By enacting laws to regulate development, by enforcing those laws, and by creating programs that help government, industry, and individuals do what's right for our environment.

During the past twenty years, North Carolina's environmental record has included such successes as creation of the Coastal Area Management Act in 1974, Outstanding Resource Water classifications in 1986, and the new High Quality Water classifications in 1989. We have tough laws, and we have proven our willingness to enforce them.

During the past five years, the Martin administration has issued more fines against polluters, and collected more dollars from those fines, than during any previous ten-year period. The most obvious example is our $1 million penalty against Texasgulf, in 1989, for violating air-quality standards. The best part of that story doesn't often get told. After paying the fine, Texasgulf agreed to install, on its own, a waste-water recycling system that removes at least 90 percent of the phosphate discharge in the waste-water before it enters the Pamlico River. Combined with the Best Management conservation practices on our farms, and state requirements for phosphate removal by cities and towns through chemical or biological technologies, North Carolina is doing what is needed to cut the phosphate loading of our surface waters.

In more recent years, I'm proud to point to the consolidation of all our health and environmental agencies into one Department of Environment, Health, and Natural Resources. This consolidation makes our environmental bite at least as bad as our bark. Now our watchdog agencies can communicate more easily and respond more quickly to protect our storehouse of natural resources, and both developers and their opposition can get quicker answers to what can be done and what can't.

We can point with pride to our successes on the regulatory front, but today, as we continue the Earth Day celebration, I want to make a few special announcements that will keep North Carolina clean and beautiful, as we like to say, while she moves forward into the 1990s.

The New Office of Waste Reduction

I have asked Secretary Bill Cobey, of the Department of Environment, Health, and Natural Resources, to create the new Office of Waste Reduction, a brand-new agency that ensures our long-term commitment to reducing the waste flow in North Carolina. This new Office of Waste Reduction, which will soon have its own director, will include the ongoing work of the Pollution Prevention Pays program, our waste minimization efforts, and our recycling activities.

In North Carolina, all three of those efforts—pollution prevention, waste minimization, and recycling—have become top priorities. The new Office of Waste Reduction will coordinate that work and serve as the centerpiece for the diverse projects going on in other cabinet agencies. I want this new office to report directly to Secretary Cobey. That way, he will be able to monitor its work personally and to implement priority projects as needed.

More than a paper change, this reorganization represents a strategic management change by Secretary Cobey that will bring new focus on our waste-reduction efforts and bring more visibility to that work within the agency—and more clout. By strengthening our efforts through this waste-reduction office, we will save literally millions in landfilling and managing our excess wastes. Most important, in keeping with this Earth Day 1990 theme, we begin to change the thinking of our citizens, our businessmen and -women, and yes, our leaders. We all must take up the mantle of waste minimization. I believe this new Office of Waste Reduction is an important part of that reorganization of our personal and governmental priorities.

There's another important part of this process. That element is education. With that transition, let me offer another new proposal.

Office of Environmental Education

For months, we have been talking—brainstorming, if you will—about ways to carry the environmental banner into all our communities in North Carolina. While all of us at this event know of the increased attention given to the environment, there are others who do not realize the importance of these issues, still others who would trivialize them, and others yet who would undermine our efforts by ignoring real progress.

I believe we can reach every corner of every community with this message of conservation, of balanced regulation and of careful use of our resources. That's why I have asked Dr. Linda Little to set up North Carolina's first Office of Environmental Education.[4] This office will be charged with broad-based environmental education across North Carolina, in the small towns, in the communities, in the businesses, in the gas stations and convenience stores across the state, and of course, in the schools.

Like Earth Day itself, which started in 1970 without much acclaim, this program will begin without a massive budget. In fact, I will ask Dr. Little to use her staff at the Governor's Waste Management Board to get the program started. But I expect great things, and I know you do, as we begin this coordinated approach to teaching North Carolinians the importance of protecting our environment.

The Governor's Project Tomorrow Awards

The future of this program—indeed, the future of this planet—lies in our classrooms, and that is where I believe this Office of Environmental Education will be most effective. To make sure that process gets off to a good start, I have asked Dr. Little to help with another new idea: the Governor's Project Tomorrow Environmental Awards. One year from now, on Earth Day 1991, a single school in North Carolina will be designated as the first winner of the 1991 Project Tomorrow Environmental

Award for excellence and creativity because of its work to improve the environment in its community.

It is my hope that the Office of Environmental Education will present perhaps a dozen regional awards across North Carolina, on Earth Day 1991, and designate one school as the statewide winner. At one school, for example, they might choose a recycling project; another a stream or waterway clean-up. Another might be so creative as to use an industrial by-product for some educational use. The only limitation, of course, is the creativity of the students.

The benefits are obvious: Schoolchildren learn the importance of the environment while their schools and communities benefit from the projects. As adults, we have learned too slowly the importance of simple acts of environmental protection: recycling our aluminum and glass, taking old oil to recycling centers. But our children will learn these lessons early and, as is always the case, teach their parents the lessons of the 1990s.

Taken together, these new programs offer us a pathway toward environmental progress through waste reduction, through environmental education, and through challenge awards for our schoolchildren. An old Kenya proverb speaks eloquently to the value of this Office of Environmental Education and the Governor's Project Tomorrow Awards. It goes, "Treat the earth well. It was not given to you by your parents; it was lent to you by your children."

You will never hear me talk about environmental programs without mentioning balance and responsibility, on both sides, as we continue to work for a cleaner home and workplace. I hope these new programs will embody that principle of balanced education and responsible positions.

The Challenges Ahead

No major discussion of the environment in North Carolina will be complete without a tight-lipped look at the future. We face tough decisions in the immediate future. Acres of lifeless trees stand in silent testimony to the devastation caused by sulfur dioxide emissions from other upwind states, carried over the mountains and dumped in North Carolina.

We've paid the extra cost to reduce sulfur dioxide emissions in North Carolina by burning low-sulfur coal. We've also joined with sixteen other states and President Bush in a coalition to fight acid rain. We've done our part. Now it's time for polluting states to do theirs.

I will not tolerate acid rain poisoning the life out of our mountains, but neither can I agree to our people having to pay for clean-up costs for other states who don't want to accept responsibility for their actions. Our utility customers are already paying for the cost of reduced SO_2 [sulfur dioxide] discharges in our state. We should not be required to pay for other state[s], too.

Waste management is another item which dominates the news this spring. Within thirty days, the state will announce final sites for a low-level radioactive waste storage facility and a chemical-waste incinerator.[5] I ask for your support for these very difficult siting decisions. You can surely understand that no one, and no county, wants such facilities nearby, but no one knows better than you the serious need for such facilities to properly manage these kinds of waste. Surely the worst possible environmental policy is to oppose any and all waste treatment technologies, but that's all North Carolina has ever really done about it.[6]

As I have said many times, I support the empirical processes that [are] being used in the selections of these sites. Most important, I believe we must convince our citizens that without these facilities, we risk illegal and harmful toxic dumping in populated areas or, worse, in our water supplies.

President Bush has said that, "Through millions of individual decisions—simple, everyday, personal choices—we are determining the fate of the earth." He's right. Dottie and I, and the staff at the Executive Mansion, have started a recycling project there with aluminum and glass. Humble as it may be, it is a start. During the months it's been in place, we've saved a few cubic feet in a landfill—and so could you! All the laws in the books won't make much difference in the environmental arena until we first make individual decisions about responsible, personal environmental actions. By doing so, we honor the spirit of Earth Day 1990.

---

[1]Mark Twain, *Letter to an Unidentified Person* [1908], quoted in Bartlett, *Familiar Quotations*, 764.

[2]The quotation is from an essay, written by Greer C. Tidwell, that appeared in the April 20, 1990, edition of the Raleigh *News and Observer*. Tidwell was administrator of the southeastern region, U.S. Environmental Protection Agency.

[3]MarketSearch Corp. of Columbia, South Carolina, polled 1,500 North and South Carolinians on the relationship between the environment and economic development. The results of the survey, conducted during October 1989, were announced April 16. *News and Observer*, April 17, 1990.

[4]Linda West Little (1937–), born in Kinston; resident of Raleigh; B.A., Woman's College, University of North Carolina (later University of North Carolina at Greensboro), 1958; M.S.P.H., 1962, Ph.D., 1968, University of North Carolina at Chapel Hill. Assistant professor, 1971–1974, associate professor, 1974–1977, and adjunct associate professor, since 1977, of environmental biology, University of North Carolina at Chapel Hill; administrative judge-environmental sciences, U.S. Nuclear Regulatory Commission, 1974–1988; biologist-water pollution control specialist, Research Triangle Institute, 1977–1979; environmental consultant, 1979–1983, and since 1994; executive director, Governor's Waste Man-

agement Board, 1983–1993; director, Office of Environmental Education, 1990–1993; author. Linda West Little, letter to Jan-Michael Poff, March 31, 1994.

[5]No final determination on the site of either the low-level radioactive waste storage facility or the hazardous waste incinerator was forthcoming by the end of May 1990. However, two potential homes for the incinerator were named early that month: a tract of land on the Iredell-Rowan border, and 580 acres in central Granville County, near Oxford; see *News and Observer*, May 2, 1990. The decision on the location of the low-level radioactive waste disposal plant was not announced until December 1993, almost a year after Martin concluded his second term; see "Press Release: Governor Martin's Statement on Site Area Announcements by Low-Level Radioactive Waste Authority," pages 188–189, above.

[6]The international environmental movement Greenpeace helped stoke local opposition to the proposed sites for the state's hazardous-waste incinerator. Said an irritated Martin of Greenpeace, "This radical organization of bogus pseudo-environmentalists has launched a campaign to block North Carolina from meeting its responsibility for proper waste treatment. They are irresponsibly calling on North Carolina to refuse to build a waste incinerator, and to ship our wastes to South Carolina and Alabama—while at the very same time stirring up South Carolinians and Alabamians to refuse waste from North Carolina, on the grounds that we can't be trusted to do our share of the waste treatment. They didn't think we would check up on them. Despite such phony, fraudulent hypocrisy by . . . Greenpeace, the real environmentalists are the people in this room, whom we honor for doing something constructive about waste management, instead of just promoting more membership dues." Governor's Hazardous Waste Management Awards, Raleigh, May 17, 1990, Governors Papers, James G. Martin.

FORBES MAGAZINE ANNOUNCEMENT

CHARLOTTE, MAY 9, 1990

It is an honor and a privilege for me to be here today with such an outstanding group of business leaders from North Carolina. It is also a pleasure for me to have the opportunity to spend the day with former secretary of defense and current publisher of *Forbes* magazine Caspar Weinberger, and with Christopher Forbes, the magazine's vice-chairman.[1]

Before we begin, I would like to thank Terry Orell and the Charlotte Chamber of Commerce for helping the North Carolina Department of Economic and Community Development coordinate this event. Charlotte is a great place to start in talking about North Carolina's economic success. Spirit Square is a wonderful example of the growth that the Queen City has enjoyed, serving as a center for cultural activity for uptown Charlotte's business community; and I'm equally proud of our North Carolina Department of Economic and Community Development, just yesterday rated by Conway Data Publications to be in the top-ten economic development forces in America, the only state to be so honored.[2]

Our Department of Economic and Community Development has teamed up with *Forbes* magazine to produce a special supplement on North Carolina in their October 15 issue.[3] That's the reason we're here:

to introduce that opportunity to boost North Carolina and your own business. This supplement is a great opportunity for us to show off North Carolina and our quality products to the rest of the country, and to the world, and to explain the many reasons why our state is the "better business climate."

As many of you know, North Carolina again led the nation in the number of new manufacturing plant announcements in 1989, for the third year in a row. We tied for first place with the state of Florida, with a total of 106 announcements of new manufacturing facilities. During the past three years, our state has welcomed a total of 320 new manufacturing facilities, far and away the best in the nation. We should take great pride in these economic accomplishments, but this is no time to rest on our laurels.

Today, at three press conferences across the state, I am announcing North Carolina's economic development figures for 1989. North Carolina recorded its second-highest amount of new investment dollars in 1989, totaling over $5.8 billion. That figure is slightly lower than the all-time record of $6.2 billion that was invested in our state in 1988.

What these figures represent to me is consistency. For the past five years, we have averaged almost $5.4 billion in new investment, and this year's above-average number of $5.8 billion is another link in the chain of progress we are forging. That strong vote of confidence, along with strong retail sales, including exports, and low unemployment coupled with rising per-capita income, confirm the strength of North Carolina's economy.

Then why are we looking at a $500 million shortfall in taxes? Well, it's not because of any shortfall in the economy. It's mainly because of a high jump, or an attempted pole vault, in revenue overestimate when the General Assembly adopted its budget last August without consulting my budget office. Revenue collections didn't go down—they just didn't rise near as sharply as their happy forecast.

The North Carolina economy is still strong, but we want to keep it that way; and as economic competition in the United States and the world grows in both size and complexity, North Carolina must respond by diversifying our economic development campaign. We need greater emphasis on the quality of our products and services, to advance the competitiveness and the growth of the employers we've already got in North Carolina. That goal, for example, is why we are working with manufacturers and food processors to stop being defensive and attack world markets, to export more. That's why we were thrilled by the analysis just reported by economists at UNC-Charlotte that North Carolina exports last year grew to $6.6 billion. That gave us an all-time high trade surplus of exports $1 billion over imports.[4] The way to get America to do that, Cap, is for North Carolina doing more [*sic*]. *Forbes* has given us an excellent opportunity to reach out to new markets, to highlight our successes and advantages in an international forum.

At this time, I would like to turn the program over to the youngest participant in today's events. At the ripe old age of thirty-nine, Christopher Forbes has an outstanding record of achievement. A fellow Princeton alumnus, Mr. Forbes graduated *magna cum laude*. Since 1970, Mr. Forbes has been working with the Forbes organization, and he is now in his second year as vice-chairman of the magazine. Mr. Forbes is a member of one of America's most famous families.

His late father, Malcolm Forbes, Sr., who had begun planning this day's program of activities with us, brought new meaning to the word *entrepreneur*.[5] I am certain that Mr. Forbes will honor his father's legacy in fine fashion, and we are privileged to have him with us today. It is my pleasure to introduce to you Mr. Christopher Forbes.

---

[1]Caspar Willard (Cap) Weinberger (1917–), born in San Francisco; A.B., 1938, LL.B., 1941, Harvard University; U.S. Army, 1941–1945. Attorney; Calif. legislator, 1952–1958; chairman, Calif. Republican Central Committee, 1962–1964; Calif. state finance director, 1968–1969; chairman, Federal Trade Commission, 1970; deputy director, 1970–1972, director, 1972–1973, U.S. Office of Management and Budget; counsel to President Nixon, 1973; U.S. health, education, and welfare secretary, 1973–1975; general counsel, vice-president, director, Bechtel Power Corp., Bechtel, Inc., and of Bechtel Corp., 1975–1980; U.S. defense secretary, 1981–1987; publisher, 1989–1993, chairman, from 1993, *Forbes* magazine. *Who's Who in America, 1994*, II, 3604.

Christopher (Kip) Forbes (1950–), born in Morristown, N.J.; B.A., Princeton University, 1972. Curator, Forbes Magazine Collection, 1970–1980; advertising salesman, 1972–1976, associate publisher, vice-president, 1978–1989, secretary, 1981–1992, vice-chairman, since 1989, *Forbes* magazine; Republican. *Who's Who in America, 1994*, I, 1131.

[2]"Twenty Success Stories from the Development World: 1989's Top Groups and Top Deals," *Site Selection and Industrial Development*, April 1990, 305, 314–316.

[3]See "North Carolina: The State of Innovation Today," *Forbes*, October 15, 1990, 141–160.

[4]The figures the governor cited actually were compiled by North Carolina State University and First Wachovia Corporation. State products showing the largest export gains in 1989 were industrial and electronic equipment, cigarettes and other tobacco products, chemicals and pharmaceuticals, and agricultural crops. *News and Observer*, March 13, May 8, 1990.

[5]Malcolm Stevenson Forbes (1919–1990), born in New York City; A.B., Princeton University, 1941; honorary degrees; U.S. Army, 1942–1945. Associate publisher, 1946–1954, publisher, editor-in-chief, 1957–1990, *Forbes* magazine; vice-president, 1947–1964, president, 1964–1980, chairman, chief executive officer, 1980–1990, Forbes, Inc.; N.J. state senator, 1952–1958; GOP candidate for N.J. governor, 1957. *Who Was Who in America, 1989–1993*, 117.

PRESS RELEASE: GOVERNOR ANNOUNCES APPROVAL BY EPA
OF STATE'S HAZARDOUS WASTE PLAN

Raleigh, May 16, 1990

Governor Jim Martin announced Thursday that North Carolina has become the first state in the nation to receive approval from the U.S. Environmental Protection Agency for a state capacity assurance plan (CAP) for the management of hazardous waste. EPA required each state to prepare a capacity assurance plan by October 17, 1989, to certify its ability to manage its hazardous waste for the next twenty years. Approval of the plan allows the state to remain eligible for Superfund money to clean up hazardous waste sites.

"We're pleased that our plan has been approved and that we were the first state to receive approval without the addition of supplemental data," Governor Martin said. The governor said North Carolina's plan is based on reducing hazardous waste by 36 percent by the year 2009. The plan outlines arrangements for exporting some wastes that cannot be prevented and for constructing in-state facilities to deal with other hazardous wastes generated by North Carolina and four other southern states.[1]

In December 1989, the General Assembly overwhelmingly endorsed an agreement that Governor Martin worked out with the governors of Alabama, Kentucky, South Carolina, and Tennessee. Under that agreement, the states will share treatment operations rather than have each construct all the facilities needed to dispose of its hazardous waste. The agreement permits North Carolina to continue using facilities in the other four states, including the disposal facilities in Alabama and South Carolina, as long as North Carolina complies with its schedule for building hazardous waste management facilities as outlined in the agreement and in the capacity assurance plan.

---

[1]Eight percent of the hazardous waste generated in North Carolina was transported off-site for treatment and disposal. That amount was to be cut to 5 percent under the new capacity assurance plan. Governor's Hazardous Waste Management Awards, Raleigh, May 17, 1990, Governors Papers, James G. Martin.

PRISON COMPROMISE AGREEMENT

Raleigh, June 26, 1990

I am pleased to join today with legislative leaders of both parties in announcing an agreement, on a compromise package, for a $275 million bond financing package for construction of new, expanded, and replacement of prisons over a three-year period. When completed, this will not only complete the commitments we have made to make our prisons constitutionally defensible, and replace a few outdated facilities which are too costly to operate, but also will expand our prison capacity from its present population of about 18,000 to 24,300.

This agreement represents the midpoint between my earlier proposal to expand prison capacity to 27,500, and that of Representative Anne Barnes and Senator David Parnell to expand it to 21,000. If enacted and approved by the voters, this will provide funding for the first three years, essentially, of my five-year program, then allow the administration and General Assembly then in office to consider whether and when to proceed with additional facilities. The first $75 million would be made available via legislative bonds, limited by the constitution not to exceed two-thirds of the bonds retired during the preceding year. Specific projects have been identified for this first phase.[1] The remaining $200 million in general obligation bonds would then be submitted to a referendum this November.

If approved in November, the bonds would be issued and allocated to specific projects at the further direction of the General Assembly. The specific nature of such improvements is outlined in summary form, to indicate the type and size of such facilities that I would recommend for allocation if the bonds are approved.

Six months ago, in an address to the Criminal Justice Forum, sponsored by the North Carolina Center on Crime and Punishment, I proposed a major new program of expansion for our overcrowded prison system. After four years of a bipartisan collaboration to meet federal court standards for the approximately 18,000[-inmate] prison population in North Carolina, I had concluded that it was vitally important that we now make the same commitment to increase the capacity to 27,500 over a five-year period.

Having supported expansion of a variety of alternative sentences, including regular and intensively supervised probation and parole, electronically monitored house arrest, BRIDGE and Impact programs for youthful offenders, community service, and victim restitution, I had come to realize that those valuable and less-expensive alternatives were being undermined due to insufficient prison capacity. In recent years, the rate of active prison sentences from our courts had increased dramatically. That caused the average time served to decrease by about one-third, even though the number of misdemeanants in prison had been greatly reduced. That eroded respect for the discipline and integrity of our criminal justice system, among both criminals and victims.

This agreement, if enacted, will get us moving to meet our responsibility to both criminals, victims, and to society at large. It will give our corrections department a far better opportunity to live up to its name and mission. Rehabilitation will have a better chance of succeeding. Punishment will be more certain, and prisons will pose a more credible alternative to the alternative sentences.

It gives me great personal satisfaction to commend legislative leaders who have worked together with my administration to prepare this agreement. Certainly Representative Barnes and Senator Parnell deserve congratulations for their willingness to negotiate between our earlier positions. They have also persuaded members of their select committee on prisons to invite us, for the first time, to submit a proposal for a 500-bed, privately built-and-operated, treatment and detention facility for inmates with alcoholism and drug addiction problems.

Other members, of both parties, contributed many good ideas and gave us the encouragement we needed to succeed. Senators Barnes, Bryan, Kincaid, Royall, Smith, and Bryan [sic]; and representatives Craven, Esposito, Huffman, Sam Hunt, Justus, Mavretic, Rhyne, and Sizemore should all be commended.[2] Without their help, and that of Lieutenant Governor Gardner, we would not be here.

Corrections secretary Aaron Johnson, and prisons director Joe Hamilton,[3] and Secretary Joe Dean, and their staff deserve so much credit for helping build support, both for my initial proposal and for this compromise. Secretary of Human Resources Dave Flaherty convinced all of us of the need to include badly needed attention to youth services facilities without waiting for litigation. And very special commendation should go to supreme court justice Burley Mitchell, who gave us outstanding leadership with my Advisory Board on Prisons and Punishments, in conducting public hearings to gauge the sentiment of the people of North Carolina and recommending an even more farsighted concept.

With this three-year plan to raise the number of prison beds to 24,315, it will also give us some breathing room to take a fresh look at our sentencing laws, to be sure they are meeting the needs of society. For that reason, I have agreed to endorse legislation to establish a sentencing commission.[4] They will review again the needs which we and other boards have spoken to, will examine the fairness and credibility of sentencing laws and practices, including the active time normally served as a percentage of sentence, and make recommendations for our General Assembly to consider. In that way, the momentum needed for expansion and reform can be sustained and assured.

---

[1]Seventy-five million dollars in two-thirds bonds were authorized under the "Prison Facilities Legislative Bond Act of 1990," ratified July 16; section 6 listed approved projects. *N.C. Session Laws, Extra Session, 1989, Extra and Regular Sessions, 1990,* c. 933.

[2]Senator Henson Perrymoore Barnes, Senator Kenneth Claiborne Royall, Jr., and Representative Josephus Lyman Mavretic were identified earlier in this volume.

Howard Franklin Bryan (1942–), born in Bladenboro; resident of Iredell County; B.A., Davidson College, 1966; U.S. Army Reserve, 1969–1973. President, Piedmont Realty of Statesville; chairman, Iredell County Republican Party, 1973–1975; mayor pro tem, Statesville City Council, 1985–1987; member, state Senate, since 1987. *North Carolina Manual, 1991–1992,* 246.

Donald R. Kincaid (1936–), native, resident of Caldwell County; B.S., Appalachian State Teachers College (later Appalachian State University), 1959; served with N.C. National Guard. Schoolteacher; owner, Kincaid Insurance Agency; member, state House of Representatives, 1967–1971; member, since 1973, minority leader, 1977–1990, state Senate; Republican. *North Carolina Manual, 1991–1992,* 261.

Paul Sanders Smith (1927–), member, since 1981, minority whip, since 1985, state Senate; Republican. Previously identified in Poff, *Addresses of Martin,* I, 602n; see also *North Carolina Manual, 1991–1992,* 239–240.

James M. Craven (1930–), born in Pine Bluff; was graduated from Ellerbe High School, 1948; U.S. Army, 1948–1969. Board chairman, New South Industries; Moore County commissioner, 1980–1982; member, state House, 1981–1990. *North Carolina Manual, 1989–1990,* 343.

Theresa Harlow Esposito (1930–), born in Washington, D.C.; resident of Forsyth County; G.P.N., National Institute of Practical Nursing, 1957; was also educated at Prince George Community College and Salem College. Former federal employee; member, since 1985, minority whip, since 1991, state House; Republican. *North Carolina Manual, 1989–1990,* 316, 359, *1991–1992,* 311–312.

Doris Rogers Huffman, born in Burke County; resident of Newton; was educated at Catawba Valley Technical College. Homemaker; chairwoman, Catawba County Republican Party, 1982; member, state House, 1985–1992; GOP candidate, nomination for lieutenant governor, 1992. *News and Observer,* May 6, 1992, October 5, 1993; *North Carolina Manual, 1991–1992,* 380.

Rector Samuel Hunt III (1941–), born in Burlington; A.B., East Carolina University, 1965; U.S. Army, 1966–1969, and Reserve, 1970. President, Hunt Electric Supply Co.; former director, Alamance County Chamber of Commerce; member, state House, 1985–1992; Democrat. *News and Observer,* February 8, 1992; *North Carolina Manual, 1991–1992,* 383.

Larry T. Justus (1932–), born in Hendersonville; was educated at University of North Carolina at Chapel Hill; U.S. Air Force and Reserve, 1954–1982. Owner-operator, Justus Sand and Stone, 1957–1978; real estate broker; three-term chairman, Henderson County Republican Party; member, state House, since 1985. *North Carolina Manual, 1991–1992,* 396–397.

Johnathan Laban Rhyne, Jr. (1955–), member, 1985–1992, minority leader, 1989–1992, state House; Republican. Previously identified in Poff, *Addresses of Martin,* I, 107n; see also *News and Observer,* February 2, 1992; *North Carolina Manual, 1989–1990,* 314, *1991–1992,* 309.

Frank J. "Trip" Sizemore III (1946–), born in High Point; resident of Greensboro; B.A., 1968, J.D., 1971, Duke University. Attorney; member, state House, 1985–1990; chairman, Corrections Subcommittee of House Judiciary Committee; GOP candidate, nomination for lieutenant governor, 1992. *News and Observer,* April 28, May 6, 1992; *North Carolina Manual, 1989–1990,* 426, 450.

[3]Joseph L. Hamilton (1950–), born in Fayetteville; resident of Raleigh; B.A. and graduate study, N.C. State University. Various positions with N.C. Dept. of Correction, since 1973, included assistant director of prisons-administrative services, 1982–1986, deputy director of prisons, 1986–1987, and prisons director, 1987–1992; was appointed deputy director, Division of Prisons, 1992. Joseph L. Hamilton, letter to Jan-Michael Poff, June 20, 1994.

[4]The General Assembly ratified "An Act to Create a Sentencing and Policy Advisory Commission and to Establish a Uniform Standard for the Development of Criminal Justice Policy" on July 28, 1990. *N.C. Session Laws, Extra Session, 1989, Extra and Regular Sessions, 1990,* c. 1076.

PRESS RELEASE: GOVERNOR MARTIN'S STATEMENT ON
ATTORNEY GENERAL'S REQUEST TO SEND THE HIGHWAY
PATROL TO PHYSICALLY REMOVE PROTESTERS

RALEIGH, JUNE 28, 1990

Governor Jim Martin issued the following statement yesterday concerning the recommendation from the Attorney General's Office on the demonstrations at the prospective hazardous waste site in Iredell-Rowan counties.

"Yesterday I received a recommendation from the Attorney General's Office that I order thirty to forty Highway Patrol officers onto the prospective hazardous waste site on the border of Iredell and Rowan counties to physically remove the 500-or-so demonstrators who have gathered there to oppose test drilling. After reviewing this with Secretary Joseph Dean, who has line responsibility for the Highway Patrol, I have decided not to make such an order.

"The people who have gathered there are good people and have taken great care to show that they are not threatening the safety of anyone else. It would not serve any necessary purpose at this time to use force to remove them from private property. Instead, I will ask the Hazardous Waste Management Commission to consider what other alternatives are available to them, so that we can meet our responsibilities for proper treatment of these wastes."

INTERSTATE 40 DEDICATION

NEWTON GROVE, JUNE 29, 1990

[The ribbon-cutting in Newton Grove opening the Benson-Magnolia portion of Interstate 40, on June 29, 1990, was a proud moment for Governor Martin. The ceremony marked the completion of the final link of the highway, which stretched 2,554 miles from Wilmington, North Carolina, to Barstow, California. *News and Observer*, June 29, 1990; *Wilmington Morning Star*, June 30, 1990.]

How sweet it is! Thank you, Tommy, and thank you, Sampson County, for extending such a warm welcome to all of us.[1] Let me add my personal greetings to our good friends who live just down the road a piece: the mayor of Barstow, California, Bill Pope, and Mayor Pro Tem Manuel Gurule. And welcome, too, to Senator Jesse Helms who is also here today to help celebrate.[2]

Our friends from Barstow have already proven that they are good neighbors. During the summer of 1986, when North Carolina was suffering through a terrible drought, the city of Barstow sent our Rowan County farmers 300 tons of hay. We won't forget your generosity. Welcome to North Carolina, and thank you for being here to share this momentous occasion with us.

I've said it before many times, and I'm going to say it again today. When I ran for governor in 1984, I made one highway campaign promise to the people of North Carolina: that Interstate 40 from Raleigh to Wilmington would be under contract in four years. We made good on that in three and one-half years, and today we even keep our schedule for completion by July 1990! We fulfilled that promise with one day to spare, just in time for Fourth of July holiday travelers.

But it could not have been done on time had I promised everybody every other highway at the same time. By making only this one commitment in that campaign, I asked you to believe I could get it done—and what an accomplishment completing this highway represents. It's more than just a symbol of a promise made and a promise kept. This modern freeway is a vital strategic corridor that will provide major dividends to our state in terms of safety, efficiency, and economic development.

Your local leaders are busy preparing for the economic impact that I-40 is already having on your communities. Businesses in more than thirty communities along this newest 120-mile corridor between Raleigh and Wilmington are participating in the I-40 economic impact study conducted by the state Division of Community Assistance. Through strategic planning sessions, state and local governments will cooperatively examine and pursue responsible economic growth and environmental planning.

But you and I know that the benefits of I-40 extend far beyond this 120-mile corridor. With the completion of I-40, we continue a tradition of excellence in road building that has earned North Carolina its reputation as the "Good Roads State." After thirty-two years and $880 million, 418 miles of I-40 now connect Wilmington and the southeast to the piedmont and our mountains. Today, we deliver on the promises of six previous governors.

We celebrate the opening of this highway at a time when North Carolina is commemorating the diamond jubilee anniversary of the establishment of the old Highway Commission. As we all learned in science class, sustained high energy and pressure can turn a lump of graphite into a sparkling diamond. Well, in the same way, high energy and high pressure are what created this diamond we celebrate today.

During the past seventy-five years, the North Carolina Department of Transportation has undergone a similar visionary transformation, moving from dirt paths, to farm-to-market roads, to award-winning highway designs. The State Highway Commission, as it was first called, began piecing together the fragments of that dream when it was first created by the General Assembly in 1915. With a first-year budget of only $10,000, the commission was determined to pave the way for progress in North Carolina.

That new Highway Commission had a number-one priority: to link every county seat with a system of strategic roads, a system that would crisscross the state and promote growth and economic development along the way. This same idea remains strong in my vision of North Carolina as one united state, linked by a strategic network of four-lane, limited-access, divided highways reaching within ten miles of over 96 percent of our entire population. Now, without any campaign promise, that commitment has been made. As I've often said, unpaved promises are never as good as unpromised pavement! This system we now call the intrastate system will bring economic prosperity to all of North Carolina.

As a critical component of that intrastate system, I-40 links our port at Wilmington to the rest of the nation. This superhighway stretches 2,554 miles, from North Carolina through Tennessee, Arkansas, Oklahoma, Texas, New Mexico, and Arizona, all the way to Barstow, California. Of all the states I-40 passes through, however, North Carolina is unique. In 1958, the nation's first construction on this freeway began along the Pigeon River in Haywood County. Today we've come full circle as we celebrate the completion of the last unfinished section in the nation in Sampson and Duplin counties.

Interstate 40 is a tribute to the thousands of men and women of the Department of Transportation, and the highway construction industry, who have toiled for more than thirty-two years to construct North Carolina's "main street." We are privileged that one of our very own, DOT division engineer Verlin Edwards, was a member of the first crew in the nation to begin work on I-40. Mr. Edwards is here with us today, and what a special reward it must be for him to witness this historic event.

As we look with satisfaction at this opening of what for too long was the "missing link," let's remember the strong help we got from our congressional delegation in Washington and the Federal Highway Administration, as well as the cooperation and encouragement of state and local officials and business leaders. But I hope you will not soon forget that had I fallen into the temptation to promise every county every highway project, this one could not have been finished. It now stands as a completed, vital asset for North Carolina, and I am very proud of it.

---

[1]Thomas J. Harrelson, state transportation secretary.

[2]Helms's presence at the ribbon-cutting rankled the *Wilmington Morning Star*. Its lead editorial of July 3, 1990, criticized, "Sen. Helms was never a friend of I-40. On one of the rare occasions when he bothered to get involved with the project, it was to oppose it." Congressman Charles G. Rose III, state representative Harry Payne, former governor James B. Hunt, Jr., and Governor Martin earned the newspaper's praise for their support of the highway.

PRESS RELEASE: GOVERNOR ANNOUNCES OPPOSITION TO OFFSHORE DRILLING, SAYS COMPANY HAS NOT SUPPLIED ENOUGH ENVIRONMENTAL ASSURANCES

RALEIGH, JULY 17, 1990

[On June 26, 1990, President Bush announced a ten-year moratorium on off-shore exploration for oil and natural gas. Although North Carolina was not included in the declaration, the president's surprise decision, combined with less-than-reassuring reports from Mobil Oil and the federal Minerals Management Service, galvanized Governor Martin's opposition to Mobil's plan to drill a test well northeast of Cape Hatteras. He registered his disapproval of the project, below, and in related press releases; see "Governor Martin Asks that Oil Drilling Site in North Carolina Be Included in President Bush's Moratorium on Off-shore Drilling," Raleigh, June 26, 1990, and "Governor Formally Opposes Mobil Proposal," Raleigh, September 21, 1990, Governors Papers, James G. Martin.

Congress delighted Mobil's adversaries by augmenting the presidential moratorium with the Outer Banks Protection Act. That legislation, contained in the Oil Pollution Act of 1990, established a five-person scientific panel to review Mobil's proposal and postponed any chance of federal approval of the plan until October 1, 1991. Drilling was further delayed by the earlier memorandum of understanding that limited such activity to the months of May through October; see page 134, above.

The Mobil test rig never sprouted off Cape Hatteras during Martin's second term. Opposition from state authorities, coastal residents, and environmentalists played a role. Perhaps more important, the combination of falling oil and gas prices, mounting planning and equipment development costs, and the less stringent offshore drilling regulations of other nations made the project untenable as a business decision. Unable to benefit from the undersea petroleum leases it purchased from the Reagan administration in 1981, Mobil announced its intention, in October 1992, to sue the federal government to buy them back. *Congressional Quarterly Almanac, 1990,* 283, 284, 287, 312, 872; Donna D. Moffitt, former director, Outer Continental Shelf Office, interview with Jan-Michael Poff, July 27, 1994; *News and Observer,* August 9, 1990, October 28, 1992; P.L. 101–380, "Oil Pollution Act of 1990" (short title), *United States Statutes at Large,* Act of August 18, 1990, 104 Stat. 555–558.]

Representatives of Governor Jim Martin informed Mobil Oil Company on Tuesday that the governor will oppose the company's offshore exploration plan for two reasons:

1) The company and the federal government have failed to provide adequate information about the safety or the environmental impact of

the drilling off the North Carolina coast.

2) President Bush's announcement of a change in national energy policy, through his national moratorium on offshore drilling, indicates there is no need to search for additional energy reserves in the ocean.

Secretary of Administration Jim Lofton, Director of the Outer Continental Shelf Office Donna Moffitt, Associate Attorney General Clark Wright, and others met Tuesday with Mobil project manager James Martin and Deputy Director Ed Cassidy of the Minerals Management Service. The North Carolina representatives delivered a four-page statement from Governor Martin to company officials. The two paragraphs below are excerpted from the governor's statement:

> Because we are not getting the level of environmental and socioeconomic information commensurate with the level of those OCS [outer continental shelf] areas under the president's ten-year moratorium and the president's change in national policy, I will not support drilling for oil or gas off the North Carolina coast and will do all that I can to prevent it from occurring. Drilling off the coast of North Carolina for natural gas is not needed at this time for national energy security. The 5 trillion cubic feet of natural gas that Mobil says it has a one-in-ten chance of finding is trivial in comparison to the known U.S. natural gas reserves listed in the president's fact sheet released with his moratorium announcement.
>
> If the other two parties to the memorandum of understanding—Mobil and the Minerals Management Service—continue to operate under the terms of the agreement, I will honor it also. However, I am putting both parties on notice that when the environmental review process established by the memorandum of understanding is completed, I will take all the steps within my power to see that drilling does not take place off the coast of North Carolina.

In a related but separate development, North Carolina coastal management officials on Tuesday refuted Mobil Oil's claim that its proposed discharge activities off the North Carolina coast are consistent with provisions of the N.C. Coastal Management Program. Mobil's permit request for discharging drilling wastes on the site as a part of the test drilling process has been rejected by the Division of Coastal Management. This decision prevents EPA from issuing the permit to Mobil and effectively halts the process unless it is successfully challenged in an appeal to the U.S. Department of Commerce.[1]

---

[1]Citing the environmental damage that offshore drilling would cause, the U.S. Commerce Department turned down Mobil's appeal in 1994. The action further blocked undersea exploration for natural gas off Cape Hatteras and confirmed the initial decision made by state coastal management authorities. The oil company, however, still had the

option to file a motion for reconsideration with the Commerce Department or take its case to federal court. *News and Observer*, September 16, 1994.

TESTIMONY BEFORE U.S. HOUSE SUBCOMMITTEE ON SURFACE TRANSPORTATION

Durham, September 21, 1990

[The U.S. House Subcommittee on Surface Transportation scheduled a number of regional hearings, between March 8 and September 21, 1990, on the reauthorization of post-interstate surface transportation programs. Governor Martin addressed the last such forum, held in Durham. Information presented in testimony across the country contributed to the composition of P.L. 102–240, the "Intermodal Surface Transportation Efficiency Act of 1991" [short title], *United States Statutes at Large*, Act of December 18, 1991, 105 Stat. 1914–2207.

P.L. 102–240 authorized highway and mass transit programs for seventy-two months, beginning in fiscal year 1992. North Carolina received $147.9 million for "special road and bridge projects." President Bush and members of Congress hailed the act as the only legislation passed during 1991 to generate employment. *Congressional Quarterly Almanac, 1991*, 137–151.]

I want to welcome all of you to North Carolina. To our distinguished guests, let me extend to you warm greetings from the Tar Heel State. Now, North Carolina has been called the Tar Heel State since the War Between the States. This goes back to the days when our forefathers would pick up pine tar on their bare feet during the war. Our $9.2 billion, state-funded highway construction program passed last year gives the slogan even more credence, so if you notice a little fresh asphalt on your heels, remember it's mostly state tar—with maybe just a little federal tar mixed in.

Seriously, I do want to thank Chairman Mineta, congressmen Tim Valentine and David Price, for coming to this region and particularly to our state.[1] I'm pleased to be with you, this morning, as we begin to deal with an issue which affects every one of us at some time or another: transportation. I want to say that the importance of what we are trying to accomplish was said very well a few days ago, and I quote,

> I believe that the United States must enter the twenty-first century with a transportation network that is second to none in an increasingly competitive world. That means we must first redefine our transportation programs to meet the challenges of the 1990s. I believe we must look at the reauthorization of the federal transportation programs from a broader perspective than we have in the past. I believe we must define our efforts in terms of how they aid our international competitiveness, foster domestic economic

development, improve public safety, enhance our overall quality of life, and provide a stable, consistent level of funding.[2]

These comments are attributed to Chairman Mineta, recently, as he announced a new initiative for the national surface transportation reauthorization policy. Let me say, Norm, I couldn't agree with you more.

There's much to talk about, there are many people who are scheduled to speak, and time is short, so I'll get right to the point. Through state, federal, and local government partnerships, North Carolinians have invested an estimated $66 billion in our extensive highway system; and yet, we recognized several years ago that to cope with our current economic success and prepare to meet the challenges of the twenty-first century, we needed to invest even more. We needed a program that addressed our most pressing, immediate needs and one that planned for North Carolina's future.

Last year, our state made that kind of commitment to transportation with the enactment of the largest public works program in its history: $9.2 billion over thirteen and a half years, all state money, and this was in addition to our normal highway and transportation improvement budget. It will pave all our dirt roads and complete a 3,000-mile, uninterrupted network of four-lane, divided, limited-access, intrastate highways that will reach within ten miles of 96 percent of our people. What we are doing is making North Carolina a better place to live and to work. We're making it easier and safer for people to get to work, for buses to transport children to school, for farmers to get their produce to market, for businesses to move their products, and for people to enjoy their leisure time.

On the state level, we are trying to do our part. However, a fair federal transportation program is essential to the success of any state's transportation plan. One element of a fair federal transportation program would be the orderly "spend down" of the trust fund balances. More than $10 billion is sitting in the U.S. Treasury in an effort to disguise the true level of the federal fund deficit. Taxpayers have contributed to the federal trust fund thinking their money would be used to address transportation problems nationwide. This money would be well spent on a backlog of critical transportation needs such as unsafe bridges, congestion relief in our cities, and better access to our rural areas. The Highway Trust Fund should be removed from the unified federal budget process so that its surplus is not used to balance the deficit. The trust fund is a dedicated revenue source for transportation programs and projects and should be taken off budget and made independently accountable.

The new federal program also would be well served to omit so-called demonstration projects altogether. Among the states and within the American Association of State Highway and Transportation Officials, opposition to the practice is virtually universal. However, once started, this pork barrel initiates a free-for-all among the states and their congressional delegations. The process distorts the distribution of funds at the national level and detracts from the decision making at the state level. If Congress insisted upon continuing the practice, I would recommend that any demonstration projects come out of a state's normal allocation.

Highway safety will be another important element in the new federal program. I see the key to a national safety program to be more local, and state flexibility in using safety money, as well as dedicated and secure sources of funding for long-term development of projects and requests.

As far as the current total federal program is concerned, North Carolina has a dubious distinction. Our state has received the smallest proportion of federal highway funds over the cumulative history of the highway trust fund. We are not a wealthy state, but you have made us a donor state! North Carolina is also a fast-growing and populous state and should not receive fewer federal dollars than taxes contributed. A fair federal program ought to ensure a more equitable distribution of funds—and while we are on the subject of equity, I can't help but mention the fact that North Carolina contributes $40 million a year to the mass transit account and gets back $2 million. The $38 million difference is money that could be spent getting more handicapped people to the store and to the doctor. It's money that could be spent getting more elderly citizens to places they need and want to go when they are no longer able to drive. It's money that could be spent on a variety of mass transit alternatives. It's money that should be returned for use by its contributors. We only ask for a fair share.

The public transportation need in North Carolina is different from many states of similar size. Our low-density, cluster-type cities are not suited for billion-dollar, mass-transit rail projects, but we do own, as a state, the railroad from Charlotte to Greensboro, to Raleigh, to Morehead City on the coast, and are promoting rail passenger service with our own money. A fair federal program would provide more flexibility in how the money could be spent.

If there is a theme for the new federal transportation program, it should be fairness and flexibility. Without those two vital elements, we have no interest in a federal program.

I know from the days I spent in your midst that the decisions you must make will be difficult in many respects. But working together, we can develop a new federal surface transportation program to help meet the needs of the future. Just be fair.

---

[1]Norman Yoshio Mineta (1931–), native of San Jose, Ca.; B.S., University of California at Berkeley, 1953; U.S. Army, 1953–1956. Insurance business; city councilman, 1967–1971, vice-mayor, 1968–1971, and mayor, 1971–1974, of San Jose; elected to U.S. House of Representatives, 1974, and returned in subsequent elections; chairman, House Surface Transportation Subcommittee; chairman, House Public Works Committee, since 1993; Democrat. Barone and Ujifusa, *Almanac of American Politics, 1994*, 125–126; *Biographical Directory of Congress*, 1510.

Itimous T. Valentine, Jr. (1926–), born in Nashville; A.B., The Citadel, 1948; J.D., University of North Carolina, 1967; U.S. Army Air Force, 1944–1946. Attorney; member, state House of Representatives, 1955–1960; legal advisor, 1965, and legislative counsel, 1967, to Governor Dan K. Moore; chairman, state Democratic Executive Committee, 1966–1968; elected from North Carolina's Second Congressional District to U.S. House of Representatives, 1982, and returned in subsequent elections; retired from Congress in 1994. *North Carolina Manual, 1991–1992*, 511.

David Eugene Price (1940–), born in Johnson City, Tenn.; resident of Chapel Hill; B.A., University of North Carolina at Chapel Hill, 1961; B.D., 1964, Ph.D., 1969, Yale University. Assistant professor, political science and American studies, Yale University, 1969–1973; professor of political science and public policy, Duke University, 1973–1986; executive director, 1979–1980, chairman, 1983–1984, N.C. Democratic Party; elected from North Carolina's Fourth Congressional District to U.S. House of Representatives, 1986, 1998, 1990, 1992; author. *News and Observer*, November 9, 1994; *North Carolina Manual, 1991–1992*, 513.

[2]The lines attributed to Mineta appear to be a partial summary of his opening remarks on the first day of hearings, held March 8, 1990, in Washington, D.C. He stated, "In the past, some have chosen to view our transportation programs as a collection of individualized concerns. But, I strongly believe that we must look at our federal transportation programs from a broader perspective. I believe that we must define our efforts in terms of domestic economic development, our international competitiveness, public safety, quality of life, and a stable, consistent funding source." *Reauthorization of the Post-Interstate Surface Transportation Programs, Hearings before the Subcommittee on Surface Transportation, Committee on Public Works and Transportation, House of Representatives, One Hundred First Congress, Second Session* (Washington: U.S. Government Printing Office, 1991), 1. The transcript of Martin's testimony was recorded on pages 3118–3125.

CELEBRATION NORTH CAROLINA FINANCE COMMITTEE

ASHEVILLE, SEPTEMBER 27, 1990

Welcome to our fall briefing here in the beautiful mountains of Asheville, the home of George Cecil, a member of our Celebration North Carolina Finance Committee and an active supporter of our Celebration activities.[1] I'd like to thank all of you for attending our first briefing. Each of you represents what Celebration North Carolina is all about: working together, as a team, to strengthen our communities so that North

Carolina can become an even better place to live, work, and play.

By sharing your time, money, resources, and expertise, each of you is helping to meet some of our state's most pressing challenges. Glaxo, Incorporated, for example, has generously contributed to reducing the state's infant mortality rate. Duke Power, IBM, and R. J. Reynolds are also donating their time and financial resources to improve our state's educational system. Several have expressed an interest in our important new math-science initiative.

I applaud these efforts, and thank each of you for the example of community service you set and for your personal contributions making North Carolina the best state in the nation. Already you are helping us to achieve the goals of our Celebration mission. That mission is for Celebration North Carolina to provide a catalyst for community action throughout the state. That's a tall order, but ensuring a strong, stable future for North Carolina must begin at the grass-roots level.

To accomplish this mission, we've established several goals for Celebration North Carolina. First, we want to herald 1991 as the "celebration year" in which we celebrate North Carolina as the best state in the nation to live, work, and play. Let's not forget all the reasons we have to celebrate that make us the envy of other states. After all, we can boast about:

—an excellent business climate;

—outstanding colleges and universities;

—a strong commitment to reform our public schools to get better results;

—an efficient transportation system, with a historic commitment to improve it;

—the ability to create jobs for our citizens and maintain a low unemployment rate;

—growing investment in high technology;

—ranking number one in manufacturing;

—excellent recreational facilities from the mountains to the coast;

—and a population with a can-do attitude.

With this "celebratory" backdrop, Celebration North Carolina looks toward addressing some of our most pressing needs to make this state better tomorrow than it is today.

The second goal we've established is to identify community programs across our state that have proven to be successful, to expand them, and to raise public awareness about them. Third, we want to provide the resources necessary to bring those successful programs to areas where there is a demonstrated need and a commitment to achieve results. Fourth, we want to recognize and publicize the outstanding corporate involvement in our communities and [the] good corporate citizenship which has blessed us statewide. And finally, we want to develop partnerships between the private and public sectors and community organizations, who are working together as a team, to solve our problems.

Let me share with you an example of the Celebration program at work. Some of you may be familiar with Motheread, a nationally recognized family literacy program. Motheread: that's one word with one *r*.

Motheread was founded right here in North Carolina by Nancy Gaj (pronounced Guy) and Patric Dorsey, my secretary of cultural resources and [a] member of Celebration's Board of Directors, with crucial support from Correction Secretary Aaron Johnson. Motheread was begun in our prison system originally, helping female inmates to improve their reading skills and requiring that they read to their children during family visits. The program has been so successful it now has been expanded outside the prison system into several communities, in libraries and churches.[2]

Motheread is an example of how Celebration North Carolina capitalizes on an excellent program and replicates it in other communities across the state. Thanks to a gift from Duke Power Company, Celebration North Carolina will double Motheread's current outreach by expanding the program into five new counties across the state. When word of the Duke grant went out to the public, Celebration received over eighty applications from seventy-eight different counties asking to establish Motheread in those communities. That response certainly demonstrates the need for this Motheread-Celebration-Duke Power partnership.[3]

In addition to Motheread, Celebration is also looking forward to working with IBM and R. J. Reynolds to identify and implement other successful educational programs.

The first Celebration gift from Glaxo has united communities all over the state to bring prenatal care and nutrition to expectant mothers, to reduce our infant mortality rate. Already we are seeing improvement from 12.6 per thousand, in 1988, to 11.5 per thousand. Some don't think that's significant progress, but I do. It came down with a bigger improvement in one year than it had gone up in two years, slippage combined, and it reached the lowest rate ever—so let's celebrate.

Moore and Van Allen is also working with us to protect our environmental resources through the well-known Adopt-A-Stream initiative, which is based on a project I started back when I was a county commissioner, called Martin's Mecklenburg Monitors.

With that kind of support, Celebration North Carolina is moving forward to address those crucial issues that will affect us for years to come. Celebration also makes good business sense, because addressing those issues now will enable us to remain competitive in the years ahead. About the future: We have a two-year agenda, with its main emphasis next year, and at the end of 1991 we will sit down, review our progress, and evaluate what steps should be taken next. Right now we are off to a great start, and I have every reason to believe we will achieve our goals.

The essence of Celebration North Carolina was stated best by President Bush when he said, "What millions of Americans need is not another government program, but a set of meaningful relationships that results in the conviction that their future is not limited by their present circumstances." Your presence here tonight, and your continuing support, makes [sic] it possible for us to mold and shape North Carolina's future so that our citizens' future will not be limited by their present circumstances.

I look forward to seeing you again at our next Celebration event. If you want to mark your calendars, that will be held at the Governor's Mansion, in Raleigh, on Tuesday, December 18. We've just finished extensive renovations of the mansion, and you won't want to miss seeing it decorated in all its Christmas finery. Between now and then, let me challenge you to bring at least one additional colleague from another corporation in your community into the Celebration fold. They can enjoy [the] Christmas season at the Executive Mansion with us and, more importantly, help us to design and build a long-lasting future of progress and opportunity for our state—so we can celebrate.

---

[1]George H. V. Cecil (1925–), native of Biltmore; was educated in Europe; served in Royal Naval Volunteer Reserve during World War II. President, The Biltmore Co., 1962–1979; president, 1979–1992, chairman, since 1992, Biltmore Dairy Farms, Inc.; director, First Union Corp., 1958–1993, of Multimedia, Inc., since 1975, and of Carolina Power and Light Co., since 1976. Letter, George H. V. Cecil to Jan-Michael Poff, June 30, 1993.

[2]Martin summarized the founding of Motheread as follows: "Secretary Dorsey was concerned for mothers who had been separated from their children while serving time in prison. That concern matched Ms. Gaj's personal and professional interest in literacy. Secretary Dorsey therefore asked Ms. Gaj to design a literacy program to reach out to these mothers, and the Motheread program was born." Established in Wake County in 1987, Motheread had been adopted in Durham, Guilford, Halifax, and Mecklenburg counties by 1990. Its staff also aided the development of similar programs sponsored by the Minnesota Humanities Council and Vermont's EvenStart. Celebration North Carolina Press Conference, Raleigh, August 30, 1990, Governors Papers, James G. Martin, hereinafter cited as Celebration North Carolina Press Conference.

[3]Duke Power Company offered Celebration North Carolina a $50,000 matching grant to broaden the availability of the Motheread program. Celebration North Carolina Press Conference.

DIVISION OF AGING AWARDS PRESENTATION

WILMINGTON, OCTOBER 10, 1990

Today we honor those outstanding people who have generously contributed their time and talents to programs and services for older adults in our state. These honorees have shown us what it means to be committed, to have the vision and the determination to help older adults meet the challenges that face them. I want personally to commend these individuals, and every one of you, for these efforts, because together we are making a difference in North Carolina.

But now is no time to rest on our laurels. Despite what we've done in the past, we must continue to improve programs and services for older adults if we hope to meet their future needs. Meeting those needs is going to be quite a challenge, because citizens sixty-five and older make up one of the fastest-growing segments of our population.

Between 1980 and 2010, the number of older adults living in North Carolina will almost double. During that same period, we expect the number of people eighty-five and older to more than triple. That kind of rapid growth is changing the way we live and respond to the needs of older adults.

More than 6 million elderly Americans need help with daily activities. In many cases, families provide that help, caring for older relatives as part of an extended family. *Newsweek* magazine reports that the average American woman now spends about the same amount of time caring for her parents as she does for her own children.

As our older adult population continues to increase, our society will have to accept greater responsibility for meeting the special needs of both older adults and their families. We can't wait for another ten years to get started. We have to start now, planning for and building a secure future for older adults in North Carolina.

I'm proud to say we're already moving forward. As a result of the budget requests I submitted to the General Assembly, state funding for aging programs and services has grown from $1.6 million, in 1985, to $9.8 million in 1991. That's an increase of 612 percent, and I don't mind telling you, that's an increase I'm proud of.

We put the focus on aging, and in 1987, the General Assembly joined us in our support for older adults by approving our Aging Policy Plan.[1] That plan offers a strategic, detailed agenda for addressing the needs of older adults in seven major areas: income, employment, retirement, housing, transportation, continuum of care services, and health care. As part of that plan, the Division of Aging applied to the Federal Administration on Aging and received a three-year grant to expand housing options for older adults—one of only three such grants awarded. Those grant monies helped us learn about the types and conditions of housing options currently available. The project is also helping to develop regulatory standards for lenders and adequate consumer protection for older adults.

Having a decent place to live is important, but for older adults with vision or other health problems, transportation can become a major obstacle to maintaining a comfortable life-style. To help overcome that obstacle, the Americans with Disabilities Act, recently passed by Congress and signed by President Bush, requires all newly purchased mass-transit vehicles, including buses and railcars, to be readily accessible to persons with disabilities. The act also requires communities with fixed-route transportation systems to operate a paratransit system, serving persons with disabilities who are unable to use fixed-route transportation. In addition, telephone companies will soon be required to provide relay services for persons who are deaf, hearing-impaired, or speech-impaired.

But when living at home and traveling independently are no longer options because of declining health, we still must make sure that older adults receive proper care. That's why we established the Long-Term Care Ombudsman Program in 1989 as part of the Older Americans Act. By resolving grievances through an ombudsman, this advocacy program ensures that our older adults in long-term care facilities receive the highest quality care possible. The program also educates the public and promotes community involvement and volunteerism in long-term care facilities.[2]

Health care is always important, but becomes even more critical as we enter our sixties, seventies, and eighties. Recognizing that fact, the General Assembly authorized funding, in 1988, that expanded chore services in fifty-six counties and homemaker health aide services in twenty-nine counties. Funds from this legislation have been used to expand adult day care, adult day health, case management, home-delivered meals, and mental health counseling. In addition, those state funds have paid to develop and maintain North Carolina's 125 senior centers in eighty-five counties.

Yes, we've put the focus on aging—so much so that in 1989, Secretary Flaherty elevated state aging services to division-level status within the Department of Human Resources. That same year, the General Assembly designated our new Division of Aging as the lead state agency for maintaining and expanding our strategic plan for serving older adults in North Carolina. To help in its work, our Division of Aging has received grants from the Kate B. Reynolds Health Care Trust Fund to conduct aging policy forums, to train local officials, to finance grants for local planning models, and to address the special needs of frail older adults. The division staff have also compiled county aging service profiles that keep track of money spent [for] aging services by each county.

We are moving forward. We are focusing on aging, and we are getting results. Caring for older adults is their right, and it is our responsibility. Each generation is indebted to the one that came before—indebted to the care they have given us, to our sense of family and our shared heritage that we experience only through them.

Today's older adults are yesterday's pioneers. Just think of the miracles they have seen. An eighty-five-year-old has seen the miracle of flight at Kitty Hawk grow into supersonic flight and the space shuttle. They've witnessed two world wars and a changing map of political and social alliances that continue to rewrite modern society.

These pioneers have built this state and our nation with their caring, their hard work, and their dedication. Now, as they age, they deserve our caring, our hard work, and our dedication to preserve for them the quality of life they have worked so hard for us to enjoy. Thanks to you and your continued efforts, we can and will provide a comfortable, secure life for our older adults well into the 1990s and beyond. Thank you for coming, and thank you for caring about our older adults in North Carolina.

Now it is my privilege to present two awards from the North Carolina Division of Aging to two very special legislators who have done great things for older adults in this state. Under the leadership of Senator James Richardson and Representative C. R. Edwards, the North Carolina Study Commission on Aging made precedent-setting contributions to our older North Carolinians. Senator Richardson, Representative Edwards, and other committee members were the architects of Senate Bill 1559, passed by the General Assembly in 1988. This landmark legislation provided the first significant state appropriation to the Division of Aging.[3]

With that money, the division has funded more in-home health services for older adults. For the first time, over eighty counties were able to provide respite care services to family caregivers. Over fifty senior centers have received money for capital improvements, and seventeen new senior centers have been developed. Our councils of government and area agencies on aging have received crucial support, and under this legislation, service delivery systems for older North Carolinians have been simplified. I want to commend Senator Richardson and Representative Edwards for their vision and their notable achievements on behalf of older adults in our state. Thank you for making a difference.[4]

[1]"An Act to Establish an Aging Policy Plan for North Carolina," *N.C. Session Laws, 1987*, I, c. 289, was ratified June 4, 1987.

[2]See *N.C. Session Laws, 1989*, I, c. 403, and P.L. 89–73, "Older Americans Act of 1965," *United States Statutes at Large*, Act of July 14, 1965, 79 Stat. 218.

[3]James Franklin Richardson (1926–), native of Charlotte; B.S., Johnson C. Smith University, 1949; U.S. Navy, 1944–1946. Former postmaster; member, state House, 1985–1986; member, state Senate, since 1987, majority whip, since 1991; chairman, Senate Appropriations-Human Resources Committee; Democrat. *North Carolina Manual, 1991–1992*, 237.

Chancy Rudolph Edwards (1925–), born in Nash County; resident of Fayetteville; B.A., 1946, M.Div., 1949, Shaw University. Pastor, Spring Garden Baptist Church, Washington, 1948–1953, and of First Baptist Church, Fayetteville, since 1953; president, General Baptist State Convention of N.C., Inc., 1970–1974; member, state House, 1983–1990, and chairman of its Education Committee; chairman, Fayetteville City Board of Education; Democrat. Chancy Rudolph Edwards, letter to Memory F. Mitchell, Historical Publications administrator, Division of Archives and History, April 5, 1981; *North Carolina Manual, 1989–1990*, 358.

S.B. 1559 was ratified July 11, 1988, as c. 1095, *N.C. Session Laws, 1987, Regular Session, 1988*. The measure was entitled "An Act to Provide for the Urgent Needs of Older Adults, to Begin Building an In-Home and Community-Based System of Services for Older Adults, and to Appropriate the Necessary Funds."

[4]Richardson also accepted the award for Edwards, who was unable to attend the ceremony.

ADVISORY BUDGET COMMISSION

RALEIGH, OCTOBER 15, 1990

Before we launch into departmental budget presentations, I'd like to describe to you a new planning process I've set in motion. . . [incomplete]. At a recent meeting of the Executive Cabinet, including Council of State and cabinet secretaries, we discussed possible ways to improve the process of decision making in state government and to devise better methods of accountability. As a result of that discussion, I've asked department heads to develop a legislative and executive management plan that will help us deal with long-term budget issues. That document should be available in January. My hope is that stronger planning will help us to rethink the way we make budgetary decisions in state government. The seriousness of our current fiscal situation makes this move necessary.

Charles Dickens may have described our situation best with the opening lines of *A Tale of Two Cities*: "It was the best of times; it was the worst of times." For a few months last fall, the national economy posted the highest quarterly growth rates since the end of World War II. But this past spring, despite continued economic growth, we faced an unprecedented shortfall in state tax revenues along with increased demands for government services. Now the potential for war in the Middle East and the threat of economic recession at home add to the uncertainty of predicting future revenue growth. Prudence requires that we begin making strategic choices that will remain viable in a rapidly changing environment.

Painful though it may be, our current situation gives us a golden opportunity to take stock of where we are and where we need to be. As Pogo the comic-strip character said, "If you don't know where you're headed, you may end up somewhere else."

We don't want to end up somewhere else. We want to end up right where we plan to be: with a strong, healthy, and growing economy. But to do that, we must overcome a number of special challenges that the 1990s are likely to present.

As state government leaders, it's our responsibility to define our goals, make responsible decisions, and accept accountability for their results. We may disagree on what issues we consider to be most important. We may also disagree on how to address those issues. Whether we agree or disagree, we need a common framework that will help us resolve our conflicts and guide us toward making responsible, long-term decisions.

First, our departments must define specific goals for which they expect to be held accountable. The General Assembly must then determine whether those departmental goals reflect voter concerns and priorities. It will then prescribe the intended results, measures that tell managers and legislators whether programs are making a difference. If legislators and program managers agree on departmental priorities, we would hope to be allowed to develop procedures that will allow managers to have the flexibility, within legislated limits, to use their personnel and budget resources in the best ways possible.

For these reasons, under the provisions of G.S. 143A-17, which directed us to develop a planning process, I have asked all departments and the university system to prepare their own executive management plans. I've asked them not to give us mountains of data and excess verbiage that would mainly cloud the issue. I'm asking for departmental plans that are concise and focused—so that these plans can be compiled in a single volume and submitted to the General Assembly along with my proposed budget.

This planning process is well under way. I have asked Dr. Sheron Morgan, director of the Office of Policy and Planning in the Department of Administration, to coordinate departmental efforts.[1] We've also set up a working group of departmental representatives to decide on a format for the final document and to guide departments in developing their plans. On Wednesday, department and university representatives will discuss how work on their plans is proceeding.

In the process of working on their individual plans, some departments have also discussed common challenges. Early in this process, for example, staff members in the four criminal justice agencies decided it was important for them to collaborate. I commend them for their initiative in taking this extra step.

The members of the General Assembly have received a briefing on this process. In addition, some departmental staffs have met to discuss how legislative committees might use this document in the early stages of the legislative session beginning in late January.

After this process has been tested and fine tuned, I intend to make it a permanent part of state government to help us take a long-term view on major issues. By requiring department heads to put on paper and publish our major goals, we will establish a system that ensures state government accountability to the General Assembly and to the public. It's important that this commission review this document and listen to department heads discuss the major goals they've identified for the next four years, even during a time of uncertain revenue projections. Levels of expenditure may change, but goals, if they are sound and forward looking, ought to remain unchanged. They should, in fact, serve as a steadying influence even in the midst of uncertainty.

In the future, these departmental plans will be available well before we begin to consider the budget. But because this is a new approach to an old problem, the plans being prepared will not be available to us until early January. That means we may not be able to use all of them to guide us in making decisions for inclusion in the biennial budget which I must submit in early February.

These plans may still be useful, however, in providing this commission with an overview of the departments' major policy and program commitments in the budget. Let me ask your opinion: If you would like to receive an early draft copy of the departmental plans, we could schedule a commission meeting, perhaps in mid-January, to discuss them and perhaps hear brief presentations by department heads. Do you have any reaction to that?

(Discussion)

As I said earlier, we all have different perspectives on the issues, and each of us has different responsibilities. My administration will no doubt choose to focus on three or four specific issues that may or may not be high on your list of priorities, but I want you to join in this discussion by raising those issues that are of primary importance in your perspective. I believe these departmental plans can help us reach that consensus for the good of both state government and the public. With your help, we can reach that goal.

[1]Sheron Keiser Morgan (1942–), director, from 1988, Office of Policy and Planning, N.C. Dept. of Administration. Previously identified in Poff, *Addresses of Martin*, I, 892n–893n.

BUSINESS COMMITTEE FOR EDUCATION
AWARDS PRESENTATION

RALEIGH, OCTOBER 15, 1990

It's a pleasure to be here again to honor those outstanding teachers and businesses who have given so much of [their] time, talent, and support to improve education in North Carolina. We honor these award winners for their commitment and energy, for doing what it takes to encourage our young people to stay in school to learn how to be successful adults.

Of course, one of the most difficult things about education is that you don't often see immediately how your efforts have shaped a future of opportunity for individual students. There's a story Nat Wyeth once told about his brother, the famous artist Andrew Wyeth.[1] Andrew was working on a picture of Lafayette's quarters, which were built next to the spreading branches of a beautiful sycamore tree in Chadd's Ford, Pennsylvania. While the painting was in progress, Andrew showed his brother countless drawings of the tree's trunk and gnarled roots, parts of the tree that were hidden behind the building. Confused, his brother asked, "Where's all that in the picture?"

Andrew answered, "It's not in the picture, Nat. For me to get what I want in the part of the tree that's showing, I had to know thoroughly how it's anchored in the back of the house." The same is true of educating students. After our young people graduate, no one will see the roots of education that shape their view of the world and their potential for success. All people will see are the spreading branches.

But whether those former students spread their branches in success will be due in great part to how deeply and strongly their roots are anchored in the education they receive from us. So I want those strong foundations to be acknowledged and appreciated. We won't make much progress, though, until we give our students more rigorous academic training and better reasoning skills. With so many distractions in a typical school day, it's time for us to reaffirm and return to the main purpose of learning. Confucius once said, "He who learns, but without thinking, will waste his learning; but he who thinks without learning is utterly lost!"[2]

I'm proud to say that the state is working with you to enrich our educational programs in North Carolina: both basic skills and thinking skills. By now, most of you will be familiar with the Governor's Commission on Workforce Preparedness that I created back in February of this year. I charged my commission members, led by Tom Smith, president of Food Lion, to find ways to get business and education talking to one another, to find successful programs that meet the needs of business and education, and to recommend those programs to be spread statewide. This way we hope to improve the skills of adults in the workforce and ensure that our high school graduates are also ready and able to work.

The final commission report, due November 8, will focus on improving secondary education through business-education partnerships like Tech Prep, originated in Richmond County and Lincoln County, and upgrading the skills of our existing workforce through training programs like those already set up through our community colleges. The Governor's Commission on Workforce Preparedness will show us what ideas and programs are working and what new ones should be developed and expanded.

Fortunately, as many of the award winners here today demonstrate, business has already heeded the call to get involved through financial incentives, equipment, teacher training programs, employee loan programs, and other creative and successful ideas. One example of a successful public-private partnership in education is the Cities in Schools, sometimes called the Communit[ies] in Schools, program which Graeme Keith has just described.[3]

Cities in Schools brings an entire range of community involvement into local schools to serve at-risk children and keep them from dropping out. With volunteers from the business community serving as tutors and mentors, students can take advantage of any health, mental health, social services, or youth and child services available in the community. These services are taken directly to the students in their own schools.

Cities in Schools also works with the children's parents, encouraging them to invest their time and energy in their child's education. Superintendent Etheridge is pushing to increase parental awareness and involvement in their children's education. This is a must, and we must all help him by supporting this effort.

Last December, the North Carolina Business Committee for Education opened a state office [for] Cities in Schools in Raleigh to coordinate expansion of this program statewide. Even in a time of budget restraint, we were able to take the lead—thanks in particular to the help of BellSouth and Southern Bell. The state office for Cities in Schools has already opened three new programs in Wake, Transylvania, and Nash counties.[4]

The Communities in Schools program in Transylvania County is a special success. Because of a grant from R. J. Reynolds, students in that system are able to receive comprehensive health and prenatal care services that extend all the way through the adult graduation equivalent diploma. That's what I call commitment. The Cities in Schools office is working now with twenty-three other communities across the state to begin similar programs in their areas.

We're moving forward on other fronts, as well. For example, we've established [a] new partnership between businesses and schools, called the Science and Math Alliance, to improve science, math, and technology education in the classroom. My staff just completed a proposal for a $10-million, five-year grant from the National Science Foundation to fund expansion of this science and math education project. Some businesses have generously offered to help with the nonfederal costs of the project, and more sponsors are needed. The prototype is already a success, utilizing a two-way exchange: Some businesses offer teachers the opportunity [to] work as interns in various local businesses, to learn how they actually use math and science, and to take that knowledge back to the classroom. Other programs flow the other way, offering industry employees [a chance] to come to the classroom as visiting teachers.

These programs should make the students' experiences more meaningful, improving their mastery of the basic skills they need to compete in the high-tech workplace. Hopefully, this should also encourage more students to choose careers in math and the sciences. That's particularly true of women and minorities who are currently underrepresented in those fields. The California Achievement Tests show that, in grades 3, 6, and 8, females consistently out-perform males in math. Yet, of the eleventh and twelfth graders who indicated engineering as their career preference on the SAT, only 16 percent were females. It is expected that the number of women and minorities in the workforce will increase dramatically by the twenty-first century. They can, and they must, be encouraged to choose careers in math and the sciences.

We want to give those children strong, deep roots in education, stretching their minds so that they can blossom and grow into successful adults. That process begins now, by teaching our children the skills they need to succeed in the high-tech, highly competitive workplace of the future. For the immediate future, we should emphasize mastery of learning. Their learning must demonstrate mastery of communication, problem solving, and applied knowledge skills.

We are moving forward, but all the outstanding programs in the world won't mean anything without you—our parents, our teachers, our business and our community leaders. If we can continue to work together, innovate and support an emphasis on excellence, there is no doubt that success will be ours, and all North Carolina will praise you for it. Thank you all, and congratulations.

---

[1]Nathaniel Convers Wyeth, an engineer, was the older brother of painter Andrew Wyeth and the son of artist Newell Convers Wyeth. *Current Biography Yearbook, 1981*, 446–450.

[2]"Learning without thought is labor lost; thought without learning is perilous." Confucius, *The Confucian Analects*, 2:15, quoted in Bartlett, *Familiar Quotations*, 71.

[3]Graeme M. Keith (1932–), born in Greenwood, S.C.; resident of Charlotte; bachelor's degree, Davidson College, 1954; U.S. Army, 1954–1956. Career with First Union National Bank, 1956–1973, included positions as city executive in Durham, Greensboro, Charlotte, and regional executive vice-president, Charlotte; president, Georgia Railroad Bank and Trust Co., 1973–1981; vice-chairman, First Railroad and Banking Co., 1981–1983; president-chief executive officer, 1983–1984, chairman-chief executive officer, 1984–1988, BarclaysAmericanCorporation; chairman, The Keith Corp. real estate development, since 1989; chairman, Cities in Schools in N.C. Graeme M. Keith, letter to Jan-Michael Poff, November 8, 1993.

[4]North Carolina was the first state to open a statewide coordinating office for Cities/ Communities in Schools projects, Martin told a luncheon audience during Capital for a Day festivities in Wilkesboro, April 17, 1990.

SOUTHERN GROWTH POLICIES BOARD

New Orleans, Louisiana, October 22, 1990

What a fine and productive conference, with its focus on literacy. How important it is to stay focused, even amid the legendary revelry of "N'Yawlins'" famous [French] Quarter, and Governor Roemer[1] and all the speakers have kept us in focus and on target.

At a time with our own state and local budgets hard pressed; with the federal budget process uncertain; with far too many unmet needs which we simply can't afford; we did [not] and must not fall into the temptation of just seeking more federal grants to meet our needs. We stayed focused on what we are doing, and can do, as states and as a region. That is the value of regional organizations like the Southern Growth Policy Board, its allied organizations like [the] Southern Regional Education Board, the Southern States Energy Board, and the Southern Legislative Conference, and Southern Governors' Association, which started us on this regional approach to problem solving some fifty years ago—the cause then being to combat unfair railroad freight rates. Since its own founding, our Southern Growth Policies Board has promoted economic growth through regional approaches among our member states—to share ideas, and resources, and crusades for the benefit of our people.

Our region has been blessed with many advantages: a beautiful climate, with many natural and historic attractions; hardworking people, whose work ethic arises out of their religious convictions; our low cost of living, with favorable utility rates and good agricultural yields; an agreeable, friendly, neighborly way of life; and low taxes. I'm talking about basic tax rates for all businesses, not special tax favors—five-year holidays—for new employers. I think that's a dangerous practice. It raises taxes on existing businesses to help finance new competitors.

We have also had to face honestly many disadvantages: a legacy of strained race relations, low per-capita income, and lower education levels, per capita, than the rest of the country; an earlier disparity of economic development and diversity, relatively greater health and housing deficiencies—yet, the best we could afford, with low tax rates and low wage rates. The latter half of this century has seen us working, together and as rivals, to build the South, so that "when the South shall rise again," it will be many degrees different from what that phrase originally contemplated.

The earlier half of this century had developed paved roads, and fuel deposits, timber and agricultural resources, and of course, major military bases. All of which added to our depressed regional economy. Entry-level manufacturing—textiles, furniture, food packaging—gave us jobs that required more craftsmanship and less manufacturing skills. This improved our earning power and buying power, relative to what we had before, but left us far behind the nation.

Then began a strategy of economic development which has driven us to a level where we know we have the capacity to catch up and lead America. The first stage, in the fifties, was industrial recruitment. Runaway, low-wage industry was better than no industry at all. This was an improvement and fit nicely with our low taxes, low power rates, low wage rates, and it helped us finance improved public works, infrastructure: sewers, roads, seaports, airports, power plants. That continues with fiber-optic telecommunications and just-in-time deliveries.

The second stage of concerted southern development was the growth of travel and tourism in the fifties and sixties. While this favored some with investments, it did little to raise wages and left pockets of seasonal unemployment. That, too, continues with state-funded advertising and promotion.

Next came a great and strategic phase of the seventies, with major new public and private levels of support for our colleges and universities. Driven politically by our Southern Regional Education Board, world-class research universities emerged. We also revolutionized our laconic community colleges into strategic centers for remedial and advanced training for our workers; that, too, must continue, for this is our super-structure. This set the stage for our Southern Growth Policies Board and Southern Technology Council to become the catalyst for addressing both the high end and the low end of our economy, to make the South a leader in new technologies while leaving no one behind.

The seventies and eighties have seen a flourishing of research parks, with campus-like research and development facilities, space explora-tion, microelectronics and biotechnology research centers, and supercomputers, and interstate banking. Now as we enter the nineties, we are near completion of what may later appear to have been a grand strategy for positioning the South to be competitive for the twenty-first century.

Many components and ingredients are in place, functioning smoothly. Our favorable assets are widely recognized and acclaimed. They have attracted a far greater diversity of manufacturing and nonmanufacturing investments.

One more great strategy is needed. One piece is not yet in place. Too many of our people are not ready. The next stage must develop the hu-man resource of half our population: those who do not go to college; those who may not have finished high school or, if they did, have little to show except a diploma of uncertain warranty; those whom our em-ployers and new prospects view as an unqualified, undeveloped re-source.

Many of our people did have the skills to fill those jobs, and so we found prosperity. But too many of our people could not qualify; thus, our challenge. Hence the recurring, repetitious theme of literacy, both language and mathematics; adult literacy, to retrieve a great resource; functional workplace literacy, emphasizing job requirements; workforce preparedness, the higher order of listening now to what our employers need, but can't find, and shaping education to that standard; develop-mental preschool for those four-year-olds at risk of becoming dropouts. All this, keyed to education reforms based on measurable, important goals for improved student achievement and stricter accountability for those schools which do not meet such goals. This is a performance-based reform of a school system that is still fashioned for the early twentieth century.

There is a tendency for organizations such as ours to leap from one cause to another. New leadership tends to set new targets different from those of the previous administration. This may be good for style points, but does little for sustained progress.

I am proud that Governor Roemer was not distracted by fads, but stayed focused on the goal of literacy for all our people. Louisiana has chosen for itself a leader of uncommon gifts, but with the common touch and the common sense to listen even as he leads. With enormous budgetary challenges, Louisiana chose a young man with an understanding of fiscal prudence and integrity—and chose for us a leader who would stay focused on the needs of the rising, emerging South.

Both I and Mississippi's governor, Ray Mabus,[2] who is to follow me, could set no higher standard than to sustain this emphasis on literacy, workforce preparedness, and all that is necessary to bring that great, but too often forgotten, half of our people—so that no one is left behind; so that no human resource is neglected; so that we reach our fullest potential together.

One of my priorities as your chairman will be to continue the fine visionary work begun by Governor Roemer, Governor Bill Winter, and Bill Friday, chairman of the Southern Regional Literacy Commission, and complete with them the development of a regional literacy forum.[3] Through that forum, we will build for our states a resource to ensure that every southerner will be literate and can compete, head-to-head, for a job that can provide them and their families with a good and decent living.

I also intend to continue the board's work on other issues contributing to workforce preparedness that will move our region to the forefront of action and help us build a world-class workforce. A number of our states have special initiatives addressing workforce preparedness. I'm proud to say that North Carolina is among those states. I expect to receive the recommendations of my Commission on Workforce Preparedness on November 8.

We need to coordinate these and other workforce preparedness efforts going on in our southern states. We need to learn from each other and put the best of our ideas to work for us as a region. That's why I'm asking the staff of the Southern Growth Policies Board to review what our member states are doing, to identify and inform us about common elements, and to help us generate support in our legislatures for those shared priorities. At the same time, I want them to keep track of unique innovations and keep all of us informed on those which succeed.

I also hope that through the board we can begin a dialogue between economic development and environmental interests, with the idea of developing a partnership for progress and preservation, much like those already evolving across our region between economic development and education. Progress and preservation should be made mutually supportive. Protecting our natural resources and neighborhoods is crucial to the future economic development and attractiveness of the region.

At the same time, a sound economic base is absolutely critical to our ability to protect and enhance our environment. It's time to work together, as a region, to build that balance between preservation and progress for our future growth.

Yes, we have many challenges to address—some would call them problems—but we also have tremendous assets in our region. I want us to take stock of our progress since publication, in 1986, of the report, *Halfway Home and a Long Way to Go.*[4] We've moved well beyond that, both in education reform and rural economic development. Why not say so?

As we work toward next year's Commission on the Future of the South, let us take credit for some of our successes. This is my final point. After all, if we continue to move our region forward a few steps at a time, we will ultimately reach the top. We won't get there by dwelling on the intimidating problems. We need to celebrate more, as an organization.

Let's stop criticizing our traditional industries, like textiles and furniture, with their entry-level jobs. They came along when entry-level jobs were what we needed and [were] all we were qualified for—and if you don't like that, then remember that bad breath is better than no breath at all. Today they are modernizing and automating, too, and their jobs are becoming more technical.

I happen to believe we can achieve more, and overcome more problems, if we focus more attention on the positive steps being taken. If we continue moaning about low per-capita income and high infant mortality rates, that will obscure and undercut efforts among us which have been successful. If we continue self-flagellation over the previous decade's statistics of rural economic decline, we overlook the positive message of what some of our states have done, and are doing, to recruit jobs to rural areas. That doesn't show up in contemporary learned research, which is designed to "discover" again and again the old rural-urban dichotomy of the previous decade. It's designed to ignore progress.

What I'm saying is this: We need to identify problems as benchmarks and target them for solutions, surely, but do it without discrediting ourselves. Instead, let's make some effort to accentuate the positive, and learn from our successes, and praise those who achieve them—both in hopes that they will achieve more and as a good example, to others, that success is possible and that it does not go unnoticed. That's the world's greatest management principle: Reward or praise good behavior, and you'll get more of it.

Stay focused. Stay positive. Come the millennium, 2000 A.D., we'll be ready.

[1]Charles Elson (Buddy) Roemer III (1943–), born in Shreveport, La.; resident of Bossier City, La.; B.A., 1964, M.B.A., 1967, Harvard University. Businessman, banker, farmer; member, U.S. House of Representatives, from La., 1981–1988; governor of Louisiana, 1988–1992; Democrat. *Biographical Directory of Congress*, 1735; *Current Biography Yearbook, 1990*, 528–531.

[2]Raymond Edwin Mabus, Jr. (1948–), born in Starkville, Miss.; B.A., University of Mississippi, 1969; M.A., Johns Hopkins University, 1970; J.D., Harvard University, 1976; U.S. Navy, 1970–1972. Attorney; legal counsel, U.S. House of Representatives, 1977–1978; governor's legislative aide, 1980–1983, state auditor, 1984–1988, governor, 1988–1991, of Mississippi; chairman, Southern Regional Education Board, 1988–1989; Democrat. *Who's Who in America, 1994*, II, 2166.

[3]Governor Martin focused his one-year term as the board's chairman on the theme "The Southerner as Global Citizen." Press release, "Martin Named Chairman of the Southern Growth Policies Board," Raleigh, October 22, 1990; see also his remarks to the National Governors Association, February 5, 1991. Governors Papers, James G. Martin.

William Forrest Winter (1923–), born in Granada, Miss.; B.A., 1943, LL.B., 1949, University of Mississippi; honorary degrees; U.S. Army, 1943–1946, 1951. Attorney practicing in Granada, 1949–1958, and Jackson, Miss., since 1968; member, Miss. House of Representatives, 1948–1956; Miss. state tax collector, 1956–1964, state treasurer, 1964–1968, lieutenant governor, 1972–1978, and governor, 1980–1984; chairman, Southern Growth Policies Board, 1981, and Southern Regional Education Board, 1982; Democrat. *Who's Who in America, 1994*, II, 3701.

[4]Doris Betts, *Halfway Home and a Long Way to Go: Report of the 1986 Commission on the Future of the South* (Research Triangle Park, N.C.: Southern Growth Policies Board, 1986).

NORTH CAROLINA SCHOOL BOARDS ASSOCIATION

CHARLOTTE, NOVEMBER 16, 1990

[The following address largely echoes Martin's remarks to the North Carolina Workforce Preparedness Partnership Conference, November 8, 1990.]

It's great to see such a large turnout here for the annual School Boards Association Conference. I don't often get the chance to talk to you all at one time, in one place, so this is a good opportunity for me to say thank you for all the work you are doing to improve education in our North Carolina schools.

Your job has become a lot more difficult in recent years. Increasing demands on the system have left all of us scrambling to develop creative ways to keep up. Passage of Senate Bill 2 has given local school boards increased flexibility and responsibility over what and how our children learn—and if that wasn't enough, you have to struggle with making ends meet financially, with too few resources and too many needs.

All this means that you have to make some tough decisions, none of which are easy and many of which will seriously affect the way you do business. But as difficult as it sometimes can be, I believe this is a time, not just of challenge, but of real transformation in our state. For the first time in a long time, we have the opportunity to make a clean sweep, to retool and redesign, and to rebuild our educational system from the ground up if that's what it takes.

The exciting thing is that you are the architects of these new plans to rebuild the system. You have the flexibility now to make your own decisions about what needs to be done, and the decisions you make will have a real effect on countless young people for years to come. That's a big challenge. That's an exciting challenge, and it's a lot of responsibility, but I believe you can meet that challenge and fulfill that responsibility both wisely and well.

Fortunately, you are not in this alone. Educational reform has become the number-one concern in our state, as it rightfully should be, and parents, business entrepreneurs, civic and government leaders, and other educators are eager to help. For my part, I have come to believe that our educational reform must center around workforce preparedness: preparing our people to compete in the workplace.

World economic competition begins in the classroom. That's why I believe that workforce preparedness is the critical educational issue of the '90s. If we hope to maintain or improve our level of economic prosperity and retain our reputation as a ready-to-work state, we must do something, and do it now, to improve our workforce, both in the classroom and on the job.

In February, I created the Governor's Commission on Workforce Preparedness to help identify our problems in workforce preparedness and to draw us some blueprints for making repairs to the system. Under the capable leadership of Chairman Tom Smith, president of Food Lion, the commission members talked with employers and educators. Their charge was to listen, and learn, about the needs of business for productive employees and the problems our educators have in preparing those future employees to move from the classroom to the world of work. Last week, I received the commission's final report, and after some study, I believe that implementing their recommendations will go a long way toward building a knowledgeable, productive citizenry that is as ready to work as it is willing to work.[1]

Plenty of people have ideas—and good ones, too—about what needs to be done. Here in North Carolina, several major commissions have recently completed their own in-depth studies on the issue, and not surprisingly, have arrived at many of the same conclusions. Many of those conclusions are unavoidable if we are to continue to improve our competitiveness and our success in economic development.

But the time for talk is over. Now it's time to act. That's why I have proposed holding a workforce preparedness summit at the Executive Mansion, a meeting of the chairmen of the state's major educational and workforce preparedness studies. Our goal will be to develop a comprehensive legislative package on workforce preparedness.

Meeting with me at that summit would be Bob Scott and Sherwood Smith, representing the Commission on the Future of the Community College System; Bobby Etheridge and Rich Preyer, representing the Task Force on Excellence in Secondary Education; and Tom Smith and Jim Broyhill, representing the Governor's Commission on Workforce Preparedness. I have also asked several others to join us at this summit: Chairman Barbara Tapscott;[2] Bill Simpson; and John Dornan,[3] of the Public School Forum; Jerry Paschal,[4] chairman of the association of local superintendents; and former superintendent Jay Robinson, representing the University of North Carolina. I want to set all of our separate reports down, side by side, along with President Bush's national education goals, and I want us to come to a consensus on our priorities.[5] Of course, transferring recommendations from paper to the classroom takes money, something we don't have a lot of right now, but I believe that with strong bipartisan and public support, we can get the legislature to approve the most far-reaching and effective program for improving workforce preparedness that this country has ever seen.

Let me share with you a few recommendations from the governor's commission report that I find especially worthy of consideration at such a meeting of the minds. First, the commission identified five major goals that I think almost everyone in this room could support.

—Goal Number One: to improve the academic skills, thinking skills, and employability skills of the future workforce in measurable ways to ensure accountability;

—Goal Number Two: to increase the leadership role of business and industry in public education reform so that we respond to the needs of their employees;

—Goal Number Three: to expand the state's postsecondary technical training systems;

—Goal Number Four: to improve the basic skills of our contemporary adults both in and out of the workforce; and

—Goal Number Five: to establish a comprehensive and strategic planning system to respond to the impending challenge of workforce preparedness.

There's the foundation, but what about the framework? How does the commission propose to build an effective educational program on these general goals for workforce preparedness?

Surely one of the most controversial of the commission's strategies is to eliminate the general curriculum and instead offer two curriculum options by 1994–1995: a college curriculum and a career curriculum, college prep and Tech Prep. This move would focus a student's interests and abilities on a more rigorous yet effective course of study which includes academic and occupational learning. Both options would stress academic excellence, but learning methods would be tailored to individual students' needs. For example, algebra studied by Tech Prep students would be applied algebra, learned over a longer period of time if necessary. These students would be learning the same thing as students in college prep taking more theoretical-based algebra, but in a way that will be more interesting and effective for these students.

We want to prevent our schools from being dumping grounds, halfway houses where kids hang out until they can drop out. We want to make schools a place where students find training for a life of opportunity, rather than training for a life of despair. Tech Prep and similar concepts, pioneered in both Richmond County schools and Lincoln County's School of Technology, have already proven to be an outstanding success—so successful, in fact, that fifteen other school systems across the state have adopted Tech Prep, and another fifty are currently planning to do so.

That reform is already on the way. Schools must meet minimal requirements to have their programs certified as Tech Prep, but communities do have the flexibility to tailor the program to their individual needs. Tech Prep has the strong support of business leaders, educators, parents, and students, and Richmond County's success story proves the program works extremely well.

Some may be uncomfortable with the idea of splitting into two tracks, but Tech Prep has proven that it works. It also proves that it can be done while preserving the ability and right of the academic late bloomer to transfer readily to the college-bound academic curriculum at any time. The student will have a better chance to do that successfully than if he or she had been compelled to be a misfit, and dropout, by offering only one lockstep track.

The commission has also recommended requiring mandatory school attendance to age eighteen or until graduation, beginning in 1993–1994. That requirement would also demand satisfactory academic progress for all sixteen to eighteen-year-olds to obtain a driver's license, and for all twelve to eighteen-year-olds to get a work permit. The commission also supports improved comprehensive career development and guidance programs, and issuing a mastery of skills profile with each high school diploma.

Many of the commission's recommendations, and certainly the most expensive ones, relate directly to improving our community college system as the intellectual infrastructure upon which the majority of our adults in the workforce depend to help them survive in the ever-changing world of work. The commission therefore recommends that we set aside $43.4 million, over the next two years, to accommodate growth and improve instruction in our community colleges. That money would pay for, among other things, improved curriculum, new industry-focused technical training and development centers, and expanded literacy programs.[6]

Many other areas deserve further study and action, areas that the commission did not have time to study, like health insurance, child care, substance abuse, and small business financing. Among those issues is Head Start, but I'm happy to say that the federal budget recently passed by Congress includes approximately $7.5 million for a modest expansion of this program for at-risk children. This is the only federal aid program expansion that the governors uniformly supported at the summit with President Bush in Charlottesville last year.

Add that funding to the $32 million North Carolina already receives for Head Start, and we will be able to serve approximately 50 percent of the children eligible for the program. And as long as the president and Congress continue to make progress on this developmental preschool for at-risk four-year-olds, it saves us to focus on other priorities.

We've accepted quite a challenge in moving to face this workforce preparedness issue straight on. In some ways, we are like the little boy who took his new baseball and bat out to the front yard to play with it [sic] for the first time. First he threw the ball into the air, swung, and missed. Again he threw the ball up, swung, and missed. On the third try he threw the ball even higher, swung even harder, but he still missed. Bat in hand, the little boy cried out, "What a great pitcher!"

We've been tossing the educational ball in the air for too long, and no matter how hard we've swung at it with the bat of reform, we've never quite made contact. But we're perfectly capable of hitting that ball. This time, let's not throw the ball up, let's tee it up!

It's time to adjust our stance and keep our eyes on the ball. That's what my Commission on Workforce Preparedness is all about. That's what my summit proposal is all about. Working together, swinging hard and playing smart, with a positive attitude, I believe we can finally hit that ball of educational reform out of the park.

We'll have to keep our eyes on the ball and stay focused. That is my vision for North Carolina: to build an educational system and a world-class workforce second to none in the nation. Together, we can do it.

---

[1]The final report of the Commission on Workforce Preparedness, presented to Martin on November 8, 1990, offered twelve major proposals to improve the employability of the state's working-age citizens. Press release, "Governor Receives Workforce Preparedness

Report, Announces Summit Involving Workforce Leaders," Raleigh, November 8, 1990, Governors Papers, James G. Martin.

[2]Barbara M. Tapscott, native of Alamance County; A.B., Elon College, 1960; M.Ed., 1969, Ed.D., 1974, University of North Carolina at Chapel Hill. English, French, and biology teacher, Burlington City and Alamance County schools, 1960–1968; administrative posts with Burlington City Schools: principal, Glenhope Elementary School, 1969–1970, director of elementary and secondary education and federal projects, 1970–1985, and assistant superintendent for instruction (K–12), 1985–1992. Chaired N.C. Competency Test Commission, 1980–1981, and State Board of Education, 1990–1992; ad hoc professor of education, Elon College, since 1992. Barbara M. Tapscott, letter to Jan-Michael Poff, October 29, 1993.

[3]John Neill Dornan (1944–), born in Canonsburg, Pa.; resident of Raleigh; B.A., Indiana University of Pennsylvania, 1966. High school English teacher, Moon Township, Pa., 1966–1969; field representative, 1969–1970, communication specialist, 1970–1971, National Education Assn.; assistant executive secretary, Illinois Education Assn., 1971–1974; associate executive director, Coalition of American Public Employees, 1974–1976; associate executive director, N.Y. Educators Assn., 1976–1982; executive director, N.C. Assn. of Educators, 1982–1986; executive director, Public School Forum of North Carolina, since 1986. *News and Observer*, October 30, 1988.

[4]Jerry D. Paschal (1931–1993), born in Wewoka, Okla.; B.S., High Point College, 1956; master's degree, University of North Carolina at Chapel Hill, 1959; doctorate, Duke University, 1971; U.S. Army, 1954–1956. Principal, Eanes Elementary School, Lexington, 1959–1960, Chadbourn Union School, 1960–1961, and of Charles B. Aycock High School, Pikeville, 1961–1965; assistant superintendent, 1965–1966, superintendent, 1966–1972, Goldsboro City Schools; first president of N.C. Assn. of Educators, 1970–1971; associate professor, Fayetteville State University, 1972–1973; superintendent, Columbus County Schools, Whiteville, 1973–1979; principal, Whiteville Senior High School, 1979–1980; superintendent, Whiteville City Schools, 1981–1993; chairman, Division of Superintendents, N.C. Assn. of School Administrators, 1990. Fran Smith, secretary to the superintendent, Whiteville City Schools, letter to Jan-Michael Poff, October 28, 1993.

[5]Bush and governors from across the country devised six national scholastic goals during the first-ever education summit between a U.S. president and state chief executives. The meeting was held September 27 and 28, 1989, at the University of Virginia, Charlottesville; the goals, described elsewhere in this volume, became the foundation of the president's America 2000 program. The America 2000 program, in turn, provided the basis for the Goals 2000: Educate America Act, signed into law by President Clinton on March 31, 1994. As one of the Charlottesville conferees, Martin promoted the concept of increased administrative flexibility for local school districts. *Congressional Quarterly Almanac, 1990*, 18; Governor's Schedule for Weeks of September 25–October 8, 1989, Governors Papers, James G. Martin; *News and Observer*, September 27, 28, 29, October 1, 1989, March 30, April 1, 1994.

[6]The commission's proposed industry-focused technical training and development centers would "conduct applied training research, train teachers, and provide technical assistance in skills development." Press release, "Governor Receives Workforce Preparedness Report, Announces Summit Involving Workforce Leaders," Raleigh, November 8, 1990, Governors Papers, James G. Martin.

To augment the job-training programs offered by the state's community colleges, the Commission on Workforce Preparedness suggested "a tax incentive program of $20 to $25 million" that would "encourage businesses and industries to retrain their own employees. . . . In return for training their own employees, employers would receive a refund on their state unemployment insurance tax. The commission also recommends using state funds to create a North Carolina jobs training program similar to the Jobs Training Partnership Act, but with expanded support services and programs for at-risk youth and the working poor." North Carolina Workforce Preparedness Partnership Conference, Durham, November 8, 1990, Governors Papers, James G. Martin.

NOTES FOR REMARKS TO COUNCIL OF STATE

Raleigh, December 13, 1990

A Little Humor—Very Little

There is no reason to welcome you to this meeting, I suppose, because I doubt many of you truly want to be here or want to wrestle with this issue. But it is an issue of great importance to the people of North Carolina.

Recently I have heard of a new version of the NIMBY acronym that I believe is appropriate to mention here this afternoon. It is spelled N-I-M-P-F, and it stands for—are you ready for this—Not in My Political Future.

I think you all understand the humor, however black it might be. But people in our positions must demonstrate leadership, and that is what this gathering is about today: leadership, the courage to do the right thing.

The Issues We Face

To serve our citizens honorably, we must endure what I call character checks every now and again. It's easy to cut ribbons, make friendly speeches, and hear warm, sympathetic applause. It's easy to pose for photo opportunities, and greet visitors, and make them feel important. But that's not leadership. You know it isn't.

In modern North Carolina, we face enormous environmental problems that have been left undone for many years in the past. Time is passing. We need to get on with serving our people and providing leadership. The easy choice today is to vote against the land transfer and simply opt for the popular choice, killing the process that will help North Carolina treat its waste responsibly. That's the easy way. North Carolina's going nowhere by adopting that track.

The Problem Is Large—and It Is Everywhere

I hope you will remember that just two months ago, the Environmental Protection Agency pointed out 927 sites in this state that were basically illegal dump sites for hazardous waste. Those kind of numbers translate into more than just statistics. That might mean that a small community's drinking water will be poisoned in the next ten years as the chemicals leach through the soil toward an underground water supply. It might mean that farm animals eat vegetation growing up near a hazardous waste site and suddenly grow ill or pass along toxins to humans. Worse, it might mean a family living in a comfortable subdivision suddenly discovers a toxic nightmare behind the house.

The fact is, we have suffered a dismal record of handling hazardous waste. In the past, it has been dumped illegally and dangerously. All of you remember the PCBs that were dumped along highways in Johnston County. That made headlines across the South, not just in North Carolina.[1] It could have been avoided had the state offered a responsible system for handling hazardous waste.

Government has set [sic] on the sideline, twiddling its thumbs while our citizens remain at risk from the mismanagement of hazardous waste. This is an issue about protection of our people. With a modern and safe incinerator, we will be helping our people.

Ideas for the Future

Let me leave with you a few thoughts for the future before we vote. First, I would like to see North Carolina and the states in the agreement join into a kind of "compact" that would offer further protection concerning what kinds of waste can be taken [to] the incinerator. Already, ThermalKEM has assured us that no foreign waste will come to North Carolina.[2] But I want us to consider a compact, a further special protection to control the kind of waste going into the incinerator.

Second, I think this process will give us the opportunity to make sure that some of the revenue from the facility be dedicated for program and facility improvements for the mentally ill and mentally retarded at Murdoch Center and Umstead Hospital. Advocates of those programs would certainly be glad to see improvements coming their way.

The Issue of Courage

I cannot end my remarks today without calling on you to demonstrate your courage. It is easy to vote against the transfer and make some political hay. Make sure you are one who subscribes to the NIMPF philosophy.

It will be easy to soak up the cheers of the opponents of this incinerator. It will be easy to read the letters of support for voting against this incinerator. But this is an issue of courage, a test of your leadership. I am asking you to vote for the good of the future of North Carolina, to vote for our children and their children. It will be more difficult—it's certainly not the easy way out—but it is the right thing to do for North Carolina.

---

[1]The illegal disposal of PCB-laced oil along North Carolina roads in 1978 was described in Poff, *Addresses of Martin*, I, 877n. The federal government banned the manufacture of polychlorinated biphenyl (PCB), a carcinogen, in 1979. Cleanup and disposal of the contaminated oil attracted national attention; for example, see "No Dumping," *Time*, November 1, 1982, 29.

[2]Its contract with the N.C. Hazardous Waste Management Commission barred ThermalKEM North Carolina, operator of the proposed incinerator, from accepting waste material produced beyond United States borders. *News and Observer*, December 11, 1990.

PRESS CONFERENCE: FAMILY SHIELD ANNOUNCEMENTS

RALEIGH, JANUARY 17, 1991

Thank you for coming this morning. I want to make a timely and important announcement that I believe offers important assistance to the families of our servicemen in the Middle Eastern theater. As you have all reported, about one in every six soldiers in Operation Desert Shield—now Desert Storm—is from North Carolina. Our 75,000-plus figure represents 18 percent of the peace-keeping force. That's more than any other state.

Our units in place in the Middle East include the fighter wing from Seymour Johnson; tankers and transports from Pope Air Force Base; the Eighty-Second Airborne from Fort Bragg; Marines from Cherry Point and Camp Lejeune; support units, such as the National Guard Rear Area Operations Center from Morrisville, the first North Carolina group to be called to duty by President Bush. Military police and transportation units from North Carolina have joined military historians and medical officers. Our state, by the way, is second only to California in the number of medical personnel serving in the Persian Gulf.

I am proud of North Carolina's contribution, and I am thankful for the support of the public for these men. Gestures such as sending letters, care packages, and other gifts—even Christmas trees—have lifted the morale of the troops. These gifts are important, but we must also remember the families of the citizen-soldiers who are serving our country. Many of these families have been left unprepared for the financial burdens they now face. When the father or mother is called to military duty, some families are left with only part of their income. For National Guard soldiers, this is a special problem because they have been called away from full-time civilian jobs and full-time salaries.

Some families can cope on the income of [the] remaining spouse, help from parents, or other sources, but many face serious financial difficulties. That's where North Carolina's Operation Family Shield comes in. In November, the National Guard started collecting money to help families who needed financial assistance. Since November, this effort has collected more than $9,000. Just last week, Operation Family Shield sent its first relief check to a Guard-member's wife to help pay her rent. Other calls have come in, and more will come as we remain longer in the Gulf.

Here's where you come in: I am asking all North Carolinians to send money to assist this one-of-a-kind effort. Through the media, I hope we can inform residents of the importance of this project. We may prove to be the model for other states, I understand.

Now let me introduce Colonel Aubrey McLellan, the state chaplain of the North Carolina National Guard, who oversees the program.[1]

[Martin introduces Chaplain McLellan.]

I am very proud of this program—I hope we have started a national effort—and I believe it will provide critical assistance to families making enormous sacrifices. I strongly encourage North Carolinians to contribute to the fund. Operation Family Shield offers a perfect way to show support for our effort in the Gulf, and I hope you, the news media, will help in getting the word out. You will find an address for contributions in the news release that we have handed out.[2] I will tape public service announcements later today for distribution to television and radio stations.

---

[1]Charles Aubrey McLellan (1932–), born in Holmes County, Miss.; resident of High Point; B.A., Mississippi College; M.Div., Southeastern Baptist Theological Seminary; completed military education courses; was commissioned as first lieutenant, 1964, ultimately attained rank of colonel, 1985, North Carolina Army National Guard. Clergyman; served various NCARNG units as chaplain, 1964–1985; installed as state chaplain, NCARNG, 1985, retired in 1991; conceived of Operation Family Shield. CW4 Eugene R. Ray, chief, Plans and Actions Branch, North Carolina Army National Guard, letter to Jan-Michael Poff, July 13, 1993. *News and Observer*, December 7, 1991.

[2]The address to which Martin referred appeared in the press release, "Governor Urges Contributions to Operation Family Shield," Raleigh, January 17, 1991. For more on fund raising, see press release, "Operation Family Shield Raises $25,705 for North Carolina Families," Raleigh, January 24, 1991, Governors Papers, James G. Martin.

NORTH CAROLINA'S EDUCATION SUMMIT: AN EMERGING CONSENSUS THE GOVERNOR'S REPORT TO THE PEOPLE

RESEARCH TRIANGLE PARK, JANUARY 23, 1991

[The governor delivered this address to the Superintendents and North Carolina School Boards Association Winter Seminar.]

First, let me thank Superintendent Etheridge for his kind invitation to speak to you at this luncheon. During this time when our nation's attention is focused so intensely on military events in the Middle East, this is still also a time of critical attention to our responsibilities here at home. With the deepening onset of a recession, we face together our dual responsibilities for sustaining the momentum of our priorities for public education while struggling to maintain our constitutional responsibility for a balanced budget.

Before addressing the challenges we must face in developing a budget for the next fiscal biennium, let me take a few moments to review with you the immediate problem of this current fiscal year, 1990–1991. As you know, the continuing deterioration in the national economy had led to even greater reduction in current tax revenues than the earlier consensus forecast, necessitating more severe restraint on current spending than I had previously thought necessary. In addition to the General Assembly's budget amendments reducing spending this year by $338 million, we had concluded in September that another $261 million in revenue shortage would have to be offset by further limitations on spending. That estimate has now grown from $261 million to $361 million. That added $100 million shortage of revenue could partially be offset by drawing down the remaining $40 million in the so-called Rainy-Day Fund, an emergency reserve created for just that purpose, and another $28 million by halting every remaining capital facility start-up, including the fourth-quarter allocation for school construction. That left $32 million to be made up from current expenditures in the General Fund. That was why I found it necessary to order (a) an immediate hiring freeze on all vacancies, (b) a spending freeze on all purchases, and (c) an effort by all agencies and departments to identify all potential opportunities for additional savings.

I sent word to you that there would be consideration of critical needs in all departments and programs funded by the state, provided a request was made to the Budget Office, and that some relief would be allowed where there was no alternative way to fill a critical vacancy. Indeed, as of last night there were seventy such requests from schools, thirteen of which have been approved and released. From all other agencies, 137 requests for relief were received, and nine of those have been released so far and approved to be hired.

I had sought to make clear that when sufficient funds could be substituted, on the basis of other savings that could be identified, it would then be my intention to generally exempt from the freeze such positions as school bus drivers and regular classroom teachers. Then if further alternative savings could be realized, I would be able to consider other teaching positions. It is now possible to look at such exemptions, thanks to the cooperation we have received from you, and the state Department of Public Instruction, and others over the last week.

As of yesterday, specific alternative savings have been reported from schools and DPI totaling $14.5 million. In addition, I will ask you to begin looking at how another $30 million might be saved, if that later becomes necessary. As a relative frame of reference, I would want to allow you maximum flexibility in administrative discretion, by asking each system to determine how you might reduce spending by $30.00 per pupil (ADM),[1] in case that later becomes necessary. Let's hope it does not. Let me add that other departments and institutions have also identified another $18.5 million in savings to relieve our immediate problem.

That means that I can now release the freeze, effective immediately, on all vacant teaching positions and school bus drivers in our public schools—and I should add "until further notice," since it is clearly possible that the national economy could slip even worse than now expected over the next few months. All I can do about that is ask you to bear with me and stand ready to cooperate again if more extreme measures need to be taken. I will also work out with you a way to exempt psychologists and counselors at those schools near military facilities otherwise severely impacted by the war in the Persian Gulf.

That brings me to my next subject: What about next year? The severity of the shortfall in revenues is expected to flow over into the next fiscal year as well. Based upon the most recent consensus forecast from the state Budget Office and the legislative office of fiscal research, we must expect revenues to fall $507 million short of what would be required to balance the continuation level of funding for existing programs. That is $108 million less revenue than had been forecast prior to January 1 and is the result of applying to 1991–1992 the same factors that required the latest hiring freeze in the current fiscal year. By carrying forward the forced reversions and other limitations on spending throughout the next fiscal year, 1991–1992, and holding all spending at current levels—except for those mandated by the U.S. Congress—it is clear that we would still have insufficient revenue without a small tax increase or elimination of some programs. So, the situation is grim.

Even so, at such a time of strain and stress, we still must face our responsibility for [the] strategic needs of our schools. There are certain needs which must be met, lest we trade away our future ability to recover from this recession. I had concluded that was the case for Tech Prep and other workforce training programs of modest cost; and for continued forward progress on Senate Bill 2, the School Improvement and Accountability Act; as well as for early developmental preschool for those four-year-olds deemed at risk of becoming dropouts if they never quite drop in. Furthermore, there are many improvements to be made without requiring heavy budget increases. Certainly, in a time of budgetary crisis, when some tax increase may be unavoidable, we should focus our energy on how to do more with what we have and work to get better results with the generous increase in resources provided over the last seven years.

Yet, the requests for increased spending for all educational improvements would require an additional $848 million, not counting capital outlays. That's $848 million requested for all levels of education: K through 20, you might say. Clearly there is no way to add this array of needs to the forthcoming budget—not in a recession. It was for this reason that I called for a summit on education and workforce preparedness, which met in Raleigh on January 11.[2] My plan was that after presentations from each of the major educational organizations and study commissions, there would be sufficient discussions to promote the development of a consensus as to the priorities which might then be recommended on behalf of such a group, if there was a consensus.[3]

I am happy to be able to report to you that, indeed, there did emerge a clear consensus for a manageable list of priorities from the "study hall" worksheets turned in by the forty participants. First, as shown in Table 1, there were thirteen goals which received the combined endorsements of fifteen or more of the summit participants.[4] Six of the consensus priorities were listed among the top three goals of nine or more of the participants. Of these, the three most strongly endorsed priorities were improvements which would not have a major budgetary impact. In rank order, the[y] were (1) a change in governance, to have the state superintendent appointed rather than separately elected as at present; (2) greater flexibility and local control, extending to the level of the individual school unit; (3) greater academic rigor, including "Mastery of Core of Basic Skills" and increased graduation requirements.

Other low-budget reforms which were strongly agreed to were elimination of administrative tenure, which ranked sixth overall; greater parental involvement at the children's school unit; a greater degree of accountability expected of each school; and a strong training program to improve administrative leadership.

Honorable mentions included development of a career curriculum for those expecting to go to work after high school; permitting fewer interruptions during the 5.5-hour school day; and allowing parents a choice of their children's schools, with safeguards, of course, against restoring segregation.

A list of preferences that do have major funding requirements revealed that only seven items received priority support from fifteen or more participants. Heading that list, on the basis of a weighted scoring system, was the next step of Senate Bill 2, followed by major salary increases, at least completing the range of step increases which originally had been planned as a third-year improvement. After that came Tech

Prep and other workforce preparedness programs; completion of BEP [Basic Education Program], by 1995, th[at] is; and other community college needs. Rounding out this preference list for completion by 1995 were developmental preschool for at-risk four-year-olds and funding for professional staff development. Many other items were mentioned, but it was clear, as I have indicated, that the reforms and programs just mentioned were easily the consensus priorities.

The summit participants were also asked to help prioritize, for 1991–1992, those expense items which were regarded as so essential that they should not be delayed until better economic times. The purpose here was, conversely, to see if there was some degree of agreement as to program improvements which, although important, could be held until after the next fiscal year. Once again this was very helpful, because a clear consensus did emerge. Preference went to Senate Bill 2, reflecting a general agreement among thirty-five of the participants that this program, with its flexibility and accountability, was a major success and offered critically important potential for achieving better results. Almost three-fourths, a total of twenty-eight, listed this among their top three preferences! Community college program improvements also came in very strong, as did the developmental preschool for at-risk four-year-olds.

Strong support also was shown for funding pay-step increases based on seniority, so that we avoid going back to the disastrous pay freeze of 1982. A more costly general increase in the level of the pay-step schedule, i.e., a general major pay increase, finished further down the list, receiving very little support outside of the group of participants who were in the "public school" category. The Basic Education item likewise finished lower due to its cost and questions that are growing as to its cost effectiveness; even so, it finished sixth, but with a median allowance of only $30 million—less than half what the next step would require. Clearly, this indicates not abandonment of BEP, but a recognition that it would be very difficult to justify full funding in this economy, and that we need to show evidence of better results from such a major infusion of money so large as to block out many other educational needs.

In closing, before I take questions, I want to thank you for the cooperation and forbearance you have shown in this difficult time. It would be much happier for us all to have a burgeoning economy, with revenue increases to spend on many worthwhile ideas. But it is also important, in [a] time of limited resources, to work together in good faith, to adjust to necessary restraint, and concentrate on getting better results from our resources. That time is surely with us. I will continue to review this information, and your responses to it, as I complete preparation of my biennial budget message to present to the General Assembly on January 31.

[1]Average daily membership.

[2]For related press releases, see "Governor Announces Final Plans for Education Summit on January 11," Raleigh, January 4, 1991, and "Governor Sets Education Summit Agenda," Raleigh, January 10, 1991, Governors Papers, James G. Martin.

[3]Martin closed his address to the January 11 summit by listing his twelve priorities for improving education. Five recommendations not requiring new taxes, according to the governor, were 1) increase parental involvement; 2) ensure "flexibility in existing funding to reduce class sizes but not to convert teaching positions to administration"; 3) institute a "Certificate of Mastery of Core Literacy Skills"; 4) allow fewer interruptions of instructional time; and 5) raise tuition at state universities with a percentage of the increase reserved for student grants-in-aid.

Steps "which will cost taxes" included 1) moving forward on Senate Bill 2; 2) expanding Tech Prep and other workforce preparedness programs; 3) implementing developmental prekindergarten day care for at-risk four-year-olds; 4) funding step increases in the existing teacher salary schedule, lifting the freeze; 5) "community college revitalizations"; 6) "drug-free schools"; and 7) funding adult literacy and job literacy programs. Education Summit, Raleigh, January 11, 1991, Governors Papers, James G. Martin.

[4]The pair of tables attached to this speech were also appended to his 1991 State of the State message; see pages 58–59, above.

NORTH CAROLINA PRESS ASSOCIATION AWARDS

Chapel Hill, January 24, 1991

Thank you for inviting me tonight. I believe governors should always make it a point to address the reporters and editors who make it their business to nip at the heels of elected officials. That's why I have weekly news conferences, except when the legislature is not in session. The reporters told me they would prefer every other week.

I am sure you are enjoying a busy winter institute as you announce your award winners, discuss the future of the newspaper business, and make plans for your association for the coming year. But this year has a different feel, doesn't it? Our nation's attention is riveted intensely to military events in the Middle East as we follow the daily reports of sorties, bombings, and military deployment; of vocal opposition and vocal support; of rallies for peace and rallies to support an intensive war necessary to win peace for Kuwait and others threatened by Iraq.

Your pages have reflected North Carolina's distinct role in the Persian Gulf by reporting the events to family, friends, and associates of the more than 75,000 soldiers from this state now seeing duty in the Gulf. All of North Carolina['s] newspapers can be proud of their effort, but I want to point with pride to those newspapers in the eastern region of the state near military bases—Jacksonville, Fayetteville, Goldsboro, and less regularly, forgive me, Havelock—and tell you I have watched your daily coverage with great interest. Your combinations of national and local news have been outstanding; and your editorial support for the community, the global as well as local community, have given us all cause to celebrate.

It has been an interesting time for your industry. Even print journalists, I'm sure, were mesmerized by television coverage of those first few nights of the war as the networks brought live images of gas masks, fighter planes, and missiles into our living rooms. While a war fought extensively after midnight, EST, detracts from the immediacy of newspaper coverage relative to late-[night] TV, you have responded with greater depth on weapons, and strategies, and have helped to debunk false rumors which live telecasts felt obliged to circulate lest they be scooped. Just when you begin to wonder about the relevance of the newspaper medium to the theatrics of this war, the dailies in North Carolina came back with interesting special packages that have presented very thorough summaries. You have served your readers well.

I particularly want to thank those organizations that have included in your coverage comments about our Operation Family Shield. North Carolina has now raised more than $25,000 to help families pay for basic needs. Operation Family Shield funnels private contributions to the families of our National Guard and reservists who are in financial straits as a result of their family member leaving a regular job and accepting a lower salary to serve in the Gulf. While I understand your wariness of boosterism, this effort offers a unique opportunity for the media to help those families in their own communities. I would hope you might consider running a daily box with a phone number or address to help the cause. You might also want to mention similar family charitable funds at each military base. Contributions may be sent addressed to the installation chaplain at each base.

As you editors in eastern North Carolina know, these families face very real problems that threaten their sense of normal life. The rent needs to be paid; families need groceries. These programs can only help our common cause of helping families in need when our nation is at war.

Tonight also affords me my first opportunity to thank you personally for your very strong support, last year, of North Carolina Newspaper Literacy Day. Working with the U.S. Postal Service and the Governor's Advisory Council on Literacy, you reached out to thousands of people who need assistance in learning to read and write. Last year, one of the state's finest novelists—Doris Betts, who is on the English faculty here at UNC—volunteered to write a column about her experience growing up and her interest in writing and reading. Do you remember it? It began with a simple question: "What were you doing yesterday at 3 p.m.?" From there she challenged us to teach someone else to answer that question, to help someone else learn to read and write.[1]

Virtually all of the state's newspapers, from the big dailies to the small weeklies, ran her column with a toll-free number and special art packages. Many papers ran full-section fronts. It helped people. It was a good idea, and I hope you will begin planning today to run it next September. As your officers know, my staff is involved in getting this off the ground. I hope you will be in touch with the Literacy Council to get this project moving again.

As an industry, you have more than a passing interest in this issue. Literate citizens read newspapers and become better informed. I do. In fact, newspapers can be powerful allies in this effort. I hope you will continue this effort.

Finally, let me close with another request. I need your help in plotting a long-term strategy for state government as it wrestles with the fast-moving information age. You've all experienced the advantages of technology in your business, especially with computer-generated design and production. Composing rooms just aren't what they used to be a mere ten years ago.

You also know how much information you can quickly accumulate with computers. Now think about computerization in state government and appreciate for a moment, if you will, the overwhelming volume of data that state government agencies amass in short periods of time. As a part of your work, you regularly raise the issue of access to government records. I've done my part to open government—the meetings of the Council of State and Advisory Budget Commission are open, even if you do sleep through them now—and through political debates, we have opened up the General Assembly's budgeting process.

But we face more complicated questions now because of computers and the vast banks of data that have accumulated. Do citizens have any right to expect protection of their own records held by government, or is it simply a matter of making everything public? I know your point of view, but some data managers simply don't understand why they have to commit hours upon hours of time to run special programs for you, and they are fearful of letting powerful, outside computers rummage around to uncover the privacy of private individuals who must report to us. Government and the media are bumping into each other on this issue, and I want your help.

I have created the Information Technology Council, drawing together people from government and the private sector, to study this question of public access to electronic data systems and report sometime this year to the General Assembly. Perhaps this will be merely a matter of finding understanding between the press and government, but I believe technology demands that we review and clarify our statutes on this issue. As an association, I ask that you name a representative to this council, and I will ask the North Carolina Association of Broadcasters to do the same. That way, your point of view will be represented as the work proceeds. This is another chance for you to be part of the process, to join in an effort to figure out how best to define policy that will benefit you and the public we both attempt to serve.[2]

Let me close by promising you a very active two years, perhaps one of the most active times in North Carolina history from a governor's office. Many have wondered whether I achieved lame-duck status last February; others rhapsodized about it, or said that happened the day I was elected—in 1984. I think you can forget about that. Remember that, with one notable exception, North Carolina's recent governors normally completed their terms by not running for another office. What's wrong with my decision to follow the path of Luther Hodges, Terry Sanford, Dan Moore, Bob Scott, and Jim Holshouser? What's wrong with devoting my best two years to North Carolina rather than the next election?

It remains my own hope that having declared I will not be a candidate in '92—it remains my own hope that, having neutralized the main reason for partisan opposition to my proposals, such as dominated legislative opposition in 1987 and 1988. Let's hope so.

On January 31, when I present my State of the State, don't look for any crutches. I intend to outline an active, high-energy two years of progress for North Carolina! Even with a slowing economy and a desperately tight budget, there is so much that we can do with limited resources—to focus our energies on needs which don't cost big bucks, but which seem to get neglected when economic growth pours out tons of new money to spend and fight over. I will see to it that we not neglect those urgent educational needs which cannot be delayed, without which we might trade away our ability to recover [from] this recession. But if we can agree that some priorities must be funded, even if that requires a tax hike, perhaps we can also agree that other worthwhile and desirable improvements can be deferred until a bright day, when the stronger economy again generates tons of new revenue, and thus hold down tax increases to no more than absolutely necessary. I'm sure you will advise whether I get it right.

---

[1]Martin declared September 9, 1990 "North Carolina Newspaper Literacy Day." See "North Carolina Newspaper Literacy Day, 1990, by the Governor of North Carolina: A Proclamation," July 18, 1990, Governors Papers, James G. Martin.

Although Doris Betts's essay on literacy appeared under various titles in different newspapers, the body of the piece opened with the query the governor quoted; for example, see both the *Shelby Star* and *Winston-Salem Journal*, September 8, 1990, and the *Asheville Citizen-Times*, *Chapel Hill Newspaper*, *Fayetteville Observer-Times*, *Goldsboro News-Argus*, *Salisbury Post*, and the *Sunday Star-News* (Wilmington), September 9, 1990.

Doris June Waugh Betts (1932–), born in Statesville; attended Woman's College,

University of North Carolina (later University of North Carolina at Greensboro), 1950–1953; honorary degrees. Newspaperwoman in Statesville, 1950–1951, Chapel Hill, 1953–1954, and Sanford, 1956–1957; editorial staff, *N.C. Democrat*, 1961–1962; editor, *Sanford News Leader*, 1962; lecturer in creative writing, since 1962, associate professor, 1974–1978, professor, since 1978, Alumni Distinguished Professor, since 1983, English Department, University of North Carolina at Chapel Hill; award-winning author. *Who's Who in America, 1994*, I, 289.

[2]Martin revealed plans at the Executive Technology Conference, October 23, 1990, for a bipartisan task force to study the question of public access to state government computer records. The group's primary challenge was to find the "balance between public access and public privacy," according to the governor. "I will direct this task force to define 'public information' as it applies to electronic records, determine what 'public information' is currently available, and outline rules for accessibility and copying." See also press release, "Governor Announces Information Technology Task Force," Raleigh, October 23, 1990, Governors Papers, James G. Martin.

PRESS RELEASE: MARTIN ANNOUNCES HURDLE CLEARED IN PROCESS TO BUILD OREGON INLET JETTIES

RALEIGH, FEBRUARY 5, 1991

Governor Jim Martin told the North Carolina congressional delegation in Washington Tuesday that the U.S. Office of Management and Budget has cleared the way to pay for the Oregon Inlet jetty project. Governor Martin learned of the decision Monday after a White House meeting with Richard Darman, director of OMB.[1]

"They (OMB policy-makers) have looked at our new cost-benefit analysis and concluded that it works," Martin said Tuesday. "It's a major step forward. Now efforts can be directed toward getting the permit and congressional funding approved."

The decision by OMB clears one of three key hurdles remaining before jetty construction can begin. In the past, federal budget directors have refused to discuss funding for the project and would not allow formal planning to go forward. The remaining hurdles:

—U.S. Department of Interior must issue a permit allowing construction. Planners are close to getting the permit, Martin said, because of the development of a sand-bypass system. Using a pipe under the jetties, sand would be moved from where it collects on the north jetty under and past the south jetty. Martin said this design may satisfy environmental concerns about sand nourishment north and south of the jetties.[2]

—Congress must approve $80 million for the project. The U.S. Corps of Engineers has cut the cost of the project from $105 [million] to $80 million by piggybacking the southern jetty along a ridge of rocks, known as a groin, already being built to protect the island from ocean erosion.

"I will ask the congressional delegation to help us work to secure the funding when I meet with them today," Governor Martin said. "That is a critical step, and they can help a great deal." Martin praised Senator Helms, whom he described as a key ally in convincing the Office of Management and Budget to drop its objections to the jetty project.

The governor also planned to brief the members of the delegation on several other North Carolina projects:

—His request for a $250,000 planning grant from the U.S. Department of Transportation for a global air cargo and manufacturing complex, which has been the focus of planning and work by the state Department of Transportation. Martin will meet later today with U.S. secretary of transportation Samuel Skinner to brief him on the project and to lobby for the federal grant.[3] The state is now evaluating bids to conduct a feasibility study.

—Martin's work with other states and the congressional delegation for a federal compact to ensure protection for North Carolina if it builds a chemical waste incinerator.

—Martin's satisfaction with the federal budget presented by President Bush, which gives states more flexibility in managing federal programs to make their [omitted] more effective in the states.

---

[1]Richard Gordon Darman (1943–), managing director, Shearson Lehman Hutton, Inc., 1987–1988; director, Office of Management and Budget, 1989–1993. Previously identified in Poff, *Addresses of Martin*, I, 474n; see also *Who's Who in America, 1994*, I, 805. The governor met with Darman on Monday, February 4, 1991.

[2]Manuel Lujan, United States interior secretary, granted conditional land-use permits for the erection of rock jetties at Oregon Inlet in October 1992. Eight months later his successor in office, Bruce Babbitt, withdrew them. Saying the permits were "'improvidently issued,'" Babbitt explained they could not be awarded until a supplemental environmental impact statement on the jetties' effects upon Cape Hatteras National Seashore and Pea Island National Wildlife Refuge was completed. *News and Observer*, June 13, 1993; press release, "Governor Applauds Conditional Permits for Oregon Inlet," Raleigh, October 29, 1992, Governors Papers, James G. Martin.

[3]Samuel Knox Skinner (1938–), born in Chicago; B.S., University of Illinois, 1960; J.D., DePaul University, 1966; U.S. Army, 1960–1961. Attorney; chairman, Chicago Regional Transit Authority, 1984; U.S. transportation secretary, 1989–1991; White House chief of staff, 1991–1992; president, Commonwealth Edison Co., Chicago. *Who's Who in America, 1994*, II, 3193.

PRESS CONFERENCE: ECONOMIC EMERGENCY DECLARATION

RALEIGH, FEBRUARY 21, 1991

[The governor delivered a similar message at the opening of the American Watercolor Exhibit, Fayetteville Museum of Art, on the evening of February 21.]

You will remember that last Friday I met at the Executive Mansion with a number of North Carolina bankers and local representatives from

Craven, Cumberland, Onslow, and Wayne counties. We discussed the economic impact of troop deployments to the Middle East on those areas and what could be done to help ease the burden for businesses suffering from a critical loss of revenue. A number of good ideas developed from that session. My staff is currently working to organize a three-pronged approach to economic aid—I call it Project Lend-A-Hand—that includes financial counseling for troubled businesses, the Stars and Stripes Sale, and congressional legislation for federal assistance.

The bankers also said they would be willing to help businesses restructure loans and interest payments to get through the hard times. But to do that, the banks need some kind of designation that would identify those communities as areas of special need. Therefore, today I am declaring Cumberland, Craven, Onslow, and Wayne counties—home to our state's military bases—as economic emergency areas and urge all banks and businesses in North Carolina to lend a hand to businesses in these four counties that are suffering economic stress as a result of troop deployments to the Middle East.[1]

You should have copies of that declaration in front of you. Bill Graham, chairman of the North Carolina Banking Commission, is here with me today to help answer any questions you might have about the financial efforts under way. Bill Lane, assistant secretary in the Department of Economic and Community Development, is serving as my point man on this project. He would have been here today, but he is doing his job down in Havelock and Jacksonville.[2]

---

[1]"Declaration of Economic Emergency, February 21, 1991, by the Governor of the State of North Carolina," February 21, 1991, Governors Papers, James G. Martin. The counties Martin named were the locations of Fort Bragg Military Reservation and Pope Air Force Base, Cherry Point Marine Corps Air Station, Camp LeJeune Marine Corps Base, and Seymour Johnson Air Force Base, respectively.

[2]William Thomas Graham (1933–), born in Waynesboro, Va.; resident of Winston-Salem and Raleigh; A.B., Duke University, 1956; J.D., University of Virginia, 1962; U.S. Army, 1957–1958. Attorney; chairman, Forsyth County Republican Party, 1966–1969, 1973–1975; assistant general counsel, U.S. Dept. of Housing and Urban Development, 1969–1970; GOP candidate for Winston-Salem mayor, 1970; judge, N.C. Superior Court, 1975–1979; chairman, Forsyth County Board of Elections, 1985–1986; N.C. commissioner of banks, since 1987; Rules Committee member, Republican National Convention, 1992; chairman, Plan of Organization Committee, N.C. Republican Party, 1993; adjunct professor, Wake Forest University law school. Held leadership positions in over twenty local, statewide, and national political campaigns, 1963–1992, including Finance Committee member, Martin for Governor, 1984; N.C. chairman, 1988, N.C. vice-chairman, 1992, Bush-Quayle. William T. Graham, letter to Jan-Michael Poff, November 19, 1993.

William F. Lane (1933–), native, resident of Wilson; B.A., North Carolina State College (later University), 1959; U.S. Army, 1954–1956. Assistant secretary, N.C. Dept. of Commerce, 1988–1991; deputy commissioner, Division of Motor Vehicles, N.C. Dept. of Transportation, 1991–1993. William F. Lane, letter to Jan-Michael Poff, November 17, 1993.

The Salute to the Troops Celebration honored more than 75,000 members of the armed forces from North Carolina who served in Operation Desert Storm. The statewide event officially opened June 29, 1991, with ceremonies in Raleigh. Martin welcomed soldiers to dinner at the State Fairgrounds.

Sheriff L. David Huffman of Catawba County accepted a check for $209,539.40, the largest payment yet made from the controlled substance tax program, from Governor Martin on January 9, 1992. The North Carolina Department of Revenue began levying taxes on illegal drugs in 1990. Law enforcement bureaus participating in arrests that enabled the state to collect the tax were eligible for three-quarters of the money the program generated.

GLOBAL AIR CARGO AIRPORT ANNOUNCEMENT

GREENSBORO, FEBRUARY 25, 1991

[Martin unveiled plans for a global air cargo airport at the Governor's Economic Development Summit, held February 25 and 26, 1991. The conference was sponsored by the state Department of Economic and Community Development, North Carolina Citizens for Business and Industry, and the North Carolina Economic Developers Association. Press release, "Governor Announces First Annual Statewide Economic Development Summit," Raleigh, January 25, 1991, Governors Papers, James G. Martin.]

Good morning, and welcome to the economic development summit. Over the next two days, members of North Carolina's business community, economic development community, and officials with local and state governments will have an opportunity to share ideas, insights, and experiences that will eventually become our economic guide, one that truly reflects the theme of this summit, "Shaping Our Perspective for the Future."

Despite North Carolina's many successes, the face of economic development is constantly changing. To compete, we must meet many new and difficult challenges on the horizon. This summit is a part of our efforts to meet those challenges and provide North Carolina with the opportunity to successfully compete and improve our economic outlook for the future.

Providing for the state's healthy economic future cannot be done in two days, a week, a month, or even a year. It takes careful planning and analysis, a clear sense of purpose, and a well-developed foundation on which to build. One of the cornerstones of such a foundation is our state's transportation infrastructure.

North Carolina's transportation infrastructure is unique. Because of the strong multimodal transportation system we have developed, North Carolina deals from a position of strength, unlike many other states, so we can successfully compete for new businesses and industries, including a global air cargo complex.

Aviation is already an integral part of North Carolina's multimodal transportation infrastructure, with two international airports—Charlotte Douglas and Raleigh-Durham—and two domestic carriers with major hub operations: USAir in Charlotte and American at Raleigh-Durham. These two airports are among the fastest growing in the nation. All told, the state's eight major carriers and seven commuter lines offer more than nine hundred daily flights. That's a plane coming or going to North Carolina every seventy-five seconds. Direct air transportation is available to all major U.S. cities, and eighteen of the East's million-plus markets are within an hour's time.

We have before us an opportunity to take this unique and well-planned transportation infrastructure and make it the best in the world. How do we do that? By recognizing that aviation, specifically the air cargo industry, is the wave of the future that will revolutionize air transportation and the world economy.

Of course, recognizing the growing importance of air cargo is only the first step. Like the Wright brothers many years ago, we have the opportunity to shape the course of aviation. We simply must be prepared to meet the future demands for air cargo.

To ensure that North Carolina again plays a leading role in the history of aviation, the North Carolina Department of Transportation has initiated the North Carolina Air Cargo System Plan. Over the next few months, the NC DOT, along with a leading air cargo consulting firm, will map a strategy for our air cargo future. Today we take our first step toward that end. It is my pleasure to announce to you the firm and the individuals who will develop the North Carolina Air Cargo System Plan: The Transportation Management Group, Incorporated, of Raleigh, in collaboration with Leeper, Cambridge, and Campbell, Incorporated, of Alexandria, Virginia, and the Comsis Corporation of Silver Spring, Maryland.

The Transportation Management Group has a very detailed knowledge of the global air cargo market. The group also has a strong economics background and has produced a landmark analysis report of the air cargo industry. I have great confidence in their ability to develop this plan for North Carolina. Joining us today, representing The Transportation Management Group, are the company's president, Bob Bushman, and vice-president, Charles Edwards. Dr. Brian Campbell, vice-president of Leeper, Cambridge, and Campbell, is also with us.

Air cargo is the fastest-growing segment of commercial air traffic. This growth reflects structural changes in the domestic and international economy and the broadening of markets. The Transportation Management Group will assess this growth and forecast the future needs for facilities and service.

The Federal Aviation Administration and the U.S. Department of Transportation have great confidence in the uniqueness and appropriateness of this plan. We have just entered into an agreement with the federal government that this study will be financed through a joint federal-state partnership.[1]

One of the key elements of this plan is a revolutionary concept, developed by Dr. John Kasarda of the Kenan Institute, that we refer to as the Global Air Cargo Industrial Complex.[2] For the sake of North

Carolina's economic future, we must now put forth great efforts to explore this concept. It could bring to the state a wealth of jobs, knowledge, and a powerful position in the global economy. Let me take just a moment to explain to you how this concept revolutionizes the connection between transportation and industry.

[Using visual aids, the governor extemporaneously explained the air cargo complex.][3]

North Carolina's strategic East Coast location and its mild climate allow our airports to stay operational year-round. Our strategically planned multimodal transportation system also places us in the driver's seat in the competition with other states for such a complex. We can boast the largest system of state-maintained highways in the country.

North Carolina serves as a highway hub for the northeastern, Mid-Atlantic, and southeastern states, while providing rapid access to Midwest markets. That means a North Carolina air cargo complex would provide same-day access to markets from Florida to New York.

North Carolina's 10,000 manufacturing industries and excellent road network, including five interstate routes, explain why the state leads the nation in long-line truck carriers. Seventy-seven Tar Heel cities boast one or more truck terminals, and all North Carolina roads and bridges are toll free.

The recently enacted Highway Trust Fund represents one of the largest single-state investments in the country, carefully designed and planned to create a strategic network of four-lane highways that will provide safe and convenient transit routes, and facilitate economic growth and development, in every corner of the state. The trust fund was the result of years of planning, analysis, and a vision for North Carolina's future of continued economic growth and prosperity.

However, North Carolina has more to offer than a sophisticated network of strategic highways. We are at the center of an East Coast rail network linking the state's industries to suppliers and markets throughout the U.S. Modern deep-water ports in Wilmington and Morehead City provide convenient shipping for products throughout the world. Businesses can enjoy the benefits of low transportation costs by using the intermodal terminal network that links Charlotte and Greensboro to the port of Wilmington. This terminal network, the first of its kind in the nation, provides better, less expensive, and more convenient inland transportation services for cargo shipment to the port.

The intermodal network directly links the piedmont's largest manufacturing centers to the port of Wilmington. Both terminals serve as consolidation points for import and export cargo. Substantial cost savings result from the direct high-volume truck and rail transport of combined product shipments to and from the port.

I have talked to you today about the importance of planning, the importance of study, the importance of being visionary leaders in order to put the best economic foot forward for North Carolina. The air cargo industrial complex is part of my vision for a strong, progressive, and economically healthy North Carolina.

Visionaries are not dreamers. Visionaries look at today and plan for what tomorrow will bring. The visionary concept of a global air cargo industrial complex we dream about today will fulfill tomorrow's economic needs and sharpen our perspective for North Carolina's economic future.

---

[1] At this point, Martin jotted "72.6% federal $345,463 + 27.4% state/DOT $130,412 = $475,875."

[2] Martin also attributed the air cargo complex concept to Kasarda in remarks to members of the Hudson Institute, May 7, 1991.

[3] Speaking to the North Carolina World Trade Association, May 8, 1991, Martin described the proposed air cargo industrial complex as "an airport, capable of handling the biggest cargo planes flying today, coupled with a manufacturing complex surrounding the entire facility—integrated directly with taxiways." It would eliminate the need of manufacturers, located within 100 miles of the airport, to maintain massive parts inventories. "When they need a product, they can just order it from anywhere in the world and unload it at the warehouse door the next day, just in time for production. When that product is ready for distribution, they'll move it out that warehouse door, down the road to the airport, and on the way to buyers in overseas markets in a few short hours. That's speed, that's efficiency, and that's profit."

STATEMENT AT PRESS CONFERENCE

RALEIGH, MARCH 7, 1991

As the first order of business today, I would like to announce that six members of a National Science Foundation site visit team will be in Raleigh on Tuesday, March 7, to review a proposal we have submitted that would dramatically improve science and mathematics education in North Carolina classrooms.[1] The funding proposal was submitted to the National Science Foundation last October as a cooperative effort between the North Carolina Science and Mathematics Alliance and educators, business entrepreneurs, government officials, and scientists from across the state. Thirty states submitted proposals to the National Science Foundation, and thirteen have been selected for site visits. Six to ten of the thirteen proposals will receive NSF grants.

If approved, the $7.8 million in NSF monies will be used to fund administrative staff, teacher training, individual grants for science equipment to local schools, and recruitment of minorities and women to professions in the fields of science and mathematics. These programs would mean a lot to the 619,000 students in over 50 percent of our state's school systems who would benefit from improved science and math education. We plan to keep these programs going, even after NSF funding runs out after five years. At that time, these programs would be absorbed into the university system, community colleges, and the Department of Public Instruction.

You may recall that I first announced the creation of the North Carolina Science and Mathematics Alliance on February 1, 1990. Under the direction of Dr. Denis DuBay, the alliance is charged with improving science, math, and technology education in the classroom through a cooperative effort between public schools, businesses, communities, and higher education. Now I'd like to ask Denis to step forward for a few brief comments.

[Martin opened the floor to questions after DuBay concluded.]

I've got a few more announcements to make today, all of them dealing with our military personnel returning from the Middle East.

Our active-duty forces, National Guard, and reservists have been serving in the Persian Gulf for months now, separated from their families. With the end of the war, these military personnel will be returning home soon. We want to make that return to the States as easy and as memorable as possible.

Filing state taxes may be a particular problem for these returning troops. That's why, after April 15, returning military personnel have 180 days from the time of their departure from the Middle East to file their state income tax or extension requests. The state will waive any interest on tax payments for those personnel for the time they served in the combat zone, plus any time hospitalized, plus 180 days.

I've proposed legislation that would allow payment of 9 percent APR [annual percentage rate] interest on state tax refunds for combat zone military personnel if those returns are filed within the 180-day extension period. Interest will be paid from April 15, 1991, through the date the refund is made. I've also signed an executive order granting state employees who served in the National Guard or reserves an extra ten days of paid leave to settle family affairs. The leave may be taken right away when they return home, or spread out over their first year back on the job.

But that's not all we're planning. We want to show our troops that we appreciate what they've done, and so we plan to throw a statewide celebration honoring all our military personnel. Plans for that statewide celebration include prayer breakfasts, parades, the ringing of church bells, and a gala celebration at Carter-Findley Stadium. I would encourage every town in North Carolina to join us in honoring our troops in this way, with whatever means they have available. We'll be happy to organize troops for local parades, or help in any other way we can.[2]

Our troops have done a fantastic job supporting America in the Persian Gulf War. Now it's our turn to show these returning troops how much we support them and appreciate the sacrifices they have made for our country. Showing that support is especially important to us, since so many military personnel were deployed from North Carolina, more than from any other state. No date for the celebration has been set yet, but you'll be hearing a lot more about this in the future.

---

[1]March 7, 1991, fell on a Thursday. The governor's weekly schedules for the month of March do not indicate the actual date of the National Science Foundation site team's visit to Raleigh.

[2]Carter-Findley Stadium, Raleigh, was the home field of the N.C. State University football team. Press releases on the statewide festivities honoring returning military personnel include "Governor Announces Plans for N.C. Salute to the Armed Forces," Raleigh, March 8, 1991, and "Communities Prepare for 'Salute to the Troops' Celebrations," Raleigh, June 6, 1991, Governors Papers, James G. Martin.

PRESS CONFERENCE ON UPLIFT DAY CARE

RALEIGH, MARCH 20, 1991

Thank you for joining us on such short notice. Today I am pleased to announce the start of our Uplift Day Care initiative, which I outlined in my State of the State message in January. Uplift Day Care will begin ahead of schedule as a result of a $5.5 million federal grant to fund day-care services for low-income, working families. This new federal money will also ensure continued child care for families in danger of losing day-care benefits.

Recently, counties have been reporting shortfalls in their purchase of care funds, forcing them to drop children from the day-care program. This grant will keep these children in day care and their parents on the job and off welfare. It will also provide day care to more children who need it.

The Department of Human Resources tells me this grant could provide day-care services for an estimated 6,500 eligible children. That would include a number of at-risk four-year-olds as a first step in our expanded program to help this special group.

The $5.5 million in federal funds became available through the At-Risk Child Care Program, a new program under Title IV-A of the Social Security Act. Through the program, funds are available to states to provide child care for low-income working families who are at risk of becoming recipients of Aid to Families with Dependent Children. Daycare services may be provided to children younger than age thirteen in families that need day care in order to accept or maintain employment.[1]

Human Resources secretary Dave Flaherty has been notified the grant will be awarded within the next ten days from the Family Support Administration of the U.S. Department of Health and Human Services. The fact we were able to receive approval for this part of our plan this early is a testimony to the dedication of our Division of Social Services, Child Day Care Section, and the entire Department of Human Resources. And now I would like to call on Secretary Dave Flaherty for some brief comments.

---

[1]P.L. 101–508, *United States Statutes at Large*, Act of November 5, 1990, 104 Stat. 1388–236; see also Congressional Research Service, Library of Congress, *Major Legislation of the Congress: Summary Issue* (Washington, D.C.: U.S. Government Printing Office, December 1990), MLC–114.

"A NEW WORLD ORDER": THE HISTORIC CONTEXT

[This essay, written by Martin in response to a comment by former president Jimmy Carter, was reprinted in the *News and Observer*, March 24, 1991, as "New century, old idea." It was edited for publication. The original appears below.]

President George Bush has commanded the attention and admiration of the free world with his leadership through two of the most far-reaching developments in world history. By doing so, he has revitalized an old but timely idea: the realization of a "new world order."

Among President Bush's most enduring legacies will be his encouragement of democracy and liberty emerging in Eastern Europe and his command of the successful allied operation enforcing United Nations policy in the Persian Gulf War. For both, he evokes the concept of a new world order. "We have before us the opportunity to forge for ourselves and for future generations a new world order," President Bush said. "A world in which the rule of law, not the law of the jungle, governs the conduct of nations."[1]

I had accepted that as an excellent characterization of global developments until former president Jimmy Carter criticized the Reagan-Bush legacy of restoring American strength and influence during remarks he made at the Emerging Issues Forum at North Carolina State University. Challenging the description of a new world order, the former president repeated a misconception about the current president's phrasing. News accounts reported that Mr. Carter said: "We talk gloriously of a 'new world order.' Unfortunately, that was a phrase I understand was first used by Adolf Hitler."[2]

Adolf Hitler? Hardly. Like everyone, especially those of us in public life, President Carter made a very public mistake. But his error is worth pointing out so we [might] better understand the concept of a new world order.

With the assistance of the reference desk at North Carolina's State Library, a resource any citizen can use, I sorted through the history of the term. In fact, Hitler did not promote the idea of a "new world order." His idea was a "New Order," and in 1942 it did not include the world. Hitler wanted to create a new order for Europe alone, insulated from the rest of the world and dominated by his Third Reich. Hitler's command for a new order, issued from his bunker, sought to plunder and exterminate the Jews of Europe. His ugly vision deserves no place in history near the noble plan for a new world order.

Long before Adolf Hitler, President Woodrow Wilson addressed the Senate on January 22, 1917, with his vision of a new world order in which he proposed a League of Nations. Among his Fourteen Points were these objectives: to defend the territorial integrity of member nations, to promote peace, and "to make the world safe for democracy."[3]

Before Woodrow Wilson, the great Scottish libertarian philosopher, John Stuart Mill, in his influential 1859 essay, *On Liberty*, voiced fears about possible consequences of the wrong kind of new world order. Like Bush, Mill opposed socialism and advocated individual freedom. Representative democracy, Mill thought, was the best form of government to encourage the growth of individuality. He would have been comfortable with the new world order of George Bush.

As early as the very founding of our Republic, the concept of a new world order was employed by the Continental Congress when it adopted the Great Seal of the United States to authenticate official documents. The design of the Great Seal began with a most distinguished committee: Ben Franklin, John Adams, and Thomas Jefferson just prior to adjournment on July 4, 1776! Finally adopted on June 20, 1782, the two-sided Great Seal has become a strong and lasting symbol of American democracy. Not surprisingly, one side of that Great Seal refers to a new world order.

The front side, called obverse, portrays the familiar American coat of arms; the bald eagle and shield with thirteen stripes; and overhead, thirteen stars in a star-shaped constellation. The eagle holds in its talons the symbols of war and peace: on the right, a branch with thirteen leaves and thirteen olives; and on the left, thirteen arrows. The beak holds a banner proclaiming, in thirteen letters, *E Pluribus Unum*. And what of the reverse?

Never cut into a die, the back half of the Great Seal has not achieved the same general use as the obverse side, but it is as familiar as every one-dollar bill printed since 1935. In a design approved personally by Franklin Delano Roosevelt, the dollar bill representation has on its right-hand side the familiar eagle with a shield. But look at the left side. That figure is an unfinished pyramid with thirteen steps. At its apex, within a triangle surrounded by rays of light as a "blaze of glory," is the ancient representation of the eye of Providence. Above that is the Latin motto *Annuit Coeptis*, meaning "He favors our undertakings." A second motto, below the pyramid, is also derived from the Roman poet Virgil. Consider well what it says to us across these 208 years of nationhood: *Novus Ordo Seclorum*, "A new world order."[4]

Some have translated this alternatively as "A new order of the age." Charles Thomson, the venerable secretary of the Continental Congress from its first session until its last, himself first proposed the final version of the seal and its mottoes and served as keeper of the seal until the transition to constitutional government in 1789.[5] He didn't translate this motto, but explained it only by referring to "a new American era." The Latin *seculorum*, or its poetic form, *seclorum*, has several meanings, of which the ecclesiastical usage means "of the world." Hence, our derived English word, *secular*, defined as "pertaining to worldly things."

It is clear then that Hitler was not the first to call for a new world order, nor was Hitler ever among those great heroes who did. Trying to understand history can be as difficult as trying to undertake it. Ask Virgil, Thomson, Mill, Wilson, or Bush. Surely, these leaders stand as distinguished lineage to which Adolf Hitler could never rightfully claim heritage.

---

[1]President George Bush, Announcement on War against Iraq, January 16, 1991, *Congressional Quarterly Almanac, 1991*, 3–E.

[2]President Carter included the attention-getting remark in his televised speech, "America's Place in the World." He delivered the address February 14 as a participant in the sixth annual Emerging Issues Forum. *News and Observer*, February 15, 1991.

[3]Wilson proposed his Fourteen Points before a joint session of the United States House and Senate on January 8, 1918. He used the phrase, "The world must be made safe for democracy," in his April 2, 1917, request to Congress for a declaration of war against the Central Powers. Bartlett, *Familiar Quotations*, 842; George Brown Tindall, *America: A Narrative History* (New York: W. W. Norton and Co., 2 volumes, 1984), II, 969.

[4]As Martin noted, Virgil inspired both mottoes on the reverse side of the Great Seal. *Annuit Coeptis*, "He favors our undertakings" was an adaptation of the Roman poet's phrase *audacibus annue coeptis*: "Look with favor upon a bold beginning." "A new order of the age," *Novus Ordo Seclorum*, came from *magnus ab integro saeculorum nascitur ordo*, meaning "the great cycle of the ages is renewed." Bartlett, *Familiar Quotations*, 116, 117.

[5]Charles Thomson (1729–1824), born in County Derry, Ireland; died in Lower Merion, Pa. Arrived in America, 1739; educator in Philadelphia, 1750–1760; Philadelphia merchant from 1760; Pa. political activist, member Sons of Liberty; secretary, Continental Congress, 1774–1789; co-designer, with William Barton, of the Great Seal; translator; author. *Encyclopedia Americana*, 1990 ed., s.v. "Great Seal of the United States"; *Who Was Who in America, 1607–1896*, 600–601.

CELEBRATION NORTH CAROLINA QUARTERLY MEETING

CHARLOTTE, APRIL 8, 1991

A little over a year ago, I started Celebration North Carolina. It began as an idea borrowed from our neighbors in Tennessee and Alabama: Tennessee Homecoming and Alabama Reunion. I, too, wanted to launch a program that celebrated the spirit, strength, and heritage of our fine state.

When I took this idea to a group of business executives, my friend Bill Lee suggested we build a program that not only celebrates North Carolina, past and present, but also addresses some of our challenges. He convinced me that North Carolina business leaders would be interested, of course, in events to recall and celebrate the great heritage prepared for us and handed down by previous leaders—but that you would be enthusiastic about bringing corporate resources to overcome today's problems, and meet today's challenges, and then celebrate the heritage which we leave to future generations. So Bill Lee, chairman and president of Duke Power Company, became the "founding father" of our program today, Celebration North Carolina, which Duke Power has supported so generously, for programs for improved family literacy in five counties.

I would like to update you on some of the great progress we have made, the programs we have supported, and the special celebration we are planning for our troops returning from the Persian Gulf. In the course of a short year, Celebration has logged some impressive accomplishments. Recently, through a gift from R. J. Reynolds Tobacco, Celebration launched three new Tech Prep programs in Catawba, Caldwell, and Wilkes counties.[1] Tech Prep, an innovative program for non-college-bound students, was first developed in Richmond County and has proven that it can better prepare our young people for the technological challenge of today's work place.

In partnership with IBM, Celebration has enabled us to expand the North Carolina Math and Science Alliance in Orange and Durham counties. Through the generosity of Carolina Power and Light, Celebration will also expand the Cities-in-Schools program, a proven dropout prevention program which has been so successful right here in Charlotte.

In addition to education, Celebration is also actively working on environmental projects. Moore and Van Allen has helped us expand the Adopt-A-Stream program.[2] In a few short weeks, Boy Scout and Girl Scout troops in Mecklenburg and Wake counties will be out helping us clean up our rivers, learning in the process how to protect our precious natural resources. Celebration and Weyerhaeuser are also working on a reforestation project to reintroduce Atlantic white cedar, a near-extinct species native to the state.

Here in Charlotte and the surrounding area, companies like Food Lion; American Barmag; Public Service Company; Pension Plan, Inc.; Lance, Incorporated; Broadway and Seymour; AT&T; Eckerd Drug; and others have joined the Celebration team and are serving as a catalyst for community action statewide. These corporate citizens and the other individuals involved with Celebration are true patriots of North Carolina. They donate their time, money, and ideas to help strengthen our communities and make our state an even better place to live.

We share a rich heritage as North Carolinians: abundant natural resources, an excellent transportation system, strong investment in high technology, and a thriving economy, just to name a few. But we also face many challenges, like illiteracy, workforce preparedness, environmental cleanup, and infant mortality. You are leaders in business, industry, and the community. I need you to also serve as leaders in the fight to overcome the challenges we face. I need you to join with Celebration North Carolina and forge new partnerships. Help us marshal our resources. Help us rally a force of minds and ideas to meet the challenges confronting us here in North Carolina.

In his recent State of the Union Address, President Bush said, "The strength of a democracy is not in bureaucracy. It is in the people and their communities. In everything we do, let us unleash the potential of our most precious resource—our citizens. . . ."[3]

We are all citizens of the finest state in America. I am proud and honored to serve the citizens of North Carolina, but I have never been more proud than over the last months as I have watched our brave soldiers valiantly liberate Kuwait. They brought freedom to Kuwait, but they also brought a sense of renewed freedom to us here at home. Our military personnel from all branches of the service—the army, navy, marines, air force, coast guard, national guard, and including our national guard and Reserve and their families—deserve our deepest gratitude for their courageous service.

I ask each of you to join with me and others across our state to welcome home the brave men and women of our armed services. I have proclaimed the week of June 29-July 4 as North Carolina's statewide Salute to the Troops celebration.[4] It should be a matter of great pride to us that over 75,000 were deployed to the Gulf War—Desert Shield and Desert Storm—from North Carolina: That's about a fifth of the total, far more than any other state! Then we should also express that pride by having the largest patriotic celebration on the Fourth.

The leadership of Celebration North Carolina will be coordinating our statewide activities by working with communities across the state. Part of those plans include a coordinated salute to our military with a statewide Pledge of Allegiance, "Star-Spangled Banner," and tolling of bells on July 4. Mayor Myrick, the Charlotte Chamber [of Commerce], and many of you in this room will be helping to plan the Charlotte celebration. We look forward to working with you.

We've come a long way in just a year, Bill. Celebration has been working at the grass-roots level on programs that address some of our challenges, and we will continue to do so. But now we are going to celebrate. We're going to join the nation and put on the biggest celebration this state has seen to honor the brave men and women of Operation Desert Storm. Francis Scott Key must have been looking over North Carolina when he wrote "the land of the free and the home of the brave." I look forward to singing that beautiful anthem with you on the Fourth of July.

---

[1]The governor publicly accepted R. J. Reynolds Tobacco Company's donation expanding Tech Prep in late February. RJR/Tech Prep Announcement, February 22, 1991, Governors Papers, James G. Martin.

[2]The law firm of Moore and Van Allen maintained offices in Charlotte and Raleigh. *North Carolina Legal Directory, 1991* (Dallas, Texas: Directories Publishing Company, Inc., 1991), 446, 538.

[3]President George Herbert Walker Bush, State of the Union Address, January 29, 1991, quoted in *Congressional Quarterly Almanac, 1991*, 6E–7E.

[4]"North Carolina Salute to the Troops, 1991, by the Governor of the State of North Carolina: A Proclamation," March 28, 1991, Governors Papers, James G. Martin.

CHILD PROTECTIVE SERVICES ANNOUNCEMENT

RALEIGH, APRIL 18, 1991

You may have seen the report released Tuesday by the National Committee for the Prevention of Child Abuse showing that child abuse reports in North Carolina are on the rise.[1] A number of news organizations in the state have followed this issue closely and have done a fairly good job drawing public attention to this critical issue. The issue of child abuse has our attention, too. Today I want to announce several new administration initiatives that we hope will strengthen the Child Protective Services system and lessen the incidence of child abuse in our state.

Check-Off Fund

We have rekindled an old idea created by the Commission on Child Victimization under my wife['s], Dottie's, leadership as chairman. The Fund for Children and Families is designed as a check-off item on income-tax forms that would raise money through voluntary taxpayer contributions. Over a two-year period, the money would be used to strengthen child protective services by providing additional staff, training, and other program needs. Last year, the Nongame and Endangered Wildlife Check-Off raised $479,039.24 from 47,568 contributors. Just think how much more we can raise to preserve another endangered species, these abused children.[2]

Review Teams

We will be establishing child abuse-neglect and fatality review teams in every county in the state by the end of May. These review teams will strengthen supervision of the handling of child protective services by the state Division of Social Services. Other states have panels that review the deaths of abused and neglected children, and we looked at that, but when a child dies, it's already too late. That's why we want our review teams to look into the current handling of child abuse and neglect cases in addition to investigating child deaths. The review teams will include representatives of law enforcement and social services as well as child medical experts and child advocates. That means we may be able to benefit from sharing of confidential information among these agencies.[3]

Access to Information

The Division of Social Services will provide quarterly reports on child fatalities to the public. The reports will include numbers of deaths, causes of death, and DSS involvement. Access to information on child deaths and abuse will also be expanded to include law enforcement and medical professionals to the extent legally possible. In addition, county departments of social services will be allowed access to the central registry to determine if a child has been previously reported as abused or neglected while living in another county. That will help keep those children from falling between the cracks as has happened in the past.

Legislation

I have proposed three pieces of legislation that will be considered in this session. The first would place the Fund for Children and Families check-off on state tax forms. The second allows child witnesses in child-abuse cases to videotape testimony in a room away from the courtroom.[4] The third piece of legislation would close courtrooms to spectators when children testify in child-abuse cases.[5]

I support House Bill 540, sponsored by representatives Carolyn Russell and Peggy Wilson, both of whom are with us today. That bill would expand the definition of neglect to include newborns exposed to illicit drugs or alcohol prior to birth. This was a recommendation from the Drug Cabinet.[6]

I also support Representative Dave Diamont's proposal to establish a state child fatality review team to study all child deaths in the state. He was not able to join us.[7]

I must point out that the state Division of Social Services has been doing what it can to prevent the unfortunate and tragic deaths of these children. Our child protective services workers at the county level have been laboring under an extremely heavy caseload in many instances. But the laws and policies governing child abuse and neglect have not been carried out consistently in all 100 counties. That must, and will, come to an end. It must for the sake of our children.

In addition to representatives Carolyn Russell and Peggy Wilson, we also have with us today Secretary Dave Flaherty; Joan (jo-ann) Holland, assistant director for Services Administration; and Beth Osborne,[8] program manager for Child Protective Services. Ms. Deyampert and Ms. Holland will hold a press briefing this afternoon, at 1:00 in the eighth-floor conference room in the Albemarle Building, to fully brief you on these and other initiatives outlined in the press release and fact sheet in front of you.[9] I would encourage you to attend. Now I'd like to ask Dave Flaherty to come forward to make a few comments.

---

[1]The National Committee for the Prevention of Child Abuse announced, on April 16, 1991, that 52,928 abuse and neglect cases had been reported in North Carolina during 1990; the 15 percent increase over 1989 was seventh-highest in the nation. North Carolina was also among the fifteen states in which child-abuse fatalities rose. Seven children died from abuse or neglect in 1989, while ten suffered that fate the following year. Jennifer Tolle, executive director of the committee's North Carolina chapter, believed the actual number of deaths from child abuse was double the number confirmed for 1990. She said that the state's child-abuse protection system tracked only those cases of abuse that were in progress; there was no mechanism for reporting deaths from child abuse. Nationwide, child abuse complaints increased 2 percent, and deaths resulting from abuse rose 1 percent. *News and Observer*, April 17, 1991.

[2]Martin endorsed an income tax check-off to finance the North Carolina Fund for Children and Families in 1986. The next year, Senator Robert G. Shaw (R-Guilford) introduced

two bills to initiate such a mechanism, but they were not enacted. Shaw returned in 1991 with S.B. 840, "A Bill to Establish the North Carolina Fund for Children and Families, Provide for its Governance, and Permit the Allocation of Corporate and Individual Income Tax Refunds to the Fund"; meanwhile the similarly titled H.B. 1125 enjoyed bipartisan sponsorship in the House. But in 1991 as in 1987, none of the measures passed the legislature. *N.C. House Journal, 1991,* 403; *N.C. Senate Journal, 1991,* 309; Poff, *Addresses of Martin,* I, 394, 395n, 666.

[3]Executive Order Number 142, signed May 1, 1991, required each county social services department to establish a community child protection team. *N.C. Session Laws, 1991,* II, 2684–2687.

[4]Like the income tax check-off, the proposal enabling children to offer videotaped testimony was an idea the governor supported during his first term; see Poff, *Addresses of Martin,* I, 15, 21n. Revisiting the idea in 1991, Martin endorsed H.B. 1072, "A Bill to Be Entitled an Act to Provide That a Child Victim May Testify in Court in Certain Criminal Cases by Means of Closed Circuit Television." Introduced by Representative Johnathan L. Rhyne, Jr. (R-Lincoln) on April 23, 1991 and ultimately amended, H.B. 1072 passed the House on May 16. Dispatched to the Senate, the bill remained in committee through the end of the session. *N.C. House Journal, 1991,* 383, 662, 690; *N.C. Senate Journal, 1991,* 458; press release, "Governor Martin Supports Diamont Plan to Fund Additional Child Protective Services Staff," Raleigh, April 24, 1991, Governors Papers, James G. Martin.

[5]Neither H.B. 949 nor S.B. 751, House and Senate bills intended to "protect the privacy of children required to testify," was enacted into law. *N.C. House Journal, 1991,* 350; *N.C. Senate Journal, 1991,* 280.

[6]Representatives Russell and Wilson introduced H.B. 540 on April 1, 1991. That proposal, "A Bill to Be Entitled an Act to Provide that Newborns Who Were Exposed to Illicit Drug [*sic*] or Alcohol Prior to Birth Are Neglected under G.S. 7A–517," did not survive the House Appropriations Committee. *N.C. House Journal, 1991,* 217, 566.

Carolyn Barnes Russell (1944–), born in Greenville; resident of Wayne County; A.B., 1965, M.A., 1967, East Carolina University. Psychologist at Sunland Training Center; elected to state House, 1990; Republican. *North Carolina Manual, 1991–1992,* 433.

Peggy Ann Wilson (1945–), born in Anamosa, Iowa; former resident of Madison, N.C.; associate degree in science and nursing from Kirkwood Community College, Cedar Rapids, Iowa. Nurse in Kirksville, Mo., 7 years; regional manager, Modern Income Life Insurance Co., 2 years; self-employed in skin and health care business, 3 years; school nurse, Western Rockingham City Schools, 6 years; elected to state House from Rockingham County, 1988, resigned seat in 1993 to work in medical clinic in Alaska; Republican. *News and Observer,* July 6, 1993; *North Carolina Manual, 1991–1992,* 443–444.

[7]Chapter 689, s. 233, established the North Carolina Child Fatality Review Team. Representatives Wilbur B. Ethridge (D-Carteret), Howard J. Hunter, Jr. (D-Hertford), Daniel H. DeVane (D-Hoke), and Senator Robert L. Martin (D-Pitt) joined Diamont in sponsoring the measure. *N.C. Session Laws, 1991,* II.

David Hunter Diamont (1946–), born in Greensboro; resident of Pilot Mountain; B.A., Wake Forest University, 1968; M.A., Appalachian State University, 1972. History teacher, 1968–1977 and since 1990, assistant football coach, 1968–1977, head football coach, since 1990, Mt. Airy Senior High School; history teacher, head varsity football coach, East Surry High School, 1977–1989; member, 1975–1994, N.C. House, and Appropriations Committee chairman, 1989–1994; Democrat. *News and Observer,* August 22, 1993, January 22, 1994; *North Carolina Manual, 1989–1990,* 352, *1991–1992,* 347.

[8]Beth Willetts Osborne (1958–), born in Greenville; resident of Louisburg; bachelor of social work, East Carolina University, 1980; master of social work, University of North Carolina at Chapel Hill, 1983. Children's Services supervisor, Johnston County Dept. of Social Services, 1983–1985; consultant II, 1985–1987; manager II, 1987–1991, and administrator II, since 1991, Child Protective Services program, Division of Social Services, N.C. Dept. of Human Resources. Beth Willetts Osborne, letter to Jan-Michael Poff, November 8, 1993.

[9]Press release, "Governor Announces Proposals to Prevent Child Abuse," Raleigh, April 18, 1991, Governors Papers, James G. Martin.

MOUNT MITCHELL STATE PARK REDEDICATION

Burnsville, May 17, 1991

We're here today to celebrate and remember a very special event in North Carolina's history: the establishment, seventy-five years ago, of Mount Mitchell as North Carolina's first state park and the creation of the first state parks system in the Southeast. Mount Mitchell has a rich and fascinating history, ranging from the early explorations of Elisha Mitchell and "Big Tom" Wilson to the early miners and lumberjacks whose activities underscored the need to protect and preserve the highest peak east of the Mississippi.[1]

This is a relatively new idea, preserving and protecting North Carolina's natural resources. Early in the twentieth century, logging was destroying Mount Mitchell. As the magnificent forests of this mile-high peak fell to the axe of the lumberman, alarmed citizens took their concerns to the governor. Moved to action, Governor Locke Craig came to the mountain and witnessed the exploitation firsthand. Horrified by what he saw, he convinced the loggers to stop their operations until he could meet with the General Assembly.[2]

Upon his return to Raleigh, the governor waged a campaign to save Mount Mitchell, joining forces with individuals and organizations to urge the legislature to protect this area. The General Assembly complied, and on March 3, 1915, Mount Mitchell became our first state park.[3] Seventy-five years later, our state parks system, which started out as this one small plot of public land, has grown into sixty-eight properties across the state, including twenty-nine state parks, four recreation areas, fifteen state trails, four state rivers, seven state lakes, and nine natural areas. The system spans from Mount Mitchell to Jockey's Ridge, the tallest sand dune on the East Coast. Last year alone, these 129,000 acres attracted more than nine million visitors.

We have come to appreciate the beauty of our natural resources, preserved and protected through our state parks system. The many unique and valuable archaeological, geological, and biological resources protected in these lands and waters have become integral parts of our natural heritage. Yet, as stewards of these public lands, we have not lived up to the legacy established for us seventy-five years ago by Governor Craig, the General Assembly, and the visionary citizens who recognized the need for a state parks system.

State parks are too often considered luxury items and therefore don't get the funding they deserve. Years of being tossed mistakenly into the luxury category has dropped our state parks system to its current ranking of fiftieth in the country in terms of per-capita operating expenditures, dead last. In the parks system's seventy-five-year history, the state has spent only $34 million for capital improvements and $40 million on land acquisition.

Most of the facilities developed in our state parks system were built and financed through the Works Progress Administration and the Civilian Conservation Corps during the Roosevelt administration some fifty years ago. These facilities are decaying because of hard use and a lack [of] funds for regular maintenance.

Many of our other parks, which were added after the CCC and WPA era, have very few amenities for visitors. When these parks were added to the system, mostly by donation, they were not accompanied by appropriations for staffing, capital development, or additional land acquisition. This situation led to passage of the State Parks Act [in] 1987 which allows parks to be added or deleted from the system only by majority vote of the General Assembly.[4] It also requires that all legislation establishing new parks be accompanied by adequate appropriations for operations, development, and land acquisition of the park.

While this legislation prevents all future parks from being created without sufficient support, we must still recognize the shortcomings of existing parks. The North Carolina Division of Parks and Recreation has identified $121 million in capital improvements needed to complete park units which have master plans. The capital improvements would provide for very basic park facilities, such as campgrounds, visitor centers, rest rooms, and picnic areas.

The Division of Parks and Recreation estimates 18,000 acres need to be acquired to protect the resources in our state parks. That would cost an estimated $58 million.

We spend approximately $1.04 per citizen on our state parks. The national average is in excess of $4.50. This situation makes it difficult for the Division of Parks and Recreation to provide environmental education, recruit seasonal employees, and make routine repairs and renovations.

Obviously, we don't have a quick fix for this situation in our parks system. Current budget shortages and other pressing social needs, including education and health, are displacing our ability to upgrade our parks system. Yet, people across the state have learned about the funding woes of our state parks system and they are starting to act, just like they did seventy-five years ago. Our state trails, managed through our state parks system, exist because volunteers give their time, energy, and expertise to sustain them. Volunteers and support groups across our state conduct cleanups, interpretive programs, and repairs throughout the system.

Our celebration today is a fine example of people working together for our state parks. The seventy-fifth anniversary of Mount Mitchell has been coordinated through the Yancey, Mitchell, and McDowell County chambers of commerce, along with the Black Mountain-Swannanoa chamber, the Blue Ridge Parkway, state government, and a variety of local organizations and private citizens. On behalf of the people of North Carolina, I would like to thank you for your hard work and support of Mount Mitchell.

That spirit of volunteerism for stewardship of our public lands has won North Carolina national attention. For the third year in a row, North Carolina has had more finalists in the national Take Pride in America awards program than any other participating state. Take Pride in America is a public lands stewardship campaign that encourages active participation by individuals, organizations, and communities in the use and protection of our natural resources.

Through our Take Pride in America program, individuals, businesses, citizens, [and] civic, trade, and professional groups are being encouraged to speak out, write articles, "adopt" an area, organize cleanups, and conduct outdoor education programs. One such business, Carolina Power and Light Company, recently stepped forward to adopt our state parks in conjunction with the seventy-fifth anniversary. CP&L will spend $144,000, over a four-year period, to improve environmental education, cultivate grass-roots support for state parks through volunteers, and challenge other industries and businesses to get involved.

In connection with the park system's diamond anniversary, CP&L will sponsor three environmental symposiums across the state during the year. This ceremony today culminates the first of these symposiums. I know those attending have come away with a better understanding of the mission of our state parks system and our efforts to promote pride and understanding of our state's natural heritage. However, we need to do a better job preserving these resources for this and future generations. We owe it to our children, and to our ancestors who served as land stewards for our sake, to leave these treasures in better condition than we found them.

---

[1]Elisha Mitchell (1793–1857), born in Washington, Conn.; was reburied atop Mt. Mitchell, Yancey County; was graduated from Yale University, 1813. Appointed professor of mathematics and natural philosophy, 1818, professor of chemistry, mineralogy, and geology, 1825–1837, University of North Carolina; ordained as Presbyterian minister, 1821; completed geological survey of North Carolina. Discovered highest U.S. mountain (6,684 ft.) east of Rockies; U.S. Geological Survey named it in honor of Mitchell, ca. 1882. Powell, *DNCB*, IV, 281–283; S. Kent Schwarzkopf, *A History of Mt. Mitchell and the Black Mountains* (Raleigh: Division of Archives and History, North Carolina Department of Cultural Resources, 1985), 30, hereinafter cited as Schwarzkopf, *History of Mt. Mitchell*.

Thomas D. "Big Tom" Wilson (1823–1908), of Yancey County; mountain guide; found the body of Elisha Mitchell, July 7, 1857, who had fallen to his death while exploring the

peak later named for him. Schwarzkopf, *History of Mt. Mitchell*, 62–65.
[2]Locke Craig (1860–1924), governor, 1913–1917. Previously identified in Poff, *Addresses of Martin*, I, 271n; see also Schwarzkopf, *History of Mt. Mitchell*, 86.
[3]Schwarzkopf, *History of Mt. Mitchell*, 88–92.
[4]"An Act to Establish the Purposes of the State Parks System" was ratified June 2, 1987. *N.C. Session Laws, 1987*, II, c. 243.

TELECOMMUNICATIONS PRESS CONFERENCE

RALEIGH, MAY 30, 1991

[Although education spending increased during Governor Martin's tenure in office, school needs nevertheless seemed to outstrip available revenues. Statewide equity among secondary education programs in particular remained an unmet ideal. Wealthier urban school systems raised additional money to supplement state funding, but school districts serving North Carolina's widespread rural population often lacked the tax base to support the faculty, advanced coursework, and other necessities to produce sufficient numbers of college-ready or "workforce prepared" graduates. Recognizing both educational need and fiscal reality, Martin welcomed the Vision Carolina project on May 30, 1991, as a partner in teaching the state's youth.

When it began operating in the autumn of 1991, Vision Carolina was among the largest, most ambitious distance-learning projects in the country. Collaborators in the initiative included Southern Bell, Northern Telecom, state universities, community colleges, and a medical center.

Distance learning, briefly described by Martin below, employed telecommunications technology that allowed an instructor to interact simultaneously with students in his classroom and those attending other schools. Participating classrooms were equipped with cameras, microphones, and video monitors. Audio and video signals were transmitted via the public telephone system's fiber optic cables and a special video switch.

According to Southern Bell, the Vision Carolina network enabled participants "to share limited resources, enhance curriculum, and improve access to instructors." Advanced courses were made available where, under former circumstances, it was impossible for single high schools to fund them. Thus the program fostered "some leveraging of educational assets" among rural and urban students. Finally, Vision Carolina had the ability to reduce the "travel time and expense" normally associated with in-service training.

Two regions initially participated in Vision Carolina. The Cape Fear network linked the University of North Carolina at Wilmington, Cape Fear Community College, New Hanover Regional Medical Center, and John T. Hoggard and New Hanover high schools. At the time it went on-line, Cape Fear was believed to be the only project in the country to involve a regional medical facility heavily. The Southern Piedmont network joined twelve sites, including the University of North Carolina at Charlotte, Central Piedmont Community College, and Gaston College. Participating high schools included East Mecklenburg, North Mecklenburg, and Harding; Ashbrook, in Gastonia; South Point, in Belmont; and East Lincoln, West Lincoln, and the Lincoln County School of Technology. Vicki Ross, secretary, Southern Bell, letter to Jan-Michael Poff, June 1, 1993, hereinafter cited as Ross correspondence.]

Back in my real life before government, I was a chemistry professor at Davidson College. My experience in the classroom, as both a teacher and as a student, taught me just how important a quality education is for opening the doors of opportunity throughout life. As governor, I've maintained my lifelong commitment to education. With the support of the legislature, we've increased spending for education in the last six years by 76 percent—that's an increase of almost $1.5 billion in just six years.

But with tight budgets, government spending isn't enough to pre-pare our classrooms to meet the challenges of education in the next cen-tury. That's why, more and more, we are depending on private corpora-tions like Southern Bell to step in and step up the quality of education in North Carolina. During the coming school year, Southern Bell is spon-soring a pilot program that will make "distance learning" available to thousands of students through two-way, interactive video. Through dis-tance learning, students in one school will be able to take courses and use resources at other schools that would not otherwise be available to them.

This is a landmark initiative in the history of education in North Caro-lina, one that capitalizes on the leading edge of information-age tech-nology through a public-private partnership for education. We didn't have technology like this in the classroom when I was teaching. Thanks to Southern Bell, teachers in the pilot schools will be able to use these tools of technology to turn educational reform into educational oppor-tunity in North Carolina.

Without a doubt, Southern Bell is helping us to bring classrooms of the next century to life in schools of the '90s. I know you're interested in how this program will work and what systems will be included in the pilot program. For those answers, I'd like to introduce to you J. Billie Ray, Jr., president of Southern Bell's North Carolina operations.[1]

---

[1]J. Billie Ray, Jr. (1946–), born in Calhoun, Ga.; resident of Charlotte; B.S., Georgia Tech, 1968; J.D., University of Georgia, 1975; U.S. Navy, 1968–1972. Attorney in private practice, 1975–1978; attorney, 1978–1983, and solicitor, 1983–1984, with Southern Bell's Georgia operations; general attorney, 1984–1989, president, since 1990, Southern Bell's North Carolina operations; associate general counsel, BellSouth Services, Inc., 1989–1990. Ross correspondence.

EIGHTH-GRADE MATH SCORES PRESS CONFERENCE

RALEIGH, JUNE 6, 1991

This morning, the National Assessment of Educational Progress announced the results of its first math test given to eighth graders across the nation. The test was voluntary. Thirty-seven states participated along with students in the District of Columbia, Guam, and the Virgin Islands. Two thousand eighth graders were randomly selected from each state and territory representing all geographic areas and were given the test in February 1990.

Some of you may have seen the results already. They were announced an hour ago, and they're not good. For those of you who haven't seen it, North Carolina ranked thirty-sixth out of thirty-seven states, ahead of Louisiana, Guam, the District of Columbia, and the Virgin Islands. I doubt that comes as a surprise to anyone. Our neighbors in South Carolina, Tennessee, and Mississippi did not participate.

We must keep one very important point in mind in evaluating these test scores, however. I said that these tests were given in February 1990. That's sixteen months ago, before a number of new educational reforms put in place in our school systems had any chance to prove their worth. As it stands, this test does not evaluate the effects of greater flexibility and accountability given our schools through Senate Bill 2, passed in 1989. This test does not evaluate the effects of unfreezing teacher pay or of innovative new programs begun at the local level in many systems. This test does not evaluate the improvements made as a result of the statewide end-of-year testing begun during the last school year.

In the future, we should urge that such tests be graded promptly so that they more accurately reflect the current performance of our educational system. For us, this one is just a base line showing where we were a year and a half ago. But having said that, let's get back to what this ranking does tell us. It is certainly a valid base line.

Taken with other measures of student progress, including low reading and writing scores and low SAT scores, this latest test tells us, once again, we have not done a very good job of teaching the basics to our children in the past. It is another piece of solid evidence that our public schools must be reorganized for better results, and that's not the teachers' fault—it's ours.

For one thing, the test points out some significant societal factors affecting education. Across the board, it shows that children who live in homes with two parents scored higher than children living in one-parent families. The less parental supervision we have, the less math competency we get—and guess which state has nearly the lowest parental supervision. We do.

The report also shows that the number of hours children spend in front of the television set is inversely related to their academic achievement. Students who watch six or more hours of television a day had the lowest scores on the test, in every state—and guess whose students were near the top in idle time watching too much TV. Ours. That says we must encourage more homework and less TV, with more parents willing to check to see that homework is done before television.

The test also confirms that the Basic Education plan, into which we already pour $550 million a year, is not teaching basic education to our students. That should not be surprising since the misnamed Basic Education plan has nothing to do with basic skills education and, worse, drains away resources and contact time from basic education. These eighth-grade students in North Carolina were educated under the Basic Education plan about half their schooling time, and this test tells us a lot about what kind of education they have received. It wasn't strong on mathematics. Without a doubt, art, dance, and foreign languages are important and should be taught in our schools, at least to those who have [a]n aptitude for it, but not at the expense of the basics.

The basics must come first, and that's not the worst problem. The worst misappropriation in BEP is that most of the money and positions has [*sic*] gone for administration, not for teaching, and it shows. The way to fix that is to decentralize and deregulate our schools. Give them more flexibility and local control. I've been making that argument since my first year as governor.

Right now, the House is considering a move to increase funding for the BEP while reducing flexibility at the local level by increasing regulations, which will in turn force an increase in administrative staff. At the same time, the House is looking at decreasing funding for Senate Bill 2. Rather than pouring more money into a program that is too rigid to work, I would hope the General Assembly will approve Senate Bill 3 and move even farther to allow waivers from BEP regulations.[1] Central control and micromanagement is [*sic*] a failure.

Our problem isn't that we aren't putting enough money into education. In the last six years, we have increased funding for education by 76 percent, almost $1.4 billion. Sixty-seven cents out of every tax dollar pays for some level of public education in North Carolina. Adjusted for inflation, we've increased spending for education by 50 percent more than inflation. That's good, but we haven't gotten what we've paid for.

We must continue moving forward with educational reform in North Carolina. We must continue increasing flexibility, increasing accountability for student outcomes, and let teachers teach. BEP, with its rigid rules, and regulations, and its absorption of so much money, is detracting from the goals of education and crowding out basic skills education. We must also continue to support reform at the state level, supporting such worthwhile ventures [as] the Genesis Project[2] and Senate Bill 3.

I hope we've improved education in North Carolina in the sixteen months since our eighth graders took this test, and I also believe that our reforms have just begun. We've got a long way to go if we can just stay on the right course. We can count on great improvement for the future, particularly through such programs as the North Carolina Science and Mathematics Alliance, which provides for innovative curriculum development and teacher training. Through the National Science Foundation grant we recently received, that program should be available in every school system in this state by the next school year. We know what we need to do. Let's do it.

So I say, let's face the facts. These test scores show what every other test shows: Rigid, centrally controlled schools do not produce good results, no matter how much money we pour into it. The last two decades have been wasted by increasing overregulation of education by legislators trying to be a "Super Board of Education," strapping down our schools with an overload of restrictions and absentee tinkering, which has, in turn, required an overload of educational bureaucracy and detracted from teaching.

The way to fix it is to decentralize it. American business is becoming competitive again by decentralizing decision making out to the levels which deal with the customers and the products. In schools, the students are both the customers and the products. So let's transfer power to the local school buildings and teachers—and hold them accountable for how well the students do, not for how well they follow rules—and let teachers teach.

---

[1]Senate Bill 3, "A Bill to Provide the School Improvement and Accountability Act of 1991," did not emerge from the upper house of the legislature. See *N.C. Senate Journal, 1991*, 21, 506, 560.

[2]The North Carolina Public School Forum created the Genesis Project to spur innovation in education. Under the plan, competing private groups were to bid for the design and administration of individual public schools. The new schools would be exempt from many state regulations, even though they received state operating funds. Advocates hoped to launch Genesis in Cumberland, Gaston, Johnston, and Wake counties. Martin touted the concept in a May 1991 meeting with U.S. education secretary Lamar Alexander, who in turn praised the idea. *News and Observer*, May 8, 19, 1991.

Although the state Senate approved the Genesis program in 1991, the House balked— in part, according to the lead editorial in the *Charlotte Observer*, June 9, 1991, because the idea enjoyed Republican backing and the approval of the Bush administration. The following year, lawmakers authorized pilot projects in Gaston and Johnston counties under "An Act to Establish the Project Genesis Program, an Experiment with a Restructured School Approach for the Public Schools," *N.C. Session Laws, Extra Session, 1991, Regular Session, 1992*, III, c. 999; see also *N.C. House Journal, 1991*, 356, and *N.C. Senate Journal, 1991*, 747.

NORTH CAROLINA ECONOMIC DEVELOPERS ASSOCIATION

ATLANTIC BEACH, JUNE 10, 1991

It's a special pleasure for me to meet with you today. As you know, I do a lot of bragging about North Carolina: more troops deployed during Desert Storm; more college basketball teams in Indianapolis [among the] Final Four;[1] more golf courses per governor; more new factories in three of [the] last four years.

Of course, the truth [is,] it's people like you who make it possible for people like me to go out and brag about the success we've achieved as a result of your hard work and commitment. It's tough to climb the ladder of success, especially if you're trying to keep your nose to the grindstone, your shoulder to the wheel, your eye on the ball, and your ear to the ground. Try that, and you'll get a sore back. That sounds like a description of my golf stance!

But as tough as it is, you do all those things and still climb that ladder, carrying the state of North Carolina right along with you. You are the movers and shakers of industrial recruitment, the people that our state Department of Economic and Community Development works with day in and day out. You're the ones who help us to bring industry to North Carolina and to support the industries that already call North Carolina home. Thank you for allowing me to be on your team.

Our partnership has led to some important milestones for economic development in our state. The numbers tell the story:

—1990 was a record year for business investment, with new and expanding businesses investing $6.8 billion in our state and announcing plans to create more than 42,000 new jobs;

—manufacturing investment hit an all-time high of $4.2 billion in 1990;

—last year, North Carolina ranked third in the nation for the number of new plants and expansions, after being first three years in a row;[2]

—and with your support, the North Carolina Department of Economic and Community Development was ranked among the nation's top ten development groups in the nation. No other state had an agency listed in the top ten. All the others were local.

Now that's a record to be proud of, but we're not content to sit on our laurels. We can't afford to—and won't.

This past February, with your strong support, we sponsored the state's first economic development summit in Greensboro, which has helped to focus our efforts and determine our direction for economic development over the next few years. That summit was so effective that you urged us to do it again. So, if that's the way you feel about it, let's do it.

Actually, we've already made plans to hold the second economic development summit on February 24–25 in Greensboro. Mark your calendars now. We expect to see you there.

Let me tell you something else exciting. We're also moving forward with plans to site a global air cargo industrial complex in North Carolina, which I proposed at the first economic development summit—the first of its kind anywhere in the world. Air cargo shipments have increased significantly in the 1980s, and the air cargo industry will continue to expand. Take exports, for example. Already 35 percent of the dollar value of American exports goes part way by airplane.

In tomorrow's emerging global economy, the emphasis will be on speed, speed, and more speed. Businesses will also rely more and more on efficiency to reduce costs and expensive inventories. The air cargo industrial complex will provide the speed and efficiency necessary for future success in the competitive global marketplace of the future in a way that's never been done before. When built, air cargo carriers and customers will follow this facility, wherever it is located. If we build it in North Carolina, this facility could bring over 30,000 jobs and billions of dollars to our state.

Of course, building a facility like this doesn't happen overnight. It's a long-term project, requiring long-term investment and commitment. Right now, we're in the process of conducting a feasibility study and establishing an air cargo authority to manage the project. I hope you'll support us in this effort, as you have in so many others, and help us build this air cargo industrial complex for the future economic development of our state.

We've done well in the past, and we've laid the groundwork to do just as well in providing jobs and opportunities for our people well into the future. But we still face major challenges, challenges that will require our continued cooperation and commitment if we are to meet and overcome them.

You are, of course, aware of the budget problems the state is facing right now. This year, for example, revenues were flat, $729 million short of what had been appropriated. So under our constitution, I had to take severe measures to keep it balanced, even counting accrued liabilities, to satisfy the bond-rating agencies. You may have seen where the state auditor didn't like it and threatened to have me prosecuted.[3] Those with accounting backgrounds understood and approved—and Standard and Poor's looked at it and reaffirmed [our] Triple-A [rating].[4]

You are also aware that the North Carolina House has passed a massive tax package totaling $709 million for next year.[5] That is far bigger than it needs to be and could have a major depressing effect on the way we do business in North Carolina. The House package calls for a half-cent increase in the state sales tax, another half-cent local-option sales tax increase, a new 8 percent tax bracket for couples with adjusted incomes of more than $100,000, and an increase from 7 percent to 8 percent in corporate income taxes. Our income taxes already were among the ten worst in America, and aggravating that burden will surely injure our ability to attract new investment. I know you'll work hard, but that kind of anti-business, sock-it-to-the-producer attitude will give you a steep hill to climb.

It also raises taxes on the sale of boats, airplanes, train cars, and farm and manufacturing machinery, as well as cigarettes, tobacco, alcohol, and soft drinks. Evidently, the House leadership is determined to prove they're no friend to business. Except for the sales tax, all the rest is designed to discourage business investment, and it plays right into the hands of our rival neighbor states.

The Senate plan is a little bit better.[6] It would raise the sales tax by one cent, increase the corporate income surtax for two years, doubles [sic] the conveyance tax, and increases [sic] taxes on insurance, cigarettes, and tobacco. That Senate package is designed to raise $611 million in the first year of the next biennium. That's $100 million less than the House, but even at that, it's higher than it needs to be. The good news is that the feared raid on the Highway Fund did not pass.

Now, I'm not afraid to raise taxes. You will well remember that, in my "State of the State" address, I recommended that the state withhold reimbursements to counties for the repeal of the intangibles and inventory taxes, and allow the counties to make up that $240 [million] revenue [loss] with a half-cent local-option sales tax. Indeed, your association endorsed that proposal—and I know as well as anyone that since my proposal for [a] 1/2-cent local sales tax, our revenue estimates have "headed south." So there's no doubt that a bigger tax increase was needed, but it also means we've got to cut spending even more. If we ask the people to give more of their hard-earned money to the state, we also have to prove that it's absolutely necessary by reducing spending. So I sent them back to the well, again and again.

I recommended a series of additional cuts to the General Assembly aimed at reducing the shortfall in the next fiscal year by as much as $313 million—on top of $375 million they had already agreed to cut.[7] About half of those extra cuts were accepted. The rest were rejected outright in subcommittee. I have identified at least $160 million in cuts that have been ignored by the House budget bill.

In addition, the legislature has appropriated another $80 million to increase premiums in the state health plan, a plan which is universally recognized as being one of the most generous in the nation. That's simply inexcusable. That employee hospitalization insurance benefit has gone out of control, ever since legislation stripped it out of the managerial control of the Executive Branch, so they could cut themselves coverage with a lifetime retirement benefit!

Add those together and it's clear the House package calls for a tax increase that is at least $240 million too high. And who pays for that excess spending? I do, and you do. We all pay, especially if business and industry stop coming to this state because our tax structure has made it cheaper to do business elsewhere.

On another dimension, a back-room strategic consideration has to do with whether the budget will be bipartisan or partisan. Clearly, the majority party has the votes, and the responsibility, to pass whatever it wants to. Just as clearly, they don't want to pass any package alone, of course. They want bipartisan support for a tax package so the Republicans can't hold it against them in the next election. That's why all of their editorial supporters are demanding that Republicans vote for it. Well, that is not going to happen unless they accept bipartisan input. The House bill is too partisan.

I've said repeatedly that I will help build Republican support for a tax package, only if a few very important changes are agreed to. First, they must reform the budget process, including passage of gubernatorial veto. We must find a way to agree on realistic budget estimates for the next fiscal year instead of pulling numbers out of a hat and inflating estimates to suit the whims of the General Assembly, like they did in 1989 when they irresponsibly padded and fabricated $350 million more revenue than could be justified. They just falsified revenue projections that much. That has to be stopped.

And future governors must have the power to veto unjust and poorly prepared budget legislation. If I had the veto two years ago, I would have used it to strike down the overinflated budget passed by the legislature that helped to slide us down the recession hole much farther and faster than was necessary. Budget reform is the only way to ensure that we don't get into this mess again in the future.

Second, the General Assembly must initiate serious education reforms so we get better value for our money. Over sixty-seven cents out of every dollar goes to fund some level of public education in our state; 46 percent is for public schools, K–12. Despite increased spending for education, an increase of almost $1.5 billion in the last six years, our test scores in reading, writing, math, and SAT's still rank at the bottom in the nation.

Spending on schools increased 50 percent, after adjusting for inflation. It's as if we just wasted it. We didn't get 50 percent improvement, did we? Not even 10 percent better results. It takes a microscope to find any improvement in student outcomes.

If we are going to keep spending that kind of money on education, we must reform the process to get what we pay for, and we pay for improved student performance. The way to do that is decentralize the system. It's not the teachers' fault—it's ours, for piling on excessive rules and regulations and eighty-two line items in the budget, with countless layers of limitations engineered by legislators who think they were elected to be another "Superboard of Education." It's ridiculous, and it's counterproductive. Most of the new money didn't go for instruction. It had to go for bureaucratic bloat, so somebody could fill out tons of reports on all those rules, regulations, and eighty-two line items in the budget.

American business is becoming competitive again by decentralizing decision making to the levels that deal with the customers and the products. In schools, the students are both the customers and the products. So let's transfer power to the local school buildings and teachers—and then hold them accountable for how well students do, not for how well teachers follow the rigid rules set for them by the bureaucracy in Raleigh.

So, if we're going to have to have a tax increase, I say let's first cut out another $240 million—go back to the well 'til it's dry—and then let's reform the budget process to make sure we don't have to raise taxes again in another year or two. And most important of all, let's reform education to make sure the overwhelming amount of money we pay for education buys a quality product.

Things are moving fast in Raleigh. These tax bills are being pushed through the legislature like lightning. The decisions legislators make now are going to affect the way you do business in the future.

How can you help? Call or write your legislators, today, and let them know you oppose unnecessary tax increases before all options for cutting spending have been exhausted. Let them know that you oppose all these antibusiness taxes that are going to make it difficult to attract new industry and business to this state. Let them know you support spending money for education, but only if you get what you pay for. And let them know that you support veto power for the governor, so there is some check on the overwhelming power of the legislature.

With your help, we may be able to curb the tide of spending in this state, improve our education, and preserve our economic standing in the nation. I can't do all this alone. I need your help the same way I've depended on you, in the past, to make North Carolina number one in investment.

The importance of working together for a common goal reminds me of a story I once heard about a sea captain and his chief engineer, who were arguing about who was most important to the ship. Failing to agree, they decided to swap places. The chief engineer ascended to the bridge, and the captain went below to the engine room. After a couple of hours, the captain suddenly appeared up on deck, covered with oil and soot.

"Chief," he yelled, wildly waving a monkey wrench. "You'll have to come down here! I can't make her go!"

"Of course you can't," the chief engineer yelled back. "We've run aground!"

Our cooperative partnership has kept us riding high in the past. We must continue to maintain and strengthen that partnership so that we won't run aground in the future. Thank you, once again, for all your hard work and commitment, and keep up the good work.

---

[1]The "Final Four" teams remaining in the National Collegiate Athletic Association men's basketball tournament were Duke University, the University of Kansas, the University of Nevada-Las Vegas, and the University of North Carolina. Duke won the national championship by defeating Kansas, 72–65. *Charlotte Observer*, March 31, April 2, 1991.

[2]Deborah S. Fusi, "South Atlantic, Florida Top Both 1990 and 1988–1990 Analysis of New Facilities Surge," *Site Selection and Industrial Development*, February 1991, 27, hereinafter cited as Fusi, "South Atlantic, Florida Top Both 1990 and 1988–1990 Analysis of New Facilities Surge."

[3]State Auditor Edward Renfrow warned that if Martin were unable to balance the budget by the close of the fiscal year, June 30, he would move to have him "prosecuted for failure to uphold his oath of office." Said Renfrow, "'If we wind up in a deficit, statutes say and the constitution says, that's unlawful. We take an oath not to do that.'" *Greensboro News and Record*, May 4, 1991.

[4]Standard and Poor's Corporation held a "'negative'" outlook on the state's bond rating despite the Triple-A designation. See *News and Observer*, May 17, 1991.

[5]H.B. 83, "A Bill to Be Entitled An Act to Make Base Budget and Expansion Budget Appropriations for Current Operations of State Departments, Institutions, and Agencies; to Make Appropriations for Capital Improvements for State Departments, Institutions, and Agencies; to Make Appropriations for Other Purposes; and to Provide Revenues for State and Local Needs" passed the House on June 7, 1991. *N.C. House Journal, 1991*, 822–823.

[6]The Senate version of H.B. 83 cleared the upper house on June 13, 1991. *N.C. Senate Journal, 1991*, 581–582.

[7]The governor unveiled two plans, totaling $313 million, to compensate for the state's fiscal 1991–1992 budget shortfall. On May 23, 1991, he suggested cuts of $276.4 million in nineteen areas, including reducing state contributions to the state employee retirement system, an early retirement program for teachers and state workers, eliminating 1,827 nonteaching positions, halting payment of sales taxes on state government purchases, and adjustments to the AFDC and Medicaid programs. A week later, Martin proposed a further $36.9 million in budget reductions and savings. He recommended collecting unpaid taxes, automating the state Revenue Department, cutting starting salaries of new state employees—except teachers—and reducing longevity payments to judicial and legislative employees to the level earned by other state workers. Press releases, "Governor Offers Legislators Additional Budget Options for 1991–1992," Raleigh, May 23, and "Governor Offers Additional Budget Options to Legislature," Raleigh, May 30, 1991, Governors Papers, James G. Martin.

PRESS CONFERENCE: NORTH CAROLINA SALUTE TO
THE TROOPS

RALEIGH, JUNE 14, 1991

Good morning, and thank you for joining us today for this update report on the North Carolina Salute to the Troops Celebration. All across our state, communities are rolling out the banners and bunting and putting the finishing touches on their plans to honor our military personnel, from North Carolina, who served in Operation Desert Storm—over 75,000—more than from any other state. Since I first proclaimed June 29 through July 4 as the North Carolina Salute to the Troops Celebration, 120 communities from Murphy to Manteo, Aberdeen to Zebulon, have made plans to unfurl the flag at picnics and parades with concerts, military displays, and fireworks. Without a doubt, this is going to be the biggest statewide welcome home celebration and outpouring of patriotic pride this state has ever seen.

Let me give you a few examples of some of the celebrations being planned:

—Fayetteville and Fort Bragg will host a week-long schedule of joint events, from June 30 to July 5, called, appropriately, Operation Celebration;

—Goldsboro and Seymour Johnson Air Force Base will hold a parade and fly-over on June 30, with other events scheduled on the Fourth;

—Jacksonville will hold its annual Freedom Festival on July 4 in honor of the Desert Storm troops;

—Greensboro will honor the troops at a special ceremony in conjunction with its annual Fun Fourth in Greensboro;

—and Charlotte-Mecklenburg's Salute to the Troops Celebration will be held in Marshall Park, followed by evening entertainment at both Blockbuster Pavilion and Memorial Auditorium.

—The kickoff for this statewide celebration begins right here in our capital city on Saturday, June 29, with the finest military parade of the century, followed by "A Night to Remember" at Carter-Findley Stadium.[1]

North Carolina's statewide Salute to the Troops Celebration is an opportunity for communities across this state, large and small, to let their pride and their patriotism shine. It's an opportunity for us to welcome home the troops from Operation Desert Storm, to say thanks, and to honor all the men and women who have served our state and our nation so well in the armed forces. Now to give you an overview of the kickoff festivities, I'd like to introduce Bob Butler, who serves as publicity chairman for the North Carolina Salute to the Troops.

[Butler presented overview.]

Thank you, Bob. Now I'd like to ask Peter Anlyan, executive director of the North Carolina Salute to the Troops, to join me in making a special presentation to our special guests here today: Brigadier General Bobby Webb,[2] with the North Carolina National Guard, and Colonel Bill Pendleton, garrison commander at Fort Bragg. I've said this North Carolina Salute to the Troops is designed to honor the men and women who served in Operation Desert Storm. Because this is a celebration for them, in their honor, we would like to present to you, and to the commanders of all our military bases in North Carolina, 15,000 complimentary tickets to the extravaganza at Carter-Findley Stadium on June 29. These tickets are to be used by the military and their families so that they can experience firsthand "A Night to Remember" in their honor.

[Martin invited Brigadier General Webb and Colonel Pendleton to make comments. He then asked Peter Anlyan to make announcements.]

---

[1]For a related press release, see "The Capitol City Prepares to Welcome Home the Troops," Raleigh, June 27, 1991, Governors Papers, James G. Martin.

[2]Bobby Gene Webb (1942-), native, resident of Rocky Mount; B.S., New York Regents College. Career with N.C. Army National Guard: enlisted service, 1961-1965; commissioned service, from July 22, 1965; was promoted to brigadier general, November 1, 1989, and became deputy adjutant general the same month; was appointed commanding general, Troop Command, September 1990. Civilian occupation: director, restaurant systems, Hardee's Food Systems, Inc., Rocky Mount. Bobby Gene Webb, letter to Jan-Michael Poff, May 27, 1994.

SALUTE TO THE TROOPS

GOLDSBORO, JUNE 30, 1991

It's a pleasure to be here this afternoon with the citizens of Goldsboro and the men and women of Seymour Johnson Air Force Base and their families. This is truly a great event, a community event, to thank the men and women of our armed forces who risk their lives in the service of our country.

Today we also commemorate the critical role that Seymour Johnson played in Operation Desert Storm. North Carolina was "First in Flight" at Kitty Hawk. Seymour Johnson and its pilots were first in all categories of aerial combat in Korea and ever since; and we were first, once again, in sending our F-15E Strike Eagles to defend Saudi Arabia and liberate Kuwait. The airmen of Seymour Johnson flew over 1,088 combat missions, and over 1,904 air-refueling missions, to lead the war effort and help destroy weapon facilities and other hard targets in the Gulf theater. Here at home we watched together, as sortie after sortie took off in the desert to search and destroy the air and armor[ed] forces of Saddam Hussein. The F-15E Strike Eagles were also instrumental in detecting and defeating Scud attacks. Thanks to the men and women here with us today, Kuwait is a liberated nation.[1]

While there is still unrest, and oppression, and bloodshed in the Middle East for the 3,000th year in a row, our valid military objectives were achieved: 1) to halt Iraq's million-man army from conquest and destruction of all the Arab oil-producing nations, 2) to forcibly remove Iraqi invaders from annexing Kuwait, since no lesser measure would succeed, and 3) to do that without micromanagement from Washington, so that our field, and air, and naval commanders could accomplish their mission with minimum allied casualties. It is for that, and your dominant role, that we, the people of North Carolina, salute you—not to glorify war, of course not; but to honor you—and thank you, for accepting a vital and dangerous responsibility and for excellence in carrying it out.

Meanwhile, North Carolinians everywhere united to help the families and dependents of our troops as they struggled and waited for the return of their loved ones. Operation Family Shield collected hundreds of thousands of dollars for financial assistance where it is most needed. Just as in the desert and over Iraq and Kuwait, we saw the stamina, skill, and strength of our American forces; here at home, we saw the grit, grace, and strength of our families. We saw the citizens of North Carolina draw a little closer, stand a little taller, and unite in prayer for all of those risking their lives.

As the war ended, here in Goldsboro we looked again to the skies. We watched, waited, and then welcomed home our loved ones—our neighbors, husbands, wives, sons, and daughters—all those who served in the war. They are with us today, and we salute them; and yet, each of us holds close to our hearts and in our prayers the 50,000 still overseas as part of the stabilizing force, and we remember also those in support services.

North Carolina honors all our troops this week, the quiet heroes of Desert Storm, in addition to all of the veterans of the United States Armed Forces. Throughout this week, culminating on America's Independence Day, July 4, North Carolina honors all who have served our nation in uniform. Let it never again happen that we send American troops into combat without officially and properly welcoming them home with recognition and applause.

Congratulations on a job well done. We are proud of you. God bless you!

[1]The F-15E Strike Eagle was a two-seat, dual-role attack and air-superiority fighter jet built by McDonnell Douglas Corp. The Fourth Tactical Fighter Wing, stationed at Seymour Johnson Air Force Base, Goldsboro, was the first unit to receive the aircraft. The initial delivery of F-15Es occurred December 29, 1988, and the air force declared the Fourth TFW operational in October 1989. Mark Lambert (ed.), *Jane's All the World's Aircraft, 1991–92* (Coulsdon: Jane's Information Group, 1991), 436.

One of the primary duties of the F-15E crews in mid-January 1991, as Operation Desert Storm unfolded, was the destruction of Iraqi Scud missile launchers. Scud was the NATO designation for the Soviet-designed SS-1 surface-to-surface missile. Baghdad initially purchased the weapons from the U.S.S.R. and North Korea, and used them in its war against Iran during the 1980s.

Scuds were never known for their accuracy, a characteristic Iraqi engineers further aggravated as they reworked the missiles to extend their range into Iran and Israel. Incapable of striking precise targets, the Scud nevertheless had the ability to incite terror when deployed against large population areas. It could deliver conventional payloads as well as nuclear and chemical warheads. The Iraqi threat of chemical warfare made the elimination of Scud launch sites a top priority among the allied air forces during Desert Storm. *New York Times*, January 20, 1991.

EDITORIAL OPPOSING ANTI-JOBS TAXES PROPOSED BY THE GENERAL ASSEMBLY

RALEIGH, JULY 1, 1991

[Democratic lawmakers supported a business tax increase as one means of compensating for the state's $1.2 billion revenue shortfall. In response, Governor Martin submitted an editorial to major newspapers in which he emphasized the deleterious effects such a measure would have upon the North Carolina economy. His column preceded, by two days, a brief but similar letter to members of a legislative conference committee who were attempting to reconcile the differences between the House and Senate budget bills. Despite Martin's arguments to the contrary, the General Assembly ratified budget legislation on July 13 that boosted corporate income taxes from 7 percent to 7.75 percent and also included a temporary surtax. *N.C. Session Laws, 1991*, II, c. 689, secs. 257–261; *News and Observer*, July 14, 1991; "Open Letter to Finance and Appropriations Conferees," attached to press release, "Governor Urges Budget Negotiators to Hold the Line on Permanent Corporate and Personal Income Taxes," Raleigh, July 3, 1991, Governors Papers, James G. Martin.]

A few liberal legislators and editors have convinced the partisan majority in the North Carolina General Assembly that businesses don't pay enough state taxes, and that this recession is a good time to take a heavy axe to business profitability. They fail to see that business provides most of the jobs and all of the economic growth in our state. Any tax that makes it more costly to do business in North Carolina compared to other states is a tax on jobs.

The budget bills passed by the House and Senate have yet to be merged by the conference committee, but both include increases that will make North Carolina businesses face one of the heaviest tax burdens in America, and easily the heaviest in the Southeast. That is a dangerous prospect for North Carolina and for the 3.5 million people who work in our state. As soon as our neighboring states get out the word that North Carolina has decided to tax business income far more heavily than our rivals, our seven years of national leadership in economic development will come to a screeching halt.

Editorialists like to point out that in the past, site selection for new investment did not rank taxes as a major factor for choosing North Carolina. That was true only in comparison with other low-tax states that made the final cut with us. They overlook the fact that higher taxes would have been a factor in eliminating other states from consideration, a factor that will now injure us. We will no longer be among the finalists for billions of dollars of investment.

They are also trying to build revenue largess into future budgets, so that future sessions will have money to burn on a multibillion-dollar wish list. That is why this year's budget has over $200 million in excess spending that could be cut out now, and deferred for another time, but is being left in to help "justify" excessive tax increases. Tax-hungry legislators are making the same false assumption they made in 1989: that large tax increases will not change the way companies do business. But of course they will, just as heavier taxes on cars, fuel, businesses, and upper-income individuals levied in 1989 have already changed the face of business activity in North Carolina.

The lesson is clear: When word gets out that North Carolina has the most costly tax burden in the otherwise attractive southeastern United States, business interest in our state will fade, and existing businesses will be forced to look elsewhere for survival. Passage of permanently higher taxes on business means that business growth will flatten out. That will mean that revenue growth will flatten out. That, in turn, will mean that we will have no way to pay for improved education financing. Then the same legislators who prefer higher taxes in this recession will be looking for even higher taxes to make up for future economic stagnation caused by high taxes in the first place. That will only aggravate the same problem we face today.

The solution is to turn back before it's too late. If legislators have the will to make the hard decisions, enough spending can still be cut from the state budget to avoid antibusiness, antijobs taxes. It would be far better for us to wait until the recession is over, and spend revenue growth as it comes, rather than to impose excessive tax burdens that will prevent revenue growth for years to come.

PRESS CONFERENCE: 1990 INFANT MORTALITY STATISTICS

RALEIGH, JULY 11, 1991

I've got some good news to report on an issue that many of your news organizations have been following for some time. I am pleased to announce that, for the second year in a row, the rate of infant mortality in North Carolina has declined.

Most of you will remember the shock and frustration we felt a couple of years ago when we learned that our state's infant mortality rate for 1988, at 12.6 deaths per 1,000 live births, was the highest in the country. As discouraging as that news was, it served as a rallying cry to gather the private, corporate, legislative, and government resources necessary to reduce infant mortality.

According to statistics compiled by our state Center for Health and Environmental Statistics, our joint efforts lowered the 1988 rate of 12.6 to a rate of 10.6 for 1990, the lowest rate of infant death ever attained in North Carolina.[1] While the death of any baby is tragic, we are encouraged by these statistics and take some pride in knowing that we are definitely improving the odds of infant survival in our state. Also encouraging is the fact that the 1990 infant mortality rate has improved for both whites and nonwhites. The most dramatic decline has been experienced by nonwhites. Yet despite our overall improvement, the nonwhite rate of infant death remains twice as high as that experienced by the white population, but we are making progress.

The great improvement we have made since 1988 is surely the direct result of several vital programs such as the Baby Love Program, begun in 1987; the First Step campaign, begun in May 1990; the WIC [Women, Infants, Children] program; and the Rural Obstetrical Care Incentive Program. The success of these programs are [sic] outlined in your fact sheet.[2]

In December 1989, I established a Commission on the Reduction of Infant Mortality which brought together leaders of businesses, churches, schools, volunteer agencies, and health professions to stimulate community action to reduce infant death. The commission established the Healthy Start Foundation to provide private grants to communities, educated policy makers and the public about the problem of infant mortality, and encouraged the development of local task forces on infant mortality.

Many of these initiatives would not have been possible without strong bipartisan support of the General Assembly. The legislature is to be commended for the plan to reduce infant mortality developed during its

1990 session. Its full funding enabled the expansion of initiatives I've already mentioned and added new efforts, as well.

During these years and into 1991, North Carolina's commitment to this issue has continued to grow. Private foundations such as the Kate B. Reynolds Trust and the March of Dimes, together with funds from state and federal sources, are supporting many special projects at the community level. Many of these local and statewide activities have been recognized nationally as model programs.

Joining me today are a few of the people who have made these efforts and programs work. Many of you will recognize Dr. Stuart Bondurant, chairman of the Commission on Reduction of Infant Mortality, and the commission's director, Walter Shepherd.[3] I've asked Dr. Bondurant to make a few comments, but before he does, I would also like to recognize and give special thanks to Ann Wolfe, director of the Division of Maternal and Child Health, and Barbara Matula, director of the Division of Medical Assistance.[4] These folks and their staffs have worked long and hard, for many years, to reach such a milestone, and they were doing it long before infant mortality received the special attention it does today. They've been working in the trenches, and they deserve much of the credit. Thank you; I'm glad you could be here with us today. Now I'd like to ask Dr. Bondurant to step forward for a few remarks.

---

[1]The state's infant mortality rate for 1989 stood at 11.5 deaths per 1,000 live births; see press release, "North Carolina's Infant Mortality Rate Reaches Record Low for 1989," Raleigh, July 12, 1990, Governors Papers, James G. Martin. A statistical breakdown of infant deaths by region and county, between 1986 and 1990, accompanied the press release "North Carolina Infant Morality Rate Drops to Lowest Level in State History," Raleigh, July 11, 1991, Governors Papers, James G. Martin.

[2]Fact sheet attached to press release, "North Carolina Infant Morality Rate Drops to Lowest Level in State History," Raleigh, July 11, 1991, Governors Papers, James G. Martin.

[3]Stuart Bondurant (1929–), born in Winston-Salem; resident of Chapel Hill; B.S., 1952, M.D., 1953, Duke University School of Medicine; U.S. Air Force, 1956–1958. Assistant professor, 1959–1961, associate professor, 1961–1966, professor of medicine, 1966–1967, Indiana University School of Medicine; associate director, Cardiovascular Research Center, Indiana University Medical Center, 1961–1967; Medical Branch chief, Artificial Heart-Myocardial Infarction Program, National Heart Institute, National Institutes of Health, 1966–1967; professor and chairman, Department of Medicine, 1967–1974, president, dean, 1974–1979, Albany Medical College; physician-in-chief, Albany Medical Center Hospital, 1967–1974; dean, professor of medicine, University of North Carolina School of Medicine, since 1979; appointed chairman, 1989, reappointed 1992, Governor's Commission on Reduction of Infant Mortality. Stuart Bondurant, letter to Jan-Michael Poff, September 28, 1993.

Until his appointment in 1990 as executive director of the Governor's Commission on Reduction of Infant Mortality, Walter L. Shepherd was assistant dean of the East Carolina University School of Medicine. *News and Observer*, June 26, 1990.

[4]Ann F. Wolfe (1935–), born in Hazleton, Pa.; resident of Raleigh; B.S., Bucknell University, 1957; M.D., Temple University, 1961; M.P.H., University of California-Berkley, 1968. Served with Division of Health Services, state Department of Human Resources, as supervisor, Clinical Management Unit, Developmental Disabilities Branch, 1981–1987, and chief,

Maternal and Child Care Section, 1987–1989; director, Division of Maternal and Child Health, state Department of Environment, Health, and Natural Resources, since 1989. Ann F. Wolfe, letter to Jan-Michael Poff, October 5, 1993.

Barbara D. Matula (1942–), born in Hazleton, Pa.; resident of Raleigh; B.A., Rider College, 1963; M.P.A., State University of New York at Albany, 1969. Employed by state of New York, 1969–1974, as member, New York Assembly Standing Committee staff, and of Governor's Budget Office, Legislative Relations; budget-policy analyst, N.C. Office of State Budget, 1974–1978; deputy director, 1978, director, since 1979, Division of Medical Assistance, N.C. Department of Human Resources. Sarah Long, administrative assistant to Barbara D. Matula, letter to Jan-Michael Poff, September 22, 1993.

FORTIETH SOUTHERN POLICE INSTITUTE

GREENSBORO, AUGUST 2, 1991

Thank you, Chief (Sylvester) Daughtry,[1] and welcome to the great state of North Carolina. It's a pleasure to have you here with us. I expect your presence here probably makes this hotel[2] the safest place to be in the state—about as safe as the perimeter just outside a prison complex!

As a former professor, I am especially pleased to spend some time with a group of people who seized the opportunity to further their professional knowledge through the Southern Police Institute's top-notch retraining program. By coming here, you've committed to not only continue your own professional education, but also to uphold the institute's high standards so that your colleagues can receive the same high-quality education as they rise to leadership roles in law enforcement agencies across the country.

Looking at your agenda, it is obvious that you are on top of things. You are addressing issues that are certainly timely and vitally important to your profession and the citizens we serve. Issues like use of force, drug-induced violence, equal employment opportunities, and the complex problems associated with culturally diverse jurisdictions will continue to demand your attention. But you're not the only ones interested in these issues: Across the country, the executive, legislative, and judicial branches of governments at all levels will continue to be involved in these issues, as well.

You're here to learn and to take the expertise you gain here back home to your agencies, but I hope you'll go one step farther and take a leadership role in sharing your knowledge with leaders in other branches of government who are making decisions on issues that affect you. I don't suggest that any professional, especially a public law enforcement official, should use their position to be "political" in the negative sense of the word, but I do strongly encourage you to involve your associations, or your departments, in the political process concerning the laws we ask you to enforce and the limitations you are expected to abide by in waging your fight on the front lines. We seek doctors' opinions on medical issues and farmers' opinions on agricultural issues; in the same way, decision makers need to hear the law enforcement community's opinions on criminal justice issues, and your input should receive equal time with criminal defense lawyers who never refrain from putting in their two cents' worth.

To give you a good example of how law enforcement officials can and should be involved in public policy, I'd like to tell you about our efforts last year to ease overcrowding in North Carolina's prison system. In 1989, I proposed a bond referendum that would have expanded our prison system by 10,000 inmates. We based our proposal on the fact that North Carolina's crime rate had been increasing at three times the national average over the previous four years.

We also knew that the time served by inmates, as a percent of sentence, had begun to fall very steeply. Through 1985, the average time served was about 40 percent of sentence, mainly because of about 60 percent time off for relatively good behavior—good time and gain time. By 1989 it had fallen to only 14 percent for misdemeanants and, far more troublesome, to only 29 percent for the average felon. The reason was fairly obvious: The steady trend of rising criminal activity had not been matched by expanding prison capacity. Oh, we had built more prison space, just to keep the 18,000 prison population from being lopped off by the federal courts.

The 10,000-bed expansion, to take us up to 28,000 capacity, was the minimum we felt we needed to maintain the integrity of our punishment system. Our aim was to make sure that criminals being caught by the law enforcement agencies in our state would be sufficiently punished and not find their way back into the prison system once they were released.

Now 10,000 prison beds translate into a lot of money: about $400 million worth. To get that money, we had to convince the legislature to finance the project with bonds and to let the people decide, through a statewide referendum, whether or not to spend that money on prisons. We believed protecting the public safety was a nonpartisan issue, so we sought nonpartisan support for our proposal. We sought that support among law enforcement officers, judicial officials, correction experts, and even lawyers. We also established a special bipartisan study commission with members from these fields as well as legislators and private citizens. That study commission held a series of public hearings across the state and eventually endorsed our plan—and even suggested we build an additional 2,000 beds.[3]

Among the most important groups supporting our effort were the

Association of Chiefs of Police and the North Carolina Sheriffs Association, two of the major police associations in our state. We did not get much help from the criminal defense lawyers, who were joined by our own attorney general in petitioning for more "alternative sentences"—even though our experience has been that alternative sentences are worthless without adequate prison space to back up the discipline of special parole and probation. No parolee pays much attention to rules, or curfews, or off-limits, or community service when they know we don't have prison space to lock them up for more than a few weeks. They're too busy stealing to worry about idle threats and sermons.

I admire those who rose above the politics involved and supported the proposal they knew was right. Their help was probably one of the main reasons we were able to work out a compromise package with the legislature that provided for an additional 6,500 beds. That support from law enforcement associations also proved invaluable in passing our statewide referendum last November. I'm proud of the fact that North Carolina was the only state in the nation to pass a prison bond referendum last year. The sheriffs' association's effort was a prime example of how important and valuable the law enforcement community's input can be, along with the personal effort of Supreme Court Justice Burley Mitchell, who chaired our study commission; but more work needs to be done, work that will never be completed without your continuing support and that of other law enforcement personnel.

Two years ago, I established the North Carolina Drug Cabinet, led by Lieutenant Governor Jim Gardner, to coordinate our state's anti-drug abuse efforts. The drug cabinet sponsored twenty-one bills in the legislature to strengthen enforcement and improve prevention, treatment, and education efforts. One of those bills required mandatory sentences for using a handgun while committing a drug offense. That vital bill was buried in committee.

Another bill would have made it a penalty for drug dealers to fortify their houses and set booby traps to protect their operations and put your officers in danger. That bill was also buried in committee.[4] A great legislative year for the "rights" of drug dealers, and so it went for nineteen other good bills as well. All of the bills were locked up.

Two years ago we introduced legislation calling for mandatory twenty-eight-year sentences for drug dealers who ply their trade on school grounds. Our version called for no early release under any circumstances. Yes that's a harsh penalty, but it's certainly appropriate because availability of drugs on school grounds undermines our preventive efforts—including the highly successful DARE program some of you may be involved in.

Well, the civil libertarians in the General Assembly took our bill, chewed it up, and passed legislation mandating two-year sentences—that's right, two years.[5] Take 29 percent of that! That's only seven months active.

While the law enforcement community did lobby somewhat for passage of these bills, a lot more pressure might have made a difference. So, I'll call on you again in the 1992 session, next May.

That's a problem we face in North Carolina. I'm sure you face the same problem in your home states and communities.

In my twenty-five years in various elective offices, I have taken pride in listening to competent, appropriate, expert voices on a variety of issues that needed an insider's view. Obviously, some opinions stuck with me more than others, but it always helped to examine all sides of the issue. I like to think all elected officials feel the same, but if you don't speak, they can't hear you. Sometimes the key to making them listen is having the right approach, but finding the right approach isn't always easy when you're dealing with legislators who are motivated by special interests, many of whom are lawyers and who have a self-interest in maintaining the status quo.

The safety of our families and our communities should not be a partisan political issue. If we are serious about curbing the rising tide of crime, we have to be serious about supporting concrete reforms in the system. We have to be serious about supporting you, and you have to make your voice heard above the cries of special interest groups who don't have your best interests as law enforcement officers at heart.

Our law enforcement officers deserve our praise and our support. The law enforcement community has continued to grow, and improve, and has risen to every challenge, including dealing with the recent surge in the drug problem in the United States. Without a doubt, you are working hard to win the war against drugs, and you are risking yourselves in the process.

I especially want to salute the members of North Carolina's police, and sheriffs, and state law enforcement departments represented here, because we Tar Heels have a lot to be proud of. From the southwest corner of the state, including the Blue Ridge Mountains, to the Outer Banks and Cape Hatteras on the Atlantic Ocean, North Carolina is blessed with top-notch law enforcement agencies. The best ones have something in common: They send their officers to the Southern Police Institute.

I hope you enjoy your visit to North Carolina. You are always welcome here. Keep up the good work.

---

[1]Sylvester Daughtry, Jr. (1945–), B.S., North Carolina A&T State University, 1973; was graduated from four law enforcement programs, including FBI National Academy. Greens-

boro policeman since 1968, promoted through ranks to assistant chief-Field Operations Bureau commander, 1983, and appointed chief of police, 1987; vice-president, International Assn. of Chiefs of Police; past president, North State Law Enforcement Officers Assn. Sylvester Daughtry, Jr., letter to Jan-Michael Poff, June 30, 1993.

[2]Holiday Inn Four Seasons, Greensboro.

[3]The governor was referring to the Advisory Board on Prisons and Punishment.

[4]The General Assembly ultimately ratified, on July 24, 1992, "An Act to Increase the Punishment to a Felony for Fortification of a Structure Used for Illegal Controlled Substance Activity for the Purpose of Impeding Law Enforcement Entry." *N.C. Session Laws, Extra Session, 1991, Regular Session, 1992*, III, c. 1041. Martin credited the N.C. Drug Cabinet with the law's adoption; see press release, "Governor Praises Gardner, Drug Cabinet Accomplishments," Charlotte, October 17, 1992, Governors Papers, James G. Martin.

[5]"An Act to Provide that it is a Felony Offense for a Person Eighteen Years of Age or Older to Employ a Minor to Commit a Drug Violation, to Provide that a Person Twenty-one Years of Age or Older Who Hires a Minor to Commit a Drug Violation is Civilly Liable for Damages for Drug Addiction Proximately Caused by the Violation, to Increase the Sentence for the Illegal Sale or Delivery of Drugs to a Minor or a Pregnant Woman, and to Provide that a Person Twenty-one Years of Age or Older Who Commits a Drug Offense on School Property or Within 300 Feet of the Boundary of a School is Guilty of a Class E Felony," *N.C. Session Laws, 1989, Extra and Regular Sessions, 1990*, c. 1081, ratified July 28, 1990.

AIR CARGO MEETING

CHAPEL HILL, AUGUST 22, 1991

Thank you, Jack. I often wonder what it would be like if we could just get Dr. Kasarda to be somewhat enthusiastic about this project. Your attendance here, today, assures me that there are many who find this concept exciting.

Throughout American history, North Carolina and its people have defined the frontiers of our national growth. We had the first attempted English settlement. We took the first steps in conquering the frontier of education by establishing the nation's first state university system. We conquered the frontier of commerce by establishing rail transportation in the state, and we discovered the frontier of air travel with the Wright brothers' miracle of flight at Kitty Hawk. We pioneered the concept of an industrial park devoted to research facilities, all integrated with our research universities, first at Research Triangle Park. Two years ago, we committed to build a 3,000-mile network of four-lane intrastate highways which, when completed, will reach within ten miles of 96 percent of our population, tying us together as one truly united state. Our enterprising spirit as a state has not changed. Now we are preparing to conquer the frontier of what Jack Kasarda has called the "fifth wave" of economic development through the global air cargo industrial complex.

When test pilots talk about courage, they talk about "pushing the outside of the envelope." These pilots have mastered the science of flight.

They know their aircraft as well as you and I know our family car, but based on what they know, they push beyond what they know. They forge ahead into new territory.

By moving forward with plans and preparation for building a global air cargo industrial complex in North Carolina, we, too, are pushing the outside of the envelope. Like test pilots who have mastered the science of flight, we are becoming masters of the science of economic development, and now we are ready to move forward into new, uncharted territory.

We are not forging ahead blindly. When I first announced plans for this complex last February, I also announced we had retained Transportation Management Group, Incorporated, of Raleigh, to perform a feasibility study on the project. The departments of Economic and Community Development and Transportation have also been very involved in the effort to explore this project and get it moving. Secretary Estell Lee,[1] and Secretary Tommy Harrelson, and their people have been working very hard on this.

Right now we're learning as much as we can about air cargo, its current levels and capacity, and its potential for the future. We're learning about the movement of goods to and from North Carolina, the Mid-Atlantic region, the U.S., and global, international markets. Once the feasibility study is completed, sometime early next year, if it is as positive as we hope, we'll put that education to use. Through the Air Cargo Airport Authority, we'll lead the way in devising creative solutions to challenges facing this project.

Make no mistake. Other states know we've got a good thing going here in North Carolina, and they're interested in competing for this prize. Florida, South Carolina, Virginia, and a number of other states are looking at their own prospects for siting similar projects. There may or may not be room for more than one air cargo complex on the East Coast, but once the first complex is in place, it will dominate the air cargo market.

We have the talent and expertise to lead the world on a project of this type. We have impressive resources, but we can't let up. We must not become discouraged and stop working when we run up against a few roadblocks. Too many others are traveling behind, trying to overtake us.

We will be competing with other states for anchor tenants and possible FAA [Federal Aviation Administration] dollars, but we'll also be competing with ourselves. Right now we're in the lead, but our biggest competitor is time and our own commitment to move ahead with the project. Unless and until we reach a negative conclusion, unless we decide it can't be done, then we must continue to be first and retain the first-mover's advantage.

Let me bring you up to date on what we have been able to accomplish in a very short time. On May 15, we received the preliminary feasibility study from Transportation Management Group. It was a solid report, cautiously optimistic, yet realistic in its preliminary assessments. The report's conclusion? A global air cargo industrial complex will be built somewhere, by someone who is willing to take the initiative to build it, and it promises great rewards.

On the basis of that preliminary study and several briefings by staff, the General Assembly put its support behind the project. Thanks to the leadership of Senate Pro Tempore Henson Barnes, House Speaker Dan Blue, Lieutenant Governor Jim Gardner and several others, the legislature approved the creation of the Air Cargo Airport Authority and appropriated $6 million over two years to get it off the ground and allocated up to $25 million in escheat funds so we can acquire land and options. Note that's not enough to build it if it won't work; it is enough to catalyze it if it will work.[2]

Now, of course, everyone wants to know where the global air cargo industrial complex will be located. I'd like to know, too, but it will be up to the authority to develop site criteria, with guidance from the FAA and public input, and then choose the final site for the project. It will also be up to the authority to decide exactly how big the airport will be in terms of acreage or facilities. Once the site has been determined, the authority will work together with municipalities and local groups to make this complex a responsible member of the community.

As you may have seen from recent news accounts, I have announced my seven appointments to the authority. Some of those individuals are here with us today. For those of you who don't already know, I will serve as chairman of the authority. That will serve, Senator Henson Barnes has observed, to convince the FAA, and I have also appointed Lieutenant Governor Jim Gardner as a member to balance the authority's statewide representation, east and west. My other appointees are: former U.S. senator and former secretary of the North Carolina Department of Economic and Community Development Jim Broyhill; Dr. Malcolm Gillis, dean of the Faculty of Arts and Sciences at Duke University; Rusty Goode,[3] president of University Research Park; Bill Prestage,[4] president and owner of Prestage Farms; and Dr. Paul Rizzo, dean of the Kenan-Flagler Business School at the University of North Carolina at Chapel Hill.

We expect the authority will meet at least two or three times by the end of this year. The first meeting will be organizational. I expect the second will address preliminary site criteria. The authority will be housed in the Department of Transportation, with staff initially provided by that department until a permanent staff can be hired.

It was previously announced that I have asked board member Rusty Goode to serve as interim executive director, and I will recommend him to the board of directors at its first meeting. Rusty is already volunteering his time in this capacity so that the initial organizing effort will have strong direction.

The North Carolina Department of Economic and Community Development will spearhead the industrial recruiting and marketing aspects of the project. They have already developed a marketing plan. To help them in that effort, ECD is using its special $400,000 legislative appropriation, designated for marketing, to develop informational materials and brochures like the one you have in your packets.[5]

The Department of Economic and Community Development also serves as the contact agency for local groups interested in siting the project in their area, and is also in the process of recruiting air cargo industrial tenants: manufacturing, distribution, governmental, and air freight hubs. Our developers have already begun calling on air cargo companies and industries internationally to interest them in the project. As you would expect, I'm taking part in several of those calls myself.

We've found a good number of people in our state already support this project. Residents in small municipalities and urban centers, local business and industrial groups, civic organizations and local officials, and all of you here today have shown great interest in the complex. So far, some interest has been expressed by officials and others in no less than thirty-five counties, many of them aligning in coalitions to promote their attractiveness.

You reaffirm the high hopes we have for this complex. Discussions like those we have here today could have a profound impact on North Carolina's future. We will also need to listen carefully to the reasoning and evidence presented by those who may oppose it, or think it can't be done, or who want it with qualified limitations. I believe the global air cargo industrial complex can have the kind of impact for North Carolina that the Research Triangle Park has had, and more. I know that's saying a lot.

The park has received worldwide recognition. Its economic impact in the Raleigh-Durham-Chapel Hill area has been enormous, with a positive ripple effect across the state. I don't know exactly what the small group of men and women who launched the park felt as they made plans for what was then an undeveloped area, but I'm sure they believed as strongly as I do that their concept would one day bring great benefits to North Carolina. They were right: It was just a matter of time until the Research Triangle Park blossomed into the local and international success story it is today.

Many resources are available to help make this complex work. We have the interest, support, and talent of residents like you. We have the manpower resources and the brainpower. We have the universities and our community colleges. We have an existing and planned transportation infrastructure that will perfectly accommodate the air cargo complex, including two major air passenger hubs, two seaports, and rails and highways in place and yet to be built.

We have the political will. We have uniquely strong banking and utility assets, and we have a positive sociopolitical climate for manufacturing and distribution. Best of all, we have the workforce, trainable and ready to work, and we have everything to gain. We have a bright economic future that can provide for generations of North Carolinians.

We have at stake a leading role in tomorrow's global economy. We have a project here that could bring to our state about 56,000 new jobs and $2.8 billion a year in production increases, according to estimates by our consultants. That's a lot to consider as the board of the Airport Authority takes up its responsibilities.

As I see it at this point, the board will have strategic decisions to make. The first and most crucial is to decide if the evidence is convincing that the project is feasible. Can it succeed, and do we have the ability to do it? All I have seen and heard I have expressed very positively in my opening remarks, but the board must review everything and reach its own judgment: Go? or don't go? We may spend $6 million to find out, but before much more is invested in land and improvements, a shared judgment must be reached that there is more than vision and enthusiasm.

While weighing that fundamental question, the board will prepare to make the next most crucial decision about criteria for site selection. The FAA will provide a lot of guidance, since they have major responsibility and power in this project. Consideration will be given as to how this project can benefit less-developed areas of North Carolina, but at the same time, whether assets in those areas can enhance the attractiveness of the related industrial park for prospective business executives, their engineers, and professional staffs.

The criteria will probably include the relative strength of existing and planned highways, rails, waste treatment and water supply, community colleges, land-use attitudes, and their proximity to larger residential and market centers. It will also take into account terrain, and soil, and ground water characteristics that our marvelous Geographic Information System will help us to map out. The recent change in federal wetlands definitions will probably open up many counties which otherwise would have been totally excluded by the old definition, but we must consider that and the value of other ecological resources. As soon as these criteria are in hand and under discussion, we will make every effort to publish and circulate them so that timely comment can be received, for or against various criteria, before the board decides.

Next, the board must arrange to receive proposals from individuals and local officials, including groups of counties. We will ask them to rate their strengths and weaknesses in accordance with the site selection criteria. We will expect them to undertake to privately contact and persuade major landowners to offer a land package at a reasonable price. We will expect to negotiate the willingness of groups of counties to serve as a "special taxing district" for the purposes of bond financing. And then the board will choose the site.

Along the way, the board will consider how to build the facility and finance it with maximum private participation. We will consider how best to combine and separate the functions of managing the airport and promoting development of the surrounding industrial park. One suggestion is to create a 501(c)6 nonprofit organization to run and develop the industrial park, as is done both at the Research Triangle and Charlotte's University Research Park. Whether the airport itself is operated by the authority, or by a contract with an experienced airport management company, will have to be determined and may depend on whether a major landowner prefers to take that responsibility, as is the case with Ross Perot's Alliance Airport, in Texas.[6]

There is so much to be done. Are we visionaries? I hope so. Visionaries look at today and plan for what tomorrow will bring. The visionary concept of a global air cargo complex we initiate today will fulfill tomorrow's economic needs and sharpen our perspective for the future.

Are we also practical? I hope so. Only through practical analysis and decisions can we make it work. Otherwise, all we have is a field of dreams. With your support, we can make today's dreams tomorrow's realities.

---

[1]Estell Carter Lee (1935–), born in Loris, S.C.; resident of Wilmington; A.A., Wilmington College (later University of North Carolina at Wilmington), 1955. Various managerial positions with Almont Shipping Co., 1969–1990, including president, 1980; president, chairwoman, Seacor, Inc., holding and management firm, and of The Lee Co., specializing in retail sale of doors, windows, and building trusses; first woman to hold post of secretary, N.C. Dept. of Economic and Community Development, appointed 1991; vice-chairwoman, New Hanover Republican Party. *North Carolina Manual, 1991–1992*, 156–157; press release, "Governor Martin Names Estell Lee Secretary of Economic and Community Development," Raleigh, April 4, 1991, Governors Papers, James G. Martin.

[2]"An Act to Create the North Carolina Air Cargo Airport Authority, to Authorize the Issuance of Revenue Bonds to Finance Airport and Industrial Facilities, to Authorize Units of Local Government to Take Certain Actions Related to Cargo Airport Complexes, and to

Make Conforming Changes to Other Statutes" was adopted July 16, 1991. *N.C. Session Laws, 1991*, II, c. 749. Section 8 of that law allocated the escheat funds; the $6 million appropriation was awarded under *N.C. Session Laws, 1991*, II, c. 689, s. 183.

[3]Seddon (Rusty) Goode, Jr. (1932–), president, director, University Research Park, since 1981; president, director, N.C. Global TransPark Authority, since 1991. Previously identified in Poff, *Addresses of Martin*, I, 167n; see also Martha Borden, N.C. Global TransPark Authority, letter to Jan-Michael Poff, September 23, 1994.

[4]William H. Prestage (1935–), born in Kalamazoo, Mich.; resident of Clinton. Former regional sales manager, Central Soya Co.; held 50 percent ownership in Carroll's Foods, Inc., 1967–1983, pork and poultry producer located between Clinton and Warsaw; president, National Turkey Federation, 1982; founder, 1983, Prestage Farms, in Sampson County, one of America's largest commercial pork and poultry producers; winner, Industrial Conservationist Award, N.C. Soil and Water Conservation Society, 1988; board member, Clinton-Sampson Airport Authority. William H. Prestage, letter to Jan–Michael Poff, November 10, 1993.

[5]*N.C. Session Laws, 1991*, II, c. 689, s. 210.2.

[6]The Alliance Airport, Fort Worth, was an all-cargo facility backed by the family of Texas financier H. Ross Perot. Completed in 1988, it had been unable to attract any airfreight carriers away from existing passenger airports by late 1992. *News and Observer*, December 6, 1992, reprint of *Wall Street* (N.Y.) *Journal* article.

PRESS RELEASE: GOVERNOR LIFTS HIRING FREEZE, DIRECTS CREATION OF RESERVE FUND

RALEIGH, SEPTEMBER 5, 1991

Governor Jim Martin today announced that he has lifted the hiring freeze on state government positions that had been in effect since January 9, 1991. The governor has also directed department heads to manage vacancies within their agencies as part of an effort to establish a $150 million reserve fund in the state budget.

"It's critical that we establish a reserve fund that can be used to offset future revenue shortfalls or a natural disaster that requires emergency assistance," Martin said.

"We used up almost all of our available funding options managing last year's budget crisis," Martin said. "Lifting the hiring freeze will enable us to fill much-needed positions while also helping to create a contingency fund as insurance against the unexpected."

Governor Martin had requested that the legislature establish a $165 million rainy-day fund in his 1991–1993 biennial budget, but only $400,000 was approved.[1] The state's $141 million rainy-day fund established in fiscal year 1990–1991 was used in combination with other options to offset last year's budget shortfall of $729 million.

---

[1]*N.C. Session Laws, 1991*, II, c. 689, s. 346, established the savings reserve account; s. 182 authorized the $400,000 appropriation.

PRESS RELEASE: GOVERNOR ISSUES JUDGES EIGHT-YEAR
COMMISSIONS

Raleigh, September 9, 1991

Governor Jim Martin today announced that he will issue eight-year judicial commissions for six judges currently serving on both the North Carolina Court of Appeals and Superior Court. Judges on the Court of Appeals receiving commissions are: Jack Cozort; John B. Lewis, Jr.; Robert F. Orr; and James A. Wynn. W. Russell Duke, Jr., and Quentin T. Sumner, both judges on the North Carolina Superior Court, will also receive eight-year commissions. Each of these judges was either elected to a position they had previously been appointed to, or won election to a position previously held by an appointed judge.[1]

The six judges requested the commissions from Governor Martin in April of this year, stating that judges who are elected to office following appointment to fill a vacancy are elected to an eight-year term as provided for in the North Carolina Constitution. The North Carolina General Statutes provide that judges who win election to office following an appointment to fill a vacancy are elected to the unexpired portion of the vacating judge's term.[2]

"In late June of this year, on the advice of my general [counsel],[3] I requested an advisory opinion from the North Carolina Supreme Court on this subject," Governor Martin said. "In August, the court declined to render an opinion.[4]

"After much deliberation, I have concluded that these judges were elected to eight-year terms," the governor continued. "Terms of constitutional offices are determined by the North Carolina Constitution, not the General Statutes. Our constitution also sets terms for judges, not judgeships."

The two provisions of the North Carolina Constitution reviewed by Governor Martin are Article IV, Section 16, and Article IV, Section 19. Article IV, Section 16 provides that "judges" of the Court of Appeals and "regular judges" of the Superior Court are elected for eight-year terms. The constitution refers to "judges," not "judgeships," and provides for eight-year terms after elections to office. It does not provide for elections for the remainder of unexpired terms. Article IV, Section 19 of the North Carolina Constitution provides that judges who are appointed to fill vacancies serve until the next election at which time they are to run for election to the office.

The commissions for each of the six judges will extend for eight years from the date that they became certified to take office by the state Board of Elections. Those dates are:

Court of Appeals

Jack L. Cozort, term begins November 25, 1986, ends November 24, 1994;

John B. Lewis, Jr., term begins November 29, 1988, ends November 28, 1996;

Robert F. Orr, term begins November 29, 1988, ends November 28, 1996;

James A. Wynn, Jr., term begins November 27, 1990, term ends November 26, 1998.

Superior Court

W. Russell Duke, Jr., term begins November 27, 1990, ends November 26, 1998;

Quentin T. Sumner, term begins November 27, 1990, ends November 26, 1998.

---

[1]Jack Lowell Cozort (1950–), born in Valdese; B.A., North Carolina State University, 1972; J.D., Wake Forest University, 1975. Associate attorney general, N.C. Dept. of Justice, 1975–1977; legal counsel to Governor James B. Hunt, Jr., 1977–1985; judge, state Court of Appeals, since 1985. *North Carolina Manual, 1991–1992,* 486.

John Baker Lewis, Jr. (1936–), born in Farmville; A.B., 1958, LL.B., 1961, University of North Carolina at Chapel Hill; U.S. Navy, 1961–1966, and Reserve, since 1966; military judge. Special Superior Court judge, 1982–1988; elected judge, state Court of Appeals, 1988. *North Carolina Manual, 1991–1992,* 489.

James Andrew Wynn, Jr. (1954–), born in Robersonville; B.A., University of North Carolina at Chapel Hill, 1975; J.D., Marquette University, 1979; U.S. Navy JAG Corps, 1979–1983, U.S. Navy Reserve, since 1983. N.C. assistant appellate defender, 1983–1984; attorney in private practice, 1984–1990; judge, state Court of Appeals, since 1991. *North Carolina Manual, 1991–1992,* 490.

Wilton Russell Duke, Jr., born in Louisburg; resident of Greenville; bachelor's and law degrees from Wake Forest University. Farmville mayor, 1981–1983; District Court judge, 1988–1990; Superior Court judge, since 1990; senior resident Superior Court judge, District 3A, Pitt County, since December 1992. Wilton Russell Duke, Jr., letter to Jan-Michael Poff, October 21, 1993.

Quentin T. Sumner (1950–), born in Rocky Mount; bachelor's degree, 1972, J.D., 1975, N.C. Central University. Attorney practicing in Wilson, 1975–1977, and Rocky Mount, 1977–1983; district representative for Congressman I. T. Valentine, Jr., 1983; District Court judge, District 7, 1983–1990; senior resident Superior Court judge, District 7A, since 1990. Quentin T. Sumner, letter to Jan-Michael Poff, October 28, 1993.

[2]G.S. 163–9.

[3]James R. Trotter (1923–), general counsel to Governor Martin since 1985. Previously identified in Poff, *Addresses of Martin,* I, 153n.

[4]The North Carolina Supreme Court offered no advisory opinion, in August 1991, on whether the state constitution or the General Statutes held the answer to the governor's question regarding elections to unexpired judgeships. While the justices' position afforded Martin the option to proceed as he thought necessary, they also told him that a matter of such significance was best resolved through the attendant processes and scrutiny of a regular court case.

A suit brought by Superior Court judge Anthony M. Brannon early in 1992 provided the opportunity for just such an extensive evaluation of the issue. Brannon intended to run for the Court of Appeals in that year's general election, and challenged the validity of the eight-year commission Martin awarded to Judge Robert F. Orr. Orr had been elected in 1988 to an unexpired term that ended in 1992, according to Brannon, and had to stand for reelection if he hoped to continue to serve on the bench. Naturally, Orr defended Martin's decision and claimed that the state constitution entitled him to serve a full eight years on the Court of Appeals—ending, in his case, in 1996.

The Supreme Court settled the issue in May 1992, finding that a judge elected to fill a predecessor's unexpired term was entitled to occupy that position only for the remainder of the term. The decision upheld the constitutionality of the state statute and voided the eight-year commissions Martin issued. Although Brannon won his case, final victory proved elusive: Orr defeated him in a close Court of Appeals contest the following November. *Brannon v. N.C. State Board of Elections*, 331 N.C. 335, 416 S.E. 2d 390 (1992); Louise Stafford, librarian, N.C. Supreme Court, letter to Jan-Michael Poff, September 22, 1994; *News and Observer*, July 18, August 30, September 10, 13, 1991, February 13, May 9, November 25, 1992.

WORKFORCE SAFETY PRESS CONFERENCE

RALEIGH, SEPTEMBER 11, 1991

[One of the worst industrial accidents in North Carolina history occurred September 3, 1991, when a fire swept through the Imperial Food Products chicken-processing factory in Hamlet, killing twenty-five people. Plant management refused to halt production while repairs were being attempted on a hydraulic line; flammable hydraulic fluid sprayed onto a hot poultry fryer, igniting the blaze and filling the building with choking black smoke. The factory was equipped with neither smoke alarms nor a sprinkler system. Their escape barred by locked and blocked emergency exits, the victims suffocated.

The tragedy focused national attention on workplace safety issues. In North Carolina, it raised general questions about the administration of the state Department of Labor and specific concerns over its understaffed and underfunded safety inspection program. Imperial opened in 1980; not once during the plant's eleven years of operation did state officials evaluate its compliance with safety regulations.

In the aftermath of the fire, the General Assembly adopted new workplace safety legislation. Incumbent labor commissioner John C. Brooks lost the 1992 Democratic primary, denying him the opportunity to seek a fifth term. Emmett J. Roe, Imperial's owner, pleaded guilty to twenty-five counts of involuntary manslaughter and was sentenced to nineteen years in prison. *News and Observer*, September 4, 5, 7, 13, 17, 18, 19, 24, 28, October 15, 30, November 13, 14, 15, December 3, 4, 31, 1991, January 12, April 25, May 4, 6, September 15, 16, 1992. Martin mentioned the Hamlet tragedy in his September 19, 1991, announcement of an open meeting of the state Building Code Council.]

One week ago, on Tuesday, September 3, I met with town officials in Hamlet and visited with a few of the victims caught in the tragedy of the fire at Imperial Food Products. From them I heard stories of great heroism—of fire fighters, coworkers, neighbors, and friends fighting to save their fellows and offering what comfort was possible to the families of those who were lost. I also saw the anxiety and anguish of families, friends, and a community rocked by both the speed and enormity of such a disaster and by the injury and loss of so many who were their friends and loved ones.

That day, I told the officials in Hamlet that I would do everything I could to help them get through this disaster, and our state Emergency Management team has been doing just that, installing a response line for victims and families, establishing a victim's assistance center, and offering any and all forms of help it is in their power to give. Just yesterday, Hamlet's mayor, Abbie Covington, officially expressed to me her appreciation for this.

We cannot change what happened. We cannot restore lives lost. But we can share in the grief of that community and learn from this tragedy what we can do to ensure that it is not repeated here or elsewhere in our state.

Ongoing investigations by the Department of Insurance, the Department of Labor, federal OSHA [Occupational Safety and Health Administration] personnel, local officials, and other groups have uncovered a number [of] concerns about workplace safety in our state. I share those concerns and am determined to take positive action toward eliminating some of the problems that have been identified. I have therefore developed eight proposals that I believe are positive steps toward improving workplace safety in North Carolina.

First, I have today directed my Office of Citizen Affairs to establish an 800 number that can be used by employees to report suspected fire, safety, or health hazards in their workplace. We will require that this number be posted conspicuously in every workplace, with the assurance that the caller's identity will be confidential, to relieve any fear of reprisal. Outside business hours, the "Safety-Line" will be connected to an answering machine to record relevant information. The Office of Citizen Affairs will refer all complaints to the appropriate agency for follow-up inspections and will request confirmation that the inspection was done.

Second, I will use our newly created reserve fund to provide for additional safety inspectors. Instead of the nineteen positions I had earlier requested for this biennium, which were denied by the General Assembly, I will fund twenty-seven additional inspector positions. That will increase our total number of inspectors from thirty-seven to sixty-four, the minimum number of safety inspectors required by the federal OSHA program. The state budget office estimates this would cost an additional $1.4 million.

As you know, the General Assembly has restricted this administration so that if additional positions were requested, but for any reason not funded, I could not then subsequently do anything to create those positions even in an emergency—even if I had nonstate money to pay for it. Fortunately, this session I persuaded them to provide a waiver or deviation clause for just such emergencies. Because of what we have learned from this tragedy, compliance with federal OSHA requirements is currently impossible. These budget complications were not foreseen in the last session of the General Assembly. Therefore, I have the authority to waive legislative budget restrictions, subject to ten-day notification to Senator Barnes, Speaker Blue, and Lieutenant Governor Gardner. Because of the $150 million reserve we are currently building up, we have sufficient appropriations of nonstate monies to cover the cost of these additional inspectors for nine months.

Meanwhile, third, I will direct the North Carolina commissioner of labor to fill those safety inspector positions currently vacant.[1] I will also ask him to identify and reform any departmental policies that stand in the way of hiring inspectors and let me know any budgetary restraint he faces from any source so that I can help him overcome that. If this is not done, if we do not provide for these vital positions, we may have to consider turning the administration of the Occupational Safety and Health program back over to the federal agency.

Fourth, I will also propose that a new fire safety inspection division be established in the North Carolina Department of Insurance. Its immediate responsibility will be to inspect for fire code violations and hazards in every workplace and other indoor gathering places. I will ask Commissioner Long to work with the state budget office to perfect this proposal. Initially, the new division will employ forty inspectors at a cost of $1.6 million a year. This number might be reduced if the new inspectors can coordinate their work with fire insurance company inspectors across the state and as we train more local inspectors.

The first duty of this new division would be to prioritize communities needing inspections, particularly targeting areas which rely upon volunteer fire departments to fight fires and have no professional fire inspectors. The staff will confer with mayors, volunteer fire department chiefs, and county fire marshalls to prepare that initial priority list.

Fifth, to further aid inspections, I have asked that the U.S. Occupational Safety and Health Administration offer cross-training to inspectors from other departments so they can recognize and report any major problem they discover while carrying out their routine job responsibilities.

Sixth, I have also asked the U.S. Department of Labor to expedite that department's annual review of our state-administered program so that their report can be shared with me as early as December 31, 1991, rather than the normal target date of July 1, 1992. This afternoon, U.S. Secretary of Labor Lynn Martin called me to confirm that these two requests would be done.[2]

Seventh, I will ask all federal, state, and local agencies with responsibilities for investigating different aspects of this tragedy to cooperate with me so that we can produce one complete report on all the things we have learned from the Hamlet fire. This will not delay publication of any one part of any agency's findings, but will ensure that the total picture is coordinated so that we will then have in one place all that is known about what happened and what could have been done.

These initial steps can significantly strengthen our efforts to improve health and safety procedures in the workplace.

Eighth, I will urge businesses across our state to voluntarily police their own facilities and make whatever changes are necessary to ensure the health and safety of their employees. They should take their own initiative to establish in-house safety and health teams of workers to make regular patrols, and surveys, and recommendations. Many are already doing some of this out of concern for their workers. All should accept the painful lesson of Hamlet and get their house in order.

I will ask the North Carolina Advertising Council to assist me in preparing a powerful message for public service announcements to get out this word and the 800 number. I would also encourage workers, or anyone else who know[s] of safety violations, to call our toll-free Safety-Line and report those violations immediately.

These actions cannot prevent what happened in Hamlet, but I believe they can help prevent what happened in Hamlet from happening anywhere else in our state. If anybody has a better idea, I want to hear it. And to ease the pain of those still caught in the grief and anger of that painful tragedy, I would encourage our citizens all across North Carolina to send a donation to the Hamlet Victims Assistance Fund established through the Richmond County United Way. The address and phone number are listed on your press release.[3]

Now I would be happy to answer any questions you might have.

---

[1] John Charles Brooks (1937–), born in Greenville; A.B., University of North Carolina at Chapel Hill, 1959; J.D., University of Chicago, 1962. Attorney; elected N.C. labor secretary, 1976, reelected 1980, 1984, 1988; defeated in Democratic primary election by Rep. Harry Payne, 1992. *News and Observer*, May 6, 1992; *North Carolina Manual, 1991–1992*, 103–104.

[2] Lynn Martin (1939–), born in Evanston, Ill.; B.A., University of Illinois, 1960. Public schoolteacher in Illinois, 1961–1975; member, Illinois House of Representatives, 1977–1979, and Senate, 1979–1981; member, U.S. House of Representatives from Illinois Sixteenth Congressional District, 1981–1990; national cochairwoman, Bush-Quayle Presidential Campaign, 1988; appointed U.S. labor secretary, 1991; Republican. Louise Mooney (ed.),

Newsmakers, The People Behind Today's Headlines: 1991 Cumulation (Detroit: Gale Research, Inc., 1991), 266–268.
    [3]See press release, "Governor Outlines Plans to Improve Workplace Safety," Raleigh, September 11, 1991, Governor's Papers, James G. Martin.

TESTIMONY BEFORE U.S. HOUSE COMMITTEE ON EDUCATION AND LABOR

WASHINGTON, D.C., SEPTEMBER 12, 1991

[The House Education and Labor Committee hearing on the Imperial Food Products fire was conducted in conjunction with its discussion of H.R. 3160, the "Comprehensive Occupational Safety and Health Reform Act."]

Chairman Ford[1] and Members of this Distinguished Committee:

It is my deep regret that such a tragedy as the September 3 fire at the Imperial Food Products plant in Hamlet, North Carolina, would happen in my state or anywhere. I have asked Chairman Ford to permit me to come, today, as a witness in the hope that my testimony will help you in your timely deliberations. You will also hear from our commissioner of labor, who is independently elected under our constitution. I provide for the record a copy of the subsequent fire investigation by the independently elected commissioner of insurance.

The good people of Hamlet have suffered deeply. All of us share in their grief and want to do right out of respect and as our tribute to those twenty-five who were killed and fifty-four injured in this terrible fire.[2] Your commitment to address the lessons of the Hamlet tragedy is deeply appreciated.

Let me tell you that we know that our safety enforcement program was far from adequate. It was disgracefully deficient. Instead of what Commissioner Brooks and I believe to be the minimum standard of sixty-four safety inspectors, our General Assembly has authorized only thirty-seven. I want you to know that even in this recession, my January budget request included nineteen additional inspectors, but it was turned down by our legislature. But it is not likely that it would have saved us from this disaster had it passed. Right now, our program has a backlog of complaints from other workplaces. Even if we had sixty-four inspectors, they would probably have devoted their time to that backlog and would not have known to go to Imperial Food Products.

The crucial point is that the state Department of Labor had received no complaint about this plant, nor had our state Insurance Department. The same concerns which led you to draft the pending legislation, calling for mandatory safety and health committees of employees, were tragically illustrated at Imperial Food Products. There are reports that some workers knew about the locked doors—which are illegal in our state—and other problems, but were afraid to speak out about it for fear of losing their jobs.

There can be no question that our response to what we have learned here must include elements which can solve that communication bridge for the future and revise our priority list of workplaces. Let me tell you what we are going to do, so that you will know. I just regret it comes too late for twenty-five of my people.

I have announced a six-point program, which does include key features relevant to what we have found:

1. We have established a free 800 number—a Safety-Line for workers or anyone else, to call with information about any safety or health concern. Their information will be received in confidence and relayed to the appropriate agency for investigation. I've just been advised we got our first call this morning.

2. Using the leeway that I have as budget director in such an emergency, I will transfer $1.4 million from a reserve to employ twenty-seven additional safety inspectors to get us up to the sixty-four level.

3. A new state law required local governments to have fire safety inspectors as of July 1, but many are not yet able to comply, such as smaller municipalities which rely on volunteer fire fighters. So, as an interim, partial response, I am asking our state insurance commissioner to provide forty fire inspectors to assist in such cases.

4. Our food processing industries all have food hygiene inspectors from the U.S. Department of Agriculture. At Hamlet, they either did not know the workers' concerns, even though their own lives were in danger, or did not know what to do about it. At my request, Secretary Lynn Martin has agreed to provide cross-training for inspectors from other agencies, so they will know what to look for and report, and that Agriculture Secretary Ed Madigan has agreed to this.[3] Incidentally, our state Agriculture Department inspects food processors whose markets are intrastate only; and a year ago, they started to check doors, fire extinguishers, and first-aid kits in these businesses.

5. Secretary Martin has also agreed to expedite OSHA's annual review of our state-administered program. Instead of the normal July report date, she will see that we get it by December 31, so that we can compile all of the state, local, and national investigations of Imperial Food Products into one volume. This way, we will have all that has been learned from this tragic experience in one place.

6. Finally, I will send an urgent message, to all North Carolina employers, to recommend that they review their own fire safety situation

and procedures, and set up an in-house workers' committee on safety and health on their own initiative. Clearly that would have helped in the Imperial Food Products plant. That part of your bill therefore has merit. There would still be a concern as to how to safeguard effectively against reprisals without creating unintended consequences. I respectfully suggest that the simultaneous availability of a free, 800-number, Safety-Line for people to call to report their concerns confidentially will offer the kind of security you seek.

Mr. Chairman and members of the committee, we are a sadder and hopefully wiser people in North Carolina. We have been severely hurt and have to carry the deep grief of both the loss of twenty-five lives and a shared burden of responsibility for it. We will deal with the issue of weighing blame and liability in due process and time, but we will deal immediately with trying to fix the error before it happens again. That must be our respectful tribute to those who died and suffered.

Now, this hearing is also to examine your legislative remedy, H.R. 3160. While I have not drawn any conclusion regarding all the sections of this bill, I would like to comment favorably regarding the general principle of establishing health and safety committees in the workplace. It is clear to me that such a requirement, or the 800 line which I have established, or a combination of both, could very well have led to a correction of the conditions which cost the lives of twenty-five good people in Hamlet. It is also evident that without such mechanisms for communication, the other changes which we had earlier proposed and have now made resolving our state program deficiency by increasing the number of inspectors alone, very well might not have made a real difference in Imperial Food Products.

I expect that you will hear helpful testimony as to how to perfect this plan so as to achieve the intended employee committee while minimizing the burden of any nonessential requirements. You should try to accommodate that. But if there is any lesson from what we have learned after the tragedy in Hamlet, it is that our workers are at risk if we do not provide some secure means for them to participate with employers in preparing a safer workplace, and if that fails, to be able to call for help without fear of reprisals.

You have my best wishes in fixing this serious flaw in our workplace safety policies. I'm sorry it comes too late.

---

[1] William D. Ford (1927–), born in Detroit; resident of Ypsilanti, Mich.; B.S., 1949, J.D., 1951, University of Denver; U.S. Navy, 1944–1946; U.S. Air Force Reserve, 1950–1958. Attorney; Taylor Township justice of the peace, 1955–1957, township attorney, 1957–1964; Melvindale city attorney, 1957–1959; member, Michigan Senate, 1963–1965, elected to U.S. House, 1964, and returned in subsequent elections; chairman, House Education and La-

bor Committee; Democrat. Barone and Ujifusa, *Almanac of American Politics, 1994,* 666–668.

[2]Fifty-six people were injured in the Imperial Food Products fire. *News and Observer,* December 31, 1991.

[3]Edward R. Madigan (1936–1994), born in Lincoln, Ill.; was graduated from Lincoln College, 1955; honorary degrees. Member, Illinois House of Representatives, 1967–1972; member, U.S. House of Representatives, 1973–1991, from Illinois Fifteenth Congressional District; U.S. agriculture secretary, 1991–1993; Republican. *News and Observer,* December 9, 1994; *Who's Who in America, 1994,* II, 2182.

NORTH CAROLINA 2000 ANNOUNCEMENT
NORTH CAROLINA BUSINESS COMMITTEE FOR
EDUCATION AWARDS

RALEIGH, SEPTEMBER 27, 1991

[The governor preceded his announcement regarding the North Carolina 2000 program by recognizing Lamar Alexander, United States secretary of education and former governor of Tennessee, who was in attendance. Much of the information provided in the following address appeared in Martin's text, "North Carolina 2000: Education Reform for the Twenty-first Century," which was published in the September 29, 1991, edition of the *Charlotte Observer.*]

Today we honor excellence in education. There can be no better time, then, to announce a new plan that will expand that commitment to excellence found in the boardrooms and classrooms represented here today, to boardrooms and classrooms found in every community in every corner of this state. We can't impose it from the top.

Lamar Alexander has outlined six national goals for educational excellence, created by President Bush and our nation's governors.[1] Together, united in a sweeping bipartisan effort, they have called upon every community in America to achieve those national education goals by the year 2000. These goals are ambitious, but they can be achieved.

They are not the president's goals, or the governors' goals. They are the nation's goals. They are the beginning of a process designed to involve every citizen, in every community, of every state, in a national effort to give our children a world-class education.

Many important initiatives to improve education are already in place in North Carolina. Thanks to the General Assembly, a lot more money is allocated and a lot more staff are in place. Many more initiatives are being developed and are in the pilot stages. What we lack is a comprehensive statewide focus for bringing educational excellence to every school and every classroom in the state—not just for more resources, but for better results; not just more inputs, but better outcomes. We've been holding schools accountable, for what? Accountable for rules, regulations, requirements, and restrictions as if that's the 4 *R*'s. We lack an organized commitment to reaching our national goals.

Legislative reforms are under way. S.B. 2 has been enacted by our General Assembly, and S.B. 3 is being perfected to further decentralize and deregulate public education and put less emphasis on central micromanagement and more on goals and results. What is needed now is a way to energize and organize locally to accept that challenge and responsibility.

If the citizens of North Carolina pledge to focus all their resources, talents, and energies into making these goals a reality, nothing can stand in our way. I believe that North Carolina is ready to respond to that challenge. We are ready to declare our dedication to excellence in education, and I have a plan that will lead us on the journey to educational excellence in North Carolina. It's not a collection of new ideas to be debated; rather, it's a new way of organizing and harnessing public support for the best ideas which have already been debated too long.

I have established a program, called North Carolina 2000, that is designed to help us meet our educational goals by the year 2000. This statewide effort will focus local community energy on making education a priority, and on achieving our state and national goals in every school in this state.[2]

Let's begin by agreeing that North Carolina will be a strong participant in the national reform campaign, America 2000. The first requirement of this program will be to adopt our national goals as goals for the state of North Carolina. These goals will be the destination of our journey to excellence. Achieving these goals will be the focus of our efforts. I have committed myself, my staff, and my cabinet officials to the task of making sure:

—That all our children enter school ready to learn;

—That students stay in school and are adequately prepared to go to work or on to further study. That's expressed as a goal of [a] 90 percent graduation rate, which means cutting our dropout rate dramatically;

—That our children attend safe and drug-free schools;

—That we provide literacy education for all those who are undereducated; and

—That our mathematics and science programs are nothing less than world class.

I ask all other state leaders to commit the time and resources of their organizations to help communities set and meet these goals in their schools. Choosing a proper direction to follow in reaching those goals will be the responsibility of a statewide steering committee I have already created by executive order. The members of this bipartisan committee will be the visionaries who will develop strategies to help communities become "North Carolina 2000 Communities" in our state.

Members of that steering committee will include the governor, educators, legislators, civic leaders and business executives, government officials, and parents. The North Carolina 2000 Steering Committee will:

—Work with the state board to officially adopt our national goals as goals for North Carolina;

—Establish an action plan making those goals a state priority and challenging communities to organize community action teams;

—Develop the capability to distribute information statewide describing strategies and activities created by other community action teams;

—Develop and implement a reporting system to evaluate the program's progress and to publish those results in an annual statewide report; and

—To select North Carolina 2000 Communities eligible to seek grant funding for a "New American School" from the United States Department of Education.

Clearing a path in the direction set by the statewide steering committee will be the responsibility of six statewide goal teams, each of which will work to help meet one specific goal. These teams will be the guides to our goals. Their members will be experts in the areas relating to each particular goal. These six goals teams will:

—Advise the state steering committee on technical issues and progress being made toward each goal;

—Merge any additional state goals into the national goals as needed;

—Prepare materials and information to distribute to local goal teams; and

—Develop statewide strategies for implementing and distributing ideas created by other community action teams.

The state steering committee and goals teams will be organized and meeting by early November. We will keep you informed as to their progress and encourage you to share with them your ideas for achieving educational excellence in our state.

To achieve our goals, it must be done community by community. That is why North Carolina 2000 focuses on community organizations with support at the state level. We challenge local leaders to develop community action teams dedicated to implementing school reform based on these six goals, but also on the specific educational needs unique to their community.

My staff will help to develop and distribute goal materials to local communities. We will meet with community leaders who want to develop community action teams, and we will help them become North Carolina 2000 Communities. Technical expertise for this effort will be available from goal team members; from the Department of Public

Instruction and its technical assistance centers; the local and state offices of our community colleges, universities, and colleges; and departments of state government with expertise in specific areas.

Communities that join this effort will be designated a North Carolina 2000 Community if they have:

—Set up a community action team;

—Adopted the national education goals in a way that most clearly meets the special needs and circumstances of that community;

—Outlined a plan for action that involves the entire community using existing resources for ideas and technical assistance;

—Developed a method of both measuring and reporting programs to the entire community;

—Created a plan for one of the first New American Schools to be funded by the United States Department of Education; and

—Ask[ed] to be declared a North Carolina 2000 Community.[3]

The state steering committee will help decide whether a community has met all these requirements. After earning the title, the new North Carolina 2000 Community will be eligible to apply for a limited number of million-dollar federal grants to fund fourteen New American Schools in North Carolina.

Of course, setting a goal, determining a direction, and clearing a path don't mean much without a map for others to follow. North Carolina 2000 comes with a map in the form of a state report card to be issued each year in September. That report will assess initiatives under way in the state and focus on accountability, but our report will also celebrate our success. We will encourage local and state officials, schools, community groups, and business leaders to recognize and applaud those individuals, groups, and activities that are truly breaking down barriers to learning for our students.

Together we can make educational opportunity a priority in North Carolina for the young child, the elementary and secondary student, the young adult, and all those who are undereducated and underemployed. Together we can create a new generation of better and more accountable schools for tomorrow's students. We can transform North Carolina into a "state of students," a place where lifelong learning is celebrated, and we can make our communities places where learning will happen.

This is our commencement. Our statewide process commences with today's announcement and call to action. I call on leaders in education, business, and government to join me on this journey toward educational excellence. I encourage them, and all of you, to adopt the North Carolina 2000 proposal as your own. If it becomes your commitment, only then will it succeed.

[1]Martin recounted the six national goals for education later in this speech and in re-marks to North Carolina 2000 Steering Committee, Raleigh, January 30, 1992; see pages 410–411, below.

Andrew Lamar Alexander (1940–), governor of Tennessee, 1979–1987; chairman, Lead-ership Institute, Belmont College, 1987–1988; president, University of Tennessee, 1988–1991; U.S. education secretary, 1991–1993; Republican. Previously identified in Poff, *Ad-dresses of Martin*, I, 271n; see also *Who's Who in America, 1994*, I, 41.

[2]See Executive Order Number 153, "North Carolina 2000," signed September 24, 1991. *N.C. Session Laws, Extra Session, 1991, Regular Session, 1992*, 1279–1282.

[3]Of the seventy-nine communities in fifty-eight counties that applied for the North Carolina 2000 designation, six succeeded: Catawba County, Charlotte-Mecklenburg, Hickory, New Hanover County, Perquimans County, and Rosman. Press release, "Gover-nor Names First North Carolina 2000 Communities," Raleigh, August 11, 1992, Governors Papers, James G. Martin.

INVESTMENT BREAKOUT SESSION
SOUTHEAST UNITED STATES-JAPAN ASSOCIATION

Tokyo, Japan, October 7, 1991

As I said in my opening remarks this morning, I am excited to be participating in this session to talk about mutual direct investment pro-motion. For our two nations to build lasting relationships, with great benefits to both sides, we need less *bashing* and more *bashi*, i.e., more bridges. Investment is one important bridge for this SEUS-*Nihon bashi*.[1]

Mr. Yahiro has talked about promotion of American investment in Japan.[2] My assignment is to talk about how we promote Japanese in-vestment in the southeastern states. As Mr. Yahiro stated, goodwill be-tween our two peoples is the most important part of our friendship. He is correct. Goodwill is the basis, the foundation on which we must build our efforts for other mutually beneficial relations such as trade and investment.

North Carolina and our sister states are proud of the very special relationship we share with Japan. We value the friendship and exchanges that have expanded our understanding and appreciation of each other. Our region also enjoys an excellent economic partnership, with many impressive Japanese business investments and operations, which are good for both sides.

Japanese people and businesses have grown and prospered in our states. Our American people benefit from a stronger economy with a stronger job market. Part of the success is due to the favorable costs of doing business. Moderate taxes, low construction costs, low utility rates, reasonable labor costs are certainly important factors and favor the south-east United States as a good climate for business investment. But if that's all an investor considers, we know there are cheaper economies. So, obviously, there must be other factors that make our region so attract-ive. I believe the personal attributes make the difference. You find that we share many values and appreciate many of the same things.

The South has a tradition of courtesy, with social behavior reflecting the personal respect that has flourished in our warm, gracious southern hospitality. It's sometimes been romanticized as easy living, but that's not correct. When we talk about quality of life, we stress the quality. We're committed to family, business, community, church, and friends, and we work hard doing our very best. But the South has a more gentle way and pace about living. Traditions are still strong, such as welcom-ing newcomers and making them feel comfortable and at home. We make a point to stop and talk to our neighbors and associates.

There is a genuine friendliness which helps investors and managers feel truly welcome. Unlike those Americans who seem to resent your wish to invest, we in the Southeast prefer to see it as a compliment—and as an advantage. We know from experience that when you build a factory, you build it to succeed. When you buy a golf course, you don't move it, you keep it where it was. Remember those who seemed upset when Mitsubishi acquired Rockefeller Center in New York City? Well, I visited New York two weeks ago and noticed that Rockefeller Center was still there![3]

This spirit of working together in trust and friendliness is the key to how the southeastern United States made our phenomenal transition from a predominantly agricultural economy into manufacturing and a more stable, more diversified economy. A major element of our outstand-ing success is our can-do spirit, our work ethic, and the willingness and ability of management and workers to work together. There is an un-written but most effective loyalty of employee to company and com-pany to employee in the South. There is simply no need or room for a labor union to come between managers and workers who work together as partners. Southerners value self-satisfaction, doing well what we choose to do.

Just as we like to work hard, we also enjoy our free time and recre-ation. Our states have scenic beauty and entertainment delights, com-bined with a mild climate, for year-round pleasure. We have water sports in abundance at our oceans, lakes, rivers, and fishing holes. We have every kind of terrain imaginable: majestic mountains, rolling hills, flatlands, bayous, coastal sand dunes, and much more—and we have golf courses everywhere! Japanese and Americans share an avid inter-est in golf, and together our southeastern states have thousands of courses at affordable prices for all our citizens.

It's true that we have much to promote and have found many ways in which to promote the southeastern United States as the best place for

Japanese companies to call home and do business. We're so proud of our message that we've taken it directly to you. Six of our seven states have established offices in Japan so we can maintain day-to-day contact. The staffs of these international offices are important liaisons between the United States and your businesses, and they keep us at home abreast of happenings in your country. This shows we're serious in our interest in you, and we want to do business!

All of our states make direct contact with leaders of Japanese industry and government through trade missions. Several times each year, state and community groups visit and talk with your company executives. These visits provide us with the opportunity to learn how we can help each other through trade and investment.

Many of our states keep in touch with their Japanese counterparts through the mail. Newsletters, annual reports, and special announcements are a good source of information about what is happening in our region of the United States. Few states do regular mass mailings, but most do send information they think will be helpful to you. To help Japanese investors better understand all the positive things our states have to offer, many of our materials are translated. We also have videos in Japanese.

Some of our states buy advertisements to promote our offerings to Japan, but most often you will find that, as southerners, we value the personal contacts we can make in preference to communicating through an ad you might see on TV or in a publication. We value the one-on-one experience and know you do, too. Our states have programs that educate Japanese executives about our better business climate and show them how and why they can best benefit by locating in our area. Ours is a probusiness attitude, where fair taxes and competitive costs for land, construction, utilities, and labor combine for an overall positive environment for investment. We are home to national centers for finance and banking. Indeed, our southeastern states pioneered interstate banking in America, which other states have not yet discovered. That's another advantage for business investment in SEUS.

Among us we have excellent transportation systems with international airline hubs, deepwater ports, and expansive rail and road networks. One example of how we're continuously making improvements and exploring new ideas to keep our competitive advantage is the concept of an air-cargo facility. I believe this can be developed into a new, attractive force for promoting investment, especially in this age of just-in-time manufacturing and distribution—and global markets.

While many nations and states are interested in this concept of international air shipments, North Carolina proposes to add a unique new dimension. Earlier this year, I launched a major project to build a global air-cargo complex with manufacturing facilities located adjacent to the taxiways, as shown in this brochure. Just think how that can maximize just-in-time delivery of materials, direct shipment, and overnight delivery of products anywhere in the world. Think of this as a new kind of major industrial park, one which features a unique attraction: its own air cargo airport. In an industrial era in which markets are global; and suppliers of components are global; and where quality must be matched by speed, speed, and more speed, just think how favorable such an industrial site could be.

As governor and as chairman of the board for this airport, I intend to spread the word, and gauge the interest, and move forward. I believe this facility could benefit the South and world trade. Just as North Carolina was successful in building Research Triangle Park from an innovative vision in its day, we intend to take this idea of a global air-cargo industrial complex and make it a reality. If you want to know more about this idea and how it can fit into your plans, just see me after the session.

As you know, Japanese investment in our region is extensive. In terms of dollar value, Japan ranks first, or second, or third in most of our states as the largest international investor. The manufacturing industries you have established in our states are diverse and include telecommunications, electronics, automobiles and automotive parts, pharmaceuticals, chemicals, steel, food, and much more.

We also want to let you know that once you come to our states and invest in our communities and in our people, we support you in every way. North Carolina and several other states have established Saturday Japan schools so that Japanese children can maintain the educational curriculum and cultural traditions of their homeland. The schools enable Japanese children to more easily move between our two countries. To further this spirit of communication, the Saturday Japan school in my state capital of Raleigh also offers lessons in basic Japanese to non-Japanese children of any age. That is a great attraction for a school.[4]

Our states value and celebrate the great cultural interaction that our ties with Japan have brought. Several states, including North Carolina, have established Japan centers, usually housed in our universities, to be an important focal point of these exchanges. The Japan centers help prepare both Japanese and American industry leaders on what it takes to do business. Knowing the differences in culture and work-style are important in order for a potential relationship to be successful. Along the same lines, several states also have founded Japanese-American societies where Japanese newcomers can make friends, easily learn customs and language, and share their heritage with Americans.

In all of these ways, we are telling you one very important thing: The southeastern United States is open for business, and we want you to come over and test the waters. We favor business and promote it. Talk to those who have already invested in us, and I believe they will tell you we speak the truth.

---

[1]"We are all sensitive and alert to the attitude of some in America to engage in 'Japan bashing,' blaming Japanese business success and growth as though that were the cause of America's economic difficulties," Martin told the audience gathered for the opening of the sixteenth annual SEUS-Japan Association meeting. "At these conferences, we have learned that it is much more productive and beneficial to build bridges: bridges of cooperation and mutual understanding, and bridges of two-way flow of trade and ideas. This annual conference has thus become our bridge to Japan, and your Japanese word for that is *Nihon-bashi*, Japan bridge. So we grow together, to our shared mutual benefit, not by Japan bashing but by Nihon-bashi, this Japanese bridge."

[2]Toshikuni Yahiro, adviser to the board of Mitsui and Company, Limited. Nancy Jo Pekarek, letter to Jan-Michael Poff, January 20, 1995.

[3]Japan had more direct foreign investment in American commercial real estate in 1988 than any other country, and the increasing acquisition of landmark properties by Japanese businesses, such as Sony Corporation's $3.4 billion purchase of Columbia Pictures in September 1989, elicited howls of protest across the United States. Voices of anger and disbelief echoed again the following October, when Mitsubishi Estate Company obtained 51 percent interest in New York's Rockefeller Group for $846 million in cash. Rockefeller Group owned Rockefeller Center, Radio City Music Hall, and other midtown Manhattan property. Mitsubishi was one of Japan's two largest real estate developers and one of the world's wealthiest investment institutions. *New York Times*, October 31, November 1, 1989.

[4]Besides Raleigh, Saturday Japan schools also operated in Greensboro and Charlotte. Opening Ceremonies, SEUS-Japan Association Meeting, October 7, 1991, Governors Papers, James G. Martin.

NEWSPAPER COLUMN: ECONOMIC DEVELOPMENT FOR THE FUTURE—NORTH CAROLINA'S GLOBAL TRANSPARK

RALEIGH, NOVEMBER 15, 1991

Less than a year ago, we began studying the possibility of building a unique, futuristic industrial park in North Carolina that would revolutionize the way business is conducted in the global economy of the twenty-first century. This project—known as the Global TransPark, or GTP—clusters an industrial park facility around an intermodal transportation network that includes an airport capable of handling international cargo flights. That network would integrate the production and distribution demands of our U.S. industrial base, and that of a worldwide market, with the latest improvements in air, sea, and land transportation. The Global TransPark would combine the most up-to-date equipment in aviation and cargo handling, industrial production, and telecommunications to improve our access to worldwide markets. The three main qualities of this state-of-the-art distribution system would be speed, access, and reliability.

History has taught us a very clear lesson: Transportation plays an extremely important role in commercial development. For North Carolina, the Global TransPark and its promise of a state-of-the-art intermodal transportation system makes sense, especially since our state is already blessed with a very good network of highways, airports, rails, and seaports.

Aviation is a rapidly expanding method of distribution for industrial goods, leading to the rise of what many refer to as "just-in-time" production. With just-in-time production, an order is received and processing begins the same day. The product can then be delivered to any point on the globe in a matter of hours. The access, speed, and reliability offered by the Global TransPark's transportation infrastructure of highways, rails, seaports, and other airports would immediately answer the needs of growing JIT businesses—American and foreign alike—as well as a wide array of manufacturers who rely on less-immediate delivery.

Our Global TransPark has been mistakenly compared to existing cargo airports in Texas and Alabama, but those comparisons are inaccurate. Though elements of our proposed facility have been implemented elsewhere, no facility anywhere in the world incorporates all the features we propose.

Yet, if we are to compete in international markets, the United States must develop a better understanding of how government and the private sector can work together to improve U.S. commerce. The success of joint efforts between private enterprise and government in European and Pacific Rim countries show[s] that we must continue our efforts to develop similar partnerships. Global TransPark is a good example of how we can work together to bring vast opportunities to the American economy and transform American business enterprise.

North Carolina has a proposal on the table that will strengthen American business by improving cooperation between government and the private sector. We are continuing to study the proposal. We have not worked out every detail. We have not foreseen every problem. But we are working hard to market the project and prove its feasibility.

We face many challenges in building this facility in North Carolina. For example, about 2,000 bilateral agreements currently determine what routes are flown by international carriers. The framework for these bilateral agreements was laid in 1945 and needs to be drastically modified. These bilateral agreements severely hinder the ability of American business to compete in a global economy.

Yet the Global TransPark concept, with its many facets, holds great promise. For North Carolina alone, early projections show that this facility could create almost 55,000 new jobs and bring $2.8 billion into the state economy each year. The Global TransPark is also symbolic. It marks a new turn that American government and business can take toward renewed prosperity and competitiveness in a global market. Our plan for the Global TransPark sets a new agenda that integrates a highly expensive, and highly fragmented, intermodal transportation system to strengthen the economic future of both our state and nation.

UPLIFT DAY CARE

Raleigh, November 18, 1991

[Notes for an editorial describing the Uplift Day Care program, reprinted below, very nearly duplicate the first section of the booklet "Martin Administration Initiatives Outlined in the 1991 State of the State Message" (n.p., January 31, 1991), 1–2.]

Mission

The goal of the Martin administration Uplift Day Care initiative is to provide more and better day care to the working poor of our state through the new federal funding sources. The program emphasizes parental choice, building on existing programs, public-private partnerships, and maximizing existing resources. Uplift Day Care is designed to allow parents the choice of where they want their child to receive day-care services and to expand the availability of quality day-care services across the state.

Elements of the Initiative

1. Provides "wrap around" or extended day care for eligible Head Start children.
Uplift Day Care will extend the Head Start program from the current six hours of service daily for nine months to ten hours a day, year-round. Extending services will enable parents to become gainfully employed through educational, training, and employment opportunities. Services will be provided by Community Action agencies and Head Start programs and will cover education, health care, nutrition, handicap services, parent involvement, mental health care, and social services. For their children to be eligible, parents must be working or enrolled in an education/training program and meet income eligibility requirements. Three thousand, two hundred children will be served by the program at a total cost of $3,892,052 in federal funds.

2. Serves more than 14,000 children on the current state day-care waiting list.

More than 14,000 children were enrolled on county waiting lists for child day-care assistance in November 1990. Most of those children were waiting for day-care funds to become available. If day-care assistance were provided for all these children, most of the parents would be able to work, complete high school, or enter a job-training program. All of these children are either economically disadvantaged or live in families in crisis. Some of the children are also developmentally disabled. The additional day-care services would be provided through the existing state day-care and Family Support Act child care system for 14,440 children at a total cost of $15,885,071.

3. Expands state day-care coverage for AFDC recipients who are working or engaged in education/training.

The federal Family Support Act provides day-care funds to support AFDC [Aid to Families with Dependent Children] recipients who are working, participating in the Job Opportunities and Basic Skills program, or enrolled in an education/training program which will lead to a job. It also provides up to twelve months of day care to support former AFDC recipients who have gotten jobs and left the AFDC program. The FSA day-care program has grown from a state fiscal year 1990–1991 expenditure of $7,070,549 to a projected expenditure of more than $32 million in state fiscal year 1991–1992.

4. Expands services for rural and underserved areas.

Uplift Day Care will provide: a) $588,724 to hire fourteen county day-care coordinators; b) $648,276 to support resource and referral agencies; c) $450,000 revolving fund that combines loans and grants to assist in day-care center start-up.

5. Improves the quality of state day-care services.

To improve the quality of services, Uplift Day Care will provide: a) $208,000 to reduce the infant-staff ratio by one infant; b) better training and administration: $160,000 for worker training credentials, $100,000 for a study of day-care workers' salaries, and $268,527 for additional Child Day Care Section staff.

PRESS CONFERENCE ON INFANT MORTALITY
ECONOMIC DEVELOPMENT

RALEIGH, NOVEMBER 21, 1991

[The following remarks consist of two separately issued texts, both dated November 21, 1991: Press Conference, Infant Mortality Grants/Economic Policy, and revised material, released as Economic Policy Announcement. The documents are reprinted here as the single speech Martin delivered.]

I have several important initiatives to announce to you, today, that should have a major impact on the reduction of infant mortality in our state. Before I do so, I'd like to introduce my guests: Phil Kirk, president of the North Carolina Citizens for Business and Industry, and a member of the Commission on Reduction of Infant Mortality, the Healthy Start Foundation, Celebration North Carolina, and the Healthy Mothers-Healthy Babies Coalition of Wake County; Walter Shepherd, executive director of my Commission on Reduction of Infant Mortality; Bill Austin, vice-president at Glaxo; Dr. Bob Helms, program director for a project, called Improving Quality of Life in North Carolina, at the Research Triangle Institute and a recipient of one of the grants I'm announcing today.

You may recall that almost two years ago, in December of 1989, I issued an executive order that called for the formation of a Governor's Commission on Reduction of Infant Mortality. At that time, North Carolina had the highest infant mortality in the nation. Since then, we have made great progress, as reflected by both the latest infant mortality statistics and evidence of a statewide response to the problem.

From the beginning, the business community contributed creativity and resources to the effort, led by Glaxo, Incorporated, one of the largest pharmaceutical companies in the world. At the same time, the Governor's Commission on Reduction of Infant Mortality established the North Carolina Healthy Start Foundation, a private, nonprofit organization, to implement the commission's goals and address infant mortality issues in communities throughout North Carolina. The Healthy Start Foundation is joined in this effort by Celebration North Carolina. You may remember that I created Celebration North Carolina as a nonprofit foundation to inspire our citizens to become actively involved in addressing some of the critical challenges we face, in North Carolina, and to coordinate the charitable generosity of our businesses to make a difference by focusing on a few major needs, like literacy, education, and health.

Today, the North Carolina Healthy Start Foundation and Celebration North Carolina are proud to announce the distribution of $420,000 to be awarded to twenty-four local programs across North Carolina that are actively working to reduce and prevent infant deaths.[1] Of that total, the Healthy Start Foundation is providing $293,000, and Celebration North Carolina has generated another $129,000. What makes these contributions even more significant is that all of these resources are being provided by the private sector. There are no state funds in the total. In fact, these gifts have been made possible by generous contributions from Glaxo.

At this time, it is my pleasure to introduce my good friend and colleague, Phil Kirk, to give us his perspective on this announcement.

[Kirk spoke.]

As many of you know, lack of access to medical care is frequently cited as one of the factors that contributes to infant mortality. I am pleased to also announce that, again with the help of Glaxo, the infant mortality commission and the Healthy Start Foundation are now able to address this need in areas throughout the state. Thanks to another in-kind donation from Glaxo, eleven health-care facilities across North Carolina have been selected to receive modular office units to house much-needed maternal and child health services—and a hearty thanks we offer you, Mr. Austin.

Through Celebration North Carolina and the Healthy Start Foundation, other businesses across the state have joined us to ensure a brighter future and a better quality of life for North Carolina. I'd like to ask Walter Shepherd to step forward and briefly describe our efforts and those of countless other North Carolinians in the public and private sectors.

[Shepherd spoke.]

Before I open the floor for questions, I'd also like to thank Joanie Henderson, executive director of Celebration, for her efforts on behalf of that organization. Joanie and her staff, along with the Celebration board chaired by Estell Lee, secretary of the Department of Economic and Community Development, have worked long and hard to address key issues such as infant mortality.

[Martin opened the floor for questions.]

Now for my second announcement:[2] In an effort to help bolster the state's economy, I am encouraging members of the General Assembly to pass legislation repealing the state's 20 percent surtax on businesses.

In 1987, a committee of business leaders and Employment Security Commission staff suggested that North Carolina institute a 20 percent surtax on businesses to more effectively manage the state's tax system. The tax created a reserve fund that now stands at $193 million. That fund is basically North Carolina's unemployment insurance. It can be used to pay unemployment benefits in the event that the federal trust fund becomes insolvent. The fund also can be used as collateral for federal loans or to pay interest on federal loans.

That reserve fund currently generates about $1.2 million in interest per month, or about $16 million per year. The interest from the fund is placed in the state's Worker Training Trust Fund. Those monies can be used only to enhance the labor force, through training and education, or to operate local Employment Security Commission offices. Out of this trust fund for fiscal years 1991 and 1992, the General Assembly appropriated funds to the Employment Security Commission, for the operation of local offices, and funds to the departments of Economic and Community Development, Labor, Human Resources, and Community Colleges for worker training and education.

When the tax was enacted in 1987, the chairman of the Employment Security Commission, Dave Flaherty, promised me, the General Assembly, and the business community that the tax would be repealed when the fund, combined with the federal trust fund, reached a solvency rate of $1.4 billion. ESC chairman Ann Duncan has informed me that the fund has now reached that level. A repeal of the surtax would generate a $50 million to $60 million reduction in taxes for the state's employers. This reduction will enable those employers to stimulate North Carolina's economic growth by pouring that money back into the private sector. The reserve fund remains intact, and the interest from the fund will continue to be used to fund worker training programs and employment security offices.

On another economic issue, on Wednesday I met with members of our congressional delegation to argue in support of the amended version of the Emergency Unemployment Compensation Act. The original language in the bill provided only six weeks of extended benefit payments to North Carolinians who qualify and who have exhausted their payment period as of November 15, 1991, when President Bush signed the act into law. An amendment to the bill, passed by the Senate on November 15, 1991, will allow unemployed North Carolinians to be eligible for thirteen weeks of benefits. The amended version also would allow North Carolinians who have exhausted their benefits as far back as March 1, 1991, to qualify for extended benefit payments. With the new legislation, more than 38,000 North Carolinians could qualify for additional benefit payments at an estimated cost of $34 million.[3]

---

[1]Award recipients were listed in the press release, "Governor Announces Combined Gifts to Combat Infant Mortality," Raleigh, November 21, 1991, Governors Papers, James G. Martin.

[2]Revised text substituted by the governor and issued as Economic Policy Announcement, November 21, 1991, begins here.

[3]P.L. 102–164, the Emergency Unemployment Compensation Act of 1991, shortchanged many states with regard to the distribution of extended federal benefits. The law restricted additional financial aid to six-, thirteen-, or twenty-week terms based on a state's jobless rate. Because North Carolina maintained a relatively high level of employment in spite of the national recession, P.L. 102–164 extended benefits to out-of-work Tar Heels by only six weeks.

As Martin noted, President Bush signed the controversial measure into law on November 15, 1991. That same day, the U.S. Senate approved H.R. 1724, a trade bill that included among its provisions an amendment to P.L. 102–164. As adopted, H.R. 1724 extended unemployment benefits to thirteen weeks in North Carolina and elsewhere. *Congressional Quarterly Almanac, 1991*, 301–310; P.L. 102–164, "Emergency Unemployment

Compensation Act of 1991," Act of November 15, 1991, *United States Statutes at Large*, 105 Stat. 1049–1069; P.L. 102–182, "An Act to Provide for the Termination of the Application of Title IV of the Trade Act of 1974 to Czechoslovakia and Hungary," Section 3, Act of December 4, 1991, *United States Statutes at Large*, 105 Stat. 1234. For related press release, see "Governor Urges Quick Action on Federal Extended Benefits Legislation," Raleigh, November 25, 1991, Governors Papers, James G. Martin.

STATEMENT AT PRESS CONFERENCE

Raleigh, December 5, 1991

Good morning. We've got a couple of announcements today. I know you don't like announcements, so let's pretend I'm slipping you some secret stuff, okay?

Following the fire at Imperial Food Products in Hamlet, I announced that I would establish a toll-free Safety-Line for employees to use to report safety violations if their employers failed to respond to their complaints. As you know, that line has been up and running for a couple of months now, and so far, we've logged 149 calls. Fifty-four calls were referred to the North Carolina Department of Labor and forty-eight to the Department of Insurance. Since concurrent jurisdiction went into effect, forty-seven Safety-Line calls have been referred to the U.S. Department of Labor for follow-up.

I also said that I would help publicize that Safety-Line by distributing posters with the toll-free number prominently displayed to employers in North Carolina. This poster has been sent to every business on the Employment Security payroll list that employs ten or more people. In the meantime, with the help of some very talented local production people, we've created both an audio and video PSA [public service announcement] to further publicize the number. We've got a special treat for you: the premier showing of our Safety-Line PSA.

[Video is played.]

As you can see, I didn't take that trip to Hollywood for nothing!

I'd like to thank Mr. Frank Smith, owner of Franklin Video, and Mr. Mark Harmon, account executive, for their help in producing the video.[1] I'd also like to thank Mr. Tony Burden, creative director for Sperry and Associates, for his company's help in producing the audio spots.[2] These gentlemen very kindly donated their production services to the state at no cost, and we appreciate that cooperation.

The tapes should be arriving through the mail at your TV and radio stations within the next few days, so I hope you'll encourage your public affairs people to give them plenty of air time over the next year. Does anyone have any questions?

Now I'd like to spend a few minutes talking about the economy. I think you and I can help generate some optimism that's deserved—not a lot, but some.

For the past two weeks, I've been traveling around the state, talking with bankers, economists, and business leaders from a host of different industries to get their perspective on the economy, and I've listened to chance meetings with other citizens. They're worried about their jobs, and worried about crime, and all they hear and read is negative. In the process, I've found that the idea of suspending the unemployment insurance payroll tax I announced two weeks ago has been well received even by legislative leaders, so thank you for that. I noticed that Representative Joe Hackney tried to tease me a bit.[3] He said since [we] had put on the tax in the first place, it only seemed appropriate that we should propose that it be suspended.

Well, actually, it was not a tax increase in the first place. Joe must have forgotten that the $50 million state payroll tax was designed as a companion to offset a $100 million tax reduction we initiated in the federal unemployment tax, which we control. What we actually got at the time was a net $50 million tax reduction, along with creation of a state unemployment fund. Now that the fund is solvent, we can afford to give another $50 million tax reduction, and that's good news. One thing we're looking into now is that we might be able to begin this payroll tax relief with a refund. That would have a quicker benefit. More on that later, when we get it figured out.

Let me share with you a bit more I've learned about the current economy. To a large extent, we're dependent on whatever is happening in the national economy, and as President Bush has acknowledged, it's struggling. In North Carolina, however, it's fairly definite that we hit the worst back in June [and] July when it bottomed out. The improvement has not been dramatic, but it has been steady—in the right direction.

For one thing, in North Carolina we do have a low unemployment rate—not as low as a year and a half ago, but better than six months ago—the lowest in the Southeast and lowest among all the industrial states. You will see from a table in your [press] packet that, after peaking at a rate of 6.7 [percent] in May, the state's unemployment rate is now 5.3 [percent]—as good as 1986, four years into that recovery—the best it's been since February. One very interesting fact is we've even added 14,000 manufacturing jobs to our economy since the height of the recession. Now some of those may be for a three-day work week, but that's better than no days!

One thing I discovered is that this recession has been unique, unlike any other. In '76 and '82, everybody had large inventories at the onset of the recession and a lot of production workers got laid off. Not so much this time, because of better inventory management by those with just-in-time deliveries. That also meant that those who did shut down could ease back in quicker. That's one reason North Carolina has bounced back quicker—that and our more successful industrial recruiting.

But while we were fortunate that not as many production people caught in this recession actually lost their jobs, or were laid off, as in previous recessions—not as many, this time, because of improved management efficiency—more white-collar jobs were affected, and more people became concerned for their own job security. That has led to a drop in consumer confidence. You'll note from another one of the charts in your packet that consumer confidence, as rated by the University of Michigan, is at low ebb.

Yet, I hope you'll agree it's worth reporting that the economy is picking up. Not only employment figures, but another indication is that taxable earnings bottomed out in June and July, but began picking up in August, September, and October. On the national [level], we estimate fourth calendar quarter growth at around 1 percent, with continued modest GNP growth into next year—again, not dramatic, but steady.

When you correct for the tax rate, taxable earnings and profits are not as good as they were before the recession, but what we're seeing is on the way up: slow steady growth rather than a skyrocketing recovery. According to most of the experts I've been talking to, that kind of slow, steady recovery could be better for us because it's less erratic, more stable, and helps to control inflation.

I hope you'll agree that's good news worth reporting, because it might help encourage your readers that it will be all right to go do your Christmas shopping. Old Santa Claus may be just the cure we need.

The experts also tell me the best way to promote growth at this point may be to let the economy move along as it is. They feel we've got more than enough stimulus out there right now to spur gradual growth. If Keynesian economists were right, we've got a $348 billion federal deficit to stimulate the economy. One reason it's not working is that it's so huge a deficit, it scares prudent business leaders.

But I don't want to just sit and watch, when we can do a few things that might help. For example, the construction industry has suffered most in the recession and might be given a boost by the recent reauthorization of the Federal Surface Transportation Act. We estimate that North Carolina will receive between $30 million and $50 million in additional federal funding in the first year of the program. Those funds are expected to be available in January.[4]

So I've asked Tommy Harrelson, secretary of transportation, to revise the Transportation Improvement Program in early 1992 to reflect the new funding levels. It may be possible we can accelerate some projects that are delayed now, though the funds will not be at a level that will allow the addition of many new major projects. Not only will that help the hardest hit industrial sector—construction—it will also help us to take advantage of some more bargain-priced competitive bids!

Prison construction may also offer some additional contract opportunities. We've entered Phase 6 of the prison construction plan authorized by the General Assembly, in 1991, for $103 million of the $200 million in bonds approved by the voters. Bonds for construction of 3,300 beds in fifteen locations around the state will be offered in early 1992, with funds becoming available in March. We expect to award contracts for five of the projects in April. Eight other sites should be ready for bid by early spring. In May and June, I'll ask the General Assembly to authorize the rest of the $200 million in prison bonds. That's one of the few ways to help jump start the construction industry, and the crime rate statistics prove we need to lock up the more dangerous ones longer!

For those who remain unemployed, and who are having a tough time finding a new job, we've instituted a new computer service to increase public access to state government job listings. You may remember that the State Personnel Office had to curtail open access to state job listings over in the Administration Building due to the tight budget and their own staffing shortages. We caught a little flak, deserved, over that and decided to do it better.

Actually, that same job list has been available to the public in sixty-four counties for the past two years through the State Library's North Carolina Information Network. That network is linked to public libraries, public and private academic institutions, and community colleges across the state. But the only problem with that listing is that it could only be searched by scrolling one line at a time, and was therefore very cumbersome. We've refined the system now so that job hunters can go into their local library, access the database, and search the state government job list by location, job type, position title, or department.

This expanded and more user-friendly database will soon be available in 400 library systems across the state. By the way, here's an idea that could help you sell papers. You might want to check it out and help your readers by printing your own selected list. After all, some of you have argued correctly that state databases belong to "the people." If you really want to print some state records that would really interest people who need your help, get creative; figure out a useful newsprint format so more readers will buy more papers!

In addition to job openings, the same computer network contains a listing of all state purchase and contract data from the N.C. Department of Transportation and the Division of Purchase and Contract. Updated twice a week, the network lists all state bid openings as well as equipment and highway contracts. The bids and contracts listed range from food, publications, textiles, and chemicals to hospital items and office supplies. Though this service has been available for several years, it has just been expanded into a database and can now be accessed more easily.

Several computers in the back of the room are tied into the system, and staff is available to assist any one of you who are curious about the database and want to see how it works. Here to say just a few words about this expanded system is Howard McGinn, our state librarian.[5]

[McGinn speaks.]

I'd like to thank Secretary Patric Dorsey for joining us for this announcement today and lending her support to this effort. Now, does anyone have any questions?

---

[1]Franklin H. Smith, Jr. (1952–), born in Bay City, Mich.; resident of Raleigh; B.A., Marlboro College, 1976; associate degree, Delta College, 1978. Assistant director, WUCM-TV, Bay City, 1977–1979; account executive, Mellus Newspapers, Lincoln Park, Mich., 1979–1981; commercial-promotional producer, WTVD-TV, Durham, 1981–1984; commercial producer, Dusenbury and Alban, Durham, 1984–1985; owner, president, Franklin Video, Inc., Raleigh, since 1985. Franklin H. Smith, Jr., letter to Jan-Michael Poff, July 20, 1993.

Mark Harmon (1953–), born in Buffalo, N.Y.; resident of Raleigh; B.F.A., University of Wisconsin-Milwaukee, 1985; U.S. Army, 1972–1974. Sales and marketing director, Franklin Video, Inc., since 1987. Mark Harmon, letter to Jan-Michael Poff, June 25, 1993.

[2]Anthony C. Burden, resident of Raleigh; B.A., East Carolina University. Exhibit designer, N.C. Division of Forest Resources, 1978–1979; graphic designer, N.C. Department of Cultural Resources, 1979–1981; art director, 1981–1984, creative director/copywriter, since 1987, Sperry and Associates, Raleigh; art director, associate creative director, Wilford Givens and Co. Advertising, Raleigh, 1984–1987. Tony Burden, letter to Jan-Michael Poff, June 29, 1993.

[3]John Joseph (Joe) Hackney (1945–), Democratic state representative from Orange County, first elected in 1980. Previously identified in Poff, Addresses of Martin, I, 753n.

[4]Martin likely was referring to H.R. 2950, which Congress approved on November 27, 1991. Bush signed the bill into law on December 18; see P.L. 102–240, "Intermodal Surface Transportation Act of 1991," United States Statutes at Large, 105 Stat. 1914–2207. The measure authorized highway and mass transit programs for six years, beginning in fiscal year 1992. Congressional Quarterly Almanac, 1991, 137–151.

[5]Howard F. McGinn (1943–), state librarian, 1989–1992, N.C. Dept. of Cultural Resources. Previously identified in Poff, Addresses of Martin, I, 556n; see also News and Observer, October 6, 1992.

GOVERNOR'S CONFERENCE ON CHILD ABUSE AND NEGLECT

RESEARCH TRIANGLE PARK, DECEMBER 11, 1991

We're here today because each one of us believes strongly in guarding and guiding our children along the road to adulthood. I'm glad to see that so many of you are committed to learning how we can do a better job of protecting and nurturing the young people who are the future of our state and nation.

President Bush has said that the way we treat our children reflects our values as a nation and a people. Our treatment of our children embodies our respect for ourselves and for our future. That does not obligate governments to usurp parental responsibilities. It means we are obligated to safeguard them against irresponsible adults. As adults, parents, and concerned citizens, we have a responsibility to ensure that our children can lead their lives without fear of harm from strangers, friends, or family.

The theme of this conference, "Rising to the Challenge," was selected for an important reason. Child abuse and neglect is a serious and growing problem that will take all of us, working together, to conquer. Beginning with the 1985 Commission on Child Abuse, later the Commission on Children and the Family, both chaired by Mrs. Martin, we have learned too many dreadful secrets about the desperate lives of abused children, ranging from profound neglect to torture and death.[1]

When we take time to listen, we have found many who had sad stories to be told. Consequently, in North Carolina, the increase in the number of reports of child abuse in recent years has been astronomical. In 1984, 18,456 cases were reported. That number rose to 24,418 in 1987. By the end of fiscal year 1990, county departments of social services submitted 45,617 reports of child abuse to the North Carolina central registry system.

We think most of the increase in reports is primarily the result of a change in public awareness, but we believe it also reflects actual increases in the incidence of some forms of child abuse. In any case, the number of substantiated cases has increased at a rate as shocking as the number of reported cases; and perhaps most frightening of all is the fact that we have reason to believe that number still represents but a fraction of the actual incidences of child abuse. We have not yet uncovered it all.

The child protection system, made up of the many components represented by you here today—social services, Community Action, Head Start, public health, mental health, legal-judicial, and education—has not yet been expanded adequately to meet the challenges posed by the enormous increase in reported and substantiated cases of child abuse. County directors of social services, who are charged by state law to receive and investigate reports of child abuse and neglect, have been handling these increased reports without sufficient, well-trained staff. Community resources to help children and families either are not available or may be underused due to lack of awareness or coordination.

On April 18, 1991, I announced a series of initiatives to deal with this most serious problem. The intent of these initiatives was to strengthen services for abused and neglected children and to improve the investigation of child fatalities due to suspected abuse or neglect. The responsibility for implementing the initiatives was assigned to Secretary Dave Flaherty, Department of Human Resources. Our initiatives were to:

—Establish community child protection teams in each county;

—Modify the central registry to allow on-line access to information by county departments of social services;

—Release specific information to the chief medical examiner and local law enforcement when they are investigating a child fatality in which abuse or neglect is suspected, and;

—Implement a two-level review of all cases where a decision is made not to accept a complaint alleging abuse or neglect of a child.

Not all these ideas were well received at first, but time and patience have helped reassure most early critics to come forward to help make it better.

This year, after much negotiation, the General Assembly appropriated additional resources to help meet the needs of county departments of social services. Funding was provided to increase staff, at the state level, to meet the need for training and oversight of the child protective services program.[2] I feel the[y] were appropriately generous, given the budgetary difficulties here and [in] most states, to respond to this new priority. Monies also were made available for an independent study of the child protective services system in our state.[3]

The appropriation of $3.25 million is intended to support additional child protective services staff in county departments of social services for fiscal year 1991–1992. An additional $7 million will be available for fiscal year 1992–1993.[4]

These steps alone will not prevent abuse or neglect. Interagency collaboration and coordination must be promoted and developed in the areas of planning, program design, training, funding, and referrals. County social service directors must be able to reach into their communities and receive help from community action agencies, mental health centers, health departments, law enforcement agencies, educators, the guardian-ad-litem, child advocacy leaders, judges and attorneys, the clergy, and volunteers.

These are times when pressures on families are mounting. Poverty, homelessness, joblessness, teen pregnancy, drug abuse, and lack of understanding about child development all contribute to increased abuse and neglect of our children. What a litany of problems!

Pressures are also mounting on our child protective services workers. These dedicated people have one of the most difficult jobs in government, with high pressure, overwhelming workloads, and limited resources. How well they are able to perform their duties can have serious consequences—or beautiful consequences! These professionals deserve our encouragement, our support, and our assistance, and they deserve our thanks for the many long hours of hard work they sacrifice for our children.

For the protection of our children, for the protection of our future, we must all work together to create an environment where all children have the opportunity to grow up free from neglect and abuse. The fact that you are here today shows a strong commitment from the public sector, the private sector, and the general public to "rise to the challenge" of conquering child abuse and neglect. I commend you for your dedication and thank you for your efforts to make the world a safer place for our children. Together, we can make a difference.

---

[1]According to Martin's speech to the Concerned Charlotteans group, March 21, 1988, the Governor's Commission on Children and the Family grew from the Governor's Commission on Child Victimization. Poff, *Addresses of Martin*, I, 787.

[2]*N.C. Session Laws, 1991*, II, c. 689, s. 103.

[3]*N.C. Session Laws, 1991*, II, c. 689, s. 216.

[4]*N.C. Session Laws, 1991*, II, c. 689, s. 216.

HOUSING FINANCE PRESS CONFERENCE

RALEIGH, DECEMBER 12, 1991

We're here today to mark two important milestones for the North Carolina Housing Finance Agency and our state. The first milestone is the sale of this month's mortgage revenue bonds, which closes next Thursday, December 19. That sale will provide $62.1 million in 30-year, fixed-rate mortgages for over 1,130 first-time home buyers across North Carolina.

These mortgages will be offered at 6.95 percent, the lowest interest rate ever in the history of the North Carolina Housing Finance Agency. It's also one of the lowest fixed rates available anywhere in the country. Prospective home buyers who are interested in taking advantage of this opportunity can apply for the mortgages through twenty-four participating lenders and their branches across the state; last year, Housing Finance Agency mortgages assisted families with average incomes of $25,600. I think it's worth noting that the interest rate on these mortgages is as low as it is because the North Carolina Housing Finance Agency, a self-supporting agency of state government, made a sound business decision to refinance some other bonds it held and passed its earnings on to the people of North Carolina.

Based on experience in North Carolina, approximately 30 percent of these mortgages are used to buy newly constructed homes. If that holds true for this $62 million, the new mortgages will support $18.6 million in new construction. If so, that $18.6 million would be expected to create 372 jobs in construction alone, where one job is defined as work for one person for one year. That has a ripple effect, creating additional jobs in housing-related industries, from furniture, lending, and real estate, to the sale of grass seed.

In addition to new homes, these mortgages, based on past experience, will be expected to finance $43.5 million in the sale of existing homes. That movement in the market will help support the construction of more new homes for the present owners who sell to our first-time home buyers. We expect the sale of existing homes will generate an additional $3.48 million in personal income for North Carolinians.

We would also expect this $62.1 million in mortgages will increase revenues to the state, through income and sales taxes, by nearly $1.35 million over the thirty-year period of the mortgages. Local tax revenues should also increase by more than $2.2 million. But that's not the reason we're doing this, it's just part of the total effect.

These economic impact figures are conservative. They were calculated using methods developed by the National Home Builders Association and other sources, and it's clear that it will give a much needed boost to our economy, especially to the housing sector, as we work our way out of this recession.

That brings us to our second milestone. As of this December, the Housing Finance Agency has reached the $2 billion mark in financing affordable homes and apartments using the mortgage revenue bond program. Since Governor Holshouser celebrated the first bond sale in 1976, the Housing Finance Agency has provided first home mortgages for 29,000 families; affordable apartments for 8,400 families; more than 16,000 jobs for North Carolinians; and it has generated an additional $95 million in personal income for North Carolina realtors and $150 million in local and state tax revenues.

The federal program for mortgage revenue bonds which produced this growth has been receiving year-by-year extensions in Congress. Legislation to extend the program permanently was cosponsored by every one of North Carolina's thirteen U.S. senators and representatives this year. That legislation is supported by an overwhelming majority of the full House and Senate. Nevertheless, the issue became entangled in budget negotiations this year, and the program received yet one more temporary extension—this one for six months. Congress needs to find its way clear in the next session to make the mortgage revenue bond program permanent.[1]

I think you can see what this house, purchased with one of these mortgages, means to first-time home buyers in our state. Mr. and Mrs. Sanne, Robert and Beth, and their sons Shane and Josh can explain it to you.[2]

I'd like to thank Chairman Bill Boyd, Bob Kucab, the board members, and staff at the Housing Finance Agency for reaching the $2 billion mark. In honor of this special occasion, I would like to proclaim the week of December 15 through the 21st as "Affordable Housing Week" in North Carolina.[3]

---

[1]P.L. 102–227, the "Tax Extension Act of 1991," authorized mortgage bonds and mortgage credit certificates through June 30, 1992; see *United States Statutes at Large*, Act of December 11, 1991, 105 Stat. 1688. During 1992, President Bush rejected two major budget bills that included mortgage bonds among their many provisions. H.R. 4210, the "Tax Fairness and Economic Growth Acceleration Act of 1992," vetoed on March 20, would have extended mortgage revenue bonds through June 30, 1993. H.R. 11, the "Revenue Act of 1992," vetoed on November 4, would have established the program permanently. *Congressional Quarterly Almanac, 1992*, 139, 140, 141, 144, 149.

[2]The press conference was held at the new home of Robert and Beth Sanne, Lake Woodard Drive, Raleigh.

[3]A. Robert Kucab was executive director of the North Carolina Housing Finance Agency. Martin signed "North Carolina Housing Finance Agency Affordable Housing Week, 1991, by the Governor of the State of North Carolina: A Proclamation" on December 12. Governors Papers, James G. Martin.

PROCLAMATION CALLING EXTRA SESSION OF GENERAL ASSEMBLY

RALEIGH, DECEMBER 20, 1991

I. Redistricting

The North Carolina Constitution, Article II, Section 3, requires that the "General Assembly, at the first regular session convening after the return of every decennial census of population taken by order of Congress, shall revise the Senate districts and the apportionment of Senators among those districts. . . ."[1]

Pursuant to the foregoing requirement, the 1991 General Assembly enacted Chapter 676 of the 1991 Session Laws setting forth Senate districts and the apportionment of Senators among those districts.[2]

The North Carolina Constitution, Article II, Section 5, requires that the "General Assembly, at the first regular session convening after the return of every decennial census of population taken by order of Congress, shall revise the Representative districts and the apportionment of Representatives among those districts. . . ."[3]

Pursuant to the foregoing requirement, the 1991 General Assembly enacted Chapter 675 of the 1991 Session Laws setting forth Representative districts and the apportionment of representatives among those districts.[4]

The Constitution of the United States, Article I, Section 2, as amended by Amendment XIV, provides that members of the United States House of Representatives shall be apportioned among the several states according to their respective numbers as determined every ten years in such manner as the Congress shall by law direct.[5]

Pursuant to the foregoing requirement, a census was taken in 1990 and as a result thereof the state of North Carolina is entitled to twelve members of Congress for the period of the next ten years. North Carolina law provides that the North Carolina General Assembly apportion members of the United States House of Representatives among the districts established by the General Assembly. Pursuant to said requirements, the 1991 General Assembly enacted Chapter 601 and Section 33 of Chapter 761 of the 1991 Session Laws to provide for the increase from eleven to twelve congressional districts and the 1991 redistricting plan for the congressional districts of North Carolina.[6]

As required by Section 5 of the Voting Rights Act of 1965, as amended, 42 U.S.C. 1973c, the redistricting plans for the North Carolina Senate, North Carolina House of Representatives, and the United States House of Representatives were submitted to the United States Department of Justice for pre-clearance.[7]

On December 18, 1991, the United States Department of Justice notified the state of North Carolina by letter signed by John R. Dunne,[8] assistant attorney general, Civil Rights Division, that the submitted plans do not conform to federal law and tendered objections to the North Carolina State House, Senate, and Congressional plans stating that one additional predominantly minority congressional district could have been created; that at least three additional minority districts could have been created for the state House, and that at least one additional minority district could have been created for the state Senate. The letter further referred to specific counties or geographic areas of the state in which those districts could have been created. The findings of the United States Department of Justice as set forth in the letter from John R. Dunne dated December 18, 1991, are incorporated herein by reference, and I find that additional minority districts can be created in order that election opportunities for minority citizens residing in those counties specified in findings of the Department of Justice may be enhanced.[9]

II. Date for Filing Notice of Candidacy

Filing for election to state offices and the United States Congress pursuant to North Carolina General Statutes Chapter 163–106(c), at 12:00 noon on the first Monday of January (January 6, 1992), and terminates at 12:00 noon on the first Monday in February (February 3, 1992). It appears that the General Assembly of North Carolina may not be able to convene and develop redistricting plans for the North Carolina State House, Senate, and Congressional districts within a time reasonable for potential candidates to select knowledgeably the offices for which they may desire to offer themselves considering the current statutory filing period. Therefore, I am of the opinion that there is an immediate necessity to amend current law to change the time period within which potential candidates must file for elective office.[10]

I find that there is a need to convene the North Carolina General Assembly in an extra session in order that it may amend the statutory provisions providing for the time within which potential candidates must file for office, and to fulfill its constitutional duties of redistricting and reapportionment consistent with the Voting Rights Act of 1965, as amended.

III. Economy and Employment Security Tax Surcharge

Although North Carolina's economy has shown modest but steady growth out of the current recession, the growth rate continues to be less than was expected at this time. Because of that slow growth and the inability of North Carolina and other states to fully recover from the economic downturn of the past year, employees and employers continue to struggle with personal and business financial affairs.

North Carolina's unemployment insurance trust fund was severely tested by the recessions of 1975 and 1982, causing the General Assembly in 1983 to enact legislation amending the Employment Security Law to replenish and bolster the funds held in reserve to withstand another severe economic downturn.[11] In 1987 the law was further amended so as to reach a projected trust fund balance of $1.8 billion by 1991, when only $1.2 billion to $1.4 billion would be needed for the fund to be solvent. The federal trust fund has now reached $1.35 billion, and the reserve fund now contains $193 million. Thus, these funds have exceeded all projections and have exceeded the solvency level established for the payment of unemployment insurance benefits.

Thus, I am of the opinion that immediate consideration must be given to amendments to Chapter 96 of the North Carolina General Statutes, and particularly sections 96–5 and 96–9, to repeal the 20 percent employment security tax surcharge that was enacted in 1987. In doing so, employers in North Carolina would be relieved of approximately $50 million to $60 million per year of unnecessary taxes, thereby further stimulating the economy and granting to employers an opportunity to use those funds for current expenses, maintaining employment opportunities, and expansion.

IV. Declarations

As required by Article III, Section 5(7) of the constitution, I have sought and received the advice of the Council of State concerning the need to call the General Assembly into extra session to address redistricting, the time for filing as a candidate for public office, and repeal of the employment security tax surcharge and received from them their advice that it is appropriate for the General Assembly to be convened into extra session as provided by Article III, Section 5(7) of the constitution for those purposes.[12] I have also discussed the matter with the lieutenant governor, the Speaker of the House of Representatives, and the president pro tempore of the Senate. They are of the same view.

ACCORDINGLY, pursuant to the authority granted to me by Article III, Section 5(7) of the Constitution of North Carolina, I find that the circumstances stated above constitute an "extraordinary occasion" within the meaning of Article III, Section 5(7) of the Constitution of North Carolina, and PROCLAIM that the General Assembly is hereby convened in extra session for the purpose of considering legislation (1) amending [Chapter] 163–106(c) of the North Carolina General Statutes, (2) amending 1991 Session Laws, Chapter 601, "An Act to Divide North Carolina into Twelve Congressional Districts," and Chapter 675, "An Act to Establish House of Representatives Districts and to Apportion Seats [in] the House of Representatives among Districts," and Chapter 676, "An Act to Establish Senatorial Districts and to Apportion Seats in the Senate among Districts," and Section 33 of Chapter 761, "An Act to Make Technical Corrections and Other Changes to the Law," and (3) amending Chapter 96 of the North Carolina General Statutes as necessary to repeal the employment security tax surcharge imposed in 1987.

This extra session to consider these matters shall begin the morning of December 30, 1991, at 10:00 o'clock, and shall continue as provided by law and the respective rules of the Senate and House of Representatives until both houses shall have adjourned such extra session *sine die*.

Done at Raleigh, Wake County, North Carolina, this 20th day of December, 1991.

[Signed] James G. Martin

---

[1]North Carolina Constitution, quoted in *North Carolina Manual, 1991–1992*, 622.

[2]"An Act to Establish Senatorial Districts and To Apportion Seats in the Senate among Districts," *N.C. Session Laws, 1991*, II, c. 676, was ratified July 13, 1991.

[3]North Carolina Constitution, quoted in *North Carolina Manual, 1991–1992*, 622–623.

[4]"An Act to Establish House of Representatives Districts and to Apportion Seats in the House of Representatives among Districts," *N.C. Session Laws, 1991*, II, c. 675, was ratified July 13, 1991.

[5]United States Constitution, quoted in *North Carolina Manual, 1991–1992*, 670, 683.

[6]"An Act to Divide North Carolina into Twelve Congressional Districts" was ratified July 9, 1991. *N.C. Session Laws, 1991*, I, c. 601. Chapter 761, *N.C. Session Laws, 1991*, II, is identified elsewhere in this volume.

[7]*Voting Rights Act of 1965, U.S. Code*, vol. 42, sec. 1973c (1991).

[8]John R. Dunne (1930–), born in Baldwin, N.Y.; resident of Garden City, N.Y.; A.B., Georgetown University, 1951; LL.B., Yale University, 1954. Attorney; member, 1966–1989, deputy majority leader, 1987–1988, N.Y. State Senate; appointed assistant attorney general, Civil Rights Division, U.S. Justice Department, 1990. *Federal Staff Directory, 1990*, II, 956.

[9]The extra session of the General Assembly revised state House, Senate, and congressional districts via the following legislation: "An Act to Establish Senatorial Districts and to Apportion Seats in the Senate among Districts," c. 4, ratified January 14, 1992; "An Act to Establish House of Representatives Districts and to Apportion Seats in the House of Representatives among Districts," c. 5, ratified January 14, 1992; "An Act to Divide North Carolina into Twelve Congressional Districts," c. 7, ratified January 24, 1992, *N.C. Session Laws, Extra Session, 1991, Regular Session, 1992*. The U.S. Justice Department approved the state's redrawn congressional and legislative districts on February 6, 1992. *News and Observer*, February 7, 1992.

[10]See "An Act to Delay the Opening and Closing of Filing for All 1992 Primary Elections, Except the Presidential Preference Primary so as to Allow Time for the General Assembly to Modify or Seek Enforcement of Redistricting Plans Enacted by the 1991 Regular Session and to Make Conforming Changes," c. 1, ratified December 30, 1991; "An Act to Provide that Chapter 1 of the 1991 Extra Session Does Not Affect the Filing Period for the High Point City Elections," c. 3, ratified January 14, 1992; and "An Act to Provide for Further Alteration of the 1992 Election Timetable," c. 9, ratified February 3, 1992, *N.C. Session Laws, Extra Session, 1991, Regular Session, 1992*.

[11]"An Act to Assure Unemployment Insurance Trust Fund Solvency and Compliance with Federal Law" was ratified June 22, 1983. *N.C. Session Laws, 1983*, c. 585.

[12]"The Governor may, on extraordinary occasions, by and with the advice of the Council of State, convene the General Assembly in extra session by its proclamation, stating therein the purpose or purposes for which they are thus convened." North Carolina Constitution, Article III, Section 5(7), quoted in *North Carolina Manual, 1991–1992*, 628.

AIR CARGO AIRPORT AUTHORITY BOARD OF DIRECTORS

Chapel Hill, January 7, 1992

As we approach the board's crucial decision in February–March whether to build a global air industrial complex for North Carolina, and what its features will be, it is expected and useful that we hear criticism and negative advice against which to test the evidence favoring such a dramatic proposal. The John Locke Foundation of Raleigh has published and distributed brief articles, for and against, which have been distributed for your review: one by me, in support of this project; and by Mr. Robert W. Poole, Jr., president of the Reason Foundation of Los Angeles, opposing it. Both have been reprinted in the Raleigh *News and Observer*, and in the *Greensboro News and Record*, and perhaps elsewhere. This is a valuable public service, because it helps to focus our attention on potential errors and pitfalls, and ensures that we not overlook issues about which there may be reasonable doubt. By listening carefully to such criticism, and considering how best to accommodate or overcome its negative views, we improve the chances that we reach the best possible decision for North Carolina.[1]

The original article presenting my views was not drafted to respond to Mr. Poole's critique, but was merely a positive introduction to this innovative concept based on earlier published information. Therefore, I will share with you this response as one answer to the Poole article. It is important to note that Mr. Poole does not conclude that an air cargo industrial complex should not be built. He only argues that certain questions need to be answered before that decision is made, which is essentially the same position this board has taken so far. He mistakenly asserts that we have already made a decision in haste to spend $700 million. By copy of this, I will inform him that no such decision has been made, and that we welcome his thoughtful observations regardless of the outcome. At some point, soon, you will be asked to make some strategic decisions, but not just yet.

Mr. Poole then questions the legislature's decision to "allocate millions of dollars for further work and site acquisition."[2] Without that wise appropriation, however, we would have wasted a lot of precious time with no way or means to examine and answer many questions which fall outside the scope of the feasibility study. We would have been unable to afford the marketing effort which is essential for answering some of his valid questions about willing anchor tenants, interest from cargo or passenger airlines, and site requirements other than aviation-related ones. We would have wasted valuable time, and that would have served the interests of nobody except our potential rivals in other states.

It is odd that an expert on America's airport needs would advocate unnecessary delays in the very complex decision-making process we face. Indeed, it is ironic that Mr. Poole contradicts himself when he claims that our "haste is unfortunate, because the United States definitely needs additional airport capacity over the next two decades." We won't help that by stalling. He further refutes his own position by adding: "Seventeen of our major airports are already seriously congested, and the Federal Aviation Administration [FAA] projects that as many as fifty will reach that status by the year 2000." That seems to be a rather persuasive case not for delaying tactics, but for moving ahead with all deliberate speed. Contrary to his avowed purpose, he confirms that the time is ripe, that the market is ready for us.[3]

Next, Mr. Poole trots out the FAA's 1991 "Feasibility Study of Regional Air-Cargo Airports," without noting the thoughtful response from Professor John Kasarda, which showed that this FAA study was about some other concept different from a global air cargo industrial complex. Even if the FAA study shows that another idea won't work, that's no reason for rejecting our idea—not when sixty-seven airports are, or verge upon, congestion.

As to his point that "60 percent of all air cargo is carried as belly cargo on scheduled passenger airliners,"[4] we have noted that fact very carefully, as well as the more relevant fact that 40 percent goes in air freighters. For us, it is the latter market which is not well served in all those congested passenger airports now, and is worth closer attention from somebody. He further argues that all those existing passenger airplanes are only half full,[5] but he does not seem to be aware that in less than a decade, when rapid expansion of air freight will have filled them, there will be more, not less, actual tonnage than today being carried in freighters; and it will need a convenient place to take off and to land, which is where we step forward—or somebody else will.

It is fascinating that Mr. Poole finds the Kasarda concept "dazzling" and "may eventually prove itself in the marketplace."[6] Well now, how could that ever happen if all follow his advice and no one tries it? Of course, the answer to that is that if we don't, someone else will. Then we will get little satisfaction, years from now, gloating over what a wonderful North Carolina idea [sic] had which worked so well for another state because we were too timid.

The Poole paper objects to North Carolina investing "$700 million serving a single category of user."[7] It's strange that he has decided that we are going to spend $700 million, when we haven't reached that decision ourselves. That figure is the estimated cost of developing a new "greenfield" site, including every airport feature from scratch, as well as the developmental cost of the industrial park. What if we decide to select an existing airport or joint use of a military airport? What if we decide to leave all or most of the industrial park responsibility in the private sector? What if we only have to finance one parallel runway and a parking apron to bring an existing facility up to our capacity? To what "single category of user" is he limiting us? How can he possibly pretend to know what this board will decide, when he has not even been aware of how carefully we have been considering all these factors?

Finally, in desperation lest his thoughtful questions prove inept, Mr. Poole concludes by reverting to diatribe and name-calling. What does he think he is, a politician? What he does as a last resort, his parting shot, is to throw at us the magic incantation "boondoggle"—not once, but four times! Count them![8] Does he really think that such fearful names will bring us to our knees? Or is he afraid that this state just might have a winner? He didn't say what's on his agenda. If he wants respect for his Reason Foundation, I suggest he stick to trying to reason and let the politicians trade blows with the name-calling.

We know that Mr. Poole is an ardent advocate for private ownership of airports. That's fine. I like that, and [it] may be a great idea, but all he has to do is introduce us to some private investor who will build it for us, or buy it after we build it. We should not follow his advice to back away from our hot idea while some private investor moves ahead in Kentucky or Florida.

My advice to the board is to consider carefully all the criticisms and reservations, and test our concept against what they have to say. Only then can we decide whether any negative argument is valid and, if so, whether it can be overcome. After all, one mark of every proven, successful, large-scale, innovative project is that its leaders were flexible and able to assimilate or accommodate problems which appeared late in the design of the project. One mark of large-scale failures is that they did not have the flexibility to make adjustments. In this case, with Mr. Poole's arguments, it is reassuring to observe that every valid point he has made had been recognized by our staff and consultants early in the evolution and that no irrevocable decision has yet been made.

North Carolina has no intention of investing too much in any unjustifiable project. We do not seek to waste our resources on any worthless scheme "for making North Carolina poorer," as he says.[9] We have an idea that we believe has a great potential to make North Carolina wealthier, and we have the proven track record of having successfully perfected such a pioneering concept decades ago at our Research Triangle Park. Poole would have advised against that, too, I expect. No, we will not delude ourselves into investing more than is justifiable in this concept, but neither will we be so foolish as to squander a brilliant idea and let some other state harvest what we have sown. If we not timidly stand still [*sic*] and let anything delay our bold preparations for a timely decision, that would throw away the supreme advantage we now have of being far ahead of our competition.

How often we have seen in sports the example of a talented team which could score a lot of early points, but could not hold a lead. That must not happen to us. It is vitally important that we stick to our game plan, maintain our composure, and that we not fold under pressure if we are to be worthy of the challenge given us from the General Assembly.

We must weigh all the factors carefully in order to choose the right course, the wisest course. But we must also stay focused on our objective, which is not to waste a lot of money nor waste a lot of time. Our objective is to choose what is the wisest investment for an air cargo industrial complex in North Carolina, whether it's $700 million, or nothing at all, or something in between. If we choke under pressure and avoid or delay making the right decision, that might very well "make North Carolina poorer" and somebody else richer.

---

[1]The John Locke Foundation, a conservative think-tank based in Raleigh, featured a pair of articles on the Global TransPark in its December 1991–January 1992 edition of *Carolina Journal*: Martin's essay, "State-Of-The-Art Industrial Park Holds Great Promise," appeared on pages 12–13; the assessment by Robert W. Poole, Jr., "Only the Market Can Determine Project's Feasibility," followed on pages 13–14. The *News and Observer* ran the governor's full text, and an edited version of the Poole piece, in its December 9, 1991, issue. Except for a few extremely minor differences, Martin's *Journal* article is largely identical to his "Newspaper Column: Economic Development for the Future—North Carolina's Global TransPark," November 15, 1991, reprinted on pages 385–387, above.

[2]"Even before the taxpayer-funded feasibility study is complete, the state has allocated millions of dollars for further work and site acquisition. The implicit message to the consultants is that they'd better conclude that the project is feasible." Robert W. Poole, Jr., "Only the Market Can Determine Project's Feasibility," *Carolina Journal* (December 1991–January 1992), 13, hereinafter cited as Poole, "Only the Market Can Determine Project's Feasibility."

[3]Martin correctly quoted Poole in this paragraph. Poole, "Only the Market Can Determine Project's Feasibility," 13.

[4]Poole, "Only the Market Can Determine Project's Feasibility," 13.

[5]Poole wrote that almost half the available cargo space on passenger airliners "goes unused." Poole, "Only the Market Can Determine Project's Feasibility," 13.

[6]"It's a dazzling concept, and one that may eventually prove itself in the marketplace. But as of 1991, it is also a concept fraught with risks and uncertainties. Today, firms using just-in-time systems make very little use of air freight. Because it is far more expensive than rail or truck or ocean delivery, only low-weight, high-value, very sensitive items are shipped by air. Presumably the feasibility study will identify those manufacturers for whom large-scale air shipment of components and finished products is cost effective. . . ." Poole, "Only the Market Can Determine Project's Feasibility," 13.

[7]"It is also risky to invest $700 million in an airport serving a single category of user." Referring to Alliance Airport in Fort Worth, Poole wrote that, while the facility "offers companies sites for exactly the kind of factories-alongside-taxiways being proposed for the N.C. facility, it has yet to attract any just-in-time assembly customers or all-cargo airlines." Poole, "Only the Market Can Determine Project's Feasibility," 13.

[8]"Job-creation boondoggles," according to Poole, begin as publicly funded economic development projects that promise to create employment for many—but prove to be untenable without regular infusions of tax money. Such boondoggles range from municipal sports arenas and "other buildings that sit unused the majority of the time, costing far more than they bring in," to that "classic" example of wasteful government spending, the Tennessee-Tombigbee waterway project.

"Large-scale government subsidy can create the illusion of economic development (the jobs) even when what is being developed does not really add value in economic terms," Poole wrote. "The way we distinguish proposed boondoggles from economically viable projects is not by counting the projected number of jobs but by asking whether the project can meet the test of the marketplace." If the Global TransPark feasibility study cannot furnish solid proof that the project will meet that test, "and especially if it concludes that the only way to finance the project is with large federal and state grants, it's a tipoff that what's being proposed is probably a boondoggle. Building boondoggles is a recipe for making North Carolina poorer." Poole, "Only the Market Can Determine Project's Feasibility," 13–14.

[9]See footnote 8, above.

NORTH CAROLINA 2000 STEERING COMMITTEE

RALEIGH, JANUARY 30, 1992

[The text of the address to the North Carolina 2000 Steering Committee, below, seems to have inspired the governor's remarks at Jackson Park Elementary School, Kannapolis, February 10, and Dalton McMichael High School, Madison, March 16, 1992. Martin also touted the NC 2000 program at ceremonies honoring IBM Corporation as a recipient of the North Carolina Quality Leadership Award, January 30, 1992.]

Good afternoon. Welcome to the Executive Mansion and to the first organizational meeting of the North Carolina 2000 Steering Committee. May I take a moment to introduce your chairman, Alvin P. Perkinson, better known as "Bun," a Charlotte business[man] and former president of Laurinburg's St. Andrews College. Let me also introduce my senior education adviser, Jackie Jenkins, a very innovative and creative educator who prepared us for this day.[1]

This is an important occasion, not just for me or for you, but for every child that attends school in our state and for every citizen who depends upon our educational system to better their quality of life. That's just about everybody. By joining together in this effort, you have agreed to share with me, and with thousands of other citizens across this state, the vision of what our schools and communities will be in the year 2000. What is that vision? No more and no less than this:

—That our children will enter school with strong bodies and strong minds, ready and eager to learn all that we can teach them;

—That by the time those children reach the twelfth grade, they will know how to read, they will understand history, and they will be able to find China, and Mauritania, and New Guinea on a map;

—That our young people will be the best scientists and mathematicians in the world, second to none;

—That when graduation day comes, 90 percent of our high school seniors will walk across the stage to receive a diploma that they earned, and deserve;

—That every adult in this state will be able to read, and write, and compute so they can find and keep a job and support their families;

—And that our schools will truly be places of learning, free from violence and fear, free from the pressure and threats of drug dealers.

You think all that just might be beyond our reach? Good. Let's stretch for it.

These are the six goals established by our nation's governors at President Bush's education summit two years ago in Charlottesville. These are the goals of the president's America 2000 strategy, and of our own North Carolina 2000, and of thirty-three other states, so far. And they are your goals, too, because as members of the North Carolina 2000 Steering Committee, it's your job to make these goals something much more than just words on paper—and add to them, if you wish. You can't say I haven't given you a challenge.

I'm convinced that North Carolina 2000 is the structure through which we will be able to provide a better quality education to every citizen-learner in North Carolina, of all ages. Making that happen won't be easy, but the good thing is you don't have to do it all alone. The important, the crucial thing is that we do have to do it—here in North Carolina and all over America.

I believe that just about every school, in every school system in this state, is ready for a change. Some have already forged ahead, revamping their programs, pushing and pulling and twisting them inside out to achieve better results, adapting the "total quality leadership" principles already proven in so many modern businesses. Support from communities and businesses has never been greater, but it needs to become much greater. The time for action is now.

Look at the success of the Tech Prep program. We say we need to educate a workforce capable of competing in our high-tech, highly competitive global marketplace. That's what Tech Prep is doing, and very well.

Our permanent Commission on Workforce Preparedness is also going to help build the workforce of the future, coordinating employment, vocational education, and job-training programs at the state and local levels.

What about improving science and math education? That's the goal of the North Carolina Alliance for Science and Mathematics. With a $7 million grant from the National Science Foundation already in hand, the alliance is establishing a network of regional partnerships to improve the quality of math and science education in this state, involving classroom teachers in business, and businesses in the classroom, to make math and science more timely and more relevant—so our students can see how it really is used in the workplace. I'm pleased to say that the North Carolina Alliance is ready and committed to working with us to make North Carolina 2000 a success.

What about Cities in Schools? Since that miraculously effective approach to dropout prevention began in New York City and spread to Dallas, Atlanta, and our own Mecklenburg County, we've been able to help this program expand to thirty-one schools. I'm happy to say that thirty-three other counties or school districts are working, getting ready to adopt that program. That will be close to half.

And what about our littlest people, the at-risk four-year-olds who will never enter school ready to learn unless someone is ready to read to them and lift them up to greater opportunities and a better quality of life? We're reaching out to them already through our Uplift Day Care program. Uplift Day Care uses existing state and new federal funds to integrate Head Start with day care for working parents. We're going to get those at-risk four-year-olds off the waiting list for child care and into developmental preschool programs to help them become ready to learn.

President Bush recently announced $600 million in additional federal funds for Head Start. I'm delighted, because that was the one urgent plea I made at the education summit in Charlottesville. North Carolina's share, around $12 million, will go a long way to make that program truly uplifting to even more young children.

No doubt about it, thousands of parents, teachers, principals, superintendents, and community leaders are ready for a change, and they're not just talking about change and waiting for the other guy to make the first move. No, they're stepping right in and rolling up their sleeves, making that change happen. I look around this room and see "change makers"—parents, educators, legislators, employers—people who are committed to building a quality school system in this state, and more than a few who have backed that commitment with their time and their money.

We know what works and what doesn't work in our schools. We've got plenty of demonstration projects on line and a number of proven success stories to point to, and we have stacks and stacks of studies that tell us who to talk to, what to do, and how to do it. We've got all the building materials to construct a state-of-the-art school system for the twenty-first century, but we don't have a decentralized foundation and a deregulated framework on which to nail them. That's where North Carolina 2000 comes in. You people are the architect and engineering team, upon which we'll build our goals teams and our North Carolina 2000 community action team, to design better school systems.

Building the educational system of the future will be like an old-fashioned barn raising, because it will take everyone in the community [to] come and do their part in building the future of opportunity for our children. Your job is to harness all that community energy, focus it on implementing programs that work, and build enough momentum in the project to keep everyone working hard until the job is finished. It's a big job, one that's going to demand a good deal of your energy and commitment—and I intend to be right in there with you, because I'm just as committed as you are, and I'm willing to back up that commitment with the energy of my office and the help of my cabinet secretaries. As it has been for seven years now, the education of our children will continue to be my number-one priority. I believe that North Carolina 2000 gives us the organizational structure we need to pull educational reform out of individual schools and classrooms and bring it to every school, and classroom, and social agency, and home, and workplace in the state.

I encourage you to listen well to the presentation and discussion you'll hear this afternoon. Listen, and ask questions. I also encourage you to take this message back to your communities: Spread the word that education is everybody's business. If you run into someone who doubts that, you remind them how much they rely on other people who have been educated in North Carolina—doctors, lawyers, accountants, drivers, repair services and construction workers, their own employees—the list is endless.

Remind him someone else's lack of education directly affects his ability to run his business, maintain his health, or buy goods and services for his family. I know that for a fact. A former chemistry student of mine is now my dentist. I don't know about you, but I certainly don't want anyone putting an electric drill in my mouth unless they darn well know how to use it. He made good grades.[2]

Abraham Lincoln once said that "The struggle of today is not altogether for today—it is for a vast future also." As members of the North Carolina 2000 Steering Committee, you face an awesome task: building a system of quality education in the state of North Carolina. Yet even as you struggle to meet that challenge, you will be building a vast future of opportunity for generations of North Carolinians. Thank you for joining us in this effort.

[1]Alvin P. (Bun) Perkinson, Jr. (1935–), born in Chattanooga, Tenn.; resident of Pinehurst; B.A., Davidson College, 1957; honorary degree. Charlotte real estate broker, developer, 1957–1968; development director, Rhodes College, 1968–1972; director, development and public relations, Millsaps College, 1972–1975; president, St. Andrews Presbyterian College, 1975–1987; managerial duties with Lake Norman Co., 1988–1991, included guiding the firm through Chapter 11 bankruptcy proceedings, 1990–1991; owner, Perkinson and Associates, corporate reorganization, financing and management services, since 1991. Alvin P. Perkinson, Jr., letter to Jan-Michael Poff, December 7, 1993.

Jackie Womble Jenkins (1948–), born in Louisville, Miss.; resident of Raleigh; B.S., 1971, M.S., 1972, University of Southern Mississippi; D.Ed., Duke University, 1977. Assistant professor of education and psychology, Campbell University, 1977–1979; developmental learning specialist, student personnel services director, Ravenscroft School, Raleigh, 1979–1980; private consultant in education, 1981–1987; consultant on curriculum, instruction, and testing, 1987, language arts program specialist, 1987–1990, Wake County Public School System; senior education advisor to Governor Martin, 1990–1993; executive director, North Carolina 2000 Foundation, since 1992. Jackie Womble Jenkins, letter to Jan-Michael Poff, November 8, 1993.

[2]Martin's dentist and former student was L. H. Hutchens, head of periodontics at the University of North Carolina School of Dentistry, Chapel Hill. Nancy Jo Pekarek, letter to Jan-Michael Poff, January 20, 1995.

TRAVEL AND TOURISM PRESS CONFERENCE

RALEIGH, JANUARY 31, 1992

Thanks for joining us this morning. Today I have good news—great news, in fact! As you know, we're all here to see a preview of our new television campaign for the Travel and Tourism Division. So what's the big deal? Well, this is the first time the state has developed national television commercials to attract potential visitors to our state.

Historically, North Carolina set the pace for travel advertising with its magazine and newspaper programs. But for several years, our major competitors with better-funded advertising programs have opted for television advertising. But our competitors better watch out, because if the future is any reflection on the past, North Carolina is likely to take away the competitive edge in the TV world just like we've done in the world of print. Let's see those commercials now.

[Commercials run for approximately two minutes.]

I hope that makes you want to take a North Carolina vacation! These five spots—two thirty-second and three fifteen-second commercials— were filmed all across the state: at Jockey's Ridge, Old Salem, Biltmore Estate, Bald Head Island, and Grandfather Mountain.[1] For nine weeks beginning Sunday, March 15, these commercials will be shown nineteen times a day—that's 131 times a week—on networks such as the Cable News Network, the Travel Channel, the Weather Channel, the Discovery Channel, and the Nashville Network.

When this TV blitz is over on Sunday, May 17, we will have reached millions of households. That's a lot of potential visitors, and we hope to be sharing our beautiful state with them soon. But there's more good news. The state will receive close to a half-million dollars in free air time and print media space thanks to the rigorous negotiations between the various cable stations and the division's advertising agency, Loeffler Ketchum Mountjoy. That brings our $700,000 investment in air time to more like one and a quarter million dollars.

One question may be in your minds: Why did we select cable? Because cable reaches large numbers of potential visitors and will create a rapid awareness of North Carolina as a destination. The cable viewers best match the profile of out-of-state visitors who come to North Carolina.

But these commercials are only part of a $2.2 million advertising program that also includes radio spots and print ads for national magazines and newspapers. You'll notice samples of some of the ads displayed around the room.

We decided to spend about half our ad dollars on television to help North Carolina regain lost market shares in the Southeast. Since 1980, we've seen our percentage market share decline from 11.7 percent to 11.2 percent, resulting in a loss of travel expenditures of $240 million per year from what we would have had we held 11.7 percent. In other words, travel and tourism spending rose from $3 billion to almost $7 billion, but had we held 11.7 percent it would be a quarter billion more.

North Carolina will fight our best fight to regain our position in the Southeast. After all, where else will a traveler find our great combination of beaches, mountains, and wealth of cultural and historical attractions? These commercials are only the beginning, but we know from a 1987 advertising conversion study that for every tax dollar we spend on travel advertising, we bring in more than five dollars in tax revenue. North Carolina's $7 billion travel industry stands to gain tremendously from this new television outreach program.

---

[1]The commercials, which took two weeks to produce, featured the following locations: "Ocean" (thirty seconds), Jockey's Ridge, Maggie Valley, Old Salem, Biltmore Estate, Bald Head Island, Brevard; "Country Home" (thirty seconds), Maggie Valley, Biltmore Estate, Fort Fisher State Historic Site, Grandfather Mountain, Looking Glass Falls; "Mountain" (fifteen seconds), Lake Fairfield, near Brevard, and Maggie Valley; "Coast" (fifteen seconds), Corolla, Jockey's Ridge, Fort Fisher; and "Heartland" (fifteen seconds), Winston-Salem, Guilford. Press release, "New TV Commercials Promoting NC as Travel Destination Unveiled," Raleigh, January 31, 1992, Governors Papers, James G. Martin.

CLOSING COMMENTS, AIR CARGO AIRPORT AUTHORITY

CHAPEL HILL, FEBRUARY 11, 1992

I think I speak for the rest of the Authority members when I say that it's certainly encouraging to learn we've developed a sound concept and that the Global TransPark is technically feasible.[1] The economic impact of this project could be staggering. The Global TransPark could pour as much as $3.8 billion into our economy by the year 2000 and $12.9 billion by the year 2010. That could mean 28,000 jobs by the year 2000 and almost double that—48,000—by the year 2010. If only half that, we're still looking at 29,000 jobs by 2000 and 51,000 by 2010. And the Global TransPark would improve employment numbers as well, creating as many as 59,000 additional jobs in the year 2000 and 101,200 by the year 2010.

Those are promising projections that fall squarely in the asset column when we total up all the arguments for and against going ahead with the project. More than a few questions still need to be answered, however. Now that we know the project is technically feasible, we need to determine what our siting criteria will be. The Authority has already adopted a formal process for receiving information on potential sites and will consider all potential site options. However, as I said earlier today, the selection of potential sites will also depend on financial and market concerns. The siting of this facility must be a business decision, not a political decision.

We must also move ahead with marketing the concept of the Global TransPark. The Department of Economic and Community Development has already developed and implemented an extensive marketing campaign with funds provided by the General Assembly. I've asked the department to provide us with an update on that effort at our next Authority meeting.

As you can see, we have a lot of encouraging information; we don't yet have all the answers, but we have enough answers to know that we must continue to move forward with the Global TransPark. Over the last year, we've seen more and more states beginning to follow our lead and explore this concept. Once they hear[d] about our idea for a Global TransPark, existing air cargo facilities began to change their marketing strategies to mirror ours. There will be more of that once they review this public document. That means we're in a highly competitive environment, and timing is critical if we are to retain our competitive edge. As I pointed out last August, we must not lose our "first-movers advantage."[2] We stand to lose too much if this type of facility is allowed to slip out from beneath our fingertips and locate[s] somewhere nearby on the East Coast.

The Global TransPark is not just an air cargo airport. The Global TransPark is an industrial complex designed to meet the global transportation needs of companies in North Carolina and along the East Coast far into the future. We're talking about providing the infrastructure we need for our companies to be competitive in the twenty-first century in what has already become a global economy. We have to view this whole project from more than just the exciting but oversimplified perspective of airplanes flying cargo. We have to view this project as a strategic industrial development investment in our future.

I hope all this has given you food for thought. I encourage each of you on the board to study this technical feasibility report carefully and develop your own list of questions. Together, we'll work toward getting the answers we need to determine if, when, where, and how this project should be built. If you favor [m]y timetable, you've got three more months to decide. Once a site is picked, only then can we begin the environmental studies and get firm commitments from tenants and financing.

---

[1]The governor was commenting on the outcome of the Global TransPark technical feasibility study undertaken by Transportation Management Group. TMG had just presented its findings to Martin and other members of the North Carolina Air Cargo Airport Authority. Opening Comments, Air Cargo Meeting, February 11, 1992, Governors Papers, James G. Martin.

[2]See "Air Cargo Meeting," August 22, 1991, page 362, above.

EMERGING ISSUES FORUM

RALEIGH, FEBRUARY 13, 1992

The emerging issue is education. Just a few short years from now, we will turn the corner and careen headlong into a new century. There, new marvels await us, wonders that will rival even this century's invention of the airplane, the computer, or laser surgery. But it will be the choices we make today that will determine our readiness to meet those challenges of the future. The question we must answer is this: Will we invent the marvels of the twenty-first century, as Americans so often have done in the last 100 years, or will we condemn ourselves to becoming a nation of consumers, dependent upon the energy, knowledge, and leadership of other nations to discover those marvels for us?

It's not just an issue of money choices in the budget. That's vital. You can't get what we need without it. But more importantly, we will never succeed if all we do is spend a lot more money to keep on doing what we've been doing. Over the last seven years, we've increased school funding 76 percent—three times [the] inflation rate, 50 percent more in constant dollars. You probably didn't know that because it's not newsworthy, I guess. Are we getting 50 percent better results? Twenty percent? Ten percent?

Education is the difference between innovation and stagnation, and the choice is ours. Either we reform our system of education in North Carolina and in America, now, or accept a second-class future for our citizens. Before you leave here today, do yourself a favor and talk with some of the junior high students who are here. You need to know that they are excited about what you are here to do.

Providing a quality education for every child and adult in our state is what North Carolina 2000 is all about, and North Carolina 2000 is what I'm here to discuss today. I would love to enthrall you with a report on our prospects for building the global air cargo industrial park, or excite you with a plan Dick Spangler and I have to create a North Carolina center for the study of foreign language and culture. Think what those projects will mean for business leaders, military leaders, traveling tourists. But our project is public school reform.

The emerging issue I'm talking about is a long overdue quality improvement reform in the structure and accountability of education, which I have been advocating for seven years: deregulating and decentralizing educational management and leadership of our schools, to unleash the power and skill of our teachers and schools so they can focus on student achievement—results. We've got all the plans and building materials we need to construct a state-of-the-art school system for the twenty-first century. Stacks of studies tell us what works and what doesn't work in our schools. What we have not had, until now, is a localized quality leadership delivery system to move education reform out of isolated classrooms and communities and into every classroom and community in the state.

Dr. Ravitch has outlined the focus of the president's America 2000 plan for improving education across the nation.[1] If what I have to say about North Carolina 2000 sounds familiar, that's because North Carolina 2000 builds upon the president's program—as does each of the plans of thirty-three other states with their own state "2000" commitments. North Carolina 2000 is our state plan for building educational reform from the ground up. With it, we build an organizational framework for action that will involve everyone in every community—parents, teachers, business and civic leaders—everyone.

I remember, growing up, how my own family and community supported the job my teachers were doing in educating me, my three brothers, and all the other kids in school. Education began at home, from our earliest days when Mom took us on her knee and read to us. I can easily remember evenings in the Martin household, when she and Pop would gather the family around and read us a story. Sometimes it was a passage from the Bible, sometimes Dickens's *A Christmas Carol*, but always there was a story and a joy of reading reinforced by the love and warmth of our family.[2]

At that time, the values and commitment to education of the town, neighborhood, school, church, and family were all the same. Those shared values reinforced the strength and character of young people as they grew up. Now I know that was before TV, but that's not the problem. It's that that kind of community interest and involvement is difficult to duplicate in the fragmented society in which we now live—but not impossible, for that's exactly what we plan to create through North Carolina 2000: total community schools, where education is everybody's business, everybody's entitlement, and everybody's responsibility.

So how does North Carolina 2000 propose to do that? First, the program is based on the six national education goals adopted by our nation's governors, Democrat and Republican, with President Bush at the education summit two years ago in Charlottesville. To keep things simple, the goals of the president's America 2000 strategy, and of our own North Carolina 2000, are the same. Dr. Ravitch has mentioned them, but let me tell you what those goals are:

—That our children will enter school with strong bodies and strong minds, ready and eager to learn all that we can teach them; that includes that 25-to-30 percent who today are not ready. That means Head Start for those three and four-year-olds at risk of becoming dropouts, as we have already begun for all eligible four-year-olds through our Uplift Day Care.

—That by the time those children reach the twelfth grade, they will know how to read, they will understand history, and they will be able to find China, and Lithuania, and New Guinea on a map.

—That our young people will be the best scientists and mathematicians in the world, second to none. Now that may sound like a long shot, but it is vital that we stretch our reach or we will continue to trail, badly.

—That when graduation day comes, 90 percent of those the age of high school seniors will walk across the stage to receive a diploma that they earned and deserve. That and the preschool readiness goal are our tough commitment to those who intend to go to work after high school.

—That every adult in this state will be able to read, and write, and figure so they can find and keep a job, and keep their job competitive, and support their families.

—And that our schools will truly be places of learning, free from violence and fear, free from the pressure and threats of drug dealers. Without that goal, we're not likely to reach the others.

That's a tall order. We may not achieve each of these objectives as fully as we would like, but we certainly have goals to reach for, and setting goals is the first vital step toward achieving success. Of course, setting goals is not enough. You need a plan to reach those goals, and a plan is exactly what North Carolina 2000 is designed to give us.

Next, you need total quality involvement, of all levels, of every community, and you need an attitude of continuous improvement. Sound familiar? I've named a steering committee of business, community, government, and education leaders, and parents, who will set standards for educational excellence, develop strategies for meeting those standards, and create a system of high expectations and accountability.

Stop a minute. Accountability is nothing new. For decades we've held our schools accountable, but for what? Rules and regulations, restrictions and requirements, as if they were the four *R*s of education. Now, thanks to business involvement and leadership, we're talking about stopping the micromanagement from Raleigh and just holding school teams accountable for results.

The steering committee members will also serve as leaders of goals teams, one for each goal, which will be responsible for harnessing community energy all across the state, focusing it on implementing programs that work, and building enough momentum to keep everyone working hard, like an old-fashioned barn raising, until the job of school reform reaches the ideal of continuous improvement in student outcomes. Our goals teams will support work at the local level to build what we are going to call North Carolina 2000 Communities. By building North Carolina 2000 Communities and at least fourteen "new generation" schools across the state, we will honor our goals and bring true education reform to every classroom and every citizen in North Carolina.

I expect we can all remember a special teacher in our life who made a difference. In my case, it was W. T. "Monkey" Price, my high [school] principal, school football coach, and chemistry teacher. Coach Price taught us how to block and tackle, but he also inspired us to excel in something other than football. He made chemistry and physics interesting, but took an even greater interest in developing the full potential of his students in all areas. He encouraged me to excel in sports, in music, and in all my studies. Thanks in part to his influence, I, too, sought to become a chemistry teacher—with confidence that it was within me.[3]

When I left Princeton seven years later, with a Ph.D. in chemistry, and headed back to teach at Davidson, my father reminded me of Coach Price's philosophy. Pop told me that my goal was not to teach chemistry. My goal was to teach young people. Chemistry was just one means to make a difference in their lives. Well, I accepted that distinction, as long as my students knew they were expected to master the subject of chemistry.

As it has been throughout my life, and for the past seven years as governor, the education of our children will continue to be my number-one priority. We need to support teachers like Coach Price and my English teacher, Miss Nancy Wiley, or Kathleen Lemmond in math, teachers who are truly making a difference in the lives of our young people, and build an environment that attracts more like them to teaching.[4] I believe that North Carolina 2000 gives us the organizational structure we need to do that: by putting educators, and parents, and employers in charge of education as a community commitment.

I encourage you to spread this message in your community: Education is everybody's business, everybody's responsibility, everybody's entitlement. If you run into someone who doubts that, you remind them how much they rely on other people who have been educated in North Carolina—doctors, lawyers, accountants, drivers, repair services and construction workers, their own employees—the list is endless. Remind him that someone else's lack of education directly affects his ability to run his business, maintain his health, or buy goods and services for his family. I know that for a fact. A former chemistry student of mine is now my dentist. I don't know about you, but I certainly don't want anyone putting an electric drill and a filling in my mouth who flunked chemistry.

Abraham Lincoln once said that "The struggle of today is not altogether for today—it is for a vast future also." When the mid-nineteenth-century Whigs created a new school system for their generation, they might not have expected it to still prevail in our generation. We face an awesome task: building a system of quality education in the state of North Carolina. That will meet the needs of the emerging generation as we build a vast future of opportunity for generations of North Carolinians. If each of you will join in this effort, adding your support in your communities, North Carolina will meet the challenge of this age: better schools, with better results, for a better future.

---

[1]Diane Silvers Ravitch (1938–), born in Houston, Texas; B.A., Wellesley College, 1960; Ph.D., Columbia University, 1975; honorary degrees. Historian; adjunct assistant professor, 1975–1978, associate professor, 1978–1983, adjunct professor, 1983–1991, Teachers College, Columbia University; assistant secretary, Office of Educational Research and

Improvement, U.S. Dept. of Education, 1991–1993, and counselor to U.S. education secretary, 1991–1993; visiting fellow, Brookings Institute, since 1993; author. *Who's Who in America, 1994*, II, 2821–2822.

[2] The passive joy of listening to stories being read aloud evolved into an active passion for reading. As young Jim Martin grew older, he became especially fond of the work of Sir Arthur Conan Doyle. "For an inquisitive youth, matching wits with Sherlock Holmes was mystery and excitement at its best," the governor told the Library and Information Services Conference on August 3, 1990. "But those adventures were more than just pleasant side trips into the world of imagination. They gave me real insights into psychology, observation, analysis, and solution, tools of the trade in my later career in chemistry and politics."

Even with the demands imposed by the state's highest elected office, Martin managed to find time for recreational reading. "I still relax with mystery and adventure novels, although the relaxation exhausts me by keeping me up all night. My favorite novelists are Justin Scott, who is not prolific, but understands sailboats; and Robert Ludlum, who is, but doesn't. A Mississippi legislator sent me a translation of Sun Tzu's *Art of War*. I just finished *A Time to Kill*, by John Grisham, . . . and *At Dawn We Slept*, a detailed, annotated, historical account of the attack of Pearl Harbor. Now I'm reading John Naisbitt and Patricia Aburdene's *Megatrends 2000*, unsure as yet whether it is fiction or nonfiction."

[3] Martin was a student of Price's at Mount Zion Institute, a public school in Winnsboro, South Carolina. Nancy Jo Pekarek, letter to Jan-Micheal Poff, January 20, 1995, hereinafter cited as Pekarek correspondence.

[4] Nancy Wiley and Kathleen Lemmond taught Martin as a senior at Mount Zion Institute. Pekarek correspondence.

WORLD LANGUAGE CONFERENCE

Chapel Hill, February 14, 1992

[The governor's address to the World Language Conference, February 14, 1992, focused on his proposed Center for the Study of World Languages and Cultures. Pfeiffer College donated twenty-five acres of land as a site for the center, and Governor James B. Hunt, Jr., supported the project early in his third term; see *News and Observer*, December 8, 1993. The following text is similar to messages Martin delivered to meetings of the North Carolina Education Governing Boards, March 5, and the Foreign Language Association of North Carolina, October 23, 1992.]

Before I begin, I'd like to recognize the contributions of President C. D. Spangler, the Mary Reynolds Babcock Foundation, and the Z. Smith Reynolds Foundation for being partners with my office in this conference today. I'd also like to thank you all for being here this afternoon to help develop the blueprint for a new world vision for North Carolina.

For the past few days, the world has watched the Olympics in Albertville, France. We've seen Bonnie Blair skate for the gold in the 500-meter race.[1] We've also seen the Unified Team pair of Natalia Mishkutienok and Artur Dmitriev win the eighth-straight gold medal for the former Soviet Union in the pairs figure-skating championship.

Since the first modern games were held in Athens in 1896, the Olympics have become a gathering place for the nations of the world to pit their best athletes against one another. Part of the charm of the Olympics has always been the exotic intermingling of language and cultures in a swirl of happy confusion.

Over their long history, the Olympics have also shown us how the world has changed. This year, the Unified Team competes in place of what we knew until so recently as the Soviet Union. That change has been so rapid and so complete that the team's medal winners are without a flag or anthem to honor them.

The world has changed. Foreign competition now means more than just striving for the gold in downhill skiing. Now it means striving for trade and product quality with every other nation in the world. Unfortunately, the United States is not a shoo-in for the gold in this new style of foreign competition. While Americans have generally looked toward home, many citizens of other nations have learned English, and maybe one or two other languages, in addition to their own native tongue.

How many of you saw Natalia Mishkutienok and Artur Dmitriev— or their Soviet coach, for that matter—use fluent English during interviews with U.S. television crews? How many of us in this room would be able to do a similar interview in even halting Russian, or German, or Japanese? Like it or not, as Americans, we are now also world citizens. Our playing field in this new foreign competition is now the global marketplace. Future champions will win in that arena in part because of their ability to understand and communicate with other citizens of the world. A "Center for the Study of World Languages and Cultures" is one way we can break down the culture barrier and open up a world of opportunities in business, travel, and a host of other areas.

When the state required more foreign language instruction in elementary grades, we needed a place where teachers could learn more about the foreign languages and cultures they were to teach our children. Three years ago, therefore, I established the Governor's Institutes for Foreign Language. Summer programs offered at the institutes in French, Spanish, and Latin have proven to be immensely beneficial to our teachers and the quality of education they pass on to their students.[2]

That success inspired the Governor's Language Institutes Advisory Board to develop plans for a similar program designed for business people, the military, teachers, and other citizens. The idea of a Center for World Languages and Cultures expands the target audience beyond the focus of the language institutes and places a new emphasis on economic development and international trade. We might also use the center as a place to teach English to the employees of foreign companies who are investing in North Carolina. That could make the center a big gun in our economic recruitment arsenal.

Programs at the center would vary in length, depending on the degree of mastery required by the participant. But all programs, short or long, would revolve around intense immersion in the language and culture of a number of foreign nations. With a little seed money from the General Assembly, we expect we could get such a center up and running fairly quickly. The idea is to eventually make it pay for itself through enrollment fees.

Similar centers exist and are quite successful. Middlebury College, in Middlebury, Vermont, and the Monterey Institute of International Studies, in Monterey, California, are two notable examples, but we don't have such a center located anywhere in the Southeast. I think this region is ready for such a center. I think it would benefit citizens, not just from North Carolina, but from Virginia, Kentucky, Tennessee, South Carolina, and other states in the Southeast. I also think that if the need exists, North Carolina should be the state to fill it.

Where will the center be? How will it be run, and who will run it? Who will do the teaching? What courses would be offered? Well, I don't know. We still have questions to answer. That's why we're here today: to answer a few of those questions and to help us develop a solid proposal that we can take to the General Assembly in May.

If you haven't heard me talk about this before, let me tell you, I'm enthusiastic about this idea—so enthusiastic, in fact, that I want to see this center up and running by the time I leave office next January. I expect to be one of the "world citizens" signing up to take advantage of a class or two.

Every new idea has a few critics, of course, and this idea is no different. Some say we ought to be focusing our efforts on teaching foreign languages to our young people in school. Others wonder why we worry about foreign languages at all when Johnny can't even read English.

The answer is that the state has already established an extensive foreign language program in our elementary and secondary grades. As for Johnny reading English, we've embarked on an ambitious new program for educational reform called North Carolina 2000. Programs are in place to prepare our children to compete in the global marketplace of the twenty-first century, but we also need a program to improve the language skills and understanding of our adults. I am convinced, however, that such a center can only enhance the education community in the state. That's the reason I invited so many educators to be part of this meeting today.

What about money? Should we spend state funds, in a recession, on this kind of an idea, when we have so many other critical needs? We do have critical needs, and money is tight. But an investment in this kind of a language and culture center is an investment in the future; and once again, we hope the center will eventually be self-supporting.

So why do we have to rush into it? If it's such a good idea, why won't it wait until better times? Well, a good idea today will still be a good idea tomorrow. The problem is, the world won't wait. If we hope to compete in the world marketplace, we've got to be able to speak the language and understand the culture.

Just yesterday I received a letter from a Raleigh attorney who wrote to express his views about the idea of a center for world language and culture. In part, he wrote:

"We must begin to send out representatives from this state who will be capable of understanding the opportunities available in international trade and of bringing some of those opportunities back to this state. If we do not, we can expect to fall further behind in our efforts to make progress for all of our population.

"Cultural and educational deficiencies are unquestionably obstacles which must be removed. . . . Your proposal is a welcome step toward a permanent change in the way we approach business in North Carolina."

Others have had similar ideas for developing such a center in North Carolina—Pfeiffer College, as a notable example. My hope is that we can combine our ideas, coordinate them, and unite in our support to create the finest program possible.

This is an idea whose time has come. How many of you, as managers in the public and private sectors, would prefer your employees do their work on a typewriter instead of teaching them how to use a computer? You invest in computer training for your people so they can do their jobs more efficiently and effectively, but they can't do their jobs at all if they don't have the skills to compete. Well, if you're hoping to make it in the international marketplace, you've got to have the relevant skills to compete—and that includes knowing a foreign language and understanding the culture.

I've led several economic recruitment missions to Japan and a few other Far East[ern] and European countries. The Japanese may not all speak English, but they often understand what's being said before the interpreter begins to interpret. What an advantage it would be not to have to rely on an interpreter.

President Reagan learned all about the importance of learning a foreign language back in 1984, when he and Mrs. François Mitterand were walking into a state dinner. He and Madame Mitterand had started through the tables, following the butler, when she stopped very suddenly and said something to him in French. Not understanding her comment, the president smiled and motioned for her to go forward after the butler, who was also motioning them onward. Again, she very calmly repeated something to the president. An interpreter finally explained to the president that he was standing on her gown.

If we don't move forward to learn more about foreign languages and cultures, we're going to be stepping on our own opportunities for future progress. While others are moving ahead, we'll find we've nailed ourselves to the floor. I want us to be contenders for the gold in the foreign competition for success in the global marketplace. A Center for the Study of World Languages and Cultures can help us develop the winning skills we need to compete as world citizens.

Today we begin the process. I ask each of you to share your ideas with us. Tell us what your needs are and how such a center can help fulfill them. This is your chance to help us develop this new world vision for North Carolina from the ground up. Thank you for your interest. I look forward to hearing your ideas.

---

[1]Bonnie Blair (1964–), born in Cornwall, N.Y.; attended Montana Technical University. Gold medalist, women's 500-meter speed skating, Winter Olympic Games, Calgary, Canada, 1988; gold medalist, women's 500-meter and 1000-meter speed skating, Winter Olympic Games, Albertville, France, 1992; gold medalist, women's 500-meter and 1000-meter speed skating, Winter Olympic Games, Lillehammer, Norway, 1994; first American woman to earn gold medals in consecutive Winter Olympics, and first American speed skater to win gold medals in more than one Olympics; most decorated woman Olympian as of 1995. *Who's Who in America, 1995*, I, 340.

[2]The Basic Education Program ordered intensified foreign language training by 1992. The first foreign language institutes began in 1988, a year after Martin first proposed them. See Poff, *Addresses of Martin*, I, 472–473, 474n, 897.

PRESS CONFERENCE NOTES
GOVERNOR'S ECONOMIC DEVELOPMENT SUMMIT

GREENSBORO, FEBRUARY 24, 1992

Where We Were

1991 Rankings by Site Selection *Magazine, February Issue*
Last week many of you carried the story that North Carolina ranked:
Number one, new manufacturing announcements, 110;
Number two, new and expanded facilities, 276.[1]
But there's more good news that didn't get prominent play in the news. North Carolina ranked number one with most global facilities announced in 1991. Thirty-one global facilities, 17 percent of all 182 sitings, chose North Carolina as the site for new or expanded operations.
Second: California and Ohio, 13 each;
Third: South Carolina and Georgia, 12 each;

Fourth: Indiana, 11;

Fifth: Florida, 10.[2]

North Carolina also ranked number one with the most global facilities announced from 1989–1991: 79.

Second: South Carolina, 71;

Third: Ohio, 66;

Fourth: California, 64;

Fifth: Florida, 63.[3]

This category used to be called "International Facilities." The change to "Global Facilities" reflects a change in the scope of international trade and investment.

This survey is exciting because the numbers translate into current and future growth: more and better jobs, new economic opportunities for business in the community, taxes that improve community services, and more.

This survey also makes the point that the recession's effect greatly reduced the number of facilities siting, down 34 percent from 1990's 4,731 to 1991's 3,084. There was a 17 percent drop in number of facilities from 1989 to 1990.[4]

However, North Carolina improved our rankings and our number of facilities in all categories. New: 1990—102, 1991—110; new and expanded: 1990—265, 1991—276; global: 1990—10, 1991—31.[5]

That improvement is due in large part to our ongoing efforts to further improve our economic development recruitment and our infrastructure.

ECD Top Ten Economic Recruiter

The North Carolina Department of Economic and Community Development named to national list of Top Ten Economic Development Groups for three years in a row, 1988–1990. Only state government agency. *Site Selection* praised the cooperation between state, regional, and local economic development groups, a great key to our success.[6]

Unemployment Rate

Also for 1991, North Carolina was number one with the lowest annual average unemployment rate of the eleven largest states for the third year in a row, 1989–1991.

We were also the lowest for the cumulative seven-year period, 1985–1991. In the prior seven-year period, 1977–1984, North Carolina was third, showing we have increased jobs and decreased unemployment.

While we haven't been spared the national recession—no state has—we have fared better. Our state's monthly unemployment rate was the lowest of the eleven largest for ten months of the year.

Our state unemployment rate went from a low of 3.4 percent, in March 1990, to a high of 6.7 percent in May 1991. Although it almost doubled, it's still relatively low. This is much lower than the unemployment rate during the last recession, which peaked at 11.3 percent in February 1983.

We've benefited by the industrial base we've worked so hard to expand and diversi[f]y through our targeted recruitment efforts.

We've also consistently ranked among the lowest monthly unemployment rates of the Southeastern states.

Georgia was the lowest at 4.99 percent, North Carolina was second at 5.78 percent, and Virginia was third at 5.84 percent. If rounded off it only appears Virginia tied us. We were lowest in the Southeast for the cumulative seven-year period, 1985–1991—up from third lowest for previous seven-year period, 1977–1984.

Saying that another way, our annual average unemployment rate was both the lowest of the eleven largest and of the Southeast states for the cumulative period 1985–1991, up from third lowest in the previous seven-year period. Says a lot.

Rural Investment

In 1991, 67 percent of the new manufacturing firms announced located in communities of 10,000 or less.

Sixty-nine percent of the new manufacturing jobs announced will be in communities of 10,000 or less; in 1990, it was 50 percent, so we've increased this, also.

Globalization

From 1987 to 1990, our state exports increased from $4.5 billion to $8 billion.

Export Outreach was initiated in North Carolina to walk our businesses through the process of entering export. Now used as a national model.[7]

We're one of the few states with a positive balance of trade, exporting more than we import.

National trade deficit has been decreasing as exports have grown faster than imports: 1987, $150 billion; 1990, $100 billion; 1991 fell below $100 billion for the first time in eight years, at $66.2 billion.

Where We're Going

Global Air Cargo Industrial Complex

The technical feasibility study for the GTP recently prepared by the Transportation Management Group shows the project is technically feasible. Proposals for siting are being accepted, though the current focus is on existing facilities, such as joint use of a military base.

Center for the Study of World Languages and Cultures

This new proposal would provide total immersion study in a variety of languages and cultures for business people, social service workers, teachers, travelers, interested citizens.

Right now the advisory board is conducting a needs assessment to determine who might be best served with this program and how to serve those needs.

---

[1]Tim Venable, "Florida, North Carolina and Texas: Leaders in the 1991 Chase for New and Expanded Facilities," *Site Selection and Industrial Development*, February 1992, 25, 26, hereinafter cited as Venable, "Florida, North Carolina and Texas: Leaders in the 1991 Chase for New and Expanded Facilities." The Sunshine State reported 281 new and expanded facilities for 1991, five more than North Carolina.

[2]Venable, "Florida, North Carolina and Texas: Leaders in the 1991 Chase for New and Expanded Facilities," 24.

[3]Tim Venable, "North Carolina, South Carolina and Ohio Tops in Landing Global Facilities for 1989–1991," *Site Selection and Industrial Development*, February 1992, 16.

[4]Fusi, "South Atlantic, Florida Top Both 1990 and 1988–1990 Analysis of New Facilities Surge," 23; Venable, "Florida, North Carolina and Texas: Leaders in the 1991 Chase for New and Expanded Facilities," 20.

[5]Fusi, "South Atlantic, Florida Top Both 1990 and 1988–1990 Analysis of New Facilities Surge," 23; Venable, "Florida, North Carolina and Texas: Leaders in the 1991 Chase for New and Expanded Facilities," 20.

[6]The Department of Economic and Community Development repeated its distinction as the sole state agency to earn top-ten honors in 1991; see Hoyt E. Coffee, Tim Venable, and Jack Lyne, "1991's Top Groups and Top Deals: With Competition Intensified, a Winning Hand Was All in the Numbers," *Site Selection and Industrial Development*, April 1992, 297, 312–313. For previous years' rankings as mentioned by Martin, see Jack Lyne and Deborah S. Fusi, "The Best of Development, 1988: *Site Selection* Spotlights 10 Development Groups and 10 Deals," *Site Selection and Industrial Development*, April 1989, 317, 322–323; Jack Lyne and Deborah S. Fusi, "20 Success Stories from the Development World: Top Groups and Top Deals," *Site Selection and Industrial Development*, April 1990, 305, 314, 316; Deborah S. Fusi, Tim Venable, and Jack Lyne, "1990's Top Groups and Deals: Adding Value from the Development Side," *Site Selection and Industrial Development*, April 1991, 285, 296.

[7]The Department of Economic and Community Development began the Export Outreach program in 1990. N.C. World Trade Assn., Presentation of Presidential "E" Award for Excellence in Exporting to Shuford Mills, Inc., Research Triangle Park, May 14, 1992, Governors Papers, James G. Martin.

PRESS RELEASE: CORRECTION SECRETARY AARON JOHNSON
STEPS DOWN

Raleigh, February 28, 1992

[The reports of purchasing irregularities in the Department of Correction were breathtaking. The oversupply of clothing alone was enormous. There was a 26-year reserve of white cook coats, size 38; a 113-year stockpile of brown work shirts, size XXX-large; and enough size XXX-large boxer shorts to last nearly 166 years. The department exceeded its $5.1 million budget for inmate clothing in the 1990–1991 fiscal year, ordering $12.3 million in apparel. It was $3.6 million in arrears in paying clothing bills, and one vendor had a shipment worth over $6 million ready to deliver. The purchase of other goods and services, including a $1.2 million telephone maintenance contract, was never made available for bidding. A state audit of the purchasing scandal revealed that Correction had squandered $7.2 million at a time when serious revenue shortfalls forced cutbacks throughout North Carolina government.

Top officials at the Department of Correction knew about the purchasing irregularities since 1990 but were slow to act. Secretary Aaron Johnson turned the problem over to the State Bureau of Investigation on January 27, 1992. The SBI probe targeted the activities of D. R. "Rick" Hursey, head of the Correction Department's warehouse and purchasing office. Hursey apparently circumvented state purchase and contract regulations and also had family ties to a number of the department's suppliers. He was suspended without pay January 27 and later resigned.

The publicity the department's purchasing irregularities generated, and the manner in which his subordinates addressed them, tainted Secretary Johnson. He had no choice but to step down. Standing beside Martin on February 28, the secretary told reporters, "'Certainly there has been a lot printed lately about the Department of Correction. I just didn't feel that I could overcome it. I did not want to embarrass the governor because I think so much of him.'" Johnson and six other senior administrators at the Department of Correction either resigned, retired, were transferred, or took a leave of absence as a result of the purchasing scandal. *News and Observer*, February 8, 11, 12, 13, 19, 20, 21, 22, 27, 28, 29, May 21, September 4, 1992.]

Governor Jim Martin today announced the resignation of Secretary of Correction Aaron Johnson. With Johnson at his side, Martin described the decision as a "mutual agreement that conditions within the department required new leadership in order to restore confidence and direction."

Recent months have witnessed an outpouring of allegations and disclosures regarding purchasing abuses within the department. "This has led to internal and external investigations, dismissals, and an atmosphere of damaging gossip which has made it extremely difficult for the departmental management to assert control and authority," Martin said. "Secretary Johnson has provided strong leadership in building a constitutionally defensive [*sic*] prison system and has pioneered many effective innovations as alternatives to prison for less-dangerous criminals.

"Yet, he and I have reached the regrettable conclusion that this situation can be corrected only by bringing in new leadership, with a fresh start, so the department can return to giving full attention to its important business."

Secretary Johnson will continue in his present position until a successor has been named.[1]

---

[1]V. Lee Bounds succeeded Johnson as secretary of correction on March 4, 1992. Bounds (1918–), born in Salisbury, Md.; LL.B., University of Virginia, 1949; U.S. Navy and Reserve, 1936–1952. Assistant director, professor of public law and government, Institute of Government, University of North Carolina at Chapel Hill, 1952–1965; director of prisons, N.C. Prison Dept., 1965–1967; commissioner of correction, N.C. Dept. of Correction, 1967–1973; Kenan Professor of Public Law and Administration, University of North Carolina at Chapel Hill, 1973–1986; secretary, N.C. Dept. of Correction, 1992–1993. *North Carolina Manual, 1991–1992*, 126; press release, "Governor Appoints Bounds as Correction Secretary," Raleigh, March 2, 1992, Governors Papers, James G. Martin.

ROCKINGHAM COUNTY CAPITAL FOR A DAY

EDEN, MARCH 16, 1992

[The following address is largely identical to one delivered at the economic development luncheon held February 10, 1992, in Concord, as part of Cabarrus County Capital for a Day. One major difference between the two speeches is that a segment on good government issues, included just before the conclusion of the Concord text, was omitted from the Eden version; see footnote 1, below.]

It certainly is a pleasure to be spending the day with you here in Rockingham County. This area has much to offer, and I'm pleased to have the opportunity to see some of your achievements firsthand. I had the pleasure of visiting Dalton McMichael High School, in Madison, this morning to talk a little bit about North Carolina 2000, my education initiative for 1992 and beyond. This afternoon, I'm heading over to Reidsville Intermediate School to meet with school officials to listen to their suggestions about how we can make a difference in our schools. As it has been for the past seven years, education is my number-one priority.

What I want to do right now is give you a report on what we've been doing for the past seven years, a "Report to the People!" If you know me at all, or even if you don't, you've probably heard me talk about better schools, better roads, better jobs, and a better environment for North Carolina. That's what I promised to bring to this state, and I believe I've made good on my promises.

Better Schools

You've heard a lot of talk about the need for school reform in our state. Without a doubt, our first priority is to teach our children how to read, write, and figure so they can find and keep a job in a high-tech, highly competitive, global marketplace. That's why I challenged the General Assembly to steadily increase funding for education even as a bigger percentage share of the state budget.

By making education my number-one priority, I broke a long-standing trend in which our schools' percentage share of the budget actually declined in all but two of the previous twenty-four years. In twenty-two out of twenty-four years, schools fell behind. In every administration, they fell behind, but in this administration, schools were the number-one priority.

We increased spending for public schools by 76 percent, from $1.9 billion in 1984–1985 to $3.3 billion in 1990–1991. That's three times the inflation rate. That never happened before, but most people don't know about it. I guess it just wasn't newsworthy!

The state spends almost $5 billion a year for education overall. That includes community colleges, colleges, and universities. And what about teacher salaries? How would you like it if, no matter how many years you worked, or how good a job you did, you never got anything better than a cost-of-living raise? And how would you feel if some new employee from out of state, maybe with less experience, was hired at a higher salary?

Well, that's what was happening to our teachers since 1982. That's why I persuaded the General Assembly to unfreeze teacher salaries and put teachers on a step plan to give them fair pay for their years of experience. Teacher salaries were thirty-third in the nation in 1985. Now they're twenty-ninth in the nation, and those salaries would have kept moving forward if the legislature had done what I asked, because I believed we should make some improvement—even in a tight, recessionary, budget year—and without so big a tax increase. In any case, we're spending more for education than ever before. In fact, 67 cents out of every one of your tax dollars goes toward all levels of education: 20 cents for universities and community colleges, 47 cents for public schools.

We're spending a lot more for schools than ever before, but what are we getting for our money? We all know that SAT scores are low, and that our employers are having trouble hiring skilled workers.

It's not enough to throw money at a problem. All that does is spend more for the same results! If a structure is weak, you've got to stop pouring money into patch jobs and rebuild from the inside out. That's why I've led the fight for true education reform in this state. I have fought long and hard to give local school systems the flexibility to decide where to spend their state funds, then hold them accountable for the results. That's the way the most successful businesses are reorganizing all over the country.

I established the organizational framework for putting good ideas for education reform to work in every school system in this state: We call that program North Carolina 2000. The goals of North Carolina 2000 are the same as those of President Bush's America 2000 program, which in turn, was based on the goals of the National Governors' Association. That means that by the year 2000, 90 percent of our kids will earn, and deserve, a high school diploma; we will improve adult literacy; we will free our schools of drugs and violence; and we will graduate students who are skilled in English, history, and geography, and who are first in the world in math and science.

We have already begun work on achieving those goals. We're also working to increase workforce preparedness through programs that include expanding Tech Prep and beefing up our community college system. Math and science education is on the upswing, thanks to a handsome grant from [the] National Science Foundation, administered by the North Carolina Alliance for Science and Mathematics. I have also recently unveiled plans for a North Carolina Institute for Foreign Languages and Cultures, which will offer an intensive program of study designed to help business and military people, and travelers, understand and communicate on the international scene. Better schools need that kind of leadership.

Next, let me report to you about—

Better Transportation

If you remember back in 1984, I made one highway campaign promise: that the final link of I-40, from Raleigh to Wilmington, would be under contract in four years—and it was. And by June of 1990, I-40 was completed and open to traffic from Wilmington all the way to Barstow, California. How's that for keeping a promise? For decades before, it had been promised, but not paved. And we've almost completed a new realignment of I-40 around Winston-Salem.

I also proposed, and got passed, the biggest road package in state history—thanks to the hard work and determined leadership of your senator, Bill Goldston! Together, we made history. In fifteen to twenty years, 96 percent of our state's population will live within ten miles of a four-lane expressway, part of an unbroken 3,000-mile network of limited-access, four-lane, divided highways. An intrastate system! Four-lane expressways that go somewhere. You'll never again be able to get a laugh out of that tired old one-liner about how "You can't get there from here."

Just think what that will mean for opening up our rural areas to jobs and economic development. Unpromised paving is a whole lot better than unpaved promises, and that's just what we've achieved during this administration: a whole lot of paving built on very few promises, even if it didn't seem like it was newsworthy!

Better Jobs

Thanks to these and other improvements, the future for better jobs and better wages looks a lot brighter for the working people of this state. But I want you to know we've been delivering better jobs and better wages for over seven years now, but you might not have read about it, because great news isn't very newsworthy! North Carolina has led the nation again and again as the top industrial recruiting state in four out of the last five years—more new factories than any other state, four out of five. That's like winning the NCAA [National Collegiate Athletic Association basketball tournament] four out of five times.

It's because North Carolina has become one of the nation's most favorable climates for business investment. We've added over 500,000 net new jobs to the state since 1984, from high-tech to traditional, in both urban and rural areas, too. In fact, in 1987 alone, 68 percent of the jobs announced went to communities with no more than 10,000 population. Now that's what it means to take a good program and spread it around!

Some critics have said that not all new jobs pay good wages. Maybe not, but the ones we've recruited do. That's why we've actually seen a 25 percent increase in the manufacturing wage since 1984, the highest growth rate for states in the Southeast and the eighth greatest in the nation. It may not be newsworthy, but it's good news for North Carolina workers.

Even with a record like that, we can't rest on our oars. We have to keep on keeping on! We have now embarked on our most ambitious economic development initiative yet. It's called the Global TransPark. This plan would integrate a 20,000-acre industrial complex with its own international air-freight airport and along with [sic] transportation systems to provide a futuristic North Carolina connection in the network of world trade. This is indeed a visionary proposal—as visionary as the Research Triangle Park was thirty-five years ago—and, like RTP, GTP, the Global TransPark, could create up to 50,000 jobs, and pour billions of dollars into our state economy, and keep North Carolina at the head of the class.

And a Better Environment

You might think that we're out to pave every inch of topsoil in the state and build a factory on it, but in fact, my administration has proven to be a friend and a protector to the environment. Some purists will tell you we're not perfect, but no previous administration has done better. We've strengthened environmental regulations and backed them up with some of the biggest fines for violations this state has ever seen. That get-tough policy has made North Carolina one of the ten-best states in the nation for overall enforcement of environmental laws and number one in the nation for protecting surface water. We consolidated all the state's environment, health, and natural resource agencies into one new department. We succeeded where other[s] failed.

What about all those who say we need to put more emphasis on recycling and reducing waste? Well, my administration has been forging ahead in these areas, as well. I issued a challenge to reduce the waste headed to our landfills by 90 percent by the year 2000, and created a state office to help local governments reach that goal and to coordinate the state's many ongoing pollution-prevention, recycling, and waste-minimization efforts. And I want the state to help you with the financing.

I also established the Coastal Initiative program to balance land development and environmental conservation interests. That balance is based on having the toughest storm-water runoff controls in the country, to protect our vital high-quality waters, and the best watershed protection rules in the country.

Again, the purists will say we're not perfect. For them, perfection means zero growth, and that's foolishness. It may not be perfect or newsworthy, but we're better at this [than] anybody else.

Better schools, better roads, better jobs, and a better environment for the state: That's been my vision for a better North Carolina, and I think we've done a pretty good job of getting us there. But that's not the end of our accomplishments.

In Health

When North Carolina's infant mortality began to rise two years in a row, that was newsworthy and action was needed. So, we actively worked to change that, to make sure that babies are born to live and grow up healthy in our state. Thanks to a special emphasis, through state and local efforts, our infant mortality rate has now declined to the lowest point ever in state history: 10.6 deaths per 1,000 live births in 1990.

Yes, we're working to give our littlest citizens a healthy start in life, and I've already told you a few of the things we've done to help older children make it through school and out into the working world. But what about giving young children a head start so they are ready to learn? We've established a nationally acclaimed program to give our at-risk four-year-olds a head start at learning and living healthy lives. We call it Uplift Day Care. Using existing state funds and new federal money, Uplift Day Care will soon make sure that every four-year-old who is eligible for Head Start, every child deemed at risk of becoming a high school dropout, is enrolled in a developmental preschool program.

We also continue to ensure the health and safety of all our citizens by strengthening child protective services, DWI laws, and substance-abuse enforcement, treatment, and prevention.

In Our Prison System

Part of ensuring the health and safety of our people is to make sure that those who threaten our communities and our families through violence and crime remain where they belong: behind bars. Early in my administration, I fought off a federal takeover of our prison system by expanding inmate space to meet federal guidelines. I also proposed, and won, voter approval of a $200-million bond issue to build more prison beds that will increase capacity and help relieve overcrowding, and I want to commend Representative Peggy Wilson who was one of our leaders on that.

Obviously we can't build enough cells to house all criminals all the time, but we are building enough cells to ensure that our most dangerous criminals spend more time in jail and less time in crime. What about the less dangerous criminals? We're keeping them off the streets by expanding our alternative sentencing programs, like electronic house arrest and intensive probation and parole.[1]

Conclusion

The good thing is that this administration isn't over. We are now in our "ultimate" year, as I like to call it, and we plan to govern until the lights are turned out at the close of business our very last day in office. I will keep pushing for education reform in this state. You'll hear me talk a lot about North Carolina 2000 in the future. I'll keep pushing to bring new jobs to this state, both through standard industrial recruitment efforts and by following through on plans to site the Global TransPark somewhere in North Carolina.

When historians and pundits look back on this administration, I believe it will stand up well against some of the best administrations in history, including one of our state's most progressive periods under the Whigs, from 1835–1850. The Whigs established a new constitution for the state and a new form of government that, like ours, brought stronger, healthier, more competitive, two-party politics to North Carolina. The Whigs developed and improved a statewide transportation system by building railroads, plank roads, and canals to open up the state. We're building intrastate highways to make North Carolina one united state, and we're inventing the fifth wave of world trade and transportation through the Global TransPark.

The Whigs created a public school system. We're beginning to recreate that system for the twenty-first century. The Whigs sought equality and justice, the same issues we seek both inside and outside government today.

I cannot know whether history will approve and praise our accomplishments. But I do know we have done our best to make a difference for North Carolina's future, and in this, our ultimate year, I wanted to report to you about it.

Abraham Lincoln said that "The struggle of today is not altogether for today, it is for a vast future, also"—and still it is, today.

---

[1]The section entitled "In Government" appeared at this point in the Concord speech. Martin reminded the audience of his having opened Council of State and Advisory Budget Commission meetings to the "scrutinizing eyes of the press" and public. He recalled his campaign against the "pork barrel process through which powerful senators and representatives funded more than a few of their own pet projects . . . and strong-armed less powerful colleagues into voting their way. The pork barrel dictatorship in the General Assembly was about as far away from good government as you could get. The legislature still enjoys its pork, but in far smaller portions than they had served themselves in previous years."

"Unfortunately, political arm-twisting had not been confined to the General Assembly," the governor continued. "When I took office, I promised state employees they would no longer have to contribute to someone else's idea of the 'right' candidate to get ahead. We no longer allow state employees to play politics on state time with state money and equipment, but we do allow state employees the freedom to work for the candidates of their own personal choice—on their own personal time."

Martin ended the section, saying, "We've delivered freedom for state employees from political pressure, and we've promoted opportunities for women and minorities in state government, as well. This administration employs more women in cabinet-level and other executive positions than previous administrations. That's also true for minorities, who have received more promotions to management positions than ever before."

PRESS RELEASE: GOVERNOR RESPONDS TO
ANNOUNCEMENT OF HIS CAREER PLANS IN 1993

RALEIGH, MARCH 23, 1992

Harry A. Nurkin,[1] Ph.D., president and CEO of the Charlotte-
Mecklenburg Hospital Authority, today announced that after Governor
Jim Martin completes his second term in January 1993, he will become
chairman of the Research Development Board directing the James G.
Cannon Research Center on the campus of Carolinas Medical Center in
Charlotte. The following is the governor's response to that announce-
ment:

"We are very excited about our future and look forward to living in
Charlotte next year. Dottie was born in Charlotte, we have family there,
and the people in that area have been very supportive of our twenty-
six-year career in government. We had wanted very much to stay in
North Carolina, where we could enjoy being near the many friends we've
made. I had also hoped for a position with executive leadership in a
challenging work environment. This offer fills both expectations.

"We're very fortunate to know what the future holds so that we will
not be distracted from the job at hand. We will continue to devote our
full attention to implementing my top priorities, which include education reform and siting the Global TransPark, as well as meeting the other
major challenges that lie ahead in this 'ultimate' year of my administration."[2]

---

[1]Harry Abraham Nurkin (1944–), born in Durham; resident of Charlotte; B.A., 1966,
M.H.A., 1968, Duke University; Ph.D., University of Alabama, 1983. Assistant director,
Memorial Mission Hospital, Asheville, 1971–1974; associate administrator, chief operating officer, University of Alabama Hospitals, Birmingham, 1974–1981; appointed president, chief executive officer, Charlotte Memorial Hospital, 1981; president, chief executive
officer, Charlotte-Mecklenburg Hospital Authority, since 1983; founder, Carolinas Medical Center. David Bailey, "Get 'Em Well Harry," *Business North Carolina*, July 1993, 20–33;
Who's Who in America, 1995, II, 2747.

[2]Speaking to the Charlotte Rotary Club, June 9, 1992, the governor compared his ultimate year in office to "the farewell tour of our great friend, Richard Petty, as he enjoys one
last lap around the speedway tracks of our land. To those few who urged one last competition, I hope you will accept my decision that twenty-six years is long enough. I've had
my turn, and it's time to let others enjoy the fast lane. And if that doesn't persuade you,
you have my permission to talk to Dottie about it. Just stand near a door."

Above: An eight-mile segment of U.S. 220, near his hometown of Level Cross, was named for NASCAR racing legend Richard Petty on April 14, 1992. Pictured with Petty at the dedication ceremony, Martin imitated the stock-car driver's signature attire by sporting sunglasses and a cowboy hat. *Left:* The following day, Arnold

Schwarzenegger—chairman of the President's Council on Physical Fitness and Sports, award-winning body builder, and motion-picture star—brought his national youth fitness campaign to Raleigh.

President George Bush and Governor Martin enjoy a game of softball, 1992 Fourth of July celebration, Faith, North Carolina.

GOVERNOR'S CONFERENCE ON TRAVEL AND TOURISM

ASHEVILLE, MARCH 25, 1992

Good evening! It's great to be here tonight. As a business and leisure traveler myself, it is always a pleasure to visit Asheville, one of our state's most picturesque cities and the site of our official Western Residence, and I welcome this opportunity to share with you information about our state's travel industry.

People like you—who run convention and visitor bureaus; who operate hotels, resorts, restaurants, theme parks, cultural centers, and even shopping malls—are the backbone of North Carolina's travel industry. You are why visitors return to North Carolina again and again. Your efforts, during good times or difficult times, help our state's economy stay strong.

I'd like to take this opportunity to thank all of you. You can be proud that your hard work and diligence have made tourism in 1990 a $7 billion industry in North Carolina! The 1991 statistics will be out in May, but it feels good, doesn't it, to know that because of you, North Carolina has more than 230,000 of its citizens working in travel-related jobs.

Now let's congratulate our Department of Economic and Community Development. By reallocating existing funds, the Travel and Tourism Division has created four new positions. The addition of these travel professionals to the small Travel and Tourism staff was certainly needed, and the expansion improves our ability to compete with other southeastern states, who still out-program us.

One thing our marketing study showed us is that while our competitors do have larger budgets than we do, more money is not always the best answer. Other states are spending about the same amount of money on advertising. Our competitors were capturing our market share with direct sells to tour operators, travel agents, and the media. The division's new programs, administered by these four new employees, will allow us to meet our competitors head on, and recapture our share of the Southeast market.

For the first time in the division's history, an aggressive marketing section is bringing more group travelers to our state, more sporting events, and more international visitors through North Carolina's gateway cities.

I've got some more good news. For the first time in the history of the state and the Travel and Tourism Division, we are reaching millions of households through cable television. That's right. We are in the midst of a nine-week television advertising blitz designed to increase North Carolina's share of travel to the Southeast. Our five commercials are airing on major cable stations such as the Cable News Network, the Travel Channel, the Weather Channel, and the Nashville Network, and it's working. Since the campaign began last Sunday, our toll free line has been extremely busy. And to respond to the demand for information on North Carolina, a second shift has been added at the Women's Correctional Facility in Raleigh. Secretary Lee, Assistant Secretary Pearson,[1] and other senior staff are working some evening shifts, as well, to help out in this effort.

You may recall that we began our program at the correctional facility in 1989 in order to respond more efficiently and effectively to both telephone and written inquiries. We have accomplished that and more. About 320,000 more calls came into our toll-free number in 1991, primarily as a result of year-round advertising initiated during my administration.

The program has received national attention, not only by the *New York Times*, which ran an article on its front page, but by other national leaders in the tourism industry, such as the United States Travel and Tourism Administration.[2] This program, which saves taxpayers money and provides daily job training to the inmates, should be considered a model for other programs in North Carolina and across the country.

While we've successfully generated national attention, there's always been a need to track the results to determine the actual economic impact on North Carolina. To meet the critical need for your industry, we've developed the division's first-ever new "Travel Trends Report." Earlier in the conference, you heard of the progress being made in the Travel Trends Research Project. The monitoring points are being established and the information gathering system is expanding. By now you know this data will be of tremendous value both in assessing the condition of the travel industry in your region on a quarterly basis, as well as in preparing future advertising and marketing plans.

This new Travel Trends project is only one of several new tracking methods the division is implementing. For example, press clippings generated from magazines and newspapers from around the country are currently being catalogued so we can determine how much free advertising the state is getting from its media programs. And the figures are sure to jump after Boone and Blowing Rock host the summer meeting of the Society of American Travel Writers in May. This group of 200-or-so travel journalists, photographers, [and] newspaper and magazine editors will get a firsthand look at North Carolina and its outstanding travel opportunities—along with a performance of *North Carolina is My Home*, with Charles Kuralt and Loonis McGlohon.[3] They, in turn, will then inform their newspaper and magazine readers nationwide. In fact, Jane Ockershausen, who wrote a travel guide on North Carolina, is a member of this society and was instrumental in getting this group to meet in our state.[4] The impact of these journalists' articles will be outstanding and could be felt for years to come.

We're also proud of our new consolidated travel guide. As you know, we combined the brochures for accommodations, attractions, and other travel information into one book to make it easier for our visitors. Now we are offering members of the travel industry an opportunity to market your destination, attraction, or resort in this book and further cut the cost of publication. The savings will be invested in additional advertising to generate even more travel revenue.

Other cooperative projects that help so much in getting the word about North Carolina to key travel decision makers include the recent sales blitz to Washington, D.C., where many of you met one on one with meeting planners. Another example is the countless familiarization tours you have coordinated for visiting travel agents from Germany or the United Kingdom. Thanks to these ongoing efforts, our outstanding golf courses, beautiful beaches, mountains, and historic cities are becoming recognized by tour operators and travel agents, here and abroad.

Again, you deserve the credit for your continued support of our travel division, and I thank each of you here tonight for making tourism one of the leading sources of revenue and jobs in North Carolina.

---

[1]Ernest C. Pearson (1950–), native of Charlotte; resident of Raleigh; B.A., N.C. State University, 1972; J.D., University of North Carolina at Chapel Hill, 1975; judge advocate, U.S. Army, 1977–1981. Special projects director, N.C. Dept. of Transportation, 1975–1977; attorney in private practice, Raleigh, 1981–1987, and since 1993; appointed chairman, N.C. Industrial Commission, 1987; assistant secretary, N.C. Dept. of Economic and Community Development, 1989–1993. Ernest C. Pearson, letter to Jan-Michael Poff, October 25, 1993.

[2]The article to which the governor referred, "Behind Bars, but Filling the Front Line for Tourism," appeared in the *New York Times*, November 24, 1991, page 24.

[3]Loonis McGlohon (1921–), pianist; music composer, arranger. Previously identified in Poff, *Addresses of Martin*, I, 43n–44n.

[4]Jane Ockershausen, *The North Carolina One-Day Trip Book: 150 Excursions in the Land of Dramatic Diversity* (McLean, Va.: EPM Publications, 1990).

GLOBAL TRANSPARK "SHORT LIST" ANNOUNCEMENT

RALEIGH, MAY 14, 1992

Thank you for coming here today, again. I'm sorry to put you through two press conferences in one day, but this important announcement could not be delayed until tomorrow and unfortunately was not ready to announce this morning.

I suppose you've heard me talk a time or two about our plans to build a Global TransPark in North Carolina. This project has sparked a great deal of interest, both in-state, across the country, and around the world. It's not even built yet, and this project has already provided us with opportunities to meet with corporate CEOs from around the world to talk about what a great place North Carolina is to do business.

Here in-state, interest in hosting the site was so great that the Air Cargo Airport Authority received thirteen site proposals for their consideration.[1] Ten of those proposals were reviewed by members of the authority in oral presentations last month. The proposals were very different in character, from green-field sites and noncentralized industrial locations to direct integration with major existing airports.

Each proposal was, in its own way, outstanding. But even in the best of competitions, the field has to be narrowed before a final decision can be made. After careful consideration and upon the recommendation of Rusty Goode, my CEO on the project, we have decided that the site for the Global TransPark would be best suited to an existing airport surrounded by a large tract of open land that could be developed at a reasonable cost. Only two of the thirteen proposals submitted meet that criteria and can also be developed without delay, which is an important issue to at least one prospective tenant with whom we have spoken.

We have therefore selected proposals submitted by the Kinston Regional Jetport and the Laurinburg-Maxton Airport Commission as finalists to host the Global TransPark. Each of the project directors who submitted proposals have [sic] been notified of this decision this afternoon. I have also invited the Kinston and Laurinburg project representatives to present their proposals to the full air cargo authority board at our next meeting on May 19. We hope to review these two proposals and select a final site at that meeting.

Selecting two finalists does not, however, mean that we will be turning our attention away from the other eleven proposals submitted. We received some outstanding proposals that included some truly innovative ideas. While only one site can be chosen to host the TransPark, the selection process has helped us to identify some areas of great economic potential in our state. I have directed Secretary Estell Lee to revisit each of the areas that submitted proposals to identify ways in which America's number-one economic development agency might develop state-local or public-private partnerships to maximize their development potential.

I've also asked Rusty to contact the project directors in Charlotte, Greensboro, [and] Raleigh and ask them to take [an] active role in developing the design plan for the freight operations building. The technology developed with that would then be shared with them. These areas, with their existing airport and visionary proposals, have the experience and the insight to help us plan the best possible cargo facility, so they should directly share in the benefits of the project.

I suppose you might have a question or two to ask. You have before you a copy of the letter that has been sent to each of the project directors, along with a list of those directors and an agenda for the upcoming air cargo authority board meeting. Rusty Goode, executive director of the Air Cargo Airport Authority, is here today to help me answer any questions you might ask. With that, I'll throw the floor open.

---

[1]Before site proposals were submitted, forty-four counties requested detailed information on the Global TransPark to help them determine whether or not they could attract the project. Opening Comments, Air Cargo Meeting, February 11, 1992, Governors Papers, James G. Martin.

LAKE GASTON PUBLIC HEARING

VIRGINIA BEACH, VIRGINIA, JUNE 13, 1992

[Legal maneuvering by the state of North Carolina during the Martin administration helped delay the city of Virginia Beach from fulfilling plans to build an eighty-five-mile-long pipeline to Lake Gaston. The project would have funneled 60 million gallons of water daily to the resort city. It also would have unwelcome consequences for northeastern North Carolina, as the governor explained in the following testimony, given at a hearing held by the U.S. Department of Commerce. See *News and Observer*, June 4, 5, 12, 13, 14, July 31, December 4, 1992.]

I appreciate this opportunity to speak to you on behalf of the state and people of North Carolina. As you well know, the Lake Gaston pipeline proposal is a matter of great concern to North Carolina. We understand the concerns of the citizens of Virginia Beach. We would be happy for them to continue to grow, with their own water. We, too, have communities that do not have enough water and also want to grow. But all of us—in Virginia Beach, in North Carolina, indeed in our entire country—must find ways to meet our water needs without taking water desperately needed by others.

Southeastern Virginia already has many alternative water sources available. In the late 1970s, when Virginia Beach officials first decided to expand the city's water supply, they had their choice of many sources to serve the city's needs. However, for reasons known best to them, those officials decided that the city's entire expanded water supply should come from a single source located far from the city, three river basins away! And they have no intention whatsoever of returning their treated wastewater back to the Roanoke River Basin.

We know for certain there is enough water in the Hampton Roads area to meet Virginia Beach's needs at least twice over. Maybe they want to save that for when the time comes that they cannot take any more water away from us. We say that day is at hand. Use your own water!

Earlier today you heard a technical report from Boyle Engineering Corporation, a leading national engineering firm. Boyle undertook a comprehensive, and expensive, study of alternative water supplies available to Virginia Beach. I won't repeat what was described in that engineering report, but it proves that water is available from Norfolk and Portsmouth reservoirs, from local groundwater, from sea water desalting, and from a number of other sources—if only they will use it.

Boyle showed also that tens of millions of gallons are wasted in southeastern Virginia each day. For example, an average of 10 million gallons a day can be recovered from water that is currently spilling from the Norfolk Reservoir. By simply pumping that water into the underground aquifer, then removing it in times of need, Virginia Beach can economically expand its supplies by over 30 percent. Then again, the city of Portsmouth has offered to sell Virginia Beach 6.5 million gallons of surplus water each day. Virginia Beach refused the offer.

It just doesn't make sense for the city to waste 10 million gallons of water a day, then turn down Portsmouth's offer of 6.5 million gallons a day, then demand that a neighboring state give up our much-needed water supply. Indeed, this is a matter of great concern for North Carolina. Under the present circumstances, during dry times, there already is inadequate water in the Roanoke River to meet the needs of North Carolina industry, agriculture, fisheries, and the environment. And unlike Virginia Beach, it's the only water we have; and unlike Virginia Beach, it's ours! If our water is siphoned away, we do not have any alternative! If our water is drained from Lake Gaston to serve Virginia Beach, there won't be enough left for our farmers to irrigate their crops. Already depressed fisheries will face disaster, our current industries will be restricted in their water use, and new industries will be unable to locate in the Roanoke River Basin. In each case, the people of northeastern North Carolina will lose jobs and the possibility of economic prosperity. We don't believe southeastern Virginia has a right to do that to northeastern North Carolina.

The stakes are enormous. North Carolina has committed to build a 3,000-mile unbroken network of four-lane industrial corridor expressways across our state, with our own money, so that even our depressed rural areas can offer industrial sites within ten miles of a four-lane intrastate highway. But if you take our water, you sabotage our development.

One of our major utilities now hopes to build an electric cogeneration plant within the Roanoke River Basin in Bertie County, North Carolina. Without sufficient water supplies, that plant won't be built. The citizens in this area will be deprived of possible jobs and the increased income that follows industrial development, if our water resource is pilfered by our neighbors.

The North Carolina fishing industry has long been an important part of our coastal economy. Tourism, the largest contributor to our coastal economy, also depends on our great, threatened, natural resources.

In short, for northeastern North Carolina to prosper, it must have water, and we don't have enough water now. All we ask is: At least let us keep what we've got, which is, by nature, ours. We want to bring jobs to where our water is. They want to bring jobs to where our water ain't and keep northeastern North Carolina poor forever.

Your responsibility is to decide whether there is a national interest in favoring further growth of metropolitan Virginia Beach, with our water, at the expense of direct injury to our people in northeastern North Carolina. We respectfully submit there is no such national interest to justify overriding our protection of our coastal zone. Virginia Beach wants to build a 100-mile pipeline across two river basins, directly past available and reasonably economical local water supplies, to siphon off water North Carolina desperately needs. They would tap in at a small tributary in Virginia, but would take so much more than its flow that they will make North Carolina waters in Lake Gaston flow upstream to Virginia.

Such an unnatural act must not be allowed to violate North Carolina's right to build a better life for our citizens. There is no, there can be no national interest in diverting water to foster economic growth in o[ne] area, which has alternative water resources, while depriving another, which has no alternatives. Virginia Beach has other options that enable it to meet its water resource needs without hurting its neighbors. Virginia Beach must take that course of action.

STATEMENT ON PRISON CONSTRUCTION BOND PACKAGE

RALEIGH, JUNE 18, 1992

[Martin moved the location of his weekly press conference from the Administration Building to Central Prison to underscore the legislature's obligation to allocate $87.5 million in correctional facility construction bonds.]

Good morning. Thank you all for joining us here on such short notice.

You all remember that in November 1990, the people of this state approved a $200 million bond issue for prison construction in North Carolina. With that vote, our law-abiding citizens showed that they were ready for their government to do something about keeping dangerous criminals behind bars and out of their homes. So far, only $112.5 million of that has been allocated, so I have appealed to the leaders of the General Assembly to allocate the rest so we can fulfill what the people want.[1]

Our prisons are crammed full. Yet it appears now that the General Assembly is prepared to break faith with the very people that elected them by refusing to approve the remaining $87.5 million of that $200 million prison bond package. What kind of a message does that send to the voters of this state if you disregard their vote?

I say we need those prison beds, and we need them now. By refusing to build those beds, the General Assembly is frustrating the will of the people and endangering the public safety. Every study confirms that we need m[uch] more prison space than this if we are ever going to keep the dangerous criminals locked up long enough that crime doesn't pay.

There's no reason for delay. With the initial $112 million in bonds authorized by the General Assembly, we've authorized construction at Nash Correctional Institution and Women's Prison. Several other facilities are also in the bid and design processes. We've shown we can keep faith with the people and deliver on our promises. What reason does the General Assembly have for not doing the same?

I've heard legislators' excuses. Some say they want to hold off on appropriating the $87.5 million because Secretary Bounds wants more single-cell units than the dormitories originally planned.[2] Secretary Bounds will tell you that's not a reason to hold up the appropriation. We need more of all kinds of units. All the legislators have to do is decide whether they agree with him or not and allocate the construction money. The design plans are ready. We can go either way without delay.

Other legislators say we have to wait until we develop a master plan. Well, that's another false excuse. We already have a master plan for the number of beds to be built. We did that before the bond issue. We have design plans. We can bury their desks in master plans if that will help move the project along.

I asked for 27,500-bed capacity. The committee headed by Justice Burley Mitchell concluded that over 29,000 were desperately needed. The General Assembly cut that to 24,000. Now they're trying to cut it again. What good is a master plan if they trash the one we've got? The sentencing study commission also shows that even with a restructuring of sentences to focus on dangerous criminals, even more prison capacity must be built.[3]

Others have said that the two gubernatorial candidates have much different ideas on how to manage our prisons, so this bond issue should be put on hold. Maybe that is what's behind this. Somebody wants to stop us for politics. But these prison construction bonds have already been approved by the voters and should move forward. If the next governor has other ideas, it will be up to him to develop and finance those ideas as a separate prison package of his own creation.

Some legislators have also expressed concern about approving this $87.5 million in bonds and then having to consider whether or not to support additional bond requests for education and infrastructure improvements. I say if the people can't trust the legislature to follow through on a referendum vote which passed to construct more prison space, how can they trust the General Assembly to follow through on any other bond referendum?

Those aren't reasons. They're just excuses—excuses that make me wonder what the real reason is behind this move to thwart the will of the people. Why the secret meetings and the apparent attempts to pit one prison contractor against several others? What is the real agenda here? There has been a prolonged campaign from somewhere to try to discredit the Carl Monroe firm which Cliff Cameron selected to oversee all this construction.[4] So far, only one contractor has attacked. The others have confirmed that Monroe treated everybody fairly and that the results were better than the General Assembly asked for. Construction was on time, well within budgets, and far superior to previous schedules. It makes you wonder why they want to handcuff us.

All I know is that the longer the legislature waits, more and more dangerous criminals are being let out of prison and back onto the streets because we don't have room to keep them behind bars. Right now our system is strained under a prison population emergency. This prison is full. Today there are 20,427 criminals behind bars, the seventeenth prison population emergency since the cap was instituted in March of 1987. The Parole Commission has until August 20 to reduce that population to 19,976.

Each year the courts are sending an increase of 4,500 more prisoners into our system. They can't stay long, because we don't have room. We say we manage those increased prison admissions by letting less serious offenders go after serving shorter terms. The problem is, today's relatively "less serious offenders" are very dangerous. Now we're in a situation where more dangerous criminals are being sent to prison for longer terms, because their previous time in prison was too brief to have any effect. At the very least, we've got to issue these bonds and follow through on our plans to increase prison capacity to 24,000 in North Carolina—as the people directed us to do. The General Assembly must approve the remaining $87.5 million in prison construction bonds.

Several distinguished people have agreed to join me here today to support the passage of these remaining bonds: Associate Supreme Court Justice Burley Mitchell, who served as chairman of the Commission on Prisons and Punishment; Lou Colombo,[5] chairman of the North Carolina Parole Commission; Lee Bounds, secretary of the North Carolina Department of Correction; Alan Pugh,[6] secretary of the North Carolina Department of Crime Control and Public Safety; Judge Tom Ross,[7] who chairs the legislature's Sentencing Policy Advisory Commission, was not able to join us; A. A. "Dick" Adams,[8] who serves on the commission as the incoming president of the Victims Assistance Network.

Thank you for coming today to show your support for this very important issue. Now I would like to ask Justice Mitchell if he would step forward for a few comments.

---

[1]The General Assembly allocated the initial $112.5 million of the $200 million prison bond issue under *N.C. Session Laws, 1991*, II, c. 689, secs. 239–240, ratified July 13, 1991. The remaining $87.5 million was approved under "An Act to Appropriate the Balance of the Funds from the Proceeds of the Already Authorized Two Hundred Million Dollars in General Obligation Bonds, Authorized for the Construction of State Prison and Youth Services Facilities, and to Modify the Prison Population Cap," ratified July 24, 1991; see *N.C. Session Laws, 1991, Extra and Regular Sessions, 1992*, c. 1036. The agreement between state lawmakers and Martin leading to the adoption of c. 1036 was described in the press release, "Legislature Passes Compromise on Prison Bonds," Raleigh, July 24, 1992, Governors Papers, James G. Martin.

[2]The Raleigh *News and Observer*, May 28, 29, 1991, described Bounds's prison construction recommendations. Legislators' reasons for delaying the bond issue were recounted in this speech; in the governor's July 2, 1992, press conference, below; and by the *News and Observer*, June 19, July 3, 1992.

[3]North Carolina Sentencing and Policy Advisory Commission, *Report to the 1991 General Assembly of North Carolina, 1992 Session* ([Raleigh: The Commission], May 15, 1992), 2.

[4]Carl Monroe owned the N.C. Monroe Construction Company of Greensboro, chosen in 1987 to build state prisons. *News and Observer*, May 29, 1992.

Charles Clifford (Cliff) Cameron (1923–), executive assistant to Governor Martin for budget and management, 1985–1990. Previously identified in Poff, *Addresses of Martin*, I, 153n; see also press release, "C. C. Cameron Resigns as State Budget Director; Governor Names Dorman Interim Director," Raleigh, December 20, 1990, Governors Papers, James G. Martin.

[5]Louis R. Colombo, resident of New Bern; B.A., Muhlenberg College; attended Temple University and George Washington University law schools; U.S. Navy, 1943–1946, 1951–1953. Assistant to research director, U.S. Senate Subcommittee on Internal Security, 1953–1955; positions with U.S. State Department included: staff, Office of Security and Bureau of Security and Consular Affairs, 1955–1960, supervisory and regional security officer for U.S. diplomatic and consular posts abroad, 1960–1975, and staff, Office of Security Policy and Planning, 1975. Vocational adjustment services coordinator for handicapped adults, Craven Evaluation and Training Center, New Bern, 1978–1985; chairman, Craven County Republican party; member, 1985–1989, chairman, 1989–1992, N.C. Parole Commission;

appointed to N.C. Sentencing Commission, 1990. Louis R. Colombo, letter to Jan-Michael Poff, November 3, 1993.

[6]Alan V. Pugh; resident of Asheboro; bachelor's degree, 1973, and law degree, 1976, University of North Carolina at Chapel Hill. Attorney; deputy secretary, N.C. Dept. of Administration, 1985; deputy assistant and special counsel, 1986–1988, senior assistant and special counsel, 1989–1991, to Governor Martin; secretary, Dept. of Crime Control and Public Safety, 1992–1993. Press release, "Governor Appoints New Secretary of Crime Control and Public Safety," Raleigh, May 26, 1992, Governors Papers, James G. Martin.

[7]Thomas Warren Ross (1950–), native, resident of Greensboro; B.A., Davidson College, 1972; J.D., University of North Carolina, 1975. Assistant professor of public law and government, Institute of Government, University of North Carolina at Chapel Hill, 1975–1976; attorney in private practice, 1976–1982; administrative assistant to Congressman Robin Britt (D-N.C.), 1983–1984; Superior Court judge, Eighteenth Judicial District, since 1984; appointed by Chief Justice James G. Exum to chair N.C. Sentencing and Policy Advisory Commission, 1990. Thomas W. Ross, letter to Jan-Michael Poff, October 29, 1993; Who's Who in the South and Southeast, 1991–1992, 631.

[8]Augustus A. (Dick) Adams (1935–), resident of Grifton; was graduated from Bath High School, 1953; U.S. Army, 1958–1960. Employed by E. I. du Pont de Nemours and Co., Kinston, 1953–1985, retired as supervisor; chairman, N.C. Victims Compensation Commission, 1987–1996; president, N.C. Victims Assistance Network, 1992–1993. Augustus A. Adams, letter to Jan-Michael Poff, November 4, 1993.

PRESS CONFERENCE: AN APPEAL TO THE NORTH CAROLINA GENERAL ASSEMBLY FOR MORE PRISON CONSTRUCTION

RALEIGH, JULY 2, 1992

It may well be that despite the strong appeal this administration has offered, as endorsed by all segments of our overloaded criminal justice system and all but one isolated editorial voice, the General Assembly is going to refuse to allocate the $87.5 million in prison construction bonds remaining from the $200 million approved by the voters in 1990. After many private, personal appeals, we went public with the problem two weeks ago at Central Prison.

Leaders of two major study commissions argued firmly for much greater prison expansion even than I have proposed. Secretary of Correction Lee Bounds, whom I had recruited to come out of retirement to help correct some departmental problems, made the strongest possible argument that we must move forward with every resource we have, or else we will be unable to hold the most dangerous criminals for a reasonable fraction of their sentences.

But nothing has happened. It is as if nobody cares. An issue which deserves bipartisan support is about to become a partisan political issue, because the Democrats have decided to block it. They won't listen to me or to the criminal justice system.

Secretary Bounds has appeared before the House Committee on Appropriations, but every time he has tried to raise this issue, he has been denied a hearing. The Senate Committee on Appropriations has not allowed him to testify at all. He's a respected criminal-justice expert, but they won't listen to him, either, and they won't even listen to the voters who elected them. Then they must be listening to somebody else behind the scenes. But who is calling the plays to generate such partisan opposition, and why? They don't have any valid reasons, only lame excuses. Who stands to gain? The victims and the public only stand to lose by such delays.

Ever since the number of convicts added to the prison system reached 15,000 a year, I have been pleading with the General Assembly to build an enlarged [prison] capacity so we could lock up the dangerous ones long enough to combat the crime increase. I have even tried to praise what little they have done in hopes that they would feel appreciated. But some legislators have positioned themselves to block any expansion, because they don't believe in locking up criminals, and their leaders have gone along only grudgingly, and only when the heat got too hot. Well, it's time to let 'em feel the heat. That's all they understand.

Because the expansion program has been so modest and inadequate, the cap limit adopted by the legislature has created a revolving door. With increasing frequency the cap has been exceeded, and the Parole Commission has been obliged under state law to release more and more high-risk criminals. We have warned repeatedly that we had a time bomb just waiting to explode. It exploded last Friday in Winston-Salem. It exploded again Tuesday in Fayetteville. Where will it explode again?

Lieutenant Aaron Tise of the Winston-Salem Police Department was brutally crushed to death by a motor grader which ran over his patrol car. One of the four teenagers charged would have been in prison were it not for the dangerously inadequate capacity of our prisons. Conrad Crews had been sentenced to five years for firing a weapon into a police car and entered prison last October 4. With adequate prison space, he would have served time until a year from now, next July 6, 1993. Instead, under pressure of a cap deadline, the Parole Commission had to release him on February 4. He was bad, but he was among the less worst. That's what it has come down to.[1]

Four days later, Correction Officer Leslie Becsi, a sixteen-year veteran on the staff of Sandhills Youth Center, was found murdered in his Fayetteville home. Two former inmates of that facility, both twenty-one years old, have been charged with his first-degree murder. These two men were not released because of the cap, but clearly overcrowding was a vital factor.[2]

One of the two accused, Michael Oates, had been granted conditional release, as a committed youthful offender, after serving longer than average: still only sixteen months of an eighty-four-month sentence, less than 20 percent. He fled parole supervision for a year, was sent back to prison last October, and then given another conditional release in December, only to run again on January 17. The other, Willie Ruffin, had been released just last September under the community service parole program.[3]

Let me remind you how our probation and parole officers pleaded for the prison construction bonds in 1990. They complained that all of these so-called alternative penalties have become increasingly dangerous due to the lack of adequate prison space for disciplining these offenders. Criminals cannot be forced to obey their parole supervisor under such an alternative punishment, for lack of a credible prison threat to back up the parole. We must have prison capacity as an alternative to the alternatives, they said then. They say it now.

What lesson do these young criminals learn from our overcrowded prisons? They don't learn respect. They learn the obvious lesson: that we can't keep them locked up very long. Now we've got real cop killers on our hands.

Now these are anecdotes, but they are terrible, and they are not likely to be the end of it. How many more time bombs are waiting to explode? Must we wait for more?

Let me give you the broader picture, in statistical terms, to show again why we must expand prison capacity. Look at this first graph.[4] The first line, A, shows that admissions have soared in our prisons, up from 17,500 in 1986 to over 31,000 this year. The second line, B, shows the number of people who are actually locked up on an average day. As you can see, that number has increased too, but not nearly fast enough, from 17,800 in 1986, to 20,000 in 1992. That means that for those let out in 1986, the average time actually served was down to just barely one year, 13.5 months. This year, it will be less than 10 months, and dropping fast. That is sending a dangerous message to criminals that crime pays pretty well in North Carolina.

Line C is very troubling. It shows the capacity in stricter terms, which the courts will require us to meet in July 1994. That's just two years away, and the legislature's delay will make it impossible for us to meet that date. Based on construction now authorized, plus the $87.5 million, we will have room for the 24,500 inmates expected by the voters when they approved the bond issue. Without the $87.5 million, 1,600 of those inmates will have to be set free. There is no good reason for delay.

Line D describes the effect of all this in speeding up the revolving door. It shows the average time served for those released each year, which is slightly longer than if shown for those sentenced in any given year. As admissions increase so much faster than capacity is expanded, the average time served gets shorter. I've been trying to teach that lesson for six years. Since we still aren't building prisons fast enough to keep up with the crime rate, under the cap law the Parole Commission is compelled to release more serious felons.

Look at the statement in your press kits from Lou Colombo, chairman of the Parole Commission, citing two reasons we were barely able to meet the most recent emergency exceeding the prison cap. First, he said, we got a "break" of sorts because our judges were at their annual state convention for a week, deservedly so, and sentences were briefly postponed. The second and more troubling reason was that they paroled 160 criminals who had been turned down for parole three or four times each already. These were cases convicted of rape, assault and sexual abuse of children, and numerous repeated property crimes—namely, your hardened, professional robbers.

I was shocked to learn that the available pool for release under the cap has gotten so rotten. There simply is no reserve of mild-mannered misdemeanants. They're gone, or they'll be out two weeks after they go in.

While there is no way to stop the revolving door, it is urgent that we slow it down, and the only way to do that is to build more prisons. I urge the General Assembly with all sincerity: Do not delay allocation of these bonds. The voters expect 24,500 capacity by 1994. Don't block it. Allocate the $87.5 million now, or face the consequences of irresponsibility.

There is no good reason for delay. Some Democrats balk at acting unless we draft a new master plan. That's silly. We've got master plans coming out of the kazoo. It'll take more construction than we can get for $87 million to do what we know we need without stalling while new master plans are offered, and all they will do is justify even more beds because we keep falling farther and farther behind.

Some Democrats mistakenly take Secretary Bounds's proposal for a different mix of minimum and medium custody as a reason for delay. He disputes that vigorously, because we will need far more of all kinds of facilities regardless of whether they choose to do it his way or stay with the earlier plan. The worst response to his leadership is for them to do nothing. So that's not a good reason to delay, either.

Now some Democrats are saying we aren't spending the money fast enough that was allocated last year. How will a delay help that? The truth is, the state treasurer has already explained to them his reasons for scheduling the bond sale so as to get the full amount they had authorized. Any faster bond sale, and we would have come up short $30 million.

Their latest excuse was to try to put the blame on Lieutenant Governor Gardner, saying that he and his opponent, Jim Hunt, have put forward new ideas for spending the money. That's more hogwash. The voters have already approved $200 million for prison construction, and they should expect action to carry out that mandate. No candidate has any license to thwart that expectation or divert that money for some other purpose. That's why Jim Gardner took the initiative to announce yesterday that he agrees with me and supports allocation of the $87.5 million now. If the Democrats have gotten some contrary signal from their candidate, it's time we all understand just what it is.

I hope some of you who are political reporters will ask and help us find out where does Jim Hunt stand on this issue. Has he asked his legislative "keys" to block this prison construction? If so, why? If not, I hope he will tell his fellow partisans to follow the will of the people and approve my request.

It is clear they have no *good* reason for any delay. Then maybe it's because they have some *no-good* reason. Let's see if we can find out what it is.

---

[1]Lieutenant Aaron G. Tise, Jr., was killed on the morning of June 26, 1992. Three of the four youths charged with his murder had criminal records: Conrad Crews, whom Martin mentioned; Jamarus Crews, Conrad's sixteen-year-old brother, had "outstanding felony charges of larceny of a motor vehicle and common-law robbery"; and Derrick Lamont Frierson was on "unsupervised probation" following his conviction on drug possession charges in March 1991. *Winston-Salem Journal*, June 27, 28, 1992.

[2]Willie Stanley Ruffin, Jr., and Michael Oates were charged with first-degree murder, first-degree larceny, and burglary in the beating death of Leslie Becsi. Becsi's body was discovered June 30, 1992. *Fayetteville Observer-Times*, July 1, 2, 3, 1992.

[3]According to the *Fayetteville Observer-Times*, July 1, 2, 1992, Oates received a seven-year prison term in 1988 for breaking and entering and possession of stolen property. Awarded a conditional release in May 1989, he skipped parole the following October but was apprehended and reimprisoned later that month. Ruffin's conviction on breaking and entering and larceny charges in 1989 carried a ten-year sentence. He was confined at Sandhills from July 1990 until September 1991, when he was released on parole.

[4]The governor directed reporters' attention to a chart labeled Prison Crisis, based on data compiled by the Office of Research and Planning, North Carolina Department of Correction. The following table, attached to Martin's speech, repeats that information:

Line:	A	B	C	D
				Average
			Standard	Time
Year	Admissions	Population	Capacity	Served
1986	17,554	17,804	12,082	13.5%
1987	17,316	17,545	12,682	15.1
1988	19,325	17,502	14,240	13.4
1989	22,730	17,665	15,088	12.3
1990	24,573	18,418	15,088	11.1
1991	28,510	19,049	16,136	10.4
1992	31,361	20,000	16,732	9.9
1993	34,497	22,000	16,656	9.9
1994	37,947	22,900	22,900	9.4 *
1994	37,947	24,500	24,500	10.1 **

*without $87 million in prison construction bonds
**with $87 million in prison construction bonds

Admissions increases are projected to slow down to 10 percent per year.

Population is assumed to continue to be held to "inflated" capacity, through continued early release by the Parole Commission, and to "standard" capacity in 1994, as agreed to in court settlements.

Capacity is the maximum number of inmates under the standards adopted in court agreements that become effective as of July 1994.

The *Average Time Served* is calculated each year for inmates released that year. The projected time served for 1992–1994 is that required to keep the population within limits of the cap law, assuming that the projected admission rate increases prevail.

AUTOMOTIVE INDUSTRY PRESS CONFERENCE

MEBANE, JULY 23, 1992

[Martin delivered a condensed version of the following address at the Motor and Equipment Manufacturers Association headquarters groundbreaking ceremonies, September 3, 1992, Research Triangle Park.]

I have some exciting news to share with you regarding the state's strategic marketing plan to target new and existing automotive parts manufacturers.[1] But first, I'd like to tell you a little about North Carolina's automotive industry.

In 1900, when Gilbert Waters of New Bern used gasoline to power his "Buggymobile," little did he know he had created the state's first automobile. Not too long after that, in 1925, the Ford Motor Company built a large assembly plant in Charlotte. That's how we got started in the automotive business.[2]

Today, 238 companies in North Carolina supply the automotive industry, both here in the United States and overseas. As you can see from this chart, these companies are located in many different parts of the state, from Murphy to Elizabeth City, and provide jobs for more than 48,000 of our people. The headquarters of the Motor and Equipment Manufacturers Association, the trade association of U.S. automobile and truck manufacturers, located in the Research Triangle Park earlier this year.[3] Mr. Robert Miller, [the] president, is here.

Without a doubt, the automotive industry is important to North Carolina because it provides more and better jobs for our workers. But it's also important for another reason: Automotive-related companies like GKN have helped to diversify North Carolina's industrial base. In other words, we're not relying solely on one industry to employ our workers. That's why we have such a healthy economy. We've been working hard to get these companies here, and that includes automotive part suppliers.

One thing that is going to help us attract even more automotive part suppliers to North Carolina is BMW's new facility to be built in South

Carolina.[4] This facility has already drawn a lot of positive attention to this region and has sparked even more interest in the Carolinas. [The project brings] Three great benefits: some of [the] jobs will benefit North Carolina[; it is] good for many of [the] 238 suppliers already here[;] and companies are going to want to locate near this automotive giant. So to make a good thing even better, we're going to capitalize on this excitement to intensify our recruitment efforts of automotive-related companies.

How are we going to do it? We're going to do it by following a specially designed strategic marketing plan.

Nine-Point Plan

1. A team of state developers will conduct an economic development mission to Europe this fall that will focus primarily on companies that supply the automotive industry.

2. In addition, one of our developers, Forest Rogers, is relocating to Europe this fall. His mission is to personally get to know the executives at the automotive companies there and to visit them on a regular basis.

3. On the national level, several of our state developers will travel to Detroit this fall. They, too, will focus their trip on automotive suppliers strong enough to consider expanding to new location[s].[5]

4. And Estell Lee, secretary of the Department of Economic and Community Development, is arranging a meeting with the North American headquarters of BMW to maintain our ties with the company.

5. On a regional level, we are going to strengthen our relationship with local economic developers and better coordinate our efforts to attract auto-related companies.

6. We're going to work more closely with our existing auto suppliers to help them broaden their opportunities in the automobile parts market.

7. We're also going to build new relationships with executives from Japanese and Korean companies at two conferences in October.

8. And we're going to implement a new advertising and direct-mail campaign, tailored to pique the interest of automotive executives. For example, in your press kit you'll find a "Facts in Brief" book that our developers use as marketing material; we're developing a new book similar to this, targeted specifically for the auto industry.[6] We're also going to reproduce these charts into promotional posters that our developers can display at trade shows. Some of our advertising will be aimed exclusively at attracting automotive suppliers to North Carolina. We'll be running these ads in magazines such as *Forbes, Fortune, Industry Week*, and *Handelsblatt*, a German publication.

9. And finally, we'll be expanding our mailing list of automotive suppliers to whom we will send our new marketing materials.

These elements are sure to bring a new level of intensity and depth to our current economic development efforts. They will help to further strengthen our economy, and they will position us to compete more aggressively in the global marketplace. The time is right. This region is in the spotlight. All we have to do is cash in on a golden opportunity we've been given. As you can see, we intend to do just that.

Thank you for coming. Now I'd like to answer any questions the press might have on this issue.

---

[1]At this point in the text, Martin jotted "New manufacturing—four of last five years Number One. More high-paying jobs than any previous comparable period."

[2]Actually, it is difficult to determine who completed the first gasoline-powered automobile in North Carolina. The same year Gilbert S. Waters guided his self-made Buggymobile on its maiden voyage down New Bern's Main Street—1900—Asheville bicycle merchant Eugene Sawyer constructed and drove a wood-framed, two-cylinder car. Neither Waters nor Sawyer enjoyed the success of Henry Ford and his immensely popular Model T. The brisk pace of Ford Motor Company's business in the Carolinas merited establishing a regional service depot, in Charlotte, in October 1914. Besides supplying replacement parts to Ford dealers, the facility also assembled cars from kits shipped in by rail. The operation outgrew its original facility, and Ford moved to a new, larger plant in the Queen City in 1927. Robert E. Ireland, *Entering the Auto Age: The Early Automobile in North Carolina, 1900–1930* (Raleigh: Division of Archives and History, North Carolina Department of Cultural Resources, 1990), 3–6, 16.

[3]The Motor and Equipment Manufacturers Association decided, in March 1992, to relocate its world headquarters to Research Triangle Park. Motor and Equipment Manufacturers Association, September 3, 1992, Governors Papers, James G. Martin.

[4]Bayerische Motoren Werke chairman Eberhard von Kuenheim announced on June 23, 1992, that BMW would build an automobile manufacturing plant near Greer, South Carolina. Construction of the factory was to begin later that year; vehicle production was scheduled to reach full capacity, of 50,000 units annually, in 1995. North Carolina officials attempted to win the industrial prize, which would have employed 2,000 workers by decade's end; but when it was learned that the finalists were South Carolina and Nebraska, Martin himself urged the automaker to choose the Palmetto State. BMW was the first German motor manufacturer to open an auto assembly facility in the United States since Volkswagen closed its Westmoreland, Pennsylvania, factory in 1988. *News and Observer*, May 22, June 24, 1992; *The Week in Germany*, June 26, 1992.

[5]"Take full advantage of having Motor and Equipment Manufacturers Association at Research Triangle Park," wrote Martin.

[6]"North Carolina, The Better Business Climate: Facts in Brief" ([Raleigh]: n.p., n.d.) and "North Carolina, The Better Business Climate: Automotive Industry" ([Raleigh]: n.p., n.d.) were two large, glossy, color brochures produced by the Business-Industry Development Division, North Carolina Department of Economic and Community Development.

CENTRAL AMERICA-SOUTHERN GOVERNORS' SUMMIT

Charlottesville, Virginia, July 28, 1992

[When he learned of the president of Honduras's remark to U.S. State Department officials that Central American leaders were eager to explore closer economic ties with the southeastern states, Martin sought to cultivate that inter-est. The governor, a "key player" at the Central America-southern states sum-mit, held July 28, 1992, introduced his proposal for a trade partnership between the two regions. The idea was accepted unanimously.

The daylong summit was organized by the Southern Governors' Associa-tion, the Southern Growth Policies Board, and the Agency for International De-velopment, U.S. Department of State. Along with Martin, attending dignitaries included President Rafael Calderon, Costa Rica; Governor Carroll Campbell, South Carolina; Governor Gaston Caperton, West Virginia; Governor Michael Castle, Delaware; President Violeta Chamorro, Nicaragua; Governor Lawton Chiles, Florida; President Alfredo Cristiani, El Salvador; Vice-President Guillermo Ford, Panama; Governor Kirk Fordice, Mississippi; Vice-President Jacobo Hernandez, Honduras; Juan Miron, Guatemala's minister of the economy; Prime Minister George Price, Belize; Governor William Schaefer, Maryland; and Gov-ernor L. Douglas Wilder, Virginia. Chamorro and Campbell, chairman of the Southern Governors' Association, conducted the meeting. *News and Observer*, July 28, 1992; press release, "Governor to Propose Trade Partnership at Central American Trade Summit," Raleigh, July 23, 1992, and address to Southern Industrial Development Council, Asheville, September 28, 1992, Governors Papers, James G. Martin.]

I am honored to have this chance to speak with you. Today we come together as a group united by a common goal: to promote trade and investment between the southeastern United States and Central America. We come together in an effort to create jobs, opportunities, and prosper-ity for our people. In some ways, what we do here today provides us with a link to the fifteenth-century explorers who traveled the oceans in search of a new trade route to Asia. These explorers blazed new trails and developed new relationships, marking the path of commerce for people and products between the New World and the old.

As participants in this historic summit, we, too, are explorers. We, too, can build a new relationship of trade and mark a new path of com-merce between our people. In doing this, we must recognize one major economic trend that affects all of us: The barriers to trade and invest-ment are coming down worldwide. Each of us lives and works in a glob-al economy.

As old relationships change and new relationships are forged in this global market, Central America stands out as an exciting region for trade with our equally vibrant southern states. In North Carolina, we began to actively pursue a trade relationship with Central America in 1990, when our international trade division hired a senior trade specialist as-signed to promote trade with Central and South America. At that time, Central America was becoming a more and more attractive place to do business because the region's economies were showing signs of unprece-dented growth and political stability and democracy. For the first time in years, countries in Central America were surging in their production of agricultural goods, textiles, and light industrial products for export to the United States.

On the other hand, we found that there was an excellent market for our products in Central America, products such as apparel, textiles, and textile and agricultural machinery. Other states were discovering the same thing. In 1990, four southern states—Alabama, Missouri, Virginia, and Florida—participated in a trade show in Costa Rica. The following year there was a trade show in Guatemala, but this time even more southern states participated: Delaware, Georgia, North Carolina, South Carolina, Florida, Missouri, Mississippi, and Arkansas joined the movement.

The event was a huge success, and the results have been impressive. From 1987 to 1990, exports from North Carolina to Central America nearly tripled from $51 million to more than $145 million. In 1987, the states that comprise the Southern Governors' Association were exporting approximately $2 billion worth of products to Central America; by 1990, that figure had increased by almost 50 percent, to $2.9 billion. That's almost as much as the entire United States exported to the former Soviet Union in 1990.

In recent years, we've seen a dramatic increase in world commerce and international business. Huge volumes of raw materials, product components, and finished products flow across international borders every day. That's one of the reasons North Carolina is in the process of developing a futuristic international air cargo airport that would revolutionize the way business is conducted in the twenty-first century. Manufacturing plants would be built around and integrated with this airport so that parts or finished goods could be assembled and flown to a customer half a world away within hours. With this just-in-time system, huge inventories could be eliminated, along with their huge costs. But the most important part of this concept is that the airport would combine the most up-to-date equipment in aviation and cargo handling, industrial production, and telecommunications to improve access to worldwide markets. That means improved efficiency.

But manufacturers aren't the only ones who could benefit from this state-of-the-art technology. Imagine that agriculture is your business, that you raise livestock or grow flowers—or better yet, let's say you grow the produce that many of us in the United States enjoy, particularly during our winter months. With this new air cargo airport, you could have more direct lines of distribution to your customers from a central East Coast location, allowing you to sell a fresher product faster, so you could make more money.[1]

We call this project the Global TransPark. Don't be surprised if you hear that name a good deal in the future.

My point in telling you this is that the Southeast is interested in being competitive in a global economy. We're interested in doing business with your countries. Our opportunities to prosper together involve more than the trade of our products. Opportunities abound for joint ventures among the companies in our southern states and your Central American countries—as well as cultural exchanges. For these reasons, I take pride in proposing a measure we might pursue to foster trade and investment between countries in Central America and our southern states.

Recognizing the importance of international cooperation, I propose the creation of an inter-regional economic partnership to enhance economic development opportunities between the southern states and Central America. At the conclusion of my remarks, I will move adoption of this resolution so that it will be before us for discussion for the rest of the day. Those in attendance today would be the start of this partnership, but other Central American or Caribbean countries and southern states not here today may be included later.

The details of this inter-regional partnership would be resolved in a joint planning effort. Each participating state or country would designate a representative—for example, their secretary or minister of commerce—to a working group, or task force, of this "Central American-Southern States Partnership." I envision the partnership undertaking joint cooperative activities in areas of mutual interest. This could even include an annual meeting that would alternate between regions, continuing the dialogue we begin today.

I sincerely believe this partnership will lead to bigger and better opportunities for both regions: better economies, better jobs, and a better way of life for our people. We are the explorers in this new relationship of trade between our two regions. Like the explorers of the past, we will mark the path toward a future of mutual growth and prosperity.

It is said that, at a banquet given by the grand cardinal of Spain, the great explorer, Christopher Columbus, was seated at the most honored place at the table and [was] served with great deference and ceremony. A courtier, jealous of Columbus's success, asked him rudely whether he thought that if he had not discovered the New World somebody else would have done so. Columbus did not reply at once, but taking an egg in his hand, invited the guests to make it stand on one end. All tried and failed, whereupon Columbus cracked the egg against the table in such a way as to flatten one end. Then he set it standing on the crushed part. The moral was plain to the company: Once he had shown the way, anyone could follow it.

Today we show the way, exploring new worlds of trade and opportunity for our people—and others will follow. Our prosperity depends upon our ability to build mutually beneficial economic partnerships like this one. With each step, we open new opportunities for trade and investment between our regions. If we work together, our prospects for success are unlimited. I look forward to working with you in the future. Thank you.

President Chamorro and Governor Campbell, for the southern states, I move the adoption of the resolution entitled "The Declaration of Charlottesville."

---

[1]Martin also described the potential relationship between the Global TransPark and the state's farmers in his remarks to the N.C. Farm Bureau Association, December 10, 1991, and at two "Agriculture in the Classroom" sessions, July 22, 1991, and July 27, 1992.

PRESS RELEASE: GOVERNOR REPORTS STRENGTHENING OF
FISCAL YEAR-END BUDGET RESERVE

RALEIGH, AUGUST 3, 1992

Governor Jim Martin today reported that the state ended its fiscal year June 30, 1992, with a balance of $164.8 million in the General Fund. That compares with a year-end balance of $441,000 in FY 1991. These amounts represent the amount of cash actually collected and on hand but not spent by the state.

"We ended the last fiscal year with almost nothing left in the state's coffers, especially when you consider that it costs about $50 million a day out of the General Fund to keep government operating," Governor Martin said. "This year, we have a $164.8 million balance going into fiscal year 1992–1993, which means the General Fund is much healthier than it was last year."[1]

Net operating figures for FY 1991–1992 improved substantially over FY 1990–1991. Total revenue increased by $634.3 million—8.6 percent— while expenditures increased by only $248.2 million—3.3 percent. Tax revenue for FY 1992 totaled $746 million more than in FY 1991, an 11 percent increase, primarily because of $479.1 million in increased sales and use taxes, and an increase of $161.5 million in income taxes.

Unlike previous years, revenue estimates for FY 1992 proved to be very accurate. Actual tax collections reached 100.1 percent of budget projections. All revenue, including fees, receipts, and investment income, totaled 99.9 percent of the amount budgeted. The shortfall was more than offset by reduced expenditures.

"The 1 percent sales tax increase and improvement in other tax collections, coupled with a slow-down in the growth of expenditures, made FY 1992 a much better fiscal year than FY 1991," State Controller Fred W. Talton said.[2] "The Office of State Budget and Management and the legislative fiscal research office should be commended for accurately estimating revenues for fiscal year 1992." At the recommendation of Governor Martin, the 1991 General Assembly enacted legislation requiring consensus revenue projections by these two offices to be used in adopting the state budget.

The General Assembly reduced transfers from the Highway Trust Fund to the General Fund by $61.1 million from 1991. In 1991, the Office of State Budget and Management was forced to increase transfers from other funds to the General Fund in order to overcome a $729 million revenue shortfall that year. The total amount of such transfers in FY 1992 was $112.7 million less than in FY 1991.

While current operating expenditures for both FY 1991 and FY 1992 include funds for twelve months of payroll costs, salaries earned by certain employees in June of each year are paid after the beginning of the next fiscal year. That practice was adopted in FY 1990 as a response to a $550 million revenue shortfall. The total amount of deferred salaries was approximately $329 million in FY 1992.

A condensed summary of operations for fiscal year-end 1991 and 1992 follows, expressed in millions:

	1992		1991	
	Actual	*Budget*	*Actual*	*Budget*
Revenues				
Taxes	$7,438.6	$7,433.1	$6,692.6	$7,357.4
Non-taxes	172.9	181.3	184.9	214.0
Transfers in from other funds	205.6	211.3	387.7	281.1
Bond proceeds	157.5	157.5	75.0	75.0
Total revenues	7,974.6	7,983.2	7,340.2	7,927.5
Expenditures				
Current operations	7,108.3	7,277.4	6,870.6	7,178.3
Capital improvements	157.5	157.5	181.4	282.3
Local government tax reimbursements	468.2	468.2	445.4	476.8
Debt service	75.8	79.7	64.6	71.3
Other	0.4	0.4	0.0	0.0
Total expenditures	7,810.2	7,983.2	7.562.0	8,008.7
Excess (deficiency) of revenues over expenditures	164.4	0.0	(221.8)	(81.2)
Fund Balance				
At beginning of year	0.4	0.4	222.2	222.2
At end of year	$ 164.8	$ 0.4	$ 0.4	$ 141.0

[1]For press releases on Governor Martin's budget proposals for the 1992–1993 fiscal year, see "Supplemental Budget Presented to Legislature," Raleigh, May 12, 1992, and "Governor Recommends $32 Million in Capital Improvements," Raleigh, June 11, 1992, Governors Papers, James G. Martin.
[2]Fred Wesley Talton (1927–), born in Clayton; B.S., University of North Carolina at Chapel Hill, 1950. Certified public accountant; employed by W. M. Russ and Co., 1950–1951, Sears, Roebuck and Co., 1952, Williams, Urquhart, and Ficklin, 1953–1965, and was a partner with the firm of Peat, Marwick, Mitchell and Co., 1965–1987; appointed state controller, 1988. *North Carolina Manual, 1991–1992*, 205.

NORTH CAROLINA-TENNESSEE VALLEY AUTHORITY AGREEMENT

Asheville, August 25, 1992

It's a great pleasure for me to be with you, today, on this historic occasion—even if it is late, for which I can only apologize. We gambled on the fog lifting, and lost, twice. But a hundred years from now, what will matter is that we got the right day and that what we will have done, today and subsequently, will have been good for western North Carolina and good for TVA; and I hope that will be the headline on tomorrow's editorials: "Good for TVA!"

The Tennessee Valley Authority is a unique institution in our nation. The authority was born in the Depression, in a time of crisis for our nation. When TVA was created, the Tennessee River Valley was gripped by poverty, unemployment, and outright misery. The Tennessee Valley Authority was to harness the power of the Tennessee River and its tributaries and provide flood control for communities and farms, create a navigation system that could move products efficiently, and generate electric power for economic growth.

TVA has achieved tremendous successes. The stimulus of the huge capital investment in reservoirs and other facilities, and the availability of power, have provided the foundation for the economic betterment of the valley—at least in other states. Unfortunately, some parts of the Tennessee River Valley have been left out of the picture: most of our counties have received little of its blessings. Although North Carolina's land and water resources contribute greatly to the benefit of the TVA system, these benefits have gone almost entirely to other states.

Even though North Carolina counties surrounding TVA lakes, and impacted by them, are among the poorest in our state, benefits from the TVA system have been exported to other states instead of being enjoyed locally. Legally and by geography, western North Carolina is a part of the Tennessee River Valley, but we have not been receiving a fair share of benefits created by the nation's investment in TVA. Historically, we have lost opportunities to enjoy these lakes because of rapid drawdowns during summer tourist season. In effect, that has burdened North Carolina with having to give an economic subsidy external to those in the region who get the electric power and other benefits.

Historically, until the study began in 1985, the first year of this administration, our state government had shown little interest in doing anything about it. Then when I named Bill Cobey as secretary, and Charles Taylor as chairman of the State Parks and Recreation Council, and delegated them to represent North Carolina, good things started to happen. On the other side, North Carolina owes a debt of gratitude to Chairman John Waters of TVA, and to former chairman Marvin Runyon, who saw the need to evaluate the operation of the TVA reservoir system and to make changes in the [incomplete] to get a more evenhanded system. These leaders saw that changes were needed to produce the balance of benefits needed in 1992 and to ensure that they are fairly shared.[1]

We also owe our gratitude to Congressman Charles Taylor and to Secretary Bill Cobey, who have represented North Carolina in these negotiations. They have invested their time and energy over a period of several years to get us where we are today. For Congressman Taylor, it goes back for most of his adult life.

TVA has now made a commitment to provide higher and more stable lake levels at TVA lakes in North Carolina. As North Carolina's part of the bargain, we have to obtain a congressional appropriation to cover the cost of lost power generation. In addition to the lake level improvement, TVA has made a firm commitment to work with Congressman Taylor and North Carolina on other actions to improve the recreation potential at TVA lakes. TVA will study improvements to existing recreation facilities, select potential sites for new facilities, and work with North Carolina on a long-range goal and plan for high quality recreation and tourism development.

Our ultimate goal is to create higher, more stable water levels at the North Carolina lakes until October 1. The lakes will then be reliably suitable for recreation through the whole recreation season. Only then will we be able to attract the private investment needed to create new jobs and business opportunities. This agreement is a major step toward that goal, as partners.

The strategy that we are following with TVA is right for the 1990s. We are asking TVA to manage its resources in a way that will provide a sound foundation for private initiative and prosperity. In return, North Carolina will accept responsibility to be a supportive partner and advocate before the U.S. Congress.

The agreement that we are signing today is a milestone, but not the completion of what needs to be done. Chairman Waters, we thank you for your good faith efforts, and your personal involvement, and your assurance that TVA will follow through on these commitments and that North Carolina will get its fair share of benefits from the system. North Carolina state government is committed to and will keep working toward opportunity for western North Carolina, and we look forward to a continuing partnership with TVA in that effort.

---

¹John B. Waters (1929-), native of Sevierville, Tenn.; B.S., 1952, J.D., 1961, University of Tennessee; U.S. Navy, 1952-1955. Attorney; co-chairman, Appalachian Regional Commission, 1969-1971; member, Southern Growth Policies Board, 1970-1974; member, Tennessee-Tombigbee Waterway Authority, 1978-1984; appointed board member, 1984, appointed board chairman, 1992, Tennessee Valley Authority. *Who's Who in America, 1994*, II, 3581.
    Marvin Travis Runyon (1924-), born in Fort Worth, Texas; B.S., Texas A&M University, 1948. Various engineering and management positions with Ford Motor Co., 1943-1980, including vice-president, body and assembly operations, 1979-1980; president, chief executive officer, Nissan Motor Manufacturing Corp. USA, 1980-1987; board chairman, Tennessee Valley Authority, 1988-1992; U.S. postmaster general, since 1992. *Who's Who in America, 1994*, II, 2975-2976.

STATE EMPLOYEES COMBINED CAMPAIGN KICKOFF
INTRODUCTION OF FIRST LADY BARBARA P. BUSH

RALEIGH, SEPTEMBER 2, 1992

To all of you, I want to let you know that I consider it a privilege to have served with you over the last seven and one half years as a fellow state employee. State employees as a group are hard working and, for the most part, unheralded and taken for granted. Many North Carolinians don't realize that without you, they might not receive many services they consider essential to their well-being. You make sure that the roads they drive on are safe. You protect the public health and safety. You protect the environment. You preserve and protect our cultural heritage, and you educate our children, and you do much, much more. I'm proud to have served with you, to have been one of you.

It's great to see so many of you here today as we kick off the 1992–1993 State Employees Combined Campaign! Each of us knows how much this campaign means to worthy causes here in Raleigh and all across North Carolina, and the generosity of state employees increases every year. Last year in Wake County alone, we exceeded a very impressive goal of $477,858 and raised $495,000. This year I expect we'll have no trouble at all topping last year's mark and reaching our new goal of $500,000.

Across North Carolina last year, state employees made a combined commitment to a better life for our neighbors by contributing a whopping $1.9 million. As governor, it has been my privilege to talk about North Carolina's virtues. Today I have the extra pleasure of doing that in the presence of the First Lady of the United States, Barbara Bush.

North Carolina is a state where volunteerism is second nature. Millions of our citizens give of themselves in countless ways. Giving of your money is important, too, but this year, think of ways you can give of your time as well. Be a volunteer. There are needs here in the community you could meet simply by giving of yourself a few hours a week.

Speaking of that generosity, I want to thank each of you who has already responded to the disaster in Florida and Louisiana. North Carolinians have long memories: When Hurricane Hugo ripped through South Carolina and then cut a path of destruction through Charlotte and west-central North Carolina, our neighbors helped us with food, supplies, money, and manpower. Now south Florida and Louisiana need our help, and before anyone had time to ask, North Carolinians were already on the job.[1]

So far, in just over a week's time, thousands of North Carolinians have been doing what they can to aid victims of Hurricane Andrew with their money, food, clothing—you name it. Offices, neighborhoods, churches, schools, radio stations, large and small businesses, and individuals have rallied to help people affected by Andrew. Already, many North Carolinians are in the disaster areas. Medical relief workers, National Guardsmen, Department of Transportation and Department of Crime Control and Public Safety employees, and other volunteers are there helping get relief to people who desperately need it.[2]

Some of North Carolina's businesses are lending a hand, or a truck, or a meal. ElectriCities, our association of municipalities who provide electricity services, sent manpower and equipment to south Florida shortly after the storm as part of our adoption of Homestead, Florida. Food Lion, Inc., has already sent five truckloads of food, with more on the way. Hardee's is also sending much needed food to ravaged areas. So many others—CSX railroad loaded carload after carload of equipment and supplies at terminals in Rocky Mount and Charlotte last Sunday and Monday. CSX trains transported these loads free of charge.

It's not just large businesses who are contributing. Hoke's Catering, in Garner, supplied two self-contained mobile kitchens and support vehicles for volunteers. Hoke's is also supplying free meals to hurricane victims in the Homestead, Florida, area. McCullers Ruritan Club, here in Wake County, is providing volunteers to help with this project and vehicles and RVs [recreational vehicles] for the volunteers to use and stay in so they don't place any additional burdens on the residents and city officials in Homestead.

Food for this mission, 6,000 pounds of chicken, was donated by Perdue Farms.

These are just a few of the examples of how we are responding to the disaster. I won't now, but I could go on all day listing further examples of North Carolinians' generosity. So again, thank you not only for your kind generosity to the victims of Hurricane Andrew, but also for your continued support of the Combined Campaign. Let's make this year the best ever. We can do it!

When we planned this year's kickoff, we thought of putting a few surprises into the program. This week, we got a little surprise of our own when First Lady Barbara Bush agreed to join us. Barbara Pierce Bush is known by everyone not only as the charming and gracious wife of our president, but, in her own right, also as a dedicated crusader against the cycle of illiteracy, one who has championed the cause of reading all across the United States and around the world. Her visit today is especially timely: September is "Literacy Month" in North Carolina.[3]

Everyone feels like he or she knows Barbara Bush. Her naturally friendly personality, her genuineness, and her compassion make her one of the most influential and best-loved leaders of our great country. A wife, a mother, and a grandmother, as well as a dedicated volunteer, Barbara Bush is a person our nation can look up to and be proud of. It is my pleasure this afternoon to introduce the First Lady of the United States, Barbara Bush.

---

[1]Hurricane Andrew savaged south Florida on August 24, 1992, and rocked the Louisiana coast the next day, leaving hundreds of thousands of people homeless. One of the worst natural disasters in American history, the storm caused $30 billion in damage in southern Dade County, Florida, alone. *New York Times*, August 25, 26, September 3, 1992, August 23, 1993.

[2]For related press releases, see "North Carolina to Assist Florida in Hurricane Recovery Efforts," Raleigh, August 26, 1992, and "Truck Weight Limits Waived for Carriers Aiding Hurricane Victims," Raleigh, August 28, 1992, Governors Papers, James G. Martin.

[3]"North Carolina Literacy Month, 1992, by the Governor of the State of North Carolina: A Proclamation," August 24, 1992, Governors Papers, James G. Martin.

PLENARY SESSION, INDUSTRIAL RADIATION AND
RADIOISOTOPE MEASUREMENT APPLICATIONS

Raleigh, September 9, 1992

I'm delighted to be with you this morning. I'm also happy to have the opportunity to welcome you to Raleigh for this important Industrial Radiation and Radioisotope Measurement Applications meeting. Say that three times quickly.

As governor, I've had the pleasure of traveling all over North Carolina, addressing groups such as yours that have gathered in our state for their annual meetings or conventions. But it's not often I get invited to speak to a group whose program includes discussions on "The Cross-Correlation Method of Precise Solid Particle Measurements" or "Microtomography Using an X-Ray Tube."

In real life, before I went to Congress, I was a chemistry professor at Davidson College. I've created a few funny titles of my own. My staff finds it endlessly amusing [that] they work for someone who actually wrote a thesis called the "Stereochemistry of the Diels-Alder Reaction" and who holds four patents, one in something called butyl rubber vulcanization. Somehow that doesn't fit easily into a political speech.[1]

You may remember that in the 1960s, being a Ph.D. was not a good thing if you were running for political office. When I first ran for Congress from the Ninth District in 1972, I overheard my campaign manager say that Jim Martin spent two years getting his Ph.D. and then he spent a couple hundred "thou" getting rid of it.

Back then, though, you couldn't help being inspired by the wonders of science. Americans had awakened to the need for a greater emphasis on science and math education with the former Soviet Union's launching of Sputnik in 1957. That fascination, and a determination to be globally competitive, carried over into the 1960s with the development of our own space program. Millions watched flickering black-and-white images on their television screens as John Glenn circled the globe and Neil Armstrong walked on the moon. This was front-page stuff. Every kid dreamed of being an astronaut, and every parent wanted to see that dream come true.

Now, some thirty years later, our nation needs another dream to follow. Just a few short years from now, we will turn the corner and careen headlong into a new century. There, new marvels await us, wonders that will rival even this century's invention of the airplane, the computer, or laser surgery. The choices we make today will determine our readiness to meet those challenges of the future.

The question we must answer is this: Will we invent the marvels of the twenty-first century, as Americans have so often done in the last 100 years? Or will we condemn ourselves to becoming a nation of consumers, dependent upon the energy, knowledge, and leadership of other nations to discover these marvels for us?

You and I understand the importance of science. Research into cold fusion, nuclear medicine, computer applications, and better ways to protect our environment are just a few of the ways that science provides us with a brighter future. The challenge for all of us who care about science and our nation's future is to keep students interested in science and math. Our challenge is to offer our young people the opportunity to become the most skilled mathematicians and scientists in the world.

The interest is there. I don't know how many of you had the opportunity to read a recent article in one of our local papers about the huge influx of students into introductory chemistry classes in our universities. Students know that, to be competitive, they have to be technologically smart.

It's our job to ensure that those students are ready for the challenge that college-level science and math courses provide. If our young people are well prepared in elementary, secondary, and high school—and if we can continue to offer them a stimulating learning environment—we can turn out the world's best scientists. Other nations have been investing heavily in science and math education programs for years. We, too, must make that investment. We, as interested and concerned members of the scientific community, must be willing to help put science and math programs into the forefront.

In 1988 I created the North Carolina Science and Mathematics Alliance, a program designed to make dramatic improvements across the state in science and mathematics education. This group combines the cooperative efforts of the state Department of Public Instruction, the community colleges, the University of North Carolina, and our state's industries. It involves schools in industries; industries in the schools; improvements in both pre-service and in-service education of science and mathematics instructors; enhancement of a North Carolina innovation, combining the career education resources of high schools and community colleges, called Tech Prep; and a strong recruitment of women and minorities to careers in science and technology.

The North Carolina Science and Mathematics Alliance was awarded $7.8 million as one of the first winners in the National Science Foundation's Program for Systematic Statewide Improvement in Science and Math Education. We know that reform of our educational system needs to take place in order for the United States to remain competitive in our global economy. We've begun to institute those changes.

As our nation's leaders in scientific research, you can help spread the word that science and math education needs to have a higher priority in our education system. Perhaps because of the work that we're doing today, all of us, to promote science and mathematics, a lot more of our students will follow in your footsteps and become first in the world in scientific research and discovery. Thank you for inviting me to be with you, this morning. I hope you enjoy your time here in the Capital City, and I wish you all success.

[1]All four of Martin's patents, awarded in 1957, were for butyl rubber vulcanization. Nancy Jo Pekarek, letter to Jan-Michael Poff, January 20, 1995.

STATE RURAL ECONOMIC DEVELOPMENT COUNCIL PARTNERSHIP MEETING

RALEIGH, SEPTEMBER 17, 1992

[According to a note appended to this speech, Governor Martin and Edward R. Madigan, the U.S. agriculture secretary, signed the memorandum of understanding establishing North Carolina's Rural Development Council on July 24, 1992. Council members typically included state and local officials, representatives of all federal agencies serving rural areas, educators, health care and labor interests, and individuals from the private sector. RDCs had been operating in eight other states, as part of the President's Initiative on Rural America, when federal authorities endorsed such a mechanism for North Carolina. See also press release, "U.S. Agriculture Secretary Approves Creation of Rural Development Council in North Carolina," Raleigh, February 27, 1992, Governors Papers, James G. Martin.]

It's my pleasure to be here today to participate in this first partnership meeting of the state Rural Development Council. I only regret that I must leave you to attend the funeral of the late congressman, Walter Jones, my friend of twenty years.

This is truly an important day for North Carolina and the rural communities that can use your help. Rural development is certainly one of the most important issues confronting our state today. Historically, for a long time our larger cities have been very successful in recruiting and promoting industrial development.

Four out of the past five years, more major new manufacturing facilities were announced coming to North Carolina than to any other state in the nation. Through an organized recruiting effort, industrial development has paid large dividends in terms of financial investment and, most importantly, more and better jobs for our citizens. In 1986, we began to make that effort pay off for our smaller communities. Secretary of Commerce Estell Lee was on the Economic Development Board at that time. We developed a *Blueprint for Economic Development*, which showed us that industrial development in nonmetropolitan areas was possible, and that rural counties could in fact attract industry—as long as they had good schools; good infrastructure, such as available water and sewer capacity; and a basic transportation system.[1]

To set up that magnetic attraction between business and our rural areas, we had to create a partnership between state and local officials.

Let me give you an example of how those partnerships are working.

There's a small town of about a thousand people, in Ashe County, called West Jefferson. For twenty years, from 1964 to 1984, no major companies moved to this little community. Not one. The population was much less than it is now. About ten years ago, the county even bought land for an industrial park, but couldn't attract any tenants.

Things changed for West Jefferson this year when Home Storage, a company that makes hardwood closet shelving, decided to move its company from Fort Lauderdale to Ashe County. The reason Home Storage moved to West Jefferson was because state, county, and local officials worked together to provide an outstanding package of benefits to the company—benefits such as an access road to the plant site from U.S. 221, water and sewer extensions, and a zero-percent interest loan for machinery and equipment. The move will create fifty new jobs when production starts, and one hundred more at full production.

That's what I mean when I talk about a public-private partnership. Those partnerships have helped us to better address the concerns and needs of smaller communities all across North Carolina. When you have a strong network of state and local developers and local leaders who know the assets of their community and who are committed to working together, anything is possible.

In recent years, there has been growing concern across the South that rural areas have been left out of the growth successes. Most studies have confirmed this imbalance prior to 1986, but we are doing something to change that. Last year, 69 percent of the new manufacturing firms that decided to locate in North Carolina chose sites in communities with populations of 10,000 or less, and 68 percent of new manufacturing jobs announced last year went to those smaller communities. The key is teamwork.

Teamwork will be essential to you as well in making sure the state Rural Development Council is a success. By working together, federal, state, and local governments can build partnerships that will strengthen economic opportunities in our rural areas, that will in turn strengthen the economy of our entire state. By working together, the lines of communication will be open, providing services more quickly and efficien[tl]y.

We know there's a duplication of responsibilities in various departments of state and federal government when it comes to providing services for rural development. That's the bad news, but the good news is you will be in a position to point out these duplications and get rid of them. You will evaluate local rural economic development needs and will coordinate the delivery of federal and state programs associated with rural development. You'll do that by removing barriers between government and individuals to provide the programs and services in a more timely fashion that is less costly to the taxpayers.

Think about the council as providing a road map to groups and individuals that will help them accomplish their economic development goals with the least amount of difficulty. But let me share with you an example of how this type of organization is working in Kansas. If you applied for a guaranteed loan for a small business in rural Kansas last year, you probably had to fill out half a dozen forms at half a dozen different agencies, forms all requesting the same basic information. But in April, the Kansas Rural Development Council initiated a project involving federal and state agencies in which a single application could be used for certain types of small business loans. Steve Bittel, the council's executive director, speaks highly of the program. He says it's an excellent tool that allows them to provide services faster and more efficiently.

There's another dramatic change in store for rural North Carolina. In 1988 I proposed building a continuous network of 3,000 miles of four-lane expressways to tie us together as one united state. In 1989 the General Assembly adopted such a plan, with the taxes to pay for [it]. Significantly, there's been very little complaint from taxpayers, because this time they know they'll get something for their money: a four-lane road that goes somewhere! For rural areas, it means everyone can now offer industrial sites within ten miles of a four-lane road. Let's make the most of it.

Let's take every advantage we can of what is historically and clearly a golden opportunity for rural North Carolina. You are just the right group to do that. I commend each of you for your willingness to offer your time and talents on behalf of our North Carolina citizens. I also challenge you—those who will be part of North Carolina's state Rural Development Council—to make this organization a success. I'm convinced it's a challenge we can and should meet in order to provide more opportunities for our citizens. Without a doubt, the state Rural Development Council will be a valuable asset to our future.

---

[1]*North Carolina's Blueprint for Economic Development: A Strategic Business Plan for Quality Growth* ([Raleigh: North Carolina Department of Commerce, 1986]).

OPENING CEREMONY, SOUTHEAST UNITED STATES-
JAPAN ASSOCIATION

Orlando, Florida, October 5, 1992

Good morning. How's business? Our North Carolina delegation joins
our Floridian hosts in welcoming you. We deeply appreciate the gracious hospitality you showed us last year in Tokyo, and we hope this
trip will be equally enjoyable for you.

Over the years, North Carolina has benefited greatly from the economic, cultural, and educational ties established and strengthened
through this association. First, for example, let's talk about trade. Export trade opportunities are very important to North Carolina, and Japan is our state's major trading partner, second only to Canada. In 1991,
North Carolina businesses exported more than $1 billion in manufac-
tured and agricultural products to Japan, as we enjoyed our fifth consecutive year with a net surplus of exports over imports.[1] That proves
the competitiveness of our workers, that we can compete in global markets; and in the last two years, we've seen a steady increase in shipments of many products to Japan: lumber, furniture, and fish products
are three of the main ones. We thank you—*domo arigato gozaimasu*—for
helping us do this; for helping us promote a healthier, two-way flow of
trade.

Investment is another good story. Compare the last fourteen years. In
1979, total Japanese investment in North Carolina was about $2 million,
and fewer than twenty North Carolinians worked for your firms. Since
1979, Japanese firms have invested more than $1.8 billion in North Caro-
lina. Today our state is proud to be home to 134 Japanese companies
that provide jobs for approximately 10,000 of our citizens; more than
half of those are in manufacturing.

Ajinomoto was our state's first major Japanese manufacturing investment, and this past April the company celebrated its ten-year anniversary in North Carolina. Ajinomoto's continued, indeed expanded, success is a fine example of how Japanese companies grow and prosper in
the Tar Heel State. I am so pleased to see Mr. Utada of Ajinomoto here
with us. He has been our number-one ambassador.[2]

In the year since our meeting last October in Tokyo, many other Japanese firms have announced new investments in our state. Japanese businesses enjoy a strong partnership with both North Carolina and the
southeastern United States, and I'm pleased to be on your program later
today with Mr. Tsuyoshi Kawanishi, senior executive vice-president of
Toshiba Corporation, to discuss trade promotion.[3]

I believe there are many things we can do to promote mutually beneficial exchanges between our nations. Education is essential. That's why we have established Japanese schools in three major cities, so that Japanese children can maintain their educational curriculum and the cultural traditions of their homeland while in our state. We have also established Japan Centers at colleges and universities in five cities in North Carolina. The directors of three of those centers are here today.

Now we're working on establishing a major new language institute, the North Carolina Center for the Study of World Languages and Cultures, that would further enhance our relationship with other countries. It would provide an opportunity for tourists, business travelers, students, and others for total immersion into the culture and language of the nation they are preparing to visit.

Individually and together, these schools and cultural centers serve as a bridge between our people.

As head of North Carolina's delegation to this conference, I conclude my opening remarks by once again expressing our state's collective anticipation of another positive and beneficial meeting of this association. North Carolina's delegates express their appreciation to our hosts and look forward to renewing old friendships and making new friends. *Domo arigato gozaimashita.* Thank you.

---

[1]North Carolina exports to Japan in 1987 totaled $675 million, approximately half the level reached in 1991. Breakout Session on Trade, SEUS-Japan Association Meeting, October 5, 1992, Governors Papers, James G. Martin.

[2]Katsuhiro Utada (1925–), was educated at Faculty of Law, Tokyo Imperial University; joined Ajinomoto in 1947, was appointed president, 1981, honorary chairman, 1989, and honorary chairman-senior advisor to the board, 1991; became vice-chairman, *Keidanren* (Federation of Economic Organizations), 1990. Aileen N. Peters, vice-president for public affairs, Ajinomoto U.S.A., Inc., letter to Jan-Michael Poff, May 12, 1994.

[3]During the discussion on trade promotion, Martin credited the cooperation of JETRO—the Japanese External Trade Organization—in contributing to the state's successful economic relations with Japan. Breakout Session on Trade, SEUS-Japan Association Meeting, October 5, 1992, Governors Papers, James G. Martin.

AIR CARGO AIRPORT AUTHORITY BOARD OF DIRECTORS

Kinston, October 13, 1992

It's a pleasure to be here, today. I appreciate the hospitality we've received.[1]

This is an historic meeting in several ways. Today marks the beginning of a new, important phase of this project. Until now we've been going through activities similar to a pilot's pre-flight checklist. The checklist has been an impressive one. It has included:

—Proposing the TransPark and getting support from the General Assembly;

—Carefully reviewing proposals from across North Carolina;

—Selecting Kinston and Lenoir County as the site for the TransPark;[2]

—Selecting a master planning firm;[3]

—Applying to the FAA for funding support;[4]

—Negotiating over the agreement for the transfer of the Kinston Regional Jetport;

—Creating a nonprofit development corporation.

The list goes on and on, and all of those are vital steps. Having checked off all those items, today we are moving from pre-flight to engine start-up. As we head to the runway, we're pleased that business, community, and government leadership and much of the general public of Lenoir, Kinston, and this multicounty region are on board. We will work hard with you to keep it that way.

It's taken hours, days, weeks, and months of effort by so many people in this region to make the progress possible. It would take forever to read off the list of those who have helped, but a few people must be mentioned. Their tireless work has been invaluable. So, my special thanks to Vernon (Pou) Rochelle, the point man on so many things.[5] Thanks also to Mayor Buddy Ritch and members of the city council, Chairman J. J. Langston and other members of the county commissioners.[6] Let me tell you, these folks are tough negotiators when it comes to protecting the interests of their constituents.

I've made a lot of new friends. Felix Harvey has been so important in pulling together support for this project.[7] Senator Barnes was crucial to our support from the General Assembly.

Now many more of you will be involved in determining the future of this project and your region with start-up of the master planning process. In a few minutes, you will hear more detail about the TransPark master plan. The fact that it won't be completed until a year from now is a reminder of the tremendous challenge ahead. But this process, more than any other, will begin to provide answers to many questions you have been asking. For some, the question is how this project will affect your land. This morning I met with representatives of landowners in the area. Let me assure you, as I did them, that we are going to be fair.

While the concept for the TransPark covers an area of 20,000 to 30,000 acres, initial development over the next several years will focus on 4,000 to 6,000 acres, including the nearly 1,300 acres of the Kinston Regional Jetport. We do not have to begin the process to purchase the majority of the land that will initially be required until the airport facilities portion of the master plan is done, probably in spring of 1993. As for construction of a new runway, that would likely not begin before early 1994. For land outside the initial development, the need for most of that property is many years off.

So, you can see that all of us have much to do. For the next year, the master plan will be a beacon, lighting our way to the future. This will be a very open process involving people from throughout this region. Let me add that Kinston and Lenoir County also will be represented in the planning of this project at the highest level. We look forward to representatives of Kinston and Lenoir County joining the Authority as board members at our next meeting.

Finally, two things. First, our marketing of the project has gone into second gear. We will soon have two state industrial developers working full time on taking the Global TransPark message worldwide. The response to our marketing efforts have [*sic*] continued to be extremely encouraging.

Second, my thanks to the people of this area for their vision and commitment in pursuing the Global TransPark. Yes, the next decade will be a period of change for Kinston and Lenoir. Change makes all of us a little anxious. I've got a little change of my own ahead.

Instead, you have an opportunity here for a legacy that many others wanted very badly. This is an opportunity that many states are already trying to imitate. The eyes of the country are focusing on what's happening here. Our Authority looks forward to working with you to seize this opportunity to make sure that your children are aboard this first flight into the twenty-first century on its journey to the brightest future possible.

---

[1]Martin inserted at this point: "Welcome to new board members: former governor Bob Scott, who is president of the North Carolina community college system; Dr. Richard Eakin, chancellor of East Carolina University, who is an appointee of University of North Carolina president C. D. Spangler; and P. A. Thomas, chairman of the State Ports Authority, who is unable to be with us today. These three leaders bring some very special perspectives to our board that will greatly benefit our efforts."

[2]Assets worth $220 million propelled the Kinston Regional Jetport to first place in the competition to land the Global TransPark, Martin announced on May 19, 1992. Among the site's existing attributes were a Federal Aviation Administration traffic control tower, a commercial airport rating, scheduled carrier services, a runway able to serve fully laden Boeing 727–200 cargo jets, extant FAA approval to construct a second runway, and its proximity to two military bases. Press release, "Global TransPark Site Selected," Raleigh, May 19, [1992], Governors Papers, James G. Martin.

[3]The state hired Kimley-Horn and Associates, of Raleigh, to prepare the Global TransPark master plan. Press release, "Governor Martin Announces $622,000 Grant for Global TransPark Planning," Raleigh, October 6, 1992, Governors Papers, James G. Martin.

[4]The Federal Aviation Administration awarded a grant, in early October, to aid completion of the air cargo airport's master plan. The governor noted that the FAA's gesture was "the first step in a multi-phased funding process" and that the state would seek further financial support from the agency. Press release, "Governor Martin Announces $622,000

Grant for Global TransPark Planning," Raleigh, October 6, 1992, Governors Papers, James G. Martin.

[5]Vernon H. Rochelle (1938–) native, resident of Kinston; B.A., Duke University, 1960; LL.B., University of North Carolina, 1965; U.S. Navy, 1960–1962. Attorney in private practice since 1966; attorney, city of Kinston, since 1970; secretary treasurer, Atlantic and N.C. Railroad Co., 1977–1985; president, N.C. Municipal Attorneys Assn., 1986–1987; coordinator, drafter, Kinston/Lenoir County Global TransPark proposal, 1992; liaison–coordinator between Kinston/Lenoir County and Global TransPark Authority, since 1992; appointed by Governor Hunt to Global TransPark Development Zone Commission, 1994. Vernon H. Rochelle, letter to Jan-Michael Poff, September 12, 1994; see also *News and Observer*, May 20, 26, 1992.

[6]Orice Alexander (Buddy) Ritch, Jr. (1929–), born in Mecklenburg County; resident of Kinston; B.S., University of North Carolina at Chapel Hill, 1951; U.S. Army, 1951–1954. Owner-manager, Western Auto Associate Store, Kinston, 1955–1977; commercial and rental real estate owner-manager, since 1963; member, city board of directors, BB&T bank, since 1974; organizer, board chairman, Pride of Kinston downtown revitalization project, 1983–1985; elected Kinston mayor, 1985, reelected 1989, 1993. Buddy Ritch, letter to Jan-Michael Poff, September 12, 1994.

John Jay Langston (1935–), born in Kinston; resident of Grifton area; was graduated from Contentnea High School, attended Beaufort Community College; U.S. Army, 1958–1959, 1960–1961. Member, 1984–1992, vice-chairman, 1990–1991, and chairman, 1991–1992, Lenoir County Board of Commissioners. John Jay Langston, letter to Jan-Michael Poff, November 16, 1993.

[7]C. Felix Harvey (1920–), born in Kinston; B.S., University of North Carolina, 1943; U.S. Navy, 1943–1946. Board chairman, Harvey Enterprises and Affiliates, engaged in farming and agricultural supply, ginning, terminaling, transportation, public utility contracting, real estate, and wholesale and retail petroleum distribution; founder, Life Insurance Co. of North Carolina, 1955; president and chief executive officer, 1969–1971, board chairman, 1971–1972, Georgia International Life Insurance Co.; founder, 1978, chairman, First Financial Savings Bank; became president, N.C. Global TransPark Foundation, 1993; local and state civic leader. A firm believer in the Global TransPark concept from its early stages, Harvey pledged to raise $30 million from the private sector on behalf of the project. C. Felix Harvey, letter to Jan-Michael Poff, October 3, 1994; see also biographical article on Harvey by Charlie Peek, "Looking Up Down East," *Business North Carolina*, February 1993, 36–45.

OPENING STATEMENT, NORTH CAROLINA DRUG CABINET

CHARLOTTE, OCTOBER 17, 1992

I am delighted to be with you, this morning, for this meeting of the North Carolina Drug Cabinet. It's always nice to be back in Charlotte. Dottie and I look forward to moving here in just a few short months.

Charlotte is a great city, but you and I know there is a serious drug problem here. Chief (Ronnie) Stone, I know your officers have to battle drugs and the problems they cause every day. They are the front-line soldiers in the war on drugs.

Tragically, drugs are not simply a problem found in our large cities. Small towns in every corner of the state suffer the scourge of drugs. The good people of Shallotte are just as likely to suffer from violent crime resulting from drug activity as are the good people of Charlotte. The problem is everywhere. That means all of us—law enforcement, teachers, parents—everyone must be involved in one way or another in the fight against drugs.

Each of you has joined in that fight. Despite serving under fire from the press and politicians, you remained committed and have achieved important progress in the war against drugs. Since I created this body in 1989, you developed the first statewide plan to battle illegal drug abuse in North Carolina. That took months of hard work and input from thousands of North Carolina citizens, antidrug professionals, teachers, law enforcement officials, and treatment experts. The 118 recommendations and twenty-nine pieces of legislation you developed were designed to strengthen our state's drug laws.[1]

But the Drug Cabinet didn't stop there with your good ideas. Instead, you focused on implementing the plan, passing legislative initiatives, and obtaining appropriations for much-needed education, prevention, and treatment services.[2] Our only disappoint[ment] was that some legislation got blocked for political reasons, but that's not our fault. No, that's the fault of legislators who blocked us. We asked for their help; all we got was criticism.

But you didn't stop. You looked out for our littlest ones, addressing the tragedy of infants exposed to drugs during pregnancy. Because of your concern, the Drug Cabinet sponsored the first statewide study of the prevalence of drug and alcohol abuse among pregnant women. When completed, this study will provide North Carolina with the first coordinated statewide strategic plan for preventing drug use and for helping children who are born addicts.

You've also helped to strengthen our criminal sanctions, developing legislation for user accountability and obtaining appropriations to complete the drug and alcohol prevention curriculum for kindergarten through twelfth grade. And you established a new tax, specifically a tax-stamp program to hit the drug dealers where they live: in their profits. That's one tax the majority of our citizens are happy to have on the books and would probably like to see raised even higher. The skeptics laughed, but you know what? When we caught up to a dealer, he was breaking the law! I understand we are to hear more about that program later this morning, but I did want to thank you on behalf of all North Carolinians who are grateful to you for creating this tax![3]

Lieutenant Governor Gardner, I'm glad you could be here today, because I want to thank you again for your dedicated leadership of the Drug Cabinet. You've taken a serious, nonpolitical approach to the problems of drug abuse, and all our law-abiding citizens thank you for that.

I also want to again congratulate you on receiving a special award of honor by the International Association of Narcotics Officers in 1990. You were presented this award because of your initiation of two major pro-grams to fight the war on drugs: Operation Marijuana Watch and the drug-free public housing effort. Operation Marijuana Watch has gained national attention and was developed to help our citizens eradicate a crop that earns the wrong people more than $1.5 billion a year. More than 300 landowners covering more than 2 million acres are participat-ing in this program.

You've seen firsthand the cost of drug abuse to our society, [Lieuten-ant] Governor Gardner. You've visited a number of public housing ar-eas in North Carolina to talk to the people there. You've heard their stories of pain, suffering, and violence. You listened, and you acted. To-gether with concerned residents, you and this Drug Cabinet are helping make public housing drug free.

I know you'd be the first to admit we have a long way to go in those efforts, but I'll be the first to say you've helped us come a long way toward accomplishing our goal of living in a drug-free society.

No question: We are on the offensive in the war on drugs. We need everybody on board. Because of statewide coordination, oversight and accountability for the millions of dollars of federal and state funding, and genuine, active concern of the members of the North Carolina Drug Cabinet, we are going to win this war. Thank you for letting me join you today. Thank you for caring about the citizens of North Carolina, and keep up the good work.

---

[1]The twenty-nine proposed bills, dubbed "Legislation Re-Establishing Social Control," were printed in North Carolina Drug Cabinet, *A Plan of Action for the State of North Carolina* ([Raleigh: The Drug Cabinet], March 1990), Appendix III. The 118 recommendations were offered throughout the report.

[2]For example, the N.C. Drug Cabinet was instrumental in securing the passage of the state Omnibus Drug Act of 1990, according to Martin. Press release, "Governor Praises Gardner, Drug Cabinet Accomplishments," Charlotte, October 17, 1992, Governors Pa-pers, James G. Martin; see also *N.C. Session Laws, Extra Session, 1989, Extra and Regular Sessions, 1990,* c. 1039, ratified July 27, 1990.

[3]Effective January 1, 1990, dealers in illegal drugs were required to buy excise tax stamps and attach them to all controlled substances in their possession. Failure to comply made the dealer liable for the tax, a 100 percent penalty, and accrued interest. "An Act to Impose an Excise Tax on Controlled Substances," *N.C. Session Laws, 1989,* c. 772, ratified August 12, 1989.

The controlled substance measure was "probably one of the most equitable taxes lev-ied," the governor said January 9, 1992. "It feeds off the cause of a societal problem and is applied directly to the solution of that problem. Similar to the way gasoline taxes go di-rectly toward building and maintaining our roads, controlled substance taxes go directly toward combating the drug trade. Seventy-five percent of the money collected under this tax is returned to the state and local law enforcement agencies responsible for the arrests that allow us to collect the tax." After delivering that assessment, Martin distributed $669,000 to 128 eligible law enforcement agencies, the biggest payout made under the program; the Catawba County Sheriff's Department received the largest check, which totaled $209,539. By mid-October 1992, the tax had funneled approximately $3.7 million in drug profits back into crime-fighting operations. Drug Tax Revenue Distribution Press Conference, Raleigh, January 9, 1992; press releases, "Governor Martin Announces Payments to Law Enforcement from Drug Tax Collections," Raleigh, January 9, 1992, and "Governor Praises Gardner, Drug Cabinet Accomplishments," Charlotte, October 17, 1992, Governors Papers, James G. Martin.

OPENING, INTERSTATE-40 BYPASS

WINSTON-SALEM, OCTOBER 29, 1992

What a pleasure it is to be here today. We've waited a long time for the completion of this project, and I'm going to make you wait a bit longer, because I've got some things to say, and this is kind of my swan song. I'd like to thank and congratulat[e] all the DOT [Department of Transportation] staff and contractors who worked so diligently to see this project through—and what a project it was. This 24-mile bypass consists of eight connected projects and four additional related interchange projects that tie in to the new interstate. The cost of this roadway, an impressive $191 million, means we got part of our money back! Construction began on [the] last section in 1989: the final link.

I don't have to tell you how much this bypass will help—not just the piedmont residents who will be able to travel this new corridor every day, but the thousands of others who drive through Winston-Salem to get to the mountains, the coast, or to piedmont points in between, or wherever they need to go. This bypass is a critical road for commerce and the trucking industry.

I'm sure you are all too familiar with the Hawthorne Curve on "old" I-40.[1] It was the only hairpin curve on the Interstate System! Well, this new bypass will end the traffic bottlenecks. Now you will have what you have long wanted and deserved: an efficient, east-west interstate highway that will keep North Carolina moving down the road to increased economic prosperity. It's a safer corridor that will save lives; as you know, safety has been a top priority for Secretary Harrelson and the DOT during this administration.

The bypass will also offer some relief for the portion of Interstate 40 that goes through town, the original I-40—what will now be referred to as I-40 Business. Less traffic on that road means a safer, less stressful journey for those needing to access the downtown area. For the last ten years, the traffic has been so heavy on I-40 through town that the Department of Transportation could only make emergency repairs. Anything more extensive would have tied up traffic for too long. Opening this bypass also means that DOT will finally be able to do some much needed repairs and rehabilitation work on the older section.

It is no secret that I-40 has been a priority of mine. The completion of I-40 to Wilmington was the one and only highway promise I made along the campaign trail in 1984. Every other candidate promised it, too, but they all promised every other road project, so they could never deliver on all of them. I thought if I just made one promise, I could keep it. So I did.

That missing link to our truck-dependent seaport was finished ahead of schedule. It was not the only major project completed by this administration. I hope that part of my legacy with the people was to prove that our "unpromised paving" is far better than the "unpaved promises" of previous years. The Winston-Salem Bypass is an excellent example of what I'm talking about; so are the improvements to [U.S.] 421, and [U.S.] 52, and the Greensboro connectors.

Many hurdles had to be cleared to make this road a reality. We jumped what was perhaps the biggest hurdle in October 1988, when then secretary Jim Harrington and I received word that North Carolina's application for federal discretionary funds had been approved. We had used our strong contacts with the Reagan administration to get back part of what we had lost in the 1987 highway funding bill when the Congress voted to override President Reagan's veto. The extra $114 million meant that construction of the bypass could forge ahead full force, so everybody can celebrate. It's ironic, isn't it, that the administration which got this for us is the only one with no campaign banners here today. One of the great things about America is that we can differ on politics and everyone can promote their candidate of their choice.

That funding enabled us to complete this project four years sooner than originally thought. It's not often that construction projects are completed years ahead of schedule. Not only that, we were able to free up $70 million of our other highway funds to use on other projects throughout the state, so that was a great day for North Carolina.

The "action team" that Tommy Harrelson mentioned earlier deserves a lot of credit for the success we are gathered today to celebrate. Without their hard work, we never would have received that funding, and we wouldn't be standing here today. Special thanks go to former North Carolina Department of Transportation secretary Harrington; Charles Shelton, your former DOT board member who did far more for this area than all his critics combined;[2] Bill Cobey, former deputy secretary of NC-DOT, who is now secretary of the Department of Environment, Health, and Natural Resources; Hannah Byron, the federal programs coordinator at DOT, who skillfully guided the proposal through the federal maze; Ken Bellamy, former federal highway administrator for North Carolina, who saw to it that we got treated fairly; [and] George Wells, NC-DOT's former highway administrator. Also, we received unanimous, bipartisan support from the entire congressional delegation, from congressmen Steve Neal and Bill Hefner, and especially from Senator Helms and Senator Hollings of South Carolina, who introduced the amendment to the transportation appropriation bill.[3]

But Interstate 40 has not been the only accomplishment in transportation in the last several years. Eight years ago, North Carolina's transportation program was basically bankrupt, both in terms of money and in terms of direction and purpose. The return on our federal highway taxes was just 79 cents to the dollar. The remaining 21 cents was tax money paid by our motorists that is going to support other states.

In the early '80s, the average reliability of the first year of the Transportation Improvement Program, known as the delivery rate, was 50 percent. That means that half the projects that had been promised didn't get started. At one point the rate was only a pitiful 19 percent, and between 1981 and 1984, the delivery rate never rose above 70 percent.

North Carolina's community leaders and citizens lost confidence in the TIP. No wonder: Having a project in the program didn't mean much. It was like the survey stakes along your dirt road just before an election. But, with the effort led by my two transportation secretaries, and the Board of Transportation, and support from our General Assembly, we have worked hard to change that. I wanted a transportation system and department that was reliable, one that operated with integrity, credibility, and purpose. These principles mean that the DOT would promise only what it should promise and only what it can deliver.

Following the leadership of my administration, in 1989 the General Assembly enacted the Highway Trust Fund Law to use revenue generated by highway user taxes and allow us to improve and build a sound transportation system. There's been little complaining, because our taxpayers get a lot for their money.

In 1991 and 1992, the DOT and congressional delegation linked arms and worked to increase our return on federal taxes paid by North Carolina highway users, and they did. Our federal return has climbed to about 88 percent of what we send to Washington. Not perfect, you understand, but getting better and headed in the right direction.

The delivery rate on the TIP is now an average of 94 percent and hasn't gone below 90 percent since 1986. In the last eight years, construction and maintenance work has increased by 75 percent over the previous eight years. Construction has doubled. What that means, historically, is that we have strengthened our highway construction progress by as much as all previous governors combined. That does not appear to be newsworthy, but it is true. Meanwhile the DOT work force has grown by less than 12 percent.

My overall goal for transportation was to create a program with honest, realistic goals. We've done that. You can now trust the TIP.

Ladies and gentlemen, we've really gotten the transportation ball rolling in the last eight years. Under the guidance of Secretary Tommy Harrelson and former secretary Jim Harrington, the DOT has worked hard to create a safe, sound, and sensible transportation system. Tommy, if you and Jim will stand, I'll ask the audience to join me in showing our appreciation for the outstanding transportation system you've created for North Carolina.

The I-40 Winston-Salem Bypass and the rest of I-40 is a part of that system, but there's more—much more—and I have to take a moment to tell you about [it]. Otherwise, you wouldn't know since it doesn't seem to be newsworthy.

For the first time, our state aviation, rail, and public transportation efforts now have continual funding dedicated to them that can be used to undertake worthy projects across the state. Soon the state's new passenger train, the Piedmont, will begin same-day passenger service from Raleigh to Charlotte and back, matching in reverse the Charlotte-to-Raleigh service we put together two years ago.[4]

The Global TransPark is now under way in Kinston. It's going to be a state-of-the-art manufacturing and cargo handling facility that promises to make North Carolina a world leader in the global economy of the future. It will be the kind of industrial magnet for investment and employment in eastern North Carolina such as we have long enjoyed in the piedmont.

Another: Recycled products and crumb rubber from old tires are now being used in highway construction projects, and highway work is being done with more respect for the environment. Speaking of the environment, our roads are cleaner and more beautiful thanks to the Adopt-A-Highway program and the expanded wildflower program. I have to give my wife Dottie a plug, here, and a pat on the back (a hug): She was the driving force behind the rejuvenation of the DOT wildflower program, which I understand is now one of the department's most popular efforts.

But some of our most important accomplishments have been those that increase highway safety. Both the motorists and transportation workers are safer now. I have to stop a moment and give a "hats off" to Secretary Tommy Harrelson. He's been called, and I believe even formally recognized, as DOT's safety secretary. He was instrumental in developing and installing those raised reflective pavement markers that now light the way for you on your interstate and primary routes. I'll bet there's not a person here whose drive home on a rainy or foggy night hasn't been helped by these friendly little devices.

Because of the Work Zone Safety campaign that emphasizes caution around highway construction areas, thousands of DOT employees are much more likely to return home to their families, and you are safer as you travel through work zones. Again, I commend Tommy for his insistence and promotion of safety on the roads and in the workplace.

The DOT has certainly accomplished a great deal over the past eight years. There is greater accountability at the agency and a new fairness to the way your needs are met. As I told you earlier, the Department of Transportation has emerged as an agency that is governed by those three guiding principles I mentioned earlier: integrity, credibility, and purpose. But there is still much to be done and many challenges that lie ahead. There is still a shortage of funding for safety and maintenance work, such as the maintenance work on what is now the "old I-40" through town. While the federal dollars returning to our state are up, they are still less than they should be. We shouldn't be expected to support other states with money paid by our taxpayers.

The funding equity effort is especially important to public transportation. We get mugged by the big city subway systems as our transit dollars pass through Washington, and we get a very small return. As the years go along, our rural and urban transit needs will grow and demand more funding. The best source for that funding would be the transit taxes we're already paying the federal government.

But with all its needs, what North Carolina transportation will need more than anything else in the coming year is you. You must remain interested and actively involved in transportation issues and in other issues that concern our communities and states. If you don't, we stand to lose much of what has been gained. Not everybody understands how important good roads are to your future. With your help and support, North Carolina can move forward to provide the kind of transportation system the citizens of this state need and deserve.

We need to do all we can to maintain North Carolina's reputation as the Good Roads State. This interstate, like our other strategic highways, is a key to increased economic prosperity. It is the link to our future and to the future of generations to come.

This may be my last major highway opening ceremony as governor. If it is, I can think of no better place to bring an end to this part of my job. Interstate 40 was where I began, as governor, from a transportation standpoint. I can't think of a better way to complete the circle. Thank you for being here today to share in this event. Let's open I-40!

---

[1]Winston-Salem's notorious Hawthorne Curve had been the scene of an average of one motor accident per week between 1988 and 1992. *News and Observer*, October 29, 1992.

[2]Charles M. Shelton (1935–), native of Mt. Airy; resident of Charlotte. Real estate developer; founder, Blue Ridge Enterprises, Mt. Airy; cofounder, Fortis Corp., 1962;

cofounder, The Shelton Companies, 1978; appointed to state Board of Conservation and Development, 1973, state Board of Natural and Economic Resources, 1975, and John H. Kerr Reservoir Development Commission; board member, numerous educational, humanitarian, civic, and business organizations. Charles M. Shelton, letter to Jan-Michael Poff, May 16, 1994.

Shelton resided in Winston–Salem between 1977 and 1990, and as the governor implied, his impact on the area was considerable. His commercial and industrial building projects helped "reshape" the city, and he was a major contributor to local charitable and civic groups. The reference to Shelton's detractors perhaps was prompted by reports in the *Winston-Salem Journal*, in 1989, and the *Independent Weekly* three years later, critical of his activities as a state Board of Transportation member. *Independent Weekly* (Durham), June 3, 1992.

[3]Stephen Lybrook Neal (1934–), born in Winston–Salem; A.B., University of Hawaii, 1963. Former small businessman, mortgage banker, newspaper publisher; member, U.S. House of Representatives, 1975–1994, and chairman, Subcommittee on Domestic Monetary Policy; Democrat. *News and Observer*, January 22, 1994; *North Carolina Manual, 1991–1992*, 514.

W. G. (Bill) Hefner (1930–), born in Elora, Tenn.; president, WRKB Radio, Kannapolis; first elected to U.S. House of Representatives in 1974, returned in subsequent elections; Democrat. *North Carolina Manual, 1991–1992*, 517.

Ernest Frederick (Fritz) Hollings (1922–), born in Charleston, S.C.; B.A., The Citadel, 1942; LL.B., University of South Carolina, 1947; honorary degrees; U.S. Army, 1942–1945. Attorney; member, 1948–1954, speaker pro tem, 1951–1954, South Carolina House of Representatives; lieutenant governor, 1955–1959, and governor, 1959–1963, of South Carolina; elected to U.S. Senate, 1966, returned in subsequent elections; Democrat. *Who's Who in America, 1994*, I, 1616.

[4]To help Amtrak subsidize a counterpart to the Carolinian, which began providing daily passenger service between Raleigh and Charlotte in 1990, the state purchased and rebuilt a pair of locomotives and four coaches for a new train, the Piedmont. However, difficulties in acquiring both a Raleigh maintenance site and property to turn the Piedmont in Charlotte kept the train idle until well after Martin left office. *News and Observer*, September 28, 1993, January 8, 1994.

EULOGY FOR BRAD HAYS

Charlotte, November 7, 1992

["I have lost a dear friend, a loyal champion, and a key adviser," said Martin after learning of the death of Brad Hays. The governor called him "the most knowledgeable political mind in North Carolina" and "a major political force," worthy of "a great deal of credit for developing a competitive two-party system" in the state. "Without his professional guidance," Martin asserted, "I would not have won my first campaign for Congress in 1972, nor subsequent elections to Congress and the governorship. He was the key to campaign organization, fund raising, poll taking, and advertisement for me and a host of other candidates over the years. Brad never tried to change my ideas or positions on issues, though he would often test how well I understood them. His brilliance enabled me to get across to the voters who Jim Martin was and what I planned to do for the people of North Carolina." Press release, "Governor Martin Expresses Loss at the Death of Brad Hays," Raleigh, November 5, 1992, Governors Papers, James G. Martin.

Martin delivered the following testimonial at Hays's funeral, held at Calvary Church, Charlotte.]

How often have you visited a friend who insisted on showing you his photo album or slides from a recent vacation trip? If you were not in on the trip personally, yourself, all you could do was to be polite and try to show some interest. Yes, but if the journey was one you shared, then hearing about it again, seeing those shared vistas, swapping great stories, and reliving those joyful times would surely be among the most precious moments among all the memories of a lifetime. The difference is in having good friends with whom you can share the memories, just as you had shared the experience. Well—wasn't Brad Hays just about the best trip we ever had?[1]

Now I must confess to you that I have never, ever, consented to eulogize anyone before. So many families seemed to have felt that if I attended, surely my office entitled me to make some kind of address, to say just the "right words." I believe that I was always correct to decline, and always found the right words to do so, until now. But for Brad, I found the right words to accept—realizing that after this, I may never get asked again.

Susan was right: Even in our grief, she wanted us to remember the good times we shared, and rejoice, and be glad that such a friend was ours.[2] Almost all of us are here today as friends of Brad Hays. I say "almost all," because there are surely some of his partisan adversaries who may have just come to be sure he's gone—as Brad once said irreverently of a rival from the other party, yet whom he truly admired and whose work he genuinely respected.

Many of us are here because we shared Brad's hopes and schemes for building a competitive two-party system in North Carolina and in the South. The only thing Brad would have enjoyed more would have been building a one-party political system: ours! And now, after years of preparing us, and leading and teaching us to do better than we had ever known how to do, helping us raise ourselves to a higher level of competitiveness—now our friend Brad Hays has gone to a higher glory, for which he was prepared by his faith, his devoted family, and his new active discipleship in this beautiful sanctuary and this strong Christian fellowship of Calvary Church, which meant so very much to him. All I can figure is, maybe his friend Lee Atwater needed help again![3]

Brad Hays was a hard thinker and a hard teacher. He could build rivalries within our party just as effectively as he later built unity among former rivals—all depending as the challenge of the times required, or made opportune.

He not only did not seek publicity for himself, he assiduously avoided it. He joked about legendary motives of others who hid behind the scenes, but in Brad's case, he just didn't want to become classified as "just another pretty face!"

Brad rarely attended political rallies or celebrations. Was it because he just could not bear to witness the stumbling antics of those of us he had created? We finally had to shame him into coming just so he could bring Susan, so she would not have to miss the fun and the friends.

But he faithfully came to Raleigh every Tuesday. He knew we needed his help. Now some of our more cynical reporters—usually the kind he liked the most—concluded that this was strange behavior, indeed, so surely he must be up to some foul mischief. Why else would he spend so much time with people like us?

The truth is, Brad felt it his special burden of responsibility to protect me, his innocent protégé. It was his self-appointment to ferret out mischief before it became a scandal and cauterize the wound before it festered. Yes, Brad was our guardian angel—and how well suited. No one could refuse to confess; and I remember clearly the day, during such a mission, he swooned in my office. Was it four and a half years ago?

He and Phil Kirk and I were talking about state government, and at first I thought Brad was just bored. I knew he didn't get excited about our governing nearly as much as about the intensely competitive process through which we qualified to govern. Then I realized something really was wrong and ordered him to let Phil drive him to the emergency room.

For once, obediently, he actually permitted someone to help him. But on the way, Brad recovered enough adrenaline that he tried to divert Phil from his duty—assuring him that, "It's OK now, Phil, just take me back to the hotel. I'll be all right." It would not have been the first time he avoided the treatment he needed. Thankfully, Phil saw through the stagecraft and refused, giving an even more convincing performance of his own. He told Brad: "I can't do what you want. I'll lose my job!"

Brad Hays meant a lot to us. He was our friend, our leader, our confidant, our teacher—our humorist, too. Whatever he did for us, or with us, or molding us into a team, Brad was always our special strength and our wisdom. We will surely miss him.

It would be fitting, and it is my personal wish, that we manifest our debt of gratitude for all that Brad meant to those of us who grew under his special tutelage. I want for those of us who are where we are, because of him, to unite a part of our blessings by subscribing together a scholarship trust fund. Let it be in Brad's name and for his son's college education—not out of any implied sense of need, but out of our own sense of love, with the unused remainder to be used for education programs of this, his church family.[4]

We can work that out. I didn't ask anyone for permission, because earlier, when he had heart surgery, I did ask if we could help and Brad declined. So please, Susan and Spencer,[5] just this one time? Let us do something special for Brad and for this fine young man whom he loved so devotedly.

Brad would have been amused by yesterday's nice news stories about his career and reputation. So kind! So respectful! He never accepted applause for himself; it was enough for him to see us win our accolades, so I won't ask you to make such a joyful noise in this ceremony. No, only just think of how fitting it is that our presence here today is our proper tribute of applause for this wonderful, memorable trip that he shared with us. Amen.

------

[1]Brad Hays (d. 1992, age 58), native of Oklahoma; died in Charlotte; engineering degree from Texas Tech. Engineer, Savannah River nuclear facility, until 1965, when he joined staff of National Republican Congressional Committee; chief architect of Richard Nixon's "Southern strategy," 1968, that attracted large numbers of conservative Democrats to the Republican party for the first time; director of political consulting firm, Marketing Associates, Charlotte; was instrumental in election campaigns of Jim Martin, James Holshouser for governor, U.S. representatives Alex McMillan and Howard Coble, and Charlotte mayors Sue Myrick and Richard Vinroot. *Charlotte Observer*, November 6, 1992; *News and Observer*, February 19, 1989, November 6, 1992.

[2]Susan Hays, widow of Brad Hays. *Charlotte Observer*, November 6, 1992.

[3]Harvey Leroy (Lee) Atwater (1951–1991), born in Atlanta; died in Washington, D.C.; B.A., Newberry College, 1973; M.A., University of South Carolina, 1977. Republican political consultant; managed a number of successful election campaigns, including J. Strom Thurmond for U.S. Senate, 1978, and presidential campaigns of Ronald Reagan, 1984, and George Bush, 1988; special assistant to President Reagan for political affairs, 1981–1984; chairman, Republican National Committee, 1989–1991. *Current Biography Yearbook, 1989*, 25–29, *1991*, 631. Atwater once said of Hays, "'He's legendary in Southern politics. When I was a kid, the first name I ever heard of as a Southern operative was Brad Hays. He advised me when I was in the White House. He gave me sound advice in the Bush campaign. I stopped by his home in Charlotte when I was in the state. If I want to know the nuances of North Carolina politics, he is the guy who I pick up the phone and call.'" *News and Observer*, February 19, 1989.

[4]Brad Hays had two sons: Bradford Hays, Jr., of Arlington, Texas, and Jack Hays, of Charlotte. *Charlotte Observer*, November 6, 1992.

[5]Spencer Hays, of Nashville, Texas, was Brad Hays's brother. *Charlotte Observer*, November 6, 1992.

T. J. MAXX ANNOUNCEMENT

CHARLOTTE, NOVEMBER 12, 1992

It's a pleasure to be with you today as we celebrate the announcement that T. J. Maxx will open a major distribution center here in Charlotte next June. This is indeed a significant day for T. J. Maxx; for T. J. X. Companies, Incorporated, T. J. Maxx's parent company; for the city of Charlotte; and the state of North Carolina. First and foremost, T. J. Maxx's $32 million investment will translate into quality jobs for our citizens.

At start-up, this new retail distribution center should employ about 700 people. At full production, this 630,000-square-foot facility will employ 1,050 people. That's a significant number, because that means that T. J. Maxx will effectively double the number of employees it has in North Carolina right now. Currently, thirteen T. J. Maxx retail stores are located in North Carolina. Those stores, from Asheville to Winston-Salem to Wilmington, employ about 900 of our fellow citizens.

This new investment demonstrates that you have great faith in North Carolina and in our workforce. I know we have earned your trust through our honesty, our hard work, and our reputation as the better business climate. You've seen that here in North Carolina, where we aggressively recruit business and industry—and we're quite successful at it. In fact, the North Carolina Department of Economic and Community Development was named one of the nation's top ten development groups for the last four years. It was the only state agency named to the *Site Selection and Industrial Development* magazine list.

Four out of the last five years, we led the nation as the choice location for new manufacturing plants. North Carolina was also the number-one choice last year for international firms, accounting for 17 percent of their major U.S. sitings. I'm confident that it's the way that we do business in North Carolina that encouraged you to increase your business here, too.

Back when you were still considering where to expand, T. J. Maxx was interested in knowing if we offered any incentives to businesses considering a North Carolina location. Considering our success rate, you might think we offer everything under the sun as a carrot to lure prospective investors, but we don't. We follow the same philosophy in business recruitment that T. J. Maxx does in doing business. You don't offer discounts in your stores. Instead, you offer the best product for the best price, "The Maxx for the minimum." That's how North Carolina does business, too.

The "incentives" we offer to T. J. Maxx we offer to any company, new or existing, that plans to locate or expand in North Carolina: the availability of a qualified workforce, a central East Coast location, and a better quality of life—including our own form of southern hospitality. But we don't sell the store to buy new stock. We don't have to. We offer a solid, respectable program for recruiting industry that includes a community college training program and infrastructure support. The domestic and international business communities know that North Carolina offers the "max for the minimum." We're just delighted that you decided to take us up on the offer. I know that we'll make it worth your while.

UNIVERSITY OF NORTH CAROLINA SYSTEM
BOARD OF GOVERNORS

CHAPEL HILL, NOVEMBER 13, 1992

I'm here today to ask you for your help in further enhancing North Carolina's economic future and quality of life. Let me begin by telling you something you already know and understand, just as a check to see if I've got it right.

Millions of people, representing just about all of the languages and cultures on earth, interact in a way and at a pace rarely envisioned twenty-five years ago. English has been generally accepted as the international business language, but that, too, is changing. In Sweden, for example, where students have for years learned English as a second language, students are now shifting toward learning German as the second language.

As North Carolina's successful Export Now program has flourished, with five consecutive years of trade surplus, it has been driven home that while English is satisfactory when you are buying foreign goods— money talks—if we want to sell our goods, we have to speak their language. There is, after all, much more to international commerce than paper currency transactions. The economic rise of Germany, Japan, and Latin America means that the monolingual American is going to have a hard time maintaining a competitive edge in a multilingual, multicultural world. Doing business halfway across the globe means talking to people on their turf, in their language. Yes, the international game has changed, and we must learn to play that game according to new rules based on pressing realities.

We have learned that we can't just sit out the game here in North Carolina, because we are already players in the competition for global markets. More than 1,500 North Carolina companies employing more than 435,000 workers are actively involved in international trade. Top on the list of exports from North Carolina is industrial machinery and equipment. In 1989, all those exports brought North Carolina just short of achieving a $1 billion trade surplus. We expect to break through the billion-dollar mark this year.

We've achieved unparalleled success in global business, but we cannot maintain our progress to improve the economic well-being of North Carolinians with what might be described as our nation's "island mentality." As a Southern Governors' Association report states, "There are no more guaranteed markets for our goods. We must compete—and to compete, we must communicate." The report also wryly notes that

"America is a living paradox: A nation of nations that is afraid to learn different languages."

The ability to speak fluently in other languages is manifesting itself as a tangible asset, providing an enormous edge in international competition, especially when products and services are virtually equal in quality. But business isn't the only arena where multilingual, multicultural understanding is important. Doctors, lawyers, policemen, nurses, social workers, teachers—these and other professionals in our society are also coming face to face with a need for language skills and cultural awareness.

Of course, we in North Carolina have not exactly had our heads in the sand about the need for global literacy. Foreign language courses are offered in all of our elementary and secondary schools. Three high schools offer baccalaureates in international studies, with another expected to come on board next year.

Supporting these studies is the Governor's Language Institutes, which we created five years ago. For four weeks during the summer, the institute offers public school teachers a program of intensive immersion in foreign language and culture. The program is designed to improve skills, increase awareness, and in general, recharge those teachers for the coming school year.

These programs, along with relevant curriculum at our community colleges and universities, provide opportunities for many of our citizens to learn about other languages and cultures. The Governor's Language Institutes in particular have been highly successful, but limited in scope. We need a much broader program, targeted to a more varied population, if we are to become a truly culturally literate society. That need, combined with the success of the Governor's Language Institutes model, has spawned the idea for a Center for World Languages and Cultures.

What is the Center for World Languages and Cultures? As now conceived, the center will be a noncredit, nondegree-granting institute offering intensive, results-oriented instruction in a variety of languages and cultures at a number of different locations across the state. It would be independent of any departmental structure, although it will draw upon them as needed on a contractual basis. In many respects, it will build upon the experience of such successful schools as the Monterey Institute; the Defense Language Institute; Thunderbird, in Arizona; Wharton's program for international business; and Middlebury College. Ours would be the first in the South.

Starting with a small permanent staff of five to seven professionals, the center will develop courses designed to provide practical foreign language communication skills for business, health services providers, teachers, travelers, the military, and all interested North Carolinians. Those courses will focus primarily on verbal and some written skills. Course offerings will begin on a modest scale, with the eventual expectation of satellite outreach across the state. The length of the courses will depend on the level of difficulty of the languages and the proficiency level required by the client. For example, conversational Spanish or French may take six weeks of immersion, where the same level of competence in Arabic or Japanese may take six months.

Who will this center serve? Human and health service providers; front-line workers like the police, nurses, fire fighters, and criminal-justice professionals; teachers of language, world studies, geography; North Carolina citizens, lifelong learners, senior citizens and college students; or tourists of any age. Selected military personnel may also be clients.

We hope to develop a hard base of financial support from government, businesses, foundations, and a variety of consumer—fee paying—constituencies, and related patrons. In that way, we hope to establish the center as a public-private partnership with a strong, but affordable, tuition base. The best part of the plan is that the center will strive to be financially self-sufficient within five years.

Through this Center for the Study of World Languages and Cultures, I believe we can give our businesses, entrepreneurs, professionals, and citizens the language skills and cultural understanding to communicate throughout the world and within our own increasingly diverse communities. That, in turn, will enable us to lead the nation in creating new jobs and economic development opportunities.

Recently completed needs assessments, statewide in scope, show overwhelming support for the concept. Other studies involving international businesses and language institutes are also supportive of this concept. During this past year, members of my staff, under the direction of Dr. Tom Paquin,[1] have been conducting a comprehensive study of the issues related to this center. His work includes information generated by other groups and individuals who were involved with the project in its early stages. The final report will be completed by Thanksgiving. This will be our blueprint for the project, including location and projected operational costs. I will include those results in my final budget request to the General Assembly in December.

In your handout, you will see the network of existing programs and how they will link with the center to give us comprehensive coverage of the world language and culture issue. The concept for this center is the progeny of a number of creative minds. President Spangler offered early input and support. We also received a great deal of encouragement from the Mary Reynolds Babcock Foundation and the Z. Smith Reynolds Foundation.

I am here today to propose to you that this Center for the Study of World Languages and Cultures be located administratively under the UNC-System General Administration. Due to the university's strong tradition in international studies and the personal encouragement of President Spangler, this seemed like the logical place for the center to be located—subject to your eventual approval and acceptance.

One way to look at the world languages and cultures center is to view it as a component of our overall strategy for economic and human development in the global marketplace, similar to the Global TransPark, the Research Triangle Park, our university and community college systems, and other essential institutions. The North Carolina Center for World Languages and Cultures is the piece of the puzzle that ties all of our many forays into this field together and provides the missing instructional link that we need to build a brighter future for our state.

One final bit of information for any who may doubt our need to seize the day: I invite them to look at the plan for the Japan municipal academy for intercultural training. It is a plan so grandiose, it will take your breath away. Japan is seizing the opportunity to become preeminent in international trade. Their academy's mission? "To enable Japan's cities, towns and villages to participate more fully in the international community both at home and abroad." Japan's academy is scheduled to open about two months from now, during January 1993. "At full capacity, (it) will have a full enrollment of some 2,000 trainees and conduct approximately eighteen courses a year."

Ladies and gentlemen, we are obviously way behind the curve. As it has so often in recent years, Japan is giving us a wake-up call about the urgent need to make the Center for the Study of World Languages and Cultures an integral part of North Carolina's economic development strategy. I hope you will agree to make this center part of your continuing activities under the guidance of the UNC-General Administration. Thank you for your time and attention.

---

[1]Thomas F. Paquin, native of North Adams, Mass.; bachelor's degree, Florida State University, 1965; master's degree, Salem State College, 1968; doctorate in education, University of Massachusetts, 1973. High school English teacher, Topsfield, Mass., 1965–1967; principal, Immokalee High School, Collier County, Fla., 1968–1971; director, staff development and training, Charlotte-Mecklenburg Schools, 1973–1978; associate superintendent, Brunswick County Schools, 1979–1983; appointed superintendent, St. Pauls City Schools, Robeson County, 1983; hopeful for nomination as Republican candidate for state education superintendent, 1988. *News and Observer*, April 17, May 4, 1988.

CATCH the FIFTH WAVE!

Global TransPark supporters in Kinston and Lenoir County recognized Governor Martin's tireless advocacy of the project—and their good fortune—by producing a T-shirt featuring this design. A herald of the "fifth wave" of economic development, the proposed GTP combined global manufacturing and distribution with air cargo transport. Martin revealed the selection of Kinston Regional Jetport as the GTP site in May 1992. Photograph by John Rottet, Raleigh *News and Observer*.

Governor James G. Martin and First Lady Dorothy M. Martin, Executive Mansion, Raleigh.

HEALTHY CAROLINIANS 2000

Research Triangle Park, November 18, 1992

[Martin addressed this speech to the Governor's Task Force on Health Objectives for the Year 2000. He established the group on August 6, 1991, with the signing of Executive Order Number 148. *N.C. Session Laws, Extra Session, 1991, Regular Session, 1992,* III, 1263–1266.]

Thank you, Dr. Anlyan. I want to thank you and all of the task force members for the hard work you have put into this report in such a short time.[1] I also want to thank the Kate B. Reynolds Health Care Trust for its generous support of this project. It was just a little over a year ago that my chief of staff, Nancy Temple, met with many of you and expressed my support of your efforts to take the first giant step toward making a change in the way North Carolinians approach better health. Today, just twelve and a half months later, it's somewhat amazing to realize that the report I hold in my hand is the vision—the inspiration, if you will—of an effort that has the potential to fundamentally change the way our citizens look at themselves in terms of their health and their lives.

When the task force was being created, I envisioned a panel of highly qualified health providers and concerned citizens who could speak to the health needs of our average citizens. I am pleased to see that the membership of this task force achieved that objective, and I want you to know that you certainly have every right to be proud of what you have accomplished. With this report, this very talented pool of government officials, health-care providers, educators, and civic leaders has defined eleven health objectives that, if realized, could increase our citizens' span of healthy life, reduce health disparities among the disadvantaged, and make preventive health services a matter of course by the year 2000. The results of your work will ultimately be measured in terms of the number of lives that can be saved from unnecessary deaths and illnesses, and the improvement in the quality of life of those saved.

Because this effort will be measured in terms of human life and suffering, I believe that accomplishing the health objectives will be as fundamentally important to public health as "roads to markets" was to farming. And teaching our citizens to focus on those things that will allow them to live full, healthy lives is as fundamentally necessary to our state's future as Governor Aycock's school reforms were at the turn of the century.[2] But the idea of establishing new frontiers in health is nothing new to North Carolina. We already have a proud and long public health history.

As you know, North Carolina was one of the first states to have organized local health efforts, and the gains we have made in the past decade—although greatly underrated by the media during the past eight years or so—have been tremendous. For example, in the area of human services, we now have more than 500 programs reaching people in all 100 counties. Funding for aging services is now six times more than it was just seven years ago. We now have thirty-four more senior centers than we did in 1985. Respite care, which provides temporary relief to family caregivers of frail older adults, is now available in eighty-six counties. We now have close to half again as many nursing home beds as we did in 1984; home health care has almost doubled since 1985.

Services for the visually impaired, the disabled, and the deaf and hard of hearing have been initiated or substantially increased during the past few years. We also have made great gains addressing the needs of our state's youth by establishing child protective services, by increasing funding for children with special needs, by expanding and improving daycare services, and by enforcing child support. And, by virtue of the skillful and enlightened leadership of our very intelligent First Lady, we are now helping some 25,000 adults in North Carolina improve their parenting skills through the Parent to Parent program, which trains parents to deal more effectively with drug abuse by their children.

That's just in the area of human services. If you will allow me just another minute on my soapbox, I would like to say that the gains we have made in the more traditional areas of health care have been just as significant. Since 1985 we have seen the creation of a scholarship fund for nursing students,[3] development of seven comprehensive rural health projects, and the creation of the Community Hospital Technical Assistance Program to help financially distressed rural hospitals. For the first time in North Carolina's history, we now have a unified delivery system for our mental health efforts, eliminating competition between programs for a share of mental health dollars.

But these efforts, as commendable and as worthy as they may be, represent the old approach to addressing health problems; and while there probably will always be a need for medicine and the treatment of ailments, what we are asking you to do today is to blaze a trail into an almost totally new territory of public health. What you are being asked to do today is go back to your communities and begin the difficult task of changing the way your citizens look at health, to bring about a change in their attitudes so that they can begin to understand that it is much more practical and reasonable to prevent bad health rather than to fix it. To understand how well this concept can work, take a look at our state's rate of infant mortality.

In 1985, we had an infant mortality rate of 12 deaths for each 1,000 live births. Thanks to preventive efforts like Baby Love, the First Step campaign, expansion of Medicaid coverage for pregnant teenagers who need prenatal care, and the creation of the Commission on Reduction of Infant Mortality, we have been able to reduce the infant mortality rate to 10.9 for 1991, the most recent full year for which we have statistics. And as one of the Healthy Carolinians' 11 objectives, we will be working to reduce that rate to 7.4 by the year 2000. That's below the current national average, yes, but the national average is projected to reach that level, so it's a realistic goal to stretch ourselves with.

As I said earlier, this report is the inspiration for bringing about a whole new era in public health and the way our citizens approach their lifelong well-being. As Thomas Edison once said, "Genius is 1 percent inspiration and 99 percent perspiration."[4] If the Healthy Carolinians initiative is going to be as significant as "roads to markets" and school reform, and if preventive health is going to be one of the landmarks of our era, it's going to require dedication and hard work on everyone's part.

Historically, North Carolina's approach to solving its public health problems has been unique. Most other states attempt to effect change by dictating programs to its citizens, micromanaging everything from the central capital. North Carolina has always worked from the perspective that local communities are better able to determine the solutions that are most appropriate for their specific problems and their special group of citizens. Today I am challenging you to continue this market-based approach to achieving good public health by developing local task forces to address the concerns and objectives outlined in this report.

Today I am asking you to make preventive health a priority, not only because of the tremendous savings it will create, but also because doing so will improve all of our citizens' quality of life and make good health and wellness one of our state's most valuable attributes. In short, I am asking you to convince your communities to do what only a few of our fitness-oriented citizens are already doing: to take charge of their health and keep themselves healthy. Thanks, again, to the task force for the great effort put forth, and thanks to you for being here today. You have a tremendous opportunity to participate in one of the most significant health efforts this state has seen, and I wish you the best of luck.

---

[1]William George Anlyan (1925–), born in Alexandria, Egypt; resident of Durham; B.S., 1945, M.D., 1949, Yale University. Surgeon; professor of surgery, Duke Hospital, 1961–1989; associate dean, 1963, dean, 1964–1969, vice-president for health affairs, 1983–1988, chancellor for health affairs, 1983–1988, executive vice-president, 1987–1988, Duke School

of Medicine; chancellor, 1988–1990, chancellor emeritus, since 1990, Duke University; appointed chairman, 1991, Governor's Task Force on Health Objectives for the Year 2000. Governor James G. Martin, letter of appointment to William G. Anlyan, October 17, 1991, Governors Papers, James G. Martin; *Who's Who in America, 1994*, I, 89.

Healthy Carolinians 2000: The Report of the Governor's Task Force on Health Objectives for the Year 2000 ([Carrboro, N.C.: The Task Force], November, 1992).

[2]Charles Brantley Aycock (1859–1912), governor of North Carolina, 1901–1905; Democrat. Previously identified in Poff, *Addresses of Martin*, I, 7n.

[3]Nursing scholarships were established under "An Act to Provide for the Implementation of Programs to Address the Nursing Shortage in the State," c. 560, ratified July 4, 1989, and "An Act to Establish the North Carolina Nursing Scholars Program and the North Carolina Nursing Scholars Commission," c. 594, ratified July 7, 1989, *N.C. Session Laws, 1989*. See also "An Act to Allocate Funds for Nursing Education and Training Programs," *N.C. Session Laws, 1989*, II, c. 794, ratified August 12, 1989.

[4]Thomas Alva Edison, *Life* [1932], ch. 24, as quoted in Bartlett, *Familiar Quotations*, 811.

SIXTH ANNUAL EMPLOYER AWARDS LUNCHEON

RALEIGH, DECEMBER 7, 1992

I'm delighted to be with you this afternoon and to be a part of this special occasion. Today's award presentation is very simple in its concept: employers being recognized by their peers for their vision and their commitment to North Carolina.

Employers like you, who continue to thrive during a time when many businesses have closed and thousands of individuals have become unemployed, should be commended for helping to keep your employees viable contributors to North Carolina's economy, an economy that's alive and healthy. For it is our state that has the proud distinction of having an unemployment rate that's consistently stayed below the national rate since January 1985, and it is North Carolina whose unemployment rate remains the lowest among the eleven largest states the Bureau of Labor Statistics surveys each month—and lowest in the Southeast all but one of the last eight years. You are a hero to North Carolinians. You are an employer; therefore, a job creator.

One of the challenges you face is a labor force that is changing rapidly. The days of learning one skill and finding a job that lasts until retirement are in the past. Employees are being asked to be lifelong learners, to constantly acquire new skills.

In January I appointed a Commission on Workforce Preparedness chaired by Ron Davis, a business leader from Greensboro. This group of leaders from both the public and private sector has been examining our changing labor force. The commission looked at employee education, training, and retraining efforts already under way across the state and developed ways the public and private sectors can work together to improve workforce preparedness programs. I'm proud to report the commission has just published a two-year strategic plan resulting from this analysis. It outlines some of the challenges facing North Carolina's workers, as they head into the twenty-first century, as well as suggestions for meeting those challenges.[1]

Much of the staff work for this committee was done by an Interagency Coordinating Committee, chaired by Manfred Emmrich, director of the Employment Service of the Employment Security Commission.[2] Bob Scruggs, chairman of the North Carolina Job Service Employer Committee, was also a member. Mr. Emmrich, Mr. Scruggs, and the men and women on this committee worked tirelessly to compile this comprehensive report for the commission. I would like to take just a few minutes to share some of their findings with you. The report focuses on three main areas: the workplace, the workforce, and our state's workforce preparedness system.

Whether we like it or not, North Carolina is competing in a global economy, where outside market forces have a greater impact in determining the local economy; and consumers today are demanding a wider variety of quality goods at affordable prices. This means American industries must increasingly produce goods and services through flexible networks that require fewer but more highly skilled production workers, backed up by more service workers in both the manufacturing and service industries, many of whom will also require higher skills. In this flexible organization, virtually all jobs would involve more demanding organizational and technological skills as well as people skills. This "high-performance organization" puts emphasis on quality, timely delivery, and the ability to produce customized products—demands not easily met by companies staffed and organized along traditional mass-production lines. These organizations are the keystones to economic success in our changing economy, and promoting them in North Carolina is a critical part of the commission's goal of introducing and developing such organizations, especially among small- and medium-sized employers.

If North Carolina employers are to remain competitive, they will have to depend on the existing workforce. As new technologies are introduced in the workplace, this will require an increased number of professionally and technically trained people. Equally important, front-line production workers will have to increase their skills in basic reading and math, communication with others, and in problem solving. Therefore, the commission's goal for the workforce is to increase education and training opportunities for current front-line workers and new entrants in the workforce.

Our strongest asset for reaching this goal is the North Carolina community college system, whose network of campuses across the state provides a full spectrum of education and training services needed by front-line workers. The community college system and ESC [Employment Security Commission], working together at a higher level of partnership than ever before, are also finding jobs for North Carolina's well-trained students. Currently, fifteen community colleges and three state universities now have ESC computer terminals on their campuses listing statewide jobs, both in the public and private sector, and there's an ESC employee on hand to further assist students with their job search. More community colleges are scheduled to have these terminals installed.

This partnership ESC has created with the community college system is indicative of the cooperative effort two government agencies can achieve while avoiding a duplication of services. They are working together to supply the workforce with highly skilled workers. Of course, these workers must be flexible, able to learn new skills, and adapt well to change, because they will not be in these jobs forever, which leads me to the third goal of the commission.

Our state's workforce preparedness system must meet these workers' training needs. North Carolina's workforce preparedness system is still in an early state of development, but over the next two years it must determine the best way to integrate state-level plans with local workforce and employer needs. One crucial factor in workforce planning is the difference in labor market and workforce characteristics between the urban and rural areas in a diverse state like North Carolina. Our state's many different local economies must be taken into account when shaping state policies and plans for the workforce.

There's no question that the way we work is changing, and the people making up the workforce are changing, too. In fact, dramatic changes in the number of women in the workforce, especially those with preschool and school-age children, have called on private sector employers to re-evaluate their personnel policies in light of today's new, more diverse labor force. Some concerned companies have become aware of the conflicting demands of work and family life and have designed innovative programs that are good for families and employers.

And what has government done to be a good example and to help its own employees manage the dual demands of work and family? If, in fact, government wants to encourage the adoption of family-supportive personnel policies in the private sector, should it not begin at home? Well, it has. According to a survey conducted by N.C. Equity, a private, nonprofit public-policy organization dedicated to the advancement and well-being of North Carolina women and their families, public universities and state government agencies offer more family-supportive programs and a wider variety of programs than all other sectors. Recently, the Employment Security Commission was one of nine state government agencies recognized by N.C. Equity for being a "family-friendly workplace." Congratulations, Ann.[3] Its personal and family leave policies, flexible work schedules, and family health insurance coverage were among the programs and policies lauded by the organization.

ESC also received recognition from the city of Raleigh a few weeks ago for the success of its satellite office in Chavis Heights, an inner-city neighborhood plagued by drug-related crimes. Since the Chavis Heights office opened three [blank] ago, offering job placement services to the community, it has placed more than 970 individuals in jobs. In fact, in its recent biennial summary, ESC reported to me that, statewide, it placed nearly 300,000 individuals in jobs over the past two years. Now think about that a moment: That's more than the number of people living in Forsyth County—and quite a tribute to the fine leadership of ESC's chairman, Ann Duncan.

That kind of placement activity is what Job Service is all about. The Job Service professionals that serve North Carolinians have had their collective hands full over the past couple of years. They are the ones who literally face our state's unemployed and underemployed each day. They represent hope and a better way of life for these people and their families, and they are the ones who come to you, our employers. You are the lifeblood of Job Service. Without your job orders, Job Service professionals could not do their work. That's why, earlier this year, I proclaimed the week of May 17 as "Job Service Week" in appreciation for the leadership, dedication, and compassion our Job Service professionals continually give to their fellow North Carolinians.[4]

Back in 1984, when I was first running for governor, I was actually criticized for being "pro-business." My response was not to dodge and act hostile to prove the critics wrong. I set out to prove them correct! I was for business: large, small, in-between; high-tech, low-tech. I said, "Yes, I'm for business, because that's where jobs come from." And that's why I want to commend the Employment Security Commission of North Carolina for establishing this awards program. I think it speaks well of the commission itself, and the state of North Carolina, when a tax-collecting agency pauses to recognize the taxpayer and to say, thanks for the jobs.

Someone once gave me a little book entitled *The World's Greatest Management Principle*. You know what it is? Applause: When you see a pattern of behavior you like and want to see more of it, encourage it, applaud it, and honor it. Let people know it is worthwhile and appreciated. We salute your success, your contributions to the economic well-being of North Carolinians, and for cooperating with the state's Job Service.

---

[1]Martin signed Executive Order Number 159, establishing a new North Carolina Governor's Commission on Workforce Preparedness, on January 6, 1992. The directive ended the identically named commission set up under Executive Order Number 107. *N.C. Session Laws, Extra Session, 1991, Regular Session, 1992,* 1293–1300; for related press release, see "Governor Creates Permanent Commission on Workforce Preparedness," Raleigh, February 3, 1992, Governors Papers, James G. Martin. The report to which he referred was *The 1993–1995 Strategic Plan for Workforce Preparedness,* by the Governor's Commission on Workforce Preparedness ([Raleigh: The Commission], December 1992). As Martin noted, the chairman of the permanent commission was Ronald H. Davis. Davis (1932–), vice-president for administration, Carolina Steel Corp., Greensboro, 1972–1994; Chapter 11 bankruptcy trustee from 1992, U-Filler-Up, Inc., Greensboro. Previously identified in Poff, *Addresses of Martin,* I, 481n; Ronald H. Davis, letter to Jan-Michael Poff, October 14, 1994.

[2]Manfred Emmrich, Employment Service Division director, Employment Security Commission, since 1985. Previously identified in Poff, *Addresses of Martin,* I, 654n.

[3]Ann Q. Duncan, state Employment Security Commission chief.

[4]See "Job Service Week, 1992, by the Governor of the State of North Carolina: A Proclamation," signed April 8, 1992, Governors Papers, James G. Martin.

INAUGURAL CEREMONIES: FAREWELL ADDRESS AND INTRODUCTION OF JAMES BAXTER HUNT, JR.

Raleigh, January 9, 1993

A year and a half ago, our three-year-old granddaughter, Kathren, went with her parents to a miniature golf course. She saw what she mistook for a podium: a post with a board slanted on top of it, with a pencil hanging from a string—a scoring station. Eagerly grabbing both sides of her lectern, she shouted out, "Gentlemans and Ladies, I make speech!" Then, as stunned golfers listened for her wisdom, she ma[de] this speech. She said, "God is great. Thank you. Bye-bye!"

That was it: a sermon which has been duly acclaimed by no less than Dr. Billy Graham himself. And, it is my closing message to you.

Dottie and I want you to know how grateful we are to the people of North Carolina for what has been our tremendous experience here, with the challenge, the thrill, and the satisfaction of these last eight years.

Change and continuity are all about us, continuity and change.

Governor Hunt, just as you had accomplished so many of your goals in 1984, and had begun a few for us to carry forward and complete, so, too, have we also accomplished many of our goals:

—Increased spending for schools $1.5 billion a year as our number-one priority;

—Increased highway construction about one third that much, for a major, historic, fifteen-year commitment to a network of four-lane expressways to serve the economic development needs of rural as well as urban citizens;

—Won over 100 new factories for each of five consecutive years (1992 may make it six in a row);

—Consolidated environmental enforcement and toughened it dramatically;

—And almost doubled prison capacity.

We've also left some important unfinished business which we hope will deserve your best efforts:

—The veto;

—The Global TransPark at Kinston;

—A new state responsibility for railroads;

—Deregulation and decentralization of school management;

—Uplift Day Care: developmental preschool for at-risk four-year-olds;

—And the Center for World Languages and Cultures.

It is now my honor to turn this over to you and to wish you well as you return to lead our state and its government. I am certain that you and your new team of leaders, and your enthusiastic supporters from across North Carolina, will work hard to achieve these and even greater improvements for our people.

Just as you so kindly expressed confidence in the future eight years ago, as you left this office to my care, in that same spirit I express to you the same confidence today as you return to the responsibilities of this office and we depart.

May the grace of God and the strength of the people be with you.

And now, ladies and gentlemen, as the oath of office is administered by Chief Justice James G. Exum, Jr.—assisted by our new First Lady, Carolyn Hunt—I will ask you to rise and thereafter remain standing for the official military honors which will follow.[1]

Ladies and gentlemen, the twice and future governor of North Carolina, the Honorable James Baxter Hunt, Jr.

---

[1]James Gooden Exum, Jr. (1935–), chief justice, state Supreme Court, 1986–1994. Previously identified in Poff, *Addresses of Martin*, I, 543n–544n; see also *News and Observer*, December 13, 1994.

Carolyn Leonard Hunt (1937–), native of Mingo, Iowa; attended Iowa State University; A.B., University of North Carolina at Chapel Hill, 1964; married James Baxter Hunt, Jr., 1958. Schoolteacher in Katmandu, Nepal, 1964–1966; First Lady of North Carolina, 1977–1985, and since 1993; organizer, N.C. Friendship Force program. Poff and Crow, *Addresses of Hunt*, II, 227n–228n.

OMITTED SPEECHES AND STATEMENTS, 1989–1993

[Speeches and official papers not reprinted in this volume are catalogued, by title, below. Press releases largely consisting of the governor's direct quotations also have been included. Documents either mentioned or excerpted in annotations accompanying Martin's published remarks are denoted by an asterisk. Speaking engagements, indicated on the governor's weekly agenda but for which no prepared text was provided, have been incorporated into the following list and are marked by a dagger. Existing copies of Governor Martin's addresses and other public papers are housed at the Division of Archives and History, North Carolina Department of Cultural Resources, Raleigh.]

1989

January 3, Press Release, Statement by Governor James G. Martin Concerning His Meeting with Officials of Champion International Corporation [Canton mill], Raleigh

January 7, Governor's Prayer Breakfast, Raleigh

January 10, North Carolina Drug Cabinet News Conference, Raleigh*

January 10, Welcoming Remarks, Introduction of U.S. Senator Pete Domenici, New Mexico Economic Development Delegation, Research Triangle Park

January 10, New Mexico Economic Development Delegation, Research Triangle Park

January 10, Draft Testimony, U.S. Department of Defense-U.S. Department of Transportation Hearing on Military Airspace [clear text], Fayetteville

January 11, Press Release, Statement by Governor James G. Martin Concerning the Election of Josephus L. Mavretic as Speaker of the North Carolina House, Raleigh

January 20, Press Release, Governor Martin's Reaction to the Inauguration of President George Bush, Raleigh

January 23, American Legislative Exchange Council, Raleigh [not delivered]

January 25, Press Conference with Champion International, Inc., Executives, Asheville†

January 25, Press Release, Governor's Statement Regarding Announcement of Champion International's Closing [Canton mill], Raleigh

January 26, Press Conference, Raleigh†

January 30, Park Communications Annual Awards, Raleigh

January 30, Park Communications Annual Awards [revised], Raleigh

February 2, Press Conference, Raleigh†

February 3, Kickoff, Lenoir-Rhyne College Centennial Campaign, Hickory

February 8, Announcement of Environmental Protection Agency Grant to North Carolina State University and University of North Carolina at Chapel Hill, Raleigh

February 8, Emerging Issues Forum, Raleigh*

February 8, Press Release, Governor Martin Invites Public School Leaders to "Summit Meeting" Monday to Discuss Education Issues [letter to Howard Haworth, chairman, State Board of Education, attached], Raleigh

February 9, Press Conference, Release of Report by Governor's Task Force on Aquaculture, Raleigh

February 9, Press Reception, Executive Mansion Centennial, Raleigh

February 10, Governor's Council on Alcohol and Drug Abuse among Children and Youth, Creation of Governor's Institute on Alcohol and Substance Abuse, Chapel Hill

February 13, American Airlines Southeastern Reservation Center, Cary

February 13, Press Conference, Governor's Highway Safety Program, Raleigh

February 14, North Carolina Trucking Association, Raleigh

February 15, Press Conference, Raleigh†

February 20, Bravery and Heroism Awards Ceremony, Raleigh

February 21, Press Conference on Highway Construction Proposal, Raleigh

February 23, Press Conference, Raleigh†

February 23, North Carolina Association of County Commissioners [notes], Raleigh*

February 26, North Carolina Community College "Night of the Arts," Washington, D.C.

March 1, Board of Directors, State Employees Association of North Carolina [notes], Raleigh

March 2, Human Relations Awards, Raleigh

March 3, Press Release, Governor Commutes Sentence of Sharon Anderson Cipolla [statement on commutation attached], Raleigh

March 5, Change of Command Ceremony, Announcement of Appointment of Nathaniel H. Robb, Jr., as North Carolina National Guard Adjutant General, Raleigh

March 6, Literacy Now, Raleigh

March 7, State Employees Association of North Carolina, Raleigh

March 7, Terry Sanford Distinguished Lecture Series, Duke University, Durham*

March 8, "Better Pay for Better Teachers," State Board of Education,
Raleigh*

March 8, Press Briefing on Education Plan, Raleigh†

March 8, Japanese Ambassador Nobuo Matsunaga [briefing notes],
Durham

March 9, Press Conference, Raleigh†

March 14, Press Availability, Asheboro†

March 14, Asheboro-Randolph Chamber of Commerce, Asheboro*

March 14, Randolph Correctional Center Dormitory Dedication,
Asheboro

March 14, North Carolina Zoological Park Council, Asheboro

March 15, Membership Kickoff for Area Chambers of Commerce,
Greensboro

March 15, Press Release, Governor Martin's Reaction to Republican
Legislators' Proposal [state budget], Raleigh

March 16, Press Conference, Raleigh†

March 16, Sandoz-Mallard Creek Research and Development Center
Opening, Charlotte

March 20, Adopt-A-Highway Program, Raleigh

March 20, Press Release, Statement by Governor Jim Martin on Bonner
Bridge, Raleigh*

March 22, Introduction of Wayne Calloway, North Carolina Citizens
for Business and Industry, Raleigh

March 22, Introduction of Wayne Calloway, North Carolina Citizens
for Business and Industry [revised], Raleigh

March 22, North Carolina Citizens for Business and Industry, Raleigh
[not delivered]

March 23, North Carolina Student Legislature, Raleigh [not delivered]

March 23, Presentation of North Carolina Truck Driver of the Year
Award to Charles K. Lavery, Raleigh

March 28, Reception for North Carolina Central University Men's
Basketball Team, NCAA Division II National Champions, Raleigh

March 29, Distinguished Women of North Carolina Awards, Raleigh

March 30, Acceptance of Keep America Working Award on Behalf of
North Carolina Community College System, Washington, D.C.

March 30, Charlotte-Mecklenburg Urban League Equal Opportunity
Awards, Charlotte [not delivered]

March 31, Press Conference, Raleigh†

April 3, Ribbon-Cutting, American Airlines Inaugural Flight to
Bermuda, Raleigh-Durham International Airport, Wake County

April 3, Press Release, Governor Praises Charlotte Drug Symposium,
Applauds Effort to Attack North Carolina's Drug Problems,
Raleigh

April 6, United Way of Forsyth County Leadership Circle, Presentation of Alexis de Tocqueville Society Volunteer of the Year Award to Dalton D. Ruffin, Winston-Salem

April 6, Governor's Business Council on the Arts and Humanities, Raleigh

April 7, Groundbreaking, Governor's Island Development, Lake Norman, Lincoln County

April 7, Mecklenburg County Boy Scout Council Roast of Governor Martin, Charlotte [not delivered]

April 10, Unveiling of State Capitol Portrait, Raleigh

April 11, Groundbreaking, Brevard Connector [NC 191 to I-26; draft], Mills River

April 11, Executive Mansion Benefit, Asheville

April 11, Executive Mansion Benefit [revised], Asheville

April 12, General Assembly Banquet, 200th Anniversary of North Carolina's Ratification of the United States Constitution, Fayetteville

April 13, Press Conference, Raleigh†

April 13, Organon Teknika Dedication, Durham

April 13, Groundbreaking, Environmental Management Division Laboratory, Raleigh

April 13, Society for Black Academic Surgeons, Durham

April 17, Concerned Charlotteans, Charlotte [canceled]

April 19, Presentation of North Carolina Public Service Award to Jack Laughery, Raleigh

April 19, Press Release, Governor Martin's Reaction to EPA's Announcement of Hearings on Withdrawal of Resource Conservation and Recovery Act Authority from North Carolina, Raleigh*

April 20, Oxford University Press Relocation Announcement, Raleigh

April 20, Presentation of Governor's Awards of Excellence for Outstanding Achievement in Waste Management, Raleigh

April 24, North Carolina Retail Merchants' Association, Raleigh

April 24, Press Release, Governor Martin Supports Diamont Plan to Fund Additional Child Protective Services Staff [letter to Representative David H. Diamont attached], Raleigh

April 26, Society of the Cincinnati, Raleigh

April 27, Press Conference, Raleigh†

April 27, Pinehurst Men's Member-Guest Golf Tournament, Pinehurst

April 28, Governor's Advocacy Council for Persons with Disabilities [clear text], Raleigh

April 28, Dedication, Hoots Memorial Hospital, Yadkinville
April 28, Dedication, Yadkin County Human Resources Center,
    Yadkinville
May 1, Capital for a Day, Laurinburg*
May 1, Scotia Village Dedication, Laurinburg
May 3, WestPoint Pepperell Expansion Announcement, Raleigh
May 3, Business-Industry Appreciation Dinner, Elizabeth City*
May 6, "Ambition with Integrity," North Carolina State University
    Commencement Address, Raleigh
May 8, Ribbon-Cutting, Takeda Chemical Products USA, Inc.,
    Wilmington
May 8, Luncheon Remarks, Takeda Chemical Products USA, Inc.,
    Wilmington
May 11, Presidential Disaster Declaration Recognizing Tornado
    Damage [Catawba, Cleveland, and Lincoln counties], Raleigh
May 11, Groundbreaking, Quantum Chemical Corp., Salisbury
May 11, Banquet, Quantum Chemical Corp., Salisbury
May 12, Teaches Class at Athens Drive High School, Raleigh†
May 14, Bennett College Commencement, Greensboro
May 14, Introduction of U.S. Attorney General Richard L. Thornburgh,
    University of North Carolina School of Law, Chapel Hill
May 16, North Carolina Alliance for Public Education, Raleigh*
May 17, East Davidson High School Assembly, Thomasville†
May 18, Press Conference, 1988 Investment Statistics, Raleigh
May 20, Commencement Address, Elon College
May 22, North Carolina Government Contractors Association, Raleigh
May 24, Press Release, Governor Martin's Comment on Proposed
    Substitute to Highway Trust Fund Bill by House Committee [H.B.
    399], Raleigh
May 25, Press Conference, Announcement on Alliance for Acid Rain
    Control, Raleigh [canceled]
May 26, Flue-Cured Tobacco Cooperative Stabilization Corp., Raleigh
    [not delivered]
May 26, Jerry J. Popkin Bridge Dedication, Jacksonville
May 26, Veterans Cemetery Deed Transfer, Camp LeJeune,
    Jacksonville
May 31, Press Release, Governor Martin's Response to Endorsement
    of Education Proposal by Lieutenant Governor Gardner, Raleigh*
June 1, Press Conference, Raleigh†
June 1, *Inc.* 500 Reception, Raleigh
June 2, *Inc.* 500 Breakfast, Raleigh [not delivered]
June 5, Western North Carolina Environmental Council, Raleigh

June 7, Raleigh-Durham Airport Authority Fiftieth Anniversary, Raleigh

June 8, Press Conference, Raleigh†

June 9, Commencement, Bath High School, Bath

June 10, Rockingham County Senior High School Commencement, Wentworth

June 12, Town Meeting, Snow Hill†

June 14, North Carolina Business Committee for Education, Raleigh†

June 14, Community College Roast of Governor Martin, Raleigh†

June 15, Press Conference, Raleigh†

June 15, Press Release, Governor Declines to Attend NCAE Rally, Pledges to Continue Working for Career Ladder Program, Raleigh

June 16, American Legion Convention, Raleigh

June 16, Boys' State [notes], Winston-Salem

June 16, Girls' State [notes], Greensboro

June 16, Mercury 7 Foundation, Research Triangle Park

June 20, Statement on Legislative Developments, Raleigh†

June 21, Defense-Related Industries Breakfast, Washington, D.C.

June 22, Press Conference, Raleigh†

June 23, State Games Lunch for Olympians, Raleigh

June 23, State Games Lunch for Olympians [torch ceremony; revised], Raleigh

June 23, Press Release, Governor Martin Issues Reply to Statement by Senator Barnes [Senator Rauch and highway funding], Raleigh

June 26, Albemarle Sound Bridge Ceremony [NC 32], Edenton

June 27, Reichhold Chemicals, Inc., Announcement, Research Triangle Park

June 27, Reichhold Chemicals, Inc., Announcement [revised], Research Triangle Park

June 29, Press Conference, Raleigh†

July 6, Press Conference, Raleigh†

July 7, Press Release, Governor Martin's Reaction to Announcement that South Carolina Waste Facility Will Be Reopened to North Carolina Hazardous Waste Producers, Raleigh*

July 13, Press Conference, Raleigh†

July 20, Press Conference, Raleigh†

July 21, Sears Telemarketing Center Announcement, High Point

July 21, Press Release, Governor Martin's Reaction to Proposal by Representative Cooper to Convene a Study Commission on Veto [and] Governance Issues, Raleigh

July 22, National Railroad Historical Society, Asheville

July 25, Ribbon-Cutting, Bedford Fair Industries, Wilmington

July 27, Press Conference, Raleigh†
July 27, Massey-Ferguson Tractor Unveiling, Kinston
July 28, Graduation, Love of Learning Program, Davidson College,
    Davidson
August 2, Press Release, Governor Praises Crew, Emergency Workers
    during Emergency Landing in Greensboro [Piedmont Airlines
    Flight 1489], Raleigh
August 3, Press Conference, Raleigh†
August 10, Press Release, Governor Martin's Reaction to R.J. Reynolds
    Tobacco Co. Layoffs, Raleigh
August 11, Bill Cobey Swearing-In [Secretary, Department of
    Environment, Health, and Natural Resources], Raleigh
August 11, Groundbreaking, Cogentrix of Rocky Mount, Battleboro
August 14, Burlington City Schools [notes], Burlington
August 14, Dedication, Ciba-Geigy Research Building, Greensboro
August 16, Ribbon-Cutting, Franklin Park Industrial Center,
    Youngsville
August 17, Dedication, Great Smoky Mountains Railway, Dillsboro
August 17, Old Soldiers Reunion, Newton
August 18, Dedication, Reynolds Recycling Processing Center, Raleigh
August 18, Dedication, Reynolds Recycling Processing Center,
    [revised], Raleigh
August 18, Phillips 66-U.S. Diving Outdoor Championship [notes],
    Raleigh
August 18, Press Release, Governor Announces State Recycling
    Efforts, Raleigh
August 21, Nash-Edgecombe Mental Health Center Announcement,
    Rocky Mount
August 21, Press Release, Governor Martin's Statement Concerning
    the Resignation of NCSU Chancellor Poulton, Raleigh
August 22, Dedication, North Carolina Statehood Commemorative
    Stamp, Fayetteville
August 23, Ethan Allen Factory Dedication, Spruce Pine
August 24, American Express Travel-Related Services Facility
    Expansion, Greensboro
August 24, American Express Travel-Related Services Facility
    Expansion [revised], Greensboro
August 24, Testimony, Environmental Protection Agency Public
    Hearing on Champion Paper's Canton Facility, Asheville
August 25, Press Release, Governor Martin's Reaction to Chancellor
    Spangler's Report to UNC Board of Governors [N.C. State
    University men's basketball program], Raleigh

August 28, Dedication, Lawrence Joel Veterans Memorial Coliseum, Winston-Salem

August 30, Harriet and Henderson Yarns Grand Reopening, Clarkton*

August 30, Hollywood Trade Mission Announcement, Raleigh [delivered August 31]

September 5, Status Report to Legislative Leadership on Hazardous Waste, Raleigh†

September 6, Volunteer Recognition Ceremony, Eastern Region, Kinston

September 11, Microelectronics Center of North Carolina Semiconductor Workshop, Research Triangle Park

September 11, North Carolina Wesleyan College Baseball Team Reception, NCAA Division III National Champions, Raleigh

September 12, Dedication, Clifford and Wills Telemarketing Center, Asheville

September 12, Volunteer Recognition Ceremony, Western Region, Morganton

September 13, Dedication, Konica Manufacturing USA, Greensboro

September 14, Presentation, North Carolina Farm Family of the Year Award, Elbert Ray Pitt Farm, Macclesfield

September 15, Press Release, Governor Decides Not To Call Extra Session of General Assembly on Thursday, September 21 [hazardous waste agreement], Raleigh

September 18, Press Conference on North Carolina-West German Agreement, Raleigh†

September 21, News Conference, Recognition of State Employees, Raleigh

September 21, Governor's Award for Excellence, State Employees Appreciation Day, Raleigh

September 21, Historically Black Colleges and Universities Reception [notes], Raleigh

September 23, Ceremony Honoring North Carolina Central University Men's Basketball Team, 1989 NCAA Division II National Champions, Durham

September 25, Press Release, Governor Praises EPA Decision on Champion Permit, Urges Haywood County Residents to Look Toward Future, Raleigh

September 25, Press Release, President Bush Issues Disaster Declarations for Mecklenburg, Lincoln, and Gaston Counties [Hurricane Hugo], Washington, D.C.*

September 29, Groundbreaking, GVK America, Inc., Biscoe

September 29, Swearing-in of William D. Teem as Highway Patrol Commander, Raleigh

October 6, Welcoming Ceremony, Southeast United States-Japan
Association, Tokyo, Japan*
October 12, Opening Ceremonies, Southeast United States-Korea
Association, Seoul, South Korea
October 12, Opening Ceremonies, Southeast United States-Korea
Association [revised], Seoul, South Korea
October 12, Investment Session, Southeast United States-Korea
Association, Seoul, South Korea
October 12, Investment Session, Southeast United States-Korea
Association [revised], Seoul, South Korea
October 24, "Challenge for the '90's" Conference, Raleigh*
October 24, Volunteer Recognition Ceremony, [Central] Region,
Raleigh
October 25, Grand Opening, Biltmore Square Mall, Asheville
October 25, American Defense Institute Fund Raiser, Raleigh
October 26, News Conference on Hazardous Waste, Raleigh*
October 26, Business Committee for Education Awards [typescript],
Raleigh
October 26, Press Release, Governor Asks Hazardous Waste
Management Commission to Explore Options for State Treatment
Plan [letter to Alvis G. Turner, chairman, Hazardous Waste
Management Commission, attached], Raleigh*
October 27, Charlotte Westinghouse Twentieth Anniversary, Charlotte
October 27, White Consolidated Industries, Kinston
October 27, North Carolina Awards Presentation, Raleigh
October 30, Installation of Joseph Oxendine as Chancellor, Pembroke
State University, Pembroke [delivered October 27]
November 1, Next Century Schools Program Press Conference,
Raleigh
November 15, Munich-Stuttgart Trade and Investment Round Tables,
Federal Republic of Germany
November 21, Press Conference, Raleigh†
November 22, Press Release, Governor Martin's Reaction to Inclusion
of North Carolina in Regional Hazardous Waste Treatment
Agreement, Raleigh*
November 28, Press Release, Governor Martin's Reaction to the Parole
Commission Decision Concerning John E. McCombs, Raleigh
December 1, Press Release, Governor Martin Announces Secretary
Harrington's Resignation, Raleigh
December 6, Announcement, *Inc.* Council of Growing Companies,
Raleigh*

December 7, Driving-While-Impaired Press Conference, Raleigh
December 7, Christmas Tree Lighting, Raleigh
December 7, Press Release, Governor Martin's Reaction to House, Senate Passage of Multistate Hazardous Waste Agreement, Raleigh
December 8, Infirmary Dedication, North Carolina Correctional Institute for Women, Raleigh
December 8, Housing Coordination and Policy Council, Raleigh*
December 11, Drunk and Drugged Driving Awareness Week, Raleigh
December 14, News Conference on Infant Mortality, Raleigh
December 20, Presidential Export Award Celebration, Northern Telecom, Research Triangle Park
December 20, Presidential Export Award Celebration, Thor-Lo Co., Statesville

1990

January 4, Statement at Press Conference, Raleigh†
January 8, Pinning Ceremony for Brigadier General Bobby Webb, North Carolina National Guard, Raleigh
January 11, Newspaper Column, Retrospective on Martin Administration Accomplishments during 1989, Raleigh
January 16, Concord-Cabarrus Chamber of Commerce, Harrisburg
January 17, Forestry Industry Meeting on Hugo Damage, Raleigh
January 18, North Carolina Film Industry Press Conference, Raleigh
January 18, North Carolina Press Association, Durham
January 19, "Export Now" Press Conference, Raleigh
January 22, Governor's Programs of Excellence in Education, Winston-Salem
January 23, Press Availability, Elizabeth City†
January 23, Committee of 100, Elizabeth City
January 23, Sign Unveiling [notes], Museum of the Albemarle, Elizabeth City
January 23, Grant Announcement [notes], Elizabeth City
January 23, Groundbreaking, Northside Elementary School, Elizabeth City [not delivered]
January 23, Superior Brands Expansion Dedication, Elizabeth City
January 24, Groundbreaking, North Carolina Department of Revenue, Raleigh
January 24, Press Conference, General Electric Aircraft Engines Announcement, Research Triangle Park [not delivered]
January 25, Burgaw Area Chamber of Commerce, Burgaw
January 26, Drug Summit, Raleigh

January 29, I-40 Ribbon-Cutting, Wallace

January 31, Press Release, Governor's Response to President Bush's State of the Union Address, Raleigh

February 2, Take Pride in America Awards, Raleigh*

February 2, Mayor's Award of Excellence Banquet, Research Triangle Park*

February 5, North Carolina Bus Association, Raleigh*

February 6, Hillcrest Elementary School "Leaders of Readers" Awards Ceremony [notes], Burlington

February 6, Honda Power Equipment Export Announcement, Swepsonville

February 7, Acceptance of Boy Scout Council Reports, Raleigh [not delivered]

February 7, Governor's Crime Commission, Raleigh*

February 8, Dedication, Natural Resources Research Center, North Carolina State University, Raleigh

February 8, Press Release, Governor Praises EMC [Environmental Management Commission] for Adopting Toxic Air Pollutant Controls, Raleigh

February 9, Press Release, Governor Martin Says Audit Review of Division of Executive Aircraft Confirms that State Planes Weren't Used for Political Purposes, Raleigh

February 12, Swearing-in of Allyson Duncan as Appeals Court Judge, Raleigh†

February 12, Town Meeting, Windsor†

February 16, Press Release, Governor Martin Issues Statement on Death of Judge [John] Larkins, Raleigh

February 22, Press Conference on Governor's Research Office, Raleigh†

February 23, Press Release, Governor Pleased by Exoneration of [Tommy] Pollard, Criticizes Length of SBI Probe, Raleigh*

February 23, Press Release, Governor's Response to Announcement from Attorney General [Governor's Research Office], Raleigh*

March 1, Governor's Advisory Board on Prisons and Punishment, Raleigh

March 1, North Carolina Truck Diver of the Year Award Presentation, Raleigh†

March 1, Human Relations Council Awards, Raleigh

March 5, Dedication, Texasgulf Purified Phosphoric Acid Plant, Aurora

March 6, Robeson County Chamber of Commerce [notes], Lumberton

March 6, Robeson County Chamber of Commerce [transcript], Lumberton

March 6, Press Release, Governor Praises General Assembly for Near-Unanimous Vote in Favor of Raising Prison Cap, Raleigh

March 7, Iams Co. Groundbreaking, Henderson

March 8, Introduction of First Lady Barbara Bush, University of North Carolina at Chapel Hill*

March 8, Response to Barbara Bush Speech, University of North Carolina at Chapel Hill*

March 13, Public Hearing on Governor's Prison Proposal, Charlotte [not delivered]

March 14, Principals' Executive Program Graduation, Research Triangle Park [not delivered]

March 15, Azalea Festival Announcement, Raleigh

March 16, Ribbon-Cutting, Pinehurst Hotel and Country Club Convention Center, Pinehurst††

March 19, Drug Plan Presentation, North Carolina Drug Cabinet, Raleigh*

March 20, Press Availability, Timber Damage by Hurricane Hugo, Alexander County†

March 20, Beta Sigma Gamma Distinguished Lecture, East Carolina University, Greenville*

March 20, Regional Planning Meeting, Correction Initiative, Wilson†

March 21, Workforce Preparedness Press Conference, Raleigh*

March 21, North Carolina Citizens for Business and Industry, Raleigh

March 22, Education Center Dedication, North Carolina Zoo, Asheboro

March 22, Welcoming Remarks, WalkAmerica Exec-Trek, Research Triangle Park†

March 27, Press Release, Statement by Governor Jim Martin Concerning Champion Announcement [Canton mill], Raleigh

April 2, Child Abuse Prevention Month [notes], Raleigh

April 4, Economic Development Seminar, Sylva*

April 4, Regional Planning Meeting, Correction Initiative, Asheville†

April 5, Presentation of Christa McAuliffe Award to Carolyn P. Hammond and Joyce J. Poplin, Raleigh

April 5, ProSail 1990 Press Conference [notes], New Bern

April 5, ProSail 1990 Dinner [notes], New Bern

April 10, North Carolina Victims Assistance Network, Wrightsville Beach*

April 10, Regional Planning Meeting, Correction Initiative, Wilmington†

April 11, First Meeting, Workforce Preparedness Commission, Raleigh

April 11, Press Release, Governor Urges Media to Help Census Effort [letter to news directors attached], Raleigh

April 12, Statement at Press Conference, Raleigh†
April 17, Press Availability, Wilkesboro†
April 17, Golden Needles Plant Expansion Dedication, Wilkesboro
April 17, Governor's Luncheon, Wilkesboro*
April 17, Wilkes County Airport Dedication, North Wilkesboro
	vicinity [not delivered]
April 19, Opening, International Home Furnishings Market,
	Showplace on the Park, High Point
April 20, Criminal Justice Summit, Raleigh*
April 20, North Carolina Tribute to Charles Kuralt, Research Triangle
	Park
April 23, James E. Harrington Freeway Dedication [I-40], Benson
April 24, Presentation of Bravery and Heroism Awards, Raleigh
April 24, IBM Twenty-Fifth Anniversary, Research Triangle Park
April 25, Child Support "Wanted-Poster" Press Conference, Raleigh
	[not delivered]
April 26, ASMO North Carolina Dedication, Statesville
April 26, 125th Anniversary of the End of the Civil War, Raleigh
April 27, Rocco Turkey Plant Dedication, St. Pauls
April 30, Swearing-in of Betsy Justus as Secretary of Revenue, Raleigh
May 1, Press Release, Statement by Governor Martin Regarding
	Economic Development in Haywood County, Raleigh
May 9, *Forbes* Magazine Advertising Section Kick-Off, Greensboro
May 9, *Forbes* Press Conference [notes]: Charlotte, Greensboro, Raleigh
May 10, NGK Ceramics Dedication, Mooresville
May 10, North Carolina World Trade Association, Charlotte*
May 11, Inaugural Run, Amtrak's Carolinian [notes], Rocky Mount
May 11, J. Harold Nash Depot Dedication, Kannapolis
May 14, Helikon Furniture Co. Plant Dedication, Sanford
May 14, Press Release, Governor Martin Challenges Superintendent
	Etheridge to Find Cuts in Administrative—Not Teaching—
	Positions, Raleigh*
May 15, Infant Mortality Campaign Kick-Off, Raleigh
May 15, Southern Technology Council, Research Triangle Park
May 15, European Fellows Press Conference [Hungarian and Polish
	participants in Visiting Fellows Program, North Carolina Partners
	for Democracy Foundation], Raleigh
May 16, United Way of Forsyth County Leadership Circle,
	Presentation of Alexis de Tocqueville Society Award to Ed Shelton,
	Winston-Salem
May 17, Cities In Schools Press Conference, Raleigh
May 17, Presentation, Governor's Hazardous Waste Management
	Awards, Raleigh*

May 17, Awards Presentation, Governor's Business Council on the Arts and Humanities, Durham

May 17, Press Release, Governor Chooses Option to Relieve Revenue Shortfall, Raleigh*

May 18, Southern Regional Seminar, Association of Community College Trustees, Winston-Salem*

May 19, North Carolina Jewelers Association [notes], Wrightsville Beach

May 23, Rowan County DWI Caravan, Raleigh

May 23, Wake Forest Chamber of Commerce, Wake Forest [not delivered]

May 24, Statement at Press Conference, Raleigh†

May 24, Davidson County Economic Development Commission, Thomasville

May 25, Tar Heel Junior Historian Awards Presentation, Raleigh

May 27, Veterans Memorial Dedication, Raleigh

May 29, Press Release, Governor Responds to Lieutenant Governor's Fiscal Reform Proposals, Raleigh

May 31, Statement at Press Conference, Raleigh†

June 5, American Express Merchandising Center Opening, Greensboro

June 6, Needham B. Broughton High School Commencement, Raleigh

June 7, Statement at Press Conference, Raleigh†

June 8, Press Release, Governor's Reaction to Decision by Standard and Poor's, Raleigh*

June 11, North Carolinians for Community Colleges [notes], Raleigh

June 11, North Carolina Supercomputing Center Dedication, Research Triangle Park

June 11, Town Meeting, Trenton†

June 14, Capitol Sesquicentennial Announcement, Raleigh

June 15, Boys' State [notes], Winston-Salem

June 15, Girls' State [notes], Greensboro

June 26, Press Release, Governor Martin Asks that Oil Drilling Site in North Carolina Be Included in President Bush's Moratorium on Offshore Drilling, Raleigh*

June 28, Statement at Press Conference, Raleigh†

June 29, I-40 Rest Area Dedication (Duplin County), Newton Grove

June 29, I-40 Dedication (New Hanover County), University of North Carolina at Wilmington

July 5, Press Release, Governor Martin's Reaction to House Action on Veto Bill, Raleigh

July 12, Press Conference, TEAM [Teaching Excellence and Mathematics] Announcement, Raleigh

July 12, Press Release, Governor Opposes Changing Method of
  Awarding Electoral Votes, Raleigh
July 13, Task Force on Reduction of Infant Mortality, Raleigh*
July 13, Opening, Comprehensive Beach Access Project for Disabled
  Persons, Fort Macon State Park, Atlantic Beach
July 16, School Superintendents Leadership Conference, Wilmington†
July 19, Recycling Development Plan for North Carolina, Raleigh
July 25, 100th Anniversary of Greenville Tobacco Market Opening,
  Farmers Warehouse, Greenville [not delivered]
July 26, Statement at Press Conference, Raleigh†
July 27, Opening Statement Regarding Proposed Changes in
  Hazardous Waste Commission Rules, Raleigh
July 27, Literacy Partnership Conference, Greensboro
August 1, Swearing-in of Ann Duncan as Chairwoman, North
  Carolina Employment Security Commission, Raleigh
August 1, Inaugural Lufthansa Flight to Frankfurt, Charlotte
August 1, Press Release, Governor Approves Some Changes in
  Hazardous Waste Rules, Withholds Approval for Others, Raleigh
August 3, Governor's Conference on Library and Information
  Services, Charlotte*
August 9, Press Release, Governor Martin Announces North Carolina
  Air National Guard Unit to Support United States Troops in Persian
  Gulf, Raleigh
August 22, Thad Eure Bridge Dedication [U.S. 13-158 over Chowan
  River], Gates-Hertford counties
August 24, Science and Mathematics Alliance, Charlotte
August 24, Press Release, North Carolina Army National Guard Units
  Placed on Alert Pending a Call to Federal Active-Duty Status,
  Raleigh
August 27, Science and Mathematics Alliance, Research Triangle Park
  [not delivered]
August 28, Press Release, Governor Martin Praises SAT Improvement
  Efforts, Raleigh
August 29, Governor's Awards for Safety and Health, Raleigh
August 30, National Guard Facility, Raleigh-Durham International
  Airport, Wake County [not delivered]
August 30, Press Conference, Celebration North Carolina-Motheread,
  Raleigh*
September 5, Press Conference, Ribbon-Cutting, Governors Club,
  Chapel Hill†
September 5, Governor's Conference on Rural Health, Research
  Triangle Park

September 6, Ribbon-Cutting, Landfall Club, Wilmington†
September 7, State Employees Association of North Carolina, Charlotte
September 11, Presentation of World Citizen Award to Billy Graham, Charlotte
September 12, Decision-Makers Forum on Cutting the Cost of Waste, North Carolina Board of Science and Technology, Raleigh*
September 12, State Employees Combined Campaign, Raleigh
September 13, Statement at Press Conference, Raleigh†
September 13, Presentation of National Soil and Water Conservation Award, Farm Family of the Year, Clarence Loflin and Family, Denton
September 13, Convocation for Dr. Nagai [Japanese Studies Program], Davidson College, Davidson
September 15, Terminal Complex Dedication, New Hanover County Airport, Wilmington†
September 18, Governor's Awards for Excellence, Raleigh
September 18, Oxford University Press Dedication, Cary
September 19, Family Literacy Symposium, Durham
September 21, North Carolina Medical Technology Seminar, Research Triangle Park
September 21, Western Residence Association, Asheville
September 24, Prison Bond Press Conference, Raleigh
September 25, Press Availability, Shelby†
September 25, Cleveland County Library Dedication, Shelby
September 25, Cleveland County Chamber of Commerce, Shelby*
September 26, Ribbon-Cutting, American Express Health Systems Group, Charlotte
September 27, James T. Broyhill Highway Dedication [U.S. 321], Hudson
September 28, Smoky Mountain Visitors Center Dedication [U.S. 23-441], Macon County
October 1, Red Ribbon Campaign, National Federation of Parents for Drug-Free Youth, Raleigh
October 8, Opening Ceremonies, Southeast United States-Japan Association, Atlanta
October 8, Trade Breakout Session, Southeast United States-Japan Association, Atlanta
October 9, Closing Ceremonies, Southeast United States-Japan Association, Atlanta
October 10, Visit by President George Bush, Raleigh†
October 11, Statement at Press Conference, Raleigh†

October 11, *Durham Morning Herald* Plant Dedication, Durham
October 11, Governor's Awards for Job Training, Greensboro
October 18, Glaxo Research and Development Center Dedication, Research Triangle Park
October 19, Schindler Corp. Plant Dedication, Clinton
October 19, United States Olympic Committee and Sports Development Commission Reception, Raleigh
October 22, Introduction of Thomas Sticht, Southern Growth Policies Board, New Orleans, Louisiana
October 22, Introduction of Hanna Fingeret, Southern Growth Policies Board, New Orleans, Louisiana
October 23, Executive Technology Conference, Research Triangle Park*
October 25, Press Release, Governor Asks Council of Fiscal Advisors to Review Enterprise Fund Cited in Audit of State Supreme Court, Raleigh
October 26, Sigma Xi Welcome, Research Triangle Park [not delivered]
October 27, "Give a Kid a Coat" Campaign Kick-Off, Winston-Salem†
October 29, U.S. 258-N.C. 24 Dedication, Richlands
October 30, University of North Carolina at Charlotte Silver Anniversary Campaign, Charlotte [not delivered]
November 1, Statement on Prison Construction Bond Referendum, Raleigh
November 1, Swearing-in of Wilma Sherrill as Division of Motor Vehicles Commissioner, Raleigh
November 8, Champion International Corp. Reforestation Announcement, Raleigh
November 8, Acceptance of North Carolina Workforce Preparedness Commission Report, Durham [not delivered]
November 8, North Carolina Workforce Preparedness Partnership Conference, Durham*
November 9, Inauguration of Lee Monroe as President, Florida Memorial College, Miami, Florida
November 13, North Carolina Recreation and Park Society Forum, Raleigh
November 14, North Carolina Minority Health Center, North Carolina Mutual Insurance Co., Durham
November 15, National Honor Society Induction, South Johnston High School, Four Oaks [not delivered]
November 15, Centura Banks, Inc., Donation for Celebration North Carolina, Raleigh*
November 15, Volunteer Recognition Ceremony, Western Region, Asheville

November 16, Groundbreaking for Permanent Headquarters, North
Carolina Biotechnology Center, Research Triangle Park
November 16, North Carolina Awards Presentation, Research Triangle
Park
November 19, Opening Ceremonies, Southeast United States-Korea
Association, Charleston, South Carolina
November 19, Panel Discussion on Technological Cooperation,
Southeast United States-Korea Association, Charleston, South
Carolina
November 29, Dobbs School Open House, Kinston
November 29, Kinston Rotary Club, Kinston [not delivered]
November 29, Volunteer Recognition Ceremony, Eastern Region,
Greenville
December 3, National Institute of Statistical Sciences Announcement,
Research Triangle Park
December 3, Volunteer Recognition Ceremony, Central Region,
Raleigh
December 3, Charlotte Chamber of Commerce, Charlotte
December 6, Christmas Tree Lighting, Raleigh
December 13, North Carolina Association of County Commissioners,
Pinehurst†
December 14, Statement at Press Conference, Raleigh†
December 18, Celebration North Carolina Reception, Raleigh*

1991

January 5, Centennial Celebration, Hope Mills
January 10, North Carolina Turfgrass Conference and Trade Show,
Charlotte
January 11, Education Summit, Raleigh*
January 13, "Bill of Rights" Exhibit, Raleigh
January 16, Gubernatorial Lecture, "Leading the State," Duke
University, Durham†
January 18, Memorial Tribute Honoring Dr. Martin Luther King, Jr.,
Raleigh
January 28, Press Release, Governor Praises SONAT Merger [with
North Carolina Natural Gas] as Positive Industrial Development
Decision for North Carolina, Raleigh
February 4, Press Release, Governor Praises Northampton
Commissioners' Decision, Pledges State Cooperation with
Residents, Officials [proposed site for hazardous waste incinerator/
invitation to ThermalKEM], Raleigh
February 5, National Governors' Association, Washington, D.C.*

February 7, North Carolina National Guard 1/130th Aviation
Battalion Alert, Raleigh

February 7, Press Conference: Donation of NBA All-Star Basketball
Game Tickets to Military Families; Carolina Power and Light Co.
Joins Adopt-A-Park Program, Raleigh

February 8, Tobacco Growers Association, Raleigh*

February 8, Press Release, Governor Martin's Reaction to Resolution
from UNC System Board of Trustees [tuition], Raleigh

February 11, Presentation of Rocky Mount Area Chamber of
Commerce Distinguished Citizen Award to Jack Laughery, Rocky
Mount

February 13, Education Remarks, Legislative Building, Raleigh†

February 14, North Carolina Prayer Breakfast, Introduction of Chuck
Colson, Raleigh

February 18, Kickoff, Center for World Environment and Sustainable
Development [Research Triangle Park], Durham

February 21, Opening, American Watercolor Exhibit [Transco],
Fayetteville*

February 22, RJR/Tech Prep Announcement, Hickory*

February 22, Driver License Office Dedication, Hickory

February 25, Keynote Address, Governor's Economic Development
Summit, Greensboro [not delivered]

February 25, Media Briefing on Economic Issues, Greensboro†

February 25, Introduction of Jack Kemp, Governor's Economic
Development Summit, Greensboro

February 26, Introduction of John Medlin, Governor's Economic
Development Summit, Greensboro

February 26, Governors' Round Table with Governors Martin, Hunt,
Holshouser, and Scott, Governor's Economic Development
Summit, Greensboro†

February 26, Closing Luncheon and Summit Overview, Governor's
Economic Development Summit, Greensboro†

February 28, Press Release, Governor Responds to Lieutenant
Governor's Budget Proposal, Raleigh

March 5, North Carolina Association of Women Business Owners,
Raleigh

March 7, Presentation of Truck Driver of the Year Award to James W.
Sigmon, Raleigh

March 7, North Carolina Human Relations Commission Awards,
Raleigh

March 8, Conference of District Attorneys, Raleigh [not delivered]

March 8, Welcome to Desert Storm Troops, Fort Bragg, Cumberland
County

March 19, Return of 317th Tactical Airlift Wing, Pope Air Force Base, Cumberland County

March 21, Prison Bond Bill Announcement, Raleigh

March 22, Student Legislature, Raleigh

March 22, Dedication, North Carolina State University College of Textiles, Raleigh

March 26, Concord-Cabarrus Chamber of Commerce, Raleigh†

March 27, Distinguished Women of North Carolina Award-Council on the Status of Women, Raleigh

March 28, Statement on NCAA Final Four Basketball Tournament and North Carolina Salute to the Troops Celebration, Raleigh

April 3, Presentation of North Carolina Public Service Award to Dick Daugherty, Raleigh

April 4, Press Conference on Success of State Fair Housing Act, Appointment of Estell Lee to Succeed Jim Broyhill as Economic and Community Development Secretary, Raleigh

April 5, Press Release, Governor Proclaims April as National Child Abuse Month in North Carolina, Raleigh

April 8, Rockingham-Richmond County Chamber of Commerce, Rockingham†

April 8, Monroe-Union Chamber of Commerce, Monroe†

April 8, Town Meeting, Brevard†

April 9, Forsyth County Chamber of Commerce, Winston-Salem†

April 9, Guilford County Chamber of Commerce, Greensboro†

April 9, Alamance County Chamber of Commerce, Burlington†

April 10, Catawba County Annual State Issues Seminar, Raleigh†

April 11, Statement at Press Conference, Raleigh†

April 11, Testimony on Gubernatorial Veto, North Carolina House Committee on Courts, Justice, Constitutional Amendments, and Referenda, Raleigh

April 11, Dedication, William and Ida Friday Continuing Education Center, University of North Carolina at Chapel Hill [delivered April 12]

April 12, Caterpillar, Inc., Announcement, Clayton

April 15, Air Cargo Presentation, Joint House and Senate Transportation Committee, Raleigh

April 17, Raleigh Chamber of Commerce, Raleigh†

April 18, Take Pride in America Awards, Raleigh

April 19, State Employees Association of North Carolina Headquarters Dedication, Raleigh

April 19, Press Release, Governor Martin Praises President's Education Plans, Says Same Creativity Needed in North Carolina, Raleigh

April 22, Pope Air Force Base Volunteer Week Celebration, Cumberland County

April 22, Award Ceremony, North Carolina Department of Economic and Community Development Top Ten Economic Development Groups, Raleigh

April 22, Swearing-in of Estell Lee as Secretary of Economic and Community Development, Raleigh

April 22, Sanford Chamber of Commerce, Sanford†

April 23, Presentation of Governor's Business Council Awards on the Arts and Humanities, Raleigh

April 24, Presentation of Governor's Awards for Bravery and Heroism, Raleigh

April 26, Dedication of Habitat for Humanity Home, Charlotte

April 26, Virkler Co. Grand Opening, Charlotte

April 29, Canada-U.S. Business Association, Toronto, Ontario [not delivered]

April 29, Canada-U.S. Business Association, Toronto, Ontario [revised text; not delivered]

April 29, North Carolina Tourism Breakfast, Toronto, Ontario [not delivered]

April 29, Business Seminar on North Carolina, Toronto, Ontario [not delivered]

May 1, Dedication of Rush Smith Dickson Tower, Carolinas Medical Center, Charlotte

May 1, Carolinas Medical Center Spring Physicians Symposium, Charlotte [not delivered]

May 2, Swearing-in of Ken Harris and Tom D'Alonzo to State Board of Education, Raleigh†

May 2, Christa McAuliffe Education Award Presentation, Raleigh†

May 2, Statement at Press Conference, Raleigh†

May 6, North Carolina Division of Motor Vehicles' "Quality Goes Public" Conference, Raleigh

May 7, Hudson Institute, Raleigh*

May 8, North Carolina World Trade Association, Raleigh*

May 9, Statement at Press Conference, Raleigh†

May 9, North Carolina Association of Realtors [notes], Raleigh

May 9, Governor's Conference on Travel and Tourism, Atlantic Beach*

May 10, Apparel Manufacturers, United States Olympic Committee Luncheon, Raleigh

May 14, State Employees Association of North Carolina Membership Kick-Off, Raleigh†

May 14, North Carolina Teaching Fellows, Raleigh

May 15, North Carolina PTA Legislative Conference [notes], Raleigh

May 16, Statement at Press Conference, Raleigh†
May 16, Presentation of Governor's Waste Management Awards, Raleigh
May 16, Western Carolina Industries [notes], Asheville
May 17, Mansions and Memories [notes], Raleigh
May 21, Celebration North Carolina-Carolina Power and Light Co. Cities In Schools, Raleigh
May 22, Presentation of School Beautification and Recycling Awards and Project Tomorrow Awards, Raleigh
May 29, Representatives of Eastern North Carolina Chambers of Commerce, Raleigh†
May 30, Statement at Press Conference, Raleigh†
May 30, Memorial Day Celebration, Raleigh
May 30, Press Release, Governor Opposes EPA Additions to Nonattainment Air Quality List [letter to EPA Regional Administrator Greer C. Tidwell attached], Raleigh
May 30, Press Release, Governor Offers Additional Budget Options to Legislature [memorandum to Senator Henson P. Barnes and Speaker Daniel T. Blue attached], Raleigh*
June 4, North Carolina Literacy Trust Foundation, Raleigh
June 6, Press Release, Governor Responds to Report of Low North Carolina Math Scores [National Assessment of Educational Progress], Raleigh
June 11, Acceptance of Distinguished Citizen Award from Occoneechee Council, Boy Scouts of America, Research Triangle Park [not delivered]
June 12, Boys' State [notes], Winston-Salem
June 12, Girls' State [notes], Greensboro
June 12, Presentation of State Awards, Advocacy Council for Persons with Disabilities, Greensboro
June 17, First Union Building Dedication, Raleigh
June 19, Robert A. Taft Institute Question and Answer Session [notes], Raleigh
June 20, Statement at Press Conference, Raleigh†
June 20, Grand Opening, BFI Recycling, Raleigh
June 21, Announcement, Center for a Drug-Free Workplace, Winston-Salem
June 21, Joyce Foods Headquarters Dedication, Winston-Salem
June 23, Keep North Carolina Clean and Beautiful Endowment Announcement [notes], Pinehurst
June 24, Introduction of Ambassador Robert B. Orr, World Trade Center Dinner, Research Triangle Park
June 27, *Financial World* Press Conference, Raleigh

June 28, North Carolina Federation of Business and Professional Women's Clubs, Inc., Raleigh

June 28, State Games Opening Ceremonies, Raleigh

June 29, "Salute to the Troops" Show, Raleigh

June 30, Salute to the Troops, "Operation Celebration," Fayetteville

July 2, Home Again Project, Jacksonville

July 2, Press Release, Governor Responds to Committee Vote on Veto, Raleigh*

July 3, Old Threshers Reunion, Denton

July 3, Press Release, Governor Urges Budget Negotiators to Hold the Line on Permanent Corporate and Personal Income Taxes [letter attached], Raleigh*

July 4, "Salute to the Troops" Celebration, Greensboro

July 4, Fourth of July Gala and Spirit of Freedom Parade, Asheville

July 4, "Salute to the Troops" Celebration, Welcome to Kuwaiti Ambassador Sheikh Saud Nasir Al-Sabah, Charlotte

July 4, Blockbuster Pavilion Opening, Charlotte

July 4, "Salute to the Troops" Celebration, WBTV Sky Show, Charlotte

July 12, Division of Environmental Management Laboratory Dedication, Raleigh

July 16, Press Release, Governor Expresses Condolences on the Death of Colonel Bill Teem [Highway Patrol], Raleigh

July 18, Statement at Press Conference, Raleigh†

July 22, "Ag in the Classroom" Teacher Workshop, Raleigh*

July 23, George A. Batte Center Dedication, Cabarrus Memorial Hospital, Concord

July 24, Carolina Place Grand Opening, Pineville [not delivered]

July 25, Statement at Press Conference, Raleigh†

July 29, International Lutheran Laymen's League [notes], Winston-Salem

August 1, Onslow County Committee of 100 [notes], Jacksonville

August 22, Opening Remarks, Global Air Cargo Industrial Complex Conference, Introduction of John Kasarda, Chapel Hill

August 26, Press Availability, Lexington†

August 26, "Babies Need Books," Davidson County Capital for a Day, Thomasville

August 26, Prison Construction Talking Points [notes], Lexington

August 26, Lexington Chamber of Commerce [notes], Lexington

August 27, Governor's Awards for Safety and Health, Raleigh

August 29, Newspaper Literacy Day-Literacy Month Announcement, Raleigh

September 3, Triangle Points of Light Recognition Ceremony, Research Triangle Park

October 24, Introduction of Tom D'Alonzo, Southern Growth Policies
    Board Associate Membership Breakfast, Chapel Hill
October 24, Welcoming Remarks, Keynote Address Session,
    Introduction of J. Antonio Villamil, Southern Growth Policies
    Board, Chapel Hill
October 24, Introduction of Hilary Pennington, Southern Growth
    Policies Board, Chapel Hill
October 24, Introduction of Robert Friedman, Southern Growth
    Policies Board, Chapel Hill
October 24, Introduction of Bennett Brown, Southern Growth Policies
    Board, Chapel Hill
October 24, Introduction of Robert Albright, Southern Growth Policies
    Board, Chapel Hill
October 25, Round Table Discussion, Introduction of Peter Harkness,
    Southern Growth Policies Board, Chapel Hill
October 25, Introduction of Ann Johnson, Southern Growth Policies
    Board, Chapel Hill
October 25, Introduction of Kirsten Nyrop, Southern Growth Policies
    Board, Chapel Hill
October 25, Introduction of Lawrence Framme, Southern Growth
    Policies Board, Chapel Hill
October 25, Introduction of Phil Price, Southern Growth Policies
    Board, Chapel Hill
October 25, Closing Luncheon, Southern Growth Policies Board,
    Chapel Hill
October 29, Introduction of Roger Twibell, PGA Tour Championship,
    Pinehurst
October 30, Welcoming Reception, PGA Tour Championship,
    Pinehurst
October 30, Press Release, Governor Responds to the EPA
    Announcement of Areas of Non-Attainment [air pollution], Raleigh
November 1, Ribbon-Cutting, USAir Inaugural Flight to Frankfurt,
    Charlotte/Douglas International Airport, Mecklenburg County
November 6, Lenox China Dedication, Kinston
November 6, Interstate 40 Economic Impact Study, Wilmington
November 8, Newspaper Column on Interstate 40, Raleigh
November 11, Veterans Memorial Dedication, Pinehurst
November 17, Presentation, North Carolina Quality Leadership
    Awards, Greensboro [delivered November 17, 1992]
November 19, Presentation, North Carolina Quality Leadership
    Awards, Raleigh
November 21, Announcement of Willie Gary Donation to Shaw
    University, Raleigh

November 21, AT&T Conference on Telecommunications, Wrightsville Beach

November 21, Estell Lee Roast [notes], Wilmington

November 22, Hitachi Metals, Inc., Dedication, China Grove

November 22, Presentation of National School of Excellence Award to West Rowan High School, Salisbury [not delivered]

November 22, North Carolina Awards Presentation, Raleigh

November 25, Twenty-Fifth Anniversary, Lions Clinic for the Blind, Raleigh

November 25, Presentation of Governor's Awards for Outstanding Volunteer Services, Central Counties, Raleigh

November 25, Awards Presentation, Governor's Cup Billfishing Conservation Series, Raleigh

December 2, Charlotte Chamber of Commerce Annual Meeting, Charlotte

December 3, Press Conference, Celebration North Carolina-Carolina Telephone, Tarboro

December 3, Celebration North Carolina-Carolina Telephone, Tarboro

December 5, Statement at Press Conference, Raleigh [not delivered]

December 5, Christmas Tree Lighting Ceremony, Raleigh

December 10, North Carolina Farm Bureau Federation, Asheville*

December 12, Medical Liability and Access to Obstetrical Care, Southern Regional Project on Infant Mortality, Research Triangle Park

December 12, Press Release, Governor Responds to DPI [Department of Public Instruction] Lawsuit against State Board of Education, Raleigh

December 15, "Bill of Rights" Plaque Unveiling, Raleigh

1992

January [no day], Response to Alan Janesch, Editor, "Governors Bulletin," National Governors' Association, Raleigh

January 5, Play Opening, *A Capital Idea*, Bicentennial Celebration, Raleigh

January 8, Press Release, Governor Responds to Deficiencies Found in the North Carolina Department of Labor [occupational safety and health program], Raleigh

January 9, Drug Tax Revenue Distribution Press Conference, Raleigh*

January 10, Board of Transportation Meeting, Raleigh

January 10, Introduction of Colorado Governor Roy Romer, North Carolina 2000 Partnership Conference, Research Triangle Park

January 10, Press Release, Governor Commutes Anson Maynard's
Death Sentence to Life Without Parole, Raleigh
January 30, Presentation of North Carolina Quality Leadership Award
to IBM, Research Triangle Park*
February [no day], State of the North Carolina Economy [article for
North Carolina Department of Economic and Community
Development newsletter], Raleigh
February 3, North Carolina 2000: A Promise for the Future
[newspaper column], Raleigh
February 6, UNC-Chapel Hill Bicentennial Commemorative License
Plate Presentation, Raleigh
February 10, North Carolina 2000 Workshop, Jackson Park Elementary
School, Kannapolis*
February 10, Economic Development Luncheon, Cabarrus County
Capital for a Day, Concord*
February 10, Dedication, Kirk and McWhorter Cottages, Stonewall
Jackson School, Concord
February 11, Opening Comments, Air Cargo Authority Meeting,
Chapel Hill*
February 18, Executives Club [notes], Raleigh
February 24, Keynote Address, Governor's Economic Development
Summit, Greensboro†
February 24, Introduction of Edgar S. Woolard, Jr., Governor's
Economic Development Summit, Greensboro
February 25, Introduction of Robert J. Maricich, Governor's Economic
Development Summit, Greensboro
February 25, Introduction of CEO Forum and John Kasarda,
Governor's Economic Development Summit, Greensboro
February 25, Closing Remarks, CEO Forum and Governor's Economic
Development Summit, Greensboro
February 28, North Carolina Airport Association, Pinehurst [not
delivered]
March 2, MCI Network Management Center Announcement, Raleigh
March 5, North Carolina Driver of the Year Award Presentation,
Raleigh†
March 5, North Carolina Education Governing Boards, Introduction of
Robert Stoltz, Chapel Hill*
March 5, North Carolina Human Relations Commission Awards
Presentation, Raleigh
March 5, Joseph S. Koury Convention Center Dedication, Greensboro
March 9, Presentation of North Carolina Quality Leadership Award to
Carolina Telephone, Fayetteville

March 16, Press Availability, Wentworth†
March 16, North Carolina 2000 Workshop, Dalton McMichael High
    School, Madison*
March 16, Southern Steel and Wire Groundbreaking, Madison
March 18, ITT Teves America Announcement, Morganton
March 18, North Carolina Citizens for Business and Industry, Raleigh†
March 20, Gaston County Education Summit, Gastonia†
March 20, Presentation of North Carolina Quality Leadership Award
    to Carolina Freight Corp., Cherryville
March 25, North Carolina 2000 Luncheon, Asheville†
March 25, Press Conference, Governor's Conference on Travel and
    Tourism, Asheville
March 27, Frank Kenan Reception, Research Triangle Park
April 2, Statement on NCAA Final Four Basketball Tournament,
    Raleigh [not delivered]
April 2, Dinner Honoring Paul Rizzo [notes], Chapel Hill
April 8, "A Matter of Life" Reception [Carolina Organ Procurement
    Agency], Raleigh
April 8, *Colonial Homes*\Hearst Corp. Reception, High Point
April 9, Stork Screens America Dedication, Charlotte
April 10, Marietta Street Bridge Ribbon-Cutting, Gastonia
April 10, Convention Center Groundbreaking, Charlotte
April 13, UNC Neuropsychiatric Hospital Groundbreaking, Chapel
    Hill
April 14, Richard Petty Highway Dedication [U.S. 220], Randolph
    County
April 15, Press Conference, Arnold Schwarzenegger Visit, A. B. Combs
    Elementary School, Raleigh
April 15, Assembly, Arnold Schwarzenegger Visit, A. B. Combs
    Elementary School, Raleigh
April 15, Youth Fitness Summit, Introduction of Arnold
    Schwarzenegger, Raleigh
April 21, Awards Ceremony, Governor's Business Council on the Arts
    and Humanities, Raleigh
April 23, Governor's Advocacy Council for Persons with Disabilities,
    Raleigh*
April 24, L. A. Reynolds Garden Showcase Grand Opening, Lewisville
April 24, Press Release, Governor Urges Cooperation with U.S.
    Department of Labor [N.C. Department of Labor/John Brooks],
    Raleigh
April 27, Tenth Anniversary Celebration, Ajinomoto Amino Acid
    Manufacturing, Raleigh

April 30, Dedication, Reichhold Chemicals, Inc., U.S. Headquarters and Research Center, Research Triangle Park

May 1, Novo Nordisk Plant Expansion Groundbreaking, Franklinton

May 11, Ribbon-Cutting, AT&T Manufacturing Facility, Guilford County

May 11, Ribbon-Cutting, Roche Biomedical Laboratories, Burlington

May 14, Acceptance of Paul Harris Fellow Award [notes], Research Triangle Park

May 14, North Carolina World Trade Association Awards Presentation, Research Triangle Park

May 14, Presentation of Presidential "E" Award to Shuford Mills, Inc., North Carolina World Trade Association, Research Triangle Park*

May 15, North Carolina 2000 Luncheon, University of North Carolina at Wilmington

May 15, Bryan International String Competition Reception, Raleigh

May 18, MCI First Customer Service Call, Morrisville

May 20, Dedication, James G. Cannon Medical Research Center, Carolinas Medical Center, Charlotte

May 21, DWI Advertising Campaign Announcement, Raleigh

May 21, Presentation, Governor's Awards of Excellence for Outstanding Achievement in Waste Management, Raleigh*

May 28, Bravery and Heroism Awards Presentation, Raleigh

May 30, Republican State Convention, Greensboro

June 1, Swearing-in of Alan Pugh as Secretary of Crime Control and Public Safety, Raleigh

June 1, Swearing-in of Colonel Sidney L. Jennings, Commander, and Lieutenant-Colonel Charles V. Parks, Executive Officer, North Carolina Highway Patrol, Raleigh

June 3, Thomasville and Lexington Chambers of Commerce [notes], Raleigh [not delivered]

June 9, Charlotte Rotary Club [notes], Charlotte

June 9, Charlotte Rotary Club [address], Charlotte*

June 9, New Line Activation, Matsushita Compressor Corp. of America, Mooresville

June 10, NFL Pep Rally, Charlotte

June 10, Press Release, Governor Martin Supports Call for Federal Balanced Budget Amendment [letter to Congressman T. Cass Ballenger attached], Raleigh

June 11, Statement at Press Conference, Raleigh†

June 11, Cormetech, Inc., Plant Dedication, Durham

June 11, North Carolina 2000-American Airlines Academic Achievement Awards, Raleigh

June 11, American Airlines Fifth Anniversary, Raleigh-Durham
    International Airport, Wake County
June 12, Boys' State [notes], Wake Forest University, Winston-Salem
June 12, Girls' State [notes], University of North Carolina at
    Greensboro
June 13, Twentieth Anniversary, Election of James E. Holshouser as
    North Carolina Governor, Raleigh
June 17, Klaussner Furniture Industries, Inc., Award Presentation,
    Asheboro
June 18, Japanese Business Reception, Raleigh
June 24, Highway Safety Exposition Dedication, Raleigh
June 24, Acceptance of Official Copy, *Addresses and Public Papers of
    James Grubbs Martin, Governor of North Carolina*, Volume 1 [notes],
    Raleigh
June 29, ABB Transmission Technology Institute Grand Opening,
    North Carolina State University, Raleigh
July 3, Press Release, Governor Supports Presidential Visit to Faith,
    North Carolina, Raleigh
July 4, Fourth of July Celebration, Faith
July 7, Southeastern States Summit on Violent Crime, Charlotte
July 9, North Carolina Business Committee for Education, Raleigh
July 24, John Locke Foundation, Raleigh†
July 27, "Ag in the Classroom" Teacher In-Service Workshop, Raleigh*
July 31, Raleigh Chamber of Commerce Planning Conference,
    Pinehurst [not delivered]
August 5, Alpha Sigma Phi National Conference, Charlotte
August 16, Luncheon Address to North Carolina Delegation,
    Republican National Convention, Houston, Texas
August 24, Morganite, Inc., Expansion Announcement, Dunn
August 25, "Vision Carolina" Reception, Northern Telecom, Research
    Triangle Park
August 26, Governor's Minority Executive Council [notes], Raleigh
August 31, Habitat for Humanity House Dedication, Charlotte
September 1, Presentation, Governor's Awards for Outstanding
    Volunteer Services, Piedmont and Eastern Groups, Raleigh
September 2, North Carolina Scholars-North Carolina 2000 Reception,
    Raleigh [not delivered]
September 3, Motor and Equipment Manufacturers Association
    Groundbreaking, Research Triangle Park*
September 9, North Carolina 2000 Communities Ceremony, Raleigh
September 14, Portrait Unveiling, Martin Chemistry Building,
    Davidson College, Davidson†

September 14, Dinner Honoring Hugh McColl [revised], Charlotte
September 14, Dinner Honoring Hugh McColl [notes], Charlotte
September 14, Dinner Honoring Hugh McColl [transcript], Charlotte
September 15, Press Release, Governor Expresses Sympathy at the
    Death of Walter Jones, Raleigh
September 16, Presentation, Governor's Awards for Excellence,
    Raleigh [not delivered]
September 18, Governor's Crime Commission [notes; October 1991
    progress report attached], Raleigh
September 18, Presentation of Farm Family of the Year Award to
    C. L. White and Family, Surry County
September 22, Dedication of Superintendent's House in Honor of
    David Young, Dorothea Dix Hospital, Raleigh
September 25, Presentation, Governor's Awards for Outstanding
    Volunteer Service, Western Group, Asheville
September 28, Southern Industrial Development Council, Asheville*
October 1, Heritage and Promise Dinner, Wake Forest University,
    Winston-Salem
October 3, U.S.S. *Charlotte* Christening, Newport News, Virginia
October 5, Breakout Session on Trade, Southeast United States-Japan
    Association, Orlando, Florida*
October 8, Governor's Council on Alcohol and Drug Abuse [notes],
    Raleigh
October 9, Dedication, State Revenue Building, Raleigh
October 16, Preview, North Carolina Museum of History Building,
    Raleigh
October 16, Press Release, Governor Denies Clemency for John
    Sterling Gardner, Raleigh
October 17, Closing Statement, North Carolina Drug Cabinet Meeting,
    Charlotte
October 20, High Speed Rail Corridor Press Conference, Raleigh
October 23, Foreign Language Association of North Carolina,
    Greensboro*
October 23, Dedication, North Carolina Blumenthal Performing Arts
    Center, Charlotte
October 26, Transamerica Reinsurance Group, Charlotte [not
    delivered]
November 5, Press Release, Governor Martin Expresses Loss at the
    Death of Brad Hays, Raleigh*
November 10, Presentation of Inaugural National Living Treasure
    Award, University of North Carolina at Wilmington
November 13, University of North Carolina Board of Governors
    [typescript], Chapel Hill

November 13, North Carolina Awards Presentation, Raleigh
November 17, Riding Lawn Mower Production Announcement,
    Honda Power Equipment Manufacturing, Inc., Swepsonville
November 17, Presentation, North Carolina Quality Leadership
    Awards, Greensboro [erroneously dated 1991]
November 25, Production of One-Millionth Dishwasher, WCI-
    Frigidaire, Kinston
December 4, Naming of Western Vocational Rehabilitation Facility in
    Honor of David T. Flaherty, Morganton
December 8, Capitol Christmas Tree Lighting, Raleigh
December 10, Operation Lifesaver Awards Presentation, Cary†
December 10, Carroll's Foods Center Dedication, Warsaw
December 21, Building a Framework for the Future: Accomplishments
    of the Martin Administration, 1985-1993, Raleigh [Reprinted in
    Charlotte Observer, January 3, 1993, as "Framework for the Future:
    Schools, Roads, Jobs; The Martin Team's Major Accomplishments,
    1985-93."]

1993

January 4, Governor James G. Martin Highway Dedication [I-485],
    Charlotte
January 5, Senator Bill Goldston Highway Dedication [N.C. 14],
    Rockingham County
January 6, Tommy Harrelson Highway Dedication [U.S. 17],
    Brunswick County*
January 6, S. Thomas Rhodes Bridge Dedication [U.S. 421 over Cape
    Fear River], Wilmington
January 6, Frank H. Kenan Bridge Dedication [I-40 over Cape Fear
    River], Wilmington

EXECUTIVE ORDERS

[Governor Martin issued 106 executive orders during his second term in office. Although space limitations prohibit the inclusion of these items in their entirety in this documentary, a listing of titles has been provided below. The complete texts of Martin's executive orders, promulgated during the period from 1989 to 1993, are located as follows: numbers 80 through 96, *Session Laws of North Carolina, 1989*, II, 3094–3144; numbers 97 through 123, *Session Laws of North Carolina, Extra Session, 1989, Extra and Regular Sessions, 1990*, 1004–1125; numbers 124 through 146, *Session Laws of North Carolina, 1991*, II, 2637–2695; numbers 147 through 173, *Session Laws of North Carolina, Extra Session, 1991, Regular Session, 1992*, III, 1257–1343; numbers 174 through 186, *Session Laws of North Carolina, 1993*, II, 3097–3165.]

1989

Executive Order Number 80, established North Carolina Drug Cabinet, January 10

Executive Order Number 81, amended Executive Order Number 80, North Carolina Drug Cabinet, January 12

Executive Order Number 82, extended expiration date of Executive Order Number 1, North Carolina Board of Ethics, January 29

Executive Order Number 83, established Office of State Printing, February 8

Executive Order Number 84, amended Executive Order Number 79, North Carolina Small Business Council, February 10

Executive Order Number 85, amended Executive Order Number 53, Governor's Interagency Advisory Team on Alcohol and Other Drug Abuse, March 1

Executive Order Number 86, directive on minimizing solid, hazardous, and infectious waste and control of toxic air pollutants, March 1

Executive Order Number 87, amended Executive Order Number 75, North Carolina Wildlife Resources Commission, April 27

Executive Order Number 88, established Columbus Voyages Quincentenary Commission, May 8

Executive Order Number 89, transferred State Employees' Advisory Group from Department of Administration to Office of State Personnel, May 8

Executive Order Number 90, established Governor's Advisory Council on Literacy, superseded Executive Order Number 32, Governor's Literacy Council, May 18

Executive Order Number 91, established North Carolina Motor Carrier Advisory Council, May 18

Executive Order Number 92, established Western North Carolina Environmental Council, May 31

Executive Order Number 93, reissued the following executive orders: Number 8, Governor's Advisory Committee on Travel and Tourism; Number 12, Governor's Highway Safety Commission; Number 36, Governor's Task Force on the Farm Economy; Number 39, State Employees Deferred Compensation Fund Board of Trustees; Number 43, North Carolina Emergency Response Commission; Number 45, Governor's Language Institutes Advisory Board; Number 47, North Carolina Fund for Children and Families Commission; and Number 49, Governor's Advisory Commission on Military Affairs. Executive Order Number 13, North Carolina Health Coordinating Council, and Executive Order Number 29, Governor's Task Force on Racial, Religious, and Ethnic Violence and Intimidation, were amended and reissued. June 20

Executive Order Number 94, reissued Executive Order Number 15, Juvenile Justice Planning Commission, and extended expiration date of Executive Order Number 71, Governor's Task Force on Rail Passenger Service. July 14

Executive Order Number 95, repealed Executive Order Number 57, Governor's Blue Ribbon Commission on Coastal Initiatives; created new Governor's Blue Ribbon Commission on Coastal Initiatives, July 25

Executive Order Number 96, amended Executive Order Number 92, Western North Carolina Environmental Council, July 25

Executive Order Number 97, amended Executive Order Number 80, North Carolina Drug Cabinet, September 26

Executive Order Number 98, temporary waiver of gross weight restrictions for trucks transporting disaster by-products generated by Hurricane Hugo, November 3

Executive Order Number 99, established Governor's Commission on Reduction of Infant Mortality, December 13

Executive Order Number 100, extended Executive Order Number 98, temporary waiver of gross weight restrictions for trucks transporting disaster by-products generated by Hurricane Hugo, December 14

Executive Order Number 101, extended Executive Order Number 55, Martin Luther King, Jr., Holiday Commission, December 21

Executive Order Number 102, amended Executive Order Number 88, Columbus Quincentenary Commission, December 21

1990

Executive Order Number 103, extended Executive Order Number 100, temporary waiver of gross weight restrictions for trucks transporting disaster by-products generated by Hurricane Hugo, February 6

Executive Order Number 104, amended Executive Order Number 90, Governor's Advisory Council on Literacy, February 8

Executive Order Number 105, extended Executive Order Number 3, North Carolina Advisory Council on Vocational Education, February 8

Executive Order Number 106, extended Executive Order Number 66, State Employee Combined Campaign, February 22

Executive Order Number 107, established North Carolina Governor's Commission on Workforce Preparedness, March 14

Executive Order Number 108, reestablished North Carolina Drug Cabinet and rescinded Executive Orders Number 80, 81, and 97, March 19

Executive Order Number 109, established North Carolina Sports Development Commission, March 29

Executive Order Number 110, established Governor's Advisory Council on International Trade, March 29

Executive Order Number 111, amended and extended Executive Order Number 45, Governor's Language Institutes Advisory Board, April 12

Executive Order Number 112, restructured and reestablished Governor's Advisory Commission on Travel and Tourism, April 12

Executive Order Number 113, established Governor's Conference on Library and Information Services Committee, April 20

Executive Order Number 114, budget administration, 1989–1991 biennium, May 8

Executive Order Number 115, amended Executive Order Number 92, Western North Carolina Environmental Council, May 22

Executive Order Number 116, amended and extended Executive Order Number 78, Governor's Task Force on Injury Prevention, May 22

Executive Order Number 117, amended Executive Order Number 108, North Carolina Drug Cabinet, May 30

Executive Order Number 118, extended Executive Order Number 79, North Carolina Small Business Council, June 12

Executive Order Number 119, established North Carolina Quality Leadership Awards Council, June 18

Executive Order Number 137, placed contributions to Teachers' and
State Employees' Retirement System into escrow, March 22
Executive Order Number 138, amended Executive Order Number 37,
Teachers' and State Employees' Retirement System, March 28
Executive Order Number 139, established Governor's Volunteer
Advisory Council, March 28
Executive Order Number 140, appointed special commission to
investigate Northampton County school finances, April 22
Executive Order Number 141, amended Executive Order Number 90,
Governor's Advisory Council on Literacy, April 17
Executive Order Number 142, required that each county department
of social services establish a community child protection team,
May 1
Executive Order Number 143, established North Carolina Advisory
Council on Vocational and Applied Technology Education and
rescinded Executive Order Number 3, North Carolina Advisory
Council on Vocational Education, May 1
Executive Order Number 144, amended and extended Executive
Order Number 53, Governor's Interagency Advisory Team on
Alcohol and Other Drug Abuse, May 3
Executive Order Number 145, reallocated Community Penalties
Program from Department of Crime Control and Public Safety to
Department of Correction, May 30
Executive Order Number 146, supplemented Executive Order
Number 145, Community Penalties Program, June 28
Executive Order Number 147, established Geographic Information
Coordinating Council and transferred Center for Geographic
Information and Analysis to the Office of the Governor, July 30
Executive Order Number 148, established Governor's Task Force on
Health Objectives for the Year 2000, August 6
Executive Order Number 149, rescinded Executive Order Number 79,
North Carolina Small Business Council, August 15
Executive Order Number 150, established North Carolina Human
Service Transportation Council, August 21
Executive Order Number 151, reestablished Governor's Advisory
Commission on Military Affairs, September 11
Executive Order Number 152, established Persian Gulf War Memorial
Commission, September 11
Executive Order Number 153, established North Carolina 2000
Steering Committee, September 24
Executive Order Number 154, amended Executive Order Number 53,
Governor's Interagency Advisory Team on Alcohol and Other Drug
Abuse, September 30

Executive Order Number 167, amended Executive Order Number 152, Persian Gulf War Memorial Commission, and established Persian Gulf War Memorial Advisory Committee, May 26

Executive Order Number 168, established North Carolina Interagency Council for Coordinating Homeless Programs, May 29

Executive Order Number 169, authorized criminal record checks of applicants for direct care positions within the Department of Human Resources, June 26

Executive Order Number 170, amended Executive Order Number 151 and Number 163, Governor's Advisory Commission on Military Affairs, June 29

Executive Order Number 171, reissued and extended Executive Order Number 45, Governor's Language Institutes Advisory Board, July 13

Executive Order Number 172, increased recycled product procurement and expanded solid waste reduction activity by state agencies, July 24

Executive Order Number 173, extended Executive Order Number 106, State Employees Combined Campaign, July 24

Executive Order Number 174, amended Executive Order Number 162, Council on Health Policy Information, July 30

Executive Order Number 175, Hurricane Andrew relief, August 28

Executive Order Number 176, extended and amended Executive Order Number 148, Governor's Task Force on Health Objectives for the Year 2000, September 24

Executive Order Number 177, extended Executive Order Number 175, Hurricane Andrew relief, October 1

Executive Order Number 178, temporarily waived certain penalties against vehicles transporting unprocessed yams on state highways, October 15

Executive Order Number 179, established Coordinating Committee on the Americans with Disabilities Act, October 22

Executive Order Number 180, transferred governor's extradition secretary from Governor's Office to Department of Justice, October 27

Executive Order Number 181, amended Executive Order Number 178, vehicle weight penalties, October 27

Executive Order Number 182, state agencies and accessibility of electronic equipment by persons with disabilities, November 19

Executive Order Number 183, amended and reissued Executive Order Number 175, Hurricane Andrew relief, December 7

Executive Order Number 184, transferred commutation-pardon analyst position, assigned to the Office of the Governor, from the Office of the Parole Commission in the Department of Correction to the Office of the Governor, December 22

Executive Order Number 185, extended the following executive orders: numbers 12, 51, 93, 161, Governor's Highway Safety Commission; numbers 13, 51, 93, 161, North Carolina State Health Coordinating Council; numbers 15, 59, 94, 131, Juvenile Justice Planning Committee; numbers 27, 47, 93, 161, North Carolina Fund for Children and Families Commission; numbers 29, 44, 93, 161, Governor's Task Force on Racial, Religious, and Ethnic Violence and Intimidation; numbers 39, 93, 161, North Carolina Public Employee Deferred Compensation Plan Board of Trustees; numbers 43, 48, 50, 93, 165, North Carolina Emergency Response Commission; numbers 53, 72, 85, 144, 154, Governor's Inter-Agency Team on Alcohol and Other Drug Abuse; numbers 55, 101, 161, Martin Luther King, Jr., Holiday Commission; numbers 66, 106, 173, State Employees Combined Campaign; numbers 71, 94, 125, Governor's Task Force on Rail Passenger Service; Number 99, Governor's Commission on Reduction of Infant Mortality; numbers 110, 161, Governor's Advisory Council on International Trade; numbers 121, 129, Governor's Minority, Female, and Disabled-Owned Businesses Construction Contractors Advisory Committee; numbers 126, 133, Governor's Highway Beautification Council; Number 132, Governor's Council on Alcohol and Other Drug Abuse; Number 136, North Carolina Advisory Council on Telecommunications; Number 139, Governor's Volunteer Advisory Council; Number 143, North Carolina Advisory Council on Vocational and Applied Technology Education; Number 150, North Carolina Human Service Transportation Council; numbers 151, 163, 170, Governor's Advisory Committee on Military Affairs; numbers 152, 160, 167, Persian Gulf War Memorial Commission; Number 153, North Carolina 2000 Steering Committee; and Number 156, North Carolina Committee on Literacy and Basic Skills. Executive orders 78 and 116, Governor's Task Force on Injury Prevention, were amended and extended. The following executive orders were rescinded: Number 20, Wellness Improvement for State Employees (WISE) program; Number 22, implemented certain economies in state government in response to United States legislation requiring a federal balanced budget; Number 26, Operation Hay; Number 35, transfer of State Information Processing Services from Department of Administration to the Office of State Controller; Number 86, directive on minimizing solid, hazardous, and infectious waste and control of toxic air pollutants; Number 89, transferred State Employees' Advisory Group from Department of Administration to the Office of State Personnel; Number 95, Blue Ribbon Commission on Coastal Initiatives; numbers 114, 130, 164, adjusted the 1989–1991 budget to balance the state budget; Number 122, Governor's Council of Fiscal Advisors; Number 124, Governor's Task Force on Prison Construction and Consolidation; Number 134, readjustment leave to state employees who had served in Persian Gulf War; numbers 137, 138, 158, escrow account for contributions to Teachers' and State Employees' Retirement System; Number 140, Special Commission to Investigate Shortages in the Northampton County Schools' Finances; numbers 145, 146, transferred Community Penalties Program from Department of Crime Control and Public Safety to the Department of Correction. December 29

1993

Executive Order Number 186, established North Carolina-Head Start Collaboration Project Advisory Council, January 6

APPOINTMENTS

[State law empowers the governor to appoint numerous persons to various boards, commissions, and the judiciary. This section lists most of the appointees Martin designated during his two terms as North Carolina's chief executive. Those included appear under the board on which they served; the boards, in turn, are arranged either by the department of state government in which they functioned or under a general heading, as in the case of groups not directly affiliated with agencies of the executive branch.

The names and terms of office of Executive Cabinet secretaries whom Martin appointed follow the appropriate department heading. Members of the Council of State, elected to their posts and therefore omitted from the ensuing listing, were the governor; Robert B. Jordan III (1985–1989) and James C. Gardner (1989–1993), lieutenant governor; Thad Eure (1936–1989) and Rufus L. Edmisten (1989–), secretary of state; Edward Renfrow (1981–1993), state auditor; Harlan E. Boyles (1977–), state treasurer; A. Craig Phillips (1969–1989) and Bob R. Etheridge (1989–), superintendent of public instruction; Lacy H. Thornburg (1985–1992), attorney general; James A. Graham (1964–), agriculture commissioner; John C. Brooks (1977–1993), labor commissioner; and James E. Long (1985–),insurance commissioner.

The composition of every commission presented in the following roster was assembled from information compiled from photocopies of the governor's letters of appointment. The editor and his assistants arranged this data into a standard format for each board, consisting of a heading—title, statutory citation, and identification number assigned by the Governor's Office—followed by the names, partial addresses, and dates of appointment and expiration of term of the members. A blank space under *Date of Expiration* signifies that an individual served at the pleasure of the governor. Dates employing zeros as placeholders, as in 00–00–88, indicate that Martin's letter provided incomplete term information. Instances in which a person was renamed to a commission before his or her current posting ended either reflect reassignment to a position having different term limits or resulted from the legislative restructuring of the entire board. Readers should consult the General Statutes or Session Laws for descriptions of the purpose and organization of commissions. Copies of the letters of appointment are filed among the James G. Martin Papers, State Archives, Division of Archives and History, Raleigh.

Governor Martin made over 4,500 appointments to boards and commissions during the 1985–1993 period, and a complete listing would fill a volume of its own. To conserve limited space in the current documentary, the makeup of nonstatutory boards, legislative study commissions, and federal advisory and research councils to which Martin named members has not been provided; however, a listing of such boards appears at the end of this section. Position holders also were excluded whose selection, as stated in their letter of commission, lay beyond the sole appointive power of the governor. In accordance with North Carolina law, these persons were elected, nominated, or recommended by a particular professional, legislative, or special-interest group and served with Martin's confirmation.

Every effort was made, in compiling this list, to ensure its accuracy. Where letters of commission contained discrepancies in spelling or other details, information from the one with the latest date was employed. Regrettably it must be noted that, in an undertaking of this magnitude, the potential for error exists.

Dissecting the information contained in a collection of documents occupying approximately four linear feet presents its own threat to precision. Furthermore, there is a chance that photocopies of some letters were never received. Sincere apologies are extended to those persons who served their state but whose names do not appear in this section, for whatever reason.]

OFFICE OF THE GOVERNOR

ADVISORY BUDGET COMMISSION
G.S. 143-4/Board No. 0145

Name of Appointee	Address	Date Appointed	Date of Expiration
Seddon Goode, Jr.	Charlotte	06-11-86	
W. Clay Hamner	Durham	12-03-90	
Paul S. Smith	Salisbury	06-08-87	

EDUCATION COMMISSION OF THE STATES
G.S. 115C-104/Board No. 0320

Name of Appointee	Address	Date Appointed	Date of Expiration
Bob Etheridge	Raleigh	01-31-89	
Rob Frazier	Charlotte	06-10-85	
Craig Phillips	Raleigh	06-10-85	
Elaine Poovey	Asheville	06-10-85	
Jean Powell	Clinton	06-10-85	

COMMITTEE ON INAUGURAL CEREMONIES
G.S. 143-533/Board No. 0459

Name of Appointee	Address	Date Appointed	Date of Expiration
Robert W. Bradshaw, Jr.	Charlotte	11-28-88	00-00-00
Ms. Terry Chambliss	Durham	11-18-92	00-00-00
Patric Dorsey	Raleigh	11-28-88	00-00-00
Josie E. Kite	Greensboro	11-28-88	00-00-00
Albert O. McCauley	Fayetteville	11-28-88	00-00-00
Anne S. Peden	Raleigh	11-28-88	00-00-00
Charles M. Shelton	Charlotte	11-28-88	00-00-00
		11-18-92	00-00-00
R. Edwin Shelton	Charlotte	11-25-92	00-00-00

BOARD FOR NEED-BASED MEDICAL STUDENT LOANS[1]
G.S. 143-47.21/Board No. 0639

Name of Appointee	Address	Date Appointed	Date of Expiration
Gordon L. Barnes	Burlington	11-10-86	07-01-90
Cleon F. Thompson, Jr.	Winston-Salem	11-10-86	07-01-90
Robert L. Zier	Clemmons	10-09-86	07-01-90

---

[1]G.S. 143-47.21 through G.S. 143-47.24 were repealed under *N.C. Session Laws, 1987*, II, c. 738, s. 41(c), ratified August 7, 1987.

SOUTHEAST INTERSTATE LOW-LEVEL RADIOACTIVE WASTE MANAGEMENT COMMISSION
G.S. 104F-2/Board No. 0849

Name of Appointee	Address	Date Appointed	Date of Expiration
William F. Frey	Davidson	05-09-85	
Martin P. Hines	Raleigh	02-26-85	
George W. Miller, Jr.	Durham	06-04-85	

SOUTHERN STATES ENERGY BOARD
G.S. 140D-1/Board No. 0855

Name of Appointee	Address	Date Appointed	Date of Expiration
C. Doug Culbreth	Raleigh	09-04-85	
		03-18-91	
Harold Zallen	Greenville	09-04-85	

DEPARTMENT OF ADMINISTRATION

Secretaries
Grace J. Rohrer, l985–1987
James S. Lofton, 1987–1993

NORTH CAROLINA ALCOHOLISM RESEARCH AUTHORITY
G.S. 122C-431/Board No. 0035

Name of Appointee	Address	Date Appointed	Date of Expiration
Matthew Coleridge-Taylor	Raleigh	12–07–88	02-01-92
George C. Edmonds	Apex	06-26-86	02-01-92
John A. Ewing	Wilmington	06-26-86	02-01-90
		07-02-90	02-01-96
James H. Grose	New Bern	07-02-90	02-01-96
Richard M. Miller	Franklin	06-26-86	02-01-92
Dennis F. Moore	Asheville	07-02-90	02-01-96
Samuel C. Powell	Burlington	10-30-87	01-31-88
		01-31-88	02-01-94
Jimmie C. Proctor	Pollocksville	06-26-86	02-01-92
W. J. Kenneth Rockwell	Durham	07-02-90	02-01-96
L. H. Zincone, Jr.	Greenville	10-30-87	01-31-88
		01-31-88	02-01-94

NORTH CAROLINA AQUARIUMS COMMISSION
G.S. 143B-390 16(a)/Board No. 0048

Name of Appointee	Address	Date Appointed	Date of Expiration
Michael W. Creed	Wilmington	12-04-92	07-01-96
Ted E. Haigler, Jr.	Raleigh	12-04-92	07-01-96
James S. Lofton, *chairman*	Raleigh	12-04-92	07-01-96
Walter D. Phillips	Newport	12-04-92	07-01-96

STATE BUILDING COMMISSION
G.S. 143-135.25/Board No. 0149

Name of Appointee	Address	Date Appointed	Date of Expiration
Fred C. Abernethy .... Hickory		05-12-87	06-30-90
		07-02-90	06-30-93
Henry A. Holmes .... Youngsville		05-12-87	06-30-88
		07-01-88	06-30-91
		07-01-91	06-30-94
Eugene L. Presley .... Asheville		06-30-89	06-30-92
		07-01-92	06-30-95
J. Worth Rummage .... Huntersville		05-12-87	06-30-89

COMMISSION ON CHILDREN AND YOUTH [2]
G.S. 120-70.7/Board No. 0201

Name of Appointee	Address	Date Appointed	Date of Expiration
Austin M. Allran .... Hickory		09-30-97	09-01-89
Ed Denton .... Morganton		09-30-87	09-01-89
Peggy Q. Lomax .... Lenoir		09-30-87	09-01-89
Joanne Sharpe.. Greensboro		09-30-87	09-01-89
J. Larry Simpson .... Asheboro		09-30-87	09-01-89

GOVERNOR'S ADVOCACY COUNCIL ON CHILDREN AND YOUTH
G.S. 143B-415/Board No. 0200

Name of Appointee	Address	Date Appointed	Date of Expiration
Fran Barnhart .... Charlotte		08-03-88	06-30-89
		07-01-89	06-30-93
Tommy Belle .... Asheboro		09-07-90	06-30-94
Richard W. Beyer .... Morganton		10-30-85	06-30-89
		07-01-89	06-30-93
James E. Conner .... Raleigh		07-01-89	06-30-93
Sheila Cromer... Thomasville		10-30-85	06-30-89
chairwoman		10-30-85	
Franklin D. Daniels.. Fayetteville		10-30-85	06-30-89
Frederick Frazier, Jr. .... Wilmington		09-07-90	06-30-94
Melissa R. Holden... Clayton		10-28-88	06-30-89
		07-01-89	06-30-93
J. D. Jackson .... Asheville		08-29-86	06-30-90
		09-07-90	06-30-94
John H. Miller.. Raleigh		10-31-85	06-30-90
vice-chairman		10-31-85	
		07-01-89	06-30-93
vice-chairman		07-01-89	
John G. Morris III .... Siler City		09-19-86	06-30-90
Kristi Moyer .... Wilson		09-07-90	06-30-94
Lee F. Pascasio .... Greenville		08-29-86	06-30-90
Elijah Peterson .... Rockingham		08-29-86	06-30-90
chairman		07-01-89	
		09-07-90	06-30-94
chairman		09-07-90	

---

[2]The Commission on Children and Youth was abolished; G.S. 120-70.7 through G.S. 120-70.30 were repealed under *N.C. Session Laws, 1989*, II, c. 802, s. 10.3, ratified August 12, 1989.

GOVERNOR'S ADVOCACY COUNCIL ON CHILDREN AND YOUTH
(CONTINUED)

Valerie Quinter	Charlotte	10-30-85	06-30-89
William E. Reed	Greensboro	10-30-85	06-30-89
Susannah Russell	Goldsboro	10-30-85	06-30-89
Jeffrey Samuels	Fayetteville	08-29-86	06-30-90
Kitty Simons	Durham	08-29-86	06-30-90
Alda C. Smith	Salisbury	01-03-93	06-30-94
Katherine B. Southerland	Charlotte	08-29-86	06-30-89
Gail Stewart	Lexington	07-01-89	06-30-93
Larry G. Talley	Thomasville	03-02-92	06-30-93
Meredith D. Tucker	Rocky Mount	08-03-88	06-30-90
Frank Verdi	Reidsville	08-29-86	06-30-89
		07-01-89	06-30-93
Gordon Walker	Greenville	09-07-90	06-30-94

BOARD OF STATE CONTRACT APPEALS [3]
G.S. 143-135.11/Board No. 0232

Name of Appointee	Address	Date Appointed	Date of Expiration
Paul A. DelaCourt	Raleigh	10-30-85	06-30-88
		07-01-88	06-30-92
Ross Persinger	Ayden	11-10-86	06-30-90
R. Dillard Teer	Durham	10-30-85	06-30-89
chairman		11-10-86	

NORTH CAROLINA COURTS COMMISSION
G.S. 7A-506/Board No. 0250

Name of Appointee	Address	Date Appointed	Date of Expiration
John D. Hicks	Charlotte	12-09-92	06-30-95
Arthur R. Ledford	Bakersville	07-01-85	06-30-89
Harold J. Long	Yadkinville	12-23-85	06-30-89
		11-21-89	06-30-93
Warren H. Owen	Charlotte	12-16-86	06-30-87
		07-01-87	06-30-91
		01-27-92	06-30-95
Johnathan L. Rhyne, Jr.	Lincolnton	07-01-85	06-30-89
chairman		08-15-86	06-30-87
chairman		07-01-87	06-30-89
		11-21-89	06-30-93
chairman		11-21-89	06-30-91
chairman		01-27-92	06-30-93
Clyde M. Roberts	Marshall	07-01-87	06-30-91
		01-27-92	06-30-95
Dan R. Simpson	Morganton	07-01-87	06-30-91
		01-27-92	06-30-95
Garland N. Yates	Asheboro	07-01-85	06-30-89
		11-21-89	06-30-93

---

[3]N.C. Session Laws, 1987, II, c. 847, abolished the Board of State Contract Appeals. The measure was ratified August 14, 1987 and became effective on October 1 of that year.

North Carolina Council on the Eastern Band of the Cherokee
G.S. 143B-411.1/Board No. 0192

Name of Appointee	Address	Date Appointed	Date of Expiration
Georgianna M. Carson	Bryson City	05-06-86	
George R. Hooper	Tuckasegee	07-01-92	06-30-96
Bill Lewis	Bryson City	05-09-91	06-30-92
Jack Thompson	Murphy	03-28-91	06-30-92

North Carolina Energy Development Authority
G.S. 159F-4/Board No. 0352

Name of Appointee	Address	Date Appointed	Date of Expiration
William E. Cox	Denver	10-30-85	09-30-87
		10-01-87	09-30-89
		10-19-89	09-30-91
Carson D. Culbreth	Raleigh	10-30-85	09-30-87
Harold Davis	Raleigh	10-30-85	09-30-87
chairman		10-30-85	
Vincent L. James	Charlotte	10-01-87	09-30-89
		10-19-89	09-30-91
Robert K. Koger	Raleigh	10-28-88	09-30-89
		10-19-89	09-30-91
Lonnie C. Poole, Jr.	Raleigh	10-30-85	09-30-87
		10-01-87	09-30-89
		10-19-89	09-30-91
Roger F. Rollman	Winston-Salem	10-01-87	09-30-89
		10-19-89	09-30-91
Jon Viegel	Research Triangle Park	10-30-85	09-30-87
		10-01-87	09-30-89
Jack R. Williams	Shelby	02-14-91	09-30-91

North Carolina Farmworkers' Council
G.S. 143B-426.25/Board No. 0365

Name of Appointee	Address	Date Appointed	Date of Expiration
Cheryl D. Benson, *chairwoman*	Benson	06-27-91	
John J. Collett, Jr.	Thomasville	06-27-91	
Frances F. Crofton	Durham	04-16-92	
Ronald Eaton	East Bend	05-03-85	
Bob Everett	Palmyra	05-03-85	
Sondra I. Riggs	Pollocksville	05-03-85	
W. Proctor Scarboro	Zebulon	08-17-87	
J. Emmett Sebrell	Charlotte	04-02-86	
Ralph M. Smith	Black Creek	05-03-85	
Windell L. Talley	Stanfield	09-01-87	

North Carolina Human Relations Council
G.S. 143B-392/Board No. 0440

Name of Appointee	Address	Date Appointed	Date of Expiration
Betty T. Anthony	Hickory	07-01-87	06-30-91
W. E. Banks	Thomasville	06-30-86	06-30-90
		07-02-90	06-30-94

NORTH CAROLINA HUMAN RELATIONS COUNCIL
(CONTINUED)

Ken Blankenship	Cherokee	09-15-85	06-30-89
Sonia H. Bounous	Morganton	10-23-91	06-30-95
Martin L. Brooks	Pembroke	07-01-88	06-30-92
John L. Carter III	Fayetteville	06-30-86	06-30-90
Vincent J. Colan	Hendersonville	06-30-86	06-30-87
Carolyn Cole	Pineville	12-31-92	06-30-96
Larry Fritz	Concord	04-16-92	06-30-93
Roosevelt Gardner, Jr.	Charlotte	09-24-87	06-30-89
Jack E. Gloyne	Cherokee	07-01-89	06-30-93
Rachel B. Guthrie	Sanford	07-01-87	06-30-91
Dossie M. Harrison-Goode	Roxboro	12-30-92	06-30-93
Margaret L. Hinesley	Pinehurst	03-05-90	06-30-92
		12-09-92	06-30-96
Ronald K. Ingle	Durham	09-15-85	06-30-89
		07-01-89	06-30-93
Ms. Willie J. Jennings	Goldsboro	06-30-86	06-30-90
		07-02-90	06-30-94
Aaron J. Johnson	Fayetteville	12-09-92	06-30-96
Constance H. Johnson	Winston-Salem	07-01-87	06-30-91
		10-23-91	06-30-95
chairwoman		03-04-92	
Mordecai W. Johnson	Dover	07-01-87	06-30-91
		10-23-91	06-30-95
Robert W. Kilroy	Surf City	07-01-88	06-30-92
		12-09-92	06-30-96
Robert H. Lineberger, Jr.	Lincolnton	12-27-88	06-30-92
Arnold Locklear	Pembroke	03-04-92	06-30-95
Pearl J. Logan	Greensboro	12-09-92	06-30-96
A. Parker Mills, Jr.	Monroe	07-01-88	06-30-92
William J. Moore	Fayetteville	07-22-87	06-30-89
Jimmie V. Morris	Oxford	09-16-85	06-30-89
chairman		09-16-85	
		07-01-89	06-30-93
chairman		07-01-89	
H. Dobbs Oxendine, Jr.	Lumberton	12-27-88	06-30-90
		07-02-90	06-30-94
Danita B. Parker	Durham	06-30-86	06-30-90
Angie T. Roberts	Statesville	07-01-88	06-30-92
Jimmie B. Shuler	Raleigh	12-27-88	06-30-90
		07-02-90	06-30-94
John E. Trotman	Elizabeth City	09-15-85	06-30-89
Eric White	Belmont	07-01-89	06-30-93
Steven D. Wyatt	Columbus	03-05-90	06-30-91

NORTH CAROLINA COMMISSION OF INDIAN AFFAIRS
G.S. 143B-407/Board No. 0460

Name of Appointee	Address	Date Appointed	Date of Expiration
Ms. Patrick O. Clark, *chairwoman*	Charlotte	07-30-90	
W. Lonnie Revels, Sr., *chairman*	Greensboro	05-14-85	

NORTH CAROLINA STATE INDIAN HOUSING AUTHORITY
G.S. 157-68/Board No. 0461

Name of Appointee	Address	Date Appointed	Date of Expiration
James S. Brewer	Greensboro	08-25-89	06-30-94
Sybil J. Bullard	Pembroke	12-16-86	06-30-91
		08-27-91	06-30-96
Lee R. Epps	Charlotte	12-16-86	06-30-88
		07-01-88	06-30-93
Haynes A. Graham, Sr.	Lake Waccamaw	12-09-92	06-30-97
Raymond Hammonds	Chadbourn	08-25-89	06-30-92
James A. Hardin	Fayetteville	12-16-86	06-30-87
Anthony D. Hunt	Red Springs	12-30-92	06-30-97
James A. Hunt	Red Springs	09-09-87	06-30-89
Larry P. Jacobs	Fayetteville	09-09-87	06-30-92
		12-09-92	06-30-97
Willard Locklear	Clinton	08-25-89	06-30-93
Masager T. Richardson	Hollister	12-16-86	06-30-90
William R. Richardson	Hollister	11-01-88	06-30-90
		07-02-90	06-30-95

NORTH CAROLINA INTERNSHIP COUNCIL
G.S. 143B-418/Board No. 0480

Name of Appointee	Address	Date Appointed	Date of Expiration
Belinda Bagnal	Cary	11-10-86	06-30-87
		07-01-87	06-30-89
		07-24-89	06-30-91
Anna K. Baird	Apex	08-25-89	06-30-91
		08-01-91	06-30-93
Joe S. Blair	Mars Hill	10-30-85	06-30-87
		07-01-87	06-30-89
		07-24-89	06-30-91
		08-01-91	06-30-93
Charles L. Cahill	Wilmington	07-24-89	06-30-91
		08-01-91	06-30-93
L. Raymond Camp	Cary	12-02-85	06-30-87
chairman		12-02-85	
chairman		07-01-87	06-30-89
		07-24-89	06-30-91
chairman		07-24-89	
chairman		08-01-91	06-30-93
Bruce L. Daughtry	Ahoskie	08-01-91	06-30-93
Fred B. Davenport, Jr.	Wilmington	03-13-87	06-30-87
		07-01-87	06-30-89
D. Scott Dupree	Chapel Hill	10-30-85	06-30-87
Anthony Eastman	Boiling Springs	11-20-85	06-30-87
Claude H. Farrell III	Wilmington	10-30-85	06-30-87
Roger G. Gaddis	Boiling Springs	07-01-87	06-30-89
		07-24-89	06-30-91
		08-01-91	06-30-93
Susan E. Garwood	North Wilkesboro	08-01-91	06-30-93
William H. Green	Salisbury	10-30-85	06-30-87
		07-01-87	06-30-89
John C. Hamil	Greensboro	10-30-85	06-30-87

NORTH CAROLINA INTERNSHIP COUNCIL
(CONTINUED)

Jenny Horton	Durham	10-30-85	06-30-87
		07-01-87	06-30-89
Edward Kelly	Goldsboro	11-20-85	06-30-87
		07-01-87	06-30-89
		07-24-89	06-30-91
		08-01-91	06-30-93
Ronald L. Kiziah	Hudson	08-25-89	06-30-91
		08-01-91	06-30-93
Seth T. Lawless	Franklinton	07-24-89	06-30-91
Louise W. Lewis	Raleigh	10-30-85	06-30-87
Michael Luger	Durham	10-30-85	06-30-87
Carolyn B. Meier	Raleigh	10-30-85	06-30-87
		07-01-87	06-30-89
Isaac H. Miller, Jr.	Greensboro	11-10-86	06-30-87
Caroline A. Nisbet	Durham	11-10-86	06-30-87
		07-01-87	06-30-89
		07-24-89	06-30-91
		08-01-91	06-30-93
Reeta Roy	Laurinburg	10-30-85	06-30-87
Gloria R. Scott	Greensboro	07-01-87	06-30-89
		07-24-89	06-30-91
Talbert O. Shaw	Raleigh	03-01-89	06-30-89
		07-24-89	06-30-91
		08-01-91	06-30-93
Gian Chand Sud	Charlotte	11-10-86	06-30-87
		07-01-87	06-30-89
Norma J. Thompson	Pembroke	08-01-91	06-30-93
Steven P. Wagner	Raleigh	08-15-86	06-30-87
		07-01-87	06-30-89
Beryl C. Waters	Greenville	08-01-91	06-30-93
Deil S. Wright	Chapel Hill	10-30-85	06-30-87
		07-01-87	06-30-89
		07-24-89	06-30-91
		08-01-91	06-30-93

GOVERNOR'S JOBS FOR VETERANS COMMITTEE
G.S. 143B-420/Board No. 0927

Name of Appointee	Address	Date Appointed	Date of Expiration
Michael W. Ayscue	Louisburg	04-14-86	
Charles F. Biesecker	Lexington	04-14-86	
Robert D. Brice	Maple	04-14-86	
Holland H. Chaffin	Mocksville	04-24-87	
Mr. Dorris Derrick	Fayetteville	07-02-90	
Thomas H. Fogleman	Liberty	06-16-89	
Preston F. Garris	Goldsboro	07-02-90	
Elmer E. Gordon	King	04-14-86	
Jim Harmon	Vilas	04-14-86	
Charles M. Harris, Sr., *chairman*	Charlotte	06-02-86	
Ronald B. Harrison	Weaverville	04-14-86	
Lola M. Holt	Salisbury	04-14-86	
Michael D. Lynch	Raleigh	07-02-90	
Ray V. Revels	Lumberton	06-26-86	

Governor's Jobs for Veterans Committee
(continued)

George T. Thorne, Jr.	Tarboro	06-16-89
James P. Uzzell	Goldsboro	04-14-86
Ashton P. Wiggs	Wilson	04-14-86
Coy D. Young	Lexington	07-02-90

Local Government Advocacy Council
G.S. 143-506.14/Board No. 0543

Name of Appointee	Address	Date Appointed	Date of Expiration
Cary D. Allred	Burlington	05-03-85	
Jefferson W. Brown	Charlotte	04-13-92	02-12-94
Esther M. Huntley	Elizabethtown	05-03-85	
		02-12-88	02-12-90
Betsy Justus	Cary	04-13-92	02-12-94
Bob Phillips	Taylorsville	02-12-88	02-12-90
		03-15-90	02-12-92
Robert Robertson	King	02-12-88	02-12-90
		03-15-90	02-12-92
Jim Warren	Lincolnton	03-15-90	02-12-92
		04-13-92	02-12-94

North Carolina Low-Level Radioactive Waste Management Authority
G.S. 104G-5/Board No. 0548

Name of Appointee	Address	Date Appointed	Date of Expiration
Stephen G. Conrad	Raleigh	07-25-90	06-30-94
Warren G. Corgan	Greensboro	01-15-92	06-30-94
Tenney I. Deane, Jr.	Raleigh	04-22-88	06-30-93
chairman		04-22-88	
Elizabeth H. Drury	Charlotte	08-28-87	06-30-90
		07-25-90	06-30-94
Merril Eisenbud	Chapel Hill	08-28-87	06-30-93
chairman		08-28-87	
R. Michael Jones	Raleigh	12-21-88	06-30-93
Harry E. LeGrand	Raleigh	08-28-87	06-30-90
John W. McAlister	Charlotte	08-28-87	06-30-92
		09-22-92	06-30-96
Raymond L. Murray, *vice-chairman*	Raleigh	09-25-87	
chairman		12-15-88	
Frederick L. Van Swearingen	Winston-Salem	10-03-89	06-30-92
Constance K. Walker	Durham	08-28-87	06-30-91
vice-chairwoman		01-23-89	
vice-chairwoman		10-17-91	06-30-95

North Carolina Marine Science Council [4]
G.S. 143B-390/Board No. 0555

Name of Appointee	Address	Date Appointed	Date of Expiration
Celia Bonaventura	Beaufort	11-20-85	06-30-89
John E. Bradshaw, Jr.	Wilmington	10-31-90	06-30-93
Lawrence B. Cahoon	Wilmington	11-20-85	06-30-87
		12-17-87	06-30-91
John J. Carroll	Camp Lejeune	09-29-89	06-30-93
B. J. Copeland	Raleigh	12-17-87	06-30-91
William S. Crumlish	Fayetteville	09-29-89	06-30-93
Margaret W. Curtis	Salisbury	05-17-88	06-30-91
Thomas J. Dalzell	Camp Lejeune	12-17-87	06-30-89
Harold W. Dubach	Wilmington	09-29-89	06-30-93
Gilliam S. Dunn	Sneads Ferry	09-29-89	06-30-93
Ed Foss	Wilmington	12-17-87	06-30-91
J. Webb Fuller	Nags Head	11-20-85	06-30-87
William C. Gray	Kitty Hawk	12-17-87	06-30-91
Daniel A. Hunt	Franklinton	09-29-89	06-30-93
Adrian D. Hurst	Wilmington	11-20-85	06-30-89
		09-29-89	06-30-93
Jimmy R. Jenkins	Elizabeth City	12-17-87	06-30-89
		09-29-89	06-30-93
Joseph J. Kalo	Chapel Hill	09-29-89	06-30-93
Michael K. Orbach	Greenville	03-13-86	06-30-89
chairman		03-13-86	
		09-29-89	06-30-93
chairman		09-29-89	
Graham Penny	Morehead City	12-17-87	06-30-91
Lockwood Phillips	Morehead City	09-29-89	06-30-93
Horace B. Robertson, Jr.	Durham	09-29-89	06-30-93
Arthur Smith	Charlotte	01-15-86	06-30-87
		12-17-87	06-30-91
Mary Strickland	Southport	12-30-87	06-30-91
Kenneth C. Wagner	Morehead City	01-15-86	06-30-87
		12-17-87	06-30-91
Jule D. Wheatly	Beaufort	11-20-85	06-30-87
Julian I. Wooten	Jacksonville	10-31-90	06-30-93

North Carolina Council on Ocean Affairs
G.S. 143B-39.11/Board No. 0551

Name of Appointee	Address	Date Appointed	Date of Expiration
Lawrence B. Cahoon	Wilmington	12-12-91	09-30-93
B. J. Copeland	Apex	12-12-91	09-30-95
J. E. Easley, Jr.	Raleigh	12-12-91	09-30-95
Joseph J. Kalo	Chapel Hill	12-12-91	09-30-95
Donald A. Kirkman	Pine Knoll Shores	12-12-91	09-30-93
Michael K. Orbach	Greenville	12-12-91	09-30-93
Roger N. Schecter	Wake Forest	12-12-91	
Paul A. Shumaker, Jr.	Youngsville	12-12-91	

[4]The legislation that created the North Carolina Council on Ocean Affairs also abolished the North Carolina Marine Science Council; see *N.C. Session Laws, 1991*, I, c. 320, ratified June 19, 1991.

GOVERNOR'S ADVOCACY COUNCIL FOR PERSONS WITH DISABILITIES
G.S. 143B-403.2/Board No. 0683

Name of Appointee	Address	Date Appointed	Date of Expiration
Judy W. Brooks	Andrews	09-22-89	06-30-91
Robert A. Bryan, Jr.	Garner	06-30-86	06-30-89
		09-22-89	06-30-93
William F. Bulow	Ayden	09-22-89	06-30-93
Richard B. Conoly	Fuquay-Varina	07-15-85	06-30-87
		07-01-87	06-30-91
vice-chairman		07-01-87	
Madelyn Efird	Locust	09-30-87	06-30-89
		09-22-89	06-30-93
LuAnne Forrest	Sylva	09-22-89	06-30-93
Judge W. Fowler	Huntersville	01-09-91	06-30-91
		03-02-92	06-30-93
Ruth Gibson	Maiden	07-01-87	06-30-91
Marian Grant	Raleigh	01-31-86	06-30-87
Sandra L. Grissom	Raleigh	01-30-87	06-30-87
Cynthia T. Harton	Newton	07-01-87	06-30-91
Jesse R. James	Raleigh	07-15-85	06-30-86
		06-30-86	06-30-89
Ruth S. Kadis	Goldsboro	03-02-92	06-30-93
James M. Keane	Charlotte	07-15-85	06-30-87
Pam McElhaney	Durham	06-30-86	06-30-89
Deborah C. McKeithan, *chairwoman*	Charlotte	07-01-87	06-30-91
chairwoman		03-02-92	06-30-95
Ethelyne W. Matthews	Autryville	09-22-89	06-30-93
George E. Midgett	Denver	03-02-92	06-30-93
Nancy S. Myers	Winston-Salem	09-22-89	06-30-93
Martin T. Pierson	Durham	07-15-85	06-30-87
		07-01-87	06-30-91
Mrs. Edwin S. Poole III	Charlotte	07-01-87	06-30-91
J. Stephen Ramey	Raleigh	12-30-87	06-30-89
Don M. Shanks	Pfafftown	07-15-85	06-30-86
		06-30-86	06-30-89
Lacy E. Simpson	Selma	07-15-85	06-30-86
		06-30-86	06-30-89
E. D. Smart	Newton	07-15-85	06-30-87
C. Joe Sturz	Greenville	07-15-85	06-30-86
		06-30-86	06-30-89
Cindy Teal	Weddington	07-15-85	06-30-87
		07-01-87	06-30-91
Bernadette E. Thompson	Asheville	07-15-85	06-30-86
		06-30-86	06-30-89
		09-22-89	06-30-93
		03-02-92	06-30-95
James H. Wells	Greensboro	03-13-86	06-30-87
		06-30-86	06-30-89
		09-22-89	06-30-93
vice-chairman		09-22-89	
		03-02-92	06-30-95
Durham C. White, Jr.	Saint Pauls	09-01-87	06-30-91
		03-02-92	06-30-95

Board of Trustees of the North Carolina Public Employee Deferred Compensation Plan
G.S. 143B-426.24/Board No. 3075

Name of Appointee	Address	Date Appointed	Date of Expiration
George L. Coxhead	Chapel Hill	09-15-85	
David Kepple	Winston-Salem	09-15-85	
Robert F. Newton	Raleigh	09-15-85	
		04-14-87	
Mark N. Poovey	Winston-Salem	04-14-87	
Robert N. Pulliam	Winston-Salem	05-24-89	
Donald Umstead	Raleigh	04-14-87	

Public Radio Advisory Committee
G.S. 143B-426.12/Board No. 0748

Name of Appointee	Address	Date Appointed	Date of Expiration
John Brock	Shelby	07-02-90	06-30-92
Ralph C. Burroughs, Jr.	Winston-Salem	10-17-91	06-30-93
Jack S. Childs	Raleigh	07-01-92	06-30-94
Valerie J. Daye	Raleigh	09-27-91	06-30-93
Joanne V. Latham	Cary	12-04-92	06-30-94
Robert G. Lyle	Durham	09-19-86	06-30-88
Margaret B. Murchison	Sanford	11-20-85	06-30-87
		07-01-87	06-30-89
		07-01-89	06-30-91
L. Pace Poag	Greensboro	11-20-85	06-30-87
Mrs. Lou H. Proctor	Pollocksville	09-19-86	06-30-87
		07-01-87	06-30-89
		07-01-89	06-30-91
		09-27-91	06-30-93
Vera S. Robinson	Winston-Salem	09-19-86	06-30-88
		07-01-88	06-30-90
		07-02-90	06-30-92
		07-01-92	06-30-94
Barbara J. Ryans	Asheville	09-19-86	06-30-88
Hal C. Sharpe	Nashville	07-01-88	06-30-90
		07-02-90	06-30-92
		07-01-92	06-30-94
Jan Thompson	Charlotte	11-20-85	06-30-87
		07-01-87	06-30-89
		07-01-89	06-30-91
Alfred Wright	Hickory	07-01-88	06-30-90

Board of Public Telecommunications Commissioners
G.S. 143B-426.9/Board No. 0893

Name of Appointee	Address	Date Appointed	Date of Expiration
Lawrence Behr	Greenville	08-25-89	06-30-93
		12-30-92	06-30-96
George F. Bland	Cary	01-02-87	06-30-90
Eugene H. Bohi	High Point	09-28-88	06-30-92
		12-30-92	06-30-96

BOARD OF PUBLIC TELECOMMUNICATIONS COMMISSIONERS
(CONTINUED)

Frank Bright	Durham	09-21-88	06-30-92
James T. Broyhill	Raleigh	04-10-89	04-01-90
Annette Bryant	Marion	12-23-85	06-30-87
William W. Cobey, Jr.	Chapel Hill	04-10-89	04-01-90
Arthur Cooley	Hendersonville	09-21-88	06-30-92
Joseph W. Dean	Apex	04-01-87	04-01-88
		04-01-91	03-31-92
Patric Dorsey	Raleigh	04-01-87	04-01-88
Thomas L. Drew	Durham	07-16-92	06-30-94
Allyson K. Duncan	Durham	01-09-91	06-30-94
Stuart W. Epperson	Winston-Salem	09-21-88	06-30-92
		12-30-92	06-30-96
David T. Flaherty	Raleigh	03-11-88	04-01-89
		04-22-92	03-31-93
Randall O. Fraser	Raleigh	01-02-87	06-30-90
		01-09-91	06-30-94
Wade Hargrove	Raleigh	09-21-88	
Thomas J. Harrelson	Raleigh	05-02-90	04-01-91
		12-30-92	06-30-96
James A. Heavner	Chapel Hill	01-02-87	06-30-90
John C. Hunter	Raleigh	12-30-92	06-30-96
Aaron J. Johnson	Fayetteville	04-14-86	04-01-87
		05-02-90	04-01-91
Betsy Justus	Cary	04-01-91	03-31-92
Estell C. Lee	Raleigh	04-22-92	03-31-93
Boyce C. Morrow, Jr.	Charlotte	01-02-87	06-30-88
		09-21-88	06-30-92
		12-30-92	06-30-96
D. Wayne Peterson	Tarboro	01-24-89	06-30-92
Charles W. Pickelsimer, Jr.	Brevard	09-21-88	06-30-92
Helen A. Powers	Raleigh	03-11-88	04-01-89
J. Billie Ray, Jr.	Charlotte	01-09-91	06-30-94
S. Thomas Rhodes	Raleigh	04-14-86	04-01-87
Jim Rouse	Greenville	12-30-92	06-30-96
John E. Thomas, *chairman*	Boone	01-02-87	
		09-21-88	06-30-92
Jan Thompson, *vice-chairwoman*	Charlotte	07-10-87	
		10-17-91	06-30-94

NORTH CAROLINA BOARD OF SCIENCE AND TECHNOLOGY
G.S. 143B-426.31/Board No. 0825

Name of Appointee	Address	Date Appointed	Date of Expiration
David E. Benevides	Cary	09-20-91	06-30-95
James N. Brown, Jr.	Hillsborough	10-03-89	06-30-93
James T. Broyhill	Raleigh	07-01-89	06-30-93
William Byrd	Boone	01-24-86	06-30-89
		07-01-89	06-30-93
Thomas B. Clegg	Chapel Hill	09-20-91	06-30-95
Norman R. Cohen	Charlotte	07-01-87	06-30-91
		09-20-91	06-30-95
vice-chairman		09-20-91	

NORTH CAROLINA BOARD OF SCIENCE AND TECHNOLOGY
(CONTINUED)

Mary Dell-Chilton	Raleigh	07-01-89	06-30-93
Thomas S. Elleman	Raleigh	01-24-86	06-30-89
Gerald W. Esch	Winston-Salem	07-01-87	06-30-91
		09-20-91	06-30-95
Edward B. Fort	Greensboro	09-07-90	06-30-91
Joe W. Grisham	Chapel Hill	08-29-86	06-30-87
		07-01-87	06-30-91
Charles E. Hamner	Chapel Hill	10-17-91	06-30-93
Franklin D. Hart	Cary	07-01-89	06-30-93
Howard H. Haworth	Morganton	01-27-86	06-30-89
		07-01-87	06-30-91
Matthew Kuhn	Chapel Hill	10-17-91	06-30-93
Estell C. Lee	Raleigh	06-24-91	06-30-93
Linda W. Little	Raleigh	07-01-89	06-30-93
Harold L. Martin, Sr.	Greensboro	12-30-92	06-30-93
Judy Mendenhall	High Point	01-24-86	06-30-89
Forest O. Mixon	Research Triangle Park	01-24-86	06-30-89
vice-chairman		06-25-87	
Claude E. Pope	Raleigh	03-06-87	06-30-89
Samuel C. Powell	Burlington	09-20-91	06-30-95
Charles E. Putman	Durham	07-01-87	06-30-91
vice-chairman		07-01-89	06-30-91
		09-20-91	06-30-95
John Ruffin	Durham	07-01-87	06-30-91
Ravindra P. Sinha	Elizabeth City	09-20-91	06-30-95
H. O. Williams	High Point	05-15-87	06-30-89

STATE GOALS AND POLICY BOARD
G.S. 143B-372/Board No. 0870

Name of Appointee	*Address*	*Date Appointed*	*Date of Expiration*
Marcus D. Allred	Raleigh	03-13-86	03-13-90
Charles R. Burrell	Hendersonville	03-14-90	03-13-94
Fred S. Cates, Jr.	Hillsborough	07-02-90	03-13-91
Stanley Frank	Greensboro	03-13-86	03-13-90
E. K. Fretwell, Jr.	Charlotte	02-27-87	03-13-91
M. Laney Funderburk, Jr.	Durham	09-15-85	03-13-89
Edward S. Goode	Charlotte	03-13-89	03-13-93
Ray Graichen	Pinehurst	09-15-85	03-13-89
R. Jack Hawke	Raleigh	02-27-87	03-13-91
Michael A. Heekin	Hickory	03-14-90	03-13-94
Hamilton C. Horton, Jr.,	Winston-Salem	09-15-85	03-13-89
vice-chairman		01-15-86	
		02-27-87	03-13-91
vice-chairman		02-27-87	
Eddie Knox	Charlotte	03-13-86	03-13-90
Charles R. Mosley	Asheville	12-10-86	03-15-87
		02-27-87	03-13-91
Kermit B. Nichols	Raleigh	09-30-87	03-13-90
		03-14-90	03-13-94
Kay F. Patseavouras	Greensboro	09-15-85	03-15-89
		03-13-86	03-13-90
		03-14-90	03-13-94

STATE GOALS AND POLICY BOARD
(CONTINUED)

James A. Pope	Raleigh	12-23-85	03-13-87
		02-27-87	03-13-91
Tyronza R. Richmond	Durham	03-13-86	03-13-90
		03-14-90	03-13-94
Morton D. Rochelle	Salisbury	03-13-89	03-13-93
Donald L. Smith	Raleigh	02-13-89	03-13-91
Larry N. Stern	Mars Hill	09-15-85	03-13-89
		03-13-89	03-13-93
B. Gloyden Stewart, Jr.	Wilson	09-15-85	03-13-89
		03-13-89	03-13-93
Jean Webber	Charlotte	09-15-85	03-13-89
		03-13-89	03-13-93

VETERANS' AFFAIRS COMMISSION
G.S. 143B-400/Board No. 0925

Name of Appointee	Address	Date Appointed	Date of Expiration
Granville H. Cheek	Hamptonville	08-09-89	06-30-93
Stephen T. Daniel	Morganton	11-06-89	06-30-90
Thomas Dlugos	Hickory	06-30-86	06-30-90
Daniel W. Fouts	Greensboro	10-30-87	06-30-91
Harvey W. Hall	King	02-26-86	06-30-89
		08-09-89	06-30-93
Ben B. Halterman	Wilmington	08-09-89	06-30-93
chairman		08-09-89	
Edward A. Hirst	Salisbury	08-09-89	06-30-93
T. Clay Houston	Newland	08-09-89	06-30-93
J. Reid Lawrence	Morganton	11-07-90	06-30-93
Hoyt R. Moore	Yanceyville	08-09-89	06-30-93
J. Van Myers	Greensboro	11-06-89	06-30-91
		08-27-91	06-30-95
Otto W. Ritter	Holly Ridge	08-09-89	06-30-93
Betty H. Rowland	Pittsboro	08-09-89	06-30-93
Edward M. Tetterton	Washington	08-09-89	06-30-93

NORTH CAROLINA COUNCIL FOR WOMEN [5]
G.S. 143B-394/Board No. 0967

Name of Appointee	Address	Date Appointed	Date of Expiration
Judith S. Abbott	Camden	07-21-86	06-30-88
		07-01-88	06-30-90
		07-25-90	06-30-92
		08-04-92	06-30-94
Jo Ann Bishop	Fayetteville	07-30-87	06-30-89
		07-01-89	06-30-91
		10-17-91	06-30-93
Elsie R. Blice	Forest City	04-16-92	06-30-92
		08-04-92	06-30-94
Brenda B. Bright	Morehead City	07-21-89	06-30-91
		10-17-91	06-30-93
Brenda B. Campbell	Charlotte	07-30-87	06-30-89
		07-01-89	06-30-91
		10-17-91	06-30-93

[5]*N.C. Session Laws, 1991*, I, c. 134, ratified May 27, transformed the Council on the Status of Women into the North Carolina Council for Women.

North Carolina Council for Women
(continued)

Doris Conoly	Greensboro	07-30-87	06-30-89
Mary A. Crocker	Elizabeth City	04-16-92	06-30-92
		08-04-92	06-30-94
Betty W. Ellen	Wilmington	07-01-88	06-30-89
		07-01-89	06-30-91
		10-17-91	06-30-93
Marilyn C. Flanary	Durham	07-21-86	06-30-87
		07-30-87	06-30-89
		07-01-89	06-30-91
		10-17-91	06-30-93
Margot M. Flood	Durham	08-04-92	06-30-94
Donna M. Foster	Southern Pines	10-03-88	06-30-89
		07-01-89	06-30-91
Susan W. Good	Rutherfordton	11-06-89	06-30-90
		07-25-90	06-30-92
Edgar B. Gregory	Wilkesboro	10-28-88	06-30-90
Karen B. Hastings	Boone	07-21-86	06-30-88
chairwoman		07-30-87	
Teresa A. Helmlinger	Clayton	07-25-90	06-30-91
		10-17-91	06-30-93
Carol H. Holder	Franklinton	08-04-92	06-30-94
Ruth B. Hoover	High Point	07-21-86	06-30-88
		07-01-88	06-30-90
L. David Huffman	Newton	07-01-88	06-30-90
		07-25-90	06-30-92
Leon D. Kay	Winston-Salem	01-24-89	06-30-89
		07-01-89	06-30-91
		10-17-91	06-30-93
Anne G. Little	Charlotte	05-15-86	06-30-87
		07-30-87	06-30-89
		07-01-89	06-30-91
		10-17-91	06-30-93
M. Grace Loftin-Hayes	Monroe	02-27-89	06-30-89
		07-01-89	06-30-91
Buck Lyda	Fairview	07-21-86	06-30-88
Irene E. Manning	Hickory	07-21-86	06-30-88
		07-01-88	06-30-90
		07-25-90	06-30-92
		08-04-92	06-30-94
Mark D. Martin	Raleigh	08-04-92	06-30-94
Nancy Miller	Asheville	07-30-87	06-30-89
Beverly R. Mitchell	Winston-Salem	07-30-87	06-30-89
Richard T. Morgan	Pinehurst	07-21-86	06-30-88
C. Louise Nelson	Davidson	07-21-86	06-30-88
		07-01-88	06-30-90
		07-25-90	06-30-92
Betty J. Pearce	Greensboro	07-30-87	06-30-89
Maxine W. Phillipi	Salisbury	07-25-90	06-30-92
		08-04-92	06-30-94
Emily O. Rankin	Raleigh	10-30-85	06-30-87
		07-30-87	06-30-89
Grace J. Rohrer	Deep Gap	07-01-88	06-30-90
		07-25-90	06-30-92
Dottie W. Salerno	Greensboro	04-16-92	06-30-92
		08-04-92	06-30-94

NORTH CAROLINA COUNCIL FOR WOMEN
(CONTINUED)

Charee C. Schulman	Asheville	10-17-91	06-30-93
Jerri Sellers	Lumberton	09-01-87	06-30-88
		07-01-88	06-30-90
Patricia D. Smithson	Wilmington	07-21-86	06-30-88
A. Leon Stanback, Jr.	Durham	07-25-90	06-30-92
Mary L. Sugg	Greenville	07-01-88	06-30-90
Timothy N. Tallent	Concord	07-01-88	06-30-90
Saravette R. Trotter	Rocky Mount	07-21-86	06-30-88
Clara F. Underwood	Raleigh	03-28-91	06-30-92
Anna M. Wagoner	Salisbury	12-27-89	06-30-90
		07-25-90	06-30-92
Mary A. Warren	Winston-Salem	07-21-86	06-30-88
		07-01-88	06-30-90
Barbara G. Washington	Greensboro	07-25-90	06-30-92
chairwoman		02-22-91	
chairwoman		08-04-92	06-30-94
Karen H. Watford	Thomasville	03-02-92	06-30-93
Geraldine M. Weeks	Elizabeth City	09-01-87	06-30-89
		07-01-89	06-30-91
		10-17-91	06-30-93

STATE YOUTH ADVISORY COUNCIL
G.S. 143B-386/Board No. 0970

Name of Appointee	Address	Date Appointed	Date of Expiration
Michael W. Baker	Lincolnton	02-13-89	06-30-89
		11-21-89	06-30-91
		08-26-91	06-30-93
Valerie Ballance	Warrenton	10-01-90	06-30-91
Wanda A. Barnard	Moyock	08-26-91	06-30-93
Iris Battle	Charlotte	07-01-85	06-30-87
		09-15-87	06-30-89
Clyde Benedict	Winston-Salem	07-01-85	06-30-87
		09-15-87	06-30-89
Lea A. Boykin	Wrightsville Beach	07-14-92	06-30-93
Amy M. Brann	Wake Forest	10-01-90	06-30-91
Milledge T. Brodie IV	Charlotte	10-01-90	06-30-91
Jonathan Brooks	Dunn	09-15-87	06-30-88
Carla A. Byrd	Wilmington	08-26-91	06-30-92
		07-14-92	06-30-93
Michelle Carawan	Knightdale	09-15-87	06-30-88
Andrea M. Cashion	Thomasville	08-15-88	06-30-89
		11-21-89	06-30-90
Harold B. Cloud	Wilmington	08-26-91	06-30-93
chairman		12-02-91	
Dana R. Cockrell	Plymouth	03-13-86	06-30-86
		06-30-86	06-30-87
William C. Corriher	Boone	12-02-91	06-30-93
Michael D. Crouse	Yadkinville	01-15-86	06-30-87
Carol L. Darr	Archdale	09-15-87	06-30-89
		11-21-89	06-30-91
Cosmos N. George II	Warrenton	08-26-91	06-30-92

State Youth Advisory Council
(continued)

Timothy N. Goodman	Rockwell	11-21-89	06-30-91
Carol A. Harrington	Rocky Mount	07-01-85	06-30-87
		09-15-87	06-30-89
Lee Hartsell	Concord	08-26-91	06-30-92
		07-14-92	06-30-93
Robert Hede	Rockingham	07-01-85	06-30-87
		09-15-87	06-30-89
chairman		09-15-87	
Elizabeth P. Hedgecoe	Fayetteville	03-25-88	06-30-89
		11-21-89	06-30-91
Jonathan C. Hickman	Charlotte	08-15-88	06-30-89
Jenny P. Horton	Durham	11-21-89	06-30-91
		08-26-91	06-30-93
Richard L. Houghton III	Jacksonville	09-15-87	06-30-88
Reggie Hundley	Belmont	07-01-85	06-30-87
		09-15-87	06-30-89
Shelby M. Johnson	Greensboro	11-21-89	06-30-90
Eddie Jones	Rocky Mount	11-21-89	06-30-90
John R. Little	Raleigh	01-15-86	06-30-86
Ralph E. Lowrance	Belmont	07-01-85	06-30-87
		09-15-87	06-30-89
Bob Mazzoni	Salisbury	07-01-85	06-30-86
David Miner	Washington, D.C.	07-01-85	06-30-87
Douglas V. Moon	Hendersonville	09-15-87	06-30-89
		11-21-89	06-30-91
chairman		11-21-89	
Robert G. Morgan	Carrboro	07-01-85	06-30-87
Teresa L. Nash	Avon	08-26-91	06-30-92
Terry E. Osborne	Salisbury	08-26-91	06-30-93
Charles R. Poole	Atlantic Beach	11-21-89	06-30-90
		10-01-90	06-30-91
Thomas M. Powe III	Winston-Salem	06-30-86	07-30-87
Tina Ruffin	Blanch	07-14-92	06-30-93
Thomas W. Simmons	Raleigh	11-21-89	06-30-91
		08-26-91	06-30-93
Jeffrey B. Smith	Asheville	06-30-86	07-30-87
Benny Stewart	Raleigh	09-15-87	06-30-88
		08-15-88	06-30-89
Miss Benji F. Taylor	Raleigh	06-30-86	07-30-87
Mrs. Peter K. Thompson	Charlotte	07-01-85	06-30-87
Betty J. Toler	Princeton	09-15-87	06-30-89
Kathryn M. Virkler	Charlotte	08-16-88	06-30-89
J. LaTerrie Ward	Goldsboro	08-26-91	06-30-93
Hildred T. Watkins	Lewisvlle	11-21-89	06-30-91
Mary A. Weiss	Swansboro	02-13-89	06-30-89
		11-21-89	06-30-91
		08-26-91	06-30-93
Richard J. White III	Chapel Hill	01-15-86	06-30-86
		01-30-87	06-30-87
		09-15-87	06-30-89
Walter Zelasko	Winston-Salem	11-21-89	06-30-91
		08-26-91	06-30-93

DEPARTMENT OF AGRICULTURE

Board of Agriculture
G.S. 106-2/Board No. 0010

Name of Appointee	Address	Date Apppointed	Date of Expiration
D. Bruce Cuddy	Marshville	07-15-85	05-04-91
		06-04-91	05-04-97
Rena M. I. Danieley	Burlington	03-17-87	05-04-91
J. Reid Gray	Stony Point	05-16-89	05-04-95
William E. Holliday	Snow Camp	06-04-91	05-04-97
John C. Howard, Jr.	Deep Run	05-04-87	05-04-93
Pete Lovette	Wilkesboro	05-04-87	05-04-93
Sam McLawhorn	Grifton	05-16-89	05-04-95
G. Earl Rountree	Sunbury	05-04-87	05-04-93
Windell L. Talley	Stanfield	06-04-91	05-04-97
Sherry S. Thompson	Hendersonville	06-04-91	05-04-97
Richard W. Vaughan	Lasker	05-16-89	05-04-95

North Carolina Agricultural Finance Authority
G.S. 122D-4/Board No. 0009

Name of Appointee	Address	Date Appointed	Date of Expiration
W. Henry Hayes	Mebane	10-09-86	06-30-89
Josephus D. Jacobs	Charlotte	08-03-89	06-30-92
		07-01-92	06-30-95
William W. Linville	Kernersville	10-09-86	06-30-89
		08-03-89	06-30-92
		07-01-92	06-30-95
William L. Powell II	Windsor	09-14-92	06-30-95
Zeno O. Ratcliff	Pantego	10-09-86	06-30-89
		08-03-89	06-30-92
		07-01-92	06-30-95

North Carolina Agricultural Hall of Fame Board of Directors
G.S. 106-568.14/Board No. 0015

Name of Appointee	Address	Date Appointed	Date of Expiration
C. Dwight Howard	Kinston	04-30-87	01-27-93
Patricia C. Jones	Raleigh	02-15-89	01-27-95
Joe L. Kiser	Vale	11-20-85	01-27-91
Kenneth H. Roberson	Robersonville	06-25-87	01-27-91
Gene F. Sears	Apex	12-31-91	01-27-97

Gasoline and Oil Inspection Board
G.S. 119-26/Board No. 0395

Name of Appointee	Address	Date Appointed	Date of Expiration
David A. Wheatly	Beaufort	01-30-87	

GENETIC ENGINEERING REVIEW BOARD
G.S. 106-769/Board No. 0401

Name of Appointee	Address	Date Appointed	Date of Expiration
Stephen Dumford	Summerfield	10-19-89	10-01-92
		12-09-92	10-01-95
Hassell Thigpen	Tarboro	03-05-90	

ADVISORY COMMISSION FOR THE MUSEUM OF NATURAL HISTORY
G.S. 143-370/Board No. 0630

Name of Appointee	Address	Date Appointed	Date of Expiration
Zack C. Allen III	Asheville	10-22-86	08-31-87
		09-01-87	08-31-89
		11-21-89	08-31-91
		12-12-91	08-31-93
Betsy Bennett	Raleigh	12-12-91	08-31-93
Ken Blankenship	Cherokee	10-22-86	08-31-87
		09-01-87	08-31-89
Mae H. Block	Mount Pleasant	03-02-92	08-31-93
William W. Cobey, Jr.	Chapel Hill	02-10-89	08-31-89
		11-21-89	08-31-91
Stephen G. Conrad	Raleigh	10-22-86	08-31-87
		09-01-87	08-31-89
		11-21-89	08-31-91
Renee H. Coward	Sylva	11-21-89	08-31-91
		12-12-91	08-31-93
Cherrylle Deal	Raleigh	12-12-91	08-31-93
James Ferguson	Gastonia	12-12-91	08-31-93
Dirk Frankenberg	Hillsborough	10-22-86	08-31-87
		09-01-87	08-31-89
		11-21-89	08-31-91
		12-12-91	08-31-93
Rita G. Fuller	Durham	12-12-91	08-31-93
Charles R. Fullwood	Raleigh	10-22-86	08-31-87
		09-01-87	08-31-89
		11-21-89	08-31-91
		12-12-91	08-31-93
John B. Funderburg	Raleigh	10-22-86	08-31-87
		09-01-87	08-31-89
Charles H. Gardner	Chapel Hill	10-11-90	08-31-91
		12-12-91	08-31-93
Leland "D" Gottschalk	Warrenton	10-22-86	08-31-87
		09-01-87	08-31-89
		11-21-89	08-31-91
James A. Graham	Raleigh	11-10-86	08-31-87
		09-01-87	08-31-89
		11-21-89	08-31-91
		12-12-91	08-31-93
Alexandra M. Hightower	Raleigh	10-22-86	08-31-87
		09-01-87	08-31-89
Joyce Hilliard-Clark	Raleigh	10-22-86	08-31-87
		09-01-87	08-31-89
		11-21-89	08-31-91

ADVISORY COMMISSION FOR THE MUSEUM OF NATURAL HISTORY
(CONTINUED)

Eloise K. Howard	Greenville	12-10-86	08-30-87
		09-01-87	08-31-89
		11-21-89	08-31-91
		12-12-91	08-31-93
Nancy J. Iseley	Burlington	10-22-86	08-31-87
		09-01-87	08-31-89
Gifford S. Nickerson	Raleigh	09-01-87	08-31-89
		11-21-89	08-31-91
		12-12-91	08-31-93
Ann M. Pugh	Asheboro	02-24-89	08-31-89
		11-21-89	08-31-91
S. Thomas Rhodes	Raleigh	10-22-86	08-31-87
		09-01-87	08-31-89
Ernest C. Sanders, Jr.	Tabor City	10-22-86	08-31-87
Thomas A. Stevens	Smithfield	12-12-91	08-31-93
Morris Thompson	Rocky Mount	10-22-86	08-31-87
		09-01-87	08-31-89
		11-21-89	08-31-91
		12-12-91	08-31-93
Betty Wallace	Raleigh	11-10-86	08-31-87
		09-01-87	08-31-89
		11-21-89	08-31-91
Helen M. Weaver	Greenville	04-13-92	08-31-93

NORTH CAROLINA PESTICIDE BOARD
G.S. 143-436/Board No. 0685

Name of Appointee	Address	Date Appointed	Date of Expiration
Jerry Coker	Plymouth	07-01-87	06-30-91
		08-01-91	06-30-95
Ray Forrest	Raleigh	02-27-87	07-01-89
		09-01-89	06-30-93
Melvin H. Hearn	Raleigh	11-20-85	07-01-89
Rudolph W. Jones	Benson	07-01-87	06-30-91
		08-01-91	06-30-95
Ronald H. Levine	Raleigh	11-20-85	07-01-89
		09-01-89	06-30-93
Edythe M. McKinney	Raleigh	09-01-89	06-30-93
Robert E. Ogle, Sr.	Raleigh	07-01-87	06-30-91
		08-01-91	06-30-95
Mary J. Pugh	Raleigh	12-04-88	06-30-89
S. Thomas Rhodes	Raleigh	11-20-85	07-01-89
John C. Stuart	Raleigh	02-21-86	06-30-89
Lu Ann Whitaker	Raleigh	10-31-90	06-30-91
		08-01-91	06-30-95
Carolyn P. Williams	Raleigh	07-01-87	06-30-91

NORTH CAROLINA PLANT CONSERVATION BOARD
G.S. 106-202.14/Board No. 0703

Name of Appointee	Address	Date Appointed	Date of Expiration
Wilbert W. Johnson	Raleigh	02-12-88	09-30-91
		12-02-91	09-30-95

NORTH CAROLINA PLANT CONSERVATION BOARD
(CONTINUED)

Jamie H. King, Jr.	New Bern	10-22-86	09-30-89
		11-06-89	09-30-93
Harry F. Layman	Raleigh	02-27-87	09-30-87
		02-12-88	09-30-91
Lorraine B. Spencer	Cary	04-13-92	09-30-95
Fred M. White	Durham	12-02-91	09-30-95
Peter S. White	Chapel Hill	11-10-86	09-30-89
		11-06-89	09-30-93

NORTH CAROLINA RURAL REHABILITATION CORPORATION
BOARD OF DIRECTORS
G.S. 137-31.3/Board No. 0800

Name of Appointee	Address	Date Appointed	Date of Expiration
R. Anderson Cain	Greensboro	03-17-87	11-30-89
Lewis C. Dozier	Supply	03-17-87	11-30-89
		03-15-90	11-30-92
		12-04-92	11-30-95
Dennis Meyers	Brasstown	03-17-87	11-30-89
		03-15-90	11-30-91
		12-12-91	11-30-94
Shirley Perry	Hertford	03-17-87	11-30-89
		03-15-90	11-30-92
		12-04-92	11-30-95
Stanley H. Staton	Dana	09-22-89	11-30-90
		12-01-90	11-30-93
James G. Tilley	Walnut Cove	12-01-87	11-30-90
Henry B. Winslow	Hamilton	03-15-90	11-30-91
		12-12-91	11-30-94

STRUCTURAL PEST CONTROL COMMITTEE
G.S. 106-65.23/Board No. 0875

Name of Appointee	Address	Date Appointed	Date of Expiration
W. Harden Blackwell	Greensboro	07-01-89	06-30-93
Charles A. Cooper	Raleigh	02-27-87	06-30-90
David R. Nimocks, Jr.	Fayetteville	07-31-85	06-30-89
Michael D. Philbeck	Shelby	11-19-91	06-30-93
J. W. Taylor III	Wilmington	07-25-90	06-30-94

DEPARTMENT OF COMMUNITY COLLEGES

STATE BOARD OF COMMUNITY COLLEGES
G.S. 115D-2.1/Board No. 0212

Name of Appointee	Address	Date Appointed	Date of Expiration
Royce N. Angel	Wilmington	07-30-87	06-30-93
U. James Bennett	Monroe	07-01-89	06-30-95
Ben M. Boddie	Rocky Mount	10-01-91	06-30-95
Joanne W. Bowie	Greensboro	07-01-85	06-30-91
Asa B. Dail	New Bern	07-01-85	06-30-91
		10-01-91	06-30-97

BEAUFORT COUNTY COMMUNITY COLLEGE BOARD OF TRUSTEES
G.S. 115D-12/Board No. 2025

Name of Appointee	Address	Date Appointed	Date of Expiration
Barry L. Gutfeld	Washington	06-01-85	06-30-89
		07-21-89	06-30-93
Warren S. Lane	Washington	12-30-92	06-30-93
Milan J. Muzinich	Washington	07-01-87	06-30-91
Frances J. Ratcliff	Pantego	02-24-89	06-30-91
		07-01-91	06-30-95
Allen T. Rhodes	Washington	07-14-92	06-30-96
Helen W. Sommerkamp	Aurora	07-14-92	06-30-93
		12-30-92	06-30-96
William M. Stephenson	Washington	12-27-89	06-30-90
		07-02-90	06-30-94

BLADEN COMMUNITY COLLEGE BOARD OF TRUSTEES
G.S. 115D-12/Board No. 2030

Name of Appointee	Address	Date Appointed	Date of Expiration
Nile Brisson, Jr.	Elizabethtown	07-21-89	06-30-93
D. M. Campbell, Jr.	Elizabethtown	08-01-91	06-30-95
Levy C. Pait	Bladenboro	07-01-87	06-30-91
		07-01-92	06-30-96
Essic M. Williams	Elizabethtown	07-02-90	06-30-94

BLUE RIDGE COMMUNITY COLLEGE BOARD OF TRUSTEES
G.S. 115D-12/Board No. 2035

Name of Appointee	Address	Date Appointed	Date of Expiration
Charles R. Burrell	Hendersonville	08-27-91	06-30-95
Robert H. Dowdeswell	Flat Rock	07-01-87	06-30-91
		07-01-92	06-30-96
Margaret L. Milroy	Hendersonville	01-09-91	06-30-94
Philip R. Milroy	Hendersonville	07-02-90	06-30-94
William S. Prim	Hendersonville	08-25-89	06-30-93

BRUNSWICK COMMUNITY COLLEGE BOARD OF TRUSTEES
G.S. 115D-12/Board No. 2037

Name of Appointee	Address	Date Appointed	Date of Expiration
William T. Bradsher	Shallotte	07-01-87	06-30-91
Malcolm Grissett	Shallotte	04-03-91	06-30-93
Jimmy Hobbs	Holden Beach	08-27-91	06-30-95
Mr. Kelly Holden	Shallotte	07-21-89	06-30-93
James H. Milliken	Shallotte	07-02-90	06-30-94
Albert Q. Wooten	Calabash	10-11-90	06-30-92
		07-01-92	06-30-96

LENOIR COMMUNITY COLLEGE BOARD OF TRUSTEES
G.S. 115D-12/Board No. 2145

Name of Appointee	Address	Date Appointed	Date of Expiration
Nancy Barwick	Kinston	09-14-90	06-30-94
Marilyn M. Cogdell	Kinston	07-01-85	06-30-89
A. Jack Harrell III	Kinston	07-01-87	06-30-91
		07-14-92	06-30-96
James A. Hodges, Jr.	Kinston	08-01-91	06-30-95
Cameron W. McRae	Kinston	07-14-92	06-30-95
Paul E. Porterfield	Grifton	08-03-89	06-30-93

McDOWELL TECHNICAL COMMUNITY COLLEGE BOARD OF TRUSTEES
G.S. 115D-12/Board No. 2150

Name of Appointee	Address	Date Appointed	Date of Expiration
Joyce M. Ellis	Old Fort	07-30-90	06-30-94
Hermon M. Huffman	Marion	07-01-85	06-30-89
Judi W. Jarvis	Marion	07-01-87	06-30-91
		07-01-92	06-30-96
C. Randy Pool	Marion	09-13-91	06-30-95
Donna C. Shaw	Marion	08-03-89	06-30-93

MARTIN COMMUNITY COLLEGE BOARD OF TRUSTEES
G.S. 115D-12/Board No. 2155

Name of Appointee	Address	Date Appointed	Date of Expiration
Joe R. Ayers	Oak City	09-27-91	06-30-95
Stan L. Crowe	Williamston	09-07-90	06-30-94
Henry C. Dunstan	Windsor	09-24-87	06-30-89
William M. Green	Robersonville	04-02-86	06-30-87
		07-01-87	06-30-91
		07-01-92	06-30-96
David L. Jennette, Sr.	Windsor	11-10-86	06-30-89
Joseph L. Mizelle, Jr.	Windsor	08-03-89	06-30-93

MAYLAND COMMUNITY COLLEGE BOARD OF TRUSTEES
G.S. 115D-12/Board No. 2160

Name of Appointee	Address	Date Appointed	Date of Expiration
J. Todd Bailey	Burnsville	03-13-87	06-30-87
		07-01-87	06-30-91
Janice E. Buchanan	Green Mountain	07-16-92	06-30-96
Louise H. Buchanan	Newland	09-26-90	06-30-94
Pat V. Eller	Newland	07-01-87	06-30-89
Betty H. Fox	Burnsville	08-25-89	06-30-93
Hal G. Harrison	Spruce Pine	06-11-86	06-30-89
Lois D. Hughes	Newland	10-19-89	06-30-90
Joyce S. Masters	Bakersville	08-01-91	06-30-95
Dudley Robertson	Burnsville	07-01-87	06-30-89
Ms. Myrle Slagle	Burnsville	02-12-88	06-30-89

PITT COMMUNITY COLLEGE BOARD OF TRUSTEES
G.S. 115D-12/Board No. 2190

Name of Appointee	Address	Date Appointed	Date of Expiration
William C. Byrd	Greenville	08-25-89	06-30-93
G. Henry Leslie	Greenville	07-02-90	06-30-94
Richard J. McKee	Greenville	07-01-85	06-30-89
Lorraine G. Shinn	Greenville	07-01-92	06-30-96
Joan B. Warren	Greenville	08-01-91	06-30-95
A. B. Whitley, Jr.	Greenville	07-01-87	06-30-91

RANDOLPH COMMUNITY COLLEGE BOARD OF TRUSTEES
G.S. 115D-12/Board No. 2195

Name of Appointee	Address	Date Appointed	Date of Expiration
Robert B. Davis	Sophia	08-31-85	06-30-89
		07-21-89	06-30-93
Joan S. Redding	Asheboro	07-01-87	06-30-91
		07-01-92	06-30-96
Joseph D. Ross, Jr.	Asheboro	07-01-91	06-30-95
Mrs. Ernest C. Watkins	Ramseur	07-02-90	06-30-94

RICHMOND COMMUNITY COLLEGE BOARD OF TRUSTEES
G.S. 115D-12/Board No. 2200

Name of Appointee	Address	Date Appointed	Date of Expiration
Richard G. Buckner	Rockingham	11-19-91	06-30-95
Ruth F. Inman	Rockingham	09-01-87	06-30-91
		07-14-92	06-30-96
Walter F. Long IV	Rockingham	07-02-90	06-30-94
James R. McLester	Rockingham	07-01-85	06-30-89
		07-21-89	06-30-93

ROANOKE-CHOWAN COMMUNITY COLLEGE BOARD OF TRUSTEES
G.S. 115D-12/Board No. 2205

Name of Appointee	Address	Date Appointed	Date of Expiration
Melvin L. Clayton	Murfreesboro	07-01-85	06-30-89
Joyce S. Daughtry	Ahoskie	08-27-91	06-30-95
Joyce Elliott	Sunbury	08-24-90	06-30-94
Susan H. Joyner	Ahoskie	07-21-89	06-30-93
John R. Lewis	Jackson	09-15-92	06-30-96
Dan T. Phillips	Murfreesboro	03-13-87	06-30-87
		07-01-87	06-30-91

ROBESON COMMUNITY COLLEGE BOARD OF TRUSTEES
G.S. 115D-12/Board No. 2210

Name of Appointee	Address	Date Appointed	Date of Expiration
H. Franklin Biggs, Sr.	Lumberton	07-01-87	06-30-91
		07-01-92	06-30-96
Sue W. Brown	Lumberton	08-01-91	06-30-95
Donald E. Metzger	Lumberton	07-10-90	06-30-94

SOUTHEASTERN COMMUNITY COLLEGE BOARD OF TRUSTEES
G.S. 115D-12/Board No. 2235

Name of Appointee	Address	Date Appointed	Date of Expiration
James C. Masten	Whiteville	07-02-90	06-30-94
Kenneth L. Miller, Jr.	Whiteville	07-14-92	06-30-96
Angus H. Monds	Whiteville	07-21-89	06-30-93
John E. Thompson	Whiteville	07-01-87	06-30-91
Alice S. Wright	Tabor City	08-26-91	06-30-95

SOUTHWESTERN COMMUNITY COLLEGE BOARD OF TRUSTEES
G.S. 115D-12/Board No. 2240

Name of Appointee	Address	Date Appointed	Date of Expiration
Orville D. Coward, Jr.	Franklin	08-01-91	06-30-95
Mary J. Ferguson	Cherokee	07-01-87	06-30-91
		09-18-92	06-30-96
Mrs. M. F. McDonald	Sylva	07-30-90	06-30-94
W. Calvin Myers	Bryson City	08-03-89	06-30-93
Judith G. Revis	Whittier	02-21-91	06-30-93

STANLY COMMUNITY COLLEGE BOARD OF TRUSTEES
G.S. 115D-12/Board No. 2250

Name of Appointee	Address	Date Appointed	Date of Expiration
Darrell E. Almond	Norwood	12-09-92	06-30-96
Jerry W. Almond, Sr.	Norwood		
		07-01-87	
			06-30-91
Thomas D. Hawkins	New London	07-30-90	06-30-94
Leon D. Parker	New London	07-21-89	06-30-93
G. Foreman Rushing	Oakboro	10-23-91	06-30-95

SURRY COMMUNITY COLLEGE BOARD OF TRUSTEES
G.S. 115D-12/Board No. 2255

Name of Appointee	Address	Date Appointed	Date of Expiration
Harris W. Bradley	Mount Airy	08-25-89	06-30-93
James A. Everett	Elkin	07-01-87	06-30-91
Dallas P. Nance	State Road	04-10-89	06-30-91
		07-01-92	06-30-96
Floyd E. Rees	Mount Airy	07-01-91	06-30-95
Betty K. Vaughn	Mount Airy	08-25-89	06-30-90
		01-09-91	06-30-94

TRI-COUNTY COMMUNITY COLLEGE BOARD OF TRUSTEES
G.S. 115D-12/Board No. 2260

Name of Appointee	Address	Date Appointed	Date of Expiration
Lyle Carringer	Murphy	08-27-91	06-30-95
Gene P. Farmer, Sr.	Murphy	10-09-86	06-30-89
William A. Hoover, Jr.	Murphy	07-01-87	06-30-91
		07-14-92	06-30-96
Joyce C. Jenkins	Robbinsville	07-25-90	06-30-94
Jack R. Rogers	Hayesville	08-25-89	06-30-93

WILKES COMMUNITY COLLEGE BOARD OF TRUSTEES
(CONTINUED)

William L. Fowler	Millers Creek	07-02-90	06-30-94
John V. Idol	North Wilkesboro	07-01-85	06-30-89
		07-21-89	06-30-93
William H. McElwee III	North Wilkesboro	11-19-91	06-30-92
		07-01-92	06-30-96
Edwin H. McGee	Ferguson	07-01-87	06-30-91
Gordon E. Rhodes	North Wilkesboro	11-20-85	06-30-87

WILSON COUNTY TECHNICAL COLLEGE BOARD OF TRUSTEES
G.S. 115D-12/Board No. 2285

Name of Appointee	Address	Date Appointed	Date of Expiration
U. H. Cozart III	Wilson	08-23-89	06-30-93
Donald I. Evans	Wilson	10-17-91	06-30-95
Hugh H. Ingram, Jr.	Wilson	07-01-87	06-30-91
		07-01-92	06-30-96
Mrs. Melrose W. Rogerson	Wilson	08-28-90	06-30-94

OFFICE OF THE STATE CONTROLLER [6]

Fred W. Talton, 1988-1993

INFORMATION RESOURCE MANAGEMENT COMMISSION [7]
G.S. 143B-426.21(a)/Board No. 0469

Name of Appointee	Address	Date Appointed	Date of Expiration
William W. Cobey, Jr.	Raleigh	09-01-92	06-30-95
Rufus L. Edmisten	Raleigh	09-01-92	06-30-93
Bob Etheridge	Raleigh	09-01-92	06-30-93
James C. Gardner	Raleigh	09-01-92	06-30-93
Thomas J. Harrelson	Raleigh	09-01-92	06-30-95
Jim Long	Raleigh	09-01-92	06-30-93

DEPARTMENT OF CORRECTION

Secretaries
Aaron Johnson, 1985-1992
V. Lee Bounds, 1992-1993

BOARD OF CORRECTION
G.S. 143B-265/Board No. 0235

Name of Appointee	Address	Date Appointed	Date of Expiration
Bruce Briggs	Mars Hill	05-10-85	
Henry B. Burton	Durham	05-10-85	

---

[6]The General Assembly created the Office of State Controller in 1986. Subject to legislative confirmation, the state controller was an appointee of the governor. He was responsible for overseeing the state's accounting system during a seven-year term. *N.C. Session Laws, 1985, Extra and Regular Sessions, 1986,* c. 1024, ratified July 15, 1986.

[7]Legislation establishing the Information Resource Management Commission became effective September 1, 1992. Although the governor made appointments to the body, time constraints prevented its activation. Martin's second administration was nearing its end, and there was little opportunity for the board to organize and accomplish any of its goals. Susan Myrick, Boards and Commissions, Office of the Governor, telephone conversation with Jan-Michael Poff, December 3, 1992.

BOARD OF CORRECTION
(CONTINUED)

M. E. Doud	Wrightsville Beach	05-10-85
Bethany B. Floan	Jacksonville	01-15-86
Sam C. Gouge	Bakersville	01-15-86
Samp C. Hopkins, Jr.	Albemarle	01-15-86
Bob Keen	Graham	11-10-87
James C. Lyons	Boone	05-10-85
Howard E. Manning, Jr.	Raleigh	02-06-89
Don M. Pendleton	Lincolnton	05-10-85
Mary Randolph	New Bern	05-10-85
James D. Riddick III	Como	04-28-89
Donald L. Smith	Raleigh	05-10-85
R. Tracy Walker	Wilkesboro	05-10-85
Arthur Wilson	Fayetteville	04-28-89

GRIEVANCE RESOLUTION BOARD
G.S. 148-118.6/Board No. 0407

Name of Appointee	Address	Date Appointed	Date of Expiration
Stephen R. Berlin	Winston-Salem	01-11-88	06-30-91
chairman		10-03-89	
chairman		08-27-91	06-30-95
James R. Bruner	Greenville	02-05-88	06-30-90
		07-02-90	06-30-94
Christine Longoria	Asheville	01-11-88	06-30-91
		08-27-91	06-30-95
John W. Lunsford	Roxboro	10-03-89	06-30-93
N. Hector McGeachy	Fayetteville	01-11-88	06-30-89
chairman		01-11-88	
J. Howard Sherman, Sr.	Charlotte	01-11-88	06-30-88
		07-01-88	06-30-92
		07-01-92	06-30-96
James D. Yorker	Charlotte	12-04-92	06-30-96

INMATE GRIEVANCE COMMISSION [8]
G.S. 148-101/Board No. 0465

Name of Appointee	Address	Date Appointed	Date of Expiration
Irving L. Joyner	Durham	09-15-85	06-30-86
		12-16-86	06-30-90
N. Hector McGeachy, chairman	Fayetteville	12-02-85	06-30-89
Cornelia McGee	Raleigh	09-15-85	06-30-89

PAROLE COMMISSION
G.S. 143B-267/Board No. 0675

Name of Appointee	Address	Date Appointed	Date of Expiration
Bruce B. Briggs	Mars Hill	09-16-85	06-30-89
chairman		09-16-85	

---

[8]The Inmate Grievance Commission was replaced by the Grievance Resolution Board, effective January 1, 1988; see N.C. Session Laws, 1987, II, c. 746.

Parole Commission
(continued)

Louis R. Colombo	New Bern	07-01-85	06-30-89
		09-01-89	06-30-93
chairman		09-01-89	
Charles L. Cromer	Cary	07-13-92	06-30-93
Wanda J. Garrett	Durham	09-25-89	06-30-93
Katrena B. Horton	Raleigh	09-25-89	06-30-93
Jeffrey T. Ledbetter	Skyland	07-01-85	06-30-89
Arlene C. Pulley	Raleigh	06-01-89	06-30-89
		09-25-89	06-30-93
Joseph E. Slate, Jr.	Cary	09-01-89	06-30-93
Samuel A. Wilson III	Raleigh	08-17-87	06-30-89
chairman		08-17-87	

Substance Abuse Advisory Council
G.S. 143B-270/Board No. 0877

Name of Appointee	Address	Date Appointed	Date of Expiration
Robert Goodale	Charlotte	10-01-87	09-30-91
Bradford V. Ligon	Salisbury	10-01-87	09-30-89
		10-01-89	09-30-95
Shirley D. Lowder	Albemarle	10-01-87	09-30-91
Donald S. McMillan	Charlotte	01-27-92	09-30-95
George H. Roberts	Pinehurst	02-15-89	09-30-91
		01-27-92	09-30-95

DEPARTMENT OF CRIME CONTROL AND PUBLIC SAFETY

Secretaries
Joseph W. Dean, 1985-1992
Alan Pugh, 1992-1993

Governor's Crime Commission
G.S. 143B-478/Board No. 0257

Name of Appointee	Address	Date Appointed	Date of Expiration
Larry W. Adams	East Bend	04-24-87	03-01-90
J. B. Allen, Jr.	Burlington	05-17-88	03-01-91
		04-02-91	03-01-94
Sherry F. Alloway	Greensboro	04-24-87	03-01-90
		05-02-90	03-01-93
Michael A. Ashburn	Millers Creek	04-02-91	03-01-92
		04-16-92	03-01-95
Wilhelmina Bratton	Asheville	03-01-86	03-01-88
		05-17-88	03-01-91
		04-02-91	03-01-94
Diane W. Buchanan	Burlington	03-01-89	03-01-92
		04-16-92	03-01-95
Edward E. Carter	Greenville	12-30-87	03-01-90
Laurence A. Cobb	Charlotte	03-01-86	03-01-89
chairman		03-01-86	
chairman		03-31-89	
Sylvester Daughtry, Jr.	Greensboro	05-02-90	03-01-93
John M. Dolan	Wilmington	04-24-87	03-01-90

GOVERNOR'S CRIME COMMISSION
(CONTINUED)

John O. Dunn, Jr.	Wilmington	05-02-90	03-01-93
Bruce R. Eckard	Conover	05-02-90	03-01-93
Samuel C. Evans	Sparta	03-01-86	03-01-89
William C. Fann	Salemburg	03-01-86	03-01-89
		03-01-89	03-01-92
Arlene G. Fonorow	Greensboro	03-01-86	03-01-89
Chuck Forrester	Greensboro	04-24-87	03-01-90
Gerald G. Fox	Charlotte	03-01-86	03-01-89
		03-01-89	03-01-92
		04-16-92	03-01-95
Angel Green	Raleigh	04-02-91	03-01-94
Paul S. Helms	Robbins	10-18-89	03-01-91
		04-02-91	03-01-94
Coy Hollifield	Bakersville	03-01-86	03-01-88
		05-17-88	03-01-91
		04-02-91	03-01-94
William T. Justice III	Hampstead	04-02-91	03-01-94
Thomas J. Keith	Winston-Salem	12-30-92	03-01-95
Joe L. Kiser	Vale	05-26-87	03-01-88
		05-17-88	03-01-91
Floyd W. Lucas, Jr.	Hickory	11-20-85	03-01-87
		04-24-87	03-01-90
Thomas P. McNamara	Raleigh	03-01-86	03-01-89
vice-chairman		08-21-87	
vice-chairman		03-01-89	03-01-92
vice-chairman		04-16-92	03-01-95
Robert R. Mason	Asheboro	07-31-85	03-01-86
		03-01-86	03-01-89
		03-01-89	03-01-92
Lisa P. Morgan	Raleigh	07-01-92	03-01-94
William M. Neely	Asheboro	05-17-88	03-01-91
		04-02-91	03-01-94
Felicia L. Redmond	Raleigh	05-17-88	03-01-91
Thomas S. Royster, Jr.	Oxford	08-15-86	03-01-89
		03-01-89	03-01-92
		04-16-92	03-01-95
James T. Rusher	Boone	03-01-86	03-01-89
		03-01-89	03-01-92
Fred A. Spruill	Edenton	10-18-89	03-01-92
		04-16-92	03-01-95
Bettie S. Stem	Wilson	05-17-88	03-01-91
D. Ronald Stone	Charlotte	05-10-85	03-01-88
		05-17-88	03-01-91
		10-18-89	
chairman		04-02-91	03-01-94
chairman		04-02-91	
Thomas H. Thompson	Dana	03-01-89	03-01-92
		04-16-92	03-01-95
Carl L. Tilghman	Beaufort	07-22-88	03-01-90
		05-02-90	03-01-93
Robert N. Wesley, Jr.	Winston-Salem	04-24-87	03-01-90
Gary Whitener	Hickory	03-01-86	03-01-88
vice-chairman		03-01-86	
James W. Wise	Aberdeen	01-10-91	03-01-92
		04-16-92	03-01-95

GOVERNOR'S CRIME COMMISSION
(CONTINUED)

J. Hugh Wright	Winston-Salem	05-02-90	03-01-93
Thomas C. Younce	Wilson	04-24-87	03-01-90
		05-02-90	03-01-93

CRIME VICTIMS COMPENSATION COMMISSION
G.S. 15B-3/Board No. 0258

Name of Appointee	Address	Date Appointed	Date of Expiration
L. Louis Pippin	Grifton	09-30-87	06-30-91
		08-27-91	06-30-95

MILITARY AIDES-DE-CAMP
G.S. 127A-18/Board No. 0580

Name of Appointee	Address	Date Appointed	Date of Expiration
Dolores D. Adams	Fuquay-Varina	02-21-91	01-05-93
Bruce H. Baker, Jr.	Greenville	02-10-89	01-05-91
Vance K. Bishop, Jr.	Parkton	06-01-87	01-05-89
Mary E. Buley	Chapel Hill	06-01-87	01-05-89
Julia C. Byrd	Cary	01-31-89	01-05-91
Bernard Coleman	Raleigh	06-01-87	01-05-8?
		02-21-91	01-05-93
John H. Creech	Garner	02-21-91	01-05-93
Chester C. Davis	Winston-Salem	01-31-89	01-05-91
		02-21-91	01-05-93
Forrest D. Earley	Morganton	02-21-91	01-05-93
Irvin R. Ellington, Jr.	Apex	02-21-91	01-05-93
James T. Ellis III	Ramseur	01-31-89	01-05-91
Larry L. Eudy	Albemarle	06-01-87	01-05-8?
James H. Everette	Belhaven	07-24-89	01-05-91
Kelly F. Gonitzke	Raleigh	06-01-87	01-05-89
Terry R. Henderson	Gastonia	01-31-89	01-05-91
Baron G. Hignite	Raleigh	02-21-91	01-05-93
Joseph D. Hughes, Jr.	Benson	01-31-89	01-05-91
		02-21-91	01-05-93
David L. Jennette, Jr.	Windsor	01-31-89	01-05-91
		02-21-91	01-05-93
Jaylon Jones	Raleigh	06-01-87	01-05-89
Stephen M. Jones	Apex	06-01-87	01-05-89
Richard D. Kingsberry	Charlotte	01-31-89	01-05-91
		02-21-91	01-05-93
Dana N. Lewis	Apex	06-01-87	01-05-89
		01-31-89	01-05-91
James R. Martin	Eden	06-01-87	01-05-89
Billy J. Reid	Charlotte	06-01-87	01-05-89
James H. Spell	Roseboro	06-01-87	01-05-89
		01-31-89	01-05-91
Arnold W. Torbert	Pittsboro	02-21-91	01-05-93
Bobby G. Webb	Rocky Mount	01-31-89	01-05-91
William H. White	Raleigh	01-31-89	01-05-91
		02-21-91	01-05-93
Lewis A. Wilson	Charlotte	06-01-87	01-05-89

DEPARTMENT OF CULTURAL RESOURCES

Secretary
Patric G. Dorsey, 1985-1993

ARCHAEOLOGICAL ADVISORY COMMITTEE [9]
G.S. 143B-66/BOARD No. 0043

Name of Appointee	Address	Date Appointed	Date of Expiration
Lindley S. Butler	Wentworth	11-20-85	06-30-89

NORTH CAROLINA ART SOCIETY, INCORPORATED, BOARD OF DIRECTORS
G.S. 143B-89/Board No. 0070

Name of Appointee	Address	Date Appointed	Date of Expiration
Carolyn M. Bechtel	Charlotte	12-27-89	06-30-92
Joseph M. Bryan, Jr.	Greensboro	09-19-86	06-30-89
		07-01-89	06-30-92
		08-04-92	06-30-95
Jeanne L. Cummings	Asheville	09-19-86	06-30-89
Anne S. Davis	Hickory	11-19-91	06-30-92
Patric Dorsey	Pinehurst	12-30-92	06-30-95
Katrena B. Horton	Raleigh	09-19-86	06-30-89
Mrs. Chris B. Link	Raleigh	12-30-92	06-30-95
Charlotte M. Martin	Raleigh	11-19-91	06-30-92
		08-04-92	06-30-95
Mrs. Kenneth E. Martin	Raleigh	09-19-86	06-30-89
Miriam S. Mayo	Tarboro	09-19-86	06-30-89
Tula C. Robbins	Raleigh	11-10-87	06-30-89
		07-01-89	06-30-92
		08-04-92	06-30-95
Dorothy M. Shelton	Winston-Salem	07-01-89	06-30-92
Emily P. Smith	Charlotte	09-19-86	06-30-89
		07-01-89	06-30-92
Mrs. Billy J. Stallings	Rocky Mount	04-25-90	06-30-92
Nancy J. Ward	Raleigh	08-12-88	06-30-89
		07-01-89	06-30-92
		08-04-92	06-30-95

NORTH CAROLINA ARTS COUNCIL
G.S. 143B-88/Board No. 0060

Name of Appointee	Address	Date Appointed	Date of Expiration
James G. Aycock	Fremont	10-20-87	06-30-90
		07-10-90	06-30-93
Ruth F. Barnett	Henderson	07-10-90	06-30-93
Ronald H. Bayes	Laurinburg	09-09-87	06-30-90
Mollie Blankenship	Cherokee	09-09-87	06-30-90
		07-10-90	06-30-93
Cynthia Bringle	Penland	11-20-85	06-30-88
		07-22-88	06-30-91
		12-12-91	06-30-94

---

[9] *N.C. Session Laws, 1985, Extra and Regular Sessions, 1986*, c. 1028, s. 10, abolished the Archaeological Advisory Committee.

NORTH CAROLINA ARTS COUNCIL
(CONTINUED)

Chuck Davis	Durham	12-12-91	06-30-94
Mollie Faison	Charlotte	11-20-85	06-30-88
Albert S. Gooch, Jr.	Hendersonville	09-09-87	06-30-90
		07-10-90	06-30-93
Jean L. Griffing	Wilkesboro	09-19-86	06-30-89
		07-21-89	06-30-92
Pegge L. Haywood	Concord	12-12-91	06-30-92
Marianne B. Hayworth	High Point	09-19-86	06-30-89
		07-21-89	06-30-92
		09-16-92	06-30-95
Edward O. Hill	Advance	09-09-87	06-30-90
		07-10-90	06-30-93
Claude F. Howell	Wilmington	03-31-88	06-30-88
		07-22-88	06-30-91
Ira J. Jackson III	Raleigh	03-01-88	06-30-90
		07-10-90	06-30-93
Paul H. Jeffrey	Durham	11-20-85	06-30-88
		07-22-88	06-30-91
Frank W. Kiker	Charlotte	09-19-86	06-30-89
		07-21-89	06-30-92
		09-16-92	06-30-95
Richard D. Levy	Greensboro	12-12-91	06-30-94
Robert Lindgren	Winston-Salem	11-20-85	06-30-88
Keith T. Martin	Charlotte	03-02-92	06-30-94
Lavie G. Michael	Asheville	09-19-86	06-30-89
		07-21-89	06-30-92
Stephanie A. Mitchell	Raleigh	09-19-86	06-30-89
		07-21-89	06-30-92
		09-16-92	06-30-95
David W. Moore	Gastonia	09-16-92	06-30-95
Clarence E. Morgan	Greenville	09-09-87	06-30-90
		07-10-90	06-30-93
Katherine A. Phillips	High Point	05-06-86	06-30-87
		09-09-87	06-30-90
		07-10-90	06-30-93
Deborah A. Pirotte	Raleigh	09-19-86	06-30-89
		07-21-89	06-30-92
Milton R. Pollock	Kinston	11-20-85	06-30-88
Susie R. Powell	Durham	05-06-86	06-30-88
		07-22-88	06-30-91
Moselle M. Puett	Murphy	09-09-87	06-30-90
Dorothy S. Redford	Creswell	12-12-91	06-30-94
Ruth L. Revels	Greensboro	09-19-86	06-30-89
		07-21-89	06-30-92
		09-16-92	06-30-95
Lorraine H. Robinson	New Bern	09-09-87	06-30-88
		07-22-88	06-30-91
		12-12-91	06-30-94
Jane B. Rouse	Emerald Isle	09-19-86	06-30-89
		07-21-89	06-30-92
Harley F. Shuford, Jr.	Hickory	11-20-85	06-30-88
chairman		09-09-87	
chairman		07-22-88	06-30-91
chairman		12-12-91	06-30-94

North Carolina Arts Council
(CONTINUED)

Bradley R. Smith	Durham	09-16-92	06-30-95
William Stevens	Winston-Salem	09-09-87	06-30-88
		07-22-88	06-30-91
		12-12-91	06-30-94
Hellena H. Tidwell	Charlotte	12-09-92	06-30-95
James C. Walker, Jr.	Statesville	09-16-92	06-30-95
Mark L. Woods	Charlotte	11-20-85	06-30-88
		07-22-88	06-30-91

North Carolina Composer Laureate
N.C. Session Laws, 1991, c. 56/Board No. 3100

Name of Appointee	Address	Date Appointed	Date of Expiration
Hunter Johnson	Benson	06-11-91	

Edenton Historical Commission
G.S. 143B-98/Board No. 0300

Name of Appointee	Address	Date Appointed	Date of Expiration
Marcia K. Crandall	Edenton	12-09-92	
R. Dillard Dixon III	Edenton	07-22-88	
Frances D. Inglis	Edenton	07-31-85	
John C. Morehead	Edenton	07-31-85	

Executive Mansion Fine Arts Committee
G.S. 143B-80/Board No. 0360

Name of Appointee	Address	Date Appointed	Date of Expiration
Claudia W. Belk	Charlotte	06-30-86	06-30-90
		07-02-90	06-30-94
Janet Bradshaw	Charlotte	07-01-89	06-30-93
Faye A. Broyhill	Lenoir	07-01-89	06-30-93
Ms. Carson J. Clark	Raleigh	09-14-92	06-30-96
Chalmers G. Davidson	Davidson	08-05-87	06-30-90
Joanne S. Dickson	Charlotte	07-01-88	06-30-92
		09-14-92	06-30-96
Betty B. Godwin	Rocky Mount	06-30-86	06-30-90
Sandra Henson	Kinston	03-28-91	06-30-94
Meredythe J. Holmes	Durham	06-30-86	06-30-90
		07-02-90	06-30-94
Dorothy C. Howard	Winston-Salem	08-05-87	06-30-91
Nancy M. Jenkins	Greenville	07-01-88	06-30-92
Karen L. Johnston	Greensboro	11-10-87	06-30-91
		08-26-91	06-30-95
Thomas S. Kenan III	Chapel Hill	07-01-88	06-30-92
		09-14-92	06-30-96
Edward G. Lilly, Jr.	Raleigh	09-07-90	06-30-94
Anne S. Peden	Raleigh	08-05-87	06-30-91
		08-26-91	06-30-95
Libby Pope	Raleigh	07-01-89	06-30-93

EXECUTIVE MANSION FINE ARTS COMMITTEE
(CONTINUED)

Betty Y. Powell	Burlington	08-05-87	06-30-91
		08-26-91	06-30-95
Sidney Schrum	Goldsboro	07-01-89	06-30-93
Mary D. B. T. Semans	Durham	07-01-88	06-30-92
chairwoman		07-01-88	
		09-14-92	06-30-96
Sandra G. Shelton	Charlotte	04-03-89	06-30-91
		09-20-91	06-30-95
Dennis Toney	Rutherfordton	06-30-86	06-30-90
		07-02-90	06-30-94

HISTORIC BATH COMMISSION
G.S. 143B-102/Board No. 0120

Name of Appointee	Address	Date Appointed	Date of Expiration
Jane Alligood	Washington	07-01-87	06-30-92
		07-01-92	06-30-97
Robin C. Arnold	Washington	07-10-90	06-30-95
George C. Bailey	Washington	07-01-87	06-30-92
Anna D. Biggs	Elizabeth City	07-01-87	06-30-92
		07-01-92	06-30-97
Marian D. Booth	Washington	07-01-91	06-30-96
Alice H. Bost	Greenville	07-21-86	06-30-91
		07-01-91	06-30-96
Rebecca M. Boyd	Washington	07-01-89	06-30-94
Mary A. Browning	Greenville	07-01-89	06-30-94
Jesse Crisp	Chocowinity	07-01-92	06-30-97
Toni S. P. Doub	Greenville	07-01-87	06-30-92
Mary A. Edwards	Bath	07-01-91	06-30-96
Gino Giusti	Stamford	07-01-89	06-30-94
Ira M. Hardy II	Bath	06-30-86	06-30-91
		07-01-91	06-30-96
Hackney High	Washington	07-01-92	06-30-97
Faleese M. Jenkins	Elizabeth City	06-30-86	06-30-91
Edward H. Jones	Washington	07-10-90	06-30-95
Ned M. Kinsey	Washington	07-01-92	06-30-97
W. Larry Kinsey	Washington	07-10-90	06-30-95
Joseph C. Leary	Washington	06-30-86	06-30-91
Loonis McGlohon	Charlotte	07-01-89	06-30-94
Margaret S. McMicken	Aurora	07-22-88	06-30-93
John F. Redding	Asheboro	07-10-87	06-30-89
		07-01-89	06-30-94
Dorothy S. Redford	Creswell	07-22-88	06-30-93
Henry M. Shaw, Jr.	Raleigh	07-22-88	06-30-93
Wilton W. Smith, Jr.	Bath	07-10-90	06-30-95
Janet B. Stephenson	Washington	07-10-90	06-30-95
Melinda C. Wall	Greenville	07-22-88	06-30-93
Christina Williams	Washington	07-01-87	06-30-92
Jean D. Winstead	Bath	07-22-88	06-30-93
William M. Zachman	Washington	06-30-86	06-30-91
		07-01-91	06-30-96

Historic Hillsborough Commission
G.S. 143B-106/Board No. 0427

Name of Appointee	Address	Date Appointed	Date of Expiration
J. Adam Abram	Research Triangle Park	12-23-85	10-01-91
Josephine H. Barbour	Hillsborough	03-12-85	10-01-89
		11-06-89	10-01-95
Eleanor P. Bell	Hillsborough	12-23-85	10-01-91
Saragene G. Boericke	Hillsborough	10-01-87	10-01-93
		12-02-91	10-01-97
J. L. Brown, Jr.	Hillsborough	12-23-85	10-01-91
Kenneth D. Carden	Hillsborough	12-27-89	10-01-95
Refford Cate	Reidsville	11-06-89	10-01-95
Dianne Cates-Cantrell	Hillsborough	12-09-92	10-01-93
Nellie D. Cheshire	Hillsborough	11-06-89	10-01-95
E. Wilson Cole	Hillsborough	12-23-85	10-01-91
Alonzo B. Coleman, Jr.	Hillsborough	12-09-92	10-01-93
Lida L. Coleman	Chapel Hill	12-02-91	10-01-97
Betty P. Converse	Chapel Hill	10-01-87	10-01-93
Ellyn G. Courts	Chapel Hill	12-23-85	10-01-91
Bonnie Davis	Hillsborough	12-23-85	10-01-91
		12-02-91	10-01-97
James F. Davis	Hillsborough	12-23-85	10-01-91
Caroline Donnan	Chapel Hill	10-01-87	10-01-89
		11-06-89	10-01-95
Nancy S. Ellis	Ramseur	12-02-91	10-01-97
Suzanne Faulkner	Hillsborough	12-09-92	10-01-93
Donna Freeland	Hillsborough	10-01-87	10-01-93
Mary S. Gattis	Hillsborough	10-20-87	10-01-93
Harold R. Grunewald	Hillsborough	12-02-91	10-01-97
Stephen H. Halkiotis	Hillsborough	12-23-85	10-01-91
Alex Jones	Durham	12-02-91	10-01-97
Craig D. Leonard	Cary	11-06-89	10-01-95
Evelyn P. Lloyd	Hillsborough	12-23-85	10-01-91
		12-02-91	10-01-97
Jack R. Martin	Hillsborough	10-01-87	10-01-93
H. W. Moore	Hillsborough	12-23-85	10-01-91
		12-02-91	10-01-97
Mrs. Pat S. Moore	Hillsborough	11-06-89	10-01-95
Robert J. Page	Chapel Hill	12-23-85	10-01-91
Evelyn B. Patterson	Hillsborough	10-01-87	10-01-89
		11-06-89	10-01-95
Millicent C. Rainey	Hillsborough	12-09-92	10-01-95
Grace J. Roberts	Hillsborough	07-02-90	10-01-93
Tom Roberts	Hillsborough	04-28-89	10-01-93
Jane Rogers	Chapel Hill	10-01-87	10-01-93
Connie M. Sessoms	Hillsborough	11-06-89	10-01-95
Faye Swanson	Hillsborough	12-02-91	10-01-97
Mary Frances A. Vogler	Chapel Hill	10-01-87	10-01-89
Geneva W. Warren	Prospect Hill	10-01-87	10-01-93
Norma B. White	Hillsborough	12-02-91	10-01-97
Peachee Wicker	Chapel Hill	10-01-87	10-01-93
Hilda J. Winecoff	Hillsborough	11-06-89	10-01-95
Jack C. Woodall	Hillsborough	10-01-87	10-01-93

Historic Murfreesboro Commission
G.S. 143B-110/Board No. 0615

Name of Appointee	Address	Date Appointed	Date of Expiration
Roger A. Askew	Ahoskie	06-04-92	03-01-97
Danny M. Blowe	Murfreesboro	04-28-89	03-01-90
		03-15-90	03-01-95
Grace B. Boone	Weldon	03-15-90	03-01-95
Earl T. Brown	Greenville	03-15-90	03-01-95
Mary J. Burkette	Ahoskie	04-03-87	03-01-92
		06-04-92	03-01-97
Helen R. Cain	Raleigh	10-09-86	03-01-90
Marie V. Cooke	Murfreesboro	05-31-88	03-01-93
Margaret B. Daly	Windsor	06-04-92	03-01-97
Barbara Dixon	Ahoskie	06-11-91	03-01-96
Dudley E. Flood	Raleigh	10-09-86	03-01-91
Joseph A. Futrell	Winton	05-31-88	03-01-93
Faye Gaudette	Murfreesboro	04-14-87	03-01-92
Edna Hammel	Murfreesboro	04-14-87	03-01-92
		06-04-92	03-01-97
Jack L. Harper	Raleigh	06-11-91	03-01-96
Helen E. Henry	Ahoskie	06-11-91	03-01-96
Rita P. Hoggard	Windsor	06-11-91	03-01-92
		06-04-92	03-01-97
Maria H. Jennette	Windsor	06-11-91	03-01-96
Brenda M. Jordan	Raleigh	11-10-86	03-01-91
Mildred F. Lackey	Murfreesboro	10-09-86	03-01-91
Kevin N. Lewis	Ahoskie	03-15-90	03-01-95
Mrs. Lester V. Lowe, Jr.	Wilson	12-10-86	03-01-91
		06-11-91	03-01-96
Timothy L. Minton	Murfreesboro	05-31-88	03-01-93
John R. Moore, Jr.	Ahoskie	07-31-85	03-01-90
Ms. Lindsay S. Newsom	Raleigh	07-31-85	03-01-90
		03-15-90	03-01-95
Thomas Parramore	Raleigh	05-31-88	03-01-93
Thilbert H. Pearce	Franklinton	06-11-91	03-01-96
Daniel T. Phillips	Murfreesboro	10-09-86	03-01-91
Charles L. Revelle III	Murfreesboro	03-01-89	03-01-94
Gertrude J. Revelle	Murfreesboro	03-01-89	03-01-94
James D. Riddick III	Como	05-31-88	03-01-93
Mrs. Charles L. Smith, Jr.	Raleigh	04-03-87	03-01-92
		06-04-92	03-01-97
Frank Stephenson, Jr.	Murfreesboro	03-01-89	03-01-94
Joseph H. Stutts	Murfreesboro	05-31-88	03-01-93
Maurice A. Sullivan	Harrellsville	03-01-89	03-01-94
Benjamin C. Sutton	Murfreesboro	03-01-89	03-01-94
Harry L. Thompson	Windsor	03-15-90	03-01-95
Ethleen V. Underwood	Murfreesboro	04-03-87	03-01-92
William S. Vann	Murfreesboro	03-01-89	03-01-94
Harry W. Whitley, Sr.	Murfreesboro	10-09-86	03-01-91
Bobbi B. Wooten	Murfreesboro	04-14-87	03-01-92

NORTH CAROLINA HISTORICAL COMMISSION
G.S. 143B-63/Board No. 0430

Name of Appointee	Address	Date Appointed	Date of Expiration
Millie M. Barbee	Beaufort	09-07-90	03-31-91
		04-01-91	03-31-97
Ralph W. Donnelly	Washington	04-14-87	03-31-93
Helen G. Edmonds	Durham	05-13-85	03-31-91
Frances A. Fanjoy	Statesville	05-02-89	04-01-95
T. Harry Gatton	Raleigh	05-13-85	03-31-91
chairman		09-07-90	
chairman		03-28-91	03-31-97
Ms. Gerry F. Johnson	Raleigh	04-14-87	03-31-93
H. G. Jones	Chapel Hill	05-02-89	04-01-95
Mrs. Rome Jones	Newton	05-02-89	04-01-95
Danny G. Moody	Fuquay-Varina	05-13-85	03-31-91
Percy Murray	Durham	04-14-87	03-31-93
William S. Powell	Chapel Hill	05-02-89	04-01-95
Mary B. Sherwood	Murphy	11-20-85	03-31-87
		04-14-87	03-31-93
Alan D. Watson	Wilmington	05-02-89	03-31-91
		04-01-91	03-31-97
W. Buck Yearns	Winston-Salem	10-03-89	03-31-93

JOHN MOTLEY MOREHEAD MEMORIAL COMMISSION
G.S. 143B-115/Board No. 0595

Name of Appointee	Address	Date Appointed	Date of Expiration
Ronald Barbee	Greensboro	07-22-88	06-30-94
William G. Barbour	Greensboro	02-06-86	06-30-88
		07-01-88	06-30-94
Judy M. Carter	Greensboro	02-06-86	06-30-88
Bonnie D. Cordes	Greensboro	02-06-86	06-30-89
		07-01-89	06-30-95
Mrs. Robert H. Edmunds	Greensboro	02-06-86	06-30-91
		07-01-91	06-30-97
Grace B. Hunt	Greensboro	07-01-91	06-30-97
Mrs. Joseph M. Hunt, Jr.	Greensboro	02-06-86	06-30-91
Sally K. Millikin	Greensboro	02-06-86	06-30-88
		07-01-88	06-30-94
Betty Y. Powell	Burlington	01-09-91	06-30-91
		07-01-91	06-30-97
Anne A. Rawls	Greensboro	02-06-86	06-30-91
Becky Rucker	Greensboro	02-06-86	06-30-89
		07-01-89	06-30-95
Henry C. Zenke	Greensboro	02-06-86	06-30-89
		07-01-89	06-30-95

NORTH CAROLINA MUSEUM OF ART BOARD OF TRUSTEES
G.S. 140-5.13/Board No. 0049

Name of Appointee	Address	Date Appointed	Date of Expiration
William T. Barnett	Henderson	09-13-91	06-30-97
Alfred O. Canon	Montreat	06-30-86	06-30-92

North Carolina Museum of Art Board of Trustees
(continued)

Adair M. Graham	Wilmington	07-07-89	06-30-95
Marcus T. Hickman	Charlotte	02-24-88	06-30-89
		07-07-89	06-30-95
Karen L. Johnston	Greensboro	12-10-92	06-30-98
Lynn Lail	Conover	12-10-92	06-30-98
Jeanne G. Rauch	Gastonia	06-30-86	06-30-92
Linda C. Shaw	Greensboro	06-30-86	06-30-92
Elizabeth H. Smith	Durham	01-15-86	06-30-91
Kathi L. Smith	Sanford	12-10-92	06-30-98
Charles B. Sutton	Winston-Salem	01-15-86	06-30-91
chairman		07-22-87	
chairman		09-13-91	06-30-97
Mrs. Edward T. Taws, Jr.	Southern Pines	07-07-89	06-30-95
Elizabeth O. Taylor	Brevard	12-10-92	06-30-98
Jeanne B. Teagarden	Cullowhee	03-02-92	06-30-92
Mrs. Ricky H. Thornton	Elizabeth City	01-15-86	06-30-91
		09-13-91	06-30-97
Philip R. Tracy	Raleigh	07-07-89	06-30-95
Barbara G. Washington	Greensboro	01-03-93	06-30-98
Ruby S. Wilkerson	Goldsboro	06-30-86	06-30-92
Mr. Sylvania Wilkerson, Sr.	Goldsboro	10-17-91	06-30-92

North Carolina Awards Committee
G.S. 143B-84/Board No. 0095

Name of Appointee	Address	Date Appointed	Date of Expiration
Anthony S. Abbot	Davidson	05-10-85	
John Ehle	Winston-Salem	06-11-85	
George W. Hill	Durham	05-10-85	
James E. Holshouser, Jr.	Southern Pines	04-14-86	
Anne Peden	Raleigh	05-10-85	
A. P. Perkinson, Jr.	Davidson	07-09-91	
David C. Sabiston, Jr.	Durham	04-03-87	
Terry Sanford	Durham	05-10-85	

U.S.S. North Carolina Battleship Commission
G.S. 143B-74/Board No. 0125

Name of Appointee	Address	Date Appointed	Date of Expiration
Helen A. Alford	Charlotte	04-01-87	04-01-89
		04-01-89	04-01-91
Ben W. Blee, *chairman*	Jacksonville	04-01-87	04-01-89
chairman		04-01-89	04-01-91
Norwood E. Bryan, Jr.	Fayetteville	03-17-92	04-01-93
Donald B. Canupp, *vice-chairman*	Hickory	05-15-86	
vice-chairman		04-01-87	04-01-89
vice-chairman		04-01-89	04-01-91
Gordon L. Carpenter	Durham	04-01-87	04-01-89
		04-01-89	04-01-91
Charles E. Couns	Raleigh	10-28-88	04-01-89
		04-01-89	04-01-91
Patrick C. Dorsey	New Bern	04-01-87	04-01-89
		04-01-89	04-01-91

PUBLIC LIBRARIAN CERTIFICATION COMMISSION
G.S. 143B-68/Board No. 0750

Name of Appointee	Address	Date Appointed	Date of Expiration
Martha H. Davis	Reidsville	06-30-86	06-30-89
		07-24-89	06-30-93
Nancy G. Gibson, *chairwoman*	Bryson City	09-16-85	06-30-89
		07-24-89	06-30-93
chairwoman		07-24-89	
Martha R. Plaster, *chairwoman*	Shelby	01-15-92	06-30-93
Benjamin F. Speller, Jr.	Durham	06-30-86	06-30-89
		07-24-89	06-30-93

ROANOKE VOYAGES AND *ELIZABETH II* COMMISSION
G.S. 143B-131/Board No. 0781

Name of Appointee	Address	Date Appointed	Date of Expiration
Martha B. Austin	Buxton	01-22-91	10-01-94
Bill Booker	Manteo	11-10-86	10-01-90
William D. Burrus	Hatteras	11-10-86	10-01-90
Cheryl L. Byrd	Waves	12-09-92	10-01-94
Deborah P. Davenport	Roper	10-01-88	10-01-92
		12-09-92	10-01-96
Amelia Frazer	Eden	01-22-91	10-01-94
		12-09-92	10-01-96
Wallace W. Harvey, Jr.	Manteo	01-30-91	10-01-94
John F. Hohmann	Manteo	01-22-91	10-01-94
Melvin L. Jackson	Manteo	01-22-91	10-01-94
Patsy R. Miller	Williamston	10-01-88	10-01-92
		12-09-92	10-01-96
Mrs. Heilig H. Pittard	Oxford	01-30-87	10-01-88
Marlene Roberts	Manteo	11-10-86	10-01-90
		01-22-91	10-01-94
Sharon C. Robinson	Elizabeth City	12-22-88	10-01-92
Sandra G. Shelton	King	10-01-88	10-01-92
Rex E. Simpson	Wanchese	11-10-86	10-01-90
David Stick	Kitty Hawk	11-10-86	10-01-90
Dennis W. Swain	Columbia	10-01-88	10-01-92
		12-09-92	10-01-96
Nancy Y. Thorp	Rocky Mount	12-31-92	10-01-96
Jeanine D. Tillett	Manteo	11-10-86	10-01-90
Rozelle R. Wicks	Maysville	10-01-88	10-01-92
		12-09-92	10-01-96

NORTH CAROLINA STATE LIBRARY COMMISSION
G.S. 143B-91/Board No. 0535

Name of Appointee	Address	Date Appointed	Date of Expiration
Pauletta B. Bracy	Durham	10-17-91	06-30-95
Thomas H. Folwell, Jr.	Buies Creek	08-05-87	06-30-93
Mary A. Hamil	Greensboro	07-01-91	06-30-93
Betty A. Lennon	Raleigh	01-01-93	06-30-93

NORTH CAROLINA STATE LIBRARY COMMISSION
(CONTINUED)

Leland M. Park	Davidson	08-05-87	06-30-93
chairman		07-21-89	06-30-91
chairman		07-01-91	06-30-93
William H. Roberts III	Winston-Salem	10-17-91	06-30-93
Ms. Gorda Singletary	Wilmington	07-21-89	06-30-93
Elinor H. Swaim	Salisbury	09-16-85	07-01-91
chairwoman		09-16-85	
		07-01-91	06-30-97
		09-27-91	06-30-95
Barbara M. Walser	Greensboro	09-16-85	07-01-91
Carol H. Wilson	Shelby	07-21-89	06-30-93

TRYON PALACE COMMISSION
G.S. 143B-72/Board No. 0910

Name of Appointee	Address	Date Appointed	Date of Expiration
Merle L. Bergstrom	Pinehurst	10-25-89	
Charles C. Collins	New Bern	12-09-92	
Mrs. Phillip R. Dixon	Greenville	08-15-86	
Lynn L. Dunlea	Wilmington	03-02-92	
Alyce F. Grant	Emerald Isle	06-19-89	
Nancy C. Lilly	Raleigh	05-17-88	
Frenise A. Logan	Greensboro	01-30-87	
Margaret Manooch	Raleigh	05-17-88	
Armistead J. Maupin	Raleigh	10-25-89	
Dale T. Millns	New Bern	09-24-87	
Mrs. J. Samuel Mitchener	Raleigh	07-31-85	
Corneille Sineath	Wrightsville Beach	06-20-91	
W. Keats Sparrow	Greenville	03-02-92	
Mrs. Andrew B. Stoney	Morganton	08-31-85	
J. Harold Talton	New Bern	12-10-86	
John A. J. Ward	New Bern	11-06-89	

VETERANS' MEMORIAL COMMISSION [10]
G.S. 143B-133/Board No. 0923

Name of Appointee	Address	Date Appointed	Date of Expiration
William C. Cox	Raleigh	09-15-87	
Jake LaBar	Rocky Mount	09-15-87	
Danny G. Moody	Fuquay-Varina	09-15-87	
Clifford L. Roberts	Vass	09-15-87	
Lawrence O. Walser, Sr.	Lexington	09-30-87	

---

[10]The Veteran's Memorial Commission was established to oversee the design, placement, and construction of a monument on the Capitol grounds, honoring veterans of the two world wars and the Korean conflict. The legislation authorizing the commission expired with the dedication of the monument on May 27, 1990. *N.C. Session Laws, 1987,* II, c. 779.

DEPARTMENT OF ECONOMIC AND COMMUNITY DEVELOPMENT

Secretaries
Howard H. Haworth, l985-1987
Claude E. Pope, 1987-1989
James T. Broyhill, 1989-1991
Estell C. Lee, 1991-1993

NORTH CAROLINA ALCOHOLIC BEVERAGE CONTROL COMMISSION
G.S. 18B-200/Board No. 0030

Name of Appointee	Address	Date Appointed	Date of Expiration
Franklin R. Anderson	Durham	01-11-85	
Larnie G. Horton, Sr.	Raleigh	07-14-89	
Fred S. Hutchins, Jr.	Winston-Salem	11-24-87	
Charles E. Knox, *chairman*	Charlotte	01-11-85	
		03-31-88	
Robert F. Orr	Asheville	01-11-85	
William P. Powell, Jr.	Lake Junaluska	10-09-86	
chairman		02-16-88	

STATE BANKING COMMISSION
G.S. 53-92/Board No. 0110

Name of Appointee	Address	Date Appointed	Date of Expiration
J. Cooper Adams	Mount Airy	06-30-86	04-01-87
		04-17-87	04-01-91
		09-27-91	04-01-95
Sue M. Adams	Wilson	04-25-88	04-01-89
		04-01-89	03-31-93
W. B. Buchanan	Graham	08-27-91	04-01-95
Richard P. Budd	Winston-Salem	04-17-87	04-01-91
E. Royden Clarke	Engelhard	10-27-92	04-01-95
Roger L. Dick	Albemarle	04-17-85	03-31-89
		04-01-89	03-31-93
Betty J. Faircloth	Clinton	02-27-89	04-01-89
		04-01-89	03-31-93
Paul E. Fisher	Granite Quarry	04-17-85	03-31-89
		04-01-89	03-31-93
Ted N. Griffin	Durham	04-16-92	04-01-93
David R. Grogan	Statesville	08-03-92	04-01-93
Alexander D. Guy	Jacksonville	04-17-85	03-31-89
Larry S. Hedrick	Statesville	09-07-90	04-01-93
Jeffrey P. Hunt	Brevard	06-03-88	04-01-91
Charles A. Hunter	Charlotte	08-27-91	04-01-93
C. Ray Kennedy	Charlotte	04-01-89	03-31-93
Joe I. Marshall	Madison	04-17-87	04-01-91
Hayes C. Martin	Asheville	04-17-87	04-01-91
Ken Martin	Raleigh	04-01-89	03-31-93
A. C. Parker	Parkton	05-17-89	04-01-91
		08-27-91	04-01-95
Gary H. Pendleton	Raleigh	04-17-85	03-31-89
William P. Pope	Statesville	04-17-85	03-31-89
		04-01-89	03-31-93

State Banking Commission
(continued)

Felix S. Sabates	Charlotte	04-17-85	03-31-89
		04-01-89	03-31-93
Julia W. Taylor	Durham	04-17-85	03-31-89
Joseph D. Teachey, Jr.	Wallace	08-23-89	04-01-91
G. Henry Temple, Jr.	Raleigh	10-27-92	04-01-95
J. Marshall Tetterton	Rocky Mount	09-27-91	04-01-95

Commissioner of Banks
G.S. 53-92/Board No. 0105

Name of Appointee	Address	Date Appointed	Date of Expiration
William T. Graham	Winston-Salem	04-28-87	03-31-91
		04-01-91	03-31-95

Cape Fear Navigation and Pilotage Commission
G.S. 76A-2/Board No. 0635

Name of Appointee	Address	Date Appointed	Date of Expiration
William P. Allen	Wilmington	07-01-85	06-30-89
		07-01-89	06-30-93
John G. Ashby	Wilmington	05-06-86	06-30-87
Lemuel L. Doss, Jr.	Wilmington	07-01-87	06-30-91
L. T. Garner, Jr.	Wilmington	10-17-91	06-30-95
Robert G. Greer	Wilmington	08-05-87	06-30-90
Edward B. Higgins, Jr.	Wilmington	10-17-91	06-30-95
William P. Rabon	Southport	07-01-85	06-30-89
chairman		08-05-87	
		07-01-89	06-30-93
chairman		07-01-89	

North Carolina Cemetery Commission
G.S. 65-50/Board No. 0177

Name of Appointee	Address	Date Appointed	Date of Expiration
J. Dean Deweese, Jr.	Asheville	09-15-85	06-30-89
Margaret B. Dixon	Lexington	07-01-88	06-30-92
		07-01-92	06-30-96
Ephraim E. Grubbs, Jr.	Surf City	02-24-88	06-30-89
Georgianne J. Harley	Norlina	07-01-88	06-30-92
		07-01-92	06-30-96
Brent F. Heffron	Hickory	07-01-88	06-30-92
		07-01-92	06-30-96
Theron H. Miller	Winston-Salem	07-01-88	06-30-89
Johnny W. Shepherd	La Grange	09-15-85	06-30-89
		07-01-89	06-30-93
Gerald K. Stephens	Morganton	09-15-85	06-30-89
		07-01-89	06-30-93
Joyce W. Summerville	Matthews	07-01-89	06-30-93
William H. Whitley, Jr.	Concord	09-15-85	06-30-89
		07-01-89	06-30-93

COMMUNITY DEVELOPMENT COUNCIL
G.S. 143B-306/Board No. 0215

Name of Appointee	Address	Date Appointed	Date of Expiration
C. Ronald Aycock	Raleigh	05-15-86	06-30-89
		12-27-89	06-30-93
Don Brady	Greensboro	06-17-87	06-30-89
Edward E. Carter	Greenville	12-27-89	06-30-93
Bill Clampett	Arden	12-27-89	06-30-93
Howard Clement III	Durham	12-30-87	06-30-89
		12-27-89	06-30-93
Carla DuPuy	Charlotte	05-15-86	06-30-89
chairwoman		05-15-86	
Homer Galloway, Jr.	Canton	05-15-86	06-30-89
		12-27-89	06-30-93
Ferd L. Harrison	Scotland Neck	05-15-86	06-30-89
		12-27-89	06-30-93
Richard Herrera	Fayetteville	05-15-86	06-30-89
		12-27-89	06-30-93
Joseph W. Icard	Hudson	05-15-86	06-30-89
Hal Mason	Shelby	12-27-89	06-30-93
chairman		12-27-89	
Nancy R. Myers	Thomasville	12-27-89	06-30-93
David E. Reynolds	Raleigh	03-06-89	06-30-89
		12-27-89	06-30-93
J. Ed Robinette	Conover	05-15-86	06-30-89
		12-27-89	06-30-93
Frederick O. Whitted	Fayetteville	05-15-86	06-30-89
S. Leigh Wilson	Raleigh	05-15-86	06-30-89
Kenneth N. Windley, Jr.	Beaufort	05-15-86	06-30-89
Thomas E. Wright	Greensboro	05-15-86	06-30-89

CREDIT UNION COMMISSION
G.S. 143B-439/Board No. 0255

Name of Appointee	Address	Date Appointed	Date of Expiration
Gregory J. Brewer	North Wilkesboro	09-22-89	07-14-93
Virginia B. Hall	Asheville	09-15-85	07-15-89
		08-25-89	07-14-93
Benjamin W. Hill III	Denver	03-06-92	07-14-93
Al King	Rutherfordton	09-15-85	07-15-89
James D. Moyer	Wilson	04-06-87	07-14-87
		07-15-87	07-14-91
		10-17-91	07-14-95
Michael R. Niday	Hickory	09-09-86	07-14-89
		08-25-89	07-14-93
Ed Pope	Durham	02-26-86	07-15-89
Ernest J. Ward	Rocky Mount	09-15-85	07-15-88
Tommy C. Welch	Winston-Salem	02-26-86	07-15-87
		07-15-87	07-14-91
		10-17-91	07-14-95
Laurie G. Worth	Manson	06-08-87	07-14-89
		08-25-89	07-14-93

CREDIT UNION COMMISSION
(CONTINUED)

Samuel T. Wyrick III	Raleigh	09-09-86	07-14-87
		07-15-87	07-14-91
		10-17-91	07-14-95

ECONOMIC DEVELOPMENT BOARD
G.S. 143B-434/Board No. 0299

Name of Appointee	Address	Date Appointed	Date of Expiration
Don G. Angell	Advance	04-30-89	06-30-91
		08-15-91	06-30-95
William T. Barnett	Henderson	03-13-87	06-30-87
		07-22-87	06-30-91
Lamar Beach	Sanford	08-15-91	06-30-95
Doug S. Boykin	Willard	03-02-92	06-30-95
James T. Broyhill	Lenoir	12-10-86	06-30-87
chairman		12-10-86	
		07-22-87	06-30-91
chairman		07-22-87	
Kent Coward	Sylva	07-01-85	06-30-87
		07-22-87	06-30-91
James B. Culbertson	Winston-Salem	07-01-85	06-30-89
		07-24-89	06-30-93
J. A. Dalpiaz	Gastonia	07-24-89	06-30-93
William P. Elmore	Dunn	07-24-89	06-30-93
John D. Enoch	Burlington	07-22-87	06-30-89
Annabelle Fetterman	Clinton	08-15-91	06-30-95
Charles L. Grace	Charlotte	02-02-90	06-30-93
David N. Henderson	Wallace	07-01-85	06-30-87
		07-22-87	06-30-91
P. Michael Hendron	Greensboro	07-22-87	06-30-91
		08-15-91	06-30-95
H. Terry Hutchens	Fayetteville	11-21-90	06-30-93
Patrick P. Joyce	Beaufort	08-15-91	06-30-95
Ronald A. Joyce	Lewisville	08-15-91	06-30-95
Ann T. Kelly	Statesville	07-22-87	06-30-91
G. Leroy Lail, Jr.	Conover	07-24-89	06-30-93
Estell C. Lee	Wilmington	07-24-89	06-30-93
John D. Lewis	Charlotte	08-05-87	06-30-89
		07-24-89	06-30-93
George W. Little	Southern Pines	07-24-89	06-30-93
vice-chairman		08-15-91	
Hayes C. Martin	Asheville	06-03-88	06-30-89
		07-24-89	06-30-93
Lewis H. Myers	Durham	07-24-89	06-30-93
James M. Peden, Jr.	Raleigh	04-11-91	06-30-93
Gary H. Pendleton	Raleigh	04-11-91	06-30-93
Earl N. Phillips, Jr.	High Point	07-22-87	06-30-91
		08-15-91	06-30-95
Jack Poole	Kinston	07-01-85	06-30-89
Claude E. Pope, chairman	Raleigh	02-07-85	07-01-87
chairman		02-10-89	06-30-91
James B. Powers	Rocky Mount	07-24-89	06-30-93
vice-chairman		07-24-89	

ECONOMIC DEVELOPMENT BOARD
(CONTINUED)

Frank A. Rouse	Emerald Isle	07-22-87	06-30-91
Fries Shaffner	Wrightsville Beach	07-22-87	06-30-91
R. Edwin Shelton	Winston-Salem	07-22-87	06-30-91
Frederick B. Starr	Thomasville	08-15-91	06-30-95
E. Stephen Stroud	Raleigh	07-24-89	06-30-93
Joseph D. Teachey, Jr.	Wallace	08-15-91	06-30-95
Benjamin T. Tison III	Charlotte	07-22-87	06-30-91
		08-15-91	06-30-95
Hans W. Wanders	Winston-Salem	07-24-89	06-30-93
chairman		07-24-89	
		08-15-91	06-30-95

EMPLOYMENT SECURITY COMMISSION
G.S. 96-3/Board No. 0345

Name of Appointee	*Address*	*Date Appointed*	*Date of Expiration*
Charles R. Cagle	Hickory	02-26-86	07-01-87
		07-01-87	06-30-91
		09-27-91	06-30-95
George B. Campbell	Greensboro	03-02-92	06-30-93
John J. Cavanagh, Jr.	Winston-Salem	07-01-89	06-30-93
Ann Q. Duncan, *chairwoman*	Cary	08-01-90	
Kevin L. Green	Asheville	07-01-87	06-30-91
		09-27-91	06-30-95
Jean H. Henshaw	Carolina Beach	07-01-89	06-30-93
Allen N. Holt	Asheboro	07-01-87	06-30-91
		09-27-91	06-30-95
Charles L. Hunley	Monroe	07-01-87	06-30-89
Betsy Y. Justus, *chairwoman*	Raleigh	05-07-87	
James W. Smith	Southport	07-01-89	06-30-93

EMPLOYMENT SECURITY COMMISSION ADVISORY COUNCIL
G.S. 96-4(e)/Board No. 0350

Name of Appointee	*Address*	*Date Appointed*	*Date of Expiration*
Elizabeth G. Anderson	Charlotte	08-03-89	06-30-93
Carson B. Annis	Raleigh	08-03-89	06-30-93
Godfrey G. Bennett, Jr.	Charlotte	04-14-86	06-30-89
		08-03-89	06-30-93
Charles Blackmon	Durham	03-28-91	06-30-93
R. L. Davis	Lumberton	08-15-86	06-30-89
Michelle M. DeLapp	Lexington	04-14-86	06-30-89
		08-03-89	06-30-93
Mrs. Jessie R. Dotson	Fletcher	04-14-86	06-30-89
Ms. Kyle G. Fraley	Fayetteville	05-06-86	06-30-89
		08-03-89	06-30-93
Hewitt Fulton	Laurinburg	08-03-89	06-30-93
Anthony C. Giordano	Greenville	08-03-89	06-30-93
Oscar A. Graham	Wilmington	04-14-86	06-30-89
James S. Harrod, Jr.	Rockingham	08-03-89	06-30-93
Dalton R. Hodges	Washington	04-14-86	06-30-89

EMPLOYMENT SECURITY COMMISSION ADVISORY COUNCIL
(CONTINUED)

Paul T. Hodul	Fayetteville	08-03-89	06-30-93
Ernest Koury, Jr.	Burlington	04-14-86	06-30-89
Bobby Langdon	Benson	04-14-86	06-30-89
Faye J. McArthur	Raleigh	08-03-89	06-30-93
L. Waldo Matthews	Franklinville	04-14-86	06-30-89
George Monk	High Point	04-14-86	06-30-89
Clyde V. Owens	Charlotte	08-03-89	06-30-93
Ted B. Owens	Columbus	08-03-89	06-30-93
A. E. Partridge, Jr.	Concord	04-14-86	06-30-89
Charles W. Pendergraft II	Raleigh	01-09-91	06-30-93
Clyde C. Poole	Granite Falls	04-14-86	06-30-89
Dennis V. Proctor, Sr.	Wilmington	08-03-89	06-30-93
Richard D. Smith	Durham	04-14-86	06-30-89
Doretha M. Stone	Castle Hayne	08-03-89	06-30-93
Thomas J. White	Durham	08-03-89	06-30-93
Kermit D. Williamson	Clinton	04-14-86	06-30-89
Chris Wrenn	Louisburg	04-14-86	06-30-89

ENERGY POLICY COUNCIL
G.S. 113B-3/Board No. 0353

Name of Appointee	Address	Date Appointed	Date of Expiration
J. T. Alexander, Jr.	Statesville	04-08-92	01-31-93
John C. Baugh	Albemarle	04-10-89	01-31-93
John B. Beall	Lenoir	06-18-85	01-31-89
		04-10-89	01-31-93
Kyle C. Boone	Asheville	04-10-89	01-31-93
Irene G. Brisson	Dublin	06-18-85	01-31-89
Robert Broady, Jr.	Hamlet	06-02-87	01-31-89
A. Leon Capel	Troy	06-18-85	01-31-89
		04-10-89	01-31-93
Winslow H. Hartford	Charlotte	06-18-85	01-31-89
		04-10-89	01-31-93
Charles C. Heath	Shelby	06-18-85	01-31-89
		04-10-89	01-31-93
N. Carnell Robinson	Dunn	01-26-90	01-31-93
Carl L. Tilghman	Beaufort	06-18-85	01-31-89
Roger N. Waud	Chapel Hill	02-06-86	01-31-89
		04-10-89	01-31-93
Annette T. West	Kinston	04-10-89	01-31-93
Emma J. Wise	Holly Springs	04-10-89	01-31-93

NORTH CAROLINA HAZARDOUS WASTE MANAGEMENT COMMISSION
G.S. 130B-6/Board No. 0410

Name of Appointee	Address	Date Appointed	Date of Expiration
Trenton G. Davis	Greenville	06-19-89	06-30-93
David E. Faircloth	Jackson	05-04-92	06-30-94
Lloyd Hise, Jr.	Spruce Pine	06-19-89	06-30-90
vice-chairman		06-19-89	
Truman L. Koehler	Charlotte	06-19-89	06-30-91
James E. Rhodes	Southern Pines	05-04-92	06-30-93

NORTH CAROLINA HAZARDOUS WASTE MANAGEMENT COMMISSION
(CONTINUED)

William W. Shingleton	Durham	06-19-89	06-30-92
Alvis G. Turner	Chapel Hill	06-19-89	06-30-93
chairman		06-19-89	

NORTH CAROLINA HAZARDOUS WASTE TREATMENT COMMISSION [11]
G.S. 143B-470.3/Board No. 0410

Name of Appointee	Address	Date Appointed	Date of Expiration
Charles Foushee, *vice-chairman*	Lenoir	04-22-85	
Joseph E. Harwood	Charlotte	03-22-85	01-31-89
chairman		03-22-85	
vice-chairman		01-15-86	
Lloyd Hise, Jr.	Spruce Pine	08-21-87	01-31-89
vice-chairman		08-21-87	
		02-01-89	01-31-93
vice-chairman		02-01-89	
Truman L. Koehler	Charlotte	01-15-86	01-31-87
		02-13-87	01-31-91
Deborah Parker, *chairwoman*	Fayetteville	04-22-85	
		02-13-87	01-31-91
chairwoman		02-13-87	
William W. Shingleton	Durham	02-15-89	01-31-91

NORTH CAROLINA HOUSING COMMISSION [12]
G.S. 147-33.12/Board No. 0433

Name of Appointee	Address	Date Appointed	Date of Expiration
H. Keith Brunnemer, Jr.	Charlotte	07-10-87	06-30-89
Benjamin H. Harding, Jr.	Yadkinville	07-10-87	06-30-89
Chandler Lee	Southern Pines	07-10-87	06-30-89
chairman		07-10-87	

NORTH CAROLINA HOUSING FINANCE AGENCY BOARD OF DIRECTORS
G.S. 122A-4/Board No. 0435

Name of Appointee	Address	Date Appointed	Date of Expiration
William T. Boyd, *chairman*	Asheboro	09-01-89	03-01-91
chairman		04-03-91	04-02-93
John Crosland, Jr., *chairman*	Charlotte	01-15-86	01-01-88
chairman		02-12-88	11-21-88
chairman		03-23-89	03-01-91
J. Edwin Hunter	Statesville	01-04-88	06-30-90
		07-02-90	06-30-94
Robert D. Kirby	Charlotte	09-15-85	06-30-89
		07-01-89	06-30-93

---

[11]The North Carolina Hazardous Waste Treatment Commission was reorganized as the North Carolina Hazardous Waste Management Commission, effective May 30, 1989; see *N.C. Session Laws, 1989*, I, c. 168.

[12]G.S. 147-33.12 through G.S. 147-33.21 were repealed on August 14, 1987, abolishing the Housing Commission; see *N.C. Session Laws, 1987*, II, c. 841.

NORTH CAROLINA HOUSING FINANCE AGENCY BOARD OF DIRECTORS
(CONTINUED)

J. Kenneth Lee .... Greensboro	09-15-85	06-30-89
vice-chairman	12-12-88	06-30-89
	07-01-89	06-30-93
vice-chairman	07-01-89	06-30-91
Melanie Wilson .... Reidsville	02-12-88	06-30-90
	07-02-90	06-30-94

NORTH CAROLINA INDUSTRIAL COMMISSION
G.S. 97-77/Board No. 0463

Name of Appointee	Address	Date Appointed	Date of Expiration
James J. Booker .... Winston-Salem	01-28-91	04-30-95
chairman	01-28-91	
Bruce B. Briggs .... Mars Hill	01-01-90	04-30-95
chairman	01-01-90	
David V. Brooks .... Raleigh	05-01-85	04-30-91
chairman	08-01-85	
J. Harold Davis .... Raleigh	05-01-87	04-30-93
Ernest C. Pearson .... Raleigh	08-21-87	04-30-91
chairman	08-21-87	
William H. Stephenson .... Garner	01-23-89	04-30-89
chairman	01-23-89	
J. Randolph Ward .... Cary	02-10-89	04-30-91
	05-01-91	04-30-97

NORTH CAROLINA MILK COMMISSION
G.S. 106-266.7/Board No. 0585

Name of Appointee	Address	Date Appointed	Date of Expiration
Charles E. McCartney, Jr. .... Shelby	07-01-89	06-30-93
W. Christopher Shields .... Mount Holly	07-15-85	06-30-89
Gary W. Smith .... Wilson	07-01-89	06-30-93
Hardy R. Watkins .... Raleigh	04-13-88	06-30-89
	07-01-89	06-30-93

MOREHEAD CITY NAVIGATION AND PILOTAGE COMMISSION
G.S. 76A-33/Board No. 3330

Name of Appointee	Address	Date Appointed	Date of Expiration
Harold A. Booth .... Beaufort	06-30-86	06-30-89
	07-01-89	06-30-92
	12-04-92	06-30-95
Warren J. Davis .... Beaufort	06-30-86	06-30-89
	07-01-89	06-30-92
	12-04-92	06-30-95
Robert G. Gaskill .... Morehead City	03-12-85	06-30-87
	07-01-87	06-30-90
	07-02-90	06-30-93
Reginald T. Styron .... Davis	07-31-85	
	07-01-88	06-30-91
chairman	07-01-88	
chairman	07-01-91	06-30-94

NORTH CAROLINA MUTUAL BURIAL ASSOCIATION COMMISSION
G.S. 58-241.7/Board No. 0155

Name of Appointee	Address	Date Appointed	Date of Expiration
William Brater	Statesville	01-09-91	11-30-95
Charles Grindstaff	Spruce Pine	11-20-85	12-01-90

NORTH CAROLINA NATIONAL PARK, PARKWAY, AND FORESTS
DEVELOPMENT COUNCIL
G.S. 143B-447/Board No. 0625

Name of Appointee	Address	Date Appointed	Date of Expiration
Gove B. Almond, Jr.	Bryson City	07-01-89	06-30-93
W. Louis Bissette, Jr.	Asheville	07-15-85	06-30-89
		07-01-89	06-30-93
Harold P. Corbin	Franklin	07-01-87	06-30-91
		08-26-91	06-30-95
R. Everett Crisp	Whittier	08-12-88	07-01-89
Phyllis A. Foxx	Sylva	07-01-87	06-30-91
		08-26-91	06-30-95
Margaret M. Hunt	Brevard	07-01-87	06-30-91
Monroe A. Miller	Waynesville	07-15-85	06-30-89
		07-01-89	06-30-93
William E. Mitchell	Bryson City	07-15-85	06-30-89
William H. Phillips	Waynesville	03-02-92	06-30-93
James M. Stump	Jefferson	03-02-92	06-30-95
Charles B. Von Canon	Banner Elk	07-01-87	06-30-91
		08-26-91	06-30-95

NORTH CAROLINA STATE PORTS AUTHORITY
G.S. 143B-452/Board No. 0715

Name of Appointee	Address	Date Appointed	Date of Expiration
Ruth A. Adams	Jacksonville	04-17-85	06-30-85
		02-21-86	06-30-91
		08-26-91	06-30-96
James M. Berry, *chairman*	Charlotte	02-01-85	06-30-85
chairman		02-21-86	06-30-91
Larry L. Brittain	Charlotte	05-01-85	06-30-85
		02-21-86	06-30-89
vice-chairman		10-03-88	
		07-01-89	06-30-95
James T. Broyhill	Lenoir	11-06-89	06-30-91
		02-14-91	06-30-93
Thomas M. Evins, Jr.	Oxford	02-21-86	06-30-87
		07-01-87	06-30-93
		07-01-89	06-30-95
Estell C. Lee	Raleigh	06-24-91	06-30-93
William F. Maready	Winston-Salem	04-17-85	06-30-89
		07-01-89	06-30-95
Coolidge Murrow	Wilmington	04-17-85	06-30-87
		07-01-87	06-30-93
Ron Perry	Lewisville	10-03-88	06-30-91

NORTH CAROLINA STATE PORTS AUTHORITY
(CONTINUED)

Perley A. Thomas	High Point	04-17-85	06-30-87
		07-01-87	06-30-93
chairman		10-03-88	
chairman		02-14-91	
		08-27-91	06-30-97

NORTH CAROLINA RURAL ELECTRIFICATION AUTHORITY
G.S. 117-1/Board No. 0795

Name of Appointee	Address	Date Appointed	Date of Expiration
Richard L. Cox	Asheboro	08-31-87	06-05-91
		09-20-91	06-30-95
Henry C. Gabriel	Sherrills Ford	02-27-87	06-05-89
		06-06-89	06-06-93
J. Wade Kincaid, Sr.	Hudson	10-30-85	06-05-89
Gerald V. Montgomery	Pineville	07-14-92	06-30-93
Bobby Pigg	Tarboro	07-31-85	06-05-89
Richard R. Robinson	Elizabeth City		
		12-22-88	06-05-89
		06-06-89	06-06-93
James L. Sheek	Mocksville	08-31-87	06-05-91
R. B. Sloan, Jr.	Statesville	07-31-85	06-05-89
		06-06-89	06-06-93
Robert L. Thornton	Clinton	09-20-91	06-30-95

NORTH CAROLINA SAVINGS INSTITUTIONS COMMISSION [13]
G.S. 54B-53/Board No. 0820

Name of Appointee	Address	Date Appointed	Date of Expiration
A. Harold Ausley, Sr.	Sanford	02-12-92	06-30-93
Edward G. Ballew, Jr.	Spruce Pine	08-15-86	07-15-90
		07-16-90	06-30-94
Norman C. Camp III	Raleigh	07-16-90	06-30-91
James T. Davis, Jr.	Elizabeth City	09-22-89	06-30-93
William A. Dunn	Raleigh	07-16-90	06-30-91
		09-27-91	06-30-95
Stedman S. Graham, Jr.	High Point	10-28-88	06-30-91
William D. Hoover	Asheboro	09-22-89	06-30-93
Betty B. Morenstein	Elkin	08-15-86	07-15-90
James K. Polk, Sr.	Charlotte	07-15-87	07-15-91
Betty S. Riddle	Ararat	07-16-90	06-30-94
John W. Sellers	Lumberton	07-15-87	07-15-91
Aaron L. Spaulding	Durham	09-27-91	06-30-95
M. E. Valentine, Jr.	Raleigh	04-14-89	06-30-89
		09-22-89	06-30-93

[13]The name of the North Carolina Savings and Loan Commission was changed to North Carolina Savings Institutions Commission under N.C. Session Laws, 1989, I, c. 76, s. 17, effective April 26, 1989.

North Carolina Seafood Industrial Park Authority
G.S. 113-315.25/Board No. 0830

Name of Appointee	Address	Date Appointed	Date of Expiration
Gerald J. Beshens	Southern Shores	04-22-92	06-30-95
Walter D. Brady	Morehead City	04-22-92	06-30-95
Nathan Cartwright, Jr.	Grandy	07-01-87	06-30-91
Lancelot M. Daniels	Wanchese	01-02-87	06-30-89
		07-24-89	06-30-93
Ward W. Daniels	Wanchese	01-02-87	06-30-89
chairman		01-30-87	
		07-24-89	06-30-93
H. Rick Gardner	Elizabeth City	07-01-87	06-30-91
		10-17-91	06-30-95
chairman		06-10-92	
chairman		09-15-92	06-30-93
Robert T. Hutchins	Elizabeth City	01-02-87	06-30-87
Clay M. Kirkman	Kitty Hawk	01-09-91	06-30-93
chairman		10-17-91	06-30-92
Levy Lilly	Newport	01-02-87	06-30-89
		07-24-89	06-30-93
Stephen H. Locke	Aurora	04-22-92	06-30-93
William J. Monti	Currituck	01-02-87	06-30-87
Leslie R. Myrie, Sr.	Southport	01-02-87	06-30-89
vice-chairman		11-24-87	
		07-24-89	06-30-93
vice-chairman		07-24-89	06-30-90
vice-chairman		07-02-90	06-30-91
Dan G. Oden	Hatteras	01-02-87	06-30-89
		07-24-89	06-30-93
Carroll U. Price	Avon	01-02-87	06-30-87
vice-chairman		01-02-87	
vice-chairman		07-01-87	07-01-91
chairman		11-23-87	
chairman		07-24-89	06-30-90
chairman		07-02-90	06-30-91
		10-17-91	06-30-95
Jean W. Williams	Swan Quarter	01-02-87	06-30-87
		07-01-87	07-01-91
vice-chairman		10-17-91	06-30-92
		10-17-91	06-30-95
vice-chairman		09-15-92	06-30-93

North Carolina Travel and Tourism Board
G.S. 143B-434.1/Board No. 3491

Name of Appointee	Address	Date Appointed	Date of Expiration
Ward K. Barnett, Sr.	Frisco	01-15-92	
Robert H. Booth, Jr.	Chapel Hill	01-15-92	
Isaac Wall	Winston-Salem	01-15-92	

NORTH CAROLINA UTILITIES COMMISSION
G.S. 62-10/Board No. 0920

Name of Appointee	Address	Date Appointed	Date of Expiration
Laurence A. Cobb	Raleigh	08-14-89	06-30-97
Allyson K. Duncan	Durham	07-01-91	06-30-99
Charles H. Hughes	Raleigh	04-03-89	06-30-89
		07-01-89	06-30-97
William W. Redman, Jr.	Raleigh	01-05-87	06-30-87
		07-01-87	06-30-95
chairman		07-01-89	06-30-93
Sarah Tate	Raleigh	07-01-85	06-30-93
Robert O. Wells	High Point	07-01-85	06-30-93
chairman		10-01-85	06-30-89
Julius A. Wright	Wilmington	07-01-85	06-30-93

NORTH CAROLINA UTILITIES COMMISSION PUBLIC STAFF
G.S. 62-15/Board No. 0921

Name of Appointee	Address	Date Appointed	Date of Expiration
Robert Gruber, *executive director*	Raleigh	07-01-89	06-30-95

DEPARTMENT OF ENVIRONMENT, HEALTH, AND NATURAL RESOURCES

Secretaries
S. Thomas Rhodes, 1985-1988
William W. Cobey, Jr., 1989-1993

ATLANTIC STATES MARINE FISHERIES COMMISSION
G.S. 113-254/Board No. 0080

Name of Appointee	Address	Date Appointed	Date of Expiration
Kenny L. Daniels	Wanchese	07-22-87	06-30-90
		07-02-90	06-30-93

NORTH CAROLINA CHILD FATALITY TASK FORCE
G.S. 143-573/BOARD NO. 0203

Name of Appointee	Address	Date Appointed	Date of Expiration
Leah M. Devlin	Raleigh	12-04-92	
Edward R. Inman	Burlington	10-17-91	
John S. Niblock	Raleigh	10-17-91	
Richard R. Nugent	Raleigh	10-17-91	

COASTAL RESOURCES COMMISSION
G.S. 113A-104/Board No. 0207

Name of Appointee	Address	Date Appointed	Date of Expiration
David A. Adams	Raleigh	08-25-89	06-30-92
		07-01-92	06-30-96
R. Page Ayres	Washington	08-28-86	06-30-90
Daniel V. Besse	New Bern	08-28-86	06-30-90
chairman		08-28-86	
		07-02-90	06-30-94
Grace H. Bonner	Aurora	07-01-92	06-30-96

Coastal Resources Commission
(continued)

Percy E. Bunch	Murfreesboro	07-01-92	06-30-96
Ernest A. Carl	Wilmington	12-09-92	06-30-94
L. Reginald Caroon	Lowland	08-28-86	06-30-90
		07-02-90	06-30-94
Arthur W. Cooper	Raleigh	08-29-88	06-30-92
Courtney T. Hackney	Rocky Point	09-27-89	06-30-90
		07-02-90	06-30-94
James W. Hamilton	Jacksonville	08-28-86	06-30-90
		07-02-90	06-30-94
Richard J. Hargitt	Kinston	07-01-92	06-30-96
James E. Harrington	Raleigh	07-02-90	06-30-94
chairman		07-02-90	
T. Erie Haste, Jr.	Hertford	08-29-88	06-30-92
		07-01-92	06-30-96
David L. Jennette, Sr.	Windsor	07-02-90	06-30-94
Paula A. Kirby	Jacksonville	07-01-92	06-30-96
Myra S. Ladd	Kill Devil Hills	08-29-88	06-30-92
M. Kent Mitchell	Wilmington	08-29-88	06-30-92
W. Lawrence Robertson	Wilmington	08-29-88	06-30-92
Ronnie E. Rose	Moyock	08-28-86	06-30-90
J. Bowen Ross, Jr.	Morehead City	07-02-90	06-30-94
Martha B. R. Simpson	Roper	08-29-88	06-30-92
John T. Thornton	Elizabeth City	08-29-88	06-30-92
		08-24-92	06-30-96
Eugene B. Tomlinson, Jr.	Southport	08-29-88	06-30-92
		07-01-92	06-30-96
Ronnie O. Watson	Emerald Isle	08-28-86	06-30-90
John G. Wood IV	Edenton	12-23-85	06-30-86
		08-28-86	06-30-90

Environmental Management Commission
G.S. 143B-283/Board No. 0355

Name of Appointee	Address	Date Appointed	Date of Expiration
Edwin E. Andrews III	Raleigh	09-27-91	06-30-95
Charles L. Baker	Charlotte	11-20-85	06-30-91
chairman		07-08-86	
chairman		09-27-91	06-30-97
Thomas W. Bradshaw, Jr.	Raleigh	09-11-86	06-30-89
Charles A. Brady III	Lenoir	09-01-87	06-30-93
Carla E. DuPuy	Charlotte	07-14-89	06-30-95
William S. Farabow	High Point	08-25-89	06-30-95
Robert W. Griffith, Jr.	Morehead City	07-30-87	06-30-93
Thomas J. Harrelson	Southport	07-01-85	06-30-91
Michel A. Ibrahim	Chapel Hill	07-14-89	06-30-95
Jerry D. Lewis, chairman	Shallotte	03-14-85	
		07-08-86	06-30-91
Dennis Loflin	Denton	09-27-91	06-30-97
Virgil L. McBride	Advance	07-30-87	06-30-93
Duncan Malloy III	Lumber Bridge	07-01-85	06-30-91
Miguel A. Medina, Jr.	Durham	07-14-89	06-30-95
Charles H. Peterson	Morehead City	07-14-89	06-30-95
Charles A. S. Phillips	Pinehurst	09-02-86	06-30-89
Terry F. Turner	Wilmington	01-02-87	06-30-89

ENVIRONMENTAL MANAGEMENT COMMISSION
(CONTINUED)

Gladys S. Van Pelt	Greensboro	07-01-85	06-30-91
Richard V. Watkins	Conover	09-27-91	06-30-97
Candler A. Willis	Morehead City	07-30-87	06-30-93
Lawrence R. Zucchino	Raleigh	09-27-91	06-30-97

FORESTRY ADVISORY COUNCIL
G.S. 143B-309/Board No. 0385

Name of Appointee	Address	Date Appointed	Date of Expiration
Robert J. Beason	Wilmington	05-28-85	06-30-88
chairman		05-28-85	
		06-30-88	06-30-92
chairman		06-30-88	
		12-09-92	06-30-96
chairman		12-09-92	
Charles T. Cone	Tarboro	02-27-87	06-30-90
		10-19-90	06-30-94
Jocille B. Eddleman	New Bern	02-27-87	06-30-90
		10-19-90	06-30-94
Daniel H. Gelbert	Durham	10-19-90	06-30-94
James L. Gundy	High Point	12-30-87	06-30-88
		06-30-88	06-30-92
		12-09-92	06-30-96
Lislott D. Harberts	Statesville	12-30-87	06-30-88
		06-30-88	06-30-92
		12-09-92	06-30-96
David L. Jennette	Windsor	02-27-87	06-30-90
Gene M. Linney	Taylorsville	02-27-87	06-30-88
		06-30-88	06-30-92
		12-09-92	06-30-96
D. Hilbert Lovette	Lumberton	02-27-87	06-30-90
J. Parker Lumpkin II	Louisburg	03-09-89	06-30-90
		10-19-90	06-30-94
Forney A. Rankin	Gastonia	02-27-87	06-30-90
		10-19-90	06-30-94
Willie E. Rich	New Bern	02-27-87	06-30-88
		06-30-88	06-30-92
		12-09-92	06-30-96
John B. Veach	Asheville	02-27-87	06-30-90
		10-19-90	06-30-94
J. Max Yates	Jefferson	01-27-92	06-30-94

STATE COMMISSION FOR HEALTH SERVICES
G.S. 143B-143/Board No. 0420

Name of Appointee	Address	Date Appointed	Date of Expiration
G. Shuford Abernethy	Hickory	08-31-85	05-01-89
		04-30-89	04-30-93
Imagean V. Adams	Andrews	01-09-91	04-30-93
Paul Bissette	Wilson	05-22-91	04-30-95
Frank C. Cockinos	Charlotte	04-30-89	04-30-93
Harold V. Day	Spruce Pine	05-01-87	04-30-91
Walter W. Dickson	Gastonia	05-01-87	04-30-91

STATE COMMISSION FOR HEALTH SERVICES
(CONTINUED)

Frances P. Digh	Denver	04-30-89	04-30-93
Victor H. Hoffman	Thomasville	04-30-89	04-30-93
Beverly Malone	Greensboro	10-19-90	04-30-94
H. Wayne Mohorn	Greensboro	04-30-89	04-30-93
Leigh F. Sugg	Goldsboro	05-15-86	05-01-90
John W. Thuss, Jr.	Lenoir	01-24-89	04-30-91
		05-22-91	04-30-95

NORTH CAROLINA MARINE FISHERIES COMMISSION [14]
G.S. 143B-289.5/Board No. 0552

Name of Appointee	Address	Date Appointed	Date of Expiration
Thomas S. Bennett, *chairman*	Morehead City	10-30-87	09-30-93
Ray J. Boleman, Jr.	Rocky Mount	10-17-91	09-30-97
JoAnn M. Burkholder	Raleigh	05-29-92	09-30-93
Cashwell B. Caroon	Southport	11-20-85	06-30-91
		10-30-87	09-30-89
		10-18-89	09-30-95
chairman		05-29-92	
James S. Carson, Jr.	Charlotte	10-30-87	09-30-93
George T. Clark, Jr.	Wilmington	10-17-91	09-30-93
J. D. Costlow	Beaufort	02-05-85	06-30-88
Ford A. Cross	Beaufort	02-05-85	06-30-87
		10-30-87	09-30-93
Rodney E. Everhart	Wilmington	11-10-86	06-30-87
Paul B. Forsberg	Wilmington	01-16-91	09-30-95
William A. Foster	Hatteras	10-17-91	09-30-97
Dirk Frankenberg	Hillsborough	02-22-91	09-30-93
Mr. Jodie E. Gay	Hampstead	12-30-92	09-30-95
Tilman R. Gray	Avon	11-10-86	06-30-91
		10-30-87	09-30-91
Jerry W. Hardesty	Clemmons	10-30-87	09-30-91
		10-17-91	09-30-97
Garvin Hardison	Arapahoe	11-20-85	06-30-91
		10-30-87	09-30-93
M. R. Hewett	Shallotte	03-03-88	09-30-89
Maughan Hull	Elizabeth City	10-30-87	09-30-91
Franklin B. Johnston	Washington	10-30-87	09-30-91
Gordon W. Meekins, Jr.	Englehard	11-20-85	06-30-91
		10-30-87	09-30-89
		10-18-89	09-30-95
P. Clinton Midkiff	Elizabeth City	05-18-89	09-30-91
Pete Moffitt, Jr.	High Point	10-17-91	09-30-97
Murray L. Nixon, Sr.	Edenton	10-30-87	09-30-89
		10-18-89	09-30-95
Michael K. Orbach	Greenville	11-10-86	06-30-92
		10-30-87	09-30-91
		10-17-91	09-30-97
Francisco Perez	Wilmington	11-10-86	06-30-90
		10-30-87	09-30-93

---

[14]The North Carolina Marine Fisheries Commission was reorganized under *N.C. Session Laws, 1987*, I, c. 641, which accounted for the overlapping terms served by some individuals. The revised membership guidelines, addressed in Section 2 of the law, became effective October 1, 1987.

NORTH CAROLINA MARINE FISHERIES COMMISSION
(CONTINUED)

Charles H. Peterson	Morehead City	11-10-86	06-30-92
James I. Piner	Beaufort	11-10-86	06-30-92
Lena S. Ritter	Holly Ridge	10-30-87	09-30-89
Carson Varnam	Supply	10-06-88	09-30-89
		10-18-89	09-30-95
Mr. Jule D. Wheatly	Beaufort	10-30-87	09-30-89
		10-18-89	09-30-95

NORTH CAROLINA MINING COMMISSION
G.S. 143B-291/Board No. 0587

Name of Appointee	Address	Date Appointed	Date of Expiration
Edwin E. Andrews III	Raleigh	12-02-91	06-30-93
Harold J. Andrews	Gastonia	08-26-91	06-30-97
Charles L. Baker	Charlotte	12-10-85	06-30-91
		08-26-91	06-30-97
John R. Bratton	Raleigh	10-16-92	06-30-93
W. Stephen Brier	Salisbury	11-23-87	06-30-93
Henry S. Brown	Raleigh	08-03-89	06-30-95
G. Douglas Carroll	Winston-Salem	08-26-91	06-30-97
Sherrod B. Clarke, Jr.	Winston-Salem	08-26-91	06-30-97
Thomas S. Elleman	Raleigh	07-01-86	
William E. Isler	Raleigh	01-12-90	
Joseph A. Phillips	Raleigh	10-11-90	06-30-93
James W. Smack	Winston-Salem	12-09-92	06-30-97
chairman		12-09-92	
Gladys S. Van Pelt	Greensboro	12-10-85	06-30-87
		11-23-87	06-30-93
Charles H. Wallschleger	Pfafftown	10-16-92	06-30-97
W. W. Woodhouse, Jr.	Raleigh	11-23-87	06-30-93

MINORITY HEALTH ADVISORY COUNCIL
G.S. 130A-33.44(a)/Board No. 0591

Name of Appointee	Address	Date Appointed	Date of Expiration
Cherry M. Beasley	Lumberton	10-16-92	10-15-94
Pedro A. Castillo	Winston-Salem	10-16-92	10-15-93
Mary K. Deyampert	Fayetteville	10-16-92	10-15-93
Henry E. McKoy	Raleigh	10-16-92	10-15-95
Maliston Stanley	Shallotte	10-16-92	10-15-94

BOARD OF NATURAL RESOURCES AND COMMUNITY DEVELOPMENT [15]
G.S. 143B-280/Board No. 0627

Name of Appointee	Address	Date Appointed	Date of Expiration
Charles A. Brady	Lenoir	07-01-85	
Alexander T. Davison	Hillsborough	07-01-85	
Rodney E. Everhart	Wilmington	07-01-85	
Tilman R. Gray	Avon	07-01-85	
Rhonda Innes	Davidson	07-01-85	
Thomas E. Strickland	Goldsboro	09-30-87	

---

[15]N.C. Session Laws, 1989, II, s. 2, abolished G.S. 143B-275 through G.S. 143B-281, effective July 1, 1989.

NORTH CAROLINA ON-SITE WASTEWATER SYSTEMS INSTITUTE
BOARD OF DIRECTORS
G.S. 130A-344(b)/Board No. 0650

Name of Appointee	Address	Date Appointed	Date of Expiration
Richard K. Rowe	Raleigh	09-15-92	06-30-95

NORTH CAROLINA PARKS AND RECREATION COUNCIL
G.S. 143B-312/Board No. 0673

Name of Appointee	Address	Date Appointed	Date of Expiration
Philip W. Babcock	Hendersonville	03-13-87	06-30-90
		03-06-92	06-30-94
U. James Bennett	Monroe	03-13-87	06-30-90
		03-06-92	06-30-94
Philip E. Berger	Eden	02-12-88	06-30-90
Patrick Campbell	Hickory	03-13-87	06-30-90
W. G. Clark III	Tarboro	03-13-87	06-30-90
Sue T. Dean	Carolina Beach	03-13-87	06-30-90
		03-06-92	06-30-94
David Drexel	Southern Pines	03-13-87	06-30-90
Steven H. Everhardt	Buies Creek	03-13-87	06-30-90
Phillip E. Fleming	Fuquay-Varina	03-06-92	06-30-94
Jack Frauson	Wilmington	01-19-88	
Zeb F. Hanner	Thomasville	02-12-88	06-30-90
		03-06-92	06-30-94
Marc T. Latta	Raleigh	03-06-92	06-30-94
Jon Leatherwood	Huntersville	12-09-92	06-30-94
William Lopp	Jefferson	03-13-87	06-30-90
Jeannie R. Martin	Columbus	03-06-92	06-30-94
G. Douglas Massey	Goldsboro	04-17-87	
Earnest L. Morris	Winston-Salem	12-09-92	06-30-94
Ann B. Orr	Raleigh	06-03-88	06-30-90
James F. Parnell	Wilmington	12-09-92	06-30-94
Phil Rea	Raleigh	03-13-87	06-30-90
		03-06-92	06-30-94
Kent Robinson	Boone	06-03-88	06-30-90
Keith Rouse	Goldsboro	03-13-87	06-30-90
James E. Swofford	North Wilkesboro	05-15-87	
Charles H. Taylor	Brevard	02-11-87	06-30-90
chairman		02-11-87	
R. Frank Timberlake, Jr., *chairman*	Zebulon	12-23-85	
		03-13-87	06-30-90
Mike Waters	Wilmington	04-17-87	
Andy Wells	Hickory	03-06-92	06-30-94
chairman		03-06-92	

GOVERNOR'S COUNCIL ON PHYSICAL FITNESS AND HEALTH
G.S. 130A-33.40/Board No. 0697

Name of Appointee	Address	Date Appointed	Date of Expiration
Nancy C. Boland	Asheville	07-01-88	06-30-92
Walton W. Curl	Winston-Salem	10-17-91	06-30-92
		08-03-92	06-30-96

GOVERNOR'S COUNCIL ON PHYSICAL FITNESS AND HEALTH
(CONTINUED)

William J. Fletcher, Jr.	North Wilkesboro	01-15-86	06-30-87
		07-01-87	06-30-91
		09-27-91	06-30-95
Stedman S. Graham	Chicago	07-10-90	06-30-92
Isaac B. Grainger, Jr.	Burlington	01-15-86	06-30-87
		07-01-87	06-30-91
Bishop T. Harris	Cary	08-03-92	06-30-96
Carolyn B. Hughes	Manteo	01-15-86	06-30-86
		06-30-86	06-30-90
Daniel M. Lotz	Raleigh	09-21-90	06-30-94
Angela Lumpkin	Raleigh	01-15-86	06-30-88
		07-21-88	06-30-89
		07-01-89	06-30-93
Angus M. McBryde, Jr.	Charlotte	01-15-86	06-30-88
		07-01-88	06-30-92
chairman		09-21-90	
Jeff Mullins	Charlotte	01-15-86	06-30-89
Dave Rowe	Asheboro	10-17-91	06-30-95
chairman		10-17-91	
Susan W. Stankavage	Durham	02-21-91	06-30-94
Roger G. Thrift	New Bern	01-15-86	06-30-89
		07-01-89	06-30-93
Mr. Shirley S. Wilson	Durham	01-15-86	06-30-86
chairman		02-21-86	
		06-30-86	06-30-90
		09-21-90	00-00-94

NORTH CAROLINA RADIATION PROTECTION COMMISSION
G.S. 104E-8/Board No. 0752

Name of Appointee	Address	Date Appointed	Date of Expiration
G. Shuford Abernethy	Hickory	02-26-86	
Vicky C. Best	Fletcher	07-01-87	06-30-91
		11-19-91	06-30-95
Mary L. Birch	Charlotte	07-21-89	06-30-93
Charles B. Burns	Chapel Hill	07-01-87	06-30-91
		11-19-91	06-30-95
Robert G. Cockrell	Greensboro	03-17-87	06-30-90
		09-21-90	06-30-94
David E. Crisp	Raleigh	02-26-86	
Ronald S. DeMars	Greensboro	11-19-91	06-30-95
William S. Farabow	High Point	01-08-90	
Eugene A. Lewis	Greensboro	01-15-86	06-30-87
		07-01-87	06-30-91
Lionel Lewis	Charlotte	01-15-86	06-30-89
R. William McConnell	Greenville	01-15-86	06-30-89
		07-21-89	06-30-93
David Mallette, Jr.	Raleigh	06-02-87	
Stephen R. Matteson	Chapel Hill	01-15-86	06-30-89
C. Jeff Mauney	Kings Mountain	03-17-87	06-30-90
		09-21-90	06-30-94
H. Wayne Mohorn	Greensboro	04-10-89	
Raymond L. Murray	Raleigh	07-01-87	06-30-91

North Carolina Radiation Protection Commission
(continued)

James A. Oppold	Raleigh	06-30-86	
Ernest C. Pearson	Raleigh	09-25-87	
Charles A. S. Phillips	Pinehurst	05-17-88	
John M. Syria	Raleigh	04-03-91	
Wayne R. Thomann	Chapel Hill	01-15-86	06-30-89
		07-21-89	06-30-93
Donald A. Tyndall	Chapel Hill	09-23-88	06-30-89
		07-21-89	06-30-93
William F. Walker	Raleigh	09-16-92	06-30-94
J. Randolph Ward	Cary	03-03-89	
James E. Watson, Jr.	Chapel Hill	06-02-87	06-30-90
		09-21-90	06-30-94
Billy H. Webster	Cary	04-03-91	06-30-93
Charles W. Welby	Raleigh	05-17-88	06-30-91
		11-19-91	06-30-95
Julius A. Wright	Raleigh	06-30-86	

Recreation and Natural Heritage Trust Fund Board of Trustees
G.S. 113-77.8/Board No. 3361

Name of Appointee	Address	Date Appointed	Date of Expiration
Hamilton C. Horton, Jr.	Winston-Salem	03-04-88	01-01-94
chairman		03-04-88	
Thomas W. Reese	Hickory	01-01-88	01-01-92
		01-27-92	01-01-98
Dewey W. Wells	Winston-Salem	01-01-88	01-01-90
		01-26-90	01-01-96

State Board of Sanitarian Examiners
G.S. 90A-55/Board No. 0815

Name of Appointee	Address	Date Appointed	Date of Expiration
Paul M. Andrews	Ayden	12-27-89	12-15-93
David R. Baxley, Sr.	Taylorsville	02-27-87	12-15-90
Gary G. Cole	Pfafftown	02-26-86	12-15-89
		12-27-89	12-15-93
Trenton G. Davis	Greenville	02-26-86	12-15-89
		12-27-89	12-15-93
Judy R. Daye	Burlington	03-17-92	12-15-95
Audy R. Dover	Concord	02-24-88	12-15-91
Ruby T. Hooper	Morganton	02-26-86	12-15-89
Donnie R. McFall	Durham	12-31-92	12-15-93
Thomas F. Owens	Colfax	02-26-86	12-15-89
		12-27-89	12-15-93
Terry L. Pierce	Brevard	12-31-92	12-15-94
Charles E. Powell	Goldsboro	02-26-86	12-15-89
John F. Renfro	Burnsville	03-17-92	12-15-95
David L. Rust, Jr.	Valdese	01-16-91	12-15-94
Linda C. Sewall	Clayton	07-02-90	12-15-93
Marjorie O. Strawn	Lenoir	02-27-87	12-15-90
		01-16-91	12-15-94
Gerald Strickland	Pembroke	02-24-88	12-15-91
Dennis R. Wilson	Garner	04-13-88	12-15-91

Sedimentation Control Commission
G.S. 143B-299/Board No. 0835

Name of Appointee	Address	Date Appointed	Date of Expiration
Sam Ballou	Morehead City	12-09-92	06-30-95
Gregory Bethea	Durham	12-11-87	06-30-90
Ronald M. Bost	Denver	12-31-91	06-30-92
		12-09-92	06-30-95
Philip H. Bracewell	Hickory	12-11-87	06-30-90
		02-21-91	06-30-93
Joshua F. B. Camblos	Asheville	11-10-87	06-30-90
		02-21-91	06-30-93
G. Douglas Carroll	Winston-Salem	02-21-91	06-30-93
Thomas F. Dabney, Jr.	Asheville	11-10-86	06-30-89
Daniel E. Dawson	Wilmington	12-31-91	06-30-94
Robert Hege III	North Wilkesboro	09-29-89	06-30-92
Hal C. Johnson	Asheboro	04-17-91	06-30-93
Patrick P. Joyce	Beaufort	11-10-86	06-30-89
		08-09-89	06-30-92
H. Joseph Kleiss	Cary	02-21-91	06-30-93
Duncan Malloy III	Lumber Bridge	12-23-85	07-01-86
		11-10-86	06-30-89
		08-09-89	06-30-92
William E. Mangum	Raleigh	11-10-86	06-30-89
David H. Moreau, *chairman*	Chapel Hill	04-17-91	
Charles H. Peterson	Pine Knoll Shores	12-30-92	06-30-95
Joseph A. Phillips	Raleigh	11-10-87	06-30-90
		12-09-92	06-30-94
Ralph D. Stout, Jr.	Greensboro	08-09-89	06-30-92
Albert F. Troutman, Jr.	Aberdeen	11-10-87	01-01-88
		01-01-88	01-01-91
		04-17-91	01-01-94
		12-09-92	06-30-95
W. W. Woodhouse, Jr.	Raleigh	11-10-87	06-30-90
Lawrence R. Zucchino	Raleigh	12-31-91	06-30-92

North Carolina Council on Sickle Cell Syndrome
G.S. 130A-131/Board No. 0840

Name of Appointee	Address	Date Appointed	Date of Expiration
Dora Atlas	Asheboro	03-19-86	
		07-24-89	07-30-91
Alice M. Barbee	Greensboro	03-19-86	
		07-24-89	07-30-91
		01-27-92	07-30-94
Ivestia H. Beckwith	Charlotte	05-16-91	07-30-91
		01-27-92	07-30-94
Alvin B. Blount, Jr.	Greensboro	03-19-86	
		07-24-89	07-30-90
Robert Broady, Jr.	Hamlet	02-22-91	07-30-93
Sallie W. Brown	High Point	03-19-86	
Roger D. Camp	Asheville	03-19-86	

NORTH CAROLINA COUNCIL ON SICKLE CELL SYNDROME
(CONTINUED)

Evelyn J. S. Carter	Greenville	07-24-89	06-30-92
		08-01-92	07-31-95
Joan E. Cockburn	Raleigh	02-22-91	07-30-92
		08-01-92	07-31-95
Gloria H. Davis	Raleigh	03-19-86	
Nellie B. Fields	Willard	07-24-89	07-30-92
Martina E. Goode	Norlina	03-19-86	
		07-24-89	07-30-90
		02-22-91	07-30-93
Gina H. Gore	Greensboro	03-19-86	
		07-24-89	07-30-91
		03-02-92	07-30-94
Clarice R. Greene	Warrenton	03-19-86	
Lillie L. Gregory	Fayetteville	03-19-86	
		02-22-91	07-30-93
C. Tate Holbrook	Greenville	05-16-91	07-30-93
John James	Gastonia	03-19-86	
Shirley W. Johnson	Durham	07-24-89	07-30-92
		08-01-92	07-31-95
L. E. Latour	Elm City	08-01-92	07-31-95
Mary E. McAllister, *chairwoman*	Fayetteville	03-19-86	
		07-24-89	07-30-91
chairwoman		07-24-89	
David L. Moore	Washington	08-01-92	07-31-95
Donald T. Moore	Durham	03-19-86	
Ralph Parker	Southport	03-19-86	
Harold R. Roberts	Chapel Hill	07-24-89	07-30-90
		02-22-91	07-30-93
Gladys A. Robinson	Pleasant Garden	03-19-86	
		07-24-89	07-30-91
chairwoman		02-22-91	
		01-27-92	07-30-94
Cleo M. Rollins	Fayetteville	02-22-91	07-30-91
		01-27-92	07-30-94
Lillie J. Solomon	Enfield	07-24-89	07-30-92
Marcia M. Wright	Jacksonville	02-22-91	07-30-93

SOIL AND WATER CONSERVATION COMMISSION
G.S. 143B-295/Board No. 0847

Name of Appointee	Address	Date Appointed	Date of Expiration
William M. Allen	Hamptonville	03-26-90	01-01-93
H. Gray Ashburn	North Wilkesboro	02-25-85	01-00-86
Tom Burns	Elizabeth City	03-26-90	01-01-93
William A. Butler	Bladenboro	01-24-89	01-01-92
James Ferguson	Clyde	04-17-91	01-01-94
John W. Finch	Spring Hope	01-15-86	01-08-89
E. Foy Gann	Asheboro	03-02-92	01-01-95
William V. Griffin	New Bern	02-13-87	01-01-90
Mr. Fernie C. Laughinghouse	Pantego	02-25-85	01-01-88
		01-19-88	01-01-91

Soil and Water Conservation Commission
(continued)

G. C. Palmer, Jr.	Clyde	02-13-87	01-01-90
John Y. Phelps, Jr.	Raleigh	01-15-86	01-08-89
		01-24-89	01-01-92
Rebecca H. Rhyne	Dallas	01-19-88	01-01-91
David W. Sides	Stoney Point	03-26-85	01-01-88
Charles W. Snipes	Hillsborough	03-02-92	01-01-95
John Stallings	Windsor	04-17-91	01-01-94
Albert F. Troutman, Jr.	Aberdeen	09-25-87	01-01-88
chairman		09-25-87	
		01-01-88	01-01-91
chairman		01-01-88	
chairman		04-17-91	01-01-94

Southeastern Interstate Forest Fire Protection Compact
Advisory Committee
G.S. 113-60.14/Board No. 0380

Name of Appointee	Address	Date Appointed	Date of Expiration
McCarroll Alston	Warrenton	05-10-85	
J. Marshall Hall	King	05-10-85	
Wallace W. Wicks	Maysville	05-10-85	

Governor's Waste Management Board
G.S. 143B-285/Board No. 0949

Name of Appointee	Address	Date Appointed	Date of Expiration
Joe E. Beck	Cullowhee	02-12-88	11-01-90
		02-21-91	11-01-93
William H. Briner	Durham	03-09-87	11-01-89
		01-02-90	11-01-92
		12-09-92	11-01-95
David A. Craft	Asheville	04-22-92	11-01-94
Linda S. Craig	Blowing Rock	04-10-87	11-01-89
James K. Ferrell	Raleigh	12-12-91	11-01-93
Ray Forrest	Raleigh	03-09-87	
Edward Garner, Jr.	Raleigh	02-12-88	
Martin P. Hines	Raleigh	03-09-87	11-01-89
		01-02-90	11-01-92
chairman		03-04-92	
		12-09-92	11-01-95
chairman		12-09-92	
Harold Imbus	Greensboro	03-09-87	11-01-89
Paul A. Jordan	Raleigh	03-04-92	
Harold A. Ladwig	Wilson	07-08-88	11-01-89
		01-02-90	11-01-92
		12-09-92	11-01-95
William F. Lopp	Jefferson	05-26-87	
Ralph M. McAlister	Albemarle	11-01-88	11-01-91
chairman		11-01-88	
Jerry A. McMahon	Morganton	01-15-86	11-01-88
Jennifer B. Martin	Raleigh	03-01-88	
Michael A. Martin	Charlotte	02-12-88	11-01-90
Timothy L. Minton	Apex	08-05-92	

Governor's Waste Management Board
(CONTINUED)

Kathleen G. Moyer	Wilson	12-09-92	11-01-93
Gretchen W. Peed	Hickory	05-23-88	11-01-88
		01-01-88	11-01-91
		12-12-91	11-01-94
Philip J. Penn	Charlotte	04-03-91	11-01-93
Nathaniel H. Robb, Jr.	Raleigh	04-14-86	
James L. Self, Sr.	Durham	02-17-89	
Douglas T. Story	Greenville	02-12-88	11-01-90
		02-21-91	11-01-93
Gil T. Vinzani	Chapel Hill	04-20-88	
Ms. Lynn Wheeler	Charlotte	12-30-92	11-01-95

Water Treatment Facility Operators Board of Certification
G.S. 90A-21/Board No. 0945

Name of Appointee	Address	Date Appointed	Date of Expiration
Phillip W. Boles	Robbins	08-27-91	06-30-94
Frank L. Bradham	Farmville	10-30-87	01-01-89
Shoou-Yuh Chang	Greensboro	12-09-92	06-30-95
Joe H. Clayton	Morehead City	10-11-90	06-30-93
William E. DeJarnette	Stony Point	10-24-86	10-24-89
Thomas W. Elliott	Lake Waccamaw	07-21-89	06-30-92
		12-09-92	
			06-30-95
Thomas C. Flowers	Fayetteville	09-19-86	06-10-87
		07-01-88	06-30-90
Ray Fogelman	Graham	09-19-86	06-30-88
		07-01-88	06-30-91
William S. Galler	Raleigh	09-19-86	06-30-89
		07-21-89	06-30-92
Gregory A. Knowles	Greenville	07-21-89	06-30-92
Cheryl McClary	Asheville	12-09-92	06-30-95
John C. McFadyen	Raleigh	06-30-86	03-09-87
		07-01-87	06-30-90
		10-11-90	06-30-93
Joe C. Stowe, Jr.	Charlotte	09-19-86	06-30-88
		07-01-88	06-30-91
		08-27-91	06-30-94
L. Roger Swann	Mars Hill	07-21-89	06-30-92
G. Michael Tardif	Liberty	10-11-90	06-30-92
		12-09-92	06-30-95
Marshall T. White	Riegelwood	02-27-87	06-30-89
Steve Wyatt	Chadbourn	09-19-86	01-01-89

North Carolina Wildlife Resources Commission
G.S. 143-241/Board No. 0965

Name of Appointee	Address	Date Appointed	Date of Expiration
R. Reed Allen, Jr.	Lake Waccamaw	07-01-87	06-30-93
J. Chalmers D. Bailey	Rocky Mount	04-01-85	03-31-89
Robert E. Barnhill, Jr.	Tarboro	04-14-87	04-01-89

NORTH CAROLINA WILDLIFE RESOURCES COMMISSION
(CONTINUED)

Ferrell L. Blount III	Bethel	04-25-89	04-25-93
Richard P. Budd	Advance	04-25-89	04-25-95
Ovide E. de St. Aubin	Siler City	04-26-91	04-25-97
William H. Drummond	High Point	05-01-92	04-25-93
Robert C. Hayes	Concord	12-19-90	04-25-93
Robert W. Hester	Fairfield	07-01-87	06-30-93
Russell M. Hull, Jr.	Elizabeth City	04-25-89	04-25-95
E. Richard Jarrett	Haw River	04-25-89	04-25-91
O. L. Leatherman, Jr.	Concord	12-10-92	04-25-93
Ted B. Lockerman	Clinton	04-25-89	04-25-95
William H. McCall	Asheville	07-01-85	06-30-91
		04-25-89	04-25-93
Allan D. Miles, Sr.	Concord	07-01-85	06-30-91
Joseph A. Neisler, Jr.	Kings Mountain	04-25-89	04-25-91
Stuart R. Paine	Southern Pines	04-01-85	03-31-89
		04-25-89	04-25-93
John W. Parks III	Gastonia	04-26-91	04-25-97
Eugene Price	Dudley	07-01-85	06-30-91
		04-25-89	04-25-93
R. G. Sowers III	Burgaw	04-25-89	04-25-91
		04-26-91	04-25-97
Howell W. Woltz	Advance	07-01-87	06-30-93

NORTH CAROLINA ZOOLOGICAL PARK COUNCIL
G.S. 143B-336/Board No. 0980

Name of Appointee	Address	Date Appointed	Date of Expiration
Jerry V. Blackwelder	Greensboro	09-26-90	06-30-91
		10-17-91	06-30-97
David Blust	Boone	09-20-89	06-30-95
Edna F. Cobb	Raleigh	12-04-92	06-30-93
Murray C. Greason, Jr.	Winston-Salem	09-20-89	06-30-93
Ernest W. Greup	Durham	07-15-85	06-30-91
		10-17-91	06-30-97
James C. Hastings	Boone	09-01-87	06-30-93
Susan W. Hays	Charlotte	10-17-91	06-30-97
Lottie M. High	Rocky Mount	09-01-87	06-30-93
Mary C. Hoey	Pine Knoll Shores	09-01-87	06-30-93
Mitchell L. Hunt	Greensboro	12-30-87	06-30-91
		10-17-91	06-30-97
James L. Lassiter	Winston-Salem	09-01-87	06-30-93
S. Dave Phillips	High Point	04-11-91	
J. M. Ramsay, Jr.	Asheboro	02-13-89	
James M. Rich, Jr.	Asheboro	09-20-89	06-30-95
C. J. Snow	Pilot Mountain	09-20-89	06-30-95
Paul W. Stephanz	Greensboro	01-08-86	01-08-92
James E. Swofford, *chairman*	Wilkesboro	09-01-87	06-30-93
		12-04-92	06-30-97
chairman		12-04-92	
Cullie M. Tarleton	Charlotte	10-17-91	06-30-97
Brenda S. Thomas	Asheboro	09-20-89	06-30-95

NORTH CAROLINA GENERAL ASSEMBLY

COMMISSION ON CHILDREN WITH SPECIAL NEEDS
G.S. 120-58/Board No. 0197

Name of Appointee	Address	Date Appointed	Date of Expiration
Ann B. Clark	Charlotte	09-01-87	00-00-89
		09-22-89	00-00-91
		01-27-92	07-31-93
Julia F. Green	Zebulon	09-22-89	00-00-91
		01-27-92	07-31-93
Nancy S. Haines	Elizabeth City	10-01-85	00-00-87
Harriett S. McDonald	Raeford	10-01-85	00-00-87
		09-01-87	00-00-89
		09-22-89	00-00-91
		01-27-92	07-31-93
J. Stephen Ramey	Raleigh	10-01-85	00-00-87
Susan C. Snipes	Gibsonville	11-26-86	06-30-87
		09-01-87	00-00-89
Elaine J. Woodruff	West End	09-01-87	00-00-89
		09-22-89	00-00-91
		01-27-92	07-31-93

COMMISSION ON THE FAMILY
G.S. 120-70.72/Board No. 0356

Name of Appointee	Address	Date Appointed	Date of Expiration
Connie A. Davies	Forest City	05-29-92	
Dorothy M. Martin	Raleigh	09-10-89	
Lynda B. Middlemas	Charlotte	09-10-89	
Ashton P. Wiggs	Wilson	08-24-90	

ADVISORY COMMITTEE TO THE NORTH CAROLINA MEMBERS OF THE
LOW-LEVEL RADIOACTIVE WASTE MANAGEMENT COMPACT COMMISSION
G.S. 104F-4/Board No. 0546

Name of Appointee	Address	Date Appointed	Date of Expiration
Mary L. Birch	Charlotte	08-25-89	07-14-91
Lionel Lewis, *chairman*	Charlotte	02-21-86	07-15-87
chairman		07-15-87	07-14-89
Wayne R. Thomann	Chapel Hill	02-21-86	07-15-87
		07-15-87	07-14-89
		08-25-89	07-14-91
chairman		08-25-89	
		12-02-91	07-14-93
Billy H. Webster	Cary	12-02-91	07-14-93

NORTH CAROLINA RAILROAD NEGOTIATING COMMISSION [16]
N.C. *Session Laws, 1985*, c. 792, secs. 13.1-13.26/Board No. 0754

Name of Appointee	Address	Date Appointed	Date of Expiration
George T. Clark, Jr.	Wilmington	04-01-86	

---

[16] The commission terminated June 30, 1988. *N.C. Session Laws, 1985*, c. 792, s. 13.6.

NORTH CAROLINA RAILROAD NEGOTIATING COMMISSION
(CONTINUED)

William J. Godfrey, Jr.	Whittier	04-01-86
Walker F. Rucker, Sr.	Greensboro	08-15-86

NORTH CAROLINA STATE GOVERNMENT COMPLEX COMMISSION
N.C. Session Laws, 1985, c. 792, sec. 18.1/Board No. 0406

Name of Appointee	Address	Date Appointed	Date of Expiration
James F. Hughes	Linville	10-30-85	06-15-86
Libby Pope	Raleigh	10-30-85	06-15-86
E. Stephen Stroud	Raleigh	10-30-85	06-15-86

JOINT LEGISLATIVE COMMISSION ON SEAFOOD AND AQUACULTURE
G.S. 120-70.61/Board No. 0829

Name of Appointee	Address	Date Appointed	Date of Expiration
William D. Adams	Southport	11-06-89	
Cashwell B. Caroon	Southport	10-17-91	
James H. Carson, Jr.	Charlotte	10-17-91	
John D. Costlow	Beaufort	10-17-91	
Michael Daniels	Wanchese	11-06-89	
J. M. Holleman	Raleigh	10-17-91	
Phillip M. Prescott, Jr.	Bayboro	11-06-89	

DEPARTMENT OF HUMAN RESOURCES

Secretaries
Phillip J. Kirk, Jr., 1985-1987
Paul T. Kayye, 1987 (interim)
David T. Flaherty, 1987-1993

GOVERNOR'S ADVISORY COUNCIL ON AGING
G.S. 143B-181/Board No. 0005

Name of Appointee	Address	Date Appointed	Date of Expiration
Vera A. Burch	Pinehurst	07-02-90	06-30-93
Sam W. Colerider, Jr.	Concord	07-01-85	06-30-89
		07-01-89	06-30-93
Stokes F. Craver	Lexington	07-02-90	06-30-94
Priscilla M. Cunningham	Raleigh	07-01-92	06-30-96
Horace E. Faulkner	Dover	07-01-85	06-30-89
		07-01-89	06-30-93
Otis Fenn	Fayetteville	07-02-90	06-30-94
Edna S. Goshorn	Whittier	07-02-90	06-30-94
Sophese L. Hawkins	Warrenton	08-15-86	06-30-90
Joe H. Hege, Jr.	Lexington	01-04-93	06-30-94
Lucy B. Hinshaw	Yadkinville	07-01-88	06-30-92
		07-01-92	06-30-96
Ruby T. Hooper	Morganton	07-01-92	06-30-96
Sherman Lillard	Cherokee	02-21-86	06-30-86
		08-15-86	06-30-90

GOVERNOR'S ADVISORY COUNCIL ON AGING
(CONTINUED)

Frank P. McCloskey	Pittsboro	08-15-86	06-30-90
		07-02-90	06-30-94
Lois M. McManus	Greensboro	07-01-85	06-30-89
chairwoman		10-30-85	
		10-09-86	06-30-90
chairwoman		10-09-86	
		07-02-90	06-30-94
J. T. McMillan	Winston-Salem	12-10-86	06-30-90
R. A. Mabry	Raleigh	02-21-86	06-30-89
		07-01-89	06-30-93
chairman		07-02-90	
Isabelle C. Miller	Ahoskie	07-01-87	06-30-91
		07-01-91	06-30-95
Jean S. Muller	Charlotte	07-01-85	06-30-89
		07-01-89	06-30-93
Martha S. Nicholson	Thomasville	02-21-91	06-30-93
Chester W. Nixon	Whispering Pines	07-01-88	06-30-92
Marie Rowe	Charlotte	07-01-85	06-30-89
Annie C. Shaw	Asheboro	10-20-87	06-30-90
		07-02-90	06-30-94
Martha D. Stevens	Smithfield	09-09-86	06-30-90
Fred A. Stone	Raleigh	07-01-89	06-30-93
Geraldine R. Taylor	Charlotte	07-01-91	06-30-93
A. J. Turner	Raleigh	08-15-86	06-30-90
John H. Williams	Valdese	07-01-85	06-30-89
		07-01-89	06-30-93
chairman		09-14-92	06-30-93

NORTH CAROLINA COMMISSION FOR THE BLIND
G.S. 143B-158/Board No. 0130

Name of Appointee	Address	Date Appointed	Date of Expiration
Harry N. Baldwin	North Wilkesboro	07-30-87	06-30-93
A. Buford Caudle	Winston-Salem	08-25-89	06-30-95
Wilford R. Dowe	Winston-Salem	07-30-87	06-30-93
Robert G. Frye	Hickory	07-15-85	06-30-91
chairman		07-15-85	
chairman		08-01-91	06-30-97
W. Herbert Hollowell, Jr.	Edenton	08-25-89	06-30-95
Andrew S. Holt III	Hillsborough	07-30-87	06-30-93
Marcus V. Ingram	Durham	08-25-89	06-30-95
Hattie M. Jones	Raleigh	08-15-86	06-30-92
Quentin A. Krause	Kitty Hawk	08-15-86	06-30-92
J. Oattley Lee	Fayettevlle	08-25-89	06-30-95
George D. Murphy	Hickory	08-15-86	06-30-92
		08-03-92	06-30-98
Paul H. Starling	Durham	08-03-92	06-30-98
Joseph L. Sullivan	Asheville	03-02-92	06-30-92
		08-03-92	06-30-98

BUSINESS AND CONSUMER ADVISORY COUNCIL
DIVISION OF VOCATIONAL REHABILITATION SERVICES
G.S. 143-548(a)/Board No. 0159

Name of Appointee	Address	Date Appointed	Date of Expiration
Ulrich Alsentzer	Greenville	12-04-92	09-30-95
Mark E. Brown	Raleigh	12-04-92	09-30-95
Jeannie Darquenne	Cary	12-04-92	09-30-95
Cynthia T. Harton	Newton	12-04-92	09-30-95
Debbie C. Jackson	Raleigh	12-04-92	09-30-95
Vickie M. Taylor	Claremont	12-04-92	09-30-95
Dennis H. Troy	Tarheel	12-04-92	09-30-95

CENTRAL ORPHANAGE OF NORTH CAROLINA BOARD OF DIRECTORS
G.S. 115C-135/Board No. 0180

Name of Appointee	Address	Date Appointed	Date of Expiration
Sidney C. Cutts, Jr.	Oxford	10-30-85	03-10-89
Daniel O. Leatherberry	Oxford	07-01-85	05-10-89
Jimmie V. Morris	Oxford	07-01-85	05-10-89
I. W. Murfree	Oxford	08-15-86	05-10-89
Robert D. Smith, Jr.	Oxford	07-01-85	05-10-89

CHILD DAY-CARE COMMISSION
G.S. 143B-168.4/Board No. 0195

Name of Appointee	Address	Date Appointed	Date of Expiration
Ruby L. Atkinson	Charlotte	07-28-89	06-30-91
		08-27-91	06-30-93
Donna D. Ballenger	Hickory	06-30-86	06-30-88
		07-29-88	06-30-90
		07-10-90	06-30-92
Charles Bright	Youngsville	07-10-90	06-30-92
		11-13-92	06-30-94
Geraldine L. Daniels	Goldsboro	08-17-87	06-30-89
		07-28-89	06-30-91
John C. Fonville, Jr.	Lincolnton	11-13-92	06-30-94
Kenneth H. Koontz	Charlotte	08-17-87	06-30-89
John W. Morris	Smithfield	06-30-86	06-30-88
		07-29-88	06-30-90
		07-10-90	06-30-92
Joan T. Perry	Kinston	07-28-89	06-30-91
		08-27-91	06-30-93
J. Phillip Reid	Shelby	11-13-92	06-30-94
John Rosemond	Gastonia	09-15-85	06-30-87
Dixie Sebastian	Thomasville	06-30-86	06-30-88
Barry Shearer	Charlotte	06-30-86	06-30-88
		07-29-88	06-30-90
Thomas A. Stith III	Durham	08-27-91	06-30-93
Ms. Pat M. Strawbridge	Louisburg	07-29-88	06-30-90
		07-10-90	06-30-92
		11-13-92	06-30-94
Lorey H. White, Jr.	Monroe	08-17-87	06-30-89

Board of Directors of the North Carolina Schools for the Deaf [17]
G.S. 143B-173/Board No. 0280

Name of Appointee	Address	Date Appointed	Date of Expiration
Richard C. Best	Spring Hope	03-05-86	07-15-89
Janice Branstrom	Morganton	01-15-86	07-15-89
Paul R. Givens	Pembroke	01-15-86	07-15-89
chairman		03-05-86	
Marylin M. Gordon	Morganton	01-15-86	07-15-89
Ralph E. Hester	Wilson	01-15-86	07-15-89
Ms. Bobbie D. McKenzie	Charlotte	01-15-86	07-15-89
Janice M. McMahon	Morganton	01-15-86	07-15-89
Bobby Parrish	Durham	01-15-86	07-15-89
Herbert O. Piper	Marion	01-15-86	07-15-89
John M. Scoglio	Greensboro	01-15-86	07-15-89
Catherine S. Turner	Raleigh	01-15-86	07-15-89

Council for the Deaf and Hard of Hearing
G.S. 143B-216.32/Board No. 0277

Name of Appointee	Address	Date Appointed	Date of Expiration
Dorothy D. Allen	Southern Pines	02-09-90	06-30-92
Teresa Alphin	Dunn	02-09-90	06-30-92
Kathleen Beetham-Gury	Durham	01-27-92	06-30-95
David Binning	Cary	09-15-92	06-30-96
Joan P. Black	Durham	02-09-90	06-30-93
Amy Branscome	Charlotte	02-09-90	06-30-92
		09-15-92	06-30-96
Mary Clark	Hot Springs	02-09-90	06-30-94
Florence P. Corpening	Winston-Salem	03-26-90	06-30-91
		01-27-92	06-30-95
Martha Downing	Raleigh	09-15-92	06-30-96
Craig L. Fields	Oxford	09-15-92	06-30-96
Terry R. Jones	Saint Pauls	03-26-90	06-30-91
Kurt L. Klinepeter	Winston-Salem	02-09-90	06-30-93
Glenn T. Lloyd	Morganton	08-24-90	06-30-93
Ms. Bobbie D. McKenzie	Charlotte	02-09-90	06-30-94
Ms. Jona Maiorano	Charlotte	02-09-90	06-30-91
Ms. Tambrey Oettinger	Durham	02-09-90	06-30-93
Brenda S. Patton	Morganton	09-15-92	06-30-96
Ms. Jackie P. Pope	Clinton	02-09-90	06-30-92
John M. Scoglio	Greensboro	02-09-90	06-30-94
J. Sterling White	Winston-Salem	02-09-90	06-30-94
Kathleena Whitesell	Morganton	02-09-90	06-30-93
Carole Williamson	Chapel Hill	09-15-92	06-30-93

Council on Developmental Disabilities
G.S. 143B-179/Board No. 0285

Name of Appointee	Address	Date Appointed	Date of Expiration
James O. Abrahamson	Chapel Hill	01-15-86	06-30-89
Cynthia P. Boykin	Burlington	02-22-91	06-30-93

[17]G.S. 143B-173 through G.S. 143B-176 were repealed under N.C. Session Laws, 1989, I, c. 533, s. 3, ratified June 30 and effective July 1, 1989.

COUNCIL ON DEVELOPMENTAL DISABILITIES
(CONTINUED)

Al Boyles	Raleigh	02-15-89	
Raymond A. Brockway	Hendersonville	03-05-86	06-30-88
		08-01-88	06-30-92
Howard F. Bryan	Statesville	04-24-87	
Ralph C. Burroughs	Winston-Salem	12-09-92	06-30-96
Robert C. Carpenter	Franklin	08-01-88	06-30-89
		09-22-89	06-30-93
Dino D. Cimma	Greensboro	01-15-86	06-30-89
		09-22-89	06-30-93
Laurie M. Collins	Winston-Salem	03-02-92	06-30-93
Richard B. Conely	Fuquay-Varina	07-15-85	06-30-87
		11-20-85	06-30-89
Ms. Jessie S. Crosswhite	Statesville	08-01-88	06-30-92
Ed Denton	Morganton	12-09-92	06-30-96
Theodore Drain	Raleigh	05-13-85	
Theresa H. Esposito, *chairwoman*	Winston-Salem	03-08-91	
Mrs. A. Donald Evans	Raleigh	01-15-86	06-30-89
Bill Franklin	Raleigh	05-13-85	
Patricia A. Gibbs	Greensboro	08-01-88	06-30-92
Ruth Gibson	Maiden	08-01-88	06-30-89
Marilea Grogan	Charlotte	02-21-86	06-30-86
Victor Hall	Raleigh	01-15-86	06-30-89
		09-22-89	06-30-93
E. Lowell Harris	Raleigh	02-22-91	
Richard A. Harrop	Raleigh	01-23-89	
Jack B. Hefner	Maggie Valley	12-16-86	06-30-90
		08-20-90	06-30-94
Joan C. Holland	Cary	05-13-85	
		04-16-92	
Ruby Hooper	Raleigh	05-13-85	
Juanita Howard	Goldsboro	01-15-86	06-30-89
Mr. Terry Ingram	Four Oaks	12-09-92	06-30-96
Ken Jacobs	Maxton	12-16-86	06-30-90
Kenneth G. Jens	Chapel Hill	10-17-91	06-30-94
Larry Justus	Hendersonville	05-13-85	
chairman		01-30-87	
George E. Kelly III	Raleigh	09-22-89	06-30-93
Angela V. Langley	Durham	11-07-90	06-30-94
Annette M. Lauber	Raleigh	08-01-88	06-30-89
		09-22-89	06-30-93
Stephanie D. McFadyen	Pinehurst	12-16-86	06-30-90
		08-20-90	06-30-94
Martha R. Macon	Kannapolis	02-22-91	06-30-92
		12-09-92	06-30-96
Suzanne P. Merrill	Raleigh	12-08-88	
Joanne E. Murray	Raleigh	12-16-86	06-30-90
		08-20-90	06-30-94
Emily C. O'Hara	Morehead City	01-15-86	06-30-89
John G. Patseavouras	Raleigh	05-13-85	
Paul Peruzzi	Raleigh	05-13-85	
Robert Philbeck	Raleigh	05-13-85	
Patricia B. Porter	Chapel Hill	08-01-88	

COUNCIL ON DEVELOPMENTAL DISABILITIES
(CONTINUED)

Rosa A. Sampson	Pembroke	01-15-86	06-30-89
		09-22-89	06-30-93
Wendell Sawyer	Greensboro	05-13-85	
Nancy B. Seymour	Asheville	08-01-88	06-30-92
Carrie C. Shoffner	Weldon	02-22-91	06-30-92
		12-09-92	06-30-96
Lacy E. Simpson	Selma	08-17-87	06-30-89
Sally C. Sloop	Raleigh	12-30-92	06-30-93
Jeanne Spangler	Rocky Mount	12-09-92	06-30-96
Mary H. Sugioka	Chapel Hill	01-30-87	06-30-90
		08-20-90	06-30-94
John M. Syria	Raleigh	10-14-88	
Don Taylor	Raleigh	05-13-85	
Cindy M. Teal	Weddington	10-03-89	06-30-93
Isaiah Thornton	Morrisville	08-01-88	06-30-92
		12-09-92	06-30-96
Dorothy R. Triplett	Charlotte	09-22-89	06-30-93
Charles F. Tyson, Jr.	New Bern	08-17-87	06-30-89
		09-22-89	06-30-93
Thomas Vitaglione	Raleigh	05-13-85	
Mary L. Warren	Durham	08-01-88	06-30-92
James H. Wells	Greensboro	04-16-92	06-30-93
Jerry W. Wiley	Raleigh	07-08-92	
Michael C. Wilson	Gastonia	01-15-86	06-30-89
Donald G. Wiseman	Fuquay-Varina	12-16-86	06-30-90
		08-20-90	06-30-94

ADVISORY COMMITTEE ON FAMILY-CENTERED SERVICES
G.S. 143B-150.7/Board No. 0196

Name of Appointee	Address	Date Appointed	Date of Expiration
Michael D. Atkinson	Durham	01-27-92	06-30-95
Peter S. Brunstetter	Winston-Salem	01-27-92	06-30-92
		12-04-92	06-30-96
Diane W. Buchanan	Graham	01-27-92	06-30-92
		12-04-92	06-30-96
Gwendolyn C. Chunn	Raleigh	01-27-92	06-30-92
		12-04-92	06-30-96
Mary K. Deyampert	Raleigh	01-27-92	06-30-95
Ms. Lynn Gurkin	Smithfield	01-27-92	06-30-95
Joan C. Holland	Cary	01-27-92	06-30-94
Shirley D. Lowder	Albemarle	01-27-92	06-30-92
		12-04-92	06-30-96
Laura Mast	Raleigh	01-27-92	06-30-94
Patricia B. Porter	Chapel Hill	01-27-92	06-30-93
John Y. Powell	Greenville	01-27-92	06-30-94
M. Harold Rogerson, Jr.	Chapel Hill	01-27-92	06-30-94
Rufus H. Stark II	Raleigh	01-27-92	06-30-95
Anna M. Wagoner	Salisbury	01-27-92	06-30-93
Gwyndella Wilson	Mount Olive	01-27-92	06-30-93
Loretta Worrell	Lillington	02-05-92	06-30-93

Governor Morehead School Board of Directors
G.S. 143B-174/Board No. 0590

Name of Appointee	Address	Date Appointed	Date of Expiration
Bertram W. Coffer	Raleigh	03-25-88	05-01-93
William F. Fairley	Southport	06-20-91	05-01-97
Barry L. Gardner	Rocky Mount	08-27-91	05-01-93
John P. Gore	Clinton	06-16-89	05-01-95
Malcolm Grissett	Shallotte	03-25-88	05-01-91
Andrew S. Holt III	Hillsborough	04-07-88	05-01-91
		05-22-91	05-01-97
chairman		07-02-91	
Mrs. Ollie Kearns-Gore	Aberdeen	03-25-88	05-01-91
		05-22-91	05-01-97
Paula R. Newsome	Charlotte	03-25-88	05-01-91
		05-22-91	05-01-97
Wanda D. Osborne	Salisbury	03-25-88	05-01-93
Robert W. Patterson	Sanford	03-25-88	05-01-93
chairman		03-25-88	
Milton S. Price	Winston-Salem	06-16-89	05-01-95
Jane Purser	Raleigh	06-16-89	05-01-95
Mary S. Styres	Lenoir	06-16-89	05-01-95
Stuart W. Teplin	Chapel Hill	09-08-92	05-01-95

Interagency Coordinating Council for Handicapped Children from
Birth to Five Years of Age
G.S. 143B-179.5(b)/Board No. 0409

Name of Appointee	Address	Date Appointed	Date of Expiration
Mrs. Robbie H. Angell	Asheville	07-01-92	06-30-94
Frank W. Ballance, Jr.	Warrenton	10-01-90	06-30-92
		07-01-92	06-30-94
Nell G. Barnes	Raleigh	10-01-90	06-30-92
		07-01-92	06-30-94
Cynthia B. Blust	Boone	10-01-90	06-30-92
Marie M. Bristol	Chapel Hill	02-15-91	06-30-92
Rick Burton	Burlington	10-01-90	06-30-92
Laurie M. Collins	Winston-Salem	10-01-90	06-30-92
		07-01-92	06-30-94
Sheila W. Cromer	Cary	10-01-90	06-30-92
Mabel O. Dillard	Raleigh	07-01-92	06-30-94
Barbara H. Doster	Charlotte	02-15-91	06-30-92
		07-01-92	06-30-94
John M. Dougherty	Greenville	01-15-92	06-30-92
		07-01-92	06-30-94
Joy English	Winston-Salem	10-01-90	06-30-92
Theresa H. Esposito	Winston-Salem	10-01-90	06-30-92
Sally L. Flagler	Chapel Hill	10-01-90	06-30-92
		07-01-92	06-30-94
Ms. Lynn F. Gurkin	Smithfield	07-01-92	06-30-94
John M. Hardy	Conover	02-15-91	06-30-92
		07-01-92	06-30-94
E. Lowell Harris	Raleigh	07-01-92	06-30-94
Joan C. Holland	Cary	07-01-92	06-30-94
Olson Huff	Black Mountain	10-01-90	06-30-92

INTERAGENCY COORDINATING COUNCIL FOR HANDICAPPED CHILDREN FROM
BIRTH TO FIVE YEARS OF AGE
(CONTINUED)

Sudesh Kataria	Greenville	07-01-92	06-30-94
Paul T. Kayye	Raleigh	10-01-90	06-30-92
Roger Langley	Garner	07-01-92	06-30-94
Larry Livengood	Goldsboro	10-01-90	06-30-92
Helen R. Marvin	Gastonia	10-01-90	06-30-92
		07-01-92	06-30-94
Patricia S. Miller	Boone	10-01-90	06-30-92
		07-01-92	06-30-94
Wilma S. Miller	Raleigh	07-01-92	06-30-94
Rufus K. Newlin	High Point	10-01-90	06-30-92
		07-01-92	06-30-94
Sammie C. Parrish	Raleigh	10-01-90	06-30-92
Sophia B. Pierce	Fayetteville	10-01-90	06-30-92
Andrea G. Price	Durham	10-01-90	06-30-92
		07-01-92	06-30-94
Sally C. Sloop	Raleigh	10-01-90	06-30-92
		07-01-92	06-30-94
Judith A. Sunder	Greenville	07-01-92	06-30-94
Betsy T. Thigpen	Goldsboro	02-15-91	06-30-92
chairwoman		02-15-91	
		07-01-92	06-30-94
Raymond M. Thompson, Sr.	Edenton	10-01-90	06-30-92
Gayle L. Underdown	Hickory	10-01-90	06-30-92
		07-01-92	06-30-94
Thomas Vitaglione	Raleigh	10-01-90	06-30-92
		07-01-92	06-30-94

NORTH CAROLINA COUNCIL FOR THE HEARING IMPAIRED [18]
G.S. 143B-214/Board No. 0426

Name of Appointee	Address	Date Appointed	Date of Expiration
Dorothy D. Allen	Chapel Hill	04-01-86	07-01-89
Mary S. Clark	Hot Springs	04-01-86	07-01-89
Robert F. Handon	Greensboro	04-01-86	07-01-89
J. Sterling White	Winston-Salem	07-21-86	06-30-90
Patricia Wilson	New Bern	07-21-86	06-30-90

NORTH CAROLINA COUNCIL ON THE HOLOCAUST
G.S. 143B-216.21/Board No. 0432

Name of Appointee	Address	Date Appointed	Date of Expiration
Gizella Abramson	Raleigh	11-20-85	06-30-87
		07-01-87	06-30-89
Arnold L. Aronson	Raleigh	11-20-85	06-30-87
		07-01-87	06-30-89
Joseph H. Call	Raleigh	10-17-91	06-30-93
Susan E. Cernyak-Spatz	Charlotte	11-20-85	06-30-87
		07-01-87	06-30-89
		08-03-89	06-30-91
		10-17-91	06-30-93

---

[18]N.C. Session Laws, 1989, I, c. 533, s. 1, repealed G.S. 143B-213 through G.S. 143B-216.5(b), effective July 1, 1989.

NORTH CAROLINA COUNCIL ON THE HOLOCAUST
(CONTINUED)

Roslyn G. Greenspon	Charlotte	11-20-85	06-30-87
		07-01-87	06-30-89
Ursula Hekler	High Point	07-01-87	06-30-89
		08-03-89	06-30-91
Henry A. Landsberger	Chapel Hill	08-03-89	06-30-91
Alan L. Novak	Raleigh	10-17-91	06-30-93
Bramy Resnick	Greenville	11-20-85	06-30-87
		07-01-87	06-30-89
Corinne S. Segal	Greensboro	11-20-85	06-30-87
Henry H. Shavitz	Jamestown	10-17-91	06-30-93
William S. Shrago	Rocky Mount	11-20-85	06-30-87
		07-01-87	06-30-89
		08-03-89	06-30-91
Runia Vogelhut	Raleigh	11-20-85	06-30-87
		07-01-87	06-30-89
		08-03-89	06-30-91
		10-17-91	06-30-93
Joseph Woodland	Raleigh	11-21-91	06-30-93
Arthur C. Zeidman	Raleigh	12-21-88	06-30-89
		08-03-89	06-30-91
		12-30-92	06-30-93

BOARD OF DIRECTORS OF THE LENOX BAKER CHILDREN'S HOSPITAL [19]
G.S. 143B-173/Board No. 0185

Name of Appointee	Address	Date Appointed	Date of Expiration
Mrs. Russell Barringer	Durham	05-15-86	07-10-91
Mrs. Claudean E. Edwards	Clemmons	05-15-86	07-10-91
Pamela L. Stanback	Greensboro	05-15-86	07-10-91

NORTH CAROLINA MEDICAL CARE COMMISSION
G.S. 143B-165/Board No. 0560

Name of Appointee	Address	Date Appointed	Date of Expiration
Mary H. Blythe	Whitsett	07-01-88	06-30-92
George H. V. Cecil	Biltmore	07-31-87	06-30-91
		10-17-91	06-30-95
Joseph D. Crocker	Hickory	07-01-88	06-30-92
		09-15-92	06-30-96
Mrs. Jo Franklin	Salisbury	09-15-92	06-30-94
Gilma B. Garrett	Durham	07-31-87	06-30-91
		10-17-91	06-30-95
Ralph M. Holt, Jr.	Burlington	10-03-89	06-30-93
Albert F. Lockamy, Jr.	Raleigh	09-19-86	06-30-90
		07-20-90	06-30-94
John F. Lynch, Jr.	High Point	07-31-87	06-30-91
chairman		07-31-87	
		10-17-91	06-30-95
Billy G. McCall	Charlotte	09-19-86	06-30-89
Louis J. Marchetti	Southern Pines	09-19-86	06-30-90
		07-20-90	06-30-94

[19]G.S. 143B-173 through G.S. 143B-176 were repealed under *N.C. Session Laws, 1989*, I, c. 533, s. 3, effective July 1, 1989.

NORTH CAROLINA MEDICAL CARE COMMISSION
(CONTINUED)

F. Maxton Mauney, Jr.	Asheville	07-31-87	06-30-90
		02-15-91	06-30-94
Otis B. Michael	Asheville	10-30-85	06-30-89
Rebecca E. Mitchell	Raleigh	09-19-86	06-30-90
		07-20-90	06-30-94
John W. Parks III	Gastonia	10-03-89	06-30-93
Tom P. Phillips	Charlotte	07-31-87	06-30-89
		10-03-89	06-30-93
John R. Powell, Jr.	Weldon	07-31-87	06-30-91
Ernest W. Reigel	Charlotte	07-01-88	06-30-92
		09-15-92	06-30-96
Dennis T. Slade	Durham	10-17-91	06-30-95
Meredith M. Smith	Durham	09-15-92	06-30-96
David T. Tayloe	Washington	09-19-86	06-30-89
		12-27-89	06-30-93
Ira O. Wilkerson, Jr.	Raleigh	10-17-91	06-30-93
John R. Willis	Raleigh	07-01-88	06-30-92
		09-15-92	06-30-96
Jere W. Witherspoon	Charlotte	10-03-89	06-30-93

COMMISSION FOR MENTAL HEALTH, DEVELOPMENTAL DISABILITIES, AND
SUBSTANCE ABUSE SERVICES [20]
G.S. 143B-148/Board No. 0570

Name of Appointee	Address	Date Appointed	Date of Expiration
Donald T. Austin, Sr.	Charlotte	09-03-92	06-30-96
Raymond A. Brockway	Hendersonville	12-14-90	06-30-91
Edith A. Brown	Warrenton	09-03-92	06-30-96
Mary M. Carter	Salisbury	08-27-91	06-30-95
Camilla P. Clark	Charlotte	01-03-93	06-30-96
Donald L. Clark	Boone	07-01-89	06-30-93
Louis R. Colombo	New Bern	09-03-92	06-30-96
Dorothy R. Crawford	Franklin	08-27-91	06-30-95
Thomas P. Davis	Yanceyville	11-23-87	06-30-91
John F. Dozier	Southport	11-23-87	06-30-91
Lewis M. Ferguson	Taylorsville	10-14-88	06-30-91
Louise Galloway	Asheboro	05-09-91	06-30-92
		09-03-92	06-30-96
Noel Garvin	Greensboro	08-15-85	06-30-89
James A. Greene	Boone	08-15-85	06-30-89
		08-09-89	06-30-91
John F. Grimes	Siler City	10-14-88	06-30-92
		09-03-92	06-30-96
Dorothy W. Hardy	Goldsboro	11-23-87	06-30-91
		08-27-91	06-30-95
Russell Harrell	Durham	08-27-91	06-30-95
Ruth L. Hines	Raleigh	08-15-85	06-30-89
chairwoman		08-21-87	
		07-01-89	06-30-93
chairwoman		07-01-89	

[20]*N.C. Session Laws, 1989*, II, c. 625, s. 23, changed the Commission for Mental Health, Mental Retardation, and Substance Abuse Services to the Commission for Mental Health, Developmental Disabilities, and Substance Abuse Services. The law was ratified July 12, 1989, and the changes to the commission became effective January 1, 1990.

COMMISSION FOR MENTAL HEALTH, DEVELOPMENTAL DISABILITIES, AND
SUBSTANCE ABUSE SERVICES
(CONTINUED)

E. Willys Hooper	Thomasville	08-15-85	06-30-89
		07-01-89	06-30-93
Adren J. Hughes	Elizabeth City	08-27-91	06-30-95
Barbara P. Israel	Hendersonville	10-14-88	06-30-92
		09-03-92	06-30-96
John A. Jarrell, Jr.	Durham	11-19-90	06-30-91
George E. Jones	Edenton	11-23-87	06-30-91
Ms. Fonda W. Kirk	Henderson	11-23-87	06-30-91
Judy L. Lewis	Charlotte	11-20-85	06-30-88
		10-14-88	06-30-92
Shirley D. Lowder	Albemarle	07-01-89	06-30-93
Hugh H. Macaulay III	Charlotte	12-17-87	06-30-91
Pat Macon	Salisbury	11-20-85	06-30-89
Carol A. Mann	Greensboro	10-03-89	06-30-91
James L. Martin	Wilmington	10-14-88	06-30-92
Richard Miller	Otto	08-15-85	06-30-89
Karen Moffitt	Southern Pines	10-14-88	06-30-89
		07-01-89	06-30-93
Emily H. Moore	Kinston	10-14-88	06-30-92
Geneva M. Moss	Fayetteville	08-27-91	06-30-95
Ms. Macon T. Newby	Raleigh	08-15-85	06-30-89
Teresa C. Nunn	Pfafftown	03-05-90	06-30-91
		08-27-91	06-30-95
Tom O. Palmer	Tarboro	07-01-89	06-30-93
Jeanie Renegar	Wilmington	08-15-85	06-30-89
John E. Robertson, Jr.	Albemarle	10-14-88	06-30-92
Edward T. Scruggs	Durham	11-23-87	06-30-91
Ricky R. Sides	Winston-Salem	07-01-89	06-30-93
M. W. Stancil	Selma	10-14-88	06-30-92
Ted G. Stone	Durham	09-03-92	06-30-96

SOCIAL SERVICES COMMISSION
G.S. 143B-154/Board No. 0845

Name of Appointee	Address	Date Appointed	Date of Expiration
Shirley Bossbach	Matthews	09-18-85	03-31-89
Myron M. Chenault	Winston-Salem	05-26-89	03-31-93
Samuel L. Cox	Lumberton	10-17-91	03-31-95
Evelyn P. Esworthy	Fayetteville	10-03-88	03-31-91
Michael P. Gore, Sr.	Clinton	10-06-88	03-31-89
		05-26-89	03-31-93
Ralph G. Hill	Arden	06-19-89	03-31-93
Charles B. McCarty	Elizabeth City	04-01-85	03-31-89
Evelyn W. McKissick	Soul City	04-17-87	03-31-91
		10-17-91	03-31-95
Jean Merson	Lillington	04-01-85	03-31-89
Dianne L. Morton	Albemarle	05-26-89	03-31-93
Ms. Macon T. Newby	Kannapolis	04-01-85	03-31-89
Larry E. Norman	Louisburg	04-01-85	03-31-89
Shirley E. Perry	Hertford	10-03-88	03-31-89
		05-26-89	03-31-93

SOCIAL SERVICES COMMISSION
(CONTINUED)

H. Sue Rawls	Wilmington	04-17-87	03-31-91
Edgar A. Readling, Jr.	Hickory	04-14-87	03-31-91
chairman		01-24-89	
chairman		10-17-91	03-31-95
Max G. Reece, Jr.	Siler City	05-26-89	03-31-93
Linda H. Reese	Asheville	05-29-92	03-31-93
Barbara A. Stevenson	Charlotte	04-17-87	03-31-91
		10-17-91	03-31-95
Judith G. Upchurch	Greensboro	04-17-87	03-31-91
		10-17-91	03-31-95
Nena W. Walker	Wilkesboro	05-29-92	03-31-93
Melvin W. Webb	Burnsville	04-01-85	03-31-89

INDEPENDENT BOARDS AND COMMISSIONS

NORTH CAROLINA BOARD OF ARCHITECTURE
G.S. 83A-2/Board No. 0045

Name of Appointee	Address	Date Appointed	Date of Expiration
Barbara E. Armstrong	Fayetteville	04-25-90	
Alan T. Baldwin, Jr.	Charlotte	09-20-91	04-01-96
Walter L. Bost	Kannapolis	04-25-90	04-01-95
Kenneth W. Burnette	Morehead City	08-15-88	04-01-92
		04-13-92	04-01-97
W. Calvin Howell	Southern Pines	07-01-89	04-01-94
Wanda H. Lewis	Charlotte	08-15-86	
James L. Padgett	Arden	08-15-86	04-01-91
Joseph T. Pegram	Statesville	02-27-87	04-01-92
Michael R. Tye	High Point	07-29-88	04-01-93

ATLANTIC AND NORTH CAROLINA RAILROAD BOARD OF DIRECTORS
G.S. 124-6/Board No. 0075

Name of Appointee	Address	Date Appointed	Date of Expiration
Benjamin K. Ball	Morehead City	07-31-87	00-00-88
		08-04-88	00-00-89
Harvey E. Beech	Kinston	07-31-87	00-00-88
		08-04-88	00-00-89
Albert R. Bell, Jr.	Raleigh	07-31-87	00-00-88
		08-04-88	00-00-89
L. Gordon Hardesty	Beaufort	07-31-87	00-00-88
		08-04-88	00-00-89
Paul W. Harrison, Sr.	New Bern	08-04-88	00-00-89
Kenneth E. Morris	New Bern	07-31-87	00-00-88
Alma G. Tilghman	Beaufort	07-31-87	00-00-88
		08-04-88	00-00-89
Arnold Tingen	Snow Hill	08-06-86	08-08-87
		07-31-87	00-00-88
		08-04-88	00-00-89
John E. Wakeley	Cullowhee	08-09-88	06-30-89
Everette L. Wooten, Jr.	Kinston	07-31-87	00-00-88
		08-04-88	00-00-89

North Carolina Auctioneers Commission
G.S. 85B-3/Board No. 0085

Name of Appointee	Address	Date Appointed	Date of Expiration
Donna M. Currie	Candor	08-17-87	06-30-90
		07-02-90	06-30-93
George R. Fuller	Raleigh	07-01-88	06-30-91
Gilbert J. Hollifield	Marion	08-26-91	06-30-94
William B. Lilly	Norwood	07-01-92	06-30-95
William R. Lutz, Jr.	Newton	08-17-87	06-30-90
		07-02-90	06-30-93
Thomas M. McInnis	Rockingham	06-30-86	06-30-89
		07-01-89	06-30-92
Mr. Bracky Rogers	Mount Airy	08-26-91	06-30-94
Tony R. Stone	Bailey	07-01-88	06-30-91

North Carolina State Bar Council
G.S. 84-17/Board No. 0119

Name of Appointee	Address	Date Appointed	Date of Expiration
Ernest H. Brown, Jr.	Lumberton	09-01-87	06-30-90
		07-30-90	06-30-93
B. E. Combs	Statesville	12-04-92	06-30-93
A. James Early III	Charlotte	09-01-87	06-30-90
		07-30-90	06-30-93
Edward Ramsey	Durham	09-01-87	06-30-90
Cornelius Smith	Charlotte	08-28-90	06-30-93

Disciplinary Hearing Commission of the North Carolina State Bar
G.S. 84-28.1/Board No. 0287

Name of Appointee	Address	Date Appointed	Date of Expiration
A. James Early III	Charlotte	07-01-92	06-30-95
J. Richard Futrell, Jr.	Rocky Mount	07-01-89	06-30-91
R. Powell Majors	Charlotte	08-31-85	06-30-88
		07-01-88	06-30-91
Donald L. Osborne	Randleman	08-29-86	06-30-89
		07-01-89	06-30-92
Emily W. Turner	Charlotte	07-01-87	06-30-90
		07-02-90	06-30-93
William H. White	Raleigh	09-20-91	06-30-94

State Board of Barber Examiners
G.S. 86A-4/Board No. 0115

Name of Appointee	Address	Date Appointed	Date of Expiration
Ms. Savada Herring	Burgaw	07-25-90	06-30-92
Alex H. Jackson	Waxhaw	04-07-88	06-30-89
		06-30-89	06-30-92
Mrs. Jimmie A. Lassiter	Robbins	12-30-92	06-30-93
Costas Melissaris	Charlotte	06-30-86	06-30-89

STATE BOARD OF BARBER EXAMINERS
(CONTINUED)

David L. Peoples	High Point	06-30-86	06-30-89
		06-30-89	06-30-92
Larry R. Pierce	Wilson	05-22-92	06-30-92
		07-01-92	06-30-95
Joan A. Shaffer	Raleigh	02-12-91	06-30-93
Lois W. Sheets	Sparta	07-01-87	06-30-90
William H. Teague, Sr.	Liberty	07-01-87	06-30-90
		07-25-90	06-30-93
Sylvester A. White, Jr.	Raleigh	05-22-92	06-30-92
		07-01-92	06-30-95

COMMISSION ON THE BICENTENNIAL OF THE UNITED STATES CONSTITUTION
G.S. 143-564/Board No. 0126

Name of Appointee	Address	Date Appointed	Date of Expiration
Juliet S. Barrus	Kinston	01-15-86	12-31-89
Elizabeth B. Fletcher	Wilkesboro	01-15-86	12-31-89
J. Wesley Jones	Flat Rock	01-15-86	12-31-89
Janice S. Ladley	Charlotte	03-05-86	12-31-89
Charles W. Lowry	Pinehurst	01-15-86	12-31-89
David Stedman	Asheboro	01-15-86	12-31-89

STATE BOARD OF CERTIFIED PUBLIC ACCOUNTANT EXAMINERS
G.S. 93-12/Board No. 0190

Name of Appointee	Address	Date Appointed	Date of Expiration
Giles K. Almond	Charlotte	06-30-86	06-30-89
Murchison Biggs	Lumberton	07-16-92	06-30-95
Stephen D. Bitter	Asheville	06-30-86	06-30-89
		07-01-89	06-30-92
William M. Butler, Jr.	Winston-Salem	12-15-87	06-30-88
		07-01-88	06-30-91
		10-17-91	06-30-94
Betty R. Faulds	Charlotte	10-17-91	06-30-94
Nathan T. Garrett	Durham	06-30-86	06-30-89
		07-01-89	06-30-92
Irwin R. Holmes	Durham	07-16-92	06-30-95
C. Richard Hubbard	Terrell	07-01-89	06-30-92
		07-16-92	06-30-95
C. Randall Isenhower	Conover	02-12-88	06-30-88
		07-01-88	06-30-91
		10-17-91	06-30-94
Steve E. Moss	Henderson	07-01-85	06-30-88
		07-01-88	06-30-91
William M. Shelton	Winston-Salem	07-01-85	06-30-88
James N. Smith	Winston-Salem	10-22-92	06-30-95
Thomas H. Woollen	Charlotte	06-30-86	06-30-89
		07-01-89	06-30-92

STATE BOARD OF CHIROPRACTIC EXAMINERS
G.S. 90-139/Board No. 0205

Name of Appointee	Address	Date Appointed	Date of Expiration
Dennis P. Cronin	Greensboro	04-14-89	03-16-92
Faye B. Eagles	Rocky Mount	04-01-86	03-06-89
		04-14-89	03-16-92
Dennis L. Hall	Concord	08-31-85	03-06-87
John J. Hawkins	Warrenton	04-01-86	03-06-89
Eugene A. Lewis	Greensboro	03-16-92	03-16-95
Joseph S. Siragusa	Charlotte	03-16-92	03-16-95
John T. Tierney	Southern Pines	03-17-87	03-16-90
		04-25-90	03-16-93
Darrell A. Trull	Kannapolis	04-01-86	03-06-89
Robert M. Vaughn	Eden	03-17-87	03-16-90
		04-25-90	03-16-93
Archie D. Williams	Macon	07-01-89	03-16-92
		03-16-92	03-16-95

STATE BOARD OF COSMETIC ART EXAMINERS
G.S. 88-13/Board No. 0245

Name of Appointee	Address	Date Appointed	Date of Expiration
Patsy T. Beckwith	North Wilkesboro	06-30-86	06-30-89
Mrs. Carroll L. Bowles	Julian	08-26-91	06-30-94
Benjamin F. Carpenter, Jr.	Charlotte	07-02-90	06-30-93
Kitty M. Pierre	Havelock	07-01-92	06-30-95
Allen R. Plummer, Jr.	Charlotte	07-01-88	06-30-90
Carol L. Richardson	Albemarle	07-28-89	06-30-92
Virginia W. Saunders	Eagle Springs	05-14-85	06-30-85
Phillip L. Shehdan	Raleigh	04-17-87	06-30-88
		07-01-88	06-30-91
Alma G. Tilghman	Beaufort	11-10-86	06-30-87
		01-04-88	06-30-90
		07-02-90	06-30-93
Mary E. Walker	Siler City	03-31-88	06-30-89

NORTH CAROLINA CREMATORY AUTHORITY
G.S. 90-210.42/Board No. 0256

Name of Appointee	Address	Date Appointed	Date of Expiration
Louis R. Bennett	Fayetteville	10-11-90	12-31-91
Frank G. Hardister	Southern Pines	10-11-90	12-31-92
Harold L. Hill	Raleigh	10-11-90	12-31-91
Thomas H. Lineberry	Greensboro	10-11-90	12-31-93
Larry E. Parker	Chapel Hill	10-11-90	12-31-92

NORTH CAROLINA STATE BOARD OF DENTAL EXAMINERS
G.S. 90-22/Board No. 0281

Name of Appointee	Address	Date Appointed	Date of Expiration
Sue M. Adams	Wilson	08-01-85	07-31-88

NORTH CAROLINA STATE BOARD OF DENTAL EXAMINERS
(CONTINUED)

Marie S. Moore	Fayetteville	03-31-88	07-31-88
		08-01-88	07-31-91
		08-27-91	07-31-94

NORTH CAROLINA BOARD OF DIETETICS/NUTRITION
G.S. 90-353/Board No. 0284

Name of Appointee	Address	Date Appointed	Date of Expiration
Beverly A. Bryant	Durham	11-21-91	06-30-93
Lauree P. Holliday	Raleigh	11-21-91	06-30-94
Betsy H. Greene	Troy	09-14-92	06-30-93
Mary B. Padgett	Hickory	11-21-91	06-30-92

EASTERN NORTH CAROLINA REGIONAL HOUSING AUTHORITY
G.S. 157-36/Board No. 0295

Name of Appointee	Address	Date Appointed	Date of Expiration
L. Dale Herring	Dunn	05-15-87	04-10-90
		04-25-90	04-10-95

STATE EDUCATION ASSISTANCE AUTHORITY BOARD OF DIRECTORS
G.S. 116-203/Board No. 0315

Name of Appointee	Address	Date Appointed	Date of Expiration
Leslie M. Baker, Jr.	Winston-Salem	02-27-89	01-16-93
James E. Burt III	Lincolnton	05-09-91	01-16-95
Fay C. Byrd	Roaring River	02-19-88	01-16-92
		03-02-92	01-16-96
John A. Campbell	Charlotte	08-31-85	01-16-88
Ovide E. de St. Aubin	Siler City	08-31-85	01-16-86
		04-14-86	01-16-90
		01-26-90	01-16-94
George S. Erath	High Point	08-31-85	01-16-87
		01-15-87	01-16-91
Dick Futrell	Rocky Mount	08-31-85	01-16-89
Cicero M. Green, Jr.	Durham	08-31-85	01-16-88
		01-18-88	01-16-92
		03-02-92	01-16-96
John Parks	Gastonia	08-31-85	01-16-87
James W. Perkins	Greensboro	10-10-88	01-16-92
Robert M. Pittenger	Charlotte	01-26-90	01-16-94
Richard B. Roberts	Winston-Salem	01-26-90	01-16-93
Betty T. Suttles	Franklin	08-31-85	01-16-86
		04-14-86	01-16-90
Richard Vaughn	Mount Airy	10-30-85	01-15-87
Ben T. Vernon	Denver	12-09-92	01-16-96
Paula R. Warlick	Lewisville	05-15-86	01-15-87
		01-15-87	01-16-91
		05-09-91	01-16-95

STATE BOARD OF ELECTIONS
G.S. 163-19/Board No. 0330

Name of Appointee	Address	Date Appointed	Date of Expiration
Gregg O. Allen	Southern Pines	05-12-89	04-30-93
Robert R. Browning	Greenville	05-01-85	04-30-89
M. H. Ellis	Edenton	12-11-87	04-30-89
		05-12-89	04-30-93
Thomas A. Farr	Wake Forest	08-04-86	04-30-89
Robert N. Hunter, Jr.	Greensboro	05-01-85	04-30-89
Margaret R. King	Charlotte	05-01-85	04-30-89
William A. Marsh, Jr.	Durham	05-12-89	04-30-93
Ruth A. Turner	Morehead City	05-12-89	04-30-93
June K. Youngblood	Arden	08-12-87	04-30-89
		05-12-89	04-30-93

STATE BOARD OF EXAMINERS OF ELECTRICAL CONTRACTORS
G.S. 87-39/Board No. 0335

Name of Appointee	Address	Date Appointed	Date of Expiration
William T. Easter	Cary	04-15-88	04-15-95
George T. Glenn II	Greensboro	08-27-91	04-15-93
Robert E. Linton	Greensboro	05-06-86	04-15-93
Edward H. Marrow, Jr.	Tarboro	05-06-86	04-15-93
William H. Roberts	Fayetteville	04-15-87	04-14-94
J. Michael Silver	Bakersville	05-24-89	04-15-96

NORTH CAROLINA BOARD OF ELECTROLYSIS EXAMINERS
G.S. 88A-5/Board No. 0336

Name of Appointee	Address	Date Appointed	Date of Expiration
Charlene Bell-Taylor	Charlotte	10-17-91	08-31-94
Susan S. Everett	Raleigh	09-14-90	08-31-92
Christine S. Glasgow	Rocky Mount	09-14-90	08-31-91
		10-17-91	08-31-94
Laurinda L. Queen	Raleigh	01-09-91	08-31-93
Stuart Tafeen	Greensboro	09-13-91	08-31-93

NORTH CAROLINA STATE BOARD OF EXAMINERS OF FEE-BASED PRACTICING
PASTORAL COUNSELORS
G.S. 90-385/Board No. 0366

Name of Appointee	Address	Date Appointed	Date of Expiration
Robert E. Johnston	Davidson	11-21-91	09-30-95
Barbara H. Price	Cary	11-21-91	09-30-93
Charles Van Wagner II	Raleigh	11-21-91	09-30-93

STATE BOARD OF REGISTRATION FOR FORESTERS
G.S. 89B-3/Board No. 0375

Name of Appointee	Address	Date Appointed	Date of Expiration
T. Paul Davis	Lattimore	07-21-89	06-30-92
		09-14-92	06-30-95

Douglas J. Frederick	Raleigh	11-06-89	06-30-91
		08-01-91	06-30-94
Samuel M. Hughes	New Bern	07-21-89	06-30-90
		07-02-90	06-30-93
Carl Jones	Columbia	07-21-86	06-30-89
		07-21-89	06-30-92
Richard M. Keyes	Lenoir	09-14-92	06-30-95
George L. Pace	Nashville	12-18-85	06-30-88
		07-26-88	06-30-91
Donald H. J. Steensen	Raleigh	07-26-88	06-30-91
Derryl L. Walden	Cary	08-01-91	06-30-94
John Weatherly	Kings Mountain	07-01-87	06-30-90

STATE LICENSING BOARD FOR GENERAL CONTRACTORS
G.S. 87-2/Board No. 0230

Name of Appointee	Address	Date Appointed	Date of Expiration
D. Bruce Armstrong	Gastonia	05-15-86	12-31-86
		01-01-87	12-31-91
		01-15-92	12-31-96
Nathaniel E. Clement	Greensboro	01-01-89	12-31-93
Arthur C. Flood	Durham	01-01-87	12-31-91
		07-31-87	12-31-90
		01-09-91	12-31-95
Robert A. Harvell	Willard	01-01-89	12-31-93
John A. Kuske	Wilmington	01-15-92	12-31-95
Douglas A. Lopp	Thomasville	08-17-87	12-31-91
		01-15-92	12-31-96
Dean B. McClatchey	New Bern	03-05-86	12-31-90
		07-31-87	12-31-87
		01-01-88	12-31-92
		12-31-92	12-31-97
Carolyn W. Thomasson	Charlotte	01-15-92	12-31-94

NORTH CAROLINA BOARD FOR LICENSING OF GEOLOGISTS
G.S. 89E-4/Board No. 0403

Name of Appointee	Address	Date Appointed	Date of Expiration
Edwin E. Andrews III	Cary	08-15-85	06-30-88
		07-01-88	06-30-91
George L. Bain	Asheboro	07-01-91	06-30-94
John E. Callahan	Boone	08-15-85	06-30-86
		06-30-86	06-30-89
		07-01-89	06-30-92
William A. Caster	Wilmington	09-16-92	06-30-95
Ronald A. Crowson	Greenville	08-15-85	06-30-87
John M. Dennison	Chapel Hill	12-30-92	06-30-95
Neil J. Gilbert	Charlotte	08-15-85	06-30-87
		07-01-87	06-30-90
		07-02-90	06-30-93
Mr. Lynn E. Graham	Durham	01-01-88	06-30-89
		07-01-89	06-30-92
Lewis J. Hash	Spruce Pine	08-21-87	06-30-90
		07-18-90	06-30-93

NORTH CAROLINA STATE HEARING AID DEALERS AND FITTERS BOARD
G.S. 93D-3/Board No. 0425

Name of Appointee	Address	Date Appointed	Date of Expiration
L. Ashby Adams	Wilson	01-02-87	06-30-89
Harlan S. Cato	Greensboro	01-15-86	06-30-87
		07-01-87	06-30-90
Trudy P. Cloyd	Murfreesboro	08-01-91	06-30-94
Stanley B. DeWeese	Waynesville	03-05-86	06-30-87
		07-01-87	06-30-90
		07-02-90	06-30-93
William S. Fisher III	Winston-Salem	10-31-90	06-30-91
		08-01-91	06-30-94
Shelby M. Freeman	Morehead City	01-15-86	06-30-88
		07-01-88	06-30-91
Donald E. Irwin	Charlotte	01-15-86	06-30-86
		06-30-86	06-30-89
		07-01-89	06-30-92
Robert E. Jay	Durham	06-30-86	06-30-89
Thomas S. Joseph	Haw River	07-14-92	06-30-95
Robert I. Kohut	Winston-Salem	01-31-89	06-30-91
Gerard A. McCall	Goldsboro	07-14-92	06-30-95
John R. Mills	Asheville	07-02-90	06-30-93
Stephen A. Mitchell	Rocky Mount	01-15-86	06-30-86
		06-30-86	06-30-89
James R. Moore	Rocky Mount	11-04-92	06-30-94
G. Don Roberson	Charlotte	07-01-88	06-30-91
Nancy H. Schiltz	Greensboro	08-01-91	06-30-94
Howard T. Shell	Raleigh	01-15-86	06-30-88
		07-01-88	06-30-91
Kathleen A. Tuomala	Southern Pines	12-08-88	06-30-89
		07-01-89	06-30-92

NORTH CAROLINA JUDICIAL STANDARDS COMMISSION
G.S. 7A-375/Board No. 0505

Name of Appointee	Address	Date Appointed	Date of Expiration
Margaret H. Almond	Charlotte	01-09-91	12-31-96
Albert E. Partridge, Jr.	Concord	01-01-88	12-31-93

NORTH CAROLINA BOARD OF LANDSCAPE ARCHITECTS
G.S. 89A-3/Board No. 0520

Name of Appointee	Address	Date Appointed	Date of Expiration
John A. Broadbooks	Asheville	01-02-87	07-01-89
		08-25-89	07-01-93
Charles A. Fountain	Greensboro	01-02-87	07-01-89
		08-25-89	07-01-93
Admah Lanier, Jr.	Wilmington	10-19-87	06-30-91
		08-27-91	07-01-95
Lee R. McLaren	Charlotte	07-21-88	07-01-92
		07-01-92	06-30-96
Roy H. Pender	Danbury	07-21-88	07-01-92
		07-01-92	06-30-96

NORTH CAROLINA BOARD OF LANDSCAPE ARCHITECTS
(CONTINUED)

Larry J. Ragland	Raleigh	10-19-87	06-30-91
		08-27-91	07-01-95
Owen L. Williams	Durham	10-19-87	06-30-91
		08-27-91	07-01-95

NORTH CAROLINA LANDSCAPE CONTRACTORS' REGISTRATION BOARD
G.S. 89D-4/Board No. 0521

Name of Appointee	Address	Date Appointed	Date of Expiration
Louise J. Ballew	Kings Mountain	07-21-86	12-01-88
		02-06-89	12-01-91
Martha S. DuBose	Kinston	03-11-88	12-01-90
		12-01-90	11-30-93
Doris G. Hagler	Concord	03-02-92	11-30-94

NORTH CAROLINA MARITAL AND FAMILY THERAPY CERTIFICATION BOARD
G.S. 90-270.50/Board No. 0558

Name of Appointee	Address	Date Appointed	Date of Expiration
Anne H. Beachum	Raleigh	11-26-86	09-30-89
Jackie W. Bohenstiel	Winston-Salem	12-27-89	09-30-93
RaVonda Dalton-Rann	Greensboro	11-26-86	09-30-90
Edith S. Delaine	Charlotte	10-01-87	09-30-91
		12-12-91	06-30-95
Mary T. Desmond	Durham	01-09-91	09-30-94
Gordon N. Diem	Durham	03-02-92	09-30-93
Nancy T. Edwards	Raleigh	11-26-86	09-30-90
		01-09-91	09-30-94
Elizabeth F. Little	Gastonia	11-26-86	09-30-89
Edgar B. Mackie	Granite Falls	10-01-87	09-30-91
chairman		12-30-87	
		12-12-91	09-30-95
Edward Markowski	Greenville	12-27-89	09-30-93
chairman		12-12-91	09-30-93
Martha H. Mozley	Lincolnton	05-15-87	09-30-90
Maynard L. Rich	Salisbury	12-27-89	09-30-93
Mary E. Smith	Charlotte	11-26-86	09-30-89

STATE BOARD OF MEDICAL EXAMINERS
G.S. 90-2/Board No. 0561

Name of Appointee	Address	Date Appointed	Date of Expiration
Eben Alexander, Jr.	Winston-Salem	11-01-87	10-31-90
George C. Barrett	Charlotte	12-04-92	10-31-95
John T. Daniel, Jr.	Durham	02-05-85	10-31-86
		11-01-86	10-31-89
		01-26-90	10-31-92
Harold L. Godwin	Fayetteville	11-01-88	10-31-91
		12-04-92	10-31-95
Hector H. Henry II	Concord	11-01-86	10-31-89
		01-26-90	10-31-92
George Johnson, Jr.	Chapel Hill	12-04-92	10-31-95

STATE BOARD OF MEDICAL EXAMINERS
(CONTINUED)

John W. Nance	Clinton	11-01-88	10-31-91
		01-15-92	10-31-94
F. M. Simmons Patterson, Jr.	Pinehurst	11-01-86	10-31-89
		01-26-90	10-31-92
Walter M. Roufail	Winston-Salem	01-09-91	10-31-93
Ernest B. Spangler	Greensboro	01-15-92	10-31-94
Nicholas E. Stratas	Raleigh	11-01-87	10-31-90
		01-09-91	10-31-93
Kathryn Willis	Zirconia	11-01-87	10-31-90
		01-09-91	10-31-93

NORTH CAROLINA BOARD OF MORTUARY SCIENCE
G.S. 210.18(b)/Board No. 0600

Name of Appointee	Address	Date Appointed	Date of Expiration
Stuart L. Cozort, Jr.	Murphy	07-31-85	12-31-88
		02-06-89	12-31-91
Randy Mears	Wake Forest	01-04-93	12-31-95
Mrs. Billie C. Wilson	Asheboro	01-15-92	12-31-94
Celia R. Winters	Shallotte	01-04-93	12-31-95

NORTH CAROLINA CENTER FOR APPLIED TEXTILE TECHNOLOGY
BOARD OF TRUSTEES [21]
G.S. 115D-68/Board No. 0935

Name of Appointee	Address	Date Appointed	Date of Expiration
John W. Copeland	Gastonia	07-01-87	06-30-91
John M. Harney	Charlotte	07-01-85	07-01-89
		08-25-89	06-30-93
		10-17-91	06-30-93
William D. Holt	Greensboro	07-01-85	07-01-89
William F. Huckaby	Pilot Mountain	07-01-87	06-30-91
		10-17-91	06-30-95
W. Giles Hunnings	Eden	08-25-89	06-30-93
		10-17-91	06-30-93
Harold D. Kingsmore	Kannapolis	01-15-86	07-01-88
Vilma D. Leake	Charlotte	09-19-86	06-30-88
		07-06-88	06-30-92
		10-17-91	06-30-94
James H. Martin, Jr.	Linville	07-01-85	07-01-89
Thomas A. Novinc	Concord	03-26-85	06-30-87
		07-01-87	06-30-91
		10-17-91	06-30-95
John F. Redding	Asheboro	06-30-86	06-30-88
D. Harding Stowe	Charlotte	09-09-86	06-30-89
		08-25-89	06-30-93
		10-17-91	06-30-93
William W. Temple	Monroe	07-20-88	06-30-92
		10-17-91	06-30-94
Sabert S. Trott II	Kannapolis	10-17-91	06-30-95

---

[21]The North Carolina Center for Applied Textile Technology succeeded the North Carolina Vocational Textile School effective July 1, 1991; see *N.C. Session Laws, 1991*, I, c. 184. The change resulted in the overlapping of board members' terms.

NORTH CAROLINA CENTER FOR APPLIED TEXTILE TECHNOLOGY
BOARD OF TRUSTEES
(CONTINUED)

Horst Wagner	Gastonia	07-06-88	06-30-92
		10-17-91	06-30-94

NORTH CAROLINA CENTER FOR NURSING BOARD OF DIRECTORS
G.S. 90-171.71/Board No. 0642

Name of Appointee	Address	Date Appointed	Date of Expiration
Ruth L. Bailey	Selma	10-17-91	06-30-94
Donna D. Bost	Wilmington	10-17-91	06-30-93
Madine H. Fails	Charlotte	09-14-92	06-30-95
V. Diane Gibbs	Rocky Mount	10-17-91	06-30-92
		07-01-92	06-30-95
Jeanne R. Ross	Charlotte	10-17-91	06-30-92

NORTH CAROLINA RAILROAD BOARD OF DIRECTORS
G.S. 124-6, 147-12(7)/Board No. 0755

Name of Appointee	Address	Date Appointed	Date of Expiration
Jerome Bolick	Conover	07-11-85	07-09-86
		07-22-87	00-00-88
		08-15-88	00-00-89
George T. Clark, Jr.	Wilmington	07-11-85	07-09-86
William K. Davis	Winston-Salem	08-15-86	07-10-87
Jane S. Doby	Raleigh	07-11-85	07-09-86
		07-22-87	00-00-88
		08-15-88	00-00-89
Marilyn Gideon	Greensboro	07-11-85	07-09-86
		07-22-87	00-00-88
		08-15-88	00-00-89
William Godfrey	Whittier	07-11-85	07-09-86
William H. Kincheloe	Rocky Mount	07-22-87	00-00-88
		09-23-88	00-00-89
Richard D. Messinger	Salisbury	07-11-85	07-09-86
		07-22-87	00-00-88
		08-15-88	00-00-89
John K. Patterson	Burlington	07-11-85	07-09-86
		07-22-87	00-00-88
		08-15-88	00-00-89
Russell M. Robinson II	Charlotte	07-25-86	07-10-87
C. Reitzel Smith	Asheboro	07-25-86	07-10-87
		07-22-87	00-00-88
		08-15-88	00-00-89
H. Glenn White, Jr.	Raleigh	07-10-86	07-10-87
		07-22-87	00-00-88
		08-15-88	00-00-89

NORTH CAROLINA BOARD OF NURSING
G.S. 90-171.21/Board No. 0640

Name of Appointee	Address	Date Appointed	Date of Expiration
C. Edwin Allman	Winston-Salem	01-01-89	12-31-91

NORTH CAROLINA BOARD OF NURSING
(CONTINUED)

David J. Conroy	Asheville	02-26-86	01-01-89
David T. Flaherty	Raleigh	01-01-93	12-31-95
Joyce T. Hardesty	Salisbury	03-28-91	12-31-91
		01-15-92	12-31-94
Charlotte B. Hoelzel	Wilmington	06-15-87	12-31-89
Phail Wynn, Jr.	Durham	02-27-87	12-31-89
		12-27-89	12-31-92

NORTH CAROLINA STATE BOARD OF EXAMINERS FOR NURSING HOME ADMINISTRATORS
G.S. 90-277/Board No. 0645

Name of Appointee	Address	Date Appointed	Date of Expiration
Ms. Jency L. Abrams	Sanford	07-01-88	06-30-91
Donald C. Beaver	Hickory	07-01-88	06-30-91
		11-19-91	06-30-94
Nolan G. Brown	Yadkinville	11-20-85	06-30-87
		08-17-87	06-30-90
		08-24-90	06-30-93
Gary K. Farlow	Greensboro	11-20-85	06-30-87
		08-17-87	06-30-90
William T. Graham, Jr.	Winston-Salem	11-19-91	06-30-94
Wanda A. Holt	Raleigh	11-19-91	06-30-94
B. B. Pearce	Charlotte	03-06-92	06-30-93
Gene B. Tarr	Yadkinville	12-30-92	06-30-94
Sara P. Titchener	Dunn	08-24-90	06-30-93
Anthony R. Triplett	Wilkesboro	07-01-88	06-30-91
Vanda S. Viehman	Kernersville	08-17-87	06-30-90
		08-24-90	06-30-93
George E. Wilson	Clinton	08-17-87	06-30-90
		08-24-90	06-30-93
Gary D. Witte	Raleigh	03-06-92	06-30-94

NORTH CAROLINA NURSING SCHOLARS COMMISSION
G.S. 90-171.60/Board No. 0646

Name of Appointee	Address	Date Appointed	Date of Expiration
Diane Fogleman	Hickory	10-03-89	07-01-93
Jo Franklin	Salisbury	10-03-89	07-01-93
Marion F. Gooding	Durham	10-03-89	07-01-93

NORTH CAROLINA BOARD OF OCCUPATIONAL THERAPY
G.S. 90-270.68/Board No. 0810

Name of Appointee	Address	Date Appointed	Date of Expiration
Cindy S. Beal	Durham	03-09-90	10-01-93
Dorothy H. Cameron	Kinston	02-13-87	10-01-89
Judy C. Colditz	Raleigh	10-01-88	10-01-92
Mansfield M. Elmore	Sanford	02-13-87	10-01-90
		10-11-90	10-01-94
Alice Gilbert	Concord	11-25-87	10-01-91

NORTH CAROLINA BOARD OF OCCUPATIONAL THERAPY
(CONTINUED)

Name	Address	Date Appointed	Date of Expiration
Walter S. Hunt, Jr.	Raleigh	08-05-87	10-01-88
		10-01-88	10-01-92
Kathleen A. H. Jones	Asheville	03-09-90	10-01-93
Ms. Ellis A. Kehoe	Durham	12-30-92	10-01-96
William S. Ogden	Whiteville	03-06-87	10-01-88
Karen H. Smith	Gastonia	03-06-87	10-01-89
Judy H. Stevenson	Morganton	01-09-91	10-01-91
		03-02-92	10-01-95

NORTH CAROLINA STATE BOARD OF OPTICIANS
G.S. 90-238/BOARD NO. 0655

Name of Appointee	Address	Date Appointed	Date of Expiration
A. Lyle Boyd	Fletcher	08-20-90	07-01-91
		09-13-91	07-01-94
Kent Carver	Charlotte	03-01-89	06-30-90
		07-02-90	06-30-93
Judy R. Driver	Winston-Salem	07-01-92	06-30-95
Ronald S. Graves	Hendersonville	07-15-85	07-01-88
		07-01-88	07-01-91
Richard C. Hamilton	Durham	07-01-88	07-01-91
Deborah A. Hardy	Vass	07-15-85	07-01-88
Clifford J. Lopp	Lexington	07-22-87	06-30-90
		07-02-90	06-30-93
F. Milo McBryde	Fayetteville	08-15-86	07-01-89
		09-22-89	06-30-92
Robert T. Morris, Sr.	Raleigh	07-22-87	06-30-90
Debra N. Newell	Wake Forest	09-13-91	07-01-94
Nicholas I. Obayuwana	High Point	08-15-86	07-01-89
Sharon J. Parks	Hubert	08-15-86	07-01-89
Sharon J. Pearse	Newport	09-22-89	06-30-92
H. Russell Tolar, Jr.	Carrboro	07-01-92	06-30-95
Augusta B. Turner	Raleigh	09-22-89	06-30-92
		07-01-92	06-30-95

NORTH CAROLINA STATE BOARD OF EXAMINERS IN OPTOMETRY
G.S. 90-116/BOARD NO. 0660

Name of Appointee	Address	Date Appointed	Date of Expiration
L. Sidney Christian	Williamston	10-09-86	05-01-91
Steven H. Eyler	Charlotte	09-20-91	05-01-96
Alfred M. Goodwin	Louisburg	08-15-86	05-01-91
W. Paul McBrayer	Forest City	05-31-88	05-01-91
		09-20-91	05-01-96
Mrs. Charles I. Martin	Winston-Salem	08-15-86	05-01-91
Daniel Mottola	Wilmington	08-04-92	05-01-97
Olee J. Olsen	Charlotte	07-21-89	05-01-94
William B. Rafferty	Winston-Salem	07-08-88	05-01-93
John D. Robinson	Wallace	06-11-86	05-01-90
James N. Rowland	Oxford	07-22-87	04-30-92
Janet L. Schonhofen	Winston-Salem	07-02-90	05-01-95
Gloria M. Smith	Southport	09-20-91	05-01-96

State Personnel Commission
G.S. 126-2/Board No. 0680

Name of Appointee	Address	Date Appointed	Date of Expiration
F. Douglas Biddy	Durham	08-01-91	06-30-97
Ray C. Corbett	Macclesfield	07-01-85	06-30-91
Garland S. Edwards	Eden	04-17-87	06-30-87
		07-30-87	06-30-93
chairman		07-01-89	
Robert M. Frazer	Charlotte	05-07-90	06-30-95
Vivian W. Fuse	Fayetteville	07-01-89	06-30-95
Malachi J. Greene	Charlotte	07-01-89	06-30-95
Jeffrey P. Hunt	Brevard	07-01-89	06-30-95
Joyce O. Lawing	Lenoir	07-30-87	06-30-93
Angela R. Massengill	Smithfield	08-01-91	06-30-97
Marlene S. Safrit	Raleigh	07-01-85	06-30-91
vice-chairwoman		01-15-86	
Hal L. Scott	Graham	08-01-91	06-30-93

North Carolina Board of Pharmacy
G.S. 90-85.7/Board No. 0695

Name of Appointee	Address	Date Appointed	Date of Expiration
William R. Adams, Jr.	Wilson	05-01-87	04-30-90
William T. Biggers	Asheville	02-12-88	04-30-90
		05-01-90	04-30-95
Harold V. Day	Spruce Pine	05-01-86	04-30-89
		05-17-89	04-30-92
		12-04-92	04-30-97
Albert F. Lockamy, Jr.	Raleigh	05-01-90	04-30-95
Evelyn P. Lloyd	Hillsborough	05-01-86	04-30-89
William W. Moose	Mount Pleasant	05-01-87	04-30-90
		05-01-90	04-30-95
William H. Randall, Jr.	Lillington	05-01-88	04-30-91
		05-01-91	04-30-96
Jack G. Watts	Burlington	05-17-89	04-30-92
		12-04-92	04-30-97

North Carolina Board of Physical Therapy Examiners
G.S. 90-270.25/Board No. 0700

Name of Appointee	Address	Date Appointed	Date of Expiration
James R. Bacon	Durham	01-09-91	01-01-93
		01-01-93	01-01-96
Priscilla G. Beckwith	Hope Mills	01-15-92	01-01-95
Phil Benfield	Statesville	01-26-90	01-01-93
A. Griswold Bevin	Chapel Hill	01-26-90	01-01-93
David S. Caldwell	Durham	01-30-87	01-01-90
Donna A. Creech	Wilson's Mills	01-19-88	01-01-91
Elisha Denny	Chapel Hill	03-19-86	01-01-89
Shirley C. Fisher	Chapel Hill	01-19-88	01-01-91
		01-09-91	01-01-94
Rebecca B. Hamilton	Charlotte	01-19-88	01-01-91
		01-09-91	01-01-94

NORTH CAROLINA BOARD OF PHYSICAL THERAPY EXAMINERS
(CONTINUED)

Angela B. Hunter	Rocky Mount	09-08-92	01-01-93
Dianne Lindsey	Chapel Hill	01-30-87	01-01-90
Maria G. Little	Charlotte	01-15-86	01-01-88
		01-19-88	01-01-91
		01-09-91	01-01-94
Leah M. Sneed	Banner Elk	01-01-89	01-01-92
		01-15-92	01-01-95
Sheree B. Watson	Hickory	03-19-86	01-01-89
		01-01-89	01-01-92

STATE BOARD OF EXAMINERS OF PLUMBING, HEATING, AND FIRE SPRINKLER CONTRACTORS [22]
G.S. 87-16/Board No. 0705

Name of Appointee	Address	Date Appointed	Date of Expiration
Perry G. Davis	Etowah	04-25-92	04-25-99
William E. Garrett, Jr.	Greensboro	04-28-87	04-25-94
Malachi Goforth	Hendersonville	07-01-85	04-25-92
Ronnie J. Hahn	Clayton	08-28-90	04-25-91
		04-25-91	04-25-98
Rhyn H. Kim	Charlotte	04-25-88	04-25-95
David J. Lombardi	Apex	06-18-91	04-25-95
Brian C. Miller	Rural Hall	04-26-86	04-25-93
Stuart M. Shinn	Greenville	04-30-89	04-30-96
John A. Ward, Jr.	Raleigh	04-25-90	04-25-97

BOARD OF PODIATRY EXAMINERS
G.S. 90-202.4/Board No. 0710

Name of Appointee	Address	Date Appointed	Date of Expiration
Thomas M. Hampton	Charlotte	07-22-87	06-30-90
		07-10-90	06-30-93
John H. Hodges	Winston-Salem	08-31-85	06-30-88
Lena H. Jones	Winston-Salem	07-22-87	06-30-90
Jimmy E. Keith	Raleigh	12-21-88	06-30-90
		07-10-90	06-30-93
Edwin B. Martin, Jr.	Fayetteville	07-22-88	06-30-91
C. Jeff Mauney	Kings Mountain	09-09-86	06-30-89
		07-21-89	06-30-92
James Mothershed	Clemmons	04-25-90	06-30-91
		08-27-91	06-30-94
H. Lisle Snyder	Blowing Rock	09-14-92	06-30-95

NORTH CAROLINA PORTS RAILWAY COMMISSION BOARD OF DIRECTORS
G.S. 143B-469/BOARD NO. 0717

Name of Appointee	Address	Date Appointed	Date of Expiration
J. Street Brewer	Charlotte	09-15-85	03-15-86
		06-20-86	03-15-90
		03-26-91	03-15-94
Paul G. Burton	Wrightsville Beach	04-16-92	03-15-96

---

[22]The State Board of Examiners of Plumbing and Heating Contractors was reorganized as the State Board of Examiners of Plumbing, Heating, and Fire Sprinkler Contractors under N.C. Session Laws, 1989, Extra and Regular Sessions, 1990, c. 842, effective October 1, 1990.

NORTH CAROLINA PORTS RAILWAY COMMISSION BOARD OF DIRECTORS
(CONTINUED)

Jyles J. Coggins .... Raleigh	09-15-85	03-15-88
chairman	11-20-85	
chairman	03-15-88	03-15-92
chairman	04-16-92	03-15-96
Millard S. Jones .... Whiteville	02-26-86	03-15-88
	03-15-88	03-15-92
O. Elwood Mixon.. Rocky Mount	09-15-85	03-15-87
	02-27-87	03-15-91
	04-03-91	03-15-95
George H. Spencer .... Asheville	11-20-85	03-15-89
	04-14-89	03-15-93

NORTH CAROLINA STATE BOARD OF EXAMINERS OF PRACTICING PSYCHOLOGISTS
G.S. 90-270.6/Board No. 0720

Name of Appointee	Address	Date Appointed	Date of Expiration
Margery F. Adams .... Conover	10-30-87	06-30-89
		08-25-89	06-30-92
		07-01-92	06-30-95
Paul Babiak .... Raleigh	07-22-88	06-30-91
Susan M. Bennett .... Troy	04-20-88	06-30-89
William V. Burlingame .... Hillsborough	08-15-85	06-30-88
John W. Edgerly .... Chapel Hill	09-20-91	06-30-94
Robert D. Gregory .... Wilson	08-15-85	06-30-88
Anne B. Harris... Hendersonville	09-30-87	06-30-90
Craig A. Iversen .... Waynesville	09-30-87	06-30-90
		08-24-90	06-30-93
Mary Lewis .... Fayetteville	10-30-87	06-30-88
		07-22-88	06-30-91
		09-20-91	06-30-94
Thea Monroe .... Raleigh	08-15-86	06-30-89
Mary A. Olsen .... Raleigh	07-01-92	06-30-95
Julian A. Powell.. Greenville	01-26-90	06-30-90
		08-24-90	06-30-93
Rodney E. Realon................................... Morganton	08-15-86	06-30-89
J. William Spakes, Jr. .... Maiden	07-22-88	06-30-91
Carol M. Speas .... Raleigh	04-10-89	06-30-91
		09-20-91	06-30-94
Chester Throckmorton .... Danbury	08-31-85	06-30-88
Michael E. Wells .... Dobson	08-25-89	06-30-92

STATE BOARD OF REGISTRATION FOR PROFESSIONAL ENGINEERS AND LAND SURVEYORS
G.S. 89C-4/Board No. 0354

Name of Appointee	Address	Date Appointed	Date of Expiration
Ray E. Anders .... Asheville	01-01-88	12-31-92
		12-31-92	12-31-97
J. Albert Bass .... Raleigh	01-01-87	12-31-91
		01-15-92	12-31-96
J. Richard Cottingham .... Raleigh	01-26-90	12-31-94
R. Larry Greene .... Marion	01-01-89	12-31-93
Bobby M. Long .... Shallotte	11-20-85	12-31-90
		01-01-91	12-31-95

STATE BOARD OF REGISTRATION FOR PROFESSIONAL ENGINEERS AND LAND SURVEYORS
(CONTINUED)

Helen Merritt	Hampstead	07-02-90	12-31-94
Geraldine A. Overby	Snow Hill	01-26-90	12-31-94
James N. Poole	Cary	06-11-86	12-31-88
Dana H. Rucker III	Davidson	11-20-85	12-31-90
		01-01-91	12-31-95
William T. Steuer	Wilmington	02-15-89	12-31-93
Frank L. Turner	Raleigh	01-01-89	12-31-93

REAL ESTATE APPRAISAL BOARD
G.S. 93A-78/Board No. 0766

Name of Appointee	Address	Date Appointed	Date of Expiration
William G. Brown, Sr.	Charlotte	07-15-91	06-30-95
Robert L. Byrd, Jr.	Mount Pleasant	07-15-91	06-30-94
Tom J. Keith	Fayetteville	07-15-91	06-30-95
John P. Robinson, Jr.	Salisbury	07-15-91	06-30-94
Beryl J. Stevenson	Charlotte	11-19-91	06-30-94

NORTH CAROLINA REAL ESTATE COMMISSION
G.S. 93A-3/Board No. 0765

Name of Appointee	Address	Date Appointed	Date of Expiration
Ann M. Allen	Greensboro	08-31-85	06-30-88
Oliver W. Alphin	Durham	09-01-87	07-31-89
Charles F. Biesecker	Lexington	10-17-91	07-31-94
Gilbert L. Boger	Mocksville	08-31-85	06-30-88
		08-01-88	07-31-91
		10-17-91	07-31-94
Patrice P. Carter	Raleigh	08-23-89	07-31-92
Patricia B. Casey	Raleigh	08-01-88	07-31-91
Elmer C. Jenkins	Blowing Rock	12-16-86	07-31-88
		08-01-88	07-31-91
Chandler B. Lee	Southern Pines	11-10-87	07-31-89
June P. Mooring	Goldsboro	08-01-87	07-31-90
Ernest C. Pearson	Raleigh	08-01-86	07-31-89
James K. Polk, Sr.	Charlotte	08-24-92	07-31-95
Brantley T. Poole	Raleigh	10-31-90	07-31-93
J. Edward Poole	Spring Lake	08-01-86	07-31-89
		08-23-89	07-31-92
		08-24-92	07-31-95
William A. Smith, Jr.	Cary	10-17-91	07-31-94
Grace T. Steed	Randleman	08-01-87	07-31-90
		09-26-90	07-31-93
Patricia C. Wilson	Wilson	08-31-85	06-30-88

STATE BOARD OF REFRIGERATION EXAMINERS
G.S. 87-52/Board No. 0775

Name of Appointee	Address	Date Appointed	Date of Expiration
Jack M. Bailey, Sr.	Walnut Cove	02-12-88	01-01-95
Calvin E. Dae	Raleigh	03-27-87	01-01-94
Ralph G. Jaeggli	Asheville	01-15-87	01-01-93

State Board of Refrigeration Examiners
(CONTINUED)

Thomas A. Newber	Hampstead	03-02-92	07-01-99
George Ramsey	Concord	02-15-91	01-01-98
Parker C. Reist	Chapel Hill	03-28-89	01-01-96
Clarence L. Smith, Jr.	Raleigh	08-17-87	01-01-90
		01-26-90	01-01-97

North Carolina Board of Registered Practicing Counselors
G.S. 90-333/Board No. 0718

Name of Appointee	Address	Date Appointed	Date of Expiration
David C. Arledge	Hendersonville	11-26-86	06-30-88
		07-01-88	06-30-91
		10-17-91	06-30-94
Ray V. Beatty	Lumberton	11-26-86	06-30-87
		12-30-87	06-30-90
		07-02-90	06-30-93
Keith G. Lewis	Fayetteville	04-25-90	06-30-92
Ann Z. Sandler	Charlotte	11-26-86	06-30-87
		12-30-87	06-30-90
		07-02-90	06-30-93
Susan A. Scott	Asheboro	11-26-86	06-30-89
Virginia G. Sykes	Charlotte	12-30-87	06-30-89
		07-01-89	06-30-92
		07-01-92	06-30-95
S. Cecelia Ferguson Taylor	Greensboro	11-26-86	06-30-88
		07-01-88	06-30-91
		10-17-91	06-30-94
Barnetta M. White	Durham	12-30-87	06-30-88
		07-01-88	06-30-91
		10-17-91	06-30-94
D. Clifton Wood	Charlotte	03-04-92	06-30-92
		07-01-92	06-30-95

North Carolina Certification Board for Social Work
G.S. 90B-5/Board No. 0677

Name of Appointee	Address	Date Appointed	Date of Expiration
Andrea T. Benfield	Newton	07-01-92	06-30-95
Lee M. Bruner, Jr.	Concord	09-13-91	06-30-94
Lutritia Darr	Trinity	10-20-85	06-30-87
Connie A. Davies	Forest City	09-13-91	06-30-92
William G. Hamby, Jr.	Concord	11-20-85	06-30-88
		07-01-88	06-30-91
Ms. Frankie E. Hedrick	Lexington	07-22-87	06-30-89
		08-03-89	06-30-92
Helen L. Keyes	Asheboro	07-22-87	06-30-90
		07-02-90	06-30-93
Constantine Kledaras	Raleigh	07-02-90	06-30-93
Jane C. Moorman	Durham	07-01-92	06-30-95
R. Carl Mumpower	Asheville	10-20-85	06-30-87
		07-22-87	06-30-90
		07-02-90	06-30-93
Sandra Page	Gastonia	04-14-87	06-30-89

North Carolina Certification Board for Social Work
(continued)

Sandra J. Roberts	Greensboro	11-20-85	07-01-88
		07-01-88	06-30-91
Ms. Billie W. Shelton	Winston-Salem	07-01-89	06-30-92
Nancy Wilkerson	Charlotte	07-01-89	06-30-91
		09-13-91	06-30-94
Wilma P. Wilkins	Raleigh	07-22-87	06-30-90

Southern Growth Policies Board
G.S. 143-492/Board No. 0850

Name of Appointee	Address	Date Appointed	Date of Expiration
John A. Allison	Wilson	12-07-88	
John C. Fennebresque	Charlotte	08-25-89	
Joseph B. Martin III	Charlotte	03-26-85	
A. P. Perkinson, Jr.	Laurinburg	04-24-85	

Board of Examiners for Speech and Language Pathologists and Audiologists
G.S. 90-303/Board No. 0863

Name of Appointee	Address	Date Appointed	Date of Expiration
Sabrina A. Bass	Fayetteville	11-23-87	06-30-90
Doris S. Blackwell	Roxboro	11-23-87	09-30-90
		11-07-90	09-30-93
Patricia A. Chase	Chapel Hill	10-17-91	09-30-94
Shelia W. Cothran	Marion	06-21-88	06-30-90
		07-02-90	06-30-93
Valeria W. Edwards	Greensboro	10-09-86	06-30-89
Berrylin J. Ferguson	Durham	02-06-91	09-30-93
Gregg D. Givens	Greenville	01-15-86	09-30-88
		09-21-88	09-30-91
G. Carroll Jordan, Sr.	Statesville	12-04-92	06-30-93
LuVern H. Kunze	Durham	10-09-86	09-30-88
		09-21-88	09-30-91
Robert Muzzarelli	Greenville	10-09-86	06-30-88
David C. Pillsbury	Winston-Salem	12-30-92	09-30-94
G. Don Roberson	Charlotte	01-15-86	09-30-87
		11-23-87	09-30-90
Stephanie H. Rogister	Raleigh	10-17-91	09-30-94
Ms. Thayle M. Sanderson	Pembroke	11-23-87	06-30-89
		07-01-89	06-30-92
		07-01-92	06-30-95
John E. Sexton	Greensboro	09-21-88	09-30-91
		10-17-91	09-30-94
Robert C. Williams	Hickory	12-30-92	09-30-93

Board of Trustees, Teachers' and State Employees'
Comprehensive Major Medical Plan
G.S. 135-39, 120-22/Board No. 889

Name of Appointee	Address	Date Appointed	Date of Expiration
Charles W. Crutchfield	Cary	07-01-92	06-30-94
Frank Fishburne, Jr.	Waynesville	12-16-86	06-30-88

Board of Trustees, Teachers' and State Employees'
Comprehensive Major Medical Plan
(continued)

Lawrence C. Gardner	Forest City	03-04-88	06-30-88
		07-01-88	06-30-90
		07-02-90	06-30-92
		07-01-92	06-30-94
Edward L. Minnich	Fayetteville	10-17-91	06-30-93
J. Larry Peters	High Point	07-31-85	06-30-87
		12-16-86	06-30-88
		07-01-88	06-30-90
		07-02-90	06-30-92
Charles W. Stone	Goldsboro	07-01-87	06-30-89
		07-01-89	06-30-91

Technological Development Authority, Inc.
G.S. 143B-471.1/Board No. 0891

Name of Appointee	Address	Date Appointed	Date of Expiration
H. Keith Brunnemer, Jr.	Charlotte	11-06-89	06-30-91
John J. Cavanagh, Jr.	Winston-Salem	10-23-91	06-30-95
chairman		11-19-91	
Joe K. Cochrane	Advance	06-09-88	06-30-91
William O. Cordes	Greensboro	07-01-87	06-30-91
J. C. Cousar	Charlotte	11-19-91	06-30-95
Tom Dillon	Monroe	01-31-86	06-30-87
S. E. Douglass	Raleigh	07-01-87	06-30-91
Gloria B. Faulk	Cary	11-19-91	06-30-95
Robert M. Freeman	Concord	10-23-91	06-30-95
David A. Harlow	Durham	10-23-91	06-30-95
Lee P. Hedgecoe	Fayetteville	07-01-87	06-30-91
Walter C. Holden	Southern Pines	10-03-89	06-30-91
Lawrence M. Kimbrough	Davidson	07-02-90	06-30-91
Steven M. Kincaid	Lenoir	07-01-87	06-30-91
Frank P. Meadows III	Rocky Mount	10-23-91	06-30-95
Ralph W. Peters, Jr.	Raleigh	12-27-89	06-30-91
chairman		08-28-90	
Edward P. Pickett	Charlotte	10-23-91	06-30-95
Robert E. Rupert	Dunn	07-01-87	06-30-91
chairman		07-01-87	
Carlton C. Schmidt	Chapel Hill	03-13-86	07-01-87
		07-01-87	06-30-91
Ricky G. Slade	High Point	08-15-86	07-01-87
		07-01-87	06-30-91
Mrs. Glenn G. Sumner	Chapel Hill	03-13-86	07-01-87
		07-01-87	06-30-91
		10-23-91	06-30-95

North Carolina State Board of Therapeutic Recreation Certification
G.S. 90C-5/Board No. 0812

Name of Appointee	Address	Date Appointed	Date of Expiration
James L. Barrett	Greenville	11-23-87	06-30-88
		07-01-88	06-30-91
Theodore A. Manly	Durham	02-12-88	06-30-90

NORTH CAROLINA STATE BOARD OF THERAPEUTIC RECREATION CERTIFICATION
(CONTINUED)

E. Ron Mendell	Dudley	08-25-89	06-30-90
		07-02-90	06-30-93
Peggy H. Pruett	Rural Hall	10-17-91	06-30-94
Ms. Sandy Smith	Beaufort	07-01-89	06-30-92
Wilfrenia W. Smith	Goldsboro	09-08-92	06-30-95
Nancy R. Ward	Beaufort	11-23-87	06-30-89

UNIVERSITY OF NORTH CAROLINA CENTER FOR PUBLIC TELEVISION BOARD OF TRUSTEES
G.S. 116-37.1/Board No. 0749

Name of Appointee	Address	Date Appointed	Date of Expiration
Gregory L. Edmond	Raleigh	07-02-90	05-31-94
J. Alex McMillan III	Charlotte	05-31-86	05-31-90
		07-02-90	05-31-94
Clifton Metcalf	Waynesville	11-28-88	06-30-89
James G. Patterson	Greensboro	09-19-86	05-31-90
Venita Peyton	Raleigh	10-20-87	05-31-90
Nancy H. Temple	Raleigh	01-08-93	05-31-96
Joyce White	Raleigh	09-19-86	05-31-88
		07-21-88	05-31-92
J. Edgar Williams	Pittsboro	07-21-88	05-31-92
		09-16-92	06-30-96

VETERINARY MEDICAL BOARD
G.S. 90-182/Board No. 0930

Name of Appointee	Address	Date Appointed	Date of Expiration
Mitchell K. Barnes	Hampstead	07-02-90	06-30-95
Walter W. Dickson	Gastonia	07-01-88	07-01-93
Nellie P. Jones	Winston-Salem	06-30-86	06-30-91
		08-01-91	07-01-96
James D. Peeples	Hickory	08-03-89	07-01-94
William E. Plummer	Goldsboro	03-19-86	07-01-90
Benjamin S. Turner	Rocky Mount	02-10-89	07-01-93

DEPARTMENT OF INSURANCE

BUILDING CODE COUNCIL
G.S. 143-136/Board No. 0150

Name of Appointee	Address	Date Appointed	Date of Expiration
John R. Andrew	Wilmington	09-09-85	07-31-91
chairman		09-09-85	
		08-01-91	07-31-97
James G. Andrews, Jr.	Winston-Salem	08-01-90	07-31-95
Clifton N. Bishop	Huntersville	09-09-85	07-31-91
		08-01-91	07-31-97
Robert C. Bowness	Linville	09-09-85	07-31-91
James H. Byrd	Cary	03-06-87	07-31-87
		08-01-87	07-31-93
Ralph P. Cochrane	Charlotte	09-09-85	07-31-89
Louis R. Dickerson	Raleigh	08-01-87	07-31-93

BUILDING CODE COUNCIL
(CONTINUED)

Earl Driggers	Charlotte	07-14-89	07-31-95
Barry W. Gardner	Clemmons	12-08-89	07-31-91
		08-01-91	07-31-97
Larry C. Hayes	Mocksville	12-30-92	07-31-98
Clayton S. Lineberger	Charlotte	08-01-87	07-31-93
Jack F. Neel	Albemarle	12-30-92	07-31-98
Robert C. Pierce	Charlotte	07-14-89	07-31-95
James W. Smith II	Asheboro	04-25-88	07-31-91
		08-01-91	07-31-97
Sam T. Snowdon, Jr.	Laurinburg	08-01-87	07-31-93
H. K. Stewart	Wingate	09-09-85	07-31-91
Ellis P. Thomas	Durham	08-01-90	07-31-95
Edward L. Woods	Charlotte	08-01-91	07-31-97

NORTH CAROLINA CODE OFFICIALS QUALIFICATION BOARD
G.S. 143-151.9/Board No. 0208

Name of Appointee	Address	Date Appointed	Date of Expiration
W. P. Davis	Marshville	10-09-86	07-01-90
Earl F. Fowler	Raleigh	08-27-91	06-30-95
John J. Gaitten	Murfreesboro	02-20-89	06-30-91
		08-27-91	06-30-95
J. Franklin Goode	Rutherfordton	02-20-89	06-30-90
		07-02-90	06-30-94
Hubert Jefferson	Charlotte	08-16-88	06-30-92
		07-01-92	06-30-96
Virginia W. Johnson	Creston	07-24-89	06-30-93
Ronald R. Kimble	Greenville	07-02-90	06-30-94
Howard H. King, Jr.	Fayetteville	07-01-87	06-30-91
Stephen R. Little	Marion	10-09-86	07-01-87
		07-01-87	06-30-91
Willis H. Overby	Danbury	12-04-92	06-30-93
Joseph D. Wheliss	Thomasville	08-16-88	06-30-92
		07-01-92	06-30-96
Kenneth N. Windley, Jr.	Beaufort	10-09-86	07-01-90
John B. Yorke	Lincolnton	06-02-87	07-01-88

STATE FIRE AND RESCUE COMMISSION [23]
G.S. 58-27.30/Board No. 0367

Name of Appointee	Address	Date Appointed	Date of Expiration
David L. Cope	Durham	09-15-85	10-01-88
		11-09-88	09-31-91
		11-19-91	09-30-94

---

[23]N.C. Session Laws, 1989, II, c. 750, effective July 1, 1989, changed the name of the State Fire Commission to the State Fire and Rescue Commission. It also expanded the membership and duties of the board.

North Carolina Manufactured Housing Board
G.S. 143-143.10/Board No. 0550

Name of Appointee	Address	Date Appointed	Date of Expiration
James H. Johnson III	Henderson	10-01-90	09-30-93
Howard McGirt	Sanford	03-05-86	09-30-87
Thomas M. Tunstall	Atlantic Beach	10-01-87	09-30-90
Don L. Woodward	Raleigh	10-01-87	09-30-90
		10-01-90	09-30-93

North Carolina Medical Database Commission
G.S. 131E-211/Board No. 0564

Name of Appointee	Address	Date Appointed	Date of Expiration
Bryant T. Aldridge, Sr.	Rocky Mount	10-21-88	06-30-91
Charles J. Rothwell	Chapel Hill	09-16-85	07-01-91
Thomas E. Ryan	Burlington	01-26-90	06-30-91
Richard H. Shachtman	Chapel Hill	07-22-87	07-01-88
		07-01-88	06-30-91
		09-13-91	06-30-94
W. Joe Trogden, Jr.	Asheboro	03-11-86	06-30-87

North Carolina Rate Bureau Board of Governors
G.S. 58-124.18(b)/Board No. 0778

Name of Appointee	Address	Date Appointed	Date of Expiration
John S. Freeman	Charlotte	01-02-87	
Woodrow W. Winchester	Greensboro	01-02-87	

North Carolina Reinsurance Facility Board of Directors
G.S. 58-124.18/Board No. 0777

Name of Appointee	Address	Date Appointed	Date of Expiration
George Batten, Jr.	Cary	03-25-88	
N. Leo Daughtry	Smithfield	03-25-88	
Mary S. Eshelman	Raleigh	10-01-90	
William T. Kennedy	Smithfield	01-12-90	

JUDICIAL OFFICIALS AND RELATED APPOINTMENTS [24]

Judges of the Supreme Court
G.S. 163-9

Name of Appointee	Address	Date Appointed	Date of Expiration
Rhoda B. Billings	Raleigh	09-03-85	00-00-00
chief justice		09-03-86	00-00-00
Robert R. Browning	Greenville	09-03-86	00-00-00
I. Beverly Lake, Jr.	Raleigh	02-05-92	00-00-00
Francis I. Parker	Charlotte	09-02-86	00-00-00

---

[24]Although many of the entries in this segment on appointed judicial and court-related officials lack specific expiration dates, the following general guidelines briefly define their terms of office. Persons named to fill vacancies on the state Supreme Court, Court of Appeals, Superior Court, and District Court served until his or her successor was elected; appointed district attorneys executed their duties under the same conditions. Emergency Superior Court and emergency District Court judges presided through the last day of the month in which they reached their seventieth birthday. As always, readers are urged to refer to the General Statutes for precise information regarding terms of service.

JUDGES OF THE COURT OF APPEALS
G.S. 163-9

Name of Appointee	Address	Date Appointed	Date of Expiration
Allyson K. Duncan	Durham	02-12-90	00-00-00
Robert F. Orr	Asheville	09-02-86	00-00-00
Ralph A. Walker	Greensboro	10-01-91	00-00-00

JUDGES OF THE SUPERIOR COURT
G.S. 163-9

Name of Appointee	Address	Date Appointed	Date of Expiration
James J. Booker	Winston-Salem	05-18-89	00-00-00
Dexter Brooks	Pembroke	01-01-89	00-00-00
Leon Henderson, Jr.	Rocky Mount	11-02-89	00-00-00
Howard E. Manning, Jr.	Raleigh	06-06-88	00-00-00
Steven D. Michael	Kitty Hawk	10-01-91	00-00-00
A. Leon Stanback, Jr.	Durham	01-24-89	00-00-00
Ralph A. Walker	Greensboro	09-21-87	00-00-00
Raymond A. Warren	Charlotte	06-14-90	00-00-00
Samuel A. Wilson III	Raleigh	09-01-89	00-00-00

EMERGENCY JUDGES OF THE SUPERIOR COURT
G.S. 7A-52, -53

Name of Appointee	Address	Date Appointed	Date of Expiration
D. B. Herring, Jr.	Fayetteville	01-02-91	00-00-00
Hollis M. Owens, Jr.	Rutherfordton	01-01-91	00-00-00
Herbert Small	Elizabeth City	09-01-91	00-00-00
L. Bradford Tillery	Wilmington	08-19-88	00-00-00
Edward K. Washington	Jamestown	09-25-87	00-00-00

SPECIAL JUDGES OF THE SUPERIOR COURT [25]
G.S. 7A-45

Name of Appointee	Address	Date Appointed	Date of Expiration
James A. Beaty, Jr.	Winston-Salem	08-17-87	00-00-00
Richard D. Boner	Charlotte	04-07-87	06-30-87
		08-17-87	00-00-00
Bruce B. Briggs	Raleigh	08-17-87	00-00-00
Jack B. Crawley, Jr.	Raleigh	11-23-87	00-00-00
		01-29-88	00-00-00
Samuel T. Currin	Raleigh	08-17-87	12-31-90
Carlton E. Fellers	Raleigh	10-22-87	00-00-00
Marvin K. Gray	Charlotte	08-17-87	12-31-90
I. Beverly Lake, Jr.	Raleigh	08-17-87	00-00-00
John B. Lewis, Jr.	Farmville	08-17-87	00-00-00
Donald L. Smith	Raleigh	08-17-87	00-00-00

[25]According to their letters of commission, Beaty, Lake, Lewis, and Smith were reappointed to offices they already held; Martin initially had named Lake to the bench in 1985. G.S. 7A-45, which authorized special Superior Court judges, was repealed by *N.C. Session Laws, 1987,* I, c. 509, s. 7, effective January 1, 1989; for other legislation affecting special judges, see *N.C. Session Laws, 1987, Regular Session, 1988,* III, c. 1037, s. 4, and *N.C. Session Laws, 1989, Extra and Regular Sessions, 1990,* c. 1066, s. 124.

JUDGES OF THE DISTRICT COURT
G.S. 7A-142

Name of Appointee	Address	Date Appointed	Date of Expiration
James F. Ammons, Jr.	Fayetteville	11-01-88	00-00-00
Napoleon B. Barefoot, Jr.	Leland	01-02-91	00-00-00
Lowry M. Betts	Pittsboro	01-03-86	01-05-88
M. Alexander Biggs, Jr.	Rocky Mount	02-07-91	00-00-00
Donald L. Boone	High Point	01-16-90	00-00-00
Steven J. Bryant	Bryson City	11-21-86	12-05-86
J. Stanley Carmical	Lumberton	06-20-89	00-00-00
Gary S. Cash	Fletcher	01-22-86	12-05-86
Donald F. Coats	Marion	01-08-91	00-00-00
H. William Constangy	Charlotte	02-09-89	00-00-00
J. H. Corpening II	Wilmington	08-30-91	00-00-00
Chester C. Davis	Winston-Salem	09-01-91	00-00-00
James H. Dooley, Jr.	Salisbury	03-17-86	12-05-86
Nancy L. Einstein	Lenoir	09-12-88	00-00-00
Spencer B. Ennis	Burlington	02-05-87	12-02-88
John K. Fonvielle	Shelby	01-07-87	12-02-88
James R. Fullwood	Raleigh	01-26-89	00-00-00
Shirley L. Fulton	Charlotte	01-07-87	12-02-88
John S. Hair, Jr.	Fayetteville	07-01-86	12-05-86
Joyce A. Hamilton	Raleigh	09-24-86	12-05-86
Pattie S. Harrison	Roxboro	07-24-91	00-00-00
Ernest J. Harviel	Burlington	03-16-90	00-00-00
Michael E. Helms	Wilkesboro	08-20-86	12-05-86
Robert E. Hodges	Morganton	01-24-89	00-00-00
Shelly S. Holt	Wilmington	06-09-92	00-00-00
Philip F. Howerton, Jr.	Charlotte	07-01-92	00-00-00
		09-01-92	00-00-00
William Grady Ijames, Jr.	Mocksville	01-24-89	00-00-00
Wayne G. Kimble, Jr.	Jacksonville	02-11-86	12-02-88
Timothy Kincaid	Hickory	08-12-86	12-05-86
William C. Lawton	Raleigh	09-19-91	00-00-00
William C. McIlwain	Laurinburg	07-01-89	00-00-00
Floyd B. McKissick, Sr.	Oxford	06-28-90	00-00-00
Lawrence C. McSwain	Greensboro	09-15-86	12-02-88
William Y. Manson	Durham	03-06-89	00-00-00
Fritz Y. Mercer, Jr.	Charlotte	01-24-91	00-00-00
Fred M. Morelock	Raleigh	10-27-86	12-02-88
Thomas R. J. Newbern	Winton	05-07-91	00-00-00
Timothy L. Patti	Gastonia	08-07-86	12-02-88
James D. Riddick III	Winton	12-13-89	00-00-00
Michael A. Sabiston	Troy	03-23-92	00-00-00
Catherine A. Stevens	Gastonia	02-05-87	12-02-88
Leonard W. Thagard	Clinton	10-01-87	12-31-88
William A. Vaden	Greensboro	01-16-87	12-02-88
Jerry F. Waddell	New Bern	07-11-91	00-00-00
George L. Wainwright, Jr.	Beaufort	01-08-91	00-00-00
Owen H. Willis, Jr.	Dunn	01-16-87	12-02-88

EMERGENCY JUDGES OF THE DISTRICT COURT
G.S. 7A-52, -53

Name of Appointee	Address	Date Appointed	Date of Expiration
Abner Alexander	Winston-Salem	10-01-91	00-00-00
Robert T. Gash	Brevard	01-24-89	00-00-00
Zoro J. Guice, Jr.	Hendersonville	03-17-89	00-00-00
Robert L. Harrell	Asheville	09-24-92	00-00-00
W. S. Harris, Jr.	Graham	03-01-90	00-00-00
James O. Israel, Jr.	Chandler	11-18-85	00-00-00
Livingston Vernon	Morganton	08-24-87	00-00-00

DISTRICT ATTORNEYS
G.S. 163-10

Name of Appointee	Address	Date Appointed	Date of Expiration
Jimmie R. Barnes	Murfreesboro	10-25-89	00-00-00
Robert W. Fisher	Asheville	03-21-86	12-31-86
Thurman Hampton	Wentworth	12-01-86	12-31-86
John R. Townsend	Lumberton	01-01-89	00-00-00

NORTH CAROLINA SENTENCING AND POLICY ADVISORY COMMISSION
G.S. 164-37/Board No. 0838

Name of Appointee	Address	Date Appointed	Date of Expiration
Douglas R. Gill	Southern Pines	08-03-92	06-30-94
Mrs. Kent H. Graham	Raleigh	08-24-90	08-31-92
		08-03-92	06-30-94
William L. Osteen, Sr.	Greensboro	10-01-90	07-01-92
George P. Wilson, Sr.	Durham	08-24-90	08-31-92
		08-03-92	06-30-94

DEPARTMENT OF JUSTICE

NORTH CAROLINA ALARM SYSTEMS LICENSING BOARD
G.S. 74D-4/Board No. 0025

Name of Appointee	Address	Date Appointed	Date of Expiration
Ralph C. Brown	Statesville	10-01-86	10-01-89
John C. Ranson	Winston-Salem	02-12-88	10-01-89
		10-01-89	06-30-92
		09-14-92	06-30-95
Sylvania Wilkerson, Sr.	Goldsboro	09-14-92	06-30-95
Lorine C. Wilson	Cary	10-01-86	10-01-89
		10-01-89	06-30-92

NORTH CAROLINA CRIMINAL JUSTICE EDUCATION AND TRAINING STANDARDS COMMISSION
G.S. 17C-3/Board No. 0260

Name of Appointee	Address	Date Appointed	Date of Expiration
Charles T. Browne	Asheboro	05-23-88	06-30-90
		07-02-90	06-30-93

North Carolina Criminal Justice Education and Training Standards Commission
(continued)

Larry E. Dales	Pleasant Garden	12-09-92	06-30-93
Richard M. Holloman	Williamston	07-01-92	06-30-95
James Masters	Newton	07-01-89	06-30-92
Lee F. Pascasio	Greenville	08-31-85	06-30-86
Robert Pierce	Yadkinville	08-06-86	06-30-89
Jean D. Symmes	Greensboro	07-01-87	06-30-90
Charles Von Canon	Banner Elk	08-31-85	06-30-88

General Statutes Commission
G.S. 164-14/Board No. 0400

Name of Appointee	Address	Date Appointed	Date of Expiration
Mark C. Cramer	Charlotte	03-02-88	05-31-89
		06-01-89	06-01-91
		08-01-91	05-31-93
Garry W. Frank	Lexington	06-01-87	05-31-89
Emil F. Kratt	Charlotte	07-01-85	05-31-87
		06-01-87	05-31-89
Edward V. Zotian	Winston-Salem	06-01-89	06-01-91
		08-01-91	05-31-93

Private Protective Services Board
G.S. 74C-4/Board No. 0725

Name of Appointee	Address	Date Appointed	Date of Expiration
Stanley G. Curtis	Atlantic Beach	08-15-86	06-30-87
Jack G. Martin	Lexington	08-15-85	06-30-87
Keith S. Shannon	Charlotte	07-01-87	06-30-90
		07-02-90	06-30-93

Railroad Advisory Commission
N.C. Session Laws, 1991, c. 754, s. 3.1/Board No. 0758

Name of Appointee	Address	Date Appointed	Date of Expiration
Edward S. Goode	Charlotte	11-22-91	
John W. Smith, Jr.	Whitakers	11-22-91	

North Carolina Sheriffs' Education and Training Standards Commission
G.S. 17E-3/Board No. 0837

Name of Appointee	Address	Date Appointed	Date of Expiration
H. Eugene LeGrand	Shelby	08-15-86	09-01-87
D. Reid Sink, Jr.	Lexington	09-30-87	08-31-89
		09-01-89	08-31-91
		09-27-91	08-31-93

DEPARTMENT OF LABOR

Safety and Health Review Board
G.S. 95-135/Board No. 0805

Name of Appointee	Address	Date Appointed	Date of Expiration
Fred S. Hutchins, Jr.	Winston-Salem	11-13-92	07-31-93
Kenneth K. Kiser	Concord	08-31-85	07-30-91
chairman		08-31-85	
chairman		08-27-91	07-31-97
Philip M. Van Hoy	Charlotte	10-30-85	08-01-87
		08-01-87	07-31-93
Hugh M. Wilson	Lenoir	08-01-89	07-31-95

DEPARTMENT OF PUBLIC INSTRUCTION

State Board of Education
G.S. 115C-11/Board No. 0305

Name of Appointee	Address	Date Appointed	Date of Expiration
Amy Autrey	Charlotte	11-06-92	06-14-94
Anne Breuer	Raleigh	09-07-90	06-14-92
Fredericka C. Bryant	Charlotte	08-17-87	06-14-88
Jennifer Carroll	Denton	10-14-88	06-15-90
Crystal R. Clark	Charlotte	10-14-88	06-15-89
Thomas W. D'Alonzo	Raleigh	05-09-91	03-31-99
Jere A. Drummond	Charlotte	03-14-86	04-01-91
Maurice E. Dunn	Arden	09-19-86	06-14-87
Kenneth R. Harris	Charlotte	04-07-88	03-31-91
		05-09-91	03-31-99
Howard H. Haworth	Morganton	04-28-87	03-31-95
Natiza L. Hill	Raleigh	07-14-89	06-15-91
Allison Jonas	Lincolnton	06-15-87	06-14-89
Portia L. King	Pineville	09-19-86	06-14-88
Teena S. Little	Southern Pines	05-02-89	03-31-97
William C. Meekins, Jr.	Elizabeth City	04-28-87	03-31-95
Mary Morgan	Jacksonville	04-01-85	03-31-93
Patricia H. Neal	Durham	04-28-87	03-31-95
Jane P. Norwood	Clemmons	08-03-90	03-31-93
		11-17-92	03-31-95
Mrs. Cary C. Owen	Asheville	04-01-85	03-31-93
Donald D. Pollock	Kinston	06-25-87	03-31-93
Prezell R. Robinson	Raleigh	05-02-89	03-31-97
Barbara M. Tapscott	Burlington	05-02-89	03-31-97
Ronald D. Williams, Jr.	Gates	08-27-91	06-14-93

Annual Testing Commission [26]
G.S. 115C-191/Board No. 0042

Name of Appointee	Address	Date Appointed	Date of Expiration
Robert C. Clary	Halifax	07-31-85	06-30-87
Jean W. Davenport	Webster	07-31-85	06-30-87

[26]*N.C. Session Laws, 1985, Extra and Regular Sessions, 1986,* c. 1014, s. 74(a) abolished the Annual Testing Commission effective July 15, 1986.

ANNUAL TESTING COMMISSION
(CONTINUED)

Loraine Eason	Summerfield	07-31-85	06-30-87
Paul A. Fox	Boone	07-31-85	06-30-87
Christina R. Garratt	Goldsboro	07-31-85	06-30-87
Janie R. Hardison	Arapahoe	07-31-85	06-30-87
Peggy Johnson	High Point	07-31-85	06-30-87
Linda S. Little	Wilkesboro	07-31-85	06-30-87
John McKnight	Greenville	07-31-85	06-30-87
Roselyn Misenheimer	Rockwell	07-31-85	06-30-87
Jane Norwood	Advance	07-31-85	06-30-87
Carolyn N. Pittman	Siler City	07-31-85	06-30-87
Randy Poole	Garden City	07-31-85	06-30-87
James A. Robinson	Warrenton	07-31-85	06-30-87
Benjamin Sledge	Roanoke Rapids	07-31-85	06-30-87

NORTH CAROLINA EDUCATION COUNCIL [27]
G.S. 115C-105/Board No. 0323

Name of Appointee	Address	Date Appointed	Date of Expiration
Chester W. Crisp	Robbinsville	05-30-87	05-29-90
Vivian Fuse	Fayetteville	06-14-85	05-30-87
		05-30-87	05-29-90
Joe H. Hege, Jr.	Lexington	02-12-88	05-29-90
Jackie Manzi	Greensboro	06-14-85	05-30-87
Harold E. Mitchell	Ahoskie	06-14-85	05-30-87
		05-30-87	05-29-90
Carl L. Unsicker	Wilmington	06-14-85	05-30-87
chairman		01-15-86	
		05-30-87	05-29-90
Donald Waldo	Roxboro	06-14-85	05-30-87
		05-30-87	05-29-90

COUNCIL ON EDUCATIONAL SERVICES FOR EXCEPTIONAL CHILDREN
G.S.115C-121/Board No. 0327

Name of Appointee	Address	Date Appointed	Date of Expiration
M. Kyle Carver	Leicester	10-09-86	06-30-88
		07-01-88	06-30-90
		07-02-90	06-30-92
		07-01-92	06-30-94
Janet A. Lesser	Fremont	10-09-86	06-30-88
		07-01-88	06-30-90
		07-02-90	06-30-92
		07-01-92	06-30-94

PERSONNEL ADMINISTRATION COMMISSION FOR PUBLIC SCHOOL EMPLOYEES
G.S. 115C-328/Board No. 0681

Name of Appointee	Address	Date Appointed	Date of Expiration
Joseph N. Alexander	Norlina	02-27-87	08-30-88
		09-01-88	08-31-91
		11-19-91	08-30-94

---

[27]G.S. 115C-105 was repealed under *N.C. Session Laws, 1991*, I, c. 369, s. 2, effective June 24, 1991.

Personnel Administration Commission for Public School Employees
(CONTINUED)

Shirley C. Babson	Bolivia	02-27-87	08-30-87
		08-31-87	08-30-90
		01-29-91	08-30-93
Mary A. Chapin	Washington	02-27-87	08-30-87
		08-31-87	08-30-90
		01-29-91	08-30-93
Gary H. Fisher	Rockingham	01-29-91	08-30-91
		11-19-91	08-30-94
Garlene G. Grogan	Winston-Salem	02-27-87	08-30-89
		04-12-90	08-30-92
Susan W. Hiatt	Mount Airy	04-11-91	08-30-93
Teena S. Little	Southern Pines	02-27-87	08-30-88
		09-01-88	08-31-91
Joyce S. Masters	Bakersville	04-12-90	08-30-92
Donald L. Osborne	Randleman	10-30-92	08-30-95
Ray Ottinger	Waynesville	04-11-91	08-30-92
		10-30-92	08-30-95
Cliff Oxford	Purlear	02-27-87	08-30-87
		08-31-87	08-30-90
J. Vann Parker, Jr.	Emerald Isle	10-30-92	08-30-95
Garland F. Sailors	Matthews	11-19-91	08-30-94
Robert J. Smith	Monroe	02-27-87	08-30-88
		09-01-88	08-31-91
Ruth Stepp	Asheville	02-27-87	08-30-89
Janet H. Wilson	Lenoir	02-27-87	08-30-89
chairwoman		02-27-87	

State School Health Advisory Committee
G.S. 115C-81/Board No. 0823

Name of Appointee	Address	Date Appointed	Date of Expiration
Rebekah S. Bowden	Durham	03-25-88	06-30-88
Marjorie A. Bowman	Clemmons	09-22-89	06-30-90
		07-10-90	06-30-93
Donna Breitenstein	Boone	08-03-89	06-30-92
Sherman Brooks	Pembroke	07-10-90	06-30-93
Robert E. Chambers	Gastonia	03-31-88	06-30-90
Linda H. Charping	Flat Rock	08-27-91	06-30-94
Marcella D. Cook	Charlotte	03-25-88	06-30-89
Carol C. Davis	Raleigh	08-27-91	06-30-94
Katherine K. Glassock	Chapel Hill	03-25-88	06-30-88
		08-15-88	06-30-91
Nancy Hackett	Fayetteville	08-15-88	06-30-91
R. Keith Hartman	Cary	03-25-88	06-30-90
		07-10-90	06-30-93
Edna R. Hensey	Raleigh	08-29-88	06-30-91
R. M. Herring, Jr.	Clinton	08-03-89	06-30-92
		09-14-92	06-30-95
Paula H. Hildebrand	Wake Forest	09-14-92	06-30-95
Martha A. Keels	Chapel Hill	08-27-91	06-30-94
Beth S. Kennedy	High Point	05-22-91	06-30-93
Thomas M. McCutchen, Jr.	Fayetteville	03-25-88	06-30-89
Linda P. Nance	Wilmington	11-19-91	06-30-93
Lorraine Nicholson	Raleigh	03-25-88	06-30-88

STATE SCHOOL HEALTH ADVISORY COMMITTEE
(CONTINUED)

Carolyn L. Niemeyer	Gastonia	03-25-88	06-30-90
		07-10-90	06-30-93
Georgia Shuster	Laurinburg	08-27-91	06-30-94
Marian K. Solleder	Greensboro	03-25-88	06-30-90
Suzette Stines	Wilmington	03-31-89	06-30-91
Carlton V. Winter	Charlotte	03-25-88	06-30-88
R. Howard Yoder	High Point	08-15-88	06-30-91

NORTH CAROLINA TEACHING FELLOWS COMMISSION
G.S. 115C-363.22/Board No. 0884

Name of Appointee	Address	Date Appointed	Date of Expiration
Herbert A. Exum	Raleigh	11-09-86	07-01-90
		08-20-90	06-30-93
Linda S. Little	Wilkesboro	10-09-86	07-01-90
		08-20-90	06-30-92
		07-01-92	06-30-94
Roby F. Shore	Goldsboro	11-09-86	07-01-90
		08-20-90	06-30-94

COMMISSION ON TESTING
G.S. 115C-174.2/Board No. 0894

Name of Appointee	Address	Date Appointed	Date of Expiration
Earline A. Brooks	Greensboro	12-10-86	06-30-90
		07-25-90	06-30-94
David Broyles	Winston-Salem	09-07-90	06-30-94
Carian Clary	Winston-Salem	08-03-88	06-30-92
Linda F. Conrad	Trinity	12-10-86	06-30-88
Jean W. Davenport	Webster	12-10-86	06-30-88
		08-03-88	06-30-92
John B. Dunn	Edenton	08-03-89	06-30-90
		07-25-90	06-30-94
Esther M. Dunnegan	Morrisville	07-02-90	06-30-92
Sue R. Fairless	Colerain	07-25-90	06-30-94
Paul A. Fox	Boone	12-10-86	06-30-90
		07-25-90	06-30-94
Randal S. Garrison	Morganton	08-03-88	06-30-92
		09-18-92	06-30-96
William T. Gray	Trinity	09-09-87	06-30-88
		08-03-88	06-30-92
		09-18-92	06-30-96
Vernice M. Grigsby	Raleigh	12-10-86	06-30-90
		07-25-90	06-30-94
Janie R. Hardison	Arapahoe	12-10-86	06-30-88
		08-03-88	06-30-92
James B. Hemby, Jr.	Wilson	12-10-86	06-30-90
Kym L. Lake	Raleigh	12-10-86	06-30-88
Rosa F. Lake	Raleigh	12-10-86	06-30-88
Phyllis R. Marker	Southern Pines	12-30-92	06-30-96
David A. Martin	Mount Airy	12-10-86	06-30-90
Lenwood Padgett	Jacksonville	12-10-86	06-30-90
		07-25-90	06-30-94

Commission on Testing
(continued)

Carolyn N. Pittman	Siler City	12-10-86	06-30-88
		08-03-88	06-30-92
Amy B. Potts	Fayetteville	09-18-92	06-30-96
Alyce W. Pringle	Raleigh	09-18-92	06-30-96
Curtis R. Rains	Trenton	01-27-92	06-30-94
Joel R. Rountree	Grover	09-18-92	06-30-96
Sue W. Sams	Charlotte	12-10-86	06-30-88
		08-03-88	06-30-92
Diane Scott-Jones	Raleigh	12-10-86	06-30-90
Marcus C. Smith	Salisbury	08-03-88	06-30-90
Mary Toliver	Madison	09-18-92	06-30-96
John E. Trainer, Jr.	Hickory	12-21-88	06-30-90
Jill Via	Charlotte	12-10-86	06-30-90
		07-25-90	06-30-94
Evelyn G. Walden	Goldsboro	12-30-92	06-30-96
Jeanne Weavil-Haney	Winston-Salem	12-10-86	06-30-88
		08-03-88	06-30-92
Bert W. Westbrook	Raleigh	09-09-87	06-30-90
Dale E. Weston	Jacksonville	01-27-92	06-30-94
Le Zollinger	Hendersonville	12-10-86	06-30-90
		07-25-90	06-30-94

North Carolina Textbook Commission
G.S. 115C-87/Board No. 0895

Name of Appointee	Address	Date Appointed	Date of Expiration
Donna S. Abercrombie	Statesville	05-09-85	04-01-89
Lena C. Baynes	Greensboro	04-28-89	04-01-93
J. Breeden Blackwell	Spring Lake	05-09-85	04-01-89
Logan Darensburg	Williamston	05-09-85	04-01-89
Nancy B. Davis	Monroe	04-28-89	04-01-93
Ricky K. Davis	Robbinsville	02-27-87	04-01-89
Susan Edwards	Durham	05-09-85	04-01-89
James H. Ellerbe	Smithfield	05-09-85	04-01-89
Alexander Erwin	Wilkesboro	05-09-85	04-01-89
Scott Griffin	Mount Holly	04-28-89	04-01-93
Doris Henderson	Greensboro	05-09-85	04-01-89
		04-28-89	04-01-93
William H. Hudson III	Hendersonville	04-28-89	04-01-93
Jane H. Knox	Raleigh	05-09-85	04-01-89
		04-28-89	04-01-93
John Langley	Rockingham	05-09-85	04-01-89
Katrina Locklear	Pembroke	05-09-85	04-01-89
		04-28-89	04-01-93
Adair Massey	Charlotte	05-09-85	04-01-89
Carolyn M. Penny	Elizabeth City	04-28-89	04-01-93
Lorraine M. Robinson	Lenoir	05-09-85	04-01-89
Mary K. Robinson	Waynesville	04-28-89	04-01-93
Sandra Scott	Goldsboro	05-09-85	04-01-89
Brenda G. Sigmon	Newton	05-09-85	04-01-89
		04-28-89	04-01-93
Janice M. Smith	Fayetteville	04-28-89	04-01-93
Patricia Sutherland	Charlotte	06-03-88	04-01-89

North Carolina Textbook Commission
(continued)

Tricia N. Willoughby	Raleigh	04-28-89	04-01-93
Delano R. Wilson	Winterville	04-28-89	04-01-93
Nancy G. Wilson	Kenansville	04-28-89	04-01-93

DEPARTMENT OF REVENUE

Secretaries
Helen A. Powers, 1985-1990
Betsy Y. Justus, 1990-1992
Ward Purrington, 1992-1993

Property Tax Commission
G.S. 143B-223/Board No. 0740

Name of Appointee	Address	Date Appointed	Date of Expiration
Oliver W. Alphin	Durham	05-17-88	06-30-89
		07-01-89	06-30-93
John A. Cocklereece, Jr.	Winston-Salem	05-07-90	06-30-93
chairman		10-17-91	
William P. Pinna	Cary	07-01-87	06-30-91
chairman		01-19-88	
Robert H. Shore	Blowing Rock	07-01-89	06-30-93
James R. Vosburg	Washington	10-17-91	06-30-95
Ralph A. Walker, *chairman*	Greensboro	03-18-86	

North Carolina Tax Review Board
G.S. 105-269.2/Board No. 0883

Name of Appointee	Address	Date Appointed	Date of Expiration
Jefferson D. Batts	Rocky Mount	07-01-87	06-30-91
		10-17-91	06-30-95

DEPARTMENT OF THE SECRETARY OF STATE

Advisory Committee on Land Records
G.S. 143-345.6/Board No. 0522

Name of Appointee	Address	Date Apppointed	Date of Expiration
Robert F. Binford	Charlotte	12-12-91	06-30-95
J. Clark Brewer	Raleigh	11-10-87	06-30-89
Alice B. Brown	Gastonia	11-10-87	06-30-91
		12-12-91	06-30-95
Billy D. Chilton	Asheboro	11-10-87	06-30-89
Charles A. Clark	Asheville	12-12-91	06-30-95
Frances Dyer	Durham	11-10-87	06-30-91
Jack Freeman	Charlotte	11-10-87	06-30-91
Timothy A. Glass	Taylorsville	11-10-87	06-30-89
		02-09-90	06-30-93
Robert H. Goslee	Wilmington	11-10-87	06-30-89
Charles O. Hampton, Jr.	Fletcher	02-09-90	06-30-93

ADVISORY COMMITTEE ON LAND RECORDS
(CONTINUED)

Donald R. Hardie .... Bakersville	03-13-86	06-30-89
chairman	11-10-87	
chairman	02-09-90	06-30-93
A. Edward Holland .... North Wilkesboro	12-22-88	06-30-91
Dennis K. Hoyle .... Raleigh	11-10-87	06-30-91
James A. Jacobs .... Pembroke	02-09-90	06-30-93
Bob R. Miller .... Newton	11-10-87	06-30-91
Charles W. Ogletree .... Columbia	02-09-90	06-30-93
Philip N. Post .... Chapel Hill	12-12-91	06-30-95
Clarence A. Rickett .... Charlotte	12-12-91	06-30-95
William D. Seawell, Jr. .... Greensboro	11-10-87	06-30-89
	02-09-90	06-30-93
Barry A. Warren .... Lenoir	01-15-92	06-30-95

DEPARTMENT OF TRANSPORTATION

Secretaries
James E. Harrington, 1985-1989
Thomas J. Harrelson, 1989-1993

BOARD OF TRANSPORTATION
G.S. 143B-350/Board No. 0905

Name of Appointee	*Address*	*Date Appointed*	*Date of Expiration*
Ronald Barbee .... Greensboro	01-24-85	12-31-86
Ernest H. Barry, Jr. .... Charlotte	10-06-90	01-15-91
	02-22-91	01-15-93
John B. Beall .... Lenoir	12-06-90	01-15-91
	02-22-91	01-15-93
John E. Bishop .... Rocky Mount	01-24-85	12-31-86
	01-01-87	12-31-88
	01-05-89	01-15-91
Bruce B. Briggs .... Mars Hill	01-05-89	01-15-91
Rufus L. Brock .... Mocksville	04-01-85	12-00-86
David L. Brown .... Fairview	11-13-89	01-15-91
	02-22-91	01-15-93
W. B. Buchanan .... Graham	01-24-85	12-31-86
	01-01-87	12-31-88
	01-05-89	01-15-91
F. Hudnall Christopher, Jr. .... Winston-Salem	12-06-90	01-15-91
	02-22-91	01-15-93
J. A. Dalpiaz .... Gastonia	12-06-90	01-15-91
	02-22-91	01-15-93
Thomas F. Darden II .... Raleigh	10-06-90	01-15-91
	02-22-91	01-15-93
Randy D. Doub .... Greenville	01-24-85	12-31-86
	01-01-87	12-31-88
	01-05-89	01-15-91
Kermit Edney .... Hendersonville	01-27-92	01-15-93
Lucy C. Everett .... Elkin	01-24-85	12-31-86
	01-01-87	12-31-88

Board of Transportation
(CONTINUED)

Philip P. Godwin	Gatesville	01-01-87	12-31-88
		01-05-89	01-15-91
		02-22-91	01-15-93
Seddon Goode, Jr.	Charlotte	01-24-85	12-31-86
		07-07-87	12-31-88
		01-05-89	01-15-91
Elwood Goodson	Mount Olive	01-01-87	12-31-88
		01-05-89	01-15-91
		02-22-91	01-15-93
C. W. Hardin	Canton	12-06-90	01-15-91
		02-22-91	01-15-93
James E. Harrington	Raleigh	01-24-85	12-31-86
John W. Harris	Charlotte	01-24-85	12-31-86
		01-01-87	12-31-88
H. Terry Hutchens	Fayetteville	01-24-85	12-31-86
		01-01-87	12-31-88
		01-05-89	01-15-91
Brent B. Kincaid	Lenoir	01-24-85	12-31-86
		01-01-87	12-31-88
		01-05-89	01-15-91
W. D. Lane	Goldsboro	06-17-92	01-15-93
Jack Laughery	Rocky Mount	12-06-90	01-15-91
		02-22-91	01-15-93
Estell C. Lee	Wilmington	08-24-90	01-15-91
		02-22-91	01-15-93
Charles G. Lowdermilk	Greensboro	12-06-90	01-15-91
		02-22-91	01-15-93
Albert O. McCauley	Fayetteville	01-05-89	01-15-91
		02-22-91	01-15-93
James P. Myers, Sr.	Bryson City	01-24-85	12-31-86
		01-01-87	12-31-88
		01-05-89	01-15-91
James E. Nance	Albemarle	01-01-87	12-31-88
		01-05-89	01-15-91
		02-22-91	01-15-93
J. Kenneth Newsom	Morehead City	08-24-90	01-15-91
		02-22-91	01-15-93
Stuart R. Paine	Southern Pines	12-05-90	01-15-91
		02-22-91	01-15-93
James M. Peden, Jr.	Raleigh	01-24-85	12-31-86
		01-01-87	12-31-88
		01-05-89	01-15-91
S. Dave Phillips	High Point	12-06-90	01-15-91
		02-22-91	01-15-93
B. Thomas Pollard	Jacksonville	01-24-85	12-31-86
		01-01-87	12-31-88
		01-05-89	01-15-91
H. Dean Proctor	Hickory	01-05-89	01-15-91
		02-22-91	01-15-93
Richard K. Pugh	Asheboro	01-24-85	12-31-86
		01-01-87	12-31-88
		01-05-89	01-15-91

Board of Transportation
(continued)

Name	Address	Date Appointed	Date of Expiration
Nancy Rand	Durham	01-24-85	12-31-86
		01-01-87	12-31-88
		01-05-89	01-15-91
Kenneth H. Roberson	Robersonville	01-24-85	12-31-86
Harry L. Robertson	Taylorsville	01-24-85	12-31-86
		01-01-87	12-31-88
Ronald O. Rohadfox	Graham	02-22-91	01-15-93
G. Earl Rountree	Sunbury	12-09-85	12-31-86
Charles M. Shelton	Winston-Salem	01-24-85	12-31-86
		01-01-87	12-31-88
		01-05-89	01-15-91
Ted Smith	Swannanoa	01-24-85	12-31-86
Jefferson B. Strickland	Roseboro	12-06-90	01-15-91
		02-22-91	01-15-93
John R. Sutton, Sr.	Candler	01-01-87	12-31-88
Joseph D. Teachey, Jr.	Wallace	01-27-92	01-15-93
John Thomas, Jr.	High Point	01-01-87	12-31-88
Herman G. Thompson	Southern Pines	01-01-87	12-31-88
		01-05-89	01-15-91
Roberta Thompson	Southern Pines	01-01-87	12-31-88
C. Richard Vaughn	Mount Airy	01-05-89	01-15-91
		02-22-91	01-15-93
H. Lanier Williams	Gastonia	01-24-85	12-31-86
Marilyn W. Williams	Wilmington	04-25-91	01-15-93
J. Curtis Youngblood, Jr.	Fletcher	01-24-85	12-31-86
Ken G. Younger	Cherryville	01-01-87	12-31-88
		01-05-89	01-15-91

Aeronautics Council
G.S. 143B-357/Board No. 0001

Name of Appointee	Address	Date Appointed	Date of Expiration
Russell N. Barringer, Jr.	Durham	07-01-87	06-30-91
		10-17-91	06-30-95
Lamar Beach	Sanford	08-03-89	06-30-93
Cecil Budd, *chairman*	Siler City	07-01-87	
		08-03-89	06-30-93
chairman		08-03-89	
Thomas L. Coble	Burlington	10-17-91	06-30-95
Rob Roy M. Converse	Chapel Hill	07-01-85	06-30-89
		08-03-89	06-30-93
J. Roy Davis, Jr.	Concord	07-01-85	06-30-89
		08-03-89	06-30-93
Stanley Frank	Greensboro	07-01-87	06-30-91
Glenn C. Hilton, Jr.	Hickory	08-03-89	06-30-93
Daniel T. Lilley	Kinston	07-01-87	06-30-91
Robert H. Lineberger, Sr.	Lincolnton	07-01-87	06-30-91
		10-17-91	06-30-95
Otis B. Michael	Asheville	07-01-87	06-30-91
H. Melvin Pope	Magnolia	03-02-92	06-30-93
Carl H. Ricker, Jr.	Swannanoa	10-17-91	06-30-95
June E. Rodd	Havelock	07-01-87	06-30-91
		10-17-91	06-30-95

AERONAUTICS COUNCIL
(CONTINUED)

Joseph E. Sandlin	Lumberton	08-03-89	06-30-93
William N. Schultz, Jr.	Madison	07-01-87	06-30-91
		10-17-91	06-30-95
Herman G. Thompson	Southern Pines	10-17-91	06-30-95

NORTH CAROLINA AIR CARGO AIRPORT AUTHORITY BOARD OF DIRECTORS
G.S. 63A-3/Board No. 0002

Name of Appointee	Address	Date Appointed	Date of Expiration
James T. Broyhill	Banner Elk	08-15-91	06-30-93
S. Malcolm Gillis	Durham	08-15-91	06-30-93
Seddon Goode, Jr.	Charlotte	08-15-91	06-30-93
William H. Prestage	Clinton	08-15-91	06-30-93
Paul Rizzo	Chapel Hill	08-15-91	06-30-93

DEPARTMENT OF STATE TREASURER

EDUCATIONAL FACILITIES FINANCE AGENCY BOARD OF DIRECTORS
G.S. 74C-4/Board No. 0325

Name of Appointee	Address	Date Appointed	Date of Expiration
Harlan E. Boyles, *chairman*	Raleigh	09-30-87	
John A. Cocklereece, Sr.	Greensboro	03-23-87	03-01-90
vice-chairman		03-23-87	
		03-05-90	03-01-94
vice-chairman		03-05-90	
Stanley Green, Jr.	Raleigh	07-14-89	03-01-93
Walter M. Hall III	Belmont	04-04-91	03-01-95
Charles B. Huestis	Durham	09-30-87	03-01-91
J. J. Sansom, Jr.	Raleigh	03-23-87	03-01-89
James R. Sheridan	Charlotte	03-23-87	03-01-91
chairman		03-27-87	

BOARD OF TRUSTEES OF THE NORTH CAROLINA FIREMEN'S AND
RESCUE SQUAD WORKERS' PENSION FUND
G.S. 118-34/Board No. 0370

Name of Appointee	Address	Date Appointed	Date of Expiration
J. C. Bailey	Roxboro	08-01-91	06-30-95
Eldon Edwards	Sparta	07-01-87	06-30-91
		08-01-91	06-30-95
Dennis Foushee	Sanford	07-01-87	06-30-91
J. E. Hawkins	Rocky Mount	07-01-87	06-30-91
		08-01-91	06-30-95
Tony G. Martin	Catawba	07-01-87	06-30-91
Bobby L. Watkins	Burgaw	07-21-86	06-30-89
		07-01-89	06-30-93

BOARD OF COMMISSIONERS OF THE LAW ENFORCEMENT OFFICERS'
BENEFIT AND RETIREMENT FUND[28]
G.S. 143-166(b)/Board No. 0530

Name of Appointee	Address	Date Appointed	Date of Expiration
Jack P. Henderson	Yadkinville	04-15-85	
David Kepple, Jr.	Winston-Salem	04-15-85	

LOCAL GOVERNMENT COMMISSION
G.S. 159-3/Board No. 0540

Name of Appointee	Address	Date Appointed	Date of Expiration
Steven T. Arey	Salisbury	07-01-89	06-30-93
Larry E. Harrington	Monroe	08-31-85	06-30-89
		07-01-89	06-30-93
Donald R. Lawing	Maiden	01-27-92	06-30-93
Linwood H. Parker	Four Oaks	04-16-92	06-30-93
Melvin Pope	Magnolia	08-31-85	06-30-89
		07-01-89	06-30-93
Julian H. Scarborough, Jr.	Winston-Salem	08-31-85	06-30-89

NORTH CAROLINA LOCAL GOVERNMENTAL EMPLOYEES' RETIREMENT SYSTEM
BOARD OF TRUSTEES
G.S. 128-28/Board No. 0545

Name of Appointee	Address	Date Appointed	Date of Expiration
Koka Booth	Cary	04-01-88	04-01-92
W. G. Dinkins	Yadkinville	05-14-85	04-01-89
David L. Drummond	Clemmons	05-14-85	04-01-89
William R. McDonald III	Hickory	05-31-88	04-01-92
		04-16-92	04-01-96
Phillip M. Prescott, Jr.	Bayboro	01-09-91	04-01-92
		04-16-92	04-01-96
Joe Roberts	Sparta	03-15-86	04-01-88
Wilborn S. Swaim	Salisbury	12-16-86	04-01-89
		04-01-88	04-01-92
James W. Wise	Aberdeen	04-01-88	04-01-92
		04-16-92	04-01-96

NORTH CAROLINA SOLID WASTE MANAGEMENT CAPITAL PROJECTS FINANCING AGENCY
BOARD OF DIRECTORS
G.S. 159I-4/Board No. 0842

Name of Appointee	Address	Date Appointed	Date of Expiration
Fred W. Alexander	High Point	11-29-89	06-30-92
Carol G. Love	Raleigh	03-05-90	00-00-00
Bennett A. Macon, Jr.	Sylva	07-01-92	06-30-94
Leroy Smith	Winterville	03-05-90	00-00-00
Jefferson L. Sugg	Cary	11-29-89	06-30-90
		07-02-90	06-30-92
		07-01-92	06-30-94

---

[28]G.S. 143-166 through G.S. 143-166.04 were repealed under N.C. *Session Laws, 1985*, c. 479, s. 196(t), ratified June 27, 1985.

BOARD OF TRUSTEES OF THE TEACHERS' AND STATE EMPLOYEES' RETIREMENT SYSTEM
G.S. 135-6/Board No. 0890

Name of Appointee	Address	Date Appointed	Date of Expiration
O. K. Beatty	Raleigh	07-01-89	06-30-93
John W. Britt, Jr.	Apex	07-01-89	06-30-93
Kevin Brown	Clayton	08-01-91	04-04-95
Clyde R. Cook, Jr.	Garner	06-17-92	04-04-95
James M. Cooper	Fayetteville	04-29-88	04-01-92
		06-17-92	04-01-96
Ronald E. Copley	Wilmington	07-01-89	06-30-93
Donna A. Creech	Wilson's Mills	04-14-87	04-04-91
		08-01-91	04-04-95
James R. Hawkins	Durham	04-29-88	04-01-92
		06-17-92	04-01-96
Shirley A. Hise	Spruce Pine	04-14-87	04-04-91
		08-01-91	04-04-95
Wilma M. King	Hendersonville	07-01-89	06-30-93
W. Eugene McCombs	Faith	04-29-88	04-01-92
		06-17-92	04-01-96
Leo F. Walsh, Jr.	Southern Pines	04-14-87	04-04-91

UNIVERSITY OF NORTH CAROLINA SYSTEM

APPALACHIAN STATE UNIVERSITY BOARD OF TRUSTEES
G.S. 116-31/Board No. 1010

Name of Appointee	Address	Date Appointed	Date of Expiration
Kevin Corbin	Franklin	07-01-85	06-30-89
James C. Hastings	Boone	07-01-89	06-30-93
F. Bryan Houck	Gastonia	09-20-91	06-30-95
Fred C. Miller, Jr.	Boone	07-01-87	06-30-91
		09-20-91	06-30-95
Allene B. Stevens	Lenoir	07-01-85	06-30-89
		07-01-89	06-30-93
Kenneth Wilcox	Boone	07-01-87	06-30-91

EAST CAROLINA UNIVERSITY BOARD OF TRUSTEES
G.S. 116-31/Board No. 1035

Name of Appointee	Address	Date Appointed	Date of Expiration
William E. Dansey, Jr.	Greenville	07-01-85	06-30-89
		07-01-89	06-30-93
Max R. Joyner, Sr.	Greenville	07-01-89	06-30-93
W. Howard Rooks	Alexandria, Virginia	07-01-87	06-30-91
		08-01-91	06-30-95
J. Craig Souza	Raleigh	07-01-87	06-30-91
		08-01-91	06-30-95

NONSTATUTORY BOARDS, LEGISLATIVE STUDY COMMISSIONS, AND
MISCELLANEOUS APPOINTMENTS

Board Number	Title
0006	Adoptions/Surrogate Parenthood Study Commission
0014	Governor's Advisory Committee on Agricultural Parks
0012	Agriculture, Forestry, and Seafood Awareness Study Commission
0031	Governor's Council on Alcohol and Drug Abuse among Children and Youth (Executive Order Number 23)
0031	Governor's Council on Alcohol and Other Drug Abuse (Executive Order Number 132)
0032	Governor's Inter-Agency Advisory Team on Alcohol and Other Drug Abuse
3008	North Carolina Alternative Energy Corp. Board of Directors
0037	North Carolina Foundation for Alternative Health Programs, Inc., Board of Directors
3010	Appalachian National Scenic Trails
0044	Governor's Task Force on Aquaculture in North Carolina
3020	Governor's Business Council on the Arts and Humanities
0076	State Asbestos Study Commission
0082	Governor's Advisory Board on Athletes against Crime
0308	Legislative Study Commission on the Basic Education Program
0127	North Carolina Biotechnology Center Board of Directors
0136	Blue Ridge Parkway Committee
0137	Blue Ridge Parkway Film Advisory Committee
3011	North Carolina Blumenthal Center for Performing Arts Foundation Board of Trustees
0199	Governor's Commission on Child Victimization
0563	Christa McAuliffe Fellowship Program Selection Committee
0204	Governor's Blue-Ribbon Commission on Coastal Initiatives
3070	College Foundation, Inc., Board of Trustees
0206	North Carolina College of Chiropractic Study Committee
0211	Columbus Voyages Quincentenary Commission
0282	De Soto Trail Commission
0288	North Carolina Disability Task Force
3077	Governor's Task Force on Domestic Violence
0289	North Carolina Driver License Task Force
0298	Economic Future Study Commission
0309	Governor's Advisory Committee on Education Block Grants
0318	Education Study Commission
0311	Educational Leadership Task Force
0329	Governor's Efficiency Study Commission
0341	North Carolina Emergency Response Commission
3085	North Carolina Board of Ethics
0307	Governor's Programs of Excellence in Education Selection Committee
3154	Executive and Legislative Salary Study Commission
3087	Executive Mansion Fund, Inc., Board of Directors
0359	Governor's Commission for the Family
0361	Governor's Task Force on the Farm Economy in North Carolina
3090	North Carolina Fisheries Association, Inc., Board of Directors
0372	Flue-Cured Tobacco Cooperative Stabilization Corp. Board of Directors
0202	North Carolina Fund for Children and Families Commission
0402	Geographic Information Coordinating Council

NONSTATUTORY BOARDS, LEGISLATIVE STUDY COMMISSIONS, AND
MISCELLANEOUS APPOINTMENTS (CONTINUED)

Board Number	Title
3600	Governor's Western Residence Board of Directors
3119	State Health Coordinating Council
3115	Governor's Task Force on Health Objectives for the Year 2000
3120	Council on Health Policy Information
0428	Governor's Highway Beautification Council
3125	Governor's Highway Safety Commission
3126	Highway Study Commission
3130	State Historical Records Advisory Board
0431	North Carolina Liaison for the U.S. Holocaust Memorial Council
0450	North Carolina Humanities Council
0467	Indigent Health Care Study Commission
0464	Advisory Board, Southern Regional Project on Infant Mortality
0466	Governor's Commission on Reduction of Infant Mortality
0468	Governor's Task Force on Injury Prevention
0476	Governor's Advisory Council on International Trade
3156	North Carolina Job Training Coordinating Council
0500	Judicial Center Study Commission
3160	Judicial Selection Study Commission
0507	Juvenile Justice Planning Committee
0510	Juvenile Law Study Commission
0523	Governor's Language Institutes Advisory Board
0524	Legislative and Judicial Salary Study Commission
0229	Committee on Governor's Conferences on Library and Information Services
0538	Governor's Advisory Council on Literacy
0537	Governor's Commission on Literacy
0539	North Carolina Committee on Literacy and Basic Skills
0547	North Carolina Council of Management and Development, Inc.
0514	North Carolina Martin Luther King, Jr., Holiday Commission
0569	Mental Health Study Commission
3279	Microelectronics Center of North Carolina Board of Directors
3400	Mid-Atlantic Regional Marine Research Board
3295	Governor's Advisory Commission on Military Affairs
0588	Governor's Council of Minority Executives
0589	Governor's Minority, Female, and Disabled-Owned Businesses Construction Contractors Advisory Committee
3335	North Carolina Museum of History Associates Board of Directors
0620	National Football League Blue Ribbon Commission
0631	Natural Sciences Society Board of Directors
3114	North Carolina 2000 Steering Committee
0641	Governor's Task Force on the Shortage of Nurses in North Carolina
0672	Study Commission on State Parks and Recreation Areas
3290	Persian Gulf War Memorial Commission
0730	Governor's Task Force on Development of Private Seed Venture Capital Sources
0735	Public Engineers of North Carolina-Governor's New Product Award Program
0746	Public Health Study Commission
0742	Public School Forum of North Carolina, Inc., Board of Directors
3406	North Carolina Public Transportation Advisory Council
0757	North Carolina Quality Leadership Awards Council

NONSTATUTORY BOARDS, LEGISLATIVE STUDY COMMISSIONS, AND
MISCELLANEOUS APPOINTMENTS (CONTINUED)

Board Number	Title
0753	Governor's Task Force on Racial, Religious, and Ethnic Violence and Intimidation
0756	Governor's Task Force on Rail Passenger Service
0874	State Real Property Transfers Study Commission
3415	Governor's Commission for the Recognition of State Employees
0901	Region IV Transportation Consortium
3430	Roanoke Island Historical Association
0790	Rural Economic Development Center Board of Trustees
0723	Rural Service Delivery Area Private Industry Council
0831	Seafood Study Commission
3460	North Carolina Small Business Council
0844	Social Services Study Commission
3401	South Atlantic Regional Marine Research Board
0860	Southern Regional Education Board
0864	Southern Regional Education Board Commission on Health and Human Services
0861	Southern Regional Education Board Legislative Advisory Committee
0859	Southern Regional Education Board Legislative Work Conference Delegates
0851	Southern Technology Council
0862	North Carolina Sports Development Commission
0679	State Personnel System Study Commission
0878	North Carolina Commission on the Superconducting Super Collider
0882	Teaching Fellows Commission Regional Screening Committee
0892	North Carolina Advisory Council on Telecommunications in Education
3015	Trail of Tears National Historic Trail Advisory Council
3490	Governor's Advisory Committee on Travel and Tourism
3491	North Carolina Travel and Tourism Board
3500	National Conference on Uniform State Laws
0997	North Carolina United Nations Day Chairman
3515	Vagabond School of the Drama Board of Trustees
0922	Veterans Day Coordinator
3540	North Carolina Advisory Council on Vocational Education
0941	Governor's Volunteer Advisory Council
0000	Wake County Private-Public Recycling and Waste-Reduction Task Force
3601	Western North Carolina Environmental Council
0960	Legislative Study Commission on Wetlands Protection
0968	Women's Economic Development Advisory Council
0966	North Carolina Governor's Commission on Workforce Preparedness
3550	Chairman, North Carolina Governor's Commission on Workforce Preparedness
0876	Youth Suicide Study Commission

APPENDIX I

LETTER FROM GOVERNOR MARTIN TO CLAUDE SITTON

RALEIGH, FEBRUARY 24, 1990

[Tormented by a raging throat infection, Governor Martin nevertheless convened a news conference February 22, 1990, to defend his administration against a possible criminal probe by the State Bureau of Investigation. Attorney General Lacy Thornburg acknowledged he was considering calling in the SBI following the release, by State Auditor Edward Renfrow, of a report critical of the Governor's Research Office and the political use of state resources. See "Press Release: Governor Issues Statement on Research Office Audit," February 20, 1990, pages 235–236, above.

Martin held the floor for ninety minutes, the effects of pain and sleeplessness telling in his speech and countenance. He rambled occasionally as he awaited Thornburg, Renfrow, Democratic Party Chairman E. Lawrence Davis III, and Wake County District Attorney C. Colon Willoughby, Jr., whom he had invited for questioning, but they never arrived. Saying he was tired of political persecution and frequent criticism from the Raleigh *News and Observer*, the governor concluded the press conference by stating that he would not offer himself as a future candidate for elected office.

The revelation stunned many. The governor had been widely considered the Republican candidate for the United States Senate in 1992. However, he decided against running "some time ago," before February 22: Martin was a six-term congressman; neither he nor Dorothy desired to return to Washington. He initially intended to wait until after the 1990 elections to make his announcement, "to keep from becoming a lame-duck governor and losing some of his political influence." *News and Observer*, February 23, 24, 25, 26, 1990.

The day after the press conference, Thornburg declared that the State Bureau of Investigation would not scrutinize the research office. The governor said of the decision: "While this is a relief, I still believe the attorney general went too far in threatening me with an SBI investigation. It amazes me that these two partisan Democrat investigators (Lacy Thornburg and Ed Renfrow) cannot bring themselves to admit publicly that the Martin administration is a clean operation." Press release, "Governor's Response to Announcement from Attorney General," Raleigh, February 23, 1990, Governors Papers, James G. Martin.

Coverage of the press conference and speculation in the *News and Observer* on the permanence of Martin's withdrawal from any further political candidacy prompted the governor to write a letter to Claude Sitton, the paper's editor. He hand delivered the document to Sitton on February 24, 1990. The newspaper printed it the next day, beginning on the front page.

Martin's letter is reprinted here by permission of Frank Daniels, Jr., publisher, Raleigh *News and Observer*.]

Dear Claude:

Let me first say that your reporter's coverage of my impromptu news conference Thursday was a good piece of work.[1] He showed the background, added some contrast, but for the first time in many years, also gave my side of the story. For which I thank you. Today's sequel was a sorry piece of work.[2]

I had gotten out of sickbed not just to talk to reporters. I was too sick for that. The reason was stated clearly, so that I could respond to Attorney General Thornburg's public threat of an investigation by his State Bureau of Investigation. Had I waited until I had fully recovered, as that man has so invalorously suggested, my reputation would have long been destroyed by your repetitive coverage of his accusation before any word could be heard from me in my own defense. I've seen you do that to others.

Yes, he was within his rights to consider whether there was reason to investigate me.[3] It was unprincipled of him, though, to broadcast his threat publicly. Many times my office had privately shared with him an accusation against one or another of our ranking people, so that a discreet SBI investigation could determine whether there were any truth to it. Typically, upon finding no basis for it, the matter would then be put to rest, without unworthy publicity.

This time, however, "Judge" Thornburg was not content to undertake a quiet investigation. He needed the publicity of going after the governor (his number-one client, by the way). So he prepared and released a statement declaring that I would not be allowed to get away with a mere $15.35 payment for the election related phone calls (even though that was $15.35 more than Auditor Renfrow had asked me to pay!).[4] No, he wanted the people to know that he would protect them from me; that he would summon his warriors who had gone after Tommy Pollard, and open an investigation on me.[5]

I knew in my sickroom that all he had to do was keep talking about it until I finally was strong enough to respond, and you could be relied upon to print every leak, every mean joke, every vile accusation, every lie for that matter. After the "Old Reliable" (as you call yourself) had worked me over another week, there wouldn't have been enough left of my reputation worth defending. I knew from experience that your paper has been bitterly hostile to every Republican ever since 1896, when Governor Daniel Russell, the last Republican before Holshouser, took the state printing contract away from you. The great Republican historian Helen Edmunds [sic] nailed you on that sorry episode.[6]

I planned no prepared speech, knowing that reporters doze off when I speak from a text. I was very pleased that this time every reporter paid attention and worked hard to get a fair and balanced story in their next morning's paper.

Thankfully, I had even had the presence of mind not to take any of the cough medicine that my throat badly needed; because my doctor had mentioned that it had a codeine-like component, and I did not want to have that in my system when I spoke. My staff told reporters, who asked, that I had not taken any cough medicine, so that part of my appearance (which so delighted your editors and the Democrat consultants you quoted) was due to my agony of fighting to keep from coughing all over the assembled reporters and TV cameras.

The reason I have to write this to you is because today's paper has a front page feature speculating "that (my) thinking was clouded by medication: a prescription cough medicine. . . ."[7] I must protest that it is wicked for you to print such a false attempt at amateur psychoanalysis based on false assumptions. The same goes for WPTF-TV for showing some fool pharmacist guessing that I had taken a codeine-based cough medicine, when he did not know the truth that I had not taken any so as to keep my system cleansed.[8]

Why would you do such a thing? Were you afraid that my closing sentence that "I have lost interest in any other political office" might be retracted after I recovered?[9] Did you believe my staff, who tried to protect my future by saying that I didn't mean it?[10] Were you convinced that it was necessary to drive the stake through my heart so that I would never terrorize your beloved Democrat Party again? Were you so exhilarated that at last here was your best opportunity, as Reliable Keeper of the Redshirt Democrat Faith for a hundred years, to administer now the coup de grace to Governor Daniel Russell's successor?

That's what I believe you tried to do. You interviewed friends who had not talked to me, to show that they thought I was not thinking clearly. I can assure them that I was. You interviewed Democrat consultants, adversaries whose client candidates I had beaten, to show that they would use my sickly appearance to discredit my words, and use it against me later if I ever tried to climb back into the ring as a political candidate.[11] You even quoted Jim Hunt's press aide, of all people, gloating that I had lost control in public.[12]

In many Friday news articles (including yours) about my news conference, I was quoted as saying, "I'm getting out of control before your very eyes."[13] That surprised me. Several times during the conference, I was halted in mid-sentence by the onset of one of those coughing fits that could throw my throat into a spasm. Once, after physically choking back the screaming, inflamed nerve that was calling down a barrage of uncontrolled coughing such as I had experienced for a week, I weakly but gamely tried to squeak out that "I'm getting it under control, before your very eyes." I will listen to the transcript later (and hope you will) but that's what my brain told my tongue to say.[14]

Let me say to my friends that they must not worry or feel sorry for me. That news conference was not "the worst single day in (my) political career," as you termed it.[15] It was my best, because I stood up on wobbly legs and suppressed my illness long enough to identify the Democrat investigators and newspaper who tried to destroy me before I ran again. It was the best day, because I was strong enough to set aside any political ambition for myself and give to my wife a special, early Christmas present: that after this term she could have me back from the demands of high political office. How many noticed that I had worn my Christmas tie, so that she would remember with special meaning that I meant what I was going to say, and not wonder if I had misspoken?

It was the best day, because now I would be free of having every paper characterize every proposal I make for the good of North Carolina in terms of how it might be intended to promote a race for the United States Senate, in which I have never had any interest but could not shake without disavowing it.

Convinced that I can more effectively lead and work for a stronger North Carolina if my motives can not be misrepresented, I am happy to sacrifice any further Martin candidacy. I absolutely meant what I said, that I have lost interest in any other political office. It's too brutal for me.

Your heavy attempt this morning to convey that I was too sick or medicated to ever be allowed to run for office again did one good thing. It convinced me of the truth that I should not become a candidate again because of what you enjoy doing to my family and me.

But you were wrong about another thing: I have not "soured on politics."[16] Far from it. From now on, after 26 years of public life comes to a close, I am going to become a coach (I know you don't like coaches either). It will be my mission to work with the Republicans in office, elected and appointed, and all the candidates we can recruit, to become the strongest possible force we can become. My purpose will be to help raise our political skills to the highest level of competence and mastery we can reach.

After the way you piled on when I was down, I know for certain that the only worthwhile ambition left for me is to root you and Lacy Thornburg out of North

Carolina politics, along with any Democrats who take delight in your mischief. It would interfere with this noble purpose if it could be charged that I was only advancing my own candidacy, but I have now taken care of that distraction.

From now on, it can only be said that I am doing everything for the sole purpose of serving the people and the State of North Carolina. And that will make me your dedicated adversary.

With all the sincerity I can muster,
James G. Martin
Governor of North Carolina

---

[1]See Steve Riley, "Ailing Martin, at times incoherent, lashes out at critics," *News and Observer*, February 23, 1990.

[2]The sequel, "Echoes from remarks could haunt Martin," was written by Rob Christensen and Steve Riley. *News and Observer*, February 24, 1990.

[3]The *News and Observer* published an editorial sympathetic to the attorney general's position on February 24, 1990.

[4]"I believe it is obvious that the governor's Research Office had to be used for political purposes,' said Mr. Thornburg, a Democrat. 'It is going to take more than a $15.35 check to clear that matter up.'" *News and Observer*, February 22, 1990; see also press release, "Governor Issues Statement on Research Office Audit," pages 235–236, above.

[5]In early December 1989, the Raleigh *News and Observer* suggested a conflict of interest between B. Thomas Pollard, a member of the state Board of Transportation, and two real estate deals in his home county of Onslow. Pollard used his position, the newspaper said, to have traffic lights installed at property he owned at an intersection prior to his sale of the land, making the tract more valuable. The article also linked him to the board's endorsement to extend Western Boulevard, in Jacksonville, across acreage partially held by financial backers of Martin's 1988 reelection campaign.

Attorney General Lacy Thornburg, acting on the newspaper's story, initiated a preliminary inquiry into Pollard's activities by the State Bureau of Investigation. Presumed to take one week, the probe lasted for ten. Thornburg called it off after discovering no evidence of wrongdoing. *News and Observer*, December 3, 4, 5, 6, 7, 23, 1989, February 24, 1990; see also press release, "Governor Pleased by Exoneration of Pollard, Criticizes Length of SBI Probe," Raleigh, February 23, 1990, Governors Papers, James G. Martin.

Pollard (1941–), born in Jacksonville; self-employed, Pollard Enterprises, Inc.; elected to state Senate from Onslow County, 1990; Republican. *North Carolina Manual, 1991–1992*, 272.

[6]Democrats who controlled the General Assembly in post-Reconstruction North Carolina dispensed government printing contracts as a form of patronage, according to historian Helen Edmonds. The practice changed in 1895: Under the leadership of the Fusionists, a union of Republicans and Populists, the legislature required contracts to be awarded to the lowest bidder. Two years later, Fusion lawmakers authorized the Council of State to grant and oversee those contracts.

Josephus Daniels, ardent Democrat and publisher of the Raleigh *News and Observer*, served as state printer under several Democratic legislatures and bid for the 1897 contract. But with the Council of State in Fusionist hands and a Republican governor—Daniel Russell—in office, Daniels's overture was rebuffed. Considering the withering criticism repeatedly heaped upon Fusionists by the *News and Observer*, the council's decision was hardly surprising.

Edmonds indicated that Daniels recognized the futility of his bid but submitted it because regaining the title of state printer was less important than the publicity he sought to derive from the bid's rejection. She paraphrased one Fusionist, who wrote "that Daniels had grown to regard the job of state printer as a piece of party pie; that for seven years he had been given the job of public printer which he sublet to other printing and binding concerns while he would get a 15 percent bonus merely for subletting; that he had made on public printing alone not less than $2,500 to $3,000 a year for seven years; that now he was angry because Fusion legislatures did not continue to let him reap a rich profit; and that this anger caused him to vilify the Fusionists in his paper." Helen G. Edmonds, *The Negro and Fusion Politics in North Carolina, 1894–1901* (Chapel Hill: University of North Carolina Press, 1951), 100–101, 145.

Daniel Lindsay Russell, Jr. (1845–1908), governor of North Carolina, 1897–1901. Previously identified in Poff, *Addresses of Martin*, I, 198n.

[7]"The quick explanation is that his thinking was clouded by medication: a prescription cough medicine, an antibiotic and a decongestant. The governor had not slept the night before the news conference, and he appeared tired and woozy." *News and Observer*, February 24, 1990.

[8]WPTF-TV was Raleigh's NBC affiliate.

[9]"Ask the people of North Carolina if they understand now why I've lost interest in any other political office." *News and Observer*, February 23, 1990.

[10]"Administration officials said Mr. Martin's comments, made in the heat of the moment and while he was ill, should not necessarily be read as a firm statement of his intentions. They said he was genuinely undecided about running for the Senate." *News and Observer*, February 24, 1990.

[11]Martin was referring to the comments of R. Harrison Hickman, of Washington, D.C. Hickman, political consultant to U.S. Senator Terry Sanford and other North Carolina Democrats, said, "'The only thing I regret is we didn't have a film crew there that we could use for ads if the need arises.'" *News and Observer*, February 24, 1990.

[12]The observations of Gary Pearce, press secretary to Governor James B. Hunt from 1977 to 1984, were quoted in the *News and Observer*, February 24, 1990.

[13]*News and Observer*, February 23, 1990.

[14]A tape recording of the press conference verified the governor's version of his statement. *News and Observer*, March 17, 1990.

[15]"The worst single day in Gov. James G. Martin's political career ended before noon Thursday. But the fallout could well be felt for years." *News and Observer*, February 24, 1990.

[16]The *News and Observer*, February 23, 1990, reported that the governor "abruptly ended a 90-minute news conference by hinting that the experience had soured him on politics."

REMARKS FOR NANCY TEMPLE: MARTIN GIFT PRESENTATION

RALEIGH, NOVEMBER 20, 1992

[Staff members and other administration officials, as well as private-sector donors, met at the Executive Mansion, November 20, 1992, to present farewell gifts to the First Family. Nancy Temple, Governor Martin's chief of staff, was mistress of ceremonies for the occasion. Her largely lighthearted comments, below, provide glimpses of Martin's personality and hint at the relationship between the governor and those who worked with him daily. Nancy Jo Pekarek, note to Jan-Michael Poff, November 23, 1992.]

Good morning, everyone. Governor and Mrs. Martin, you may have guessed by now that you mean a great deal to all of us gathered here today, and to the citizens of this state that you have served so well over the past eight years. Of course, your term is not over yet. They say it's not over 'til the fat lady sings—I think I hear her now.[1] Stole one of your jokes! You've been stealing ours for years.

To show our appreciation in material terms, we've pooled our resources and gotten you a few things to remember us by. As you may know, Governor, it has become somewhat of an informal tradition for the governor's supporters to give him a car upon his departure from office. Well, we thought that would be a great idea, but we also got to thinking that we could go one better on that tradition.

We all know how much you enjoyed the "Salute to the Troops" and how much fun you had getting to know General Maxwell Thurman and some of our other military leaders in North Carolina.[2] We also know that you started a tradition of sorts yourself, presenting to your closest advisers a signed photograph of that lone individual, blocking a long line of tanks headed toward Tiananmen Square. So, instead of a car, we got you a tank.[3]

[Presents tank]

As your chief of staff, I know how hard it's going to be after January eighth when the only person you have to order around is Dottie. In the cause of preserving marital bliss, we're giving you your very own army to command. They go with the tank.[4]

[Presents army]

For eight years now, Governor, you've been able to just jump in a car and go wherever you wanted without worrying about how to get there. You may not have noticed that all this road construction you've got going on around the state, to build all these better roads, has got things pretty well torn up. In just a few short weeks, you're going to have to find your way around on your own. What you need is a map!

[Presents map]

This is an old map of Charlotte—a collector's item, in fact. Note the NCNB logo.[5] But that's OK, because we're building so many roads the new maps are outdated as soon as they're printed anyway. But you'll notice we have taken the liberty of marking on this map the way to your office, the grocery store, the mall, and a few other places so you won't get lost.

[Opens map to show highlighted details]

Before you get in the car and go, though, you're going to need something called a valid driver's license. Being efficient and devoted friends, we want to help make the licensing process as painless as possible. The troopers, in particular, want us to make sure you get a license so they don't have to drive you around anymore. Here we have a new copy of the *Driver's Handbook* for you to study.

[Presents handbook]

But since we know you're not going to have a lot of time to read this carefully, and since the troopers are so determined that you get that license, we got you a copy of the test with all the answers filled in already. Don't worry, Governor-Elect Hunt says it's perfectly legal, and he'll be sure to listen to you should the authorities decide otherwise!

[Presents test]

Once you get that license and head out on the road, you're going to become a danger to society. I guess you know that Governor Holshouser and Governor Hunt both had car accidents within a few short months after leaving office. Well, we all thought that in the interest of public safety, there should be some way to identify your car as that of an inexperienced driver. That way everyone else can get out of the way as you drive down the sidewalk.

For eight years, now, you've been our GOP Guv—code named Number 1 by the security detail. Now you'll be known all around Charlotte as the #1GOPGUV.[6]

[Presents license plate]

By the way, we've registered this plate with the patrol, so that should reduce the number of tickets on your record—if they recognize you!

At least your schedule will be lighter, so you won't have so many events to be out on the road traveling to, thank goodness. For several years now, you've been giving Denise Penny, your scheduling director, and Margot Flood before her, all kinds of grief about filling up all the available space on your schedule. Well, you won't have Margot or Denise to kick around anymore, but we don't want to let you go empty handed in the scheduling department, so here we have a 1993 desk diary. You'll note we haven't got a single appointment penciled in for you.

[Presents calendar]

By the way, this is compliments of Gary Pendleton. Any of you recognize this?[7]

There's a few other things you're going to miss when you move back into private life. One thing is this beautiful house. As a keepsake of your time in the Executive Mansion, we've obtained for you a replica of the state china for your use in your new home: dinner plate, silver, and napkins. [Holds up each as she names it.] Lenox, or Scott Paper Company, will ship the remainder of the order shortly.[8]

Then, of course, you're not going to have anyone to open doors for you anymore, either. To keep you from banging your forehead every time you try to enter a building, we've bought you a new companion: Mr. Robot Hand! It's the closest we could come to an automatic door opener. Or, you could always use it to shake hands should you decide to get back into politics.[9]

[Pulls out the robot hand]

Besides us, a few other people are going to miss having you around in the governor's chair, though they might not know it yet. I'm speaking of that beloved of all institutions, the press. I hear there's a rumor out in Charlotte so big the "Noise and Disturber" is printing an extra edition just to be the first out on the streets with the news. With all my connections, I was able to get an advance copy. Here's the headline: "Martin Goes One 'Better.' New Cough Syrup Top Priority for Carolinas Medical Center. Better Schools, Roads, Jobs, and Syrup!"[10]

[Presents paper]

Maybe Carolinas Medical can come up with a cough syrup better than that last batch you had. Anything's better than that last batch you had.

Oh, the press also asked me to give you this. [Presents egg timer.] They say you never did quite grasp the concept of the fifteen-second sound bite.[11]

I want you to know, Governor, that 225 people contributed money to your gift fund. I'm just sorry we couldn't raise enough money to get you anything more expensive.

Actually, thanks to the people in this room and all our other contributors, we were able to furnish Governor Jim and Dottie with quite a few pieces for their new home.[12] That includes a couple of sofas, three or four chairs, coffee and end tables, lamps, a clock and other accessories, including the governor's favorite, a new stereo system. Jim Sanderford, maintenance director here at the Mansion, has constructed a small house filled with items similar to those we've purchased for the Martins. The governor always says you don't raise taxes unless people can see what they've paid for. I encourage you to take a look at Jim's handiwork so you'll have at least some idea of what each of you has helped to pay for.[13]

All these people contributed to the Martin gift because they feel, as I do, that Jim and Dottie Martin are two exceptional people who have done far more than they ever promised to leave this state better than they found it. I think I can speak for everyone in this room when I say that it has been an honor to serve in the Martin administration, and a special pleasure to have known two such wonderful people. We will miss you both and wish you all the best in your new life.

We do have two additional gifts that we hope will serve as a special reminder for you as you enjoy your new home in Charlotte. Each of these gifts is engraved with the following inscription: "Governor James G. Martin, 1985–1993. In recognition of your outstanding leadership in building One United State. Friends of Dottie and Jim Martin, 1992."[14]

Thanks for eight wonderful years.

[Temple presents gifts, turns podium over to governor.]

---

[1]"The fat lady line . . . was the cue for someone on the second floor of the Mansion to play a soprano solo on the CD [compact disc player] . . . at full volume." Nancy [Temple] had to say the line a couple of times before the cue was taken." Nancy Jo Pekarek, letter to Jan-Michael Poff, January 20, 1995, hereinafter cited as Pekarek correspondence.

[2]Maxwell R. Thurman (1931–), born in High Point; B.S., chemical engineering, North Carolina State University. U.S. Army general, 1983–1991: vice-chief of staff, Dept. of the Army, 1983–1987; member, Joint Chiefs of Staff, 1983–1987; commanding general, Army Training and Doctrine Command, 1987–1989; commander-in-chief, U.S. Forces Southern Command, Republic of Panama (Operation Just Cause), 1989–1990; retired, 1991. Executive in residence, N.C. State University, 1993. Telephone conversation with Nancy Pekarek, March 2, 1995; *Who's Who in America, 1995*, II, 3685.

[3]The tank the governor received, of course, was a toy; Pekarek correspondence. Thousands of pro-democracy protesters occupied Tiananmen Square, Beijing, during May and June, 1989. The picture of a single, unarmed demonstrator halting a column of Chinese tanks was one of the most stirring images of the student-led uprising. *New York Times*, June 6, 1989.

[4]A bag of toy soldiers comprised Martin's "army." Pekarek correspondence.

[5]The Federal Reserve Board approved the merger of NCNB National Bank and C&S/

Sovran Corporation in November 1991. The resulting institution opened for business January 2, 1992, as NationsBank. *News and Observer*, November 30, December 31, 1991.

[6]Although it appeared to be authentic, the license plate was not intended to be installed on a vehicle. The tag was presented to Martin mounted on dark blue "velvet-like" material and surrounded by a wood frame. Pekarek correspondence.

[7]As president of Preferred Planning and Insurance, Inc., Raleigh, Gary H. Pendleton "used to distribute year-at-a-glance pocket calendars to large numbers of people in the administration, certainly [to] everyone in the Governor's Office. . . ." Pekarek correspondence.

Pendleton, resident of Raleigh; B.S., State University of New York; twenty-six years' military service, retired from N.C. National Guard, 1992. Commandant, N.C. Military Academy, Fort Bragg, for three years ending 1992; appointed as commander, N.C. State Defense Militia, September, 1992, and awarded state rank of brigadier general the following month. Member, State Banking Commission and State Board of Community Colleges. Press release, "Pendleton Named Head of N.C. Defense Militia," Raleigh, September 4, 1992, Governors Papers, James G. Martin.

[8]The "state china" consisted of "white paper plates with black-and-white copies of the state seal pasted on them" and plastic eating utensils, "also with small seals pasted on them." Pekarek correspondence.

[9]The "robot hand" was a child's mechanical toy: The middle was a slim rectangular plastic box, fourteen inches long and an inch thick. A plastic hand, with curved fingers molded together and an opposable thumb, protruded from one end; a handle on the opposite side, when squeezed, pulled the thumb "toward the hand so that it could grab things, albeit awkwardly, a little distance away." Pekarek correspondence.

[10]The mock-up of the *News and Observer*, which the paper's critics sometimes called the "Noise and Disturber," was purchased from "a pushcart at Crabtree Valley Mall that enabled you to print your own headlines." Pekarek correspondence. The reference to cough syrup recalled the governor's press conference of February 22, 1990; see Appendix I, above.

[11]At this point in her prepared remarks, Temple jotted the words "State Language Center."

[12]The notation "Serious" preceded this paragraph.

[13]James A. Sanderford (1940–), born in Franklin County; resident of Raleigh; was educated at Wake Forest High School, Wake Forest; U.S. Navy Reserve. Former carpenter supervisor; plant maintenance supervisor, Executive Mansion, since 1988. James A. Sanderford, letter to Jan-Michael Poff, September 14, 1994.

[14]Two gifts bearing engraved plates included a small chest of drawers and a silver box. The latter was "the size of a long, thin cigar box," shaped like a book. A painting of a ship sailing stormy seas was painted on the front of the wooden chest. Pekarek correspondence.

INDEX